Writing and Reporting News

A COACHING METHOD

From the Wadsworth Series in Mass Communication and Journalism

General Mass Communication

Biagi, *Media/Impact: An Introduction to Mass Media*, Tenth Edition

Fellow, *American Media History,* Third Edition

Hilmes, *Connections: A Broadcast History Reader*

Hilmes, *Only Connect: A Cultural History of Broadcasting in the United States*, Third Edition

Lester, *Visual Communication: Images with Messages*, Fifth Edition

Overbeck, *Major Principles of Media Law*, 2012 Edition

Straubhaar/LaRose, *Media Now: Understanding Media, Culture, and Technology*, Enhanced Seventh Edition

Zelezny, *Cases in Communications Law*, Sixth Edition

Zelezny, *Communications Law: Liberties, Restraints, and the Modern Media*, Sixth Edition

Journalism

Bowles/Borden, *Creative Editing*, Sixth Edition

Davis/Davis, *Think Like an Editor: 50 Strategies for the Print and Digital World*

Hilliard, *Writing for Television, Radio, and New Media*, Tenth Edition

Kessler/McDonald, *When Words Collide: A Media Writer's Guide to Grammar and Style*, Eighth Edition

Kessler/McDonald, *Cengage Advantage Books: When Words Collide: A Media Writer's Guide to Grammar and Style + Exercise Book*, Eighth Edition

Rich, *Writing and Reporting News: A Coaching Method*, Seventh Edition

Public Relations and Advertising

Diggs-Brown, *Strategic Public Relations: Audience Focused Approach*

Diggs-Brown, *The PR Styleguide: Formats for Public Relations Practice*, Third Edition

Drewniany/Jewler, *Creative Strategy in Advertising*, Tenth Edition

Hendrix, *Public Relations Cases*, Ninth Edition

Newsom/Haynes, *Public Relations Writing: Form and Style*, Ninth Edition

Newsom/Turk/Kruckeberg, *Cengage Advantage Books: This is PR: The Realities of Public Relations*, Eleventh Edition

Sivulka, *Soap, Sex, and Cigarettes: A Cultural History of American Advertising*, Second Edition

Research and Theory

Baran and Davis, *Mass Communication Theory: Foundations, Ferment, and Future*, Sixth Edition

Sparks, *Media Effects Research: A Basic Overview*, Third Edition

Wimmer and Dominick, *Mass Media Research: An Introduction*, Ninth Edition

SEVENTH EDITION

Writing and Reporting News

A COACHING METHOD

CAROLE RICH

WADSWORTH
CENGAGE Learning™

Australia • Brazil • Japan • Korea • Mexico • Singapore • Spain • United Kingdom • United States

Writing and Reporting News: A Coaching Method, Seventh Edition
Carole Rich

Senior Publisher: Lyn Uhl

Publisher: Michael Rosenberg

Associate Development Editor: Megan Garvey

Assistant Editor: Erin Bosco

Editorial Assistant: Rebecca Donahue

Media Editor: Jessica Badiner

Marketing Program Manager: Gurpreet Saran

Marketing Director: Talia Wise

Content Project Manager: Dan Saabye

Art Director: Marissa Falco

Print Buyer: Doug Bertke

Rights Acquisition Specialist: Mandy Groszko

Production Service: MPS Limited, a Macmillan Company

Text Designer: Anne Bell Carter, a bell design company

Cover Designer: Anne Bell Carter, a bell design company

Cover Image: AP Photo/Mark Lennihan

Compositor: MPS Limited, a Macmillan Company

For product information and technology assistance, contact us at
Cengage Learning Customer & Sales Support, 1-800-354-9706

For permission to use material from this text or product, submit all requests online at **www.cengage.com/permissions**.
Further permissions questions can be emailed to
permissionrequest@cengage.com.

Library of Congress Control Number: 2011929740

Student Edition:

ISBN-13: 978-1-111-34444-3

ISBN-10: 1-111-34444-2

Wadsworth
20 Channel Center Street
Boston, MA 02210
USA

Cengage Learning is a leading provider of customized learning solutions with office locations around the globe, including Singapore, the United Kingdom, Australia, Mexico, Brazil and Japan. Locate your local office at **international.cengage.com/region**

Cengage Learning products are represented in Canada by Nelson Education, Ltd.

For your course and learning solutions, visit **www.cengage.com.**

Purchase any of our products at your local college store or at our preferred online store **www.cengagebrain.com.**

Instructors: Please visit **login.cengage.com** and log in to access instructor-specific resources.

Printed in Canada
1 2 3 4 5 6 7 15 14 13 12 11

Brief Contents

Contents

PART FOUR
Understanding Media Issues

Preface

If you thrive on change, you've chosen the right field. The media industry is undergoing major changes due to social networks, mobile devices and economic pressures. Why study journalism in such uncertain times? It's a great choice because the possibilities for people who can communicate well are endless.

This seventh edition of *Writing and Reporting News: A Coaching Method* is a book that will prepare you for media careers now and in the future. It is a book that focuses on many ways students who study journalism can use their skills in print, broadcast, online and social media. Although thousands of journalists left newspaper and broadcast jobs in the past few years, they didn't stop using their media skills. They went into online ventures, social media and other jobs where they could use their writing and editing talents.

Ken Fuson was one of them. After 25 years at the *Des Moines* (Iowa) *Register,* he left to write books and freelance. In his farewell letter to the staff he wrote: "Human beings have always wanted and needed news and stories, whether they got it from the wall on a cave, around a campfire or on a computer screen. We're the people who can tell the news and deliver those stories. How we do that may change, but never forget that you possess a vital and important skill." You can read about him in Chapter 8, Story Organization.

In Chapter 22, Media Jobs and Internships, you'll read about the unusual jobs available for students who write well and understand social media such as this job for an online communications and community coordinator: "Develops content on the company website, manages online discussions, pitches to bloggers. Must follow AP writing style and have ability to rapidly produce editorial and technical content." That was from a national chain of pet products. Or this job ad: "Writer/editor with a nose for news. Writes news briefs for two weekly e-newletters and posts content on the association's Facebook and Twitter profiles." That was from the Society of American Florists.

The possibilities are varied and exciting. Much of the material in this seventh edition is new — focusing on social media, mobile media and convergence of print, broadcast and online media for news and public relations. And most of the features that students and teachers have praised in the past have been retained.

As in previous editions, the coaching concepts of this book are designed to help you acquire the writing and reporting skills you will need no matter which media field you choose to enter. The book also emphasizes media ethics in every chapter so that you can gain an understanding of the problems you might encounter and learn ethical principles that will help you resolve them.

The coaching method, which is the foundation of this book, is a way of helping writers discover their problems and learn techniques to solve them. The book features tips from leading writing coaches and award-winning journalists and public relations practitioners. Examples that illustrate the instructional material have been carefully chosen from professional and college news sites to appeal to the interests of students. The chapters are written in a storytelling style to make learning a pleasant reading experience.

NEW MATERIAL IN THIS EDITION

This seventh edition of *Writing and Reporting News: A Coaching Method* has been substantially revised to include an emphasis on social media, convergence and mobile media skills in every chapter and the following new material:

- Social media boxes in every chapter along with revised Convergence Coach and Ethics boxes
- A new social media chapter, which includes information from the previous Chapter 2 on Blogs but contains all new material about how to understand and write for social networks.
- A completely revised convergence chapter, which includes mobile media
- New color photographs throughout the book

Here are the other changes to chapters in the new edition:
- Chapter 1 — Changing Concepts of News has been completely revised and updated.
- Chapter 2 — The Basic News Story — This chapter, which was Chapter 4 in the previous edition, has been moved up so students can learn the basics sooner.
- Chapter 5 — Sources and Online Research incorporates the main concepts of the Beat Reporting, previously Chapter 19, which has been eliminated.
- Chapter 6 — Interviewing Techniques includes the main concepts of Curiosity and Observation, previously Chapter 5, which has been eliminated.
- Chapter 13 — Public Relations Writing has been completely revised and includes new material about how P.R. practitioners are using social media.
- Discussion of print, broadcast and online writing in all chapters
- Elimination of two chapters — Curiosity and Story Ideas and Beat Reporting — to provide space for all the new material on social and mobile media and more images throughout the book.
- Elimination of Appendix 2 — Style Guide. The major items from the guide are included in the Appendix on Grammar and Usage.
- New exercises have been added to focus on social media skills.
- The student workbook is available in both print and electronic formats. The electronic version is available for download within the book's CourseMate. Access to the CourseMate is available at *www.cengagebrain.com*. The exercises have been revised to coordinate with the revisions in the textbook.

HOW THE BOOK IS ORGANIZED

Although this textbook is arranged sequentially to take students through the steps from conceiving ideas to constructing stories, each chapter is self-contained so the chapters may be used in any order.

If you are an instructor who has used previous editions of this textbook, you will find many changes. Much of the material from the sixth edition has been retained, but because new chapters and many more images have been added, the order of the chapters has changed as follows:

Part One: Understanding News

1 Changing Concepts of News (no change)

2 The Basic News Story (was Chapter 3)

3 Convergent and Mobile Media (was Chapter 4 "Convergent Media Writing," but now includes mobile media)

Part Two: Collecting Information

4 Social Media (new chapter)

5 Sources and Online Research (was Chapter 6)

6 Interviewing Techniques (was Chapter 5; includes information from previous Chapter 3 Curiosity and Story Ideas, which was eliminated)

7 Leads and Nut Graphs (was Chapter 8)

Part Three: Constructing Stories

8 Story Organization (was Chapter 9)

9 Story Forms (was Chapter 10)

10 Storytelling and Feature Techniques (was Chapter 11)

11 Broadcast News Writing (was Chapter 12)

12 Online Journalism (was Chapter 13 and includes new material)

13 Public Relations Writing (was chapter 14 and has been completely revised)

Part Four: Understanding Media Issues

14 Media Law (was Chapter 15)

15 Media Ethics (was Chapter 16)

16 Multicultural Sensitivity (was Chapter 17 and includes new material)

Part Five: Applying the Techniques

17 Profiles and Obituaries (was Chapter 18)

18 Speeches, News Conferences and Meetings (was Chapter 20; Chapter 19 Beat Reporting was eliminated)

19 Government and Statistical Stories (was Chapter 21)

20 Crime and Punishment (was Chapter 22)

21 Disasters, Weather and Tragedies (was Chapter 23)

22 Media Jobs and Internships (was Chapter 24, includes new material about online applications)

Appendix: Grammar and Usage

SUPPLEMENTS
News Scene

The award-winning multimedia program NewsScene features 11 online interactive news assignments based on realistic news events. Through the use of extensive source material, including videotaped interviews, telephone messages, official documents and database information, News Scene can help you assign news writing projects and help students sharpen their writing skills for print, broadcast and online media. Two newly created scenarios, a sports story and a personality profile, have been included in this revised edition to reflect common reporting assignments.

A "News Scene" icon, which has been placed below the Featured Online Activities in several chapters, indicates a related exercise that is available in this program.

Student Workbook/eWorkbook

The Student Workbook, which will be available in both print and electronic formats, features several exercises in each chapter to reinforce the concepts taught in *Writing and Reporting News*, Seventh Edition. These include quizzes, exercises designed to give students more opportunities to improve their reporting and writing skills, and exercises designed to encourage critical thinking by asking students to critique news stories and analyze websites. This edition of the workbook also includes practice in using social media skills. The electronic version is available for download within the book's Course-Mate. Access to the CourseMate is available at *www.cengagebrain.com*.

Mass Communication CourseMate

The interactive teaching and learning program, CourseMate, will also be offered for the seventh edition of *Writing and Reporting News* for quick access to the electronic study resources that accompany this text, including the student eWorkbook and automatically graded quizzes. You can access the CourseMate at *www.cengagebrain.com*, using the access code that came with your book or that you bought online.

Instructor's Resource Manual

The Instructor's Resource Manual contains chapter-specific goals, teaching suggestions and answers to the textbook and workbook exercises. The Resource Manual also includes examples of original stories. As the Instructor's Resource Manual is an electronic document, the file is available for download at the Instructor's Companion Website, *login.cengage.com*.

Instructor's Companion Website

This protected website is available exclusively for instructor use, and will include a downloadable version of the Instructor's Resource Manual, the NewsScene Instructor's Manual and the eWorkbook with answers. Access is available at *login.cengage.com*.

Acknowledgments

I would like to thank many people at Cengage Learning who made the seventh edition of this textbook possible. They include: Michael Rosenberg, Publisher of the Humanities division; Megan Garvey, Associate Development Editor of Humanities; Erin Bosco, Assistant Editor; Rebecca Donahue, Editorial Assistant; Jessica Badiner, Media Editor; Gurpreet Saran, Marketing Project Manager; Dan Saabye, Content Project Manager; and Jitendra Kumar, MPS Project Manager.

I would also like to thank the reviewers, who contributed their time and advice for this edition: Paula Quinn, Western Kentucky University; Jocelyn D. Steinke, Western Michigan University; Julie Dodd, University of Florida; Judi Schoolman, New York University; Barry Hollander, University of Georgia; Noel Robinson, County College Of Morris; Wanda G. Cash, University of Texas, Austin; John Dvorak, Indiana University; and Jennifer Greer, University of Alabama.

About the Author

Carole Rich has spent 25 years teaching journalism at four universities and coaching professional writers throughout the U.S. She has taught at the University of Alaska Anchorage and has served as chair of the journalism department at Hofstra University in Long Island, N.Y. She began her teaching career at the University of Arizona in 1985 and then taught journalism at the University of Kansas from 1987 to 1998 when she was hired as the distinguished Atwood professor in Alaska. Prior to becoming a professor, she worked for 16 years in the newspaper industry. She was a reporter for the former *Philadelphia Evening Bulletin,* city editor of the *Sun-Sentinel* in Fort Lauderdale, Fla., and deputy metropolitan editor of the *Hartford* (Ct.) *Courant.*

Rich has been a visiting writing coach at newspapers throughout the U.S. and has conducted many writing seminars at journalism organizations, including a seminar for professional journalists in Spain. She is also the author of *Creating Online Media: A Guide to Research, Writing and Design on the Internet,* published by McGraw-Hill.

COACHING TIPS

Consider ways to present your story for **print, broadcast and online media.**

Ask yourself **how your story affects your readers.**

Consider whether your story needs a **photograph, graphic, audio or video.**

Plan to update your story for **online delivery.**

Use social media sites to connect with readers and viewers.

archidea/Shutterstock.com

It [convergence] used to be defined as multiple media — a newspaper and a television station and a radio station and a website working together to best tell a story. . . . To me it's much more about serving the audience however the audience wants to be served, so that they can have our content whenever they want it and however they want it.

— **ROB CURLEY,** new media division editor, *Las Vegas Sun* and Greenspun Media Group

CHAPTER 1
Changing Concepts of News

IT'S SHORTLY AFTER 1 A.M. AND THE POLICE OFFICER'S PATROL IS UNEVENTFUL, except for the man carrying a 5-inch-long rat on his shoulder. No crime; it was just a man who bought a rat at a pet store. At 5:42 a.m. a young mother wakes to the cries of her hungry 10-month-old daughter. At noon a homeless woman with a canister of pepper spray in her bra waits for lunch at the local soup kitchen, and as midnight approaches three fraternity members celebrate the last day of classes by climbing on the merry-go-round at a shopping mall.

These are just a few of the stories and photographs that chronicle one day in the life of residents in Lawrence, Kansas. The project could be done in any community. When the *Lawrence* (Kan.) *Journal-World* tackled the subject, it created a "multimedia time capsule" by producing the story in the newspaper, on television and on its website with text, photos, audio and video.

That's not unusual these days. Almost every news organization has done a 24-hour story, but what made this different was the participation from the community. In addition to reporting by reporters and photographers of the newspaper and its partner TV station, residents participated by sending in stories about their day in various forms: podcasts, blogs, video, photos and text messages via e-mail.

This project was one of several innovative methods the *Lawrence Journal-World* has produced to interact with its readers and viewers in multimedia forms. And it is an example of how the nature of news is changing.

Readers are participating much more in producing and reacting to news through social media sites such as Twitter, Facebook, YouTube and others. Mobile media and tablet computers are also affecting how news is delivered.

"Digital delivery is now a well established part of most Americans' daily news consumption," according to a study by the Pew Project for Excellence in Journalism. "Six in ten

Americans get some news online in a typical day — and most of these also get news from other media platforms as well.... Blogging is declining in frequency while 26 percent of Americans now get news on their cell phones, and half of online news consumers with social networking sites use those pages for news.

"One thing that is becoming clearer is the way people use digital technology to acquire news. The American news consumer is increasingly becoming a grazer, across both online and offline platforms. On a typical day, nearly half of Americans now get news from four to six different platforms — from online to TV to print and more."

Readers and viewers don't just receive news; they help collect and create it. They get the news when, how and where they want it on computers, mobile phones, tablet devices or social media networks. They contribute to traditional media outlets with news tips, story ideas and eyewitness reports in text, video and photos via Twitter, Facebook, Flickr, YouTube and other social media sites.

Definitions of news are also evolving, and economic factors such as mergers of media companies have changed the landscape of the news industry.

Declining newspaper circulation, increased competition from cable television news stations and access to millions of sites on the Internet are forcing news organizations to expand ways to interest readers and viewers. The days of writing for a single medium have ended at most news, public relations and advertising organizations.

MEDIA CONVERGENCE

Many of the skills you need to become a journalist are still grounded in basic reporting and writing principles, but in today's market you need to know how to present information for print, broadcast and online media. This mixture of media is called "convergence," "multimedia," "integrated media" and other terms.

In some types of convergence a print news organization will partner with a broadcast station to collaborate on a story. In other newsrooms the print and broadcast facilities are in the same building where journalists coordinate coverage of the news. Convergence can also be considered the merger of print, audio, video and interactive elements in an online form.

Rob Curley, one of the most innovative pioneers in online content, says the concept of convergence is changing. In the past a TV station would cooperate with a newspaper by telling viewers to read more about the story in tomorrow's newspaper, and the newspaper would promote something on the TV station, or they would promote something on their websites. Curley says that was the nature of convergence, but he says it was really just "cross-promotion."

At many news organizations, that concept of convergence as cross-promotion is still practiced, but more newspapers and broadcast news programs are increasing content on their websites with an emphasis on interacting with readers and viewers. The *Lawrence Journal-World* was a forerunner in this respect, due in part to Curley.

Prior to his current position as editor of the new media division for the *Las Vegas Sun* and

Convergence desk at the *Lawrence Journal-World* where editors coordinate print, broadcast and online coverage of news.

Greenspun Media Group, Curley gained national attention for the innovative websites he created at the *Lawrence Journal-World* in Kansas. Because nearly 30,000 people are students and employees of the University of Kansas in Lawrence, Curley decided to create a separate website to appeal to the college audience. This site, *www.lawrence.com,* features content such as weekly drink specials, local bands, entertainment listings and blogs, which are personal journals written by college students or members of the community.

Another site Curley created, geared to the KU sports-loving community, is *www2. kusports.com.* "We offer updates on game days every five minutes," Curley said shortly after he created the site. "We're trying to appeal to our audiences. We hire the smartest college kid we can find to do promotions." The site also features live chats with the coach of the KU Jayhawks basketball team and other sports-related personalities.

In his new position, he continues to win awards for online journalism. Although he seeks to hire people with multimedia skills, he maintains that good writing skills and knowledge of grammar are still essential. "We want solid journalists who can write their backsides off and who are not afraid of multimedia or working directly with a fairly sophisticated online content management system. . . . Above all, the students or recent graduates will demonstrate maturity and critical thinking skills, show exuberance toward the career of journalism, and embrace its values of accuracy and fairness," he wrote in a blog about what he seeks in interns.

CHANGING DELIVERY OF NEWS

Constant changes in technology have spawned an alphabet soup of new terms related to forms of delivering news. Almost all news organizations offer to deliver information via e-mail or to an iPod. With the increasing popularity of smart phones and

Rob Curley, new media division editor, *Las Vegas Sun* and Greenspun Media Group.

tablet computers like the iPad, news companies are developing applications to deliver their products to these devices. Mobile news delivery is the fastest growing trend for the media industry.

News Corporation, one of the largest media companies, is creating a national newspaper exclusively designed for tablet computers and smart phones. The company, headed by Rupert Murdoch, publishes more than 100 newspapers, including the *Wall Street Journal*, and owns 27 broadcast stations, including the Fox network. The digital newspaper will feature "short, snappy" stories that can be digested quickly, Murdoch said. "We'll have young people reading newspapers," he said when he announced his plans for the tablet news. "It's a real game changer in the presentation of news."

Other news organizations are also developing applications for mobile phone delivery, tablet computers and other devices.

USA Today has completely restructured its newsroom to take advantage of distributing news on mobile and tablet platforms. The company disbanded its universal desk and reorganized the newsroom around 15 content areas such as travel, personal finance, technology and subjects that will be geared to the audience and technology of mobile and tablet media. "This significant restructuring reflects *USA Today's* evolution from a newspaper company to a multi-platform media company, said David L. Hunke, president and publisher of the organization.

Here are some terms that describe the changing forms of news delivery:

- **Blogs:** The term "blog" is short for "Web log" because blogs are posted on the Web. A blog can be a personal journal or brief commentary about any topic and can include audio or video.

- **Podcast:** This is digital media information in audio or video form distributed over the Internet for use on a portable media player such as an iPod, an instrument developed by Apple Inc., or an MP3 player. Pod is an abbreviation for "portable on demand." You don't need an iPod to hear or view a podcast; you can receive it on your computer with the use of software.

- **RSS:** These letters stand for "Really Simple Syndication," which is probably simpler to use than to define. If you want to receive certain blogs or podcasts regularly, you can subscribe to a site using a Web feed reader called an "aggregator" that will compile them and deliver them to you. You insert a link to the site into the aggregator software. Search engines such as Google or Yahoo! offer to deliver automatic updates of news via RSS feeds. These feeds, delivered to your account, contain headlines, summaries and links to the articles.

- **Aggregator:** This is software that compiles or collects certain websites that you want delivered to you regularly and pushes them to you via e-mail or automatically downloads them for you into a portable media player. The aggregator is also known as a feed reader because it "reads" the sites it will "feed" to you. It checks them for new material and downloads updates to your account for easy access on your computer or portable media device.

SOCIAL MEDIA

SOCIAL NETWORK-ING has transformed the media, according to Clay Shirky, a New York University professor who is considered an expert in this field. "We are living in the middle of the largest increase in expressive capability in the history of the human race," he wrote in his book, *Here Comes Everybody.* "More people can communicate more things to more people than has ever been possible in the past, and the size and speed of this increase, from under one million participants to over one billion in a generation, makes the change unprecedented, even considered against the background of previous revolutions in communications tools."

Here are a few of the ways social media sites are changing journalism:

- **New job positions:** News organizations are hiring social media editors. They interact with their communities on sites such as Twitter and Facebook, train journalists in their newsrooms to use social media, maintain and contribute blogs or tweets to company sites.

- **Reporting:** Journalists are using social media to gain tips and sources and to communicate with readers and viewers especially during a breaking news event. Many government and community organizations and corporate communications agencies also post information on social media sites that reporters can follow to gain information.

- **Participation by readers and viewers:** News organizations are soliciting information from subscribers to their websites and social media sites for breaking news, eyewitness reports and feedback about stories and issues. And social media users share information about the news with each other, creating new types of communities. "The public is clearly part of the news process now. Participation comes more through sharing than through contributing news themselves," according to a report by the Pew Internet and American Life Project.

- **Social media:** News organizations are using social networks such as Facebook, Twitter, YouTube, tumblr and others to connect with readers and viewers.

CITIZEN JOURNALISM

Citizen journalism is another type of participation by people who contribute to a news organization with blogs, reporting, news stories and other information. Social media contributors sometimes perform the same functions. Other sites are operated completely by citizens who volunteer or are paid to produce content. Many of the citizen journalism sites are considered "hyperlocal," providing local news and information for a neighborhood or small community within a larger area such as *The Oakland Local (http://oaklandlocal.com). The Twin Cities Daily Planet* is a successful hyperlocal site covering neighborhoods in the Minneapolis/St. Paul, Minn., area. The site has 100 media partners and bloggers.

It was one of 55 local news projects that received grants from J-Lab: The Institute for Interactive Journalism at American University's School of Communication with funding by the Knight Foundation. In a report evaluating the projects, J-Lab concluded that there is a high churn of citizen journalists on these sites. On the other hand, the report concluded that "social media is game-changing" by ushering in a new age for community journalism by "building phenomenal capacity for recruiting readers and writers."

ECONOMIC CHANGES IN MEDIA

The changing face of the media isn't just in the content and delivery of news; it is in the ownership of the largest media organizations. Economic forces created significant changes in major media companies at the start of the 21st century. Newspaper circulation was declining and the large media companies listed on the stock exchange were under pressure because of sagging stock profits for their shareholders. Print and broadcast news organizations cut staffs and resources. Two of the largest media organizations, Knight Ridder Inc. and the Tribune Company, sold their newspapers and TV stations.

Journalists who got into the business years ago with the idealistic notion that the primary concern of media companies was content became disillusioned by the emphasis on economics, and many quit or retired. The times were changing and the news business was just that — a business that was supposed to make a profit. But journalists didn't disappear; many of them formed new online ventures and found news-related jobs in other publications, businesses, public relations organizations and government agencies. Good journalism skills have broad application.

Partnerships

News organizations that were once fiercely competitive formed partnerships to share news stories in print and video as a way to cut costs. In South Florida, *The Miami Herald,* the *South Florida Sun-Sentinel* and the *Palm Beach Post* began sharing stories, and similar arrangements were created among newspapers in Maine, Ohio and Texas. The nature of competition has changed.

John Bartosek, former editor of the *Palm Beach Post,* said that the biggest competitor is not the other newspapers in Florida but other websites that readers use. "We need to think about how much time and money and people are we going to throw at beating another newspaper when things like websites exist that are competitive with both of us," he said in an article in *Editor & Publisher.*

Partnerships with university journalism departments are another way news organizations are expanding their coverage without expanding their staffs. *The New York Times* has a partnership with City University of New York where journalism students write blogs to cover communities in Brooklyn and New Jersey and with New York University journalism students to cover other communities within the metro area.

AOL has created a partnership with several universities called "PatchU," which offers internships and coursework as well as freelance opportunities at Patch publications, which are online sites that provide news and information in hundreds of communities.

Students can write stories and cover local events in multimedia form and integrate social media for the Patch sites.

Pay walls

Would you be willing to pay for online news that you currently can get free? If your answer is "No," you are among the majority of consumers who say they would turn to other sites rather than pay for information they now get free. That's a dilemma facing news organizations that are seeking ways to pay rising costs for their online publications. With advertising revenues declining and competition rising from other websites, news organizations have discussed charging for access to some or all of their online content. Several news sites have created pay walls, which "wall off" or block access to certain content. Whether they are successful remains to be seen. The cost of applications for digital delivery to smart phones and tablets will also affect the future of charges for online information.

CHANGES IN ONLINE NEWS

The Web has changed the nature of news in other ways:

Continual Deadlines: When a news story breaks, reporters at many newspaper and broadcast organizations are expected to file the story immediately for the Web and update major stories online throughout the day. Twitter has changed the nature of breaking news as well. Reporters may tweet updates continually during a major incident.

Interactive Content: One of the main distinctions of online news is the ability to interact with readers. Web news stories often feature polls, chats and questions at the end of stories to prompt readers to express their views as well as requests to comment on a news organization's social media site. More than ever, writers need to consider how their audience will be affected by the story, regardless of the medium.

Related Links: Online news is accompanied by links to related information, so a news story may no longer be a single entity. Traditional print and broadcast news stories also refer readers and viewers to related online information. Social media sites such as Twitter also feature links to blogs, photos, videos and other media content.

Nonlinear Structure: Print and broadcast news stories are written in linear order — to be read or heard from beginning to end as if in a straight line. Because the Web features links and multimedia features, it creates a nonlinear environment, meaning readers may access content in any order they choose. Although many online news stories are still linear, original Web content is organized in more related pieces. Instead of one story containing all the information, nonlinear news might be split into separate parts for background, profiles, timelines, databases and multimedia.

Databases: Many news sites offer databases that you can search for information about health, school test scores or crime statistics in your community. For example,

The Philadelphia Inquirer (*www.philly.com/inquirer*) offers an annual report card allowing you to search a database for public and private schools in Pennsylvania and New Jersey to find out about school test scores and related facts for schools in these areas. Many other news sites also offer searchable databases for crime statistics, school test scores and other community information.

Personalized Journalism: In addition to blogs as a form of personalized journalism, online news sites are reaching out to users by asking them to contribute their personal stories on the organization's website or its Facebook or Twitter pages.

CHANGING VALUES

Several news organizations such as the Radio Television Digital News Association are developing special ethical codes for social media. With slight adjustments, these codes mirror the ones that apply to mainstream media. However, a study of executives from RTDNA and the American Society of Newspaper Editors revealed that these news leaders have some serious concerns about the effect the Internet and social networks are having on news values.

The study by the Project for Excellence in Journalism revealed that more than 62 percent of executives from print and 67 percent from broadcast media think accuracy is declining due in part to the speed of producing news and to social media. "I worry that journalistic standards are dropping in that blogging and celebrity gossip and tweets are being confused with reporting and editing that passes a rigorous standard," one broadcast executive wrote. A newspaper editor concurred and added, "There is too much emphasis, I believe, on getting information fast even at the expense of accuracy, thoroughness and fairness."

THE COACHING METHOD

Whether you are writing for print, broadcast or online media, you still need to master the basic skills of reporting and writing. The coaching method is a way of helping writers discover their problems and learn techniques to solve them. An editor may concentrate on the results of your writing and fix the story, but a coach concentrates on the process of writing. A coach doesn't stress how you failed to write a good story; a coach stresses how you can succeed.

Like a basketball coach who trains players how to improve their techniques on the court, a writing coach trains writers how to perfect their techniques in the craft. This book aims to serve as a surrogate writing coach by anticipating the problems writers might have and offering solutions. It features tips from leading writing coaches and award-winning journalists.

The coaching method in this book has four phases:

1. **Conceive the idea:** At this stage you develop the idea for the story. If you are covering an event, such as a meeting or an accident, you need to start with the idea — the main point of what occurred. If you are writing a news story about a problem in

ETHICS Plagiarism and Fabrication

THE CASE: (THIS situation is based on the case of Jayson Blair, a former reporter for *The New York Times*.) A reporter for your campus newspaper quickly becomes a star by charming editors and professors, volunteering for stories and writing prolifically. His stories are filled with descriptive details and human-interest features that gain him a reputation as an outstanding writer. But the editor of the paper is concerned because several of his stories require corrections after they are printed, and the editor can't trace some of the sources. The editor and some staffers complain to journalism professors about this reporter's inaccuracies, but the professors dismiss the complaints as jealousy over this rising star.

The reporter lands a prestigious internship with a large daily newspaper and later is hired full time even before he graduates from journalism school. He shows much promise and gets assigned to major national stories, but during his four years at the paper his stories require 50 corrections, and one of his editors thinks he should be fired. However, top management at the newspaper excuses the reporter because he says that he has had several personal problems.

His trail of deception, plagiarism and fabrication is uncovered after the newspaper is notified that he plagiarized a story written by one of his former campus newspaper colleagues, who was working at a newspaper in San Antonio. The story was only one of at least 36 articles containing plagiarized or fabricated quotes and facts. The reporter resigns, and the newspaper publishes an extensive front-page Sunday story explaining the situation and apologizing to readers.

Dilemma:

- What steps could have or should have been taken to prevent this situation from happening?
- Should a reporter be fired as soon as the first incident of plagiarism or fabrication is discovered?
- Should a reporter whose stories require numerous corrections be fired?
- What would you have done if you were the campus editor or his editor at that newspaper?
- What can be done to prevent plagiarism and fabrication in the media?

Ethical values: Accuracy, credibility.

Ethical guidelines: According to the code of ethics of the Society of Professional Journalists, "Seek truth and report it. Test the accuracy of information from all sources and exercise care to avoid inadvertent error. Deliberate distortion is never permissible."

your community, you still start with a central idea, which is the focus of your story. Once you begin reporting, you may discover some information that is more important than your original focus. Thus, you should be flexible and decide the focus for writing after you collect the material.

2. **Collect:** This is the reporting stage. Before you conduct your interview, you should look for background information: Check online sources and any available documents or clips from previous stories about your subject and your sources. Then interview sources, and gather as much information as you can about your topic. Don't rely on one source; seek several points of view. Ask more questions and take more notes than you plan to use. You should also jot down your observations and gather as many details as possible.

3. **Construct:** This is the planning and writing stage. Begin with a plan for your story developed around the focus, the main idea of your story. Then go through your notes

and mark only the information related to that focus. Like a carpenter building a house, you need a blueprint. A good writer does not write a story without a plan. Jot down a few key words to indicate how you will organize your story. Then write a first draft of your story. You may revise your original draft in the next step.

4. **Correct:** After you have written your story, read it and make any necessary changes. You may decide to add or delete information or to completely reorganize the story during this stage. You should also check the spelling of all names and the accuracy of facts, and you should correct grammar, style and typing errors.

These four steps constitute the basic process for all news stories. In the coming chapters you will learn many techniques for reporting and writing news. But first you need to understand the components of a news story.

QUALITIES OF NEWS

Definitions of news are changing. But these are some traditional qualities of news stories:

Timeliness: An event that happened the day of or day before publication or an event that is due to happen in the immediate future is considered timely. In broadcast and online media, timeliness is considered "immediacy" and is even more crucial. When stories are posted online immediately after they happen or broadcast several times a day, you have to consider how to update them frequently. Some events that happened in the past may also be considered timely if they are printed on an anniversary of the event, such as one, five or 10 years after the incident. Timeliness answers this reader's question: Why are you telling me this now? The following story was timely because it was published the day after the accident:

A bus loaded with elementary school children crashed head-on into a compact car in southwestern Jefferson County yesterday, injuring 24 students and the two drivers.

— *The* (Louisville, Ky.) *Courier-Journal*

If that story had been written for broadcast or online media, the angle would have been updated to report the current condition of the students and drivers.

Proximity: An event may be of interest to local readers because it happened in or close to the community. This story would be of particular interest to residents in the Oregon community where the man lived:

A 71-year-old former psychologist received an eight-year prison sentence Monday for running the most sophisticated indoor marijuana growing operation ever discovered in Clackamas County.

Authorities said Arvord E. Belden of Estacada may be the oldest man ever sentenced to federal prison for a drug crime in Oregon.

— DAVE HOGAN, *The* (Portland) *Oregonian*

Unusual Nature: Out-of-the-ordinary events, a bizarre or rare occurrence, or people engaged in unusual activities are considered newsworthy, as in this story:

MAN TICKETED FOR WALKING HIS LIZARD

FORT LAUDERDALE, Fla. — Walking your dog along the beach here is illegal — and so is lounging with your lizard, Chris DeMango found out. Mortimer, DeMango's 20-pound purple-tongued monitor lizard, complete with matching pink doll sweater and leash, was out for exercise Monday. DeMango said a walk makes Mortimer more docile, but police said it makes him an illegal lizard — animals are banned on the beach. DeMango was ticketed, and his lizard law violation could cost him 60 days in jail and a $500 fine, said police spokesman Ott Cefkin. DeMango was not amused. "I would think that would be the most absurd thing, if I were to go to jail for this," he grumbled.

— *St. Petersburg* (Fla.) *Times*

Human Interest: People like stories about people who have special problems, achievements or experiences; profiles of people who have overcome difficulties or who seek to improve society inspire readers. This example about a couple who spent $6,000 looking for their lost cat combines human interest and an unusual story:

Five-year-old Marble used to hide in the box springs of a spare bed in Bill and Carol Deckers' Denver home.

Now the Deckers' cat is hiding somewhere in the woods near Carthage, Mo.

Since Marble escaped from the couple's recreational vehicle Aug. 18, the Deckers have spent more than $6,000 trying to get her back.

"We taught her to live with us and we owe it to her," said Carol Decker, 41, a part-time accountant who gave up her job to look for Marble. . . .

Since losing Marble, the Deckers have put up posters and placed newspaper ads in Colorado, Missouri and Oklahoma, and contacted a psychic to locate her, to no avail.

The Deckers have returned to the site, often sleeping outdoors in the hope that their presence would draw Marble to them.

— TILLIE FONG, *Rocky Mountain* (Denver) *News*

Conflict: Stories involving conflicts that people have with government or other people are often newsworthy, especially when the conflict reflects local problems.

> LANSING — Opponents of a new law that makes it easier to obtain a permit to carry a concealed weapon in most Michigan communities are preparing a petition drive to block the law's implementation.
>
> — DAWSON BELL, *Detroit Free Press*

Here is an example of a story that combines conflict with human interest and unusual qualities:

> The family expected to mourn Anthony Romeo, who died of heart disease in September at his Seffner home. Instead, they found a stranger in his coffin.
>
> The Hillsborough Medical Examiner's Office had shipped the wrong body to the funeral home.
>
> The mix-up so upset Romeo's son Joseph that he filed suit Monday against Hillsborough County, the Brandon funeral home and the private courier that delivered the body.
>
> — RACHEL L. SWARNS, *St. Petersburg* (Fla.) *Times*

Impact: Reaction stories to news events or news angles that affect readers have impact, especially when major national stories or tragedies occur in any community. Newspapers often seek local angles by writing how people in their areas are affected by the news, as in this story following a massive tsunami that killed thousands of people in 11 Southeast Asian countries:

> Scientists at the West Coast and Alaska Tsunami Warning Center for years worked on a windy hilltop just outside downtown Palmer, far from the reach of potentially disastrous waves and public notice.
>
> But with global attention on tsunami readiness galvanized by the Indian Ocean waves that killed more than 160,000 people, the center is poised for a major upgrade that could protect Alaskans as well as coastal residents around the world, a top federal administrator told staffers at the center.
>
> — ZAZ HOLLANDER, *Anchorage Daily News*

Some additional qualities of news to consider:

Helpfulness: Consumer, health and other how-to stories help readers cope with their lives. Online news sites abound with helpful stories.

> If your head spins at the torrent of medical studies that fills newspapers, magazines and TV, join the club. It seems that each day brings another round of studies contradicting last month's hot results.

One day vitamin E is found to prevent cancer. Next, it is suspected of causing it. Margarine is good. No, it's bad.

One can almost hear a collective scream of frustration across the land.

Studies are the cornerstone of medical progress, showing doctors and patients the way to longer, healthier lives. But they can also lead us astray.

To try to help you through the hype and hustle, here's a basic outline of what studies are, how they differ, what they can tell us and where they can go wrong. Call it A User's Guide to Medical Studies. Or, How to Follow Health News Without Having a Stroke.

— PHILLIP E. CANUTO, *Knight-Ridder/Tribune News Service*

Celebrities: People who are well-known for their accomplishments — primarily entertainers, athletes or people who have gained fame for achievements, good or bad — attract a lot of attention. But celebrity news has become so popular that some journalists are concerned it is displacing news and pandering to the public's desire for entertainment.

Ted Koppel, former anchor of the TV show "Nightline," said in a "Frontline" interview: "To the extent that we're now judging journalism by the same standards that we apply to entertainment — in other words, give the public what it wants, not necessarily what it ought to hear, what it ought to see, what it needs, but what it wants — that may prove to be one of the greatest tragedies in the history of American journalism."

Entertainment: Stories that amuse readers, make them feel good or help them enjoy their leisure time have entertainment value. In a broad sense, many of the news features in sports and lifestyle sections can be classified as entertainment. These stories often involve celebrities or have human-interest qualities. But they are also controversial. The line between news and entertainment is not clear, especially in coverage of celebrities as stated in the previous item. However, this story combines qualities of human interest and unusual nature to entertain or amuse readers:

When Marjorie Clapprood opened her W-2 form from the state of Massachusetts, she was shocked.

The form said she was dead.

Boy, when you're out, you're out, said Clapprood, a former state representative who lost her bid for re-election.

But she was by no means alone.

State W-2 tax forms mailed recently listed all 199 members of last year's Legislature as dead.

Some residents of the financially troubled state suspected that all along.

But members of last year's Legislature are taking exception to their recent demise, which was caused by a clerical error.

Clapprood, for one, said she isn't about to let the IRS consider her dead.

"They owe me money, I think," she said.

Corrected forms are to be mailed to the resurrected shortly.

— TOM TOROK, *The Philadelphia Inquirer*

Issues or Problems in the Community: These stories usually include qualities such as conflict and proximity. The *St. Cloud* (Minn.) *Times* combined the trends of reader involvement with issues important to minorities in a series called "Open or Intolerant?" The newspaper sought opinions from teenagers of different races as well as from police, city leaders and residents about police treatment of young people of color.

Since moving to St. Cloud three years ago, Jacob "Cisco" Owens says he has been hassled, detained, pulled over and provoked by St. Cloud police officers more times than he can remember.

Owens, a 16-year-old Apollo High School junior, admits he's been in trouble a few times for minor things. But for every time he's done something, anything, wrong, he swears he can identify seven more times he's been confronted by police when he's done nothing at all.

"And almost all the time they ask me if I'm in a gang. It makes me angry that they just assume. It's just a given that I'm treated like that," he says. "Just because I'm young and black, I'm treated like a thug." Dozens of young people of different races in St. Cloud say it's no secret: Police here are known for targeting minority youth for bogus traffic stops, tough talk, and sometimes, rough treatment when responding to calls.

— LEE ROOD, *St. Cloud* (Minn.) *Times*

Trends: Stories may indicate patterns or shifts in issues that influence readers' lives, such as increases in crime, social issues and other forces in society.

Many Milwaukee area public libraries no longer have strict "SH!" policies.

Libraries are shedding their image as quiet, somber places for bookworms and students only. Instead, today's libraries offer a wide variety of materials and programs in an effort to appeal to more people.

— LAWRENCE SUSSMAN, *Milwaukee Journal Sentinel*

HARD NEWS AND FEATURES

News falls into two basic categories: hard news and soft news. "Hard news" includes stories of a timely nature about events or conflicts that have just happened or are about to happen, such as crimes, fires, meetings, protest rallies, speeches and testimony in court cases. The hard-news approach is basically an account of what happened, why it happened and how readers will be affected. These stories have immediacy.

"Soft news" is defined as news that entertains or informs, with an emphasis on human interest and novelty and less immediacy than hard news. For example, a profile about a man who designs model airplanes or a story about the effectiveness of diets would be considered soft news.

CONVERGENCE COACH

TRAIN YOURSELF
to think for multimedia.

- Compare online news stories with those in your local newspaper. Are they the same, or do they offer links, polls, questions and other related features? If your local TV news station has a website, compare that site with the newspaper's website.

- Learn to think interactively. Analyze interactive online features such as polls, games, message boards and databases in your local websites or others, such as CNN (*www.cnn.com*).

- Plan to update stories. Analyze how major news sites continually update their stories.

- Consider the role of blogs and social media comments. Analyze blogs for their news or entertainment value. Check journalists' blogs at *www.cyberjournalist.net*.

- Consider the nature of your audience. Compare the *Lawrence Journal-World* site, www2.ljworld.com/, with its companion site, *www.lawrence.com*.

- Become a visual thinker. Compare the visuals for a news story covered in your newspaper, on TV and online. Consider visuals for the stories you will produce.

Soft news can also be stories that focus on people, places or issues that affect readers' lives. These types of stories are called "feature stories." A story about the growing number of babies suffering from AIDS could be considered a soft-news story. It isn't less important than hard news, but it isn't news that happened overnight. However, a feature story can be based on a news event. Instead of being just a factual account of the event, it features or focuses on a particular angle, such as human-interest reactions.

If the action or event occurred the same day as or the day before publication of the newspaper, the event is called "breaking news." Here is an example of the lead of a breaking-news story from a Saturday edition:

Tornadoes rapped Topeka and southeast Shawnee County Friday afternoon, damaging seven homes and sending residents scurrying for cover.
No one was injured by the short, severe storm that struck unexpectedly.

— STEVE FRY, *Topeka* (Kan.) *Capital-Journal*

The preceding example of a hard-news story tells readers what happened. The newspaper also printed this feature story focusing on people affected by the storm:

Becky Clark of Topeka was told the tornado sirens that sounded Friday afternoon were a false alarm.
Then she got home from work and saw her back yard at 2411 S.E. Gemini Ave. in the Aquarian Acres neighborhood.
"I couldn't believe it," she said.
A tornado had lifted up the family pontoon boat, which was parked in the back yard, and tossed it into the family swimming pool, crushing part of the boat.

"It just wanted to get in the water," said Joe Clark, Becky's husband. "I guess it was tired of being in dry dock. . . ."

— JOE TASCHLER, *Topeka* (Kan.) *Capital-Journal*

The hard-news story about the storm was the main story, called a "mainbar." Because the accompanying feature story was a different angle on the same topic, it was a "sidebar" packaged with the main story.

But many other features in a newspaper do not have a breaking-news peg. They simply focus on interesting people or topics. For example, the *Boca Raton* (Fla.) *News* printed a feature story on the growing popularity of waterbeds, a topic of interest to its readers.

THE IMPORTANCE OF VISUALS

The presentation of a story with photographs or graphics is crucial. Broadcast media depend on visuals for the majority of stories. Studies by The Poynter Institute in St. Petersburg, Fla., show an increased emphasis on graphic devices and color in print media.

In one study, called "Eyes on the News," researchers measured the movements of people's eyes as they read the newspaper. The results of this study, also known as the Eye Trac study, show that readers are drawn to color photographs first, then headlines, cutlines (captions), briefs (stories abbreviated to one to three paragraphs) and a number of other graphic devices called points of entry — points where the reader enters a story. Some of those eye-catching points include sub-headlines and quotations displayed in larger type within the story.

The study also concluded that most people only scan the newspaper, looking at headlines and graphics, and that they read very few stories all the way through. The average reader skims about 25 percent of the stories in the newspaper but thoroughly reads only half of those (about 12 percent), the study concluded.

Mario Garcia, who co-authored the Poynter study and is a world-renowned consultant on newspaper design, says the majority of readers today do not remember life without television, so visual elements are crucial in a newspaper. "The marriage of visual and words has to begin early — from the first time you learn reporting," he says. Garcia now says the iPad will have a dramatic effect on news.

A subsequent study tracking eye movements of online readers determined that graphics were less important in online news. The study by The Poynter Institute and Stanford University found that online readers focused first on text in news websites rather than informational graphics. A follow-up study in 2007 of online readers revealed that online readers will read a story thoroughly if they are interested in it, contrary to earlier studies that claimed online readers had short attention spans.

Although television news depends on video, reporters in all media need to consider audio or video that may accompany a story on the Web. In addition, reporters and public relations practitioners need to consider graphic devices that will enhance the content of a news story or news release.

That is the emphasis at the *Reno* (Nev.) *Gazette-Journal,* a Gannett newspaper that makes extensive use of graphics. Reporters are expected to visualize their stories as a total package involving photos and graphics.

The emphasis is on using verbal and visual tools that will make information clear to readers. For example, a story about rare water spouts from Lake Tahoe was accompanied by the graphic shown below, which explained how water spouts are created. The information was not repeated in the text.

In this multimedia world, planning visual elements is a crucial part of any news presentation.

Graphic explaining a natural disaster.

Source: GNS research

Reprinted with permission, *Reno Gazette-Journal*

EXERCISES

1 Visual awareness: Try this experiment to test your reading habits. Bring to class a copy of a newspaper you haven't read. Read the newspaper as you would for pleasure. Place a check on the first item you look at — a picture, graphic, headline or story. Mark the stories you read, and place an X at the point in the story where you decide to stop reading. Where did your eye go first? Why are visual elements so important? Now analyze which stories you read and how much of them you read. Where did you stop on most stories? Why? Keep in mind that because you are a journalism student, you may read more than the average reader.

2 Journal: Keep a journal of your reading or viewing habits of news for three days. Write a paragraph each day about the kinds of stories you read and didn't read, how many you read all the way through, and how many you read just through the headline or the first few paragraphs. Note how you accessed the stories — online, via a mobile phone or tablet device or from a print publication or TV newscast. Analyze your preferences. Then interview three other people — students, neighbors or strangers — and ask them what kinds of stories they do and don't read in print and online. Ask where they get the majority of their news — from print, broadcast or online media. Write a summary of your findings.

3 Online news ideas: Either in small groups or as a class, brainstorm topics and ideas that you would want to read in an online newspaper or magazine. Brainstorm at least three interactive features for an online college newspaper.

4 Qualities of news: Analyze your local or campus newspaper on the front page and/or local section. Identify the qualities of news of the main stories. Now do the same for a TV news broadcast. Jot down the stories in a 30-minute telecast and identify the qualities of news in each segment.

 CourseMate

COACHING TIPS

State the focus, the main idea, of your story in one sentence.

To **find your lead,** ask yourself: What is most important or most interesting?

Write the story in a **conversational tone** as though you were telling a friend.

Consider how your story will **affect readers.**

Consider what **photographs, graphics, audio or video** your story needs for print, broadcast or online delivery.

Consider how your story could be promoted or discussed on **Twitter or other social media.**

kajakiki/Shutterstock.com

Too many stories fail to answer the reader's most challenging question: So what?

— **ROY PETER CLARK,**
writing coach and author

CHAPTER 2
The Basic News Story

THE BASIC NEWS STORY IS TOLD UPSIDE DOWN. IT USUALLY IS CALLED A hard-news story. That doesn't mean it should be hard to read — quite the contrary. It really should be called an easy-news story because the facts are presented in a direct form that makes it easy for the reader to get the most important information quickly.

A hard-news story often presents the result of a news event first, so the key facts are in the first few paragraphs. If a news story were a mystery story, you would solve the mystery in the beginning and then devote the rest of the story to telling the reader how and why it happened.

For example, if state officials who regulate higher education — often called the Board of Regents — met yesterday to discuss an increase in tuition at universities in your state, you wouldn't write that the Board of Regents met to consider a tuition increase. You would give the results. What did the regents decide? Who is affected? Here is an example:

Tuition at the University of Alaska will increase 22 percent in the next two years, according to a budget proposal approved by the university's Board of Regents.

Undergraduate fees will increase by $128 in the fall and by another $365 in the following year, raising the total tuition for in-state students to $5,754.

The board's action prompted widespread protests by students who demonstrated on the Anchorage campus and voiced their anger on Facebook and blogs.

This direct approach to news is effective in all types of media: print, broadcast, online and for news releases in public relations. It is especially important when writing for small screens on mobile media, which is an increasing form of delivery for news.

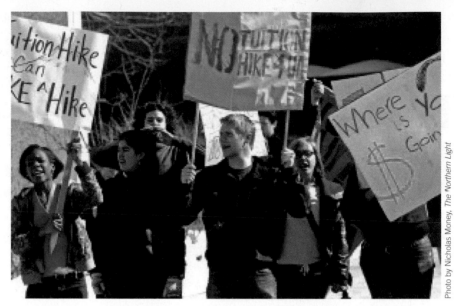

Students at the University of Alaska Anchorage protest tuition increases.

FINDING THE FOCUS

Not all basic news stories have to start with such a direct approach. Some stories start with a storytelling approach, such as an anecdote about a person or place. Regardless of how you start your story, all news stories are developed around one main point — a focus. The rest of the story should contain quotes, facts and information to support that focus. Because readers and viewers are bombarded with so much information these days, they want to know the point of the story quickly, so you need to put the focus in the first sentence or within the first few paragraphs of the story. The following questions will help you find a focus:

What's the Story About? To determine the focus of a news story, ask yourself, "What's the story about?" Try to answer that question in one simple sentence. Think of focus as a headline for your story. How would you describe the main idea in a few words? What makes this story newsworthy? How would you express the focus in a tweet of 140 characters?

How Are Readers or Viewers Affected? Why should readers or viewers care about your story? This is the "so-what" factor. Is there something important or interesting or unusual that will affect your audience? Is there something that will inspire readers to blog or tweet about your story?

How Would You Tell the Story to a Friend? Another way to determine your focus is to use the "tell-a-friend" technique. This is a natural conversational method, particularly important in broadcast writing.

Imagine that your friend asks what the story is about and what happened. Chances are that you might talk about the most interesting information first.

In this example, the focus is in the first sentence, which is the lead. It tells what the story is about and how it affects the reader. It is also written in a conversational tone. The second paragraph and the rest of the story provide facts and information to support this main idea.

| *Headline Focus in the lead* | **Eye on privacy at work** If you have a job, you have no privacy when it comes to using the office computer. | From monitoring e-mails to capturing instant messages among friends, employers can do as they see fit with the information passing through a company network. — *Chicago Tribune* | *Second paragraph supporting the lead* |

BASIC QUESTIONS

All news stories answer some basic questions: who, what, when, where, why and how?

As newspaper readership declines and competition increases because of all-day coverage in broadcast and online media, editors increasingly want answers to these questions: So what? What is the significance to readers? How can you make readers see and care about the story?

Eugene Roberts, a former editor at *The New York Times* and *The Philadelphia Inquirer,* tells this story about how his editor influenced him to write vividly enough to make the reader see. Roberts was a reporter at the *Goldsboro News-Argus* in North Carolina. His editor, Henry Belk, was blind. Many days Belk would call in Roberts to read his stories to him, and Belk would yell, "Make me see. You aren't making me see."

Advice from Roberts: "The best reporters, whatever their backgrounds or their personalities, share that consummate drive to get to the center of a story and then put the reader on the scene."

Much has changed in the media since Roberts was a reporter many years ago. But his advice is just as relevant today. Identify the center of the story, which is the focus, gather information to make the reader see, and write a compelling story to make the reader care.

ELEMENTS OF THE BASIC NEWS STORY

News stories in all media share some common elements. Every news story is based on one main idea — the focus. The basic news story structure includes a headline and three general parts: a beginning, called the "lead," a middle, called the "body," and an ending. After you determine the focus, write the lead and nut graph if needed. Here are the basic parts of a news story:

Headline

The headline is the line on top of the story that tells the reader what the story is about. The headline usually identifies the main idea of the story so the reader can decide whether to access the full story.

Online news sites and many newspapers today are using secondary headlines — called "deck heads," "summary lines" or "summary blurbs." The two headlines together give the reader a quick overview of the story's content.

Headline	**Salmon spawn a new crisis**
Deck head, summary line or summary blurb	Dwindling numbers and fading strength threaten to add the fish to the list of endangered species.

— Los Angeles Times

If you are having trouble identifying the main point of a story, think of a headline for it. Broadcast news scripts don't include headlines, but the concept will help you find focus.

Lead

At the beginning of the story, the hook that tells the reader what the story is about is called the "lead." A good lead entices the reader to continue reading. In a hard-news story, the lead usually is written in one sentence — the first sentence of the story — and gives the most important information about the event. But even a basic story can have a creative lead, called a "soft lead" or "feature lead."

Summary Leads: The most common type of lead on a hard-news story is called a "summary lead" because it summarizes the main points about what happened. It answers the questions of who, what, when, where, why and how. The rest of the story elaborates about what, why and how.

Hard-news leads do not have to answer all those questions in the first sentence if doing so would make the lead too long and difficult to read.

Shorter leads of fewer than 35 words are preferable, but that number is only a guideline. With the increasing delivery of news for mobile media, brief writing is better for readers accessing information on their smart phones.

The writer has to decide which elements are most important to stress in the first sentence. The summary lead in the following example stresses who, what, where and when; the rest of the story gives more details, such as the names of the professor and the suspect:

A Northwestern University professor of hearing sciences was shot and seriously wounded in a university parking lot Thursday.

Feature Leads: A lead that starts with a story or description about a person, place or incident, is called a "feature lead" or an "anecdotal lead." Many feature leads begin with a description of a person who is a key source in the story, and the focus of the story is explained in another paragraph.

Lead When he was a little girl, Leo said he hated wearing dresses. Today the Ball State University graduate student is sitting in his office, clad in khakis and a button shirt.

At first encounter, Leo, who asked for his last name not to be used, looks like a typical thirty-something guy; sideburns, goatee, a little pudgy but nothing out of the ordinary. In a raspy tenor voice, he talks about the store he and his wife own, about their cats and about how he quit smoking three months ago and can't live without nicotine gum.

But Leo's demure appearance betrays his extraordinary past. In 1999 he began the process of physically transitioning from a woman named Lynette into a man named Leo. . . .   *Focus*

— ADRIAN SHARP,
Ball State University

Nut Graph

The "nut graph" is a sentence or paragraph that states the focus — the main point — of the story. It should tell in a nutshell what the story is about and why it is newsworthy. The term was coined more than 50 years ago by *The Wall Street Journal* in a memo to its staff. The memo said a story must have one central theme that must be expressed in a "nutshell summary" high in the story. The concept of the nut graph has since become a standard formula for all news stories.

In a hard-news story with a direct summary lead, the lead contains the focus, so you don't need a separate nut graph. But the nut graph is crucial when a story starts with a feature lead because the reader has to wait for a few paragraphs to find out the reason for the story.

The nut graph should be placed high in the story, generally by the third to fifth paragraph. But if the lead is very compelling, the nut graph could come later. Rigid rules can ruin good writing.

Anecdotal lead SANTA CRUZ — Until Hollywood calls, film major Wesley Adkins said he's OK with being a struggling artist. But by the time he graduates, the junior may wish he was a business major. Already his student loans total $25,000.

Nut graph As the cost of attending UC Santa Cruz, or for that matter most any university, has skyrocketed over the past three years, mounting debt from student aid has kept pace. More and more students are leaving school, including many at this weekend's UCSC graduation ceremonies, with huge financial burdens.

— *Santa Cruz* (Calif.) *Sentinel*

Quotes or Sound Bites

After the lead, the body of the story should support the focus with information from sources, quotes or facts that explain the main idea. If you have a good quote or sound bite from a source, it should be placed high in the story after the lead or nut graph. The first quote that backs up the lead is called the "lead quote" or the "augmenting quote." It is usually the strongest quote you have, and it supports the concept in the lead without repeating the same information or wording. In broadcast news a good sound bite following the lead is equivalent to the lead quote.

A lead quote isn't required in all stories, but a strong quote or sound bite within a paragraph or two after the lead helps make the story more interesting. If the lead does not contain all the information about who, what, when, where, why and how, these questions should be answered in the body of the story. In this example, the lead quote is in the third paragraph:

PENSACOLA, Fla. — Soon-to-be graduate student Michael Kearney hasn't chosen a major yet — but give him time, he's only 11.

Michael will begin tackling graduate studies at the University of West Florida in Pensacola this summer.

"We don't push him," said his mother, Cassidy Kearney. "He pushes us. We just try and keep up with him."

— The Associated Press

Impact

Whenever possible, the writer should explain how the news affects readers. The "impact" sentence or paragraph should answer these questions: What is the significance of this story? What in the story makes the reader care? Sometimes the impact is explained in the lead or in the nut graph; sometimes it is lower in the story, in an explanatory paragraph.

Not all stories can show direct impact on readers, but they should all have a clear paragraph explaining the reason for the story. In some stories, such as police stories, the impact is that the news happened in the community and should be of interest to local residents.

Home users are now the top target for Internet attackers, who are launching increasingly sophisticated attacks.

That's the sobering warning from Symantec's latest Internet security threat report, released today.

— The Vancouver Sun

Online news sites provide impact in several interactive ways: Databases let readers search statistics about education, crime or property values in their communities;

interactive calculators give readers a chance to figure what a tax increase might cost them; feedback questions, polls and blogs ask readers to comment on issues. Social media sites encourage readers and viewers to interact with the news.

Attribution

Where did you get the information? Who told you these facts? How can the reader be sure what you say is true? Attribution, which identifies the source of the information, can provide those answers. With the proliferation of social media (blogs, Twitter and other sites), it is even more difficult to determine the validity of information. Attribution adds credibility for the story.

You need to attribute all quotes — exact wording of statements that people made — and much information that you did not witness. If the information is common knowledge or indisputable, you do not have to attribute it. You also need to attribute any statements that express opinions.

No attribution needed — common knowledge	Millions of people in the U.S. and other countries use cell phones.	Drivers using cell phones are four times more likely to cause a crash than other drivers, according to a Harvard University study.	*Attribution needed — not common knowledge*

The attribution should be in the lead for controversial or accusatory information, but in many other cases it can be delayed so it doesn't clutter the lead. Police stories often have attribution in the lead, especially if you get the information by telephone or if the information is accusatory:

Lead with attribution	ST. PETERSBURG, Fla. — A 15-year-old boy was stabbed twice in the chest Thursday afternoon when he apparently tried to break up a fight in a crowded parking lot at Northeast High School, authorities said.	Police and school officials said the stabbing, believed to have occurred after one student took another's hat, was the first they could recall at Pinellas County schools. — *St. Petersburg* (Fla.) *Times*	*Backup*

In the next example, general attribution is in the lead, but the specific attribution is in the third paragraph. The sources for the study are too cumbersome to use in the lead.

Lead with general attribution	A smoky bar may be more harmful to your health than a city street filled with diesel truck fumes, according to a new study.	Smoky bars and casinos have up to 50 times more cancer-causing particles than air in highways and city streets	

Backup with specific attribution

clogged with diesel trucks, the study says.

Indoor air pollution virtually disappears when smoking is banned, according to the study published in the *Journal of* *Occupational and Environmental Medicine* and partially funded by the Robert Wood Johnson Foundation of New Jersey, a philanthropic organization devoted to health care.

Context/Background

Is there any history or background the reader needs in order to understand how a problem or action occurred? Put the story in perspective. If the story is about a fire, accident or crime, how many other incidents of this type have occurred in the community recently? Most stories need some background to explain the action, as in this example:

Lead

Lock your doors.
That's the advice of University of Iowa security chief Dan Hogan in light of recent reports of a prowler slipping into unlocked dormitory rooms at night.

"I can't stress that enough," he said. "It's a very serious situation."

Nut graph

Since Aug. 24, there have been six reports of a man entering women's rooms between 3 a.m. and 5:30 a.m. Five incidents were in Burge Hall and one was in Currier Hall.

Two times the man touched the sleeping women, Hogan said. But there was no force or violence. In each instance the man ran when the woman discovered him.

Backup with lead quote

More recently, a woman in Burge Hall heard someone at her door. She opened it and saw a man running down the hall, Hogan said.

Background

— VALOREE ARMSTRONG, *Iowa City Press-Citizen*

Elaboration

Supporting points related to the main issue constitute "elaboration." These can be statements, quotes or more detail to explain what happened, how and why the problem or action occurred and reactions to the event.

In this part of the story, seek other points of view to make sure you have balance and fairness. A story based on one source can be too biased. The preceding story about the University of Iowa continued with more explanation:

George Droll, director of residence services, said main doors to the halls were locked from midnight to 6 a.m. But each resident has a key. Some floors have 24-hour visitation.

Often students feel more secure than they should because the buildings are large and are home to many of their friends, he said.

Ending

The most common type of ending includes one of these elements: future action, a statement or quote that summarizes but does not repeat the previous information or more elaboration. If the future action is a key factor in the issue, it should be placed higher in the story. Avoid summary endings that repeat what you have already said. In a basic news story, end when you have no more new information to reveal.

The ending on the Iowa story follows the residence director's comments about why students feel secure in large buildings where they have friends:

Summary quote ending   "That's a strength, but it can also be a weakness in terms of people securing their rooms," Droll said.

Fairness and Accuracy

If the story involves conflict, you should always get comments from both or all sides of an issue. Avoid one-source stories. Also, make sure you attribute your sources; including information you use from websites, other news organizations and quotes or statements from people you interview.

A common order for a news story is structured in an inverted pyramid that might look like this:

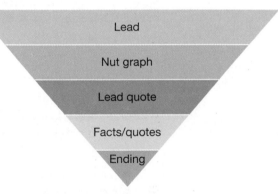

- Lead
- Nut graph (if a feature lead is used)
- Lead quote or compelling sound bite (if one is available)
- Supporting facts or impact
- More quotes and comments (or sound bites) from sources
- Additional information, facts or comments from sources
- Ending

Visuals

Visual elements such as photographs, charts and other graphic illustrations are crucial to news presentation in print and online information. Video is also a major asset for digital media. Visuals also enhance news releases or media kits in public relations. Here are some other visual elements used to enhance news stories:

Summary Blurb

A paragraph or sentence summarizing the story is called a "summary blurb." It is placed below the headline.

CONVERGENCE COACH

FOCUS IS CRUCIAL in print, broadcast and online news. If the focus of the story is unclear to broadcast viewers, they will turn to another channel. If the focus in an online story is not clear in the headline or summary blurb, readers may not even click into your online story. Ask yourself these questions:

- What is the most important idea that will entice viewers to listen to your story or online readers to click into your story?

- Before you write your story for any medium, write a focus sentence in fewer than 35 words. This also can be the lead of your story for an online site or a broadcast story. Now convert the focus into a headline of no more than six words for an online site. Here's an example:

> Headline: Campus booze arrests jump 24 percent

> Summary blurb under the headline: Sex, drug, weapons violations also increase.

- Online stories often have comment boxes or polls seeking readers' feedback. If you were seeking feedback on the main idea of your story, what question would you ask? The question may give you a clue for finding your focus.

- Have you answered the questions of who, what, where, when, how, why and explained the impact on the reader or viewer?

- If your story is about a conflict, have you contacted sources on both sides of the issue?

In online news the summary and lead of the story may be the same because the blurb may be on an index page linking to stories inside the site. But in print stories when the blurb is published directly over the story, the lead does not have to repeat the summary. It can be more creative, as in this example:

Headline *Summary* *blurb*	**Papers a lesson in criminology** *A USF professor follows a paper trail to a former student wanted on charges he sold term papers to criminology majors.* A. Engler Anderson's term papers weren't just bad. They were a crime, said one professor. Anderson, 31, is wanted on charges that he sold term papers to two University of South Florida students.	Their major? Criminology. The charge — selling a term paper or dissertation to another person — is only a second-degree misdemeanor, but if he is caught, Anderson will be held without bail because he failed to appear for a court hearing this week. — *St. Petersburg* (Fla.) *Times*

The story then explains how William Blount, chairman of the USF Criminology Department, received two papers that he thought were "awful" and then discovered they were written by Anderson, a former student.

Pull Quote A good quote might be broken out of the story, placed in larger type and used as a point of entry to entice the reader. Although a copy editor may decide which quotes to pull for graphic display, when you write your story, consider which quotes could be used to entice readers. Then use your best quotes high in your story. In a story explaining sexual harassment, this "pull quote" from an employment lawyer was used for emphasis:

> "I think what the law says is that if you hit on me, and I say, 'No way, Buster,' I'm entitled to have you accept my rejection of you, and it shouldn't interfere with my work."
>
> — JUDITH VLADECK, *Employment Lawyer*

Facts or Highlights Box Information from a story is sometimes set off in a "facts box," also called a "highlights box," for reading at a glance or providing key points in the story. A facts or highlights box can include the dates in a chronology or the main points of a proposal or meeting. It is especially useful for breaking statistics out of a story. Although some information from a facts box may be crucial to include in the story, the writer should guard against too much repetition. Facts boxes are effective in newspaper and online stories as well as in magazine and public relations articles.

CNN uses a highlights box at the top of major news stories on its website. The box contains four to five bulleted facts from the story to give readers a quick summary of the main points as in this story about the release of iPhone 4:

> **STORY HIGHLIGHTS**
> - iPhone has sharper screen, adds a gyroscope
> - Camera is improved, also has camera for video conferencing
> - Screen size stays the same; phone still requires contract with AT&T
>
> — CNN

Here is an example of a facts box that accompanied a story from *The Kansas City Star* about the dangers of lightning. These statistics were not repeated in the story:

> **LIGHTNING DEATHS AND INJURIES**
> Figures below were compiled from 35 years of U.S. lightning statistics.
>
> **Location of incident**
> - Open fields, recreation areas: 27%
> - Under trees (not golf): 14%

- Water-related (boating, fishing, swimming, etc.): 8%
- Golf/golf under trees: 5%

Month of most incidents

- July 30%

Deaths by state, top five

- Florida, Michigan, Texas, New York, Tennessee

Source: National Oceanic and Atmospheric Administration

Reprinted with permission from *The University Daily Kansan*

Infographic by Andrew Rohrback, *The University Daily Kansan*

Infographic A chart, map, graph or other illustration meant to provide information is an "infographic." Examples of infographics are diagrams of plane crashes or major accidents and illustrations explaining how something works. The most common type of infographic, called a "location map," pinpoints the location of an accident, a crime or any other major news event.

It is the reporter's responsibility to supply the information for those maps. So when you report a story that may need a map, make sure you gather information about the exact location of the event by noting the streets, the number of feet or yards from a spot where an explosion or major crime occurred, or any other crucial information that would help readers visualize the location. Stories for online delivery might use Google maps or other programs to illustrate the location.

The University Daily Kansan, the campus newspaper of the University of Kansas, used the location map and graphic shown here to accompany a story about a traffic accident in which a student was killed.

Many of the visual elements — such as headlines, boxes of information and summary sentences — are written by copy editors, and decisions about display are made by these editors or by page designers. However, reporters are expected to plan photos for their stories and to provide information for some of the graphics. When a chart, a graphic or a facts box will accompany your story, you need to consider whether the story needlessly duplicates information that could be presented visually. So in the writing process, don't just think about information to put into your story; think also about information to pull out for visual devices.

Audio and Video for Online Delivery Audio and video are crucial for television news stories, but if you are writing the story for a print publication, you still should think about sound and sight. Most news organizations have websites these days, so

SOCIAL MEDIA

YOU CAN USE social media concepts before and after you write your story.

- Use Twitter as a way to focus your story or conceive your lead by composing a tweet in 140 characters.

- Post a tweet to notify readers about the news or updates to your story.
- Consider how your story will affect readers; what tweets, blogs or posts will your story generate?
- Are there links that you should include in your tweets?
- Is there a blog that you could write about your story?
- Are there photos you might post on Flickr?

you should plan to record the interviews for posting on the organization's website. Even if you don't shoot the video yourself, you should discuss with an editor whether your story will need video so that a photographer can be assigned to the story. Also more news organizations — print and broadcast — are delivering information for mobile media in text and video forms.

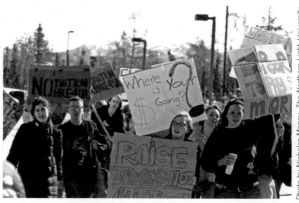

Photo by Nicholas Money, *The Northern Light*, University of Alaska Anchorage.

EXAMPLE OF BASIC NEWS STORY

The following example will show you how elements of the basic news story fit together for print or online delivery. This is a standard news story with a summary lead. The story is organized in "inverted pyramid" form, giving the most important information first and the rest in descending order of importance. This story contains most of the basic news elements described in this chapter:

Summary lead: who, what, when, where, why

'No say; we won't pay'
Participants protested through the halls of UAA

Shouts of "No say. We won't pay!" and "Chop from the top!" were heard ringing through the halls of the University of Alaska Anchorage on Wednesday, when students, teachers and community members alike grouped together to protest the proposed 23 percent tuition increase.

Many students may have heard the same protest before. Last spring a similar event was organized to protest the 22 percent increase that was proposed.

Now students are looking at a 23 percent increase, and a student group, USUAA, is hard

Backup for the lead

at work to stop this proposal. Started by an independent group of students, the protest grew into a statewide event. The universities in both Fairbanks and Juneau volunteered to start their own protests as well.

Elaboration/ background

Throughout the week, UA Chancellor Fran Ulmer sent out emails regarding the tuition increase saying, "Throughout the UA system, tuition comprises on average 11 percent of the overall UA budget. However at UAA, we rely more heavily on tuition, as it is 25 percent of our revenue. As a result, UAA's ability to support UAA programs is more reliant on tuition and tuition increases than the university as a whole."

Accompanying the chancellor's emails, were various charts and graphs depicting why the increase was necessary, and how UAA ranked compared to other schools in the country. One of the graphs showed that Alaska's 4.8 percent tuition increases for 2009–2010 were miniscule compared to that of California State University, which was a whopping 27.1 percent increase.

Even so, students still don't have the money to afford the continuously increasing tuition.

Everyone was invited to stand in front of the Student Union at 2:15 p.m. wearing black to support the cause to dismiss the 2011–2012 tuition increase. Teachers were also asked to release their classes at 2 p.m. so that students could have the chance to participate in the protest.

Standing atop a picnic bench, Amie Stanley, senior political science and marketing major, took the lead in the protest, gathering the attention of the onlookers, her voice booming into the megaphone and echoing into the crowd.

Impact

Stanley started with a straightforward introduction on how the increase is not only affecting us today, but has been affecting our upper-classmen and alumni from years past.

"Six years ago, I was paying less than a hundred dollars per credit hour. That number has almost doubled since then," Stanley said. "Our high school students are not going to want to come here to UAA continue their education if we are in a budget crisis."

Stanley continued to speak to the crowd, telling them to take pride in their education and stand up for what they believe to be wrong.

"If we can go down to the board and show that students are upset about what is happening here, if we showed that students are paying attention, we are going to be able to do a lot more to stop these increases to keep UAA affordable," Peter Finn, Speaker of the Coalition of Student Leaders, said.

The coalition is a collaborative body made up of all the student governments across the state. Finn was just one of many people who represented the students' interests at the UA Board of Regents (BOR) meeting in Juneau.

The Coalition proposed that the BOR make no revision on the already approved 2011–2012 tuition and focus on the 2012–2013 with only a 7 percent increase, which they believe is more reasonable.

Since the BOR does not accept presentations via video chat, anyone who wanted to have a say had to fly down to Juneau and present it in person, limiting the amount of voices that could be heard.

"We can send a loud message to the regents that tuition should not be increased another dollar until students are involved in the process," said Nick Moe, former Government Relations Director for USUAA.

Alaskan Senators were also invited to the protest, most of which couldn't attend, but a few sent their regards for the protest. One response was that of Senator Linda Menard, who stated she was against the tuition increase and wishes students luck in the fight against it.

State Representative, Les Gara, another guest speaker, said, "You can't have jobs and you can't have a vibrant economy unless you have a vibrant university, and that's a university that people can afford."

Each speech was accompanied by applause and cheers from the spectators, while each mention of the BOR or the tuition increase resulted in a barrage of boos.

Reaction

Over 30 people participated in the protest march, many carrying signs expressing their displeasure with the increase, reading various lines such as "Needs based scholarships now," "My money doesn't grow on trees" and "Students are not a blank check."

Starting in front of the Student Union, the group walked to the Administration Building, chanting in unison the whole time. They called to students to join

them as the troupe passed by. Even though the protestors received continuous blank stares, they didn't falter for a second, proudly holding their heads and signs high.

A few protestors even had their children with them, another gesture to show that students have families to pay for in addition to school.

Stopping once the protestors got to the flagpole, Stanley once again grasped the megaphone and gave a few words thanking everyone for their support. She then proceeded to pass out blue papers that included some outrageous facts about the increase. One said that tuition has been steadily increasing since 2001 at an average rate of 7 percent.

If this 23 percent proposal passes, the cost per semester alone will be over 500 dollars more than what students pay now, regardless of the previous nine years' increases.

Stanley's final words were asking for the assistance of student supporters to send their complaints to those members who voted yes on the tuition increase last spring, and who will most likely vote yes again.

Ending/future action

No matter what decision emanates from any of the BOR's meetings, past or future, it is inevitable that tuition will continue to rise. Students will still dig deep into their pockets to pay the rising costs because they want to complete their education, even if it means putting them further into debt in the future.

ASHLEY SNYDER, *The Northern Light,* University of Alaska Anchorage

ETHICS

ETHICAL DILEMMA: What do you do if a source tells you not to quote him at the end of an interview or after the interview but before you go to press or on the air?

Ethical values: Decency, fairness, accuracy, responsibility to readers and sources, credibility.

Ethical guidelines: The decision is more difficult when sources want to withdraw their quotes after you conduct an interview. Try to avoid this situation by making it clear at the start of your interview that you want your source to go "on the record." If you still encounter a source who wants to retract a quote, you can negotiate with the source, or you can insist that you have a right to use the information because you identified your purpose clearly. But that may not help you.

Here are some questions to consider when asked to withdraw a quote:

- Are you being fair to your source?
- Are you being fair to your readers?
- Are the quotes essential to your story?

These are tough decisions. You can read more about what constitutes "on the record" and "off the record" or "not for attribution" in the chapter on Interviewing Techniques.

QUOTES AND ATTRIBUTION

"Readers come to the newspaper the way they come to a party. They want to talk to interesting people. Long quotes usually are not very interesting."

— SUSAN AGER

Good quotes can back up your lead and substantiate information in your story. In addition, good quotes let the reader hear the speaker. But boring quotes can bog down stories. If they repeat what you have already said, it's better to paraphrase or eliminate them. In a broadcast story, sound bites take the place of quotes.

Susan Ager, a former columnist and writing coach for the *Detroit Free Press,* said reporters should consider quotes as the spice of the story, not the meat and potatoes. "Readers come to the newspaper the way they come to a party," she said. "They want to talk to interesting people. Long quotes usually are not very interesting."

When to Use Direct Quotes

Here are some guidelines for deciding when to use quotes:

- Is the quote interesting and informative?
- Can the quote back up the lead, the nut graph or a supporting point in your story?

- Ask yourself: Is the quote memorable without referring to your notes? If so, it's probably a good quote.

- Do your quotes repeat your transitions? Could the quote or the transition be eliminated? In broadcast news avoid introducing a sound bite with a transition that repeats what the source will say. That is called "parroting," a technique that should be avoided.

- Can you state the information better in your own words? If so, paraphrase.

- Does the quote or sound bite advance the story by adding emotion, interest or new information?

- Are you including the quote or sound bite for your source or for your readers or viewers? That is the most important question of all. The readers' and viewers' interests always take priority.

Here are some types of quotes or sound bites to avoid:

- Avoid direct quotes when the source is boring or the information is factual and indisputable. For example, a city official who says, "We are going to have our regular monthly meeting Tuesday night" is not worth quoting directly.

- Avoid any direct quote or sound bite that isn't clearly worded. If a government official says something in bureaucratic language that you don't fully understand, ask for clarification and then paraphrase.

- Avoid accusatory quotes from politicians or witnesses of a crime. If you intend to include any accusations, get a response from the person accused. A direct quote or sound bite does not save you from libel. If police or other criminal justice officials make accusations in an official capacity, you may use direct or indirect quotes, provided that you attribute them carefully.

- Avoid quotes that don't relate directly to the focus and supporting points in your story. Some of the best quotes a source says may have nothing to do with your focus. It's better to lose them than to use them poorly.

How to Write Quotes

On the surface, writing quotes may seem easy: You just write down what somebody else has said. The format for writing sound bites in a broadcast script differs from print style and will be explained in the broadcast chapter. For print and online delivery, you must observe the following guidelines if you want to use quotes correctly and effectively:

- Always put commas and periods inside the quotation marks: "There are no exceptions to that rule," the professor said.

- A question mark and other punctuation marks go within the quotation marks if the punctuation refers to the quoted material; otherwise, they go outside the quotation marks: He asked, "When does the semester end?" Who said, "I hope it ends soon"?

- Each new speaker must be quoted in a separate paragraph:

"Never place quotes from two speakers in the same paragraph," Professor Les Polk said.
"Even if it's short?" Janet Rojas asked.
"Yes," Polk answered.

- Don't attribute a single quote more than once. If you have two quoted sentences from the same speaker in the same paragraph, you need only one attribution:

"You must study your Associated Press Stylebook," the professor said. "You will have a test Tuesday on material in the first 30 pages."

- "When the quote is two or more sentences in the same paragraph, attribute it after the first sentence," Carol English said. "Don't make the reader wait until the end of the paragraph to discover who is speaking."

- Attribution in the middle of a quote is acceptable but not preferable if it interrupts the thought:

"It isn't the best way," he said, "to use a direct quote. But it is all right if the quote is very long. However, it's better to put it at the end of a complete sentence."

- Don't tack on long explanations for the quote. If the quote isn't clear by itself, paraphrase. For example, avoid the following:

When asked how he learned about the fire at his apartment complex, he said, "I heard the news on the television."

- Just as bad:

"I heard the news on the television," he said when asked how he learned about the fire at his apartment complex.

- Instead, introduce the quote with a transition:

He was at a friend's house when the fire broke out at his apartment.
"I heard the news on television," he said.

- Limit the use of partial quotes. They are acceptable when the whole quote would be cumbersome, but too many partial quotes make a story choppy. And the reader wonders what was left out. If you follow a partial quote with a full one, you must close the partial quote:

> McDonald says he sees the government as "weak and inept" and fraught with "major-league problems."
> "There's a crisis in our leadership," McDonald says.

- Limit the use of ellipses, which are sets of dots that indicate part of the quote is missing.

Use three dots for the middle of a sentence; four (one of which is the period) for an ellipsis at the end of the sentence. Use the ellipsis when you are condensing whole quotes or long passages from which you delete several sentences. It's useful for stories about speeches or excerpts from court rulings. Be careful not to leave out material that would change the speaker's meaning.

When to Use Attribution All quotes must be attributed to a speaker. In addition, you need to attribute information you paraphrase. In print and online writing, the attribution may follow the quote, but in broadcast writing, the attribution must come first. In many cases in broadcast news, the name and title of a speaker may be superimposed over the video on the bottom screen so you don't always need to introduce the source in a sound bite.

Plagiarism Copying the words of other writers is plagiarism, a cardinal sin in journalism. Even if you paraphrase information you receive from other publications, you are plagiarizing if you don't attribute it. Plagiarism is grounds for dismissal at most news organizations. If you take information from written or online resources, make sure you attribute it.

Plagiarism applies to blogs, tweets and other online sites as well. If you copy information from a source without needed attribution on your blog, you are still guilty of stealing information.

Here are some guidelines for material you need and don't need to attribute:

- You don't need to attribute facts that are on record or are general knowledge:

> The trial will resume tomorrow.
> A suspect has been arrested in connection with the slaying of a 16-year-old girl in Hometown last week.

- You don't need to attribute information that you observed directly:

> The protesters, carrying signs and chanting songs, gathered in the park.

- You don't need to attribute background information established in previous stories about the same subject:

> The defendant is accused of killing the three Overland Park women whose bodies have never been found.

- You do need to attribute information you receive from sources if it is accusatory, opinionated and not substantiated and if you did not witness it — especially in crime and accident stories. However, you don't always have to attribute everything in the lead. The following statement is factual, so no attribution is needed:

> A 2-year-old girl escaped injury when a mattress she was sitting on caught fire and engulfed the studio apartment in flames at Wheatshocker Apartments.

- Attribution is needed here, however, because the cause of fire is accusatory and the amount of damage is speculative:

> A 2-year-old girl playing with a lighter started the fire at the Wheatshocker Apartments near Wichita State University that caused about $400,000 in damages, fire authorities said Thursday.
>   "She was just kind of flicking it, and she caught the bedding on fire," said fire Capt. Ed Bricknell.
>
> — *The Wichita* (Kan.) *Eagle*

Wording of Attributions For most hard-news stories, the word *said* is preferable. Although there are many synonyms for *said,* they make the reader pause. *Said* does not. Don't worry about overusing the word.

- Strictly speaking, *said,* the past tense, should be used if someone said something once. If someone always says the same thing, use *says,* the present tense. However, that rule is very restrictive. You could also just use *said* for most hard-news stories and use *says* for feature stories (if *says* seems appropriate to the context). In either case, keep the tense you choose throughout the story; if you start with *says,* continue using it for the rest of the story. In broadcast writing "says" gives more immediacy.
- Avoid substitutions for *said,* such as *giggled, laughed* or *choked.* It's almost impossible to giggle, laugh or choke at the same time you are speaking. If you want to convey the emotion, write it this way: "I'm going to try out for the circus," she said, laughing.
- Use *according to* when you are referring to inanimate objects: "*according to* a study." It is acceptable to say "*according to* police" but not preferable. People talk. Use *said* or *says* when you attribute to people; *according to* is vague.

- Normal speaking order is preferable. You should place *said* after the name or pronoun. If the person has a long title, *said* can be placed before the name and title.

Awkward: "Normal speaking order is preferred," said the professor.

Preferable: "Normal speaking order is preferred," the professor said.

Overview Attribution This is a technique that allows you to attribute information to one speaker for several paragraphs without attributing each statement or each paragraph. It is useful when you are giving a chronology of events, as in a police story. But if you change speakers, you need to use attribution for the new speaker. Overview attribution is a brief statement followed by a colon.

> Police described the incident this way:
> Witnesses said this is what happened:
> Police gave this account:

Second References The second time you refer to a source in your story, use the last name only. If you have several sources — or two sources with the same last name, such as a husband and wife — use the full name again or an identifying phrase:

> James Jones, the director of public safety, was injured in a three-car crash yesterday. Jones was taken to Memorial Hospital, where he was treated for bruises and released.

If you have mentioned several other people and want to get back to Jones later in the story, remind the reader who Jones is by using his title:

> Public Safety Director Jones said he would return to work Monday.

Titles When a person's title is used before the name, capitalize it, as in the preceding example. When it is used after the name, use lowercase letters:

> Police Chief Ron Olin said the crime rate has gone down.
> Olin, police chief of Lawrence, said the crime rate has gone down.

Courtesy Titles Most newspapers and TV scripts no longer use courtesy titles — Mr., Miss, Mrs. or Ms. — before people's names. There are exceptions. *The New York Times* and *The Wall Street Journal* still use courtesy titles. Other newspapers use them in obituaries. For general purposes in this book, courtesy titles will be eliminated unless they are contained in examples from newspapers that still use them.

EXERCISES

1 Basic news story: Write a story based on the following information. Write a focus sentence before you start your story. For this story, your focus sentence should be the results of the study. If you want a lead that gets directly to the point, your focus sentence could also be your lead.

Once you have written a focus sentence, add a suggestion for visual presentation — a photograph, chart, facts box, video excerpt or other graphic illustration. Decide what facts, if any, should be duplicated in the story and the graphic. Then organize the story by placing facts, quotes and elaboration in an order with the most important information near the top of the story to the least important material and perhaps ending with a good quote. The following material is based on a story from *The* (San Bernardino, Calif.) *Sun*.

Who/what: A study comparing the death and accident rates of left- and right-handed people.

When: Study was conducted last year and was reported in today's edition of the *New England Journal of Medicine*.

Where: Study was conducted by Diane Halpern, a psychology professor at California State University at San Bernardino and Stanley Coren, a researcher at the University of British Columbia.

Why: To determine why fewer left-handed people are among the elderly population.

How: Researchers studied death certificates of 987 people in two Southern California counties. Relatives were queried by mail about the subjects' dominant hands.

Backup information: The following points are not necessarily in the order they should be used in your story.

The researchers found that the average age at death for right-handed people was 75, for left-handed people 66; left-handed people represent 10 percent of the U.S. population; right-handed females tend to live six years longer than left-handed females and right-handed males live 11 years longer than left-handed males; left-handed people were four times more likely to die from injuries while driving than right-handers and six times more likely to die from accidents of all kinds.

Halpern said, "The results are striking in their magnitude." Halpern is right-handed.

She said her study should be interpreted cautiously. "It should not, of course, be used to predict the life span of any one individual. It does not take into account the fitness of any individual." Left-handed women die around age 72; right-handed women die around age 78. Left-handed men die about age 62; right-handed men die about age 73.

"Some of my best friends are left-handed," Halpern said. "It's important that mothers of left-handed children not be alarmed and not try to change which hand a child uses," she said. "There are many, many old left-handed people. We knew for years that there weren't as many old left-handers," Halpern said. "Researchers thought that was because in the early years of the century, most people born left-handed were forced to change to their right hands. So we thought we were looking at old people who used to be left-handed, but we weren't. The truth was that there simply weren't many left-handers left alive, compared to right-handers."

"Almost all engineering is geared to the right hand and right foot," Halpern said. "There are many more car and other accidents among left-handers because of their environment."

2 Reaction story: Interview at least three students on campus who are left-handed. Ask them what problems they encounter because they are left-handed. Using the study in Exercise 1 as a focus for your story, write a reaction story with the students' comments. Make sure you get the full names of the students, their majors and year of study (freshman, sophomore and so on) so you can identify them properly in the story.

3 Find the focus: Using your local or campus newspaper or an online news site, find the focus paragraph (the nut graph) in three news stories on the front page or main screen of the online site.

4 Online focus exercise: Access an online news site for your community or for a national source, such as www.cnn.com, *www.msnbc.com or foxnews.com*, and discuss the following points:

- Do the headlines and/or summary blurbs clearly identify the main point of the story?

- Compare the headlines of major news stories in two online sites.

- Which headlines entice you to click into the story? Why?

- How long are the average online headlines?

- Do summary blurbs add or detract from your interest in reading the full story? How much information should the summary blurb reveal about the story? What type of summary blurbs do you prefer: a single sentence, a paragraph or a few paragraphs?

5 Quotes and attribution exercise: Check the appropriate column to indicate whether attribution is or is not needed:

Not Needed	Needed		
☐	☐	**a**	Two leading figures in the growing national debate about political correctness on American college campuses will be at the University of South Florida in Tampa tonight.
☐	☐	**b**	Dieting doesn't work for the vast majority of people.
☐	☐	**c**	A 40-year-old woman went berserk in her ex-boyfriend's apartment early Monday, shooting him to death with seven shots from two guns.
☐	☐	**d**	Members of a local gay rights group protested Thursday in support of a gay University of Tampa student's efforts to take an Army ROTC class.
☐	☐	**e**	City council members voted unanimously Thursday to increase city fines for prostitution.
☐	☐	**f**	A York College sophomore died early yesterday after drinking at a dormitory party.
☐	☐	**g**	Alumni members of Skull and Bones, an all-male secret society at Yale University, have voted to admit women.

6 Enterprise: Attend an event on your campus, and write a basic news story about it. (Look in your campus newspaper or your university's online site for a list of activities that will take place during the week, or check bulletin boards for notices of activities.) Talk to friends about other story possibilities. Here are some other possible topics for a news story at the start of the semester: a new course, problems that students are having enrolling in certain courses, a new club or organization on campus, a student support group.

7 Class reunion feature: This exercise will give you practice gathering and writing quotes. The scenario: Imagine you are attending a class reunion of your department 25 years from now. Interview your classmates in small groups, and rotate among the groups so you get comments from at least five different students.

Ask them their ages and occupations, and make sure you spell their names correctly. For female students who may be using a married name, include their maiden names if they were unmarried when they graduated. Even though you should never make up quotes, for this exercise students can use their imaginations about their future careers, but they must give the same information to everyone who interviews them.

Write the story as though you were a reporter for a local newspaper or news website. Do not use first-person "I" or "we"; pretend you were an observer, not part of the reunion. Give the time and place — somewhere in your school — and the number of students attending the reunion. Try a creative lead focusing on one interesting person.

Then use a nut graph: She (or he) was one of ____ students attending a class reunion of (your school). Try to get as many complete quotes as you can.

8 Social Media Assignment: Search Twitter.com for tweets on topics of stories you have written or would like to write for a college publication (in print, broadcast or online). List at least three ideas for stories you could write that would be of interest to your audience.

FEATURED ONLINE ACTIVITY Log on and visit the Writing and Reporting News CourseMate and take the interactive quiz on basic news qualities, quotes and attribution.
Access available at www.cengagebrain.com.

Check out the "Bank Robbery" scenario in NewsScene for an interactive exercise that will help to reinforce many of the themes presented in this chapter.

COACHING TIPS

Stress immediacy — the latest developments in a story.

Plan to update your story continually for mobile and online delivery.

Plan to produce your story for multimedia.

Write short versions for **mobile delivery.**

Read your story **out loud for broadcast.**

Plan audio and video elements for broadcast, the Web and mobile media.

Plan links to social media sites.

cybrain/Shutterstock.com

It's mobile, immediate, visual, interactive, participatory and trusted. Make way for a generation of storytellers who totally get it.

— **THE FUTURE OF NEWS: MEDIA, TECHNOLOGY AND SOCIETY,** report for the American Press Institute

CHAPTER 3
Convergent and Mobile Media

MOJOS ARE MAGIC CHARMS OR SPELLS, BUT IN MORE THAN 100 NEWS organizations, mojos are a new breed of journalists.

Mojos are mobile journalists equipped with notepads, cameras, recorders, cell phones and laptop computers so they can file community news stories for the Web at a moment's notice. They don't go to a newspaper office; their offices are in their cars. They don't wait for deadlines; their deadlines are whenever they get their information. As technology continues to downsize devices, reporters may accomplish all of these tasks with just a smart phone.

"We believe that most reporters will soon be mojos, producing information seamlessly across platforms," said Kate Marymont, former executive editor of *The News-Press* in Fort Myers, Fla., and now vice president of Gannett's information center content. "The most critical need is the ability to file material to online quickly and regularly."

The Gannett Co. started the mojo concept at its Fort Myers, Fla., newspaper in 2005 and has since expanded it to more than 100 of its news organizations. The company reorganized its newspapers and broadcast properties as "information centers," which develop local mobile sites for multiple platforms, including small screen and mobile devices.

In a memo to Gannett employees, Craig Dubow, the company's chief executive officer, explained the concept: "The Information Center, frankly, is the newsroom of the future. And it will be

Graphic from *The* (Fort Myers, Fla.) *News-Press* for mobile news delivery

platform agnostic: News and information will be delivered to the right media — be it newspapers, online, mobile, video or ones not yet invented — at the right time. Our customers will decide which they prefer."

In addition the company restructured its flagship newspaper, *USA Today,* to change its traditional print-centered sections such as news, sports, money and life to "content rings" with emphasis on creating information for digital products such as the iPad and mobile phones. Some of the revised content areas include "Your Life," travel, breaking news, entertainment, personal finance and technology.

"We have to go where the audience is," USA Today editor John Hillkirk told the Associated Press. "If people are hitting the iPad like crazy, or the iPhone, or other mobile devices, we've got to be there with the content they want, when they want it."

Gannett is not the only company gravitating to the mobile market. Twelve major broadcast groups, including Fox, NBC and Hearst, have formed a joint venture to develop a new national mobile content service. The group will allow member companies to share content for mobile devices, including video, local and national news from print and online sources and entertainment programming.

It is with good reason that mobile devices are generating so much attention by the media. A study from USAID (U.S. Agency for International Development) claims that 50 percent of the world's population use mobile phones, and the highest increase in cell phone ownership is in Africa, where cell phones are used by one in four people. Several studies by the Pew Internet and American Life Project also show dramatic increases in the use of mobile technology in America in the past few years:

- 85 percent of adults own a cell phone
- Six in 10 American adults use a mobile phone or wireless laptop computer to send or access information.
- More than 75 percent of all American teens own a cell phone; in the 17-year-old age group that figure increases to 83 percent and will most likely go higher.
- More than 60 percent of all teens go online for news.

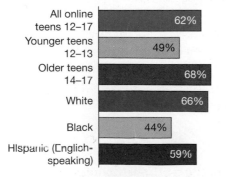

Percent of online teens in each group who get news about current events and politics online

All online teens 12–17	62%
Younger teens 12–13	49%
Older teens 14–17	68%
White	66%
Black	44%
Hispanic (English-speaking)	59%

"Social Media and Young Adults," study from the Pew Internet and American Life Project

"The mobile user population is becoming more diverse over time and more people are relying on their cell phones as their primary form of wireless connectivity," said Aaron Smith, research specialist for the Pew Internet and American Life Project.

Mobile journalism may be a wave of the future for print media, but television stations have been using mobile vans to cover breaking news for many years. The difference between mojos and traditional reporters is that these mobile journalists live, work and play in the communities they cover. The news is posted on "microsites," subsidiary sites of the newspaper's main website. These microsites contain breaking news, community profiles, searchable databases, archives and places for readers to post comments and blogs.

Mary Vorsino, a mojo for the *Honolulu Advertiser*, described her typical day: "Most days start with a check of any breaking news in my neighborhood," she said in a Gannett training session. "Many days I have interviews or events happening in my region. The difference from a conventional regional beat, however, is that throughout the day I post breaking news or update items on the *Honolulu Advertiser* website. This allows me to give readers up-to-date information on everything from car wrecks to an upcoming informational meeting happening in their neighborhood."

Mark Krzos, a mojo for *The* (Fort Myers, Fla.,) *News-Press*, files his stories from his car throughout the day. He said you need to "get it fast and get it online." In a podcast on the Gannett website, he said his stories can range from writing about a different way around traffic to telling people what concerns them.

Mark Krzoz, mojo for *The News-Press*, Fort Myers, Fla.

CONVERGENCE AND MULTIMEDIA

Convergence is defined as a mixture of media — usually print, audio, video and the Web. It is also defined as "multimedia," which often refers to a story or project that uses a combination of media. The terms can be interchangeable. But now the concept includes mobile media and social media, Web-based sites where users can interact with communities of friends and other members. These include popular sites such as Twitter, where users can post blurbs of fewer than 140 characters, Facebook, where people communicate with friends and followers and YouTube, where users can post video.

The Radio, Television Digital News Association explains convergence this way: "Communications and electronic journalism have changed dramatically in recent years and promise to change even more in years to come. The familiar lines that once marked the boundaries between radio, television, print, computers, telephones and other media are blurring. News in the future will be a fully digital broadband mix of audio, video, print, graphics and databases. In the coming years, new technology and changing market forces will completely transform the news industry."

Robert Papper, a Hofstra University professor who conducts an annual survey of the future of news in the broadcast industry, says people want news and information on demand and many want to interact with that news. "People want their news to be right up-to-the-minute," he says. "More than 90 percent of those surveyed say it's very or somewhat important, and the figure is even higher for young adults."

A Multimedia Minute

Many multimedia projects are time-consuming, in-depth reports. But graduate students at Syracuse University's Newhouse School for Communication got their first lesson in multimedia news by producing one-minute video and audio stories about people in the city's neighborhoods. Equipped with audio recorders, still and video cameras, the students produced snapshot-profiles of a gravedigger, a barber, a baker and a shoemaker and others. Then they learned how to edit their audio and video and added brief text stories, which were posted on the Web in their project, "Secs in the City," *http://secsinthecity.serramedia.com/.*

A Multimedia "Shootout"

Every year journalism students at the University of Alaska Anchorage spend their Thanksgiving weekend covering the annual basketball tournament that brings national teams to their city. The Carrs/Safeway Great Alaska Shootout also brings national attention to their coverage of the tournament. The students have been producing print, audio, video and Web stories of this event for more than 15 years — before convergence and multimedia became common terms.

Journalism students begin planning the event early in the fall when they choose a student producer, reporters, writers and photographers who will produce minute-by-minute coverage of the games, profiles of players and stories about people behind the scenes. They post stories and updates to the game statistics every few minutes on their website, *www.shootout.net.* In the past few years they added Twitter to the mix for updating information.

CONVERGENT MEDIA WRITING

Most media experts agree that the current and future state of news will involve convergent platforms and interaction with social media. But not everyone agrees that the media evolution is positive.

"The way we read and write is certainly changing," said Rebecca MacKinnon, a journalist who co-founded a global citizen media network. "Spelling and grammar have gotten worse. People don't think things through or edit as much before publishing or sending as they once did."

She was one of several media specialists who responded to a study of the future of the Internet by the Pew Internet and American Life Project. Andreas Kluth, a writer for Economist magazine, said in the study, "We are currently transitioning from reading mainly on paper to reading mainly on screens. As we do so, most of us read MORE, in terms of quantity but more promiscuously and in shorter intervals with less dedication. . . . We will be less patient and less able to concentrate on long-form texts. This will result in a resurgence of short-form texts and storytelling, in 'Haiku-culture' replacing 'book-culture.'"

©Fred Pearce

©Fred Pearce

University of Alaska Anchorage students produce multimedia news of the annual basketball tournament, the Carrs/Safeway Great Alaska Shootout.

ETHICS

YOU ARE A MOJO (mobile journalist) and you hear on the radio that there is a five-car pileup on the Interstate. You call police and confirm there is an accident, but you can't get to the scene for first-hand information because traffic is backed up for miles. However, you receive a photo and message on your cell phone from a trucker who claims he is at the scene. This is an important breaking news story, and you want to post it to your news organization's website as soon as possible. As a mobile journalist, it is part of your responsibilities to warn people about the traffic delays. Will you use the photo and description of the scene from this source? How do you know if the information is accurate?

Guidelines: The Radio Television Digital News Association says that citizens can provide valuable information, but some people try to fool news organizations with bad information or fake pictures. The association offers these ethical guidelines:

- Information gleaned online should be confirmed just as you must confirm scanner traffic or phone tips before reporting them.

- If you cannot independently confirm critical information, reveal your sources; tell the public how you know what you know and what you cannot confirm. Don't stop there. Keep seeking confirmation.

- This guideline is the same for covering breaking news on station websites as on the air. You should not leave the public "hanging." Lead the public to completeness and understanding.

With the emergence of tablet readers for books and magazines, it's possible that reading long-form books or stories on these devices will survive and even thrive. But Kluth's comments have merit for news writing in convergent media, especially on small screens.

Regardless of length, the basic elements of a news story for print, broadcast and the Web are the same. However, here are some principles that apply to writing for cross-media platforms:

Immediacy

The main point to stress in broadcast and Web stories is immediacy. What is happening now? What are the latest developments? How can you update the story, giving it a "forward spin" to tell what will happen next? Even if you are reporting a breaking news story for a newspaper, plan to report it first on the Web or on a partner television station. The days of waiting until the next publication cycle for a breaking news story in a newspaper are over. This is how print and broadcast can differ:

Print: What happened or who did what? Past tense. Fire destroyed a duplex in midtown yesterday morning, leaving two families homeless.

Broadcast and the Web: What is happening *now* or who is doing what *now*. Present tense is preferable. For example: Two families are homeless today after a fire destroyed their midtown duplex.

Conversational Style

Writing simple sentences in a conversational manner — the way you talk — is preferable for all media but essential for broadcast. Stories on the Web resemble print style.

Print: Write to be read. Sentences may be longer, and the story may include more detail.

Broadcast: Write for the ear and the eye. Write in conversational style. You are talking to the viewer. Read your story aloud. Writing for the eye means you should plan your story around the images. In most cases, broadcast stories are shorter than their print counterparts. The average TV news story is 1:30, meaning one minute and 30 seconds. Keep the sentences short and simple, structured as subject-verb-object, meaning who did what or what is happening.

Here is the print lead on a story:

> Talking on a cell phone while driving is as dangerous as driving while drunk, new federally funded research shows, and it doesn't matter whether you use a hands-free model or hold the phone up to your ear during the conversation.
>
> *— South Florida Sun-Sentinel*

Here is a conversational approach to the cell phone story for broadcast:

> How many times have you been cut off or otherwise annoyed on the road, only to find the other driver is talking on a cell phone?
> A new scientific study says it now proves that talking and driving is as dangerous as drinking and driving!
>
> — KXAN-TV *(Austin, Texas)*

Active Voice

The structure in active voice is subject-verb-object: who is doing the action. Passive voice explains what action is being done to whom. Active voice is preferable for all media but more essential for broadcast because it conveys more immediacy. In some cases the passive voice is more appropriate. For example:

Active: Police rescued the woman. (Who did what.)

Passive: The woman was rescued by police. (What was done to whom.)

Passive. The defendant was sentenced to 10 years in prison. In this case the emphasis on the defendant may be preferable.

Active: The judge sentenced the defendant to 10 years in prison. The emphasis here is on the judge, who may not be as important to stress as the defendant.

Impact

When possible, lead with the effect a story will have on viewers. In breaking news this isn't always appropriate, but explaining the impact on the audience is a good way to grab the viewers' attention. This technique also works well for print. The following example from broadcast news would work as well in print or online stories:

> Anchorage residents will able to breathe air that's a little cleaner this weekend. A new, tougher version of the citywide smoking ban goes into effect July 1.
>
> The new smoking ban effectively updates the previous ban by adding daycare centers, outdoor stadiums and bars to the list of places where smoking is against the law.
>
> — KTUU-TV *(Anchorage, Alaska)*

Attribution

Put the attribution at the beginning of the sentence in broadcast writing. In print and Web writing, the attribution may come at the end of the sentence. When you put the attribution last in a broadcast story, it sounds as though the reporter is the source of the information or opinion, which can be dangerous especially if the statement is an accusation.

Print: The blaze started in the basement, fire officials say.

Broadcast: Fire officials say the blaze started in the basement.

Consider how dangerous the following sentence would sound if the attribution is not clear at the beginning of this sentence: The suspect abused the animals, police say. A better way to say it is: Police say the suspect abused the animals.

If the information is on public records, a statement without attribution is OK as in this sentence: The suspect is charged with three counts of animal abuse.

Said vs. Says

When you attribute information in broadcast writing, "says" gives more immediacy than "said." However, if it is awkward to use the present tense, use "said." If a source said something a week ago, using "says" would be improper. In print, "said" is used more often except in features because generally the source said the quote in the past.

Print: The first firefighters arrived on the scene about three minutes later, at 7:43 a.m., the Fire Department spokesman **said**.

Broadcast: The Fire Department **says** the blaze broke out about 8 a.m., in a child's bedroom at 800 Northview Ave.

Visuals

In print publications, photos and graphics enhance a story. In television news the visual elements are crucial. In this age of convergence, many news organizations publish

CONVERGENCE COACH

WRITING NEWS FOR print, broadcast and the Web requires careful planning and reporting for more than one story. Here are some things to keep in mind:

- Plan to file breaking news immediately on the Web.

- While you are reporting, plan for the next cycle of the story. Always consider what will happen next. You will need a fresh angle for the next broadcast or the next day's newspaper.

- Plan for audio and video elements that might be posted on the website, even if you are primarily reporting the story for print publication.

stories in multiple media. As a result, if you are writing for a print publication, you should still plan photos, audio and video to post on the organization's website.

Interactivity

Try to get readers and viewers involved in all media but particularly in broadcast and online. In print and broadcast you might add a question or poll and refer your readers to the organization's website. On the Web, there are several ways to interact with the reader through questions, polls, chats, blogs or requests for readers' photos and stories. You can also encourage readers and viewers to comment on a Twitter or Facebook site.

COMPARISONS OF A NEWS STORY: P.R., BROADCAST AND PRINT

Compare the following information from a news release, a broadcast story and a print news story. The news release was issued on the Web because reporters who cover police and fire departments can't wait to receive releases for breaking news by mail. Although most print and broadcast reporters supplement news releases with their own sources, these news stories relied heavily on the releases because other sources were not available or relevant to the initial story.

Note some of these differences between the broadcast and print versions:

- The sentences in the broadcast version are much shorter than in the print version. The broadcast version is spoken over images (SOT — sound on tape).
- The Web versions for both print and broadcast were written in print style.
- The broadcast news story, which was the first to report the accident, uses present tense in the lead whereas the print version, which appeared the next day, updates the lead with newly released information.

NEWS RELEASE

Date

Contact: (Name of police spokesman and phone number)

Man in Critical Condition after Apparent Hit and Run

At about 12:04 AM on Sunday (date included) Anchorage Police mid-shift patrol officers responded to the report of a person lying in the roadway at Debarr Road and Norene Streets in East Anchorage.

Responding officers located a male adult suffering from head and torso trauma. The victim was transported to a nearby local hospital for emergency treatment. He is listed in critical condition.

Investigating officers located evidence of an apparent vehicle/pedestrian collision. The driver of the vehicle left the scene without immediate notification as required by state and municipal laws. Officers were unable to locate the suspect vehicle or the driver.

At this time, the name of the victim is unknown. The victim appears to be a white or Native male about 35–48 years of age with brown hair and eyes. The male was wearing blue jean pants, a royal blue sweat shirt and dark blue "hoodie type" sweat shirt. The male was also wearing brown leather boots.

Police are asking for anyone who has information about this incident and or the name of the victim to call the Anchorage Police Department at (number given).

Anchorage Crime Stoppers pays callers whose tip leads to the arrest of a felony crime suspect. Callers may receive a cash reward of up to $1,000 and may submit their tip anonymously by phone at (number given) or on the net at *www.anchoragecrimestoppers.com*.

NOTE — The Traffic Division reports that three vehicle/pedestrian collisions have occurred in the past few weeks. Motorists are advised to be especially alert as the prelude to winter solstice means shorter periods of daylight and extended periods of darkness. Pedestrians are advised to cross at designated, well-lit crosswalks.

Oftentimes, alcohol is a contributing factor with one or both parties involved. The Anchorage Police Department urges responsible alcohol consumption by those legally entitled to do so.

# # #

The broadcast version posted on the TV station's website featured video with the police spokesman. This is not written in broadcast two-column script style, which we will study later. Note the emphasis in the lead is on the perspective given at the end of the news release.

Police search for another hit and run driver

ANCHORAGE, Alaska — For the third time in recent weeks, police are looking for yet another hit-and-run driver. This time a driver left a seriously injured man behind as they fled the scene.

The collision happened at the intersection of DeBarr Road and Norene Street around midnight last night.

A Good Samaritan saw the man — whose identity is not known — lying in the street and tried to keep other cars from striking him.

Anchorage Police Department Spokesman Lt. Paul Honeman said the victim suffered serious head and leg injuries but is alive and in the hospital.

(Honeman sound bite — Honeman name superimposed at bottom screen)

"There's no real clear indication. Anybody who might have seen anything or knows anything about this incident is asked to call the Anchorage Police Department."
(End of sound bite)

Print version published the next morning with new information from the police department and updates on the victim's condition.

Pedestrian in critical condition after hit-and-run

A man critically injured in a hit-and-run traffic accident over the weekend is 48-year-old Garon James Koozaata, who is originally from St. Lawrence Island, police said today.

Just after midnight Sunday, Anchorage police discovered Koozaata near DeBarr Road and Norene Street. Police believe a vehicle hit him and the driver left without reporting the collision. Police are now looking for that driver.

"It's disturbing to realize that someone will mow a human being down and they'll just keep going," said Lt. Nancy Reeder.

Koozaata remained unconscious today at a local hospital, Reeder said. He was identified using his fingerprints.

Police are asking anyone with information about the hit-and-run to call 786-8900. Callers can leave tips anonymously by calling 561-7867.

Anchorage police used fingerprints to identify the victim of Sunday morning's hit and run.

Garon James Koozaata, age 48, was struck by an unknown vehicle in the area of Debarr Road and Norene Street in east Anchorage. A passing motorist discovered Koozaata shortly after midnight and notified police.

Police also want help identifying the victim. They said he looks to be 35 to 48 years old with brown hair and eyes. He appears to be white or Native descent. He was wearing blue jeans, a blue sweatshirt and a second, darker blue hooded sweatshirt. He was also wearing brown leather boots.

Police said he is in critical condition.

— JILL BURKE, KTUU-TV
(Anchorage, Alaska)

Koozaata remains at a local hospital in critical condition suffering from head and torso trauma.

Anyone with information as to the person responsible for this hit and run is asked to call Anchorage Police at (number given). Tipsters can report information anonymously by calling Anchorage Crime Stoppers at 561-STOP or submitting their tip on the internet at *www.anchoragecrimestoppers.com*. Crime Stoppers will pay cash rewards of up to $1,000 for information leading to a felony arrest. All calls and internet submissions are confidential.

— KYLE HOPKINS, *Anchorage*
(Alaska) *Daily News*

WRITING FOR MOBILE MEDIA

Access a news story on a website in your computer. Now access that story on a small-screen cell phone. Would you read more or less of the article on a small screen?

You would probably read much less. At least that's what researchers at the University of Colorado discovered when they surveyed how college students used media on their smart phones. Their findings:

- For text news stories 56 percent of students in one group read less than the first three paragraphs, and 72 percent in another group read less than 25 percent of the article.
- For video news stories 79 percent watched 59 seconds or less of each video.
- For audio news reports 81 percent listened to 30 seconds or less.

How do those findings affect the ways you should write for mobile media? The easy answer is keep your sentences and paragraphs short. But not all mobile phones are the same size, and one size does not fit all in writing styles either. If the content is compelling, readers may persevere. Good content providers will offer versions of stories formatted for mobile devices to improve readability. However, writing techniques also need to be geared for readability on mobile devices. Here are some recommendations:

- Headlines: Entice readers with clear, compelling headlines, preferably less than 25 words. Even better, write a Twitter-type headline limited to 140 characters.
- Write a summary lead that gives the most important information in a brief sentence.
- Use inverted pyramid structure–the most important information in the lead and first few paragraphs. If students and other mobile users read less than the first three paragraphs, as the Colorado researchers claim, make sure those paragraphs contain crucial information.
- Keep sentences short.

SOCIAL MEDIA

 THE U.S. CENTERS for Disease Control is an example of an extensive convergent newsroom that features multimedia and social media. Glen Nowak, Ph.D., director of the centers' news and electronic media, said the addition of social media allows the agency to reach more audiences with more varied formats. "We embedded links in our press releases; we use RSS (Really Simple Syndication) feeds to get our materials to a wider media and non-media audience; we've used content syndication to make CDC information that's on our media relations website more attractive; and we've also added social media elements to CDC's health information campaigns," he said at a conference on convergence at the University of South Carolina's College of Mass Communications and Information Studies.

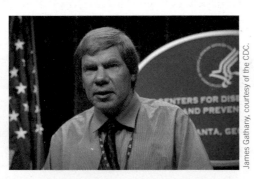

Glen Nowak, Ph.D., director of news and electronic media, U.S. Centers for Disease Control.

Nowak said that in some ways social media has made it harder to reach audiences because there are so many choices and so many places where they can go for information. "Now you have to use a lot more media to reach the same number of people."

His advice for students: Learn how to use different media. "They should also have good communication and writing skills. They should know what makes good messages. So it's not just a matter of knowing the technical elements of creating a Facebook page, but also knowing what makes a good one versus a bad one."

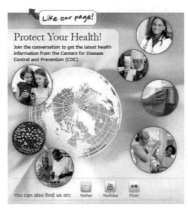

Courtesy of the CDC

Wall photo on the CDC's Facebook page.

Here are some of the ways the CDC offers convergent media (*www.cdc.gov/media/*):

- E-mail subscription to receive alerts for new information
- Audio/video resources: Online videos, podcasts and public service announcements and B-Roll for productions. Videos on YouTube and CDC-TV online
- RSS feeds of formatted articles and newsroom releases. (RSS, Really Simple Syndication, is a Web feed that automatically updates information.)
- Press releases in English and Spanish with embedded links
- Resources and stories geared to African-Americans and Hispanics
- Newsroom library with images in low to high resolution for downloading
- Mobile website
- Widgets–applications that can embed CDC information in your Web pages or blogs

- Keep paragraphs short.

- Write for readers who scan text. Put key words at the beginning or end of the sentences.

- Spacing: Some news providers insert a space between paragraphs to aid readability, but that increases scrolling. Others eliminate spaces or paragraph indentations so more text can be viewed in less space. Decide how you prefer to read; then write that way.

- Use lists to itemize information if you want to make several points in your story.

- Be concise. Edit your text carefully. Eliminate repetition. Cut extra words. Study Twitter for concise writing (but avoid the abbreviations).

- Add photos or video only if they relate to or enhance your text. Don't add to the downloading time if you aren't adding worthwhile content.

- Provide links but choose them carefully. Once you take readers to a new site, don't expect them to return to your story.

- Offer interaction. After all, this is a phone or mobile device designed for communication.

- Test how your story will look on a mobile phone or iPad. If you don't have one, use a mobile phone simulator: iPhone 4 Simulator *(http://iphone4simulator.com/)*, Iphoney *(http://www.marketcircle.com/iphoney/)* or iPad Peek *(http://ipadpeek.com/)*.

EXERCISES

1 **Convert from print to broadcast:** Take any story in today's newspaper and convert it for broadcast by updating the lead, changing the attribution to conform to broadcast writing style and condensing it.

2 **Police story — print and broadcast:** Write a brief story for print and another version for broadcast, based on the information in the following news release. Use your city's name for the police department and attribute information to Police Spokesman John Coptalker:

At about 2:54 AM on Thursday — March 22nd (use this year) Police Mid Shift Patrol Officers responded to reports of a shooting at an apartment located at the 7000 block of Walker Road.

Responding officers located two persons who had been shot. One victim, a male adult in his mid 40s was dead of the apparent gunshot wounds. Another victim, identified as Mary Pothead — age 36 — was transported to a local hospital for emergency treatment. Pothead is listed in serious condition.

Details about the incident are sketchy. Detectives believe that this incident is possibly related to illegal drug activity. Detectives are seeking a possible suspect in this case described only as an unknown male. No other information is available at this time.

Detectives are actively seeking information from any persons who may have been in the area of or have knowledge of this shooting incident. Persons with information are asked to call the (use your city) Police at 123-4567.

Persons who wish to remain anonymous may call the city's Crime Stoppers at 123-STOP or on the web at *www.crimetips.com*. Callers whose tip leads to an arrest of a Felony suspect are eligible for a reward of up to $1,000.

3 Mobile Media: Using the mobile media writing guidelines, use the previous story or another story from a newspaper or website and rewrite it for readability on a cell phone.

4 Interactivity:

a. Using the example about cell phones cited in this chapter, write a poll question for online readers.

b. Write a poll question or comment to elicit responses from readers on your website, Twitter or Facebook site about some controversial issue on your campus or in your community.

CourseMate

FEATURED ONLINE ACTIVITY Log on and visit the Writing and Reporting News CourseMate and take the interactive tutorial quiz on convergent media. *Access available at www.cengagebrain.com.*

COACHING TIPS

Keep your **blog short.**

Provide links to related articles or sources.

Write a **clear headline** for your blog.

Write a lead that gets to the **main point quickly.**

Write **short sentences.**

Use **strong verbs.**

Write in **conversational tone,** the way you would tell your reader a story.

Offer a question or comment at the end that will **elicit readers' responses.**

Michael D Brown/Shutterstock.com

SOCIAL MEDIA

Resist the temptation to tell everything you've learned; much of it doesn't matter anyway.

— **RICHARD AREGOOD,** Pulitzer Prize-winning journalist

CHAPTER 4
Social Media

THE MORE YOU KNOW, THE LESS YOU MAY HAVE TO WRITE ABOUT IT.
"Short is in.
Blogs are in.
And.
Tweets.
R.
In."

That is how Jodi Enda, a writer for *American Journalism Review*, summarized reporting and writing in this age of social media.

Social networking has changed the nature of journalism. Once a venue primarily for keeping up with friends, social networking sites are now essential tools for finding sources and sharing information with the public.

You have probably grown up with social media, but not everyone has a face on Facebook, a space on MySpace or posts on Twitter. Consider how you would explain "tweets," "blogs" and "smart phones" to someone who has never even used computers.

That is what Kathy English had to do. She is the ombudsman for the *Toronto Star*. One day she received a small, white postcard in the mail from one of her readers. He said he didn't understand the terms she used in her recent column about blogs and Twitter. "Is that a blog by a bird brain?" the reader asked. Another more sophisticated reader sent her an e-mail saying: "That the winds of change have transformed journalism of late is an understatement. I remember when tweets and twitters were birdsong, and logging on referred to forestry."

English explained the terms to her confused reader, and she tacked the reader's postcard to her bulletin board to remind her that some people still communicate by telephone and letter. "Serving the needs of traditional newspaper readers and growing online audiences means coming to terms with the reality that a digital divide still separates those who are online all the time from those yet to discover the power of this revolutionary medium," English wrote.

At the start of the 21st century, Twitter and Facebook didn't even exist. MySpace was founded in 2003, Facebook in 2004 and Twitter in 2006. Since then social media sites have mushroomed and have spawned a new vocabulary for a digital culture.

What is social media? Traditional media are print, broadcast or online forms of publication. Social media are Web-based technologies that provide ways people may connect, create and share content. With traditional media people are receivers; with social media they are contributors.

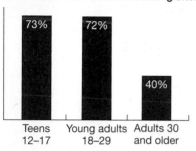

Teens and young adults converge in enthusiasm for social networking sites

- Teens 12–17: 73%
- Young adults 18–29: 72%
- Adults 30 and older: 40%

Pew Internet and American Life Project study.

Social media guru Clay Shirky, a New York University professor, says "user-generated" content revolutionizes communication by shifting power from the select few who have publishing capabilities to everyone. "The media landscape is transformed, because personal communication and publishing, previously separate functions, now shade into one another. Communications media was between one sender and one recipient. This is a one-to-one pattern — I talk and you listen, then you talk and I listen. Broadcast media was between one sender and many recipients, and the recipients couldn't talk back. This is a one-to-many pattern — I talk, and talk, and talk, and all you can do is choose to listen or tune out. The pattern we *didn't* have until recently was many-to-many, where communications tools enabled group conversation. Everyone is a media outlet," he writes in his book *Here Comes Everybody: The Power of Organizing Without Organizations.*

Here are some social media terms:

- **Apps:** Short for applications, these are programs to download to phones or tablet computers to access media, music, games or other Web-based items.
- **Blog:** The U.S. dictionary publisher Merriam-Webster defines "blog," as "a website that contains an online personal journal with reflections, comments and often hyperlinks." Also known as "Web logs," or "weblogs," blogs have proliferated to such an extent that they have their own world called a "blogosphere," which is a social network of people who post blogs (bloggers). Other blogs are more like essays commenting on news or issues with links to related articles or sources.
- **Cloud computing:** A way to securely store and retrieve your computer information and software on a Web server; the cloud is a symbol for the Internet.
- **Crowdsourcing:** Using a large group of people to help gather or produce content with social media. The technique is often used by news organizations to get information about tragedies, accidents or breaking news stories.
- **Creative Commons:** A copyright licensing system that allows content creators to specify if and how they want their material to be shared. All work is automatically copyrighted once it is in fixed form, but under this licensing system, the creator may decide if the work may be used with or without attribution, shared, used commercially, publicly or privately.
- **Facebook:** The largest social network company based on technology that allows people who join the group to interact and share information. Facebook can include personal pages, group sites and fan pages that gather "friends," people with whom you want to keep in contact.
- **Flickr:** A photo-sharing repository.

- **Foursquare:** A mobile application with a built-in GPS (Global Positioning System). After you "check in" to a location, the application can broadcast your position to other people you choose.
- **Hashtag**: A hashtag is akin to a link for Twitter. It identifies a category or similar items for the tweet (a message posted to Twitter). You can add a hashtag preceded by a pound sign anywhere in the tweet to indicate other items in that topic such as #jobs for a tweet related to job searches.
- **iPad:** A tablet computer made by the Apple Corp. Other companies also produce tablet computers.
- **iPhone:** A phone, also made by Apple, that was the first to introduce a multi-touch screen. This phone is considered a "smart phone" because with a simple touch, you can access applications. Other companies also make these phones under different names.
- **LinkedIn:** A business-oriented network generally used for professional profiles and connections.
- **Twitter:** A social network which limits messages, called "tweets," to 140 characters (including punctuation and spaces).
- **YouTube:** A video-sharing site.
- **Wiki:** A type of software that allows people to add or edit information on a website.

Reporting with Social Media

When the *Seattle Times* won a Pulitzer Prize in 2010, editor David Boardman said the newspaper reporters and editors weren't the only ones who deserved the award. "We want the whole community to share in this prize," Boardman said. The series of stories about the massacre of four police officers in the Lakewood section of Seattle relied heavily on information contributed by citizens through social media sites such as Twitter and Facebook. The *Times* was the first news organization that identified the killer who walked into a coffee shop at 8:15 a.m. and shot the four officers who were working on their laptop computers as they were about to start their shifts. Throughout the two-day manhunt that followed, the *Times* published real-time updates of the search with tips, photos and videos that members of the community contributed to social media sites that the paper set up for the stories. Reporters used smart phones to record interviews and to post streaming video on the paper's website. The search ended when a patrolman checking on a stolen car recognized the suspected killer and shot him as he was about to draw his gun.

The Pulitzer committee honored the paper for "a distinguished example of local reporting of breaking news, with special emphasis on the speed and accuracy of the initial coverage, presented in print or online or both."

Facebook

That wasn't the first time social media had been used effectively for reporting. A defining moment for social media came in the aftermath of the shooting rampage at Virginia Polytechnic Institute in 2007 when 32 people were killed in two separate attacks before

Shooting at Virginia Tech Campus

2nd shooting
Norris Hall

McBRYDE HALL

The Mall

Newman Library

Drill field

Duck Pond

Memorial Gym

West Campus Drive

Kent St.

Washington Street

Gunman's dorm room
2121 Harper Hall

1st shooting
Ambler Johnston Hall

Duck Pond Drive

Southgate Drive

Grant Jedlinsky, Chris Obrion, Rob Lunsford, Hunter Wilson, Reed Williams I The Roanoke Times

Timeline of events
Virginia Tech Campus

NEXT

7:15 a.m.: Virginia Tech police receive a 911 call about a shooting at West Ambler Johnston Hall. Within minutes, police arrive at the residence hall and find two victims, a man and a woman.

East Ambler Johnston Hall

West Ambler Johnston Hall

Room 4040

His weapons: The types of guns Police say Seung-Hui Cho used

Copyright 2009, *The Roanoke Times*, www.roankoe.com

Alvin and Earline Mudd try to salvage what is left of their home in Cameron, La., after Hurricane Rita destroyed it.

Photo by Marvin Nauman, courtesy of the Federal Emergency Management Agency.

the assailant shot himself. Telephone communication was limited that day, so students used Facebook to let friends and families know they were safe and to seek information about other students whose fate was not yet known. "To everyone I haven't talked to yet, I'm okay," one student wrote in a Facebook group called "I'm okay at VT." Journalists searched through profiles and blogs on that site and others to find sources and quotes for their stories about the massacre.

Lauren McClullough, social networks and news engagement manager for the Associated Press, said that Virginia Tech was a "pivotal moment" when the AP learned the value of social networks. "At that point Facebook was still heavily used by students. There were a lot of instances where we were looking on Facebook to find information to identify possible people who had been affected by what had happened. So this was a moment where the company realized, 'wow' these networks have some purpose. Since 2007 it has been an important part of our newsgathering process," she said in an interview on Mashable, a website for social media news.

Facebook has since become the most popular social media site with more than 500 million users. If Facebook were a country, it would be the third most populated one in the world. Although Facebook began as a network to connect with friends, it is now used by businesses, government agencies and all types of organizations as a way to establish a presence, spread a message and communicate.

Social networking sites became major sources for news during other tragedies, as well. After Hurricane Katrina in the Gulf Coast, MSNBC recruited citizens to tell their personal stories by asking these questions: "Was your home severely damaged or destroyed after Hurricane Katrina or Hurricane Rita? If you are rebuilding, tell us your story. You may also send text, pictures and video."

Twitter

Twitter has become another crucial tool to report breaking news as it happens. With the limit of 140 characters (including punctuation and spaces) allowed for a message, it may not seem as though you could convey much information. But Twitter messages, called "tweets," are like headlines, and just 10 to 20 words in a tweet can convey a lot of information.

The trial of Steven Hayes was an example. The courtroom was packed. Reporters had lined up at 5:30 a.m. to get a seat in the small New Haven, Ct., courtroom where Hayes was on trial for a grisly crime. He had invaded a physician's home, killed the doctor's wife and two daughters and set the house on fire. The trial wasn't televised. Cameras weren't allowed in the courtroom. But thousands of people witnessed the trial as reporters tapped their smart phones or computer keyboards to send minute-by-minute details of the trial to Twitter.

Consider these tweets with the hashtag #Hayes, which indicates a link to other tweets about him:

"We're in session; **#hayes** enters glaring at front row of reporters as he moves to his seat."

"Judge Blue: 'Your fate is now in the hands of others. May God have mercy on your soul.'"

"**#Hayes:** Words can never express what I feel for what I've done."

The brevity of a tweet can be deceptive. Many tweets, including the previous examples, are simply headlines that link to full stories — often posted on Facebook pages or websites. You can also use abbreviations — a form of shorthand to squeeze in more information.

Twitter is a way to get sources and eyewitness accounts quickly during a disaster, an accident or any local event. When a man jumped off an overpass on I-45 in Houston, traffic was stopped for three hours, but *Houston Chronicle* readers learned about it shortly after the incident occurred if they checked the Twitter feed at *twitter.com/@HoustonChron*. The *Chronicle* has so many Twitter subscribers that it posts a link to its twitter feed on the front page of its website. From trials to traffic, Twitter connects the community to the newsroom.

Here's how it works:

After you create a Twitter account, you can search for people whose tweets you want to read. To "follow" people or organizations, click the link under their names. That will take you to the Twitter member's home page where you can see recent tweets. When a username is preceded by the @ sign, it becomes a link to a Twitter page. When you follow certain Twitter users, you will receive their tweets on your Twitter home page. You can also "retweet" some messages by sending them to people who follow you much the same as you would send e-mail to a group of people.

Although Twitter is considered a social networking site, it is not limited to social connections. The network is used around the world by media, government agencies and corporations as a way to communicate a lot of information in a little amount of space. Twitter is considered a "microblogging" site, which is just a short form of blogging.

Writing for Twitter Twitter readers are scanners, so you need to write tweets like headlines that will grab attention. You can check your character count in a word processing program to make sure you are limited to 140 characters. Here are some writing tips:

- Read some Twitter posts before you begin to write.
- Find a focus. What are you trying to say and what is your point?
- Limit your tweet to one main point.
- Put the strongest words at the beginning of your tweet.
- Use strong verbs.
- Don't waste words — cut articles like "and," and "the."
- Use abbreviations only if they are clear. Some common ones are 2, b, u.
- Provide links or #hashtags, references to similar topics identified by the # symbol.
- Use a link shortening system such as *TinyURL.com* or *bit.ly* to abbreviate Web addresses.

New social media sites continue to develop. Some of the most popular ones include YouTube, a video-sharing site; Flickr, a photo-sharing site and MySpace, another social networking site that has trailed behind Facebook in usage. As mobile media gain popularity, more social networking sites will emerge including geolocation services, such as Foursquare, that can act like guidebooks on your smart phones. The future has no boundaries.

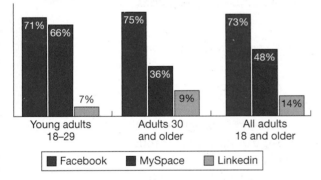

Where adult SNS users have profiles, by age group

The Pew Internet and American Life Project

BLOGS

What are the best blogs for college students? *Campusgrotto.com* claims to have them. What are the best blogs for journalism students? Your choices abound from "100 Best Blogs for Journalism Students" to "Top 50 Journalism Blogs." Do you want to improve your social life? The Positivity Blog aims to do that (*positivityblog.com*).

No matter what you are seeking, there's a blog about the topic. CNET, a website about technology news, claims a new blog is created every second — more than 80,000 a day. That's a lot of opinions.

Blogs, short for Web logs, are online journals or columns in which the writer expresses opinions or describes personal experiences. Many media blogs are commentaries about news topics. Although many blogs began as personal journals produced for friends and other people with common interests, they have become valuable ways journalists can find

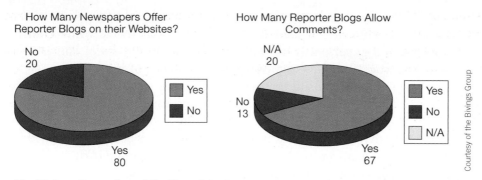

How Many Newspapers Offer Reporter Blogs on their Websites?

No 20

Yes 80

Yes / No

How Many Reporter Blogs Allow Comments?

N/A 20

No 13

Yes 67

Yes / No / N/A

Courtesy of the Bivings Group

The Bivings Group from "The Use of the Internet by America's Newspapers"

sources. The other advantage of reading blogs for news tips is that they provide insight into what readers and viewers are concerned about, much like letters to the editor.

Blogs also provide sources for human interest stories on news events. Beat reporters rely on blogs in their fields, and they can get additional help from the site, *http://beatblogging.org.* Most corporate and government agencies also offer blogs where reporters can find valuable information.

With millions of blogs on every conceivable topic, how do you find them? In addition to popular search engines such as Google and Yahoo!, which feature blog searches, these sites and programs can do the work for you:

- **Technorati:** A search engine that indexes millions of blogs and updates the references by tracking posts and links to them.
- **Permalink:** These are URLs (Web addresses) that link to comments or related sites. They are most often used in blogs.
- **RSS:** The letters stand for "Really Simple Syndication," which is a program that automatically sends information you requested to your computer or digital media player. The RSS online tool can track information that changes, whether it is in blogs or any websites, through an "aggregator," which is a program that compiles the information from the sites you have selected. It basically "feeds" the information to your computer or portable media device. It can be used for news summaries, blogs or podcasts and audio or video digital files that can be downloaded to your computer or portable media device.
- **Trackbacks:** Links at the end of a blog, like footnotes or references you might put in a term paper. Similar to permalinks. Someone who posts a comment to your blog can insert a link back to his or her comment or related sites, provided that the software for both sites supports trackbacks.

Blogs in Public Relations and Marketing

Blogs are not limited to news and personal sites. Hill & Knowlton, one of the largest public relations/marketing firms in the world, supports blogs and calls them "collective communication." On its website, the company says, "Like many other companies, we believe that blogs have the potential to become powerful communications tools.

We have created this community to optimize our consultants' participation in the blogosphere. They can listen to and learn from our audiences, while contributing their own insight and experience. All our bloggers are employees of Hill & Knowlton somewhere in the world and have signed up to a strict code of practice."

PRWeb, a wire service website that distributes news releases, also offers blogs in a blogroll, a list of links to blogs that the service recommends. The Public Relations Society of America (PRSA) offers a number of blogs, including *prnewpros* for new practitioners, a blog to foster diversity and another for professionals to share ideas. The student chapter, PRSSA, also provides a blog and a social media toolkit.

Here's some advice from PRSSA on how to write better blogs:

- Decide who your audience is and tailor the content to it.
- Consider three C's: clear, concise, compelling.
- Connect with your readers. Comment on their blog posts and encourage them to comment on yours.

"Blogs will make or break your business," according to Nora Ganim Barnes, author of the study, "Behind the Scenes in the Blogosphere: Advice from Established Bloggers." She said that consumers want to talk about products, and if they can't talk to the vendor, they will talk to others online in blogs.

FTC Rules Affecting Bloggers and Advertisers If you write a blog or post a tweet that endorses a product on a social media site, you have to disclose if you received cash, gifts or are employed by the company, according to new guidelines that the Federal Trade Commission imposed in 2009. The guidelines apply to bloggers and other users of social media. The FTC rulings require companies to disclose their relationship with celebrities or other people who endorse their products in advertisements in order to provide consumers with more knowledge about the claims that are being made. Although the FTC guidelines are not limited to social media, it was the first time in 30 years that the commission revised its guidelines regarding testimonials and endorsements for advertisements, a recognition of the impact of social media.

Citizen Journalism

The concept of involving readers and viewers in reporting and disseminating news is called "citizen journalism," "participatory journalism" or "user-generated-content." The movement is an attempt by media organizations to increase their interaction with their audience. The contributors are often called "citizen journalists," because they are not staff members of the news organization even though they may write blogs on a regular basis for the media website.

A pioneer in the user-generated-content movement is a South Korean website called OhmyNews International. Oh Yeon-ho, creator of the site, said his motto is "Every citizen is a reporter all over the world." Since its inception in 2000 with 727 citizen reporters, the organization has grown to more than 62,000 contributors with 70 full-time editors and reporters. The focus of the organization has changed to report more about citizen journalism than world news.

Courtesy of OhmyNews International.

This is how the company describes itself and its focus on citizen journalism: "We are a small team based at *OhmyNews* in Seoul, South Korea. We are international journalists. We know technology, and we are curious about the global progress of citizen journalism. And we adore coffee always. Grassroots journalism, citizen media, [and] crowdsourcing are all related terms that tackle the same question: How are regular people making and changing the news?"

How to Write Blogs

A blog is an online conversation you are having with the reader. Consider it like a telephone conversation; it's a two-way communication where you say something and hope for a response. You may use the first-person voice (I or me) because you are expressing your thoughts, but you should not insert yourself into a news story. Some blogs may just be one or two paragraphs with links to related stories, especially on news items, while others can be a complete journal entry.

You don't have to have any technical knowledge to create or publish your own blog. Wordpress does that for you. *Wordpress.org* is free Web software you can use to create your own blogs or websites, but you do need an Internet provider where you can post your blog. Although it started as a blogging system, Wordpress now offers complete content management, and many college newspapers use the program for their websites. Blogger, a free program by Google is another easy-to-learn site you can use to create and host blogs (*www.blogger.com*).

CONVERGENCE COACH

TECHNIQUES FOR incorporating blogs and comments in a news website are similar for print and broadcast news organizations. In a television newscast, the reporter or anchor will usually refer viewers to the website where links, polls or surveys and comments are posted, and print media organizations also promote additional material on their websites. To encourage reader and viewer interaction via blogs or just comments, consider using some of these techniques.

- Include a poll or quiz on the website.
- Promote added features to the news on the website such as a photo gallery, full texts of speeches or documents.
- Add multimedia features — audio and video — of news on the website.
- Update your stories frequently, especially for breaking news.
- Offer links on your website to social media sites — Twitter, Facebook and others.

Here are some tips for writing your blog:

- Be brief. Blogs are not meant to be term papers.
- Write a clear headline that will hook the reader.
- Be clear. Use simple sentences.
- Be focused. Like a news story, which should have one main idea, a blog should also contain one main topic.
- Be careful; check your spelling and grammar. Informal communication in e-mail and blogs tends to be sloppy. Errors in spelling and grammar mar credibility.
- Be interesting. Provide something new or evocative if you are writing an opinion about news. Write about a topic that would be of interest to other people in your age group or community.
- Be accurate and fair. Don't spread rumors or information that may not be truthful. The basic guidelines of accuracy and fairness that apply to news stories apply to blogs as well.
- Be conversational. Write as though you are talking to a friend.
- Target your audience. Consider the people you are trying to reach and write about topics they would want to read, especially on social network blogs. If it is a personal blog, what do your friends and family want to know? If it is a blog intended for a public audience, ask yourself why anyone would want to read your comments.
- Add links to related sites or other blogs if relevant.
- Add a question or thought at the end that would elicit readers to post their responses to your blog.
- Proofread.

PODCASTS

If you don't want to write a blog, you can hear it or see it by producing it as a podcast. Once a combination term for broadcast and iPod, podcast is now a legitimate word. It has been added to the New Oxford American Dictionary, which defines it as "a digital recording of a radio broadcast or similar program, made available on the Internet for downloading to a personal audio player."

Although the original definition was confined to audio files, definitions and uses of podcasts have expanded to include video. A video podcast is also called a "vidcast" or "vodcast," but whatever you call it, this form of media is now a common alternative format on news sites as well as social networking sites.

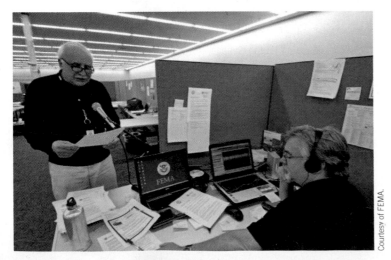

Courtesy of FEMA.

Research and Writing Specialist Ernie Martz (left) and Social Media Specialist Steve Crider (right) record a podcast for the Federal Emergency Management multimedia site (*www.fema.gov*).

You don't need an iPod, a portable digital media player by Apple Inc., or an MP3 player, which also compresses audio files into digital form, to hear or view podcasts. You can click onto a podcast in your computer and listen to it with software for hearing audio or viewing video. You can also download a podcast to your computer and listen to it or view it with free software such as iTunes, Quicktime, or Windows Media Player.

If you want to receive regularly updated information from podcasts of blogs or news, you can subscribe to a website that contains an RSS reader, the program that compiles sites you select and automatically delivers them to your computer or portable digital device.

ETHICS

BE CAREFUL WHAT you post on a blog, especially if you are seeking a job. Employers have been known to search popular sites such as MySpace and Facebook when they are interviewing job candidates. In addition, posting personal information such as telephone numbers or addresses can make it easy for sexual predators or other undesirable people to contact you, despite attempts by social networking sites to protect privacy.

Here are some other ethical issues relating to social media:

- **Plagiarism:** Don't take material from other people's blogs or websites and post the information on your blog. You can quote some of the material and attribute it, but you can't just reproduce the information as your own. That's plagiarism. It's also a copyright infringement. Everything that is produced in a fixed form (print or online) is protected by U.S. copyright laws. That includes photos and videos — unless you have permission or you receive the information under a Creative Commons license where the contributor has given permission for the material to be used. Check whether it is authorized for personal use, for use with attribution or if it is fair use, generally from a government site.

- **Inaccuracy:** How do you know if the information you get on social media sites is accurate? You don't. You have to check carefully. That's not easy to do when you are on deadline or reporting breaking news. But you should make the attempt to verify the information. If you can't confirm the source, don't use it. Avoid anonymous sources.

- **Neutrality:** Should staff reporters for TV news stations and newspapers write blogs that express their personal opinions when they are supposed to be impartial in covering the news? Several news organizations have created policies addressing this issue such as this one from *The New York Times*: "If you have or are getting a Facebook page, leave blank the section that asks about your political views. . . . Be careful not to write anything on a blog or a personal Web page that you could not write in the *Times*. Anything you post online can and might be publicly disseminated."

Even with guidelines, citizen journalism poses several ethical issues for mainstream media publications that post contributors' blogs on their sites. Some of those concerns are:

- Is the information on blogs accurate or based on rumors?

- Should journalists use sources from social networking sites without contacting the person who posted the information?

- Should blogs be edited or monitored for standards of taste?

- How should editors deal with abusive posts on websites that seek comments from readers and viewers? This issue has become a problem as interaction with readers and viewers increases on websites that seek comments, but staff to supervise the websites is limited at most news organizations.

Because blogs and other forms of citizen journalism are evolving, media organizations are still wrestling with solutions to these concerns.

TIPS FROM A PULITZER-PRIZE WINNING WRITER

Richard Aregood was an editorial writer for the *Philadelphia Daily News* when he won the Pulitzer Prize in 1985. Twitter didn't exist. Neither did Facebook. But Aregood had mastered a skill that writers of social media need today — brevity. In this article that he wrote for the American Society of Newspaper Editors several years ago, he gives advice that social media writers need today.

Writing short is simple, but it ain't easy.

What it requires is a lot of hard work before the first finger hits the key, work that answers the classic questions of just what the hell we're trying to do here. The first step of that has to come from a writer who is willing to throw out his or her best sentence if it doesn't fit. The writer must focus everything on advancing the story, not in filling space.

A piece about a cesspool overflow need not include the entire history of solid waste on the planet, complete with graphics. All it needs to tell is the basic disgusting story.

Some things that help:

Forget about all those dimwit professors who weighed blue books to determine grades and the editors who equate importance with length.

- Focus hard on the point of the story.
- Resist the temptation to tell everything you've learned; much of it doesn't matter.
- Pounce on every sentence and get rid of every word that doesn't clearly and simply say what needs to be said.
- Avoid the jargon sources use; translating it adds clarity and keeps you from getting woozy.
- Remember that you're writing for actual people.
- Let your mind wander through a story before the typing starts. I find it a lot easier in the end to write the best possible first draft because I'm one of those people who has to get it right the first time.
- Thinking a story through helps even more with the long ones, which have a tendency to grow like kudzu if there is no vision going in. Even then, advance thought can turn something that would have consumed 40 columns into merely 30.

None of this is easy. In fact, it's a lot easier to simply regurgitate everything and slap a lead on a 12-part meaningless series. The trouble is that no one will read the damn thing.

Finally, the hardest of all — convincing an editor that a really sparkling five paragraphs deserves good display.

That's all I have to say. I'm outta here.

EXERCISES

1 Word association exercise:

- Write five or 10 words that come to your mind associated with these words (one minute for each word association): snow, happy, sad, dreams, goals, pain.

- Now expand your thoughts to one paragraph (three minutes for each idea): I am afraid of . . . . I hope to be . . . . The best gift I received . . . . My worst experience . . . .

2 Six word stories: "For sale, baby shoes, never used." Those six words by Ernest Hemingway are the inspiration for a website , "Six word stories." Study the website at *www.sixwordstories.net/* and use it for inspiration to write your own six-word stories. This is practice for writing good tweets.

3 Blog: Write a blog on a personal topic that you think might be of interest to a campus audience. You can expand some of the thoughts you just wrote in exercise 1 into a blog or write about a new topic. Add a question at the end to solicit responses to your blog.

4 Twitter following: Create a Twitter account and choose at least five people you want to follow. Study their tweets. Write a critique of the tweeters.

5 Tweets Cover an event on campus (an athletic event, a lecture, a demonstration or any other event) and tweet about it in real time. If your instructor wishes, critique each others' tweets.

 CourseMate

FEATURED ONLINE ACTIVITY Log on and visit the Writing and Reporting News CourseMate and take the interactive tutorial quiz on social media and blogs. *Access available at www.cengagebrain.com.*

COACHING TIPS

dny3d/Shutterstock.com

Use the matchmaking technique: **Ask one source to recommend another** one who is knowledgeable about the subject you are researching.

Check previous stories about the subject in your organization's databases before you begin your reporting.

Check any **records** or documents related to your story.

Check the Internet for information about your sources or topic.

Check the **credibility of websites** before you use information from them.

Attribute sources; **avoid anonymous sources.**

Contact sources who have **opposing points of view.**

> Anonymous sources challenge our credibility with readers.
>
> — **PETER BHATIA,** editor, *The* (Portland) *Oregonian*

CHAPTER 5
Sources and Online Research

SOURCES FOR JOURNALISTS ARE EVERYWHERE – ON FACEBOOK, ON Twitter, on blogs and scores of social networks. In fact it is harder to keep track of sources these days than it is to find them. You can access your sources anywhere with your smart phone, iPad or other mobile device. But you shouldn't just rely on social networks for sources.

"Social networks should never be used as a reporting shortcut when another method, like picking up a phone or knocking on a door, would yield more reliable or comprehensive information," according to social media guidelines in the Associated Press Stylebook.

Good reporters still cultivate sources several ways–in person, with records and with online resources.

Mark Potter, a reporter for NBC, needs face-to-face interviews with sources who are willing to appear on television. They aren't always easy to find, especially for controversial stories. When Potter has trouble finding sources, he uses a technique called "sponsorship." This is a method of introducing yourself to a source by using a contact that the source might know.

For example, when Potter was working on a story about the problems of Haitians in Miami, the Haitian refugees were illegal immigrants who were reluctant to talk to him. Potter said they thought he was an immigration officer who might report them to authorities for deportation. So Potter asked a community social worker who had gained the refugees' trust to recommend him to a Haitian who might talk to him. The social worker introduced him to a Haitian named Pierre, but Pierre didn't have the information Potter wanted. So Pierre introduced Potter to his brother-in-law, who then "sponsored" Potter by getting other Haitians to talk to him.

Potter also cross-indexes his list of sources by their name, occupation and location. If he wants to contact an FBI agent he once interviewed in Detroit but whose name he may have forgotten, Potter looks up the agent's name under "FBI" or "Detroit." Under each listing, Potter records the source's addresses and telephone numbers and e-mail

Mark Potter, NBC reporter (third from left)

addresses. That's still good advice even if you have lists of "friends" and followers on social networks.

It's not too early in your career for you to start a list of sources. The people you interview in college, such as professors who are experts on foreign policy or the economy, may be good sources for stories later in your career. Whether you keep your source list in your cell phone, computer or mobile media device, you should back it up on a storage device. And although it may seem old-fashioned in these days of digital devices, it's a good idea to have a printed copy of your source lists.

Before you begin reporting for any assignment, check previous stories about the topic in databases and do online research. Most print and broadcast newsrooms maintain databases of stories the newspaper or television station has done, so it is easy to search for previous stories about the person or topic. If you are searching online for a source, check to make sure that the source is the person you want; many people have the same name, and the information you retrieve may not be for the correct source. For example, if you are checking a source in LinkedIn, a network often used by professional people, the profile might include a photo, which is helpful if you know the person. It will also list the person's job title.

When you are assigned to a breaking-news event, such as a fire or accident, you may not have time to check previous stories before you leave the office. But you should check them before you begin writing. The building that burned may have had problems with sprinkler systems or previous fires in the past.

The same recommendation applies to crime stories. A suspect arrested on charges may have been arrested previously for the same or other charges. If you find a story about a suspect's previous arrest, make sure that you find out if the charges were dropped or what happened in the case.

Use caution: Newsroom files and videotapes may not be up-to-date, and follow-up stories may not have been written or aired about crime suspects. Even more problematic is the Web, which can archive everything, but if the document is not dated, you may not be getting the most accurate information.

HUMAN SOURCES

News writing needs human sources to make the story credible and readable. Information from eyewitnesses and participants lends immediacy to a story, and direct quotes and sound bites make a story interesting. You can find human sources in a number of ways.

- **News releases:** All news releases list a contact person, usually a public information officer or public relations contact. Contact that person first but don't stop with that source. Whenever possible, ask to speak to the people mentioned in the news release.

- **Up and down the ladder:** Who's in charge of the organization or department? You could start at the top by contacting the department head. On many other stories, you should also go down the ladder and try to contact the person closest to the incident. For example, if you are writing a police story, try to contact the officer who was at the scene. If you are writing about a study, contact the professor or researcher who did the study.

- **Names in the news:** If you read or view a news story from a newspaper, telecast, website or social media site, don't just quote the news story. Contact the primary source — the person involved. That is particularly true when you read about a survey or a study.

- **Administrative assistants:** Get to know officials' administrative assistants, sometimes still called "secretaries." This is especially important if you have a beat — a specific area of coverage such as education, government, police or other specialties you are responsible for covering regularly. Without the cooperation of the administrative assistant, you may not get to the sources you need.

- **Community and campus leaders:** Find out who are the leaders of groups in your community and campus. Don't limit your sources to these people, but they could be valuable initial resources who can lead you to other people.

- **Self-sponsorship:** If you have reported and written a previous news story about a subject of interest to the source you are trying to contact, you can sponsor yourself. When you contact the source, introduce yourself by referring to the relevant article or newscast you reported.

- **Matchmaking:** Once you have contacted a source and want to find others, use the matchmaking technique, which is related to the sponsorship method. Ask the source who else you might contact about the situation.

- **Fairness:** If you are writing a story involving conflict, find sources who have the opposing points of view. Do not report any accusations about a person without contacting the target of those comments.

- **Primary and secondary sources:** When you are conducting an interview, if your source says something about another person, particularly if it is derogatory or controversial, make sure that you check with that other person. The first source's statements not only could be wrong; they could also be libelous. You should even check out written information about sources, especially online information, to make sure that it is accurate.

- **Blogs:** Postings on the Internet from people who have written blogs about an issue can be good sources for you to contact. Don't consider information from blogs as accurate news. Blogs are usually opinion columns and personal reflections, but they can be valuable for finding human sources.

BEAT REPORTING

Beat reporters have more sources at their fingertips than ever before. Almost all government agencies, corporations, public relations practitioners and social agencies use websites and social media to publicize information. For example, the Education Writers

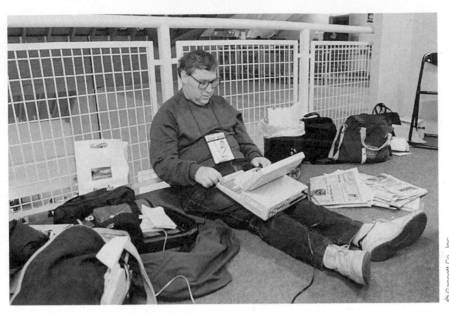

Mike Lopresti covers the sports beat for *USA Today*.

Association offers a list of Web resources including blogs, data sources from government and research agencies. It is just one of many journalism organizations that list sources for reporters. But when you establish a beat you need to develop your own sources online and in person.

When Mark McCormick first began covering the religion beat, he used the matchmaker technique similar to the sponsorship method that Mark Potter used. "I asked each person I interviewed two things: 'If you could name five or 10 people that I would need to know to do this beat well, who would they be? I amassed a large calling list." McCormick said. He also asked one source to introduce him to other people, especially those who might be skeptical about dealing with him. "That is how I made a breakthrough in the Jewish community and Muslim community."

One story can generate sources for many others. McCormick recalled a story he wrote about a hospital chapel that was closing. "I went there and talked to people about their memories, he said. "I found a woman who had spent many hours praying in the chapel 20 years ago because her husband had cancer and was supposed to die. He is still alive today." McCormick said 135 people called him or left voicemail messages to comment about the story, and many people told him similar touching stories about how faith had affected their lives. As a result, he had many sources for another story about the power of faith.

Mark McCormick, director of communications, Kansas Leadership Center.

McCormick covered the religion beat at *The Courier–Journal* in Louisville, Ky., and later covered many other beats and wrote columns for *The Wichita* (Kan.) *Eagle*. Like many former newspaper reporters, McCormick has changed jobs, but he still uses his journalism skills as the director of communications for the Kansas Leadership Center, an organization devoted to cultivating civic leadership.

ANONYMOUS SOURCES

Many people will be willing to talk to you if you promise not to use their names. An anonymous source is one who remains unnamed. (The terms "anonymous source" and "confidential source" are used interchangeably by most people.) But should you make

SOCIAL MEDIA

WHEN A SUICIDAL pilot crashed a small plane into an office building in Austin, Texas, the local newspaper gained hundreds of sources in a matter of minutes. Robert Quigley, social media editor for the *Austin* (Texas) *American–Statesman* newspaper, sent out a Twitter message asking the 20,000 people who follow the paper on its social media site if they had witnessed the incident. Photos and eyewitness accounts poured into the paper from its Twitter users. Social media sites have created opportunities for journalists to connect with the public in an unprecedented level, Quigley wrote in a column for the paper.

"We still report facts and give you the news, but the rise of social media has changed how a story is told and consumed," Quigley wrote. "For example, most of the *Statesman's* newsroom staff members use social media every day to interact with readers and sources. Thanks to these new tools, journalists can get instant feedback on their work, gather meaningful tips, track trends and build valuable relationships with the public."

That's just one example of how social media can provide instant sources for journalists on a breaking news story. Twitter, Facebook, YouTube and other social media sites are commonly used sources for journalists. As sources multiply on social media sites, keeping track of them gets more difficult. But for every problem, a new site springs up to offer solutions. These are just a few sites that will find or coordinate your sources.

- To search for people on all social network sites or blogs, a search engine called yoName will find them (*www.yoname.com*).

- To coordinate all your contacts from inboxes, e-mail address accounts, social networks and blog posts, check out Gist (*http://gist.com*).

- To find the business or professional background of a source, check LinkedIn (*www.linkedin.com*).

---

this promise? Most editors today would say no, unless there is no other way to get the information. And even then, many editors would refuse to grant that immunity from identification. The more you rely on unnamed sources, the less credibility your story has.

The Associated Press policy on anonymous sources is as follows: "Reporters should proceed with interviews on the assumption they are on the record. If the source wants to set conditions, these should be negotiated at the start of the interview. At the end of the interview, the reporter should try once again to move some or all of the information back on the record."

In the past, reporters who promised their sources anonymity had a good chance of honoring their promise even if they were subpoenaed to reveal their sources. Most news organizations successfully fought any court attempts to reveal sources. But in the last few years, judges in several courts penalized reporters by sentencing them to jail for refusing to reveal their sources.

One of the most publicized cases occurred in 2005 when Judith Miller, then a reporter for *The New York Times,* spent 85 days in jail for refusing to testify to a federal grand jury about the name of a confidential source who had revealed the identity of an undercover CIA agent, which is a federal crime. When the source gave Miller permission to reveal his name, she was released from jail and testified. An unusual factor in this case was that Miller never wrote a story about the agent. Miller claimed her refusal to reveal sources was a matter of principle. "I do not make confidential pledges lightly, but when I do, I keep them," Miller told U.S. District Court Judge Thomas F. Hogan when he sentenced her to jail. Miller resigned from the *Times* a few months after she testified because of objections from some of her colleagues about her actions and because she had become the news, she said in her resignation letter.

Matt Cooper, then a reporter for *Time*, did write a story about the same CIA agent, Valerie Plame, but he reluctantly revealed his sources to the grand jury after his appeals for immunity from testifying were rejected by the Supreme Court.

The case has prompted support for a federal shield law that would prohibit federal courts from forcing reporters to reveal their confidential sources. In 1972 the U.S. Supreme Court ruled that journalists have a duty to provide grand juries information relevant to criminal trials. Since then, all states except Wyoming offer some protection of journalist–source privileges either by shield laws or precedents from case law, but these state statutes do not apply to federal courts.

Although a federal shield bill, known as the Free Flow of Information Act, passed a committee in the U.S. Senate in 2009, the issue has become more complicated with the increase in citizen journalism and social media. Who would be considered a journalist? Would everyone who publishes news on a website be protected by such a shield law? These are some of the issues that remain to be resolved.

Despite the problems with anonymous sources, it's unlikely that news organizations will eliminate them altogether. If you must use anonymous sources because you have no other alternative, you should check the information with other sources, preferably ones who will allow use of their names, and check documents. Many sources, named or unnamed, have their own agenda and want to manipulate reporters so the sources can promote their cause. For fairness and balance, it is crucial for reporters to check with other sources to confirm, deny or provide other points of view.

Janet Cooke didn't do that. And she touched off a furor in the newspaper industry that persists years after the incident. Cooke, then a reporter for *The Washington Post,* won the Pulitzer Prize in 1981 for a story called "Jimmy's World," about an 8-year-old heroin addict. There was only one problem: Jimmy didn't exist. When Cooke first discussed the story with her editors, she said she had located the child's mother, who was reluctant to talk. Her editors said she could grant the mother anonymity. Cooke turned in a compelling story about the child and his mother. But when Cooke won the Pulitzer and was profiled in newspapers, some discrepancies in her résumé were discovered. That led to questions about her story. She ultimately admitted that she had made up the story about Jimmy and his mother. The *Post* returned the Pulitzer, and Cooke resigned in disgrace.

Cooke's story wasn't based on an anonymous source; it was a fabricated source. The impact was a crisis of credibility for the press. Newspapers throughout the country began developing policies against using pseudonyms, and many editors banned the use of anonymous sources altogether.

Fabrication of sources and other information in news stories surfaced as a problem again in the 1990s and later in several high-profile scandals. Most notorious was the case of Jayson Blair, a reporter for *The New York Times,* who made up quotes, fictionalized

ETHICS

ETHICAL DILEMMA: Should you show your story to a source before publication?

Discussion: Most journalists are opposed to prepublication review by a source because of fears that the source may recant statements or may wish to change the copy. Steve Weinberg, an author of several books and former director of the Investigative Reporters and Editors organization, strongly favors checking the story with a source because, he says, it will ensure accuracy. Other journalists have always favored reading parts of a story, especially technical or sensitive information, back to a source. In most cases, deadline pressure prevents journalists from waiting for sources to review the whole story. But if such review is possible, should it be allowed? What do you think?

Ethical guidelines: Fairness, credibility, accuracy. The Society of Professional Journalists Code of Ethics says journalists should "test the accuracy of information from all sources and exercise care to avoid inadvertent error."

When using unnamed sources, you may identify the person with a vague reference, such as "according to one official." Or you might give the person a pseudonym, a false name. Although most editors discourage pseudonyms, they are sometimes allowed in feature stories about sensitive subjects such as rape. But they are rarely used in hard-news stories. It is preferable to use no name or a first name only. If you use a full-name pseudonym, which is not preferred, you should check your local telephone directories to make sure that you aren't using the name of someone in your community. And in all cases, to protect the identity of the source, you must tell the reader that this is a false name.

scenes and plagiarized material in dozens of the stories he wrote during his four years at the newspaper. His deception was discovered after he plagiarized material from a story written by a Texas newspaper reporter with whom Blair had worked when he was a reporter on the student newspaper at The University of Maryland. Blair never graduated from the school and was hired by the *Times* after his internship there because he showed so much promise. After the discovery of this and other stories that were fabricated or plagiarized, Blair resigned in disgrace, and the *Times* published an extensive front-page story about his deception.

Blair's trail of fabrication and plagiarism mirrored the pattern of Stephen Glass, a rising star at *The New Republic,* who was fired after his editor discovered that he had fabricated sources in many of his stories. His deception was discovered when a reporter for an online site questioned a story Glass had written about a convention of hackers. The convention didn't exist, nor did the software company cited in the story. Glass even created a phony website for the nonexistent software company. A complaint from an online magazine spurred the investigation, which revealed that the article was a hoax, and several others Glass had written were also fiction. A few years later, Glass published an autobiographical novel called *The Fabulist* about a reporter who fabricates stories. The Glass story also became the subject of a movie called *Shattered Glass.*

Both Blair and Glass were reporters in their 20s with limited experience but great promise that landed them these prestigious jobs. On the other hand, Jack Kelley was a veteran reporter with 21 years of experience at *USA Today* when he resigned at age 43, after evidence surfaced that he had fabricated sources. His work was questioned after he submitted a story about a woman who died fleeing from Cuba by boat. The woman whose photo Kelley submitted with the story was a Cuban hotel worker who had neither fled from Cuba nor died. Further investigation by the newspaper revealed problems with numerous stories, including one for which he had been a Pulitzer-Prize finalist.

Patricia Smith, a former columnist for *The Boston Globe*, had also been nominated for a Pulitzer Prize. She resigned after the *Globe* discovered that she had fabricated sources and quotes in her columns. In her last column she apologized and explained why she had attributed quotes to people who didn't exist.

"I could give them names, even occupations, but I couldn't give them what they needed most — a heartbeat," she wrote. "As anyone who's ever touched a newspaper knows, that's one of the cardinal sins of journalism: Thou shall not fabricate. No exceptions. No excuses."

Despite these well-known cases and policies to prohibit plagiarism, every year more cases of it occur in all types of journalism publications — newspapers, campus publications and news sites, including social media networks. That is another reason journalists should avoid using information from unnamed sources on social media sites.

Promises: Dan Cohen made the issue of anonymous sources a legal matter that affects what journalists can promise sources. He was a public relations executive. In 1982 he gave reporters from the (Minneapolis) *Star Tribune* and the *St. Paul* (Minn.) *Pioneer Press* damaging information about a candidate for lieutenant governor in Minnesota on the condition that they would not reveal him as the source. The reporters agreed to grant Cohen anonymity. But editors of the two newspapers overruled the reporters and insisted on printing Cohen's name in the story. The editors decided that since Cohen was working for the opposing political party, the readers had a right to know the source of the information.

Cohen sued on the grounds of breach of contract. He claimed that the newspapers had violated an oral contract of confidentiality and that, as a result, he had suffered harm by losing his job. A jury at the first trial level agreed that a reporter's promise of confidentiality is as legally binding as an oral contract. The newspaper appealed and lost. The case went all the way to the U.S. Supreme Court, which ruled in 1991 that the First Amendment does not protect journalists from being sued if they break promises of confidentiality. The high court sent the case back to the Minnesota Supreme Court for a ruling on damages, and Cohen was awarded $200,000.

Before you agree to grant anonymity to a source, you should check with your editors to determine the policies of your organization.

Even when sources agree to be identified, they often ask for anonymity for portions of the interview. They'll say, "This is off the record." Sometimes they aren't even aware of what the term means.

Here are some definitions of the terms used most often to establish ground rules in an interview:

On the Record: The source agrees that all information can be used in a news story and that he can be identified as the source of it. The easiest way to establish this understanding is to identify yourself as a reporter immediately and state your purpose for the interview. If you are interviewing people who are not accustomed to dealing with the media, you may need to remind the source during the interview that you are quoting him about the material, especially if you are writing about controversial issues. Such a reminder may jeopardize your chances of using some of the material, but it is better to take that chance during the interview than later in a courtroom after you have been sued.

Off the Record: The information from this source may not be used at all. If you can get the same information from another source, you may use it, but you may not attribute it to the source who told it to you off the record.

Not for Attribution: You may use the information as background, but you may not identify the source.

Background: This is similar to the term "not for attribution." Generally, it means that you may use the information but can't attribute it. Some reporters define background as the ability to use the information with a general attribution, such as "a city official said." If you are in doubt during the interview, ask the source how you can identify him, and give the specific wording you intend to use.

Deep Background: This term is rarely used or understood by most sources except for officials in Washington, D.C. It means you may use the material for your information only but may not attribute it at all, not even with a general term, such as "government official."

MULTICULTURAL SOURCES

One of every three people in the United States is a member of a minority racial or ethnic group, according to recent U.S. Census figures. Projections indicate that by 2050 minorities will make up nearly half of the country's population, which is expected to add another million people to its current 310 million. Hispanics made up 49 percent of the children born in the U.S. in the last decade and Asians were the next fastest growing group. Do your local media reflect this diversity? Do your stories include sources from the minority members of your campus or community?

Members of minority journalism organizations have often complained that minorities are represented in the news media in stereotypical ways especially in sports pages and crime stories but not enough in the basic news stories. As this population increases, it is incumbent upon you to include diverse points of view in articles, photographs, video and other media.

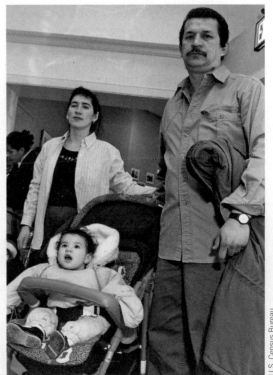

U.S. Census Bureau

Hispanic families are one of the fastest growing minorities in the U.S.

In addition to racial and ethnic diversity, there are many other minority groups such as members of the gay community and people with disabilities who are often neglected by the news media until a controversy develops or when they are subjects of a special feature story about their differences. Strive for inclusiveness in all media, including news and public relations materials. How can you develop multicultural sources?

- Identify leaders of minority groups, including religious organizations, and put them in your source list. But don't anoint them as the only spokespeople for their groups.
- Use the matchmaking technique when you are contacting these leaders and ask them to connect you with other members in their community.
- Be sensitive. Ask people of diverse backgrounds how they would like to be described. Some Hispanics prefer to be called "Chicanos," some blacks prefer the term "African-American," and people with disabilities have several preferences about how they want to be referred to in stories. The Associated Press Stylebook recommends that you avoid describing anyone as "disabled" or "handicapped" unless it is pertinent to the story. Instead describe the disability and avoid euphemisms such as "mentally challenged."
- Use racial or ethnic labels only when they are relevant to the story.
- Rely on visuals. Photographs and videos can demonstrate inclusiveness.

WRITTEN SOURCES

You can find many additional clues for human sources and other information from a variety of written sources. Even though you may rely on Google or other Internet search engines and social media, don't overlook some traditional sources, which are available in print and in searchable online form.

Telephone Directories: The white and yellow pages of telephone books are primary places to locate sources. Most local telephone books also contain information about city and county government agencies, utilities and other frequently used services.

USA Today library.

Reverse Directories: These directories, also called "city directories" or "cross-directories," list residents of a community three ways: by name, address and telephone number. Imagine that you are on deadline and have the address of a woman whose house is on fire and that you want to reach her neighbors for comments. How can you do this if you don't know the neighbors' names? You can look in the cross-directory under the address you have. The adjacent homes will be listed first by address, with names and telephone numbers of the occupants beside the address (unless they have unlisted telephone numbers). If you have a phone number but not the name, check the section for phone numbers.

The reverse directory is one of the most useful ways of locating people for comment when you can't go to the scene. These directories are published by real estate firms in most major communities and are kept in most newsrooms and libraries. Some online search engines, such as *www.reversephonedirectory.com,* will provide the same information.

Libraries: Your local public library and your college library contain a wealth of source material to help you find background about a story. Some of the most useful reference works are almanacs and other books of facts, population data and financial records of major corporations. Many of these resources are also online.

Most college and university libraries also have a section devoted to federal and state documents and publications. In this section you can find transcripts of congressional hearings, publications from federal and state agencies and reports from all sorts of government offices.

ONLINE SOURCES

You are writing a story about sexually transmitted diseases among college students. You check the Web for background by typing "sexually transmitted diseases" in a search engine such as Google. You get more than 2 million results. The first might be the U.S. Centers for Disease Control, which contains a wealth of information about these diseases. Which sites should you use? How do you know what information is credible?

Stephen C. Miller, assistant to the technology editor at *The New York Times,* offers his "trust-o-meter," a technique he uses to determine credibility of Web information. Miller says his first choice is government sources because the information is official and public. For background in the story about sexually transmitted diseases, the National Institutes of Health or the Centers for Disease Control would be considered a reliable government source. Next, Miller likes university studies because they are peer-reviewed, but he says they should be linked to university sites or research journals. He finds personal sites the least trustworthy.

You might still check personal sites for ideas or contacts, but be wary of citing them without checking the information. Even if the information is trustworthy, you can still spend needless hours wading through it if you don't search effectively.

U.S. Centers for Disease Control

CONVERGENCE COACH

HERE IS A CHECKLIST to help you determine credibility of websites and search more effectively:

- **Who:** Is an author, site owner or name of sponsoring organization listed on the site? Avoid unnamed sites.

- **What:** Is the site affiliated with a government agency, an educational institution or a nationally credible organization? Check the site index for an "about us" page for further information.

- **When:** Is the site dated? This is crucial. Use the most current information you can find.

- **Where:** Does the site have any contact information — a phone number, address or names of individuals, not just "webmaster"?

- **Why:** Does the site have a bias or promotional agenda? If so, either avoid it or get other points of view, and check the accuracy.

- **How:** Narrow your search by typing specific key words instead of a broad topic.

- **Attribution:** Print the information you plan to use so you can document it; sites frequently disappear. Copy the site name and URL (address) for a link or citation. Don't copy anything from a site without attributing it.

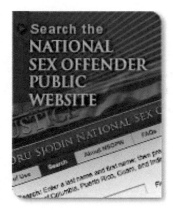

If you are writing a crime story or you just want to check a source's background to make sure that the person is not a sexual offender, all 50 states have sex offender registries with varying degrees of information available online. The U.S. Department of Justice hosts the Dru Sjodin National Sex Offender Public Website, *www.nsopw.gov*, which features a search engine for each state. Another easy way to find these registries is to start with your state site. In one case a student doing a background check on a candidate for the campus student senate found the person on a local sex offender register.

Use Journalism Directories: Several journalists have created websites with links to all sorts of valuable resources for the media. From government agencies to businesses and public records, you can find useful sources without scouring the Web yourself. For example, the Investigative Reporters and Editors organization has a website with links to topics for numerous beats in its resource center (*www.ire.org*). Another thorough directory for finding people and other sources for journalists was created by Julian Sher, a Canadian investigative journalist (*www.peoplesearchpro.com/journalism*).

Find Experts: An expert on almost every topic is willing to provide information to journalists. Profnet (*profnet.prnewswire.com*) is a site devoted to serving journalists with expert sources throughout the world. Designed for professional journalists by PRNewswire, this resource should be used for publications, not for term papers.

Find a Map: If you are seeking directions to a location for an assignment or for personal use, use a mapfinder such *www.mapquest.com* or *maps.google.com* or any other maps linked to most search engines. If you have a smart phone, chances are you have a GPS app to guide you.

Find Press Releases and Wire Services: Check *www.prnewswire.com, www.prweb.com, uwire.com* (for college wire stories) or *www.businesswire.com* (for business news).

Databases: A database is a collection of information. The term now generally refers to massive collections of information stored in computers. When you are seeking background for an in-depth story or feature, databases are worth checking. For instance, if you are working on an in-depth story about date rape on college campuses, a database check would be helpful. By reading other stories, you can get ideas for an angle on your story or find expert sources to contact.

You can access many databases online, but some of them require fees. You can probably access many databases without charge at your college library. One of the most popular databases for newspaper and magazine writers is NEXIS, a collection of newspaper, business and trade sources. It is available in some libraries but often with restrictions for users. LEXIS, the other part of this service, contains the text of court decisions, legislative records and legal resources. It is available in most law libraries. It is also available online for a fee.

PUBLIC RECORDS

Many government records, such as data from state and local agencies, may be obtained from databases consisting of public records. For example, if you want to find out who earns the highest salaries in each department at your university or college, you could spend days sifting through a printed version of the budget and trying to compare salaries. But if the budget is available on a database, you can use a computer program to analyze this information for you in minutes.

Other Public Records

An official at your university tells you that there are no serious fire safety violations on campus. But you want to be sure, so you decide to check the state fire marshal's report on the last fire safety inspection of campus buildings. The report may list many violations that the official might not have deemed serious. Records on paper or in computer form are valuable information sources.

Not only do such records as fire and police reports provide detail about investigations; they also give names of people to contact. When police officers investigate an accident or a crime, they fill out reports with details of the scene and crucial information about the people involved, including names, addresses, birth dates, physical descriptions and other material. Most of the records are public.

The following list mentions just a few of the public records that should be available to you locally or online.

Political Contributions: To check campaign contributions to candidates for state offices, you can access a searchable database for each state at *www.followthemoney.org*.

Real Estate Records: Mortgages, deeds (which record the property owners, purchase date and sale price in some states), the legal property description, indexes listing previous property owners and commercial property inventories (lists of everything the commercial property owner has, such as trucks, supplies and equipment) are available in the Register of Deeds office. This office also has maps showing all the property in the county and individual maps called "plats," which show the zoning of each piece of property. Records for tax rates and the assessed value of the property are located in the county assessor's office. If you don't have a property description or know what property your subject owns, the county clerk's office has a listing of who owns what. Some states post property records online; check your state assessor's office to see if you can access property records online.

Voter Registration Records: These records, located in the county clerk's office, list people's political party if they are registered voters, as well as their addresses and dates of birth. They also list telephone numbers. In some cases, people who have unlisted telephone numbers may have listed their numbers on these records.

Fish and Game Licenses: These are also recorded in the county clerk's office.

Salaries of County Employees: The salaries are listed by position only (usually not by employees' names) in the county clerk's office. In some counties or cities, names may be included.

County Government Expenses: These can also be found in the county clerk's office.

Corporate Records: Articles of incorporation, which list the officers of the corporation and the date the company registered with the state, are very useful if you are trying to find out who the company officers are. Articles of incorporation are located in the Register of Deeds office or in the state office that regulates corporations.

Court Records: Filings in all civil and criminal court cases, except juvenile cases, are open to the public. They are located in your county courthouse.

Military Records: You can find out the details of individuals' military service in the Register of Deeds office in some municipalities, but only for people who registered for military service in that county. Otherwise, you have to file a request under the Freedom of Information Act to the individual branch of the service.

Personal Property Loans: If a person has taken out a loan of more than $1,000 or has used credit to buy something worth more than $1,000, such as a stereo, the information could be on file under the Uniform Commercial Code listings kept in your county courthouse. Some states also have these listings online.

Tax Payments or Delinquent Tax Records: These records are kept in the county treasurer's office.

Motor Vehicle Registrations: These records and the personal property tax are on file in the county treasurer's office.

Building Inspection Records and Housing Permits: These are available in the city's building inspection and housing department. Also available are all the complaints that have been filed against a property owner, which are useful for stories on substandard housing. This office also has records on all permits issued for construction or building improvements.

City Commission Meeting Records, Local Ordinances and Resolutions: The city clerk's office keeps these records.

City Expenses: Information about purchase orders, accounts payable, the inventory of city agencies, budgets, expenditures and the like are available in the city's finance department. Records of purchase orders and accounts payable are extremely useful if you are investigating the expenditures of any city department or the actions involving any contract the city has with a vendor or builder.

Public Works Records: Plans for public works projects — such as sewers, traffic signals and traffic counts — should be available in the public works department of your municipality.

Fire Department Records: These include records of all fire alarms, calls (including response times), fire inspections and firearms owners and registration (which may be in a different location in some cities). Also on file, but not available to the public, are personnel records, including pension records and other items of a personal nature. However, salaries are public record. These are in the fire department or in your city or county clerk's office.

Police Records: Criminal offense reports, statistics of crime, accident reports and driving records are in the local police department and the sheriff's department. Records of ongoing investigations are generally not available to the public.

Utility Records: Water records — such as bacterial counts, water production, chemical usage and other items pertaining to the city's water and sewage operations — are available in the city utilities department.

School District Records: Almost all information pertaining to the expenditure of public school funds — including purchase orders, payroll records, audits, bids and contracts — is available from the school district. Personnel records of employees are also available in limited form. Names, addresses, home phone numbers, locations of employment, birth dates, dates hired and work records are available, but information about employee work performance and other personal information is not public. Information about students, other than confirmation that they are enrolled, is not public.

THE FREEDOM OF INFORMATION ACT

The Freedom of Information Act was established by Congress in 1966 to make federal records available to the public. It applies only to federal documents. In addition, the act allows for several exemptions that prohibit the release of documents. Records classified by the government because their release would endanger national defense or foreign policy are exempted. So are certain internal policies and personnel matters in federal agencies, as well as a number of records involving law enforcement investigations. If an agency refuses to release documents you have requested through the FOIA, you may appeal the decision.

In many cases, the document you request comes with information blacked out or cut out. Some documents look like paper doll cutouts by the time they are released. Another drawback to using the FOIA is that it is time-consuming. Although an agency is required by law to respond to your request within 10 working days, delays are common.

However, many reporters have found the FOIA invaluable. The documents they have received have led to major investigative stories.

Before you file an FOIA request, try the direct approach: Ask the agency for the records. You might get them. If you must file a formal FOIA request, it is a good idea to check first and make sure that you are contacting the appropriate agency for your request.

You can also access a complete online guide to the FOIA through the Internet on these sites:

- National Freedom of Information Coalition: *http://www.nfoic.org/*
- FOI Resource Center: *www.spj.org/foi.asp*
- The U.S. Department of Justice FOI site: *www.justice.gov/oip/*
- The Federal Communications Commission: *www.fcc.gov/foia/*
- The U.S. Department of Commerce: *www.osec.doc.gov/omo/foia/foiawebsite.htm*

When you file your request, be sure to write "Freedom of Information Request" on the envelope and on the letter. You do not have to explain your reason for the request. The agency may charge copying and processing fees, but if you are not using the material for commercial purposes and the material is likely to contribute to an understanding of government operations, you may be entitled to a fee waiver.

For questions or more advice, you can contact The Reporters Committee for Freedom of the Press at *www.rcfp.org/foia*. This site also offers a hotline that you can call for help and form letters to file FOIA requests.

US Department of Commerce

Freedom of Information Act & Privacy Act

The sample shown here is recommended by the Society of Professional Journalists. If you prefer to be contacted by mail, omit your telephone number.

[Date]

[Agency head or Freedom of Information Officer]
[Agency]
[City, State, Zip Code]

Freedom of Information Act Request

Dear [FOI Officer]:

This is a request under the federal Freedom of Information Act.

I request that a copy of the following documents [or documents containing the following information] be provided to me. [Identify the documents or information as specifically as possible.]

In order to help determine my status to assess fees, you should know that I am [suitable description of the requester and the purpose of the request, such as:

- A representative of the news media affiliated with the newspaper (magazine, television station, etc.), and this request is made as part of news gathering and not for a commercial use

- Affiliated with an educational or noncommercial scientific institution, and this request is made for a scholarly or scientific purpose and not for a commercial use

- An individual seeking information for personal use and not for a commercial use

- Affiliated with a private corporation and seeking information for use in the company's business]

[Optional] I am willing to pay fees for this request up to a maximum of [dollar amount]. If you estimate that the fees will exceed this limit, please inform me first.

[Recommended] I request a waiver of all fees for this request. Disclosure of the requested information is in the public interest because it is likely to contribute significantly to public understanding of the operations or activities of government and is not primarily in my commercial interest. [Include a specific explanation.]

Thank you for your consideration of this request.

Sincerely,

[Signature]
[Your name]
[Address]
[Telephone number]
[Fax number]
[E-mail address]

EXERCISES

1 Reverse directory: Imagine that the mayor of your town, another city official or a university official has disappeared. You want to talk to members of his or her family and to the neighbors. Find the missing person's telephone number in the cross-directory or an online search engine such as *www.reversephonedirectory.com.* Now find three neighbors you could interview by using the street address searches.

2 Databases: Select a topic for a feature story about an issue on your campus, such as date rape, racial tensions on college campuses, alcohol bans, political activism or a health issue such as sexually transmitted diseases among college students. Now check the Internet or go to your library and use a database to find stories about your topic. Make note of any national experts on the subject and any statistical material or reports you would find helpful in your story.

3 Primary Sources: Get copies of a police report, a university study or any other report that has been released at your school or in your community. Make note of the primary sources (officers, investigators or researchers) you would contact.

4 Record search: Conduct a record search of a person, preferably a politician or other person in your community who owns property. Your task is to construct a paper-trail profile. Try to find out all you can about the person without ever talking to him or her. However, you may drive by the person's home to observe the property and include that information in your report. Write the profile based only on records and observation.

You may be surprised how much you can write. Here are some suggestions for records that should be available to you:

- Land records, which should include a complete description of the person's house
- Court records of criminal and civil suits, possible marriage or divorce, or even birth records
- Delinquent tax records
- Corporation records for ownership of personal property or corporation papers (if applicable)
- Records of voter registration, auto registration and tax liens
- Educational background, including curriculum vitae for university employees
- Financial disclosure (for politicians)
- Check the Internet by conducting a search for your source.

5 FOIA request: Write a Freedom of Information Act request for some information from a federal agency that funds a program in your school or community.

6 Enterprise: Write a story about the people for whom buildings or landmarks on your campus are named. Using your campus library, check the archives to find the background of these people. Then conduct interviews with students who use these buildings, or who live in them if they are residence halls, and find out how much or how little the students know about these people. In the clips, try to find interesting anecdotes about the namesakes and reasons for naming the buildings for them.

CourseMate

Check out the "Basketball Scandal" scenario in NewsScene for an interactive exercise that will help to reinforce many of the themes presented in this chapter.

COACHING TIPS

Write your observations in your notes; include specific details.

Mark or **highlight important quotes or facts** that you plan to use in the story.

When interviewing athletes or people who have been interviewed frequently, try to **find a new angle or a question** they haven't been asked.

Research background of your subject in social media and websites.

Always **check the spelling** of the source's name and the wording of job titles.

Ask **follow-up questions** "why" and "how," and ask sources to elaborate.

Gather **details for graphics for maps** or other illustrations that an artist might create.

Plan to **report with audio and video** for Web publication.

withGod/Shutterstock.com

In interviewing, if you are sincere and the sources know that you have compassion, they're going to talk. A lot of the skill is just being open to what they have to say.

— **BARBARA WALSH,** Pulitzer-Prize winning reporter

CHAPTER 6
Interviewing Techniques

BARBARA WALSH WAS HAUNTED BY THE INTERVIEWS SHE CONDUCTED about children whose psychiatric problems made them scream for help or try to commit suicide. She pored over their pictures, diaries and medical files piled by her bed before she went to sleep. She dreamed about them at night and thought about them during the day.

After eight months of conducting 500 interviews and researching 4,000 pages of records, Walsh wrote "Castaway Children: Maine's Most Vulnerable Kids," a three-part series about the lack of mental care for children in her state. The series led to changes in state and federal laws and led Walsh to one of many prizes she has won in journalism.

"During those months of reporting and writing, the story simmered always in my thoughts," she wrote in a story about how she did the series published in the *Portland Press Herald/Maine Telegram*. "When I biked or ran, I did not see the ocean, the pine trees or the sky. In my mind's eye, I was seeing and thinking about the children I visited in juvenile lockups, courtrooms or psychiatric hospitals." She often thought about Joey, who began hearing voices when he was 11. He languished in a juvenile detention center, waiting for treatment and tried to drown himself in the toilet.

Joey Tracy stares at the winter moon, looming beyond the razor wire, beyond the red-brick building where the door is locked and a guard keeps watch.

The 16-year-old boy lies on his cot comforted by the thought of his mother staring at the same silver crescent illuminating the sky. He tucks his knees to his chest and whispers: "I love you, Mom." As he has done for four months, Joey cries himself to sleep, wondering if he'll ever go home.

— BARBARA WALSH, *Portland Press Herald/Maine Telegram*

Barbara Walsh, reporter

Courtesy of Barbara Walsh

One day she obtained a 15-page database about 737 of these children, including many who had been sent out of state for care for two to four years because Maine lacked treatment for them. "I remember staring at that list for hours that day. Questions came to my mind. Who were these kids? Why were they gone so long? Did anybody care about them?"

Her curiosity, compassion and ability to ask probing questions are some of the reasons Walsh achieved acclaim for her interviewing skills. She said the key to good interviewing is good listening.

That's a skill Walsh learned the hard way.

Walsh said one of the "stupidest" things she ever did almost ruined the interview that led to a Pulitzer Prize. Walsh had tried for months to get an interview with convicted murderer William R. Horton Jr. Finally, his lawyer gave her permission. She walked into the jail, met Horton and learned a painful lesson.

Horton was serving two life sentences plus 85 years in a Massachusetts prison for the murder of a gas station attendant and a subsequent crime he committed while out of prison on a furlough (a brief stay in the community). He broke into the home of a Maryland man, slashed him repeatedly and raped his fiancée twice.

Walsh, then a reporter for the *Lawrence* (Mass.) *Eagle–Tribune,* faced Horton through the window that separated them. "The first question I asked was 'How the heck did you get out on furlough?' It was the stupidest thing I've ever done," she said.

Horton wanted to terminate the interview. Walsh salvaged the interview with Horton by switching to something he wanted to discuss.

"I asked him, 'What do you want to tell me?' And he said, 'I'm not a monster. You people (the press) have made me out to be a monster,'" Walsh said.

The interview then went on for two hours, and eventually Walsh returned to the tough questions she wanted to ask Horton.

The story was one of a series about the Massachusetts furlough program that earned Walsh the Pulitzer Prize. Walsh, who later worked at newspapers in Florida and Maine and now is a freelance writer, said she was lucky that Horton talked to her, but she learned a valuable lesson about interviewing techniques: "Save your tough questions for last."

She still asks tough questions — but at the end of the interview. "I've learned to be real slow and real patient," she said. "I'm more inclined to let people talk longer. You may not use all the information, but you can offend them if you rush. In interviewing, if you are sincere and the sources know that you have compassion, they're going to talk. A lo-t of the skill is just being open to what they have to say."

But when sources were reluctant to answer her questions, she rephrased the questions and asked them again — sometimes three or four times — as in the following story about women in a Florida prison. "I asked one of the female inmates on Death Row, 'What's it like to sit there and know the state wants to electrocute you?' She skirted the question the first time. I asked it three times during the interview."

Eventually Walsh got the answer. "If you ask — not in a cold way, but sincerely ask what was it like for you — they'll answer." The result was this revealing portrait (also notice how Walsh weaves in her own observations):

Kaysie Dudley spent two years on Death Row meditating and learning more about how the state was going to kill her.

"I did a lot of research on what they were going to do to me," Dudley says. "It was very morbid, but I wanted to know." Dudley, 28, was sent to Death Row at Broward Correctional Institution in 1987 after she was convicted with her boyfriend of strangling and slicing the throat of an elderly Clearwater woman.

"My boyfriend killed her," Dudley says. "I held the woman in my arms as she took her last breath. It was a terrible experience." As she talks, Dudley sits in the cafeteria of the women's prison, nervously rubbing her fingers together, her nails raw and bitten to the quick. From her neck hangs a small silver cross.

It is cool, and Dudley wears a black sweater over her state-issued aqua dress.

"I wasn't afraid of dying," Dudley says. "But I didn't like to think about electricity running through my body. . . ." After spending two years on Death Row, Dudley says, she feels she has suffered more than enough.

"I was 22 when they locked me up in there," she says. "I feel like in a way they've already killed me. It took me almost a year to get my facial expressions back, my emotions, my ability to laugh.

"I was a zombie when I came out of there," she says, absently twisting her hair with her constantly moving fingers.

— BARBARA WALSH, *South Florida Sun-Sentinel*

OBSERVATION

Observation is also a crucial reporting skill. Walsh videotapes some of her interviews and reviews them before she starts to write so that she can include details from her observations.

These days it is even more essential to videotape interviews so you can produce audio and video that will enhance your stories for the Web and mobile media.

Observation for Breaking News

Although descriptive detail is more common in feature stories, you need the same observation techniques to gather information for hard-news stories. Stories about weather disasters, fires and other breaking news events also need details based on the reporter's observations.

Greensburg tornado aftermath.

At a protest, use observation to report what signs the protesters carried and what they were chanting. At a trial, use observation to help the reader see how the defendant and other people in the courtroom reacted.

If you are reporting a news event for television, don't depend on video to record the observations. In any disaster, fire, or similar breaking news event, the reporter needs to describe the scene and answer questions the anchor might ask. In addition reporters may be expected to post blogs to describe breaking news events.

Such was the case when a tornado wiped out the small town of Greensburg, Kan. In addition to reporting stories for print and video, the *Wichita* (Kan.) *Eagle* reporters posted their observations on blogs. Note the description based on observation in this newspaper version of the story.

This sun-baked High Plains town no longer has a grade school, a high school, a City Hall, a hospital, a water tower, a fire station, a business district or a main street.

It has people, but all 1,400 of them live elsewhere today. The homes they kept, the rooms where they were born, where they grew old together, now lie in millions of pieces, some of them as small as matchsticks. Tatters and shards of Greensburg flew for miles across the short grass and sage and yucca outside town on Friday night. Their branches now hold the shreds of housing insulation, pieces of tin, pieces of twisted roofing, crumpled family photographs, torn documents and bits and pieces of belongings.

— *Wichita* (Kan.) *Eagle*

Good writing is just as important in social media. Here are two examples of a reporter's observations in blogs posted on the *Eagle's* news site:

> HAVILAND — The street in front of Haviland High School looks like an insurance industry trade show. Major insurance companies have glitzy mobile trailers parked out front with satellite capability. High-tech toys help agents and adjusters access customer records. But the gadgets are also helping customers.
>
> "Free Internet access" signs are posted along the sidewalk for people who want to check e-mail messages.
>
> Agents are everywhere, wearing business polos with their company logos.
>
> — DEB GRUVER, *Wichita Eagle*

> In a strange juxtaposition, a full set of white and blue china — including tea service — stands on display in a storefront on Haviland's main street, perfect, while Greensburg residents' dishes are strewn across their town.
>
> People stop to hug in front of the hardware store, relieved to see one another.
>
> — DEB GRUVER, *Wichita Eagle*

GATHERING DETAILS

Like Barbara Walsh, Edna Buchanan won a Pulitzer Prize — in her case, as a police reporter for *The Miami Herald*. Buchanan recounts one of her mistakes when she didn't ask the right question. Now an author, Buchanan offers this advice in her book *The Corpse Had a Familiar Face:*

> What a reporter needs is detail, detail, detail.
>
> If a man is shot for playing the same song on the jukebox too many times, I've got to name that tune. Questions unimportant to police add the color and detail that make a story human. What movie did they see? What color was their car? What did they have in their pockets? What were they doing the precise moment the bomb exploded or the tornado touched down?
>
> Miami Homicide Lieutenant Mike Gonzalez, who has spent some thirty years solving murders, tells me that he now asks those questions and suggests to rookies that they do the same. The answers may not be relevant to an investigation, but he tells them, "Edna Buchanan will ask you, and you'll feel stupid if you don't know."
>
> A question I always ask is "What was everybody wearing?" It has little to do with style. It has everything to do with the time I failed to ask. A man was shot and dumped into the street by a killer in a pickup truck. The case seemed somewhat routine — if one can ever call murder routine. But later, I learned that at the time the victim was shot, he was wearing a black taffeta cocktail dress and red high heels. I tracked down the detectives and asked, "Why didn't you tell me?"
>
> "You didn't ask," they chorused. Now I always ask.

SENSITIVITY

The way you deal with sources can differ, depending on whether they are public or private individuals. Because public officials are accustomed to dealing with the media, you have a right to expect them to talk to you. Private individuals do not have to deal with the media, and you need to operate with more sensitivity when interviewing them. If a public official utters an outrageous quote, it's fair game. When a private individual does, you could remind the person that it will be published and make sure that the source will stand by the comment. Although many reporters believe that once they have identified themselves as members of the media, anything in an interview is fair game, reporters who display extra sensitivity often end up with more information.

All sources, public and private, want to be portrayed well in the media. Many sources, especially public officials, will manipulate reporters by revealing only information that furthers their cause. As a result, reporters need to be aware of the source's bias and ask probing questions that go beyond what the source wants to reveal. It is also crucial to check the information and seek alternative points of view.

THE PROS AND CONS OF DIGITAL RECORDERS/VIDEOTAPES

In our multimedia world, electronic equipment is invaluable. When you conduct an interview, it helps to capture images with your cell phone or record audio and video that you can use on the Web. But electronic devices are not substitutes for good notes. Machines can fail you when you need them most. They can inhibit a source. They can also prevent you from taking good notes if you rely on them too much.

If you want to get the exact wording of quotes, or if you are interviewing a source about a controversial subject, a recorder is beneficial and even crucial in investigative reporting. But you shouldn't play back the entire recording and transcribe it before you write your story. That is too time-consuming. Scan the recording for the quotes you need.

Before you begin recording your interview, follow some etiquette. Start your interview with basic introductions — who you are and why you are there — and some opening conversation. To put the source at ease, you might even ask a few questions before you ask the source if he would object to the recorder.

If you want to record a telephone interview, be aware of the laws in your state. Twelve states prohibit recorded conversations without the consent of the person being taped: California, Connecticut, Florida, Illinois, Maryland, Massachusetts, Michigan, Montana, Nevada, New Hampshire, Pennsylvania and Washington. Other states mandate that only one person must be aware of the taping, either the reporter or the person being interviewed. For a list of laws regarding taping in each state, check the Reporters Committee for Freedom of the Press at http://www.rcfp.org/taping.

You can't secretly record any conversation between two other people when you are not a part of the discourse. For example, if you are on an extension phone and neither party knows you are recording the conversation, you are violating a federal law against wiretapping. The Federal Wiretap Statute provides for penalties of up to $10,000 in fines and up to five years in prison.

The most ethical approach is to let your source know you are recording the interview, except in a very few situations. For example, if you are conducting an undercover investigation in a state where the one-party rule applies, you could record a conversation without the source's knowledge. However, most editors consider the use of deception or other undercover techniques a last resort.

LISTENING TIPS

Before you write notes or record conversations, you should develop good listening skills. Here are some tips:

Focus on the "Hear" and Now: Concentrate on what the source is saying now, not on what you will ask next. One of the major obstacles to good listening is poor concentration caused by worrying about what you will say instead of focusing on what the source is saying.

Practice Conversational Listening: Base your next question on the last sentence or thought the source expressed, as though you were having a conversation with your friend. If you want to move to another topic, you can do so either with a transition — "On another subject" — or by just asking the question.

Practice Critical Listening: Evaluate what the source is saying as you hear it. Listen on one level for facts, on another for good quotes and on a third level for elaboration and substantiation. Is the source making a point clearly and supporting it? Do you understand the point? If not, ask the source to repeat, elaborate or define the meaning.

Be Quiet: Whose interview is this anyway? Do not try to impress the source with what you know. You can't quote yourself. Let the source explain a point, even if you understand it, so you can get information in the source's words.

Be Responsive: Make eye contact frequently so your source knows you are listening. Let the source know you are paying attention. If you don't understand something, say so. "Why?" "How?" "I don't understand" and "Please explain."

Listen for What Isn't Said: Is the source avoiding a topic? Who or what isn't the source talking about — a family member (in a personal profile), a close official, a crucial part of his background? Sometimes, what is omitted from a conversation is more revealing than what is included.

Listen with Your Eyes: What kind of body language is the source displaying? Is the source smiling, frowning or exhibiting discomfort when you ask certain questions? Are these telltale signs that the source may be lying or withholding information? Observation can be a good listening tool.

Be Polite: If the source starts to ramble or give you irrelevant information, don't interrupt. Wait for the source to pause briefly, and then you can change the subject.

Block Personal Intrusions: You've had a bad day, your car broke down, you failed a test or you have some emotional concerns. Make a determined effort to block these personal thoughts that will affect your concentration. Your problems will still be there when the interview is over. The source will not.

Be Flexible: Don't go to your interview with a rigid agenda of questions. Although you may start with prepared questions, if the interview goes in another direction, follow that course if it is interesting. Listen for what you want to know and what you didn't expect to know.

NOTE-TAKING TIPS

When the late Foster Davis was a writing coach at *The Charlotte* (N.C.) *Observer,* he checked reporters' notes to determine if problems in the stories originated in the reporting process. "The quality of stories has something to do with the quality of notes," Davis once said in an interview. "Writing is the least important part of it; everything that leads up to it is what matters."

Davis said he looked at notes to see if they were legible and if they included names and dates as well as reporters' observations. "When the notes said 'trees,' were they

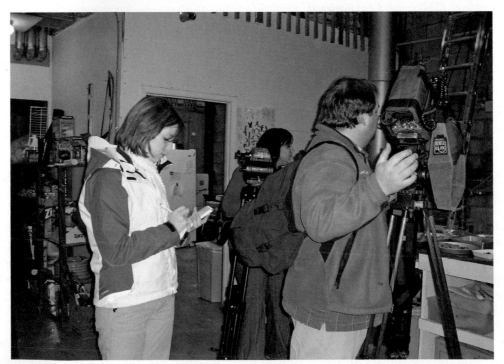

A broadcast reporter takes notes while the camera operator records the interview.

specific trees? Were the notebooks dated? Were exact titles spelled out? Detail is what makes the difference between good and bad notes," he said.

Detailed notes give you this advantage: When you begin writing your story, you may need more information than you anticipated during the reporting process. When you take notes can be as important as how you take them. Note taking can make some sources nervous. If you are dealing with people who are not accustomed to being interviewed, start your interview slowly by asking a few nonthreatening questions. After you have established some rapport with the source, take out your notebook.

Here are some tips to help you take good notes:

Be Prepared: Do not rely solely on electronic equipment for note taking. Bring extra pens and pencils. You may run out of ink, or your pencils may break. If you do an interview in the rain, you'll want to have pencils handy.

Concentrate: When you hear a good quote or the start of one, write rapidly. Concentrate on what you are hearing and block out everything else until you have written the quote. Even if you are concentrating on a previous thought, you will still hear what is being said. Thinking of your next question while you are trying to write down a complete quote will interfere with your concentration.

Use Key Words: When you are not trying to get a direct quote, jot down key words to remind you of facts and statements.

Develop a Shorthand System: Abbreviate as many words as possible.

Slow the Pace: When you are taking notes for a quote, slow the pace of the interview by pausing before your next question until you write the quote. If you think you are pausing too long, ask a question that will not require a crucial answer. You could ask the source to elaborate about the last statement. If your source is speaking too fast, politely ask him to slow down.

Request Repetition: Don't be afraid to ask your source to repeat a quote or fact you missed. Although the quote may not be worded exactly as before, it will be close enough. In fact, the repeated statement may be even better.

Make Eye Contact: Don't glue your eyes to your notes. Make sure that you look at your source during the questioning and while you are taking notes.

Mark Your Margins or Notebook Covers: When you hear something that prompts another question in your mind — a fact you want to check or the name of another source you want to contact — jot it in the margin as soon as you think of it. Don't depend on your memory to think of it later. Some reporters use the covers of their notebooks to write questions that come to mind during the interview so that they can find them easily without flipping through notebook pages. And don't forget to take notes on your observations.

Verify Vital Information: Make sure that you get the exact spelling of your source's name and his title during or at the end of the interview. Don't go by a nameplate on a door or desk. That could be a nickname. Ask the source for the name he prefers to use, and ask for the spelling even if you are sure of it. If you get this information at the end of your interview, you also could ask for a home telephone number or cell phone number and an e-mail address at this time. Even if you are reporting for television, you will need the spelling of the name, which may be superimposed on the screen during a sound bite.

Double-Check: If your source says he has three main points or reasons for running for office, make sure that you get all three. Write "3 reasons" in the margin, number them as you hear them and check before you conclude the interview.

Be Open-Minded: You may have one idea for the story when you begin taking notes. But don't limit your notes to one concept. Your story angle could change at any time during the interview. You can't always envision how you will write the story.

Use a Symbol System: To save time writing your story, mark your notes with a star or some symbol next to the information that you think will be important. Develop your own system.

Stand and Deliver: Practice taking notes while you are standing. You will not have the luxury of sit-down reporting, especially at the scene of fires, accidents, disasters and most other breaking-news stories.

Save Your Notes: You should save your notes after the story is published or aired. How long you should save them is debatable. Lawyers disagree whether notes are helpful or harmful in court cases if you are sued for libel or any other reasons. But most editors advise saving the notes at least for a few weeks after the story appears in case any questions about it arise. For this reason, it is helpful to date your notebooks.

INTERVIEWING TIPS

An important factor leading to a successful interview is that old Boy Scout motto: Be prepared. First, consider your mission. You are a reporter, not a stenographer who just receives information and transcribes it. A reporter evaluates information for its accuracy, fairness, newsworthiness and potential to make a readable story. During the reporting process, you will look for facts, good quotes, substantiation and answers to the five W's — who, what, when, where, why — and also "how" and "so what." One question should lead to another until you have the information you need.

An interview with one source is just the beginning of reporting for most stories. For credibility and fairness, you need other sources — human and written — for differing points of view and accuracy checks.

Planning the Interview

If you are sent to cover a breaking-news story, you should get to the scene quickly and find sources there or start calling sources on the phone. The planning stages described here apply only to interviews that you need to set up in advance. Most of the other reporting techniques apply to both kinds of stories.

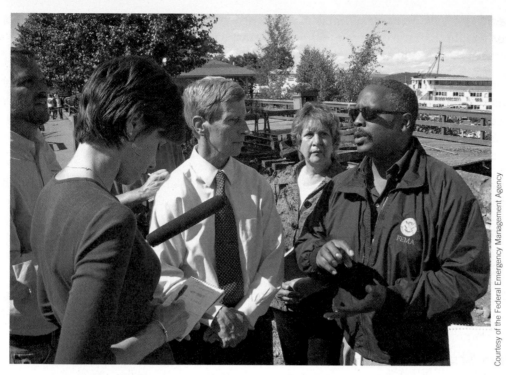

Courtesy of the Federal Emergency Management Agency

Reporters interview FEMA officials.

SOCIAL MEDIA

YOU'VE PROBABLY been using social media like Facebook to stay in touch with friends or follow topics of interest to you, but now social media sites have become a crucial part of journalism. You can use social media before and after an interview to research background, to post questions that will engage other people to post information that might be helpful and to follow links for more information. If you use information from social media, the same journalism rules apply: Check the sources for validity and don't use information without attribution. Be careful: Many people have the same names, so make sure that the information you find is about the right sources. Social media sites are proliferating; these are just a few of the popular sites you can use to find information about your sources:

- LinkedIn: Check this site as a starting point to find background about your source.

- Facebook and Myspace: Check to see if your source has pages on these sites.

- Twitter: Search comments about your sources or topics and follow hashtags.

- Blogs: Use Google, Technorati or other blog searches to find blogs by or about your sources.

- YouTube: Check to find video by or about your source.

- Flickr: Check for photos of your sources.

Identify Your Focus: What is the purpose of your interview? The focus may change after you do the interview, but you need to start with a specific reason for your story so you know what kind of information you need to get and what sources you need.

Research the Background: Check news clippings, TV footage, social media sites and available documents — court records or other relevant written and online sources. Check with secondary sources — friends and opponents — before or after you interview the subject of a story. Ask the source's friends, secretaries or co-workers to give you anecdotes and tell you about the person's idiosyncrasies.

Identify Your Goals: What kind of information are you hoping to get from this source? Is it primarily factual, as in an interview with a police officer for a story about an accident? Or do you want reaction from the source to an issue or to something some-one else said? Is the source going to be the central focus of the story, as in a profile, or just one of several people cited in the story? Get a general idea of why you need this source so you can explain briefly when you call for an interview.

Plan Your Questions: This step may seem premature, considering that you haven't even been granted an interview. However, if the person refuses to see you when you call for an interview, you might be able to ask a few questions while you have the source on the phone. If you are a good interviewer, you can prolong the conversation and wind up with a good interview.

Prepare your list of questions in two ways: Write all the questions you want to ask, preferably in an abbreviated form. Then mark the questions you must ask to get the most crucial information for your story. If your source refuses to grant you the time you need, you can switch to the crucial list during your interview.

Request the Interview: The most important point is to plan ahead. Officials, edu-cators and many other sources are busy people. They may not be able to see you on brief notice.

When you make the call, state your name and purpose. Or try the sponsorship technique: "I'm working on a story about date rape on campus, and Officer John Brown suggested that I call you."

If you are calling an official, you probably will have to negotiate through an admin-istrative assistant. Be courteous and persuasive. First, ask to speak to the source. If that's not possible, tell the assistant that you would like to interview his boss about a story you are writing. You don't need to elaborate unless you are asked to do so.

You can also try contacting a source by e-mail to set up an appointment. State your name, affiliation and purpose. Save your questions until you find out if you can get a telephone or face-to-face interview.

Dress Appropriately: If you are interviewing a source on a farm, don't wear a business suit. However, if you are interviewing corporate officials or people in more formal business settings, you should dress as though you worked there.

Arrive on Time: You could arrive 10 to 15 minutes early, but don't arrive too early because you could inconvenience people who are busy. And never come late.

Conducting the Interview

Interview questions can be classified as two types: closed-ended and open-ended. You need both types.

- **Closed-ended questions** are designed to elicit brief, specific answers that are factual. They are good for getting basic information, such as name and title; yes or no answers; and answers to some who, where, when questions. For example, these are closed-ended questions: How long have you worked here? How many people were at the rally? When did the accident occur?

- **Open-ended questions** are designed to elicit quotes, elaboration or longer responses. Avoid being judgmental in the way you frame your initial questions and follow-up questions. The more neutral you are, the more responsive your source is likely to be.

The questions that will elicit the most quotes and anecdotes start with *what, why* and *how*:

- What (What happened? What is your reaction? What do you mean by that? Can you elaborate?)
- Why (Why did you do that . . .? Why do you believe . . . ?)
- How (How did something happen? How did you accomplish that?)
- Give me an example (a follow-up question to explain how the source felt, thought, acted in a specific situation)

Keep your questions brief. Ask questions in simple sentences — one question at a time. Don't combine two questions into one sentence. A long lead-in to a question can confuse the source. Slow the pace between questions so you can take notes. Ask unimportant questions or ask for elaboration while you are writing down quotes. Remember to be responsive by making eye contact frequently during the interview.

The Dumb Factor: Beginning reporters often worry that they will appear dumb to sources. Don't worry about what you don't know. You are there to listen and learn, not to be the expert. The whole point is to get information from the source. In fact, acting dumb can give you an advantage. Even if you know the answer to a question, you should ask it anyway so that you can get the information in the source's words. If the source gives you technical or confusing information, you might ask, "Could you explain that so I can write it clearly for my readers?" Most sources enjoy taking the teaching role or showing off what they know.

Acting dumb does not mean forgetting about preliminary background work. It is dumb if you can't tell your readers something because you were afraid to ask. It's better to feel dumb during the interview than afterward when you turn your story in to an editor or when you read it in the newspaper or hear it on a broadcast.

Here are some ways to conduct the interview and some types of questions to ask. Not all of these techniques and questions apply to every story.

Start Out by Using Icebreakers: Introduce yourself and briefly state your purpose. Be friendly. Establish rapport with some general conversation. Don't pull out your notebook immediately. Try to sit at an angle to your source so you are not directly facing him in a confrontational manner.

Observe the surroundings. Do you notice something you can mention as an ice-breaker, a way to establish rapport? Don't be artificial. If an official has a picture on his desk of his family, don't get overly familiar. Use good judgment. Then explain a little more about what you are seeking in your story.

Plan Your First Question: Try to find a question or approach that would interest the source, especially if the person is a celebrity, an athlete or an official who has been interviewed often. These people often give standard answers to questions they consider boring because they have been asked the same questions so many times. If you research well, you will find some tidbit or angle to a story that might lead to an unusual question — and an interesting answer.

Put Your Questions in Nonthreatening Order: In most cases you will want to follow Barbara Walsh's advice and start with nonthreatening questions. However, if you have only five minutes with a source, you may have to ask your toughest question first or whichever one will yield you the most crucial information for your story.

Ask the Basic Questions: Who, what, when, where, why and how are the most basic. Then add the "so what" factor: Ask the significance. Who will be affected and how? This question will give you information for your impact paragraph.

Ask Follow-Up Questions: These are the questions that will give you quotes and anecdotes. Use a conversational technique. Let the interview flow naturally. When a source answers one question, follow the trend of thought by asking why and how, and asking the source to explain or give examples. Frame your next question on the information you have just heard by focusing on key words in the last answer. When you want to change the subject, ask an unrelated question or use a transition: "On another topic . . ." or "I'd like to go back to something you said earlier. Could you explain why you were at the scene where the murder occurred?" Use follow-up questions to go from the general to the specific. If the source makes a vague statement, ask for specific examples.

You may have a long list of questions, but don't let your source see them. One student reporter took out a press release during the interview. When the source saw it, he told the student to use the comments in the release and terminated the interview. It would be better to write your questions on the front or back of your notebook so you can refer to them easily without turning pages frequently.

Here are some general follow-up questions to provide context and interesting material:

- What was your reaction?
- What do you mean by that?
- How did that happen?
- How did you do that?
- What is the significance?
- Who will be affected?

Keep Quiet: Do not talk too much or try to impress your source with your knowledge. Don't insert your opinions or comments. Let the source talk. You need to quote the source, not yourself.

Be Nonjudgmental: Don't insert your comments or opinions into your questions. Nor should you judge your source's actions or answers. You should remain neutral and strive for fairness. You can get an opposing side of a dispute or other points of view from other sources. If you have to ask a controversial question, use the "blame-others" technique: Your opponent says that . . . . How do you respond?

Control the Interview: If your source rambles or prolongs an answer and you want to move the interview in another direction, don't interrupt. Wait for a natural pause and ask your next question, using follow-up question techniques.

Repeat Questions: You have asked an important or sensitive question, and the source has given you an evasive or incomplete answer. What should you do? The best tactic is to drop the question and continue the interview. After you have discussed a few other points, repeat the question you want answered, but state it in a slightly different way. Sometimes a source will recall more the second time the question is raised.

Ask Background Questions: Get the history of the issue, if applicable. How and when did the problem or program start? Why?

Ask About Developments: Go from the present to the past and to the future. What are the current concerns and developments? How did the issue evolve? What is likely to happen in the future? The answer to the question about the future may provide you with a good ending for your story. In some cases, it may give you a lead and a new focus for your story. The next step in an action is often the most newsworthy angle. Many newspapers, broadcasters and online producers prefer this approach, which is called "advancing the story." Because you may have to post your story immediately for the Web, you will need to update the news anyway for your next broadcast or newspaper edition.

Construct a Chronology: This tip is somewhat related to the previous point. When appropriate, ask questions to establish a sequence of events. You don't need to write the story in chronological order, but you need to understand the order in which events occurred.

Role-Play: If you were in the reader's place, how would you use the information? For example, if you needed to apply for a loan, what steps would you have to take, and where would you go? What does the reader need and want to know?

Ask About Pros and Cons: Ask your source to discuss both sides of an issue, when relevant. Who agrees and disagrees with his point of view? What are his responses to the opposition?

Ask for Definitions: Your job is to translate jargon for readers. Always get your source to define any bureaucratic or technical terms in language that you and your readers will understand. Don't accept or write any information that you can't explain.

To clarify, you might restate the information in your own words and ask the source if you have the correct interpretation. For example, you might ask, "Do you mean that . . . ?" or "Are you saying that . . .?"

Verify: Ask questions even if you know the answers. Always check the spelling of your source's name — first and last names and middle initial. Check the person's title and the dates of crucial events. Check the accuracy of information on a résumé or news release. You don't have to repeat everything, but you should ask the source if the information released is correct. Then ask some questions that expand on the basic information. For example, if you are interviewing the president of MADD (Mothers Against Drunk Driving), you might ask, "Have you ever been involved in an accident involving a drunken driver, or were you ever arrested for drunken driving?" Such a question may not be as insensitive as it seems because many people get involved with causes after they have had a personal experience with the problem.

Also, remember that if the source tells you something about another person, you must check it out with that person.

Use the Silent Treatment: Pause for a few seconds between questions to let the source elaborate. If the pause seems uncomfortable, the source may break the silence first. One reporter was writing a profile of a nun. He asked her if she missed having a sex life and how she coped without one. She gave a brief, expected answer that she had made a conscious choice of abstinence when she took vows of celibacy. The reporter was disappointed with the answer. He said nothing. She said nothing. For several seconds they just sat in silence. Both were slightly uncomfortable. Then she broke the silence and began elaborating about how difficult celibacy was for her at times. Sometimes the best follow-up question is no question.

Use the "Blame Others" Technique: When you have to ask tough questions, blame someone else: "Your opponent says you cheated on your income taxes. How would you respond to that?" Reporters and editors have mixed feelings about warning the source that a tough question is coming. Don't do it, they say, in confrontational interviews when you are trying to get a source to reveal information that could be damaging. It puts the source on notice and gives him a few seconds to become defensive and evasive. But do warn the source or apologize if it's going to be a tough, emotional question, especially if you are interviewing grieving people, says Jacqui Banaszynski, who won a Pulitzer Prize for a series about a man with AIDS. She tells sources that she will ask tough questions, but they don't have to answer them. "But I'll try to convince them to do so," she says.

Handle Emotional Questions with Tact: Emotional questions can be difficult. Ask your source to recall how he was thinking or feeling at the time of an incident. "Were you frightened when the train lost power? What were you thinking at the time?" Avoid insensitive questions. There's a saying in journalism that there are no stupid questions, only stupid answers. That's not exactly true. "How do you feel about the death of your three children?" is not only a stupid question; it's insensitive as well. Instead of asking such an emotionally loaded question, ask the person to recall specific memories about his children, or ask how the person is coping with the tragedy.

Ask Summary Questions: Restate information, or ask the source to clarify the key points he is making — for example: "Of all the goals you have expressed, which would you say are the most important to you? What do you think are the three major issues you face?"

Use the "Matchmaker" Technique: Ask if anyone else is involved in the issue or if there are other people the source would suggest you contact. Remember that you will want more than one source for your story so that you can strive for fairness and balance.

Ask Free-Choice Questions: Ask the source if there is anything he would like to add.

End on a Positive Note: When you have finished the interview, thank your source. Ask if you can call back if you have any further questions. At this point, you also could ask for another way to reach the source, such as an e-mail address or cell phone number.

Reporting for Visuals

Whenever you go on an assignment — especially a breaking-news story involving an accident, a disaster such as a flood or explosion, or a crime — gather information for the graphic artist or the Web. Even if you don't use all these details for a graphic, you can use many of them to make your writing more vivid. Get maps, brochures or any other written materials that might be available to help the graphics department pinpoint the location of the crime or disaster scene. Take photos with your cell phone or camera. You can also use your cell phone to gather details about your location with an application like Foursquare or GPS function.

If you have video, don't describe the scene that viewers can see for themselves. But if you don't have video, gather details so that you can describe the scene to viewers or the anchor or use in a print story.

Locations: Get the names of streets and major intersections nearest to the site of the incident. Even if you plan to use Google maps, ask details about specific measurements: yards, feet, number of city blocks or whatever else would help pinpoint locations. How many feet or yards away from the landfill is the nearest house? What buildings are in the area? When the gas pipe exploded, how many feet from the gas line was the nearest building? This information might be helpful for creating a graphic or describing the scene especially if you are broadcasting on the scene.

Chronology of Events: Get specific times or dates and other information to recount the sequence of events. For example, suppose a terrorist takes a hostage. When did the incident occur? At what time did each development occur before the hostage was released or killed?

Statistics: Think of charts for print, broadcast or public relations materials. If your city council has raised taxes, what have taxes been during the past five years? How much has tuition increased during the past several years? How does this year's enrollment compare with enrollments in previous years? Statistics like these can be boring to

CONVERGENCE COACH

THE TECHNIQUES of interviewing are similar for print, broadcast or online reporting. You still need to decide the focus or main reason for the interview, research the background and prepare good questions. But much of broadcast and online reporting may be for spot news. In a convergent media world, you need video and audio for online delivery even if you are a print reporter. Setting up cameras for TV may make your source nervous, so use that time for icebreakers or for getting background information from the source. For broadcast and online audio and video, you need good quotes, so open-ended questions are preferable. Here are some tips especially geared to broadcast interviews:

- Ask open-ended questions to elicit quotes such as how, why, what was your reaction, what were you doing at the time of the incident. Avoid questions that can be answered "yes" or "no."
- Keep questions brief in simple sentences. Don't ask two questions at one time.
- Don't ask questions that express your opinion; that works for any medium. Avoid leading questions such as "Don't you think that . . ." and similar ones that include preconceived suggestions.
- Ask questions that your audience would want answered.
- Gather information that an anchor might ask you for elaboration.
- Ask free-choice questions: At the end of the interview, ask the source if there is anything he would like to add.

read. But they are easy to understand in chart form that can be posted in print or on the Web. Charts are also effective to include in public relations news releases.

Highlights: Gather information for a facts box, such as important dates or highlights of someone's career. Suppose you are doing a profile. Instead of listing key dates and incidents in your story, could you place them more effectively in a box? Ask about interesting hobbies, favorite books, favorite movies, marital status or other personal information that might help the graphic artist — and the reader. In the past, when a reporter turned in a story that was reported and written well, editors used to say, "Your story looks good." It's up to you to make sure that it does — both verbally and visually.

E-MAIL INTERVIEWS

Although e-mail is an effective tool for contacting sources, it is not an effective method for interviewing people. However, in some cases, e-mail may be the only way you can get comments from a source. Use it as a last resort if you can't interview a source in person or by telephone.

Advantages: E-mail gives the source some time to think about responses to your questions. It also saves you from taking notes, and you can get accurate quotes when the source responds in writing.

ETHICS

ETHICAL DILEMMA: Should you accept gifts from sources? Does the value of the gift make a difference?

The case: You are working on a feature story about a new music store in your community. After you finish the interview, the store owner offers you some gifts, such as a CD case, a baseball cap and a T-shirt with the store logo and a few CDs featuring your favorite musical artists. You do not plan to write reviews of the CDs. The total worth of the gifts is about $35. Should you accept some, all or none of these gifts? If you plan to review the CDs, should you keep them after you review them?

Ethical values: Credibility, conflict of interest

Ethical guidelines: The Society of Professional Journalists Code of Ethics says journalists "should refuse gifts, favors, fees, free travel and special treatment and shun secondary employment, political involvement, public office and service in community organizations if they compromise journalistic integrity."

Disadvantages: E-mail interviews prohibit spontaneity and good follow-up questions. You also can't observe the source's reactions and body language, nor can you gather descriptive detail.

Tips for E-mail Interviews

- **Limit the number of questions:** Sources will respond better to a few questions than to a long list. Strive for a maximum of five questions.
- **Clarify your purpose:** Make it clear that you intend to use the e-mail message in a news story. Personal e-mail messages are not intended for publication.
- **Verify the source's full name and title:** E-mail addresses do not always include the source's proper name.
- **Limit your follow-up e-mail messages:** You may have to reply to the source's e-mail with another question or a request for more information. But don't badger the source with several e-mail messages.
- **Attribute to e-mail:** Although not required, it is preferable to explain in your news story that the source made the comments in an e-mail interview.

TELEPHONE INTERVIEWING

Reporters for print and television news get many of their stories by telephone — from daily checks with police about crime stories to interviews with politicians, government officials and community leaders for reaction stories, issue stories and a wide range of features.

Although interviewing people in person is preferable, it is often not practical, especially if you are on deadline. You won't be able to observe facial reactions, gestures and surroundings when you conduct telephone interviews, but you still can gather information accurately and thoroughly.

If you can arrange it, you might try to conduct a video interview with your source on Skype, a free Internet connected call.

The techniques of telephone interviewing are very similar to the methods of interviewing in person. The major difference is that you need to work harder at keeping the source's attention and focusing your questions. Researchers suggest that the average telephone interview should be limited to 20 minutes. After that, the attention span of the person responding wanes. If you call a source at home, he or she may be further distracted by children or other family concerns.

Here are some guidelines for telephone interviewing:

Identification: Immediately state your name and affiliation and the purpose for the call.

Icebreakers: These may not be necessary. Get to the point quickly. If you use any icebreaker to establish rapport, keep it very brief.

Length of Questions: Keep questions very short. Phrase each question clearly and simply. Limit questions to no more than two sentences; one is better. Limit the number of questions as well. Plan two lists: all the questions you want to ask and crucial questions. If you have time for only a few questions, switch to the crucial list. You may also want to ask your questions in a different order. Don't wait too long to ask the crucial ones. You never can tell when the source will be interrupted and will terminate the interview.

Clarification: Make sure that you understand the information you receive. It may be harder to understand information in a telephone interview, so clarify anything that is confusing. Repeat any confusing terms or information in your own words, and ask your source to verify your interpretation.

Specifics: Ask for details and examples. If you want to describe the scene, ask your source to give you the descriptive details.

Chronology: A chronology is especially important in police and fire stories you receive by telephone. If you do not understand how an event occurred, try restating the chronology: "Let me understand — is this how it happened?" Or after a source tells you the high points of what happened, you could ask him to explain the order in which events unfolded.

Control: Be mindful of the information you must get for your story. You need to control the interview by switching the subject so that you get answers to the questions you need.

Verification: Double-check the spelling of the name, title and other basic information. If you haven't heard it clearly, spell it back to the source. This basic information is crucial when dealing with police officers. They usually do not identify themselves by their full names when they answer the phone on duty, so make sure that you get first and last names and the proper rank, such as lieutenant, sergeant or captain.

At the end of the interview, thank the source and ask if you may call back if you have more questions. Use judgment here. Don't ask this of police or reluctant sources; just call back if you must have more information.

COMMON INTERVIEWING PROBLEMS

- **What do you do if the source says something is "off the record" during an interview?** Ask the source why the information should be off the record (meaning you can't use it) and try to convince the source that the information is not harmful. Ask the question another way during the course of the information to see if you can get the information on the record.

- **What do you do if the source tells you not to use his name after the interview?** Try to prevent this by making sure you identify yourself and your purpose clearly at the start of the interview. If you suspect that this might happen, set ground rules at the beginning of the interview by explaining that you cannot use anonymous sources. If this happens at the end of the interview, negotiate. Try to convince the source to be identified. If the source still refuses, ask if you can identify the source by a vague title or position such as a source in the administration.

- **What do you do if the source gets emotional and starts to cry during the interview?** Pause. Give the source a chance to regain composure. Offer to get the source a drink of water or something else that might be helpful. Be understanding and sympathetic but don't start to cry as well.

- **What do you do if the source terminates the interview abruptly before you have the information you need?** Ask if you could contact the source again for further questions.

- **What do you do if the source gives you information that is inaccurate or false?** Check your facts and if you discover inaccuracies or falsehoods, contact the source again and confront him with the problems. Ask for an explanation.

EXERCISES

1 Interview a reporter from your local newspaper, radio station or television station about his reporting techniques. Or choose a reporter whose stories you like, and interview him about techniques.

2 Icebreakers: Make a list of questions you would use as icebreakers to interview a professor or a source whose office you have visited.

3 Reporting scenarios: Develop questions for the following situations:

- You learn that there is a fire in a residence hall on your campus. List at least 10 questions you would ask. List five sources you would contact. What kind of background information do you need?

- A professor on campus has received a $1 million grant to study plagiarism among college students. List at least five questions you would ask if you were interviewing the professor. What other sources will you use to make this a good story?

- A study at another university says college students are sleep-deprived. Women students get less than six and a half hours of sleep, and men get seven to eight hours of sleep. You are writing this story for your campus newspaper. How will you localize this story? What sources (other than students) do you need to make this a credible story for your university audience? Where will you find them?

4 **Note taking:** The object of this exercise is to see how accurately you can quote sources. Tape an interview from any television news show. As you are watching the show, write down some direct quotes. If you use videotape, watch the screen periodically as though you were making eye contact with a source. Then play the tape and test your accuracy. If you do this in a classroom, you can compare your notes with classmates' notes. Analyze what caused you to be inaccurate — if you were — and how you can improve your note taking.

5 **Notes:** Submit your notes for the last story you wrote. Share your notes with another student, and critique each other's notes on the points Foster Davis recommends: Are your notes legible? Do they have names, dates, titles and details? Compare your rating of your notes with another student's evaluation of them. Discuss improvements in your note taking that might have helped your story.

6 **Technical clarity:** This exercise was suggested by Jacqui Banaszynski, Knight Chair in Journalism at the University of Missouri. Interview a source about some technical information you don't understand. The source could be anyone from an auto mechanic to a scientist. Work on clarifying jargon and other information you don't understand. Then write the results of your interview in a brief story or several paragraphs explaining the technical information clearly.

7 **Graphics:** Check a newspaper or website that uses graphic illustrations. Study the graphic, and write a list of questions you would have asked to gather the information that the artist used to design it.

8 **Social Media Research:** Choose a topic or person for an interview. Check social media sites to find out how much background information you can get. Write a blog about the most interesting information you found and which sites were the most useful.

9 **Enterprise:** Conduct an interview in order to write a news story about an issue on your campus or in your community. Here are some suggestions:

- Write a reaction story based on interviews with students or local residents about any controversial topic in the news.

- Attend a demonstration, rally, meeting or other public event on your campus or in your community.

- Check your campus and local newspapers for clubs and support groups in your community.

- Write a story about the economic or psychological impact that any unusual weather in your area may have had on businesses, agriculture or people.

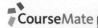 CourseMate

FEATURED ONLINE ACTIVITY Log on and visit the Writing and Reporting News CourseMate and take the interactive tutorial quiz on interviewing techniques. *Access available at www.cengagebrain.com.*

Check out the "Big Fire" scenario in NewsScene for an interactive exercise that will help to reinforce many of the themes presented in this chapter.

COACHING TIPS

iQoncept/Shutterstock.com

Keep leads short — preferably **fewer than 35 words.**

Write your nut graph as a tweet to **identify your focus in 140 characters.**

To find your lead, ask yourself: "What struck you as **most important or interesting?"**

Write a headline for your story; that could be a clue for your lead.

Points of emphasis: Place the **key words at the beginning or the end** of the sentence for emphasis.

Avoid suffering: If you can't devise your lead, **start with your nut graph** and write your lead later, or write several leads and choose one later.

Don't invent your lead. **Base it on the backup** in your notes.

The best day is the one when I can write a lead that will cause the reader at his breakfast the next morning to spit up his coffee, clutch at his heart and shout, "My God! Martha, did you read this?"

— **EDNA BUCHANAN,** former police reporter, *The Miami Herald*

CHAPTER 7
Leads and Nut Graphs

THE LEAD IS THE BEGINNING OF THE STORY THAT ENTICES THE READER, so why does renowned writing coach Don Fry write his leads last? Most writers agonize over their leads, but Fry almost never worries about what he is going to say first.

Fry says he begins the writing process long before he sits down at his computer. "I'm imagining the story while I'm reporting it," he says. Fry concentrates on what he calls the "point statement," also known as a focus graph or nut graph. He asks himself what is the story about and what is the point of the story. Any information that doesn't relate to the point statement doesn't get included in the story.

And then he starts writing. Not at the beginning, but at the paragraph containing the point statement. He continues writing until he gets to his ending, which he calls the "kicker." Then he writes his lead. After that he revises.

The point statement, which is also known as a focus statement, may end up being the lead, or it will give you the idea for the lead. You may still prefer to write your stories by starting with the lead, as most writers do. But thinking about the focus of your story first will give you a better chance of writing a good lead.

Mervin Block, a leading writing coach for broadcast journalism, has similar advice. "Think. Don't write yet. Just think," he says in his book, *Writing Broadcast News*. "Think about what you want to say and how best to say it: clearly, concisely, conversationally. . . . Start strong. Well begun is half done."

The lead is crucial in any medium, especially these days, when readers and viewers are bombarded with so much information from social media, print, broadcast and online sources. Studies show that most online readers are scanners, who just read headlines. How can your leads entice the readers, listeners or viewers to continue? Take a clue from television teasers: Does the anchor tease you about a story that makes you stay tuned after the break? Leads should entice the reader to stay tuned into the rest of the story.

Courtesy of Don Fry

Don Fry, writing coach

HARD-NEWS LEADS, SOFT LEADS AND NUT GRAPHS

The lead (originally spelled *lede* to differentiate it from "lead" type) tells the reader what the story is about. Think of the lead as a teaser or foreshadowing of what will come in the story. No matter what type of lead you write, you must back it up with information that substantiates it. If you haven't got material to support your lead, you have the wrong lead.

First determine the focus of the story. Ask yourself: What is the story about? What is the most important information? What is the point of this story? Those are the questions you need to ask yourself to write a lead or a nut graph.

Sometimes nut graphs and leads are the same; sometimes they aren't. Here's how to tell the difference:

Summary Leads: Also called a "hard-news lead," or a "direct lead," this type of lead summarizes in the first sentence what the story is about. A summary lead is usually only one sentence or two at most. It gets directly to the point.

With the increasing use of cell phones, tablet computers and other small-screen devices for news reading, the summary lead is an ideal form. Summary leads also are useful in any type of media. Public relations practitioners use summary leads in news releases, which need to be brief and newsworthy.

In these examples, note that the broadcast version uses present tense and a more current angle:

- **Print version:** A 20-year-old Franklin and Marshall College student was shot a block from campus early this morning during an attempted robbery, police said.
- **Broadcast or Web version:** A 20-year-old Franklin and Marshall College student is in critical condition today after he was shot early this morning during an attempted robbery a block from campus.

Nut Graphs: Also called the "focus graph," the nut graph is a paragraph that explains the point of the story — what the story is about. A summary lead often tells that information and takes the place of a nut graph. In this example, the lead is purposely vague to entice readers to continue, and the nut graph is in the third paragraph:

The Alpha Gamma Rho fraternity president says it was a practical joke that got blown out of proportion.

Police say it was a hazing incident that involved new AGR members preparing to have sex with a goat.

And Western officials are still trying to determine if AGR members violated university policy by having a goat in their house that may have been used to intimidate new members.

— COREY PAUL, *College Heights Herald*, Western Kentucky University

Soft Leads: Also called "feature leads" or "delayed leads," soft leads can be several paragraphs long before the nut graph. They delay telling the reader what the story is about by teasing the reader with a description or a storytelling approach as in the previous example. In these days of impatient readers and small-screen delivery, the nut graph should be early in the story — usually by the third to fifth paragraph. Here is an example of a soft lead and a nut graph:

Soft lead: who, what

SAN JOSE, Calif. — A nervous flight attendant was having trouble taking a urine drug test. So she drank a glass of water — and another — and another.

More what

After guzzling three liters in three hours, she still couldn't urinate.

Where

But hours later, the 40-year-old woman staggered into a Burlingame, Calif., hospital, her speech slurred, her thinking fuzzy.

The diagnosis: She was drunk — on water.

The unidentified San Mateo County resident is the first drug-test taker known to suffer from "water intoxication," doctors reported yesterday in the *Journal of the American Medical Association.* There have been only seven other reported cases of healthy people with the dangerous condition, which causes waterlogged brain cells and a dilution of body minerals. One died.

— *Knight-Ridder/Tribune News Service*

Nut graph: The focus is about the dangers of water intoxication in connection with drug testing.

How do you decide whether to use a direct or indirect lead? The choice depends on several factors: the significance of the news, the timing, proximity (interest to your local readers or viewers), subject matter, and in many cases, your editor's preference. If the subject is serious — death, disaster, a major change in the law — consider a summary-lead approach. Breaking news that happened yesterday or today also lends itself to a hard-news lead.

HARD-NEWS LEADS

Summary Leads

A summary lead should answer several, but not all, of the basic questions: who, what, when, where and why, plus how and so what. If you cram all of them into the lead, it could be cumbersome.

Choose the most important factors for the lead. Save the others for the second or third paragraph. This example stresses who and what, the most common type of summary lead:

Who, what, when, why

TALLAHASSEE, Fla. — A Florida law student was held Tuesday on a charge she hired a hit man to kill a secretary who found out the student had stolen an exam, police said.

This example stresses who, what and why:

> WASHINGTON (AP) — The Federal Aviation Administration said Tuesday it would hire 12,500 new air traffic controllers over the next decade to offset a wave of looming retirements.

Subject–Verb–Object Order: Summary leads are most effective when they follow subject–verb–object order (who did what or what happened). This order is also favored for broadcast writing. The following lead, which works for print, broadcast and online media, starts with who, what, why and when:

> A 22-year-old Mesa resident is accused of offering an undercover police officer $1,000 to kill a woman who appeared on her boyfriend's MySpace.com Web page.
>
> — *East Valley Tribune*, Mesa, Ariz.

Avoid writing long summary leads that begin with clauses, as in this example:

> Declaring that property owners must be protected from an arrogant government, House Republicans are nearing approval of legislation that would weaken federal efforts to protect wetlands and endangered species.
>
> — *The Associated Press*

This lead would have been clearer if it had begun by explaining who is doing what: "House Republicans are nearing approval . . . ."

Order of Information: When you write a summary lead, how do you decide which basics to include and in what order? The points of emphasis should be the first or last words in the lead. Decide which elements are the most important — who, what, where, when, why, how or so what. Usually it is safe to use a subject-verb-object format: who did the action, what happened, to whom. But sometimes the how or why is most important.

Here are some facts presented in a story:

> **Who:** Three boaters
> **What happened:** Two killed, the third injured when the boat capsized
> **When:** Sunday
> **Where:** Lake Harney near the Volusia-Seminole county line in Florida
> **Why:** High winds and waves
> **How:** Explained later in the story

The lead that appeared in the newspaper stresses who first, followed by what:

> Two boaters were killed and a third was injured Sunday when their small boat capsized in high winds and waves on Lake Harney near the Volusia-Seminole county line.
>
> — *The Orlando* (Fla.) *Sentinel*

Now look at the way the lead would read with different elements placed first:

What A small boat that capsized in high winds and waves on Lake Harney near the Volusia-Seminole county line caused the death of two boaters and injuries to a third Sunday.

When On Sunday two boaters were killed and a third was injured when their small boat capsized in high winds and waves on Lake Harney near the Volusia-Seminole county line.

Where On Lake Harney near the Volusia-Seminole county line, a small boat capsized Sunday in high winds and waves, causing the death of two boaters and injuries to a third.

Why High winds and waves on Lake Harney near the Volusia-Seminole county line caused a small boat to capsize Sunday, killing two boaters and injuring a third.

The actual lead from the newspaper seems the most logical because the point of emphasis — the important news (boaters died) — is first. The last lead, focusing on why, is the next best option; the point of emphasis (boaters died) is at the end.

If you were writing that story for broadcast news, you would update the information and use present tense:

> Two boaters are dead and a third is suffering from injuries caused when their small boat capsized today on Lake Harney near the Volusia-Seminole county line.

Point of Emphasis: Most of the time when you write a hard-news lead, you will put the most important information first. Or you might want the point of emphasis at the end of the sentence, as in this example:

> A consumer group said Thursday that some sunscreens and cosmetics contain an ingredient that can promote cancerous skin tumors, and it called on the government to halt their sale.
>
> — *The Associated Press*

Active vs. Passive Voice: Active voice is generally preferable to passive in print and always preferred in broadcast writing. Active voice stresses who is doing the action; passive voice stresses those to whom the action is done. But you may need to use passive voice when the emphasis is on what happened instead of who caused it to happen, especially in police or court stories.

Active voice is stronger for the following example, because it emphasizes the iguana as the subject; for broadcast put the attribution first:

Active	A pet iguana started a fire in a split-level house in Hillsmere Shores by knocking over a heat lamp with its tail, fire officials said.	Fire officials say a pet iguana started a fire in a split-level house in Hillsmere Shores by knocking over a heat lamp with its tail.	*Broadcast version with attribution first — active voice*
Passive	A fire in a split-level house in Hillsmere Shores was started by a pet iguana that knocked over a heat lamp with its tail, fire officials said.		

In the next example, however, passive voice is preferable because it gets to the point faster:

Passive   A former employee of the University of Pennsylvania's Van Pelt Library was sentenced to seven years of psychiatric probation yesterday for the theft of $1,798,310 worth of rare books and documents.

— The Philadelphia Inquirer

The sentence was imposed by Philadelphia Common Pleas Court Judge Russell M. Nigro, as the story later explains. The emphasis in the lead is on the employee who was sentenced. Here is how the lead would sound in active voice:

Active   Philadelphia Common Pleas Court Judge Russell M. Nigro yesterday sentenced a former employee of the University of Pennsylvania's Van Pelt Library to seven years of psychiatric probation for the theft of $1,798,310 worth of rare books and documents.

In the active version, it takes longer to get to the point of the story, and the emphasis is on the judge, not the employee.

Where to Say When: The time element can be confusing in a lead. In breaking news, when something happened yesterday, the time element usually does not come first in the sentence. But you need to place it where it is accurate, even if it sounds awkward.

Here is an example of a confusing time element:

University officials agreed to raise tuition by $100 Monday.

As written, the lead indicates the tuition will increase on Monday. Wrong. Tuition won't go up until next fall. Here's what really happened:

University officials agreed Monday to raise tuition by $100.

Delayed Identification: When the *who* in your lead is not a well-known person in your community or in the nation, you can identify the person by age, location, occupation or another modifier in the first paragraph. Then identify the person by name in the second paragraph. When you use delayed identification, even if your story involves several people, the first name you use should be the one you referred to in your lead.

All states have laws restricting the release of juvenile offenders' names, and several states prohibit the release of names of rape victims. In addition, many newspapers and television news organizations have policies to withhold names of criminal suspects until they are formally charged with crimes. Therefore, you need to use alternative forms of identification in these situations as well.

The following examples show how to say who in the lead and delay identification:

Age   An 18-year-old Tampa man was shot and killed Wednesday after he and two friends confronted a gunman who had beaten a friend of theirs, Tampa police said.

Warren Smith III, of 3524 E. 26th Ave., was shot behind his right ear at 6:40 p.m. and was pronounced dead shortly after arriving at Tampa General Hospital, police said.

— *St. Petersburg* (Fla.) *Times*

Occupation   Two Minneapolis meter monitors have been charged with stealing an estimated $35,000 worth of nickels, dimes and quarters from parking meters.

Dale Timinskis, 42, and Leroy Siner, 40, both of Minneapolis, were arrested Tuesday after police watched their activities.

— *Minneapolis Star Tribune*

Location   An Anchorage woman who embezzled more than $450,000 pleaded guilty Friday in U.S. District Court in Spokane, Wash., to charges of identity theft and filing a false tax return.

Jana J. Josey, 44, who now lives in Wenatchee, Wash., used various schemes to embezzle money while working as an accounts payable clerk for Quality Asphalt Paving, an Alaska construction company.

— *The Associated Press*

Other   A former Duke University student who posed as a wealthy French
identifier   baron was a con artist with lavish desires, said a judge who sentenced the imposter to three years in prison for fraud.

Maurice Jeffrey Locke Rothschild, 38, who changed his name from Mauro Cortex Jr., was sentenced in Greensboro, N.C., for bilking two banks by posing as a nobleman from France's wealthy Rothschild family. The charges involved $12,000 Rothschild received after submitting false information on credit card applications.

— *Newsday*

If you are writing a story about a person who has been in the news frequently, such as a suspect in a trial, you may use the name, but add a phrase or clause to identify the person, as in this example about a woman on trial for the murder of her former fiancé.

Prosecutors in the trial of former stripper Michele Linehan want the jury to watch a movie called "The Last Seduction," about a woman who tried to manipulate her lover into killing her husband for $1 million.

Updated Leads

The summary lead usually stresses basic facts about the news in the immediate past, and it is usually written in past tense. This type of breaking-news lead is often referred to as a "first-day lead," as if readers were hearing the news for the first time.

Because television and online news sites require immediacy, leads are often updated by advancing the story to the next step, a process called "forward spin" or "advancing the lead." Newspapers used to refer to updated leads as "second-day leads," but because the news breaks online or on social media sites, the second-day lead is needed more as a first-day approach in most print, broadcast and online news.

The first example is a standard summary lead that appeared in a morning paper. It stresses what happened yesterday in the search for a missing University of Arizona professor.

> Rescue workers combed a rugged area in the Tucson Mountains yesterday evening in search of a UA music professor who has been missing since Tuesday night.
>
> — *The* (Tucson) *Arizona Daily Star*

The second example appeared in a competing afternoon newspaper. It gives the story a forward spin, stressing what will happen today even though there is no new information; this would work better for broadcast:

> Deputies plan to resume a search this morning in rocky terrain in the Gates Pass area for missing University of Arizona music Professor Roy Andres Johnson, 58, who they fear was killed.
>
> — *Tucson* (Ariz.) *Citizen*

A few days later the professor's body was found; he had been murdered.

Here is an example of how you might update a lead, especially for broadcast:

| *Original version* | Princeton University officials have placed a cap on the number of A's that professors can award in an effort to crack down on grade inflation. | Students at Princeton University won't be receiving as many A's this year. School officials are cracking down on grade inflation by placing a cap on the number of A's professors can award. | *Updated version* |

Impact Leads

The "impact lead" explains how the readers and viewers will be affected by an issue. This type of lead is also good for broadcast stories. It is an excellent tool to make a story seem fresh and relevant. The impact lead is especially helpful on bureaucratic stories. It answers the questions "So what? What does this news mean to a reader?"

Impact leads can be written in a hard-news summary form or in a soft lead. The information you give must be factual, not your interpretation. If you use a soft lead, you must write a clear nut graph early in the story.

The previous updated lead is also an example of an impact lead because it starts with how students at Princeton University will be affected by the new grade restrictions.

This impact lead uses a direct summary approach:

| *Summary lead with impact* | San Francisco has become the first city in the nation to require cell phone companies to disclose how much radiation their phones emit. |

Here is an impact lead that directly addresses readers and viewers; this lead that would work equally well in print, broadcast or on the Web:

Courtesy of the Centers for Disease Control

> Are you avoiding the bathroom scale? Is it a struggle to pull on last year's clothes? If the answer is "yes," you probably need to take off some extra pounds. But what you might not know is that a little extra sleep could be the answer.
>
> Studies show that people who sleep too little are actually more likely to raid the refrigerator.
>
> — *Fairbanks* (Alaska) *Daily News Miner* webcast

Attribution in Leads

Attribution tells the reader where you got your information. Too much attribution can clutter a lead. Too little attribution can get you in trouble. For print and online stories, you may put the attribution at the beginning or the end of the sentence; for broadcast, attribution must come first. Here are some guidelines about whether you need to use attribution:

- If you know the information is factual and you witnessed it or have firsthand knowledge that it is true, you may eliminate the attribution. If you received the information by telephone, as in police or fire stories, attribute it to your source.
- Whenever you are saying anything accusatory, as in police or political stories, you must attribute the information.
- You also must attribute the quotes or partial quotes you use in a lead.

SOCIAL MEDIA

USE TWITTER AS a way to write a succinct summary lead in 140 characters, but don't use abbreviations. Search for tweets on a subject of interest to you. Then click the links and read the leads on the full post. Notice how many of the leads are summary leads, which are ideal for tweets and mobile media as these examples.

Child care costs more than food, rent and college in some metros

Pell grant and scholarship funds pay college tuition costs and fees

You can also tweet your nut graph, which will help you identify the focus of your story. You don't have to post your tweets; just use the Twitter concepts to improve your skills in writing leads and nut graphs.

To keep attribution clutter to a minimum, you may give a general reference to some sources — such as "police said" or "experts say" — if their titles are long. Then, as in delayed identification, give the specific name and title in the second reference.

In broadcast news, if the source is shown on videotape, the name and title may be superimposed under the video so you may not need to attribute by name and title. If you do use attribution, put the source's title before the name:

Right: Police Chief John Law says the suspect is in custody.

Wrong: John Law, police chief, says the suspect is in custody.

Fact vs. Opinion Here are some examples that demonstrate when to use attribution:

Fact: No attribution is needed.	An 88-year-old man died Monday afternoon when fire spread through his second-floor apartment at the Wellington Arms Apartments in north St. Louis County.	The body of a man who had been fatally stabbed was discovered Monday morning in a city trash bin in the Lewis Place neighborhood, police said. — *St. Louis* (Mo.) *Post-Dispatch*	*Attributed fact: Attribution for fact is needed because the reporter got the information secondhand (by telephone).*
Opinion: Speculation about the cause needs to be attributed.	An 88-year-old man died in north St. Louis County Monday afternoon, apparently after he started a fire while smoking in bed, authorities said.		

Accusations A person is innocent until proved guilty in court. In crime stories, attribute any accusatory statements to police or other authorities, especially when you are using a suspect's name. If the person has been charged with a crime, you may state that fact without attribution. The word *allegedly* can be used when the charges have not been proved, but direct attribution to the police is preferable. Here are some examples:

No attribution is needed.	A University of North Florida chemistry major has been charged with building a 35-pound "megabomb" powerful enough to destroy everything within a radius of 150 yards. — *The Associated Press*

Attribution is needed for an accusatory statement.	David Roger Flint killed 16-month-old Brittany K. Boyer on Monday by dangling her by the arms, swinging her side to side and beating her head against the floor and wooden furniture, police say. The 23-year-old Flint was arrested about 10:30 p.m. Tuesday and accused of murder. — JANE MEINHARDT, *St. Petersburg* (Fla.) *Times*

The word allegedly is used because it has not yet been proved that the kidnap and rape occurred.

A 38-year-old paroled murderer has been arrested in St. Croix County, Wis., for allegedly kidnapping and raping two 16-year-old girls in Minneapolis last month. . . .

Later, the lead is backed up this way.

He was charged with two counts of first-degree criminal sexual conduct and two counts of kidnapping.

— *St. Paul* (Minn.) *Pioneer Press*

This lead would be a safer alternative.

A 38-year-old paroled murderer has been charged with kidnapping and raping two 16-year-old girls in Minneapolis last month.

Quotes Whenever you quote someone directly, indirectly or partially, you need to attribute the statement.

Full quotes are difficult in leads and can be awkward. Reading a story that starts with a full quote is like coming into the middle of a conversation; it's hard to tell the context and meaning of the quote. Full quotes are also ineffective for broadcast writing.

A more effective technique is the use of partial quotes, especially when the speaker says something controversial or dramatic. Leads may also contain reference quotes, a few words referring to something controversial. Both partial and reference quotes should be backed up later in the story with the full quote or with the context in which the statement was made.

A full quote is used in this lead because it is dramatic, but it is still confusing.

"I've done everything out there," 31-year-old Gilbert Franco told his wife Thursday. "All that's left to do is learn the Bible and to die."

The next day, San Jose police say, Franco entered the C&S Market at East Julian and 26th streets and shot to death Katherine Young Suk Choe, 40, whose family owns the store.

Seconds later, 50 yards away, Franco fatally shot himself in the head.

— *San Jose* (Calif.) *Mercury News*

In this example a partial quote is used and backed up later with the full quote, a technique used more often in stories about speeches, politics and court stories:

A reference quote is used in the lead.	The University of Pennsylvania announced yesterday that it was penalizing a senior scientist for "lapses of judgment" in an experiment last April in which more than 120 people may have been exposed to a virus that can cause a fatal form of leukemia. . . .

The backup puts the partial quote in context.	The committee concluded that the professor was not guilty of research misconduct as defined in a school policy. However, the committee concluded that there were "lapses of judgment and failures of communication" in the experiment.

> — *The Philadelphia Inquirer*

Attribution First or Last The rule of thumb in the lead is to put the most important information first. If the attribution is cumbersome and will slow the lead, put it at the end. If it is brief, you can put it first. In broadcast writing, however, you need to put the attribution first. If the attribution is cumbersome, refer to the source broadly as in "a new study" or "a state official," and state the full attribution in the next paragraph.

Attribution last	Casual drug use has dropped sharply during the last five years, but the number of addicts using cocaine daily has not changed significantly, the federal government reported yesterday.

> — *The Philadelphia Inquirer*

Attribution first (acceptable, and preferable for broadcast writing)	The federal government reports that casual drug use has dropped sharply during the last five years, but the number of addicts using cocaine daily has not changed significantly.

Attribution last (because name is cumbersome and not as important as conclusions)	America's newspaper journalists want a faster transition of print to digital delivery of the news, according to "Life Beyond Print," a study of nearly 3,800 journalists by researchers at the Media Management Center of Northwestern University.

Cluttered Attribution In the example that follows, note how a long attribution at the start of the sentence clutters the lead:

Cluttered	Karen Davisson, child protection worker with the Kansas Department of Social Rehabilitation Services district office in Emporia, said Tuesday that only rarely are neglected or abused children removed from their parents' care and placed in foster homes or put up for adoption.

Uncluttered	Neglected or abused children are rarely removed from their parents' care and placed in foster homes or put up for adoption, a state social worker said Tuesday. Karen Davisson is a child protection worker with the Kansas Department of Social Rehabilitation Services district office in Emporia.

One of the most common causes of clutter in leads is too much information about where and when something was said. Put some of this material in the second paragraph. Put the location of the meeting much farther down in the story, or eliminate it altogether unless it is important to the reader.

Cluttered	Fort Riley is being considered as a possible host for the proposed joint landfill for Geary and Riley counties, Riley County Director of Public Works Dan Harden said during an informational meeting Tuesday night at the Geary County 4-H Senior Citizens Center.

Uncluttered	Fort Riley is being considered as a possible site for a landfill, a Riley County official said Tuesday. Dan Harden, director of public works said. . . .

SOFT LEADS

Coaching Tips

- Try writing many different leads instead of struggling to find the perfect one.
- Make sure that your lead is related to your focus and can be backed up in your story.
- Do not strain to "create" a lead from your head. Pull from the story, not from your head, for inspiration.

Soft leads can be fun to write and fun to read. They can also be painful. If you don't get to the point quickly, they can also be tedious. They can be as effective in broadcast writing as in print.

CONVERGENCE COACH

THE TECHNIQUES of writing leads apply to all media, but broadcast leads should stress the most current information. If you are posting the information first on the Web, you will need to update the lead for the next print edition as well as the next broadcast.

Online writing is similar to print, but summary leads are often preferred because readers are impatient to discover the main point of the story, especially for news that will be delivered to cell phones or other small-screen devices. Summary leads are also preferred for public relations writing in news releases. If you use a descriptive or anecdotal lead, make sure that the nut graph is high in the story.

Here are some guidelines for broadcast and online writing:

- Use active voice, with an emphasis on short, uncomplicated sentences. State who is doing the action rather than to whom the action was done.
- Use simple sentences, preferably in subject–verb–object order (who did what). Avoid long sentences that begin with clauses.
- Put the most important information first in the sentence.
- Use a conversational tone. Addressing the reader as "you" works well in broadcast and on the Web.
- For broadcast, place attribution first, not at the end of the sentence; either order works for the Web. If the attribution is cumbersome, put it in another paragraph, as in this example:

New research indicates that eating lots of red meat may create about as much of a certain cancer-promoting chemical in the colon as smoking does.

The findings, presented Saturday in Lyon at the European Conference on Nutrition and Cancer, were part of a study that also appears to revive the theory that fiber wards off colon cancer, the second most deadly cancer worldwide.

— The Associated Press

- Most important, get to the main point quickly. This story begins with a soft lead sentence, but the main point is still in the lead:

Never mind what the label says. The new brands of energy drinks are aimed more at marathon partiers than serious athletes. And that has health officials worried.

The drinks come in flashy cans and bottles with names like Red Bull, Adrenaline Rush and Jones Whoop-Ass Energy Drink. They don't taste great by almost universal consensus, but they're the fastest-growing segment of the beverage market because they deliver a quick punch of energy.

— The Associated Press

Although soft leads are also called "delayed leads," the lead is still first. Only the nut graph is delayed. It is preferable to place the nut graph high in the story, by the third to fifth paragraph.

There are many types of soft leads. They can be used on both news and feature stories. Most of them follow a simple concept: specific to general. Use a specific example at the beginning to illustrate the main point of the story.

ETHICS

ETHICAL DILEMMA: You want to write an anecdotal lead focusing on a person for your story, but you don't have a real source. Should you use a hypothetical person without telling the reader? Should you use a hypothetical situation at all?

Ethical values: Credibility, accuracy, truthfulness.

Ethical guidelines: The Society of Professional Journalists Code of Ethics says, "Seek the truth and report it. Avoid misleading re-enactments or staged news events."

People like to read about other people. As a result, many soft leads start with something about a person who is one of many people sharing the same problem. The idea behind these soft leads — called "anecdotal leads" — is that readers can relate better to one person's problem than to a general statement of a problem.

Little pigs could cause big problems as in the next example.

Courtesy of the Department of Agriculture

Other common types of soft leads are descriptive and narrative. "Descriptive leads" describe a person or a scene. "Narrative leads" are storytelling leads that recount the event in a dramatic way to put the reader on the scene as the action occurs.

And then there are leads that are just clever or catchy.

It's not what you call soft leads that matters; it's how you write them. The important point is to tell a good story. When writers struggle with soft leads, it is often because they think they must create something clever. All too often, the result is a cliché. It is best to look at your notes and build a lead based on something interesting in the story.

The sections that follow show a variety of ways to structure a soft lead. The basic techniques are descriptive, anecdotal and narrative.

Descriptive Leads

This type of lead describes a person, place or event. It is like the descriptive focus-on-a-person lead, but it doesn't have to focus on a person who is one of many. It can be used for news or feature stories.

In this example, the story focuses on the man who is causing the problem:

> Skippack farmer John W. Hasson stood ankle-deep in mud, pumping milk into a wooden trough as his pigs, squealing and grunting, snouts quivering, climbed over each other to get to their feed.
>
> Hasson inhaled deeply.
>
> "Does that smell sour to you?
>
> That's what they call noxious fumes," he said with a sniff toward his new neighbors, Ironbridge Estates, a subdivision of two-story colonial houses costing $200,000 plus.
>
> Ironbridge's developers say Hasson's farm smells.
>
> And his 250 pigs squeal too much.
>
> So they have filed suit in Montgomery County to force him to clean up his act. The case is scheduled to be heard May 8.
>
> — ERIN KENNEDY, *The Philadelphia Inquirer*

Anecdotal Leads

This type of lead starts with a story about a person or an event. In a sense, all soft leads are anecdotal because they are all storytelling approaches. Many combine descriptive and anecdotal techniques.

This lead is an anecdote — the story behind a woman's court case:

> Late one spring night, after drinks at a bar and a bit of protest, Elaine Hollis agreed to her boyfriend's desire to capture their passion on videotape.
>
> Inside Edward Bayliss' apartment, the video camera rolled at the foot of his bed.
>
> He promised to erase the tape.
>
> Seven years later, Hollis, who has a son with Bayliss, was in Delaware County Court accusing him of contriving to bring her into disrepute by exhibiting the tape. Bayliss, president of Philadelphia Suburban Electrical Service in Upper Darby, admitted showing the tape to one of his friends.
>
> Hollis contended he showed and distributed the tape in Delaware County and surrounding areas, as well as gave copies of it to two bar owners in Darby, who played it for customers.
>
> Last week, after three years of litigation, a county judge upheld an Oct. 15 Common Pleas Court order that mandated Bayliss pay Hollis $125,000 to settle her lawsuit.
>
> — PATRICK SCOTT, *The Philadelphia Inquirer*

This example contains another anecdotal lead that tells a story but incorporates the news in the first sentence. It is a good example of using a storytelling approach to update the news about a minor earthquake that occurred the previous day. (If the

Photo courtesy of the U.S. Geological Survey.

The 1964 earthquake in Alaska was the strongest in U.S. history. The seven-story high reinforced concrete control tower at Anchorage International Airport fell to the ground during the earthquake.

earthquake had been greater and had caused death or injuries as it did in the 1964 earthquake in Alaska, a summary lead would have been more appropriate.)

When the shock wave from a magnitude 4.7 earthquake rolled through Anchorage Wednesday morning, dentist Kendall Skinner had just inserted a 3-inch needle into the mouth of a patient and begun an injection.

"It was jarring," Skinner said. "It's such a sharp object in the back of somebody's mouth."

With a somewhat unsteady hand, Skinner finished the injection as fast and safely as he could, then pulled out. His patient, a 20-something woman who needed a filling, told him she was fine. The numbing started before the shaking, so she didn't feel a thing.

People all over Anchorage and the Matanuska-Susitna Valley were shaken but not stirred from their regular workday routine Wednesday when a quake struck beneath the Point MacKenzie area a few miles north of downtown — then triggered an afternoon of minor aftershocks.

Nut graph

— DOUG O'HARRA, MEGAN HOLLAND AND ZAZ HOLLANDER, *Anchorage* (Alaska) *Daily News*

This lead uses both anecdotal and descriptive techniques:

Dawn Clark's cat walked carefully across the lawn, then stopped suddenly, looking bewildered.

The cat sniffed tentatively, then bolted off the grass and spent the next few minutes licking its paws — trying to clean the paint flecks from them.

The lawn had recently been mowed and was green as a billiard table, because it had just been painted with a vegetable dye.

Santa Barbara residents have devised innovative ways to keep their yards green since the city, faced with an expected water shortfall of nearly 50 percent for the year, declared a "drought emergency" in late February and banned lawn watering.

Nut graph

Clark's cat had just experienced one: Several landscape companies now offer painting and local nurseries are stocking their shelves with green paint and pump sprayers.

Extension of nut graph

— MILES CORWIN, *Los Angeles Times*

Narrative Leads

Like an anecdotal lead, a narrative lead tells a story with enough dramatic action so readers can feel as if they are witnessing the event. Narrative writing uses all the techniques of fiction, including dialogue, scene setting and foreshadowing — giving the reader clues to what will happen. It takes longer to set up the nut graph for this kind of lead, but if the story is dramatic enough, the narrative approach may work.

Police Officer Juan Cabrera felt the barrel of the gun press against his head.

"I'm gonna kill you," a voice from behind said.

"I didn't see who it was. I didn't know what was happening," Cabrera said. "I just thought someone was going to kill me." Cabrera instinctively knocked the gun away, wrestled the suspect to the ground and handcuffed him.

The suspect was a 12-year-old boy.

The gun was a toy.

"It looked like a .38-caliber short-barrel revolver," said Cabrera, a five-year veteran of the force. "It was a cap gun."

The incident was no joke for the boy. He was arrested on a charge of battery on a law enforcement officer.

— KEVIN DAVIS, *The South Florida Sun-Sentinel*

Other Soft Leads

Soft leads can be written in many other ways. The following techniques are variations on the three main types of soft leads, combining features of descriptive, anecdotal and narrative leads.

Focus-on-a-Person Leads You can focus on a person in two ways: Use an anecdotal approach, telling a little story about the person, or use a descriptive approach that describes the person or shows the person in action. This type of lead can be used in profile stories about the person or in news stories about issues, where the person is one of many affected by the point of your story.

This example uses the descriptive approach:

Nita walked slowly down the narrow hall, deftly guiding her tottering 11-month-old son around the abandoned baby walkers, strollers and toys.

Inside her tiny bedroom, the 17-year-old mother pointed to photographs of her son's father and some of her friends. Cards congratulating her on her recent high school graduation were nearby. The baby's crib was crammed into an area near the door.

Nita, one of 85 residents at Florence Crittenton Services in Fullerton, is one of a growing number of teenagers having babies in Orange County — a figure that has increased 36 percent in five years.

— JANINE ANDERSON,
The Orange County (Calif.) *Register*

Nut graph: points out that this person is one of many

The focus-on-a-person lead is an effective technique for broadcast news as well, especially when the person or people used in the lead exemplify a problem shared by many other people in your community.

Residents in this flood-damaged community share problems described in the next example.

Photo by Tim Burkitt, Courtesy of the Federal Emergency Management Agency

Judy and Jose Westbrook spent the morning cleaning up the furniture in their front yard. The Blue River had overflowed its banks and forced its way into their Independence home.

More than 25 families share their predicament. Late this afternoon, all of those families were awaiting word about their flood insurance claims.

Nut graph: points out that these people are like many others

Contrast Leads This type of lead can be used to set up stories about conflicts or unusual circumstances. The two most common ways to write contrast leads emphasize circumstances and time:

But-Guess-What Contrast: Contrast leads that revolve around circumstances can be used to explain something unusual:

William Pearce, known to his patients as Dr. William J. Rick, was charming and slick, say his former associates and police detectives.

He came to town with medical degrees, numerous national board certificates and myriad other qualifications.

But the real Dr. Rick died in 1986, police say. And now William John Pearce, 57, is in jail on charges of impersonating a doctor.

— SHARON McBREEN,
The Orlando (Fla.) *Sentinel*

Nut graph

Then-and-Now Contrast: Time contrasts — then and now — are useful ways to show change. This type of lead also can be used when the background is interesting or important and is relevant to the focus.

It was March 1964 when Lewis "Hackie" Wilson, the 7-year-old son of a St. Petersburg firefighter, disappeared after stopping to pick up flowers on his way home from school.

His case received national attention a month later when a sheriff's posse on horseback, flushing out rattlesnakes ahead of a line of 80 searchers, found the child's bones in a field south of Venice.

Now the case may be revived. Prosecutors in Sarasota County have realized that Joseph Francis Bryan, a convicted child kidnapper indicted for Hackie's murder in 1965, has never been brought to trial.

— KAREN DATKO, *St. Petersburg*
(Fla.) *Times*

Nut graph

Teaser Leads These leads use the element of surprise to tease the reader into the story. The nut graph may also be a contrast, but the first sentence sets it up as a tease into something unusual. Broadcast news uses the concept of teasers before commercials to convince the audience to stay tuned after the break, but teasers are also effective in leads on broadcast stories.

BURLINGTON, Vt. — This is no ordinary public library.

For one thing, there are only four books on the shelves. For another, you won't find any of these works, or the many that are expected to join them soon, at other libraries or bookstores.

You probably never will.

That's because the Brautigan Library, which opened here last weekend, has a unique policy — it only accepts books that have never been published.

Nut graph

— STEVE STECKLOW,
The Philadelphia Inquirer

Mystery Leads Like teasers, these leads promise the reader a surprise or a treat for reading on. They set up the story like a mystery novel. They're fun to write and fun to read, but they won't work unless the subject matter lends itself to this approach. They are effective for print and broadcast writing.

One technique for writing mystery leads is to start with a vague pronoun, *it* or *they,* and to delay naming the noun to which the pronoun refers: "It began at midnight." Later you specify what "it" was. Here is an example of a mystery lead:

They know who you are, what you eat, how you procreate — and where to find you.

Do you like ice cream? The U.S. government has used that information to track down draft-dodging 18-year-olds who signed up for ice cream parlor "birthday clubs." . . .

Been turned down for a MasterCard or Visa? List Brokerage and Management, a New York list marketer, may have your name. It rents a list of 1.6 million people rejected for bank cards — obtained, the company says, from the very banks that turned you down. . . .

Computer companies are hooking up with credit bureaus and massive data banks to allow people with only a desktop computer to single you out by income, age, neighborhood, car model or waist size.

Nut graph

— STEPHEN KOFF, *St. Petersburg*
(Fla.) *Times*

This next lead uses not only the mystery approach but also the format of the novel as part of the lead:

The case has all the elements of a 1950s film noir mystery.

The characters: the scheming husband, the trusting wife, the other woman.

The story: The husband, Ray Valois, buys a lottery ticket, scratches it and finds three "Spin, Spin, Spin" symbols. That makes him eligible to win up to $2 million in the California "Big Spin" lottery, but he does not want to tell his wife, Monica, according to his statement in San Luis Obispo County Superior Court records. So he gives the ticket to another woman, waitress Stephanie Martin. She agrees to cash in the ticket, according to court records, and secretly give him half.

The inevitable plot twist: Valois and Martin turn on each other. He claims that he owns the ticket. She claims that she owns the ticket.

The conclusion: Martin spins and wins $100,000. But the wife finds out and sues both of them for fraud.

Nut graph

Now neither Martin nor Valois has the $100,000. His wife's attorney, Gary Dunlap, obtained a temporary restraining order, restricting lottery officials from awarding the winnings until a court hearing today.

— MILES CORWIN, *Los Angeles Times*

Build-on-a-Quote Leads If you have a great quote, build your lead around the quote that will back up your first sentence. But be careful not to repeat too much of the quote in your lead; that's boring and repetitious. Building on a quote is an easy and effective way to find a lead, provided that the quote is related to the focus of the story. This technique works equally well for hard-news leads. For broadcast news, however, you would not read a quote. Instead, you might start with a video of a person speaking, called a "sound on tape" (SOT).

ANDOVER, Kan. — Melinda Easterbrook knows exactly how long it took for a tornado to blast apart her comfortable home while she and her husband huddled in the basement.

"It lasted five Hail Marys and two Our Fathers, but you have to say them quickly," she said yesterday.

Nut graph

While she was praying, the concrete basement rumbled and shook. When she and her husband, Bryan, came upstairs, they were hardly prepared for the scope of the destruction that had swept through this small town about five miles east of Wichita.

— LARRY FISH, *The Philadelphia Inquirer*

The next example is the kind of build-on-a-quote lead to avoid. The backup quote says the same thing as the lead, and it's right after the lead, so it's boring. In broadcast writing this is called "parroting," when the reporter introduces a sound bite that repeats what the source says on tape. It should be avoided as well.

A commitment to high-tech learning and small classes taught by professors has made Fort Hays State University the fastest-growing university in the state Board of Regents system, FHSU's president said today.

FHSU had the largest spring semester enrollment increase among the six regents' universities — 2.4 percent compared with the previous spring.

"We've been the fastest growing of the regents' institutions over the last five years," FHSU President Edward Hammond said.

List Leads If you have a few brief examples to lead into your focus, you may list them in parallel sentences — making sure that your sentences have the same construction, such as subject–verb–object order. Three seems to be a magic number; more than three can be awkward and tedious.

Boston College has an assistant dean for alcohol and drug education. Rutgers University sets aside dorm rooms for recovering student alcoholics. The University of Nevada bars students from leaving school sports events to make alcohol runs.

Increasingly, colleges are confronting problem drinking by providing education and rehabilitation programs, alternatives to the campus bar scene and stricter regulation of on-campus parties.

Nut graph

— *The Associated Press*

Question Leads These can be effective if the reader is interested in finding the answer to the question you pose. If not, you could lose the reader. One way to test question leads is to determine if the answer would be yes or no. Those are the dangerous ones. A question that raises a more thoughtful, and more interesting, answer is preferable.

What are the odds of finding your true love by placing an ad with a telephone dating service?

About one in 40, according to Terry Ehlbert.

On April 13, Ehlbert is planning to marry Scott Anderson, who was the last of 40 guys she agreed to meet after placing a voicemail ad with the 1-976-DATE service she saw advertised on TV. . . .

The phone services work in much the same way published personal ads do.

Nut graph

— RICK SHEFCHIK, *St. Paul (Minn.) Pioneer Press*

The next example is a little dangerous. What if you don't want to buy cigarettes at all? Will you read on?

Want to buy cigarettes while at the gas station? Or while sipping a cocktail at your favorite bar?

Not in Lower Merion, if township officials have their way.

Officials there, concerned about the availability of cigarettes to minors, have proposed a municipal law prohibiting cigarette vending machines in the township. The law would be the first of its kind in Pennsylvania.

Nut graph

— *The Philadelphia Inquirer*

Cliché Leads In general, avoid clichés. But occasionally, a play on words will work as a clever lead. Consider this:

Nick Agid's workshop is just a stone's throw from the Torrance post office. Good thing, too. When Agid drops a post card into the mail, it lands with a five-pound thud.

Agid is a sculptor who carves messages on leftover chunks of marble and granite. They become postcards when he adds scratched-on addresses and slaps stamps on the slabs.

Nut graph

— BOB POOL, *Los Angeles Times*

Leads to Avoid

The leads described in this section are strained, obtuse, rambling or just plain awful. They don't work for a variety of reasons.

Cluttered Leads: Keep your leads simple, especially for broadcast. Don't try to cram all the major facts of the story in one sentence. This lead is too complex and contains the cliché, "killed two birds with one stone."

Rolling up their sleeves, 20 students from Voznesenka School, near the head of Kachemak Bay, killed two birds with one stone Saturday: they washed away the grit and grime and put a shine on more than 25 local vehicles, and they raised more than $300 to help pay for next spring's graduation expenses.

Good News/Bad News Leads: The bad news is this type of lead. They're clichés, and they're used so often that they're boring. They're also judgmental.

> Some good news for city workers: The county administration has been giving signals that it might not have to give out any pink slips, at least for now.
>
> Some bad news for city taxpayers: The county administration has shown no signs of scaling back its proposal to raise taxes for the next several years.
>
> — *Newsday*

Crystal Ball Leads: These are dream-sequence leads that foretell the future. If you were writing about psychics, perhaps you could write this kind of lead. But most people can't predict the future. "John Jones never imagined when he boarded the plane that it was going to crash." Would he have been stupid enough to board it if he had known? Leads that emphasize "if only they had known" are far-fetched. Consider the following. It's unlikely that a child who is choking is thinking about the future — much less about what he can do for someone else.

> When 10-year-old Jason Finser of Clermont was saved from choking to death at a family dinner two years ago, he never dreamed he would be able to return the favor.
>
> But luckily for his classmate, 9-year-old Abby Muick, Jason knew exactly what to do when she choked on a chocolate-and-Rice Krispies treat in the lunchroom at Minneola Elementary School.   *Nut graph*
>
> — *The Orlando* (Fla.) *Sentinel*

Nightmare Leads: These are also dream leads, usually relating to a past experience. The nightmare analogy is overused: "The past three days were like a nightmare for John Jones." For the reader, too: Every bad experience someone has does not have to be compared to a nightmare.

> The nightmare became reality for local police yesterday when a Niagara Falls drug dealer was arrested at the Greater Buffalo International Airport.
>
> Hidden in his baggage were $50,000 worth of heroin, some PCP and a sampling of a new drug he referred to as "smokable cocaine."
>
> — *Niagara* (N.Y.) *Gazette*

Plop-a-Person Leads: This type of lead is a misuse of the focus-on-a-person lead. When the writer just tops the story with a sketch of a person and does not back it up in the text, that's plopping. It's also misleading. The reader starts the story thinking that the person has something to say or do in the story. But after the lead, the person disappears.

Tuesday was a good day for psychology professor Carnot Nelson.

He spent most of it helping an honors student work on her thesis. He read another student's doctoral dissertation and two master's thesis proposals. Then he went to a meeting, which he left after an hour and a half so he could do some reading of his own.

This is the last time we hear about Nelson, despite that he was a good example.

Nelson, a senior professor at the University of South Florida, who also teaches large undergraduate classes and small graduate seminars, is a good example of the range of activity involved in teaching Florida university students.

"Education is a one-at-a-time, hand-made business," said state university spokesman Pat Riordan. "You can't mechanize it, you can't computerize it and you can't put it on an assembly line."

Nut graphs

But college professors in Florida are under increasing pressure to do exactly that. Recurring state budget cuts have made some classes larger and eliminated many others. And a political climate that says there can be no new taxes until a state government becomes "more productive" has fueled a drive to force professors to spend more time in the classroom.

— *St. Petersburg* (Fla.) *Times*

Weather-Report Leads: These leads set the scene by describing the weather: "It was a dark and stormy night." Avoid using the weather as a lead when it isn't related to the story.

It was hot and humid the day the city council decided to ban smoking from all public buildings.

The ordinance, passed unanimously, will go into effect immediately.

Stereotype Leads: These are most common in features about older people, women and groups with special interests. The writer tries hard to be complimentary but instead only reinforces stereotypes. This is the lead for a story about Senior Olympics, games for people over age 60:

At the age when most of their contemporaries are in rocking chairs, these athletes will be competing in swimming, archery, badminton, bicycle racing — just about every imaginable sport, through the long jump and shot put.

— *The Baltimore Sun*

If you look around your college campus, you're likely to see many professors in their 60s, and most of them don't spend much time in rocking chairs.

Soft leads can be enticing and creative, but they must be accurate.

REMINDERS: TIPS FOR FINDING YOUR LEAD

To find a lead that will work for you in your story, first find your nut graph. Ask yourself what the main point of the story is. Then ask some of these questions to find your lead:

Reader Interest: What did you or would the reader find most interesting about this subject?

Memorable Item: What was the most memorable impression or fact?

Focus on a Person: Is there someone who exemplifies the problem or issue? If you tell a story about this person or show the person in action, will it lead to the point in the nut graph?

Descriptive Approach: Will a description of the scene relate to the focus?

Mystery Approach: Can you tease the reader with a surprise that leads to the nut graph?

Build on a Quote: Is there a great quote to back up the lead? If so, write the lead so it refers to the quote without repeating it.

Contrast: Would a then-and-now approach work?

Problem/Solution: Can you set up a problem so the reader wants to discover the solution?

Narrative Storytelling: If you were just telling a good story, how would you start? Can you reconstruct the events to put the reader on the scene?

EXERCISES

1 Hard-news leads: Write summary leads from the following information. For the time element, use the day of the week instead of *yesterday* or *today*.

a Write this lead for a print publication: A study was released yesterday by the University of Colorado. The study was funded by the Alfred P. Sloan Foundation. The study said that 60 percent of college students who begin studying science, mathematics or engineering switch to another major. The study cited poor teaching and an aloof faculty as the cause.

b There was a fire yesterday at a pizza restaurant. It is located at 2035 Main St. Two firefighters were injured when the roof fell in. They were treated at St. Luke's Medical Center for minor injuries. The fire started in the basement of the building. The cause is under investigation. The roof collapsed, and the inside of the restaurant was destroyed. Damages are estimated at $100,000. The information comes from fire officials in your community.

c The Centers for Disease Control today released the results of a survey of nutritional supplements. Nutritional supplements include vitamins, protein supplements and products promising muscle growth. Only supplements in powder, capsule or tablet form were surveyed. "It turned out that at least half of the ingredients have no documented medical effect," said Rossane Philen, a medical epidemiologist at the National Center for Environmental Health and Injury Control. She was part of the surveying team. The survey said many nutritional supplements have no medical support for their advertised claims.

2 Broadcast versions: Convert the leads you wrote in Exercise 1 to broadcast leads.

3 Active/passive voice: Change this lead to active voice:

A 29-year-old Phoenix man was killed Tuesday when his motorcycle was struck by a car on East Ina Road.

Write a lead in passive voice from this information:

Jones County Circuit Court Judge Billy Landrum yesterday sentenced a 17-year-old high school sophomore to two consecutive life terms for the murder of two men in a convenience store.

4 Delayed identification: From the following information, write a lead using delayed identification.

Background provided by the police:
Michael Stephens, who lives in the 3700 block of North Camino Street in Tucson, was driving a flatbed truck in central Tucson early yesterday morning. He lost control of his truck, and it overturned on East 15th Street near South Kino Parkway. He died of head injuries at the scene of the accident at 2:30 a.m. He was 44 years old.

5 Updated lead: From this information, give the lead a forward spin for the next edition of your print, broadcast or online publication.

Background: Vandals broke into the Midtown Magnet Middle School at 300 Fifth Ave. just before 7 p.m. on Sunday. They broke windows and damaged 11 classrooms and an office area. They damaged computers and other equipment. The cost of the damages has not yet been estimated. Classes are scheduled to resume today. School was closed Monday while school district employees spent the day cleaning up damage to the school.

6 Impact leads: Write impact leads from this information:

a The Board of Regents (or the governing body of universities in your state) has approved an increase in rates for campus housing at your university. The biggest increase will be in residence halls, where rates will increase 14.8 percent for double-room occupancy. The current rate is $2,684, and it will increase to $3,080 next fall.

b The Rockville City Council will meet at 7 p.m. Tuesday. The council will consider adopting an ordinance that would impose penalties for false alarms that are sent to the police department from faulty or improperly operated electronic security systems. Under the proposed ordinance, an alarm system owner would be allowed six free false alarms. The owner would have to pay a $30 penalty for each additional false alarm.

7 Attribution: Write a summary lead from the following information. Decide whether you need to include attribution.

Capt. J. Randall Ogden, a spokesman for the Tucson Fire Department (or use your local fire department spokesperson): A fire destroyed a home on East 17th Street. It was started by a cigarette that was discarded in a sofa. The fire left the husband, his wife and their four children homeless. The fire started at 1 a.m. and caused $30,000 in damages.

8 Anecdotal, focus-on-a-person lead: Write an anecdotal lead with a person focus from the following information; include a nut graph. Your focus is about the frustrations that students experience trying to park on campus because the parking department has sold too many permits.

Background: Nancy Pauw is a graduate student. One morning, she circled the parking lot east of the computer center three times before she found a parking space. Last year, there were 7,565 student parking permits sold for 3,930 spaces. "I have to get here an hour early so I can get to class on time," Pauw says. She is one of many students (on your campus) who experience the daily frustration of not finding a parking space even though they have purchased $30 and $50 permits.

9 Specific to general with nut graph: Write a soft lead, including a nut graph, that uses the specific-to-general technique to convey the following information:

Background: The General Accounting Office, the investigative arm for Congress, issued a report yesterday that said record keeping at the National Park Service is defective. The report said information in the Park Service's financial statements is inaccurate and filled with accounting errors. Property owned by the Park Service is overstated by more than $90 million, the report stated. Examples of inaccurate data in the Park Service records include a vacuum cleaner that is really worth $150 but is listed in records as worth $800,000, a dishwasher worth $350 but

valued at over $700,000, and a fire truck worth $133,000 but undervalued at 1 cent.

10 Descriptive: Write a descriptive lead for a story about apartments that violate city codes and are considered hazardous but that are often rented to students anyway.

Background: You interviewed a student who lives in an attic apartment. His story is similar to the stories of many other students in this neighborhood, known as the Oread neighborhood. As you climbed the steps to his apartment, you noticed that duct tape keeps the banister in place on the stairs. You saw that the kitchen is infested with mice and roaches. The student, Ted Flis, took you to the bathroom and said it has no electricity. "It's a dump," said Flis, a senior majoring in architecture. "But it was the cheapest thing I could find." This apartment is located at 1032 Main St.

11 Narrative: Change this lead into a narrative lead:

A man threatening suicide kept police at bay for more than nine hours Sunday before he was pulled back from the ledge of a parking garage rooftop.

The man, a 36-year-old Topeka State Hospital patient and Wichita resident whose name wasn't released, threatened to jump from the south ledge of St. Francis Hospital and Medical Center's three-story parking garage at S.W. 6th St. and Mulvane.

Louis Cortez, St. Francis public safety officer, spotted the patient walking toward the ledge on the roof of the garage about 8:40 a.m. Sunday. Cortez stopped his vehicle and told the man to move away from the ledge.

The patient shook his head, "No." "I stepped out and asked him, 'Can I help you, sir?' and he said, 'I'm going to jump,'" Cortez said.

Shortly before 6 p.m. several teenagers in front of St. Francis House, 701 S.W. Mulvane, began shouting, "Don't jump!" and "It's not worth it." The patient shouted back, "You want to see me jump?"

But the teens distracted the patient just long enough for Cortez to grab him around his waist and pull him from the ledge.

12 Leads analysis: Use two or three different newspapers or online news sites. Find leads as directed, and attach copies of the leads to your report.

    a Find an example of a descriptive lead, an anecdotal lead and a narrative lead. Label each type. Analyze whether your examples are effective, and explain why or why not.

    b Find three feature news leads you like. Explain what techniques the writers used and why you like them.

    c Find three feature leads you do not like, and explain why.

13 Print to broadcast: Using your local or campus newspaper, change the leads on three newspaper stories to broadcast form.

FEATURED ONLINE ACTIVITY Log on and visit the Writing and Reporting News CourseMate and take the interactive tutorial quiz on leads. *Access available at www.cengagebrain.com.*

Check out the "Big Fire" scenario in NewsScene for an interactive exercise that will help to reinforce many of the themes presented in this chapter.

COACHING TIPS

Helder Almeida/Shutterstock.com

Write a first draft. Don't perfect every line during the drafting process; **fix it later during the revision process.**

Don't struggle to get the perfect lead. **Write a few leads** and continue writing the story; choose a preferred lead later.

Plan an order for your story: Write a **highlights box listing key points.**

Try **free-writing.** If you are stuck organizing your story, put away your notes and just write what you remember. Then plug in the facts and quotes from your notes.

Read your story aloud when you finish. You will catch errors and hear the pacing.

Plan how **social media might enhance** your story.

> I probably spend as much time on the ending as I do on the beginning. If readers remember a story I wrote, that's better than money.
>
> — **KEN FUSON,** author and freelance writer

CHAPTER 8
Story Organization

WHEN KEN FUSON WAS IN HIGH SCHOOL, HE PLAYED THE DRUMS. He still hears the beat of the drums when he writes stories. "I think a lot about rhythm," he says.

"I work at getting the tap, tap, tap. I want to make sure every paragraph doesn't sound the same." To achieve that musical quality, Fuson reads all his stories out loud.

Rhythm, also called pacing, helps readers move through the middle of a story. And Fuson wants to make sure that they read to the end. "I probably spend as much time on the ending as I do on the beginning," he says. "If readers remember a story I wrote, that's better than money."

Getting from the beginning to the end of a story isn't a haphazard process for Fuson. He carefully plans the parts of his stories. First, he thinks: "I look for ways to show conflict and to describe the mood. I think a lot about what is the right tone and the personality of the story."

Then he starts organizing his material. "I type up all my notes. I select what I want to use. Then I put that information in an order. I need to know where I'm going and what the ending will be. Once you know what you're going to say and the way you're going to say it, then you can worry about what goes first."

And worry he does. "The first paragraph has to be perfect," he says. "And the second paragraph has to be perfect. I wish I had learned a better way of writing instead of worrying about what I'm going to say first." It may not be the best writing process, but it works well for Fuson, who consistently won awards.

Fuson now uses his writing skills as a freelance writer and book author. For more than 25 years Fuson wrote award-winning stories for the *Des Moines* (Iowa) *Register*. Although the news industry has changed dramatically since Fuson started as a journalist, he still believes in its future. When he left the *Register* a few years ago, he wrote in his letter to the staff:

Courtesy of Ken Fuson

Ken Fuson, freelance writer

"Human beings have always wanted and needed news and stories, whether they got it from the wall on a cave, around a campfire or on a computer screen. We're the people who can tell the news and deliver those stories. How we do that may change, but never forget that you possess a vital and important skill."

Fuson's skill was recognized with innumerable awards, including the Ernie Pyle award for feature writing and the Distinguished Writing Award from the American Society of Newspaper Editors. Although Fuson developed a writing process that worked for him, you can use some of the following tips to develop your own process to organize stories.

STAGES OF THE WRITING PROCESS

Before you turn on your computer, you need to turn on your mind. The writing process begins long before you write your story. Here are four steps in the writing process:

- Conceive
- Collect
- Construct
- Correct

Conceive the Idea

The idea for a story may start with information from blogs, an assignment from an editor, coverage of a breaking news event or a topic you proposed. Although you may have an initial focus, that can change after you gather the information. These questions will help you determine a focus before, during and after the reporting and writing process.

- What struck you as most interesting or important?
- What is most newsworthy?
- What is the main point of the story that readers or viewers need to know or would want to know?

Collect the Information

Consider the focus as you do the reporting. What stands out in your mind as the most important or newsworthy idea?

- Get the basics: who, what, when, where, why and how.
- Take notes of your observations as well as quotes, facts and comments from your sources.
- Tape interviews for audio and video to include on the Web, but don't rely on technology to substitute for note taking.
- Note the information and background you will need to get after your interviews.

- Highlight or underline your notes for important points and good quotes to include in your story.

- Gather anecdotes — brief stories from sources about their experiences.

- Think ahead. If you will file the story on deadline for the Web or a television broadcast, gather information for the next step in the action or an updated version for the next broadcast, online or print publication.

- Collect documents or complete information for the Web.

- Verify names and spelling.

Construct the Story

Write a focus sentence on top of your story as a tool to help you select pertinent information. Here are some other ways to determine your focus:

- Write a headline for your story in fewer than 10 words.

- Express your focus as a tweet (Twitter post).

- Determine the most newsworthy, important or current information

- If you were asking readers or viewers to comment on a blog, Twitter or other interactive site, what is the main point that would elicit responses?

Plan an Order

Highlight or underline your notes for important points, good quotes or sound bites. Then jot down a preliminary order in your notes or at the top of your story document. Here are some ways to organize your story:

- *Topics:* List all the main points you want to cover. Decide which are the most important and which point naturally follows another. Arrange information from the most important to the least important points. Then insert the quotes and other information related to those topics when you write the story.

- *Highlights:* If you were writing a highlights box, what would your main points be? Use the highlights as a guide to organize your story.

- *Time Sequence:* Does the story have distinct time elements? Can it be arranged in a chronology? For example, start with the present (what is happening now), go to the past (background or how the situation developed), return to the present and end with the future.

- *Block Sources:* If you have several sources, you might organize the story with a blocking technique. Place all the comments from one source in one part of the story and then place the next source's comments in another block and so on instead of going back and forth among sources.

- *Question/Answer:* What question does one topic or paragraph raise that needs to be answered in the next paragraph?

- *Images and Sound Bites:* For broadcast writing, arrange your story around your images and sound bites. Let the video images tell the story.

- *Free-writing:* If you can't figure out an order, put away your notes and just write what you remember. Then review your draft, and arrange it in an order that seems logical. Plug in quotes and facts later.

- *Ending:* Decide how you want to end the story. Do you have a strong quote for an ending or information about a future action? What lasting impression do you want to leave?

Correct the Story

Before you turn in your story, revise and correct your work. Even if you are writing on deadline or posting to the Web, don't skip this step. These tips apply to all types of media.

- **Read your story aloud:** If you are writing for broadcast, reading the copy aloud is essential. This is also one of the best self-editing steps you can use for print or online publication.

- **Basics:** Have you covered the basics — who, what, when, where, why or how and so what (impact)?

- **Context:** Have you included background or context to help the readers and viewers understand the significance of the story?

- **Check accuracy:** Double-check the spelling and titles of names and accuracy of facts.

- **Avoid adjectives:** Show, don't tell. Let your video tell the story if you are writing for broadcast. Use observation and details to describe actions and feelings.

- **Use vigorous verbs:** Have you used strong, active verbs? Can you rearrange sentences that start with "There is" or "There are" and substitute active verbs?

- **Purge any parroting:** If your transitions repeat a quote or sound bite, rewrite or cut them. Let the quotes and sound bites move the story naturally.

- **Cut useless or excess words:** If you had to cut your story, what words, sentences or paragraphs could you eliminate?

- **Edit the pace:** Do you have a good mix of short and long sentences — most of them short? Does your story flow?

- **Check grammar:** Do your subjects, verbs and pronouns agree? Is your grammar correct?

- **Cut jargon:** Eliminate bureaucratic language and jargon (such as "hot topic") or other clichés.

Tips for Tightening Stories

The more that readers and viewers use cell phones or electronic tablets to access information, the more important it is to master the art of brevity. *USA Today* offers these guidelines to its writers for focusing, tightening and revising stories:

Squeeze a Fact on Every Line: Allow one idea per sentence.

SOCIAL MEDIA

WHEN PLANNING your story, think about how social media could be used.

- **Conceive:** Start with the conception stage. What is most newsworthy that you could promote on Twitter or Facebook?

- **Collect:** Use social media sites and blogs to gather information and sources. Ask your followers in a social media site for input.

- **Construct:** Identify your focus by writing it as a tweet or a headline you might use for a blog or post on other social media sites. Add related links at the end of your story or post a question.

- **Correct:** Check the accuracy of your social media sources and check your links. Check your share boxes or icons.

Focus Tightly: Think about what the real story is, and choose a slice of it. Emphasize what's new, what's coming and what it means to readers. Tell them the impact, how they can act on or use this information.

Use Impact Leads: Avoid rehashing what readers already know. Think forward spin. Instead of writing "A jet crashed Tuesday, killing 534 people," write "Airline takeoff procedures might be overhauled after Tuesday's crash that killed 534 people." This is especially useful in broadcast news.

Make the Story Move: Make your point early. Use only the information that helps make the point.

Keep It Tight: Propel the story with punctuation. Colons, semicolons and bullets can replace some words and help the reader move faster.

Use Specific Details Instead of Adjectives: Instead of writing "the ancient windmill," refer to "the 100-year-old windmill."

Don't Over-Attribute: You don't need a "he said" after every sentence, although it should be clear where the information came from.

Use Strong, Lively Verbs: Instead of writing "There were hundreds of people in the streets to see the pope," write "Hundreds of people lined the streets to see the pope" (or *jammed, crowded* or *thronged* the streets). Sentences that start with *there* force you to use a weak *to be* verb.

Avoid Weak Transitions: A well-organized story needs only a few transitions.

Choose Quotes that Advance the Story: Avoid quotes that merely illustrate the last point made. And don't paraphrase if you have a good quote. Be selective. Don't repeat.

ORGANIZATION TECHNIQUES

The two most common problems of professional writers are writing the lead and organizing the story. Here are some techniques to help you write well from start to finish:

Leads

Many writers insist that they can't write the rest of the story until they find their lead. That is a luxury you can't afford in these days of convergence when you need to file the story quickly for online delivery. To find your lead, ask yourself these questions:

- What will hook the reader's or viewer's attention?
- What does the reader or viewer need to know first or most to understand the story?
- What is the story about?
- Write a lead that will follow with your strongest quote.
- Start with the focus graph and write the lead later.

Transition Techniques

How do you get from one point to another smoothly? The best transition is no transition — a story so well organized that one thought follows another naturally. But if you are changing speakers or topics, you may need some of these transition techniques:

- Use cause and effect: If one paragraph raises a question, answer it in the next paragraph or elaborate with an example or quote. Try to anticipate questions the reader might have.
- To make a transition from one source to another, introduce the new source. Don't string several quotes from different sources together. For example:

A controversial proposal that would require all Temple University undergraduates to take a course related to racism drew strong support yesterday from a racially mixed group of students and faculty members who testified at a campus hearing.

Anika Trahan, a junior, said the proposed requirement would encourage more dialogue among students who come to the university from largely segregated neighborhoods.

Statement introducing speaker

"They (white students) come from communities where they are never able to interact with black people," she said.

But opinion was sharply divided on whether the course should focus on black-white relations in America or include racism against Asian-Americans and other groups.

Molefi K. Asante, chairman of Temple's African-American studies department, contended that the requirement should focus on the white racism toward African-Americans because that has been "the fundamental pattern of racism" in the United States.

Transition to new speaker

A white student, sophomore Amy Dixon, agreed. "Our predominant problem on campus is black-white relations," she said.

Transition to new speaker

— HUNTLY COLLINS,
The Philadelphia Inquirer

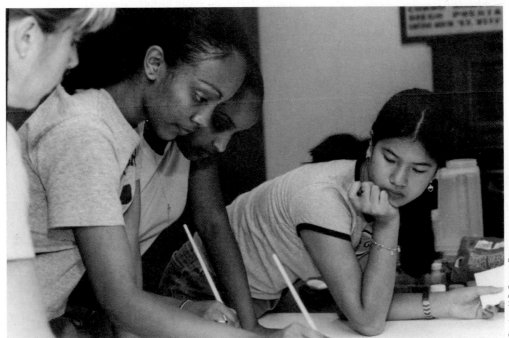

Courtesy U.S. Census Bureau

Repetition of Key Words

This is a technique that provides smooth transitions during the writing process. A word or phrase from one paragraph can be repeated in the next paragraph. The technique is also known as "stitching" because it helps stitch one paragraph to the other. In broadcast news, anchors often use repetition of key words to segue from one story to another.

As you write, look at the last sentence in each paragraph and find a key word that will trigger a question you can answer in the next paragraph, or it can will serve as a bridge for the next thought. You may either repeat the word in the next sentence as a transitional device or just use the concept of the word as a bridge to the idea in your next paragraph. Don't overuse the this technique because your writing could become boring.

In the following example, the underlined key words serve as transitions to the next thought. In some cases the writer repeats the key word, and in others he uses it as a thought bridge.

Key word drugs *serves as a bridge to the next thought*

What we need are some mandatory classes that you would attend before you attempted to move your household. These would be much more useful than those classes you go to before you have a <u>baby</u>.

When you have a <u>baby</u>, you are surrounded by skilled professionals, who, if things get really bad, give you <u>drugs</u>, whereas nobody performs any such service when you move. This is wrong.

The first thing the burly men should do when they get off the moving van is seize you and forcibly inject you with a <u>two-week supply of sedatives</u>, because moving, to judge from its effect on my wife, is far more stressful than childbirth.

— DAVE BARRY, *Syndicated columnist*

Here is another example of this technique:

With a relentless sun beating on him as he cut through fields, swamps and shaggy forests, Earl Davis always looked ahead to the next <u>leg</u> of the project.

The <u>legs</u> were long and stretched interminably. The crews made slow progress. Mosquitoes whined about their heads, and snakes thrashed away when the right-of-way crews stumbled across them. . . .

Davis, who had lived in Pinellas County for almost 50 years, sympathized and <u>suffered</u> with them (the road builders).

The <u>suffering</u> wouldn't be over for a long time.

— MARK DAVIS, *The Tampa* (Fla.) *Tribune*

Transitions for Background

To insert background, you can use words and phrases, such as *Previously* or *In the past,* or specific time elements, such as *Two months ago.* If you are going to recount part of the story chronologically, you can set it up with a phrase like *The incident began this way.*

To get from one point to another, especially in stories about meetings where several issues are discussed, you can use transitional phrases: *In another matter, On a related issue,* or *Other items discussed included.*

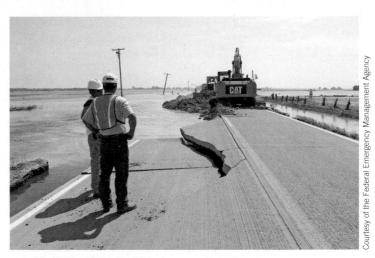

Road builders face hot and difficult conditions.

Blocking Sources

Do you get annoyed when a person's last name is mentioned in a story on a second reference but you have forgotten who the person is? After a person is identified by full name once, newspapers and online sites use only the last name if the person is mentioned again in the story. If only one or two people are mentioned in a story, this device isn't confusing. But the reader will have trouble remembering sources by their last names if the story refers to several of them.

The blocking technique helps eliminate such confusion. It is a way of organizing information by using sources in blocks instead of placing them sporadically throughout a story. The problem of last names on second reference is even more confusing for online readers when a story spans several screens or Web pages.

Here is how the blocking technique works to avoid this problem: When you have three or more sources in a story, use each source once or in consecutive paragraphs, blocking all his or her comments in one place. If you must use a source again in another part of the story, reintroduce the person by title or some reference to remind the reader of the person's identity. The exception is a well-known source, such as the mayor, the governor, the president, a celebrity or the central character in a story. The name of such a source may be placed anywhere in the story without confusing the reader.

In this example, which contains several sources, notice how each source is blocked in one or consecutive paragraphs.

A gas pipeline explosion can create a disaster like the one in the next example.

1 (first source)

Beneath the shock and the tears lies the anger.

It smoldered in Patrick Thomas' eyes as he sat holding his 15-month-old daughter, Lisa, in a Red Cross evacuation shelter set up at the Job Corps Center on Kerry Street.

Thomas was among the refugees from the neighborhood where a gas pipeline exploded Thursday morning, sending balls of fire racing through their homes. Like other residents living near the side of the May 12 train derailment on Duffy Street, he thought the worst was over.

His home at 2313 Adams St. survived the train wreck unscathed. It was situated five houses from another Adams Street house that blew up.

"I am mad," he said. "I am mad as hell — at the railroad, at whoever put that fuel line in, at whoever built those houses over a fuel line, at the city for not doing something."

Transition to new sources

Other residents focused their anger on the company that operates the pipeline, Calnev Pipeline Co.

Second source

"It makes me sick that this fire happened — especially if somebody knew it needed to be repaired. Somebody ought to be hung out to dry," said Mark Kingston.

Transition to another source

Another Duffy Street resident's fury knew no bounds.

Third source

"They had no damn business trying to patch no pipe up anyway," said Vincent Hemphill. "They should have discontinued that until they fixed it."

Hemphill, 25, grew up in the house at 2604 Duffy St. Even if his home survived, he said he won't go back.

Fourth source

Maxie Charles of 2441 San Benito Court said the federal government should step in and provide emergency relief.

"This should be declared a disaster area. And if they want to keep these pipelines, they should pay us off and we will be happy to move out," he said.

Transition to more sources

Many of the residents believe they were betrayed.

Fifth source

"If it wasn't safe for us to live, why'd they tell us it's OK to move back there?" wondered Georgia Mitchell.

Mitchell's house was destroyed and her daughter, a son-in-law and two grand-children were injured.

Sixth source

Bonita Campbell walked around in the nightgown, robe and slippers she wore when the explosion occurred.

Her family got out of their San Carlo Avenue home safely; her two dogs waited in her car.

"Right now I don't know what to think. I don't know what to do. I know I can't continue to live like this not knowing what's going to happen."

— THERESA WALKER AND CARLA WHEELER, *The* (San Bernardino, Calif.) *Sun.*

The blocking technique is only a guideline and should not be adhered to strictly when the story order would be more logical if sources were repeated in different places throughout the story.

CONVERGENCE COACH

IN A CONVERGENT media environment, where immediacy is required for posting news online or on TV before print, you may not think you have time for the correction step in the writing process. But you can actually save time writing because you can write your copy quickly if you know that you can revise it. The writing process tips in this chapter apply to all media, but here are some suggestions targeted to broadcast copy in the correction step:

- Read your copy aloud.
- Check your copy to see if the text corresponds to your video. Does the text lead smoothly to sound bites? Does the video enhance your story?

- Now read your text aloud without viewing the video. Is the text clear?
- Remove adjectives that express your opinion, such as descriptive terms — tragic, frightening, beautiful, etc.
- Do your transitions flow smoothly from the videotape to the text?
- Remove and revise any transitions that repeat sound bites.
- Rewrite any bureaucratic terms such as police lingo (perpetrator) or government jargon (infrastructure) and others.
- Check spelling and grammar and make sure names are spelled and pronounced correctly.
- Check your facts for accuracy.

MAKING MIDDLES MOVE

How do you maintain interest in the middle of the story? Transitions are one method, but these other writing techniques will help keep the middles moving:

Vary the Pace Follow long sentences with short ones. Pacing is even more important in broadcast writing when you are writing for the ear. If you use complex sentences, follow them with short, punchy ones:

> Pamela Lewiston thought she was leading a normal life as the daughter of Dr. Normal Lewiston, a respected Stanford University physician, and his wife, Diana.
>
> She thought wrong. Her father had been married to — and lived with — two women besides her mother, all at the same time. His carefully managed deception ended in a cascading series of revelations after his death from a heart attack in August.
>
> — S. L. WYKES, *San Jose* (Calif.) *Mercury News*

Parallelism Parallel sentences help the reader move quickly through the story. Parallel construction means the sentences are worded in the same grammatical order. Some of the words can be repeated for effect, especially those at the beginning of sentences. In this example, the writer uses parallelism at the beginning of the story, but you can use it anywhere:

> Rudolph Almaraz kept his battle with AIDS his personal business, even though his professional business was surgery.
>
> He didn't tell his patients. He didn't tell officials at Baltimore Johns Hopkins Hospital, where he was a cancer surgeon. He didn't tell the doctor who bought his medical practice earlier this year.
>
> But now the case of Dr. Almaraz, who died of AIDS on Nov. 16 at the age of 41, has frightened his patients.
>
> — MATTHEW PURDY, *The Philadelphia Inquirer*

Pacing Vary the length of sentences. Follow long ones with short, punchy ones.

> On New Year's Eve Lisa Botzum visited the emergency room of the Hospital of the University of Pennsylvania, complaining of nausea and vomiting. She was given a pregnancy test. She was elated by the result.
>
> Few others were.
>
> — LORETTA TOFANI, *The Philadelphia Inquirer*

Dialogue When possible and appropriate, use dialogue in your story. It works well in feature stories and especially in stories about court cases. For broadcast stories, sound bites and video constitute dialogue. In this print feature story, "13: Life at the Edge of Everything," *St. Petersburg* (Fla.) *Times* reporters spent several months reporting about the lives of middle school students. Then they wrote a series in dramatic storytelling form, making extensive use of dialogue to put the reader on the scene. In this section, Joanne, the mother of a teenage girl, Danielle, is worried about her daughter, who is starting to date:

> A few months ago, when Danielle started to show more interest in boys, Joanne cornered her.
>
> "You're not doing anything, are you?"
>
> Danielle looked at her. "What do you mean?"
>
> "You're not doing anything with that boy that calls up?"
>
> Meaning Nelson.
>
> "No," said Danielle. "We're just friends."
>
> — THOMAS FRENCH, MONIQUE FIELDS,
> DONG-PHUONG NGUYEN, *St. Petersburg Times*

BBI: Boring but Important Stuff Many stories, especially government stories, need explanation or background that could be boring. Don't put all the boring information in a long block. Break it into small paragraphs and place it where it will fit.

Also consider graphics as a way to present statistics and other information that could clog a story.

Simple Sentences for Complex Information The more difficult the information is, the simpler your sentences should be. Use short sentences with simple construction, especially for bureaucratic information that would be hard for the reader to comprehend. This excerpt is from a story explaining how the judiciary committee of the Connecticut legislature works:

> The judiciary is one of the legislature's busiest. By the end of the five-month session in June, the committee will have drafted, amended, approved or killed about 500 bills — about 14 percent of the 3,649 bills filed with the Senate and House clerks.
>
> Judiciary's 14 percent will touch nearly everyone. The committee considers matters of life and death, marriage and divorce, freedom and imprisonment.
>
> This year's issues include surrogate parenting, birth certificates and adoption. The death penalty and letting the terminally ill die. Longer prison sentences and home release. Committing the mentally ill to hospitals.
>
> — MARK PAZNIOKAS, *The Hartford* (Conn.) *Courant*

Lists Itemizing information is an excellent way to keep the flow going through the middle of your story. Lists work well in summarizing studies, statistical information or the main points in government actions. They also work well on the Web where readers tend to scan stories. You may use lists in a couple of ways:

- To itemize a group of statistics or any other cumbersome information
- To highlight key points within a story

Lists are usually preceded by a dot called a "bullet" or by some other graphic device as in this example:

> The U.S. Census Bureau reported today that more women than men are expected to occupy professions such as doctors, lawyers and college professors. They represent approximately 58 percent of young adults, age 25 to 29, who hold an advanced degree. In addition, among all adults 25 and older, more women than men had high school diplomas and bachelor's degrees.
>
> The data from the 2010 census also demonstrate the extent to which having such a degree pays off: average earnings totaled $83,144 for those with an advanced degree, compared with $58,613 for those with a bachelor's degree only. People whose highest level of attainment was a high school diploma had average earnings of $31,283.
>
> Other highlights:
>
> - Overall, 87 percent of adults 25 and older had a high school diploma, with 30 percent holding at least a bachelor's degree.
> - The number of U.S. residents with bachelor's degrees or more climbed 34 percent between 1999 and 2009, from 43.8 million to 58.6 million.

More women than men hold advanced degrees, according to the U.S. Census Bureau.

- More than half (53 percent) of Asians 25 and older had a bachelor's degree or more, much higher than the rate for non-Hispanic whites (33 percent), blacks (19 percent) and Hispanics (13 percent).
- Among young adults 25 to 29, 35 percent of women and 27 percent of men possessed a bachelor's degree or more in 2009. This gap has grown considerably in the last decade: it was only 3 percentage points in 1999 (30 percent for women, 27 percent for men).

Use Active Voice Whenever Possible Here's an example of active voice:

She will always remember her first story.

Here is the same sentence in passive voice:

Her first story will always be remembered by her.

The active voice has more impact.

Write Short Sentences On average, your sentences should have fewer than 25 words.

Write Simple Sentences Keep the subject and verb close together. This example shows what happens when you don't. It is from a story about school board approval of remodeling and construction projects at the city's two schools.

Those two projects — calling for construction of classrooms, office area and media center at Wakefield and construction of a new district-wide kitchen and computer lab plus remodeling projects at the high school — will be paid for by using approximately $800,000 of the district's special capital outlay fund.

Whew! That's a long sentence. The subject is *projects,* and the verb is *will be paid.* They are separated by too many words. Split it into three sentences:

> One project will involve construction of classrooms, an office area and a media center at Wakefield. The other includes building a new district-wide kitchen, a computer lab and remodeling projects at the high school. The $800,000 approximate cost of the projects will be paid from the district's special capital outlay fund.

Avoid Jargon Translate bureaucratic terms into simple ones; define technical terms. Here's advice from writer George Orwell:

> Never use a metaphor, simile or other figure of speech which you are used to seeing in print. Never use a long word when a short one will do. If it is possible to cut a word out, always cut it out. Never use the passive when you can use the active. Never use a foreign phrase, a scientific word or a jargon word if you can think of an everyday English equivalent. Break any of these rules sooner than say anything outright barbarous.

Here's an example of garbled writing from the U.S. federal budget:

> Funds obligated for military assistance as of September 30 may, if deobligated, be reobligated.

Write the Way You Speak Unless you speak like the bureaucrat who wrote that budget item.

ENDINGS

Call them lasting impressions. To many writers, the ending is as important as the beginning of the story. Unfortunately, many readers don't get that far. But if they do, you should reward them with a memorable ending.

The ending also is called the "kicker." Think of it as a clincher. It should give a summary feeling to your story without repeating any information you have stated previously.

For columnists, the ending is more important than the beginning. The twist or main point the writer is trying to make is at the end of the column. In many cases the lead could be an ending. And returning to your lead as a way to find your ending is an excellent technique.

Don't use the ending to summarize information as you might in a term paper. Instead of repeating information, cut the story to the last important point or last good quote.

The following sections describe some ways to form your endings.

Quote Kickers The most common type of ending is the quote kicker. Look for a quote that sums up the mood or main idea of the story. When you end with a quote, put the attribution before the quote or, in a two-quote ending, after the first sentence. Do not let the last words the reader remembers be "he said."

You might not know your sweetie is about to break up with you, but Facebook knows.

That's due to an analysis of Facebook postings compiled by David McCandless, a British journalist and graphic designer. He and a colleague scraped 10,000 Facebook status updates for the phrases "breakup" and "broken up."

The most hazardous times for romantic relationships are after Valentine's Day and before Spring Break, according to their research.

What's the day you are least likely to get dumped?

"Christmas Day," McCandless said. "Who would do that?"   *Quote kicker*

Circle kicker, which ties together the lead and the ending.

Circle Kickers When you return to your lead for an idea to end your story in a full circle, you are using a circle kicker. Ken Fuson frequently used this technique to devise his endings. In this example from a story about how families cope with Alzheimer's disease, Fuson repeats phrases from the lead — but ends with a twist:

"Mother, mother, mother, other, other, other. . . ."

The sound comes in short, grating bursts, like a children's record played at too high a speed.

Every day, relentlessly, another small slice of the person that once was Betty Jennings disappears. The brand of hell called Alzheimer's disease has reduced the 58-year-old woman to a stoop-shouldered, hand-wringing blabber of meaningless words and phrases.

She must be fed, bathed and diapered. Some mornings, after a particularly brutal night, Gordon Hanchett will look in the living room and see that his sister has attacked her plastic diaper, ripping it apart with her fingers and leaving small pieces littering the floor.

"It looks like a miniature snowstorm," he says.

The limits of devotion are stretched thinnest in the homes of Alzheimer's victims. Often operating on little or no sleep and frequently ruining their own physical health, family members witness the disintegration of a loved one's mind with the understanding that no matter what they do today, tomorrow will be worse.

The story continues with more about the family in particular and the disease in general. Here's how it ends:

> "Mother, this mother, this other . . . Daddy, daddy, daddy."
> The chatter is loud, constant and haunting. His sister's voice fills the house.
> "Oh that," says Hanchett, waving his hand. "I don't even hear that anymore."

> — KEN FUSON, *The Des Moines* (Iowa) *Register*

Future-Action Kickers Many stories end with the next step in the development of an issue. But this technique only works if the story lends itself to a future element. If the next step is crucial to the story, it should be higher in the body. But if it works as a natural conclusion, then it can be the ending. It can be in the form of a statement or a quote.

> HERRING BAY, Alaska — World attention focused Friday on the attempt to rescue birds and animals from the oil spilled in Prince William Sound. Cameras in Valdez focused on the few animals saved — fewer than 20 birds and four sea otters by evening Friday. The birds on the evening news were expensive symbols for Exxon, costing more than $1,000 apiece to rescue.
> But on the water, the rescue efforts getting all the attention stumbled along with the air of a Sunday outing. In this bay at the north end of Knight Island, a diverse and committed group of people tried to learn to perform a futile task.

Birds rescued from the Exxon tanker oil spill in Valdez, Alaska.

The story continues with detail about the rescue operation. Here is the ending:

> By Friday afternoon, about two miles of the shore of Herring Bay had been thoroughly searched.
> Only a few thousand left to go.
>
> — CHARLES WOHLFORTH, *Anchorage* (Alaska) *Daily News*

Climaxes This type of ending works on stories written like fiction, where the reader is kept in suspense until the end. It is more suited to features in narrative style or short news stories that tease the reader in the beginning and compel the reader to find out what happens.

> Scott T. Grabowski sat Tuesday in the courtroom where a federal judge would determine his future, hoping that when the words were pronounced he would hear probation and not prison.
> But Grabowski, 27, of Greenfield, is an admitted drug dealer. Early last summer, he pleaded guilty to a charge of possessing 3 ounces of cocaine that he intended to sell on behalf of an international drug network.

The story continues with the arguments from Grabowski's defense lawyer and the prosecutor. But what sentence did he receive? The reader doesn't find out until the end.

> Finally, after a 2½ hour hearing, Curran (the judge) sentenced Grabowski to 30 months in prison, to be followed by three years of parole.
> And with a nod to the parents, Curran told Grabowski: "I'm sure their hearts are aching as they sit here today."
>
> — JILL ZUCKMAN, *The Milwaukee Journal*

Cliffhanger, or suspense ending.

Cliffhangers Every day millions of people watch soap operas. The concept is a simple one: Give the readers or viewers a mystery, and make them want to find out what happens next. In writing, this kind of suspense ending is called a "cliffhanger." It is usually reserved for the endings of stories arranged in sections or series that will continue on another day. But it also can be used in the middle of stories to compel the reader to continue.

Cliffhangers are excellent devices for stories on the Web. At the end of a cliffhanger in the middle of a story, you could place a hyperlink to entice readers to click to the next section.

Not all stories lend themselves to cliffhangers. But many could be structured that way by putting the key points of the story on the front page and stopping with a question or suspenseful point in the last sentence before the story continues or "jumps" to another page.

This method is much more conducive to narrative storytelling, especially in a long feature, but it can be applied to hard news if the story stops at a crucial point.

This is only the beginning of a story that uses cliffhangers. Would you want to turn the page to continue reading?

In Fort Myers: Money, mercy and murder

Patricia Rosier's death was supposed to be peaceful and dignified.

She had made all the arrangements. Ordered food for the wake. Said a final goodbye to friends and family. Put the children to sleep.

On the nightstand rested a bottle of Seconals, powerful sedatives prescribed by her husband, Dr. Peter Rosier. Suicide would finally free Pat, 43, from the pain of invading cancer.

When the time came, she downed Seconals like "jellybeans," one witness recalled.

Cliffhanger

But something went wrong in the Rosier's stylish Fort Myers home that January night in 1985.

Pat wouldn't die.

Peter frantically began injecting doses of morphine to finish the job.

Pat's breathing slowed to a rasp.

But after 12 hours of the grim ritual, Pat would not die.

Finally, Pat's stepfather, Vincent Delman, decided something had to be done. Pat, he would later tell prosecutors, was suffering too much.

He took Pat's two half brothers into the bedroom and closed the door.

Twenty minutes later, the door opened. The Delmans walked out, their faces sullen. Peter was waiting in the living room, calming his ravaged nerves with a beer.

"Patty is dead," Vincent said.

After the funeral, the Delmans left Fort Myers. They carried with them the dark secret of what happened behind the bedroom door.

Another cliffhanger

On Monday, Peter Rosier, 47, is scheduled to go on trial for the first-degree murder of his wife of 22 years.

The Rosier story has it all — sex, love, wealth, murder and a major mystery: Who really killed Pat Rosier?

And another cliffhanger

— MARK STEPHENS AND WILLIAM SABO, *Fort Myers* (Fla.) *News-Press*

On the jump page you would find out why Peter is on trial and what kind of evidence exists to try him. You also would find out why this is an unusual case: There's no body and no autopsy report. Pat's body was cremated. There are no morphine syringes; they were thrown away when she died. And there is one other unusual twist: Peter wasn't even in the room when Pat was killed.

Court stories lend themselves to this kind of dramatic structure. But so do many others.

Factual Kickers These are strong factual statements that could sometimes substitute as leads. They are statements that summarize the mood, tone or general character of the story. They are harder to write than quote kickers, but if done well, they give the reader a powerful punch. They are truly kickers.

Strive for a very short, simple sentence that states a fact. But choose a meaningful fact that will leave a lasting impression.

Julie Sullivan is a master of the factual kicker. In the following example, she is writing about a man who lives in a run-down hotel in Spokane. This ending is a simple statement that is circular in its reference to the lead.

Here is the lead:

Joe Peak's smile has no teeth.

His dentures were stolen at the Norman Hotel, the last place he lived in downtown Spokane before moving to the Merlin two years ago.

Gumming food and fighting diabetes have shrunk the 54-year-old man's frame by 80 pounds. He is thin and weak and his mouth is sore.

But that doesn't stop him from frying hamburgers and onions for a friend at midnight or keeping an extra bed made up permanently in his two-room place.

"I try to make a little nest here for myself," he says.

The story continues with detail about the difficulties that Peak encounters living in the Merlin. It ends with factual statements. Here are the last few paragraphs:

When conditions at the Merlin began worsening three months ago, junkies and gray mice the size of baby rats moved in next door. He hated to see it, but he isn't worried about being homeless.

He's worried about his diabetes.

He's frightened by blood in his stool and sores on his gums. He wonders whether the white-staffed hospitals on the hill above him will treat a poor black man with no teeth.

— JULIE SULLIVAN, *The* (Spokane, Wash.) *Spokesman-Review*

Out-of-Gas Endings You can always just end when you have no more to say. This method is appropriate for hard-news stories, particularly those structured with a summary lead and arranged with supporting points in descending order of importance. You can end on a quote, future action or another fact in the story.

Here is a story with a factual out-of-gas ending:

TAMPA, Fla. — For the first time, a shrimper has been imprisoned for failing to use a federally mandated turtle protection device on his boat, the National Marine Fisheries Service said.

The story continues with the basic who, what, why, when and where and ends with this fact:

The government estimates more than 11,000 sea turtles drown in shrimp nets in U.S. waters each year.

— The Associated Press

BODY BUILDING FROM START TO FINISH

Here is a short story that could have been written as a routine police story. The writer made it interesting by using many of the techniques described in this chapter. Note how the writer uses good pacing, parallelism and a circle kicker:

Mystery call has police barking up wrong tree

Mystery lead

The following nail-biting police drama probably won't find its way onto the "Rescue: 911" TV show, but it's had some folks around Eldridge talking about it since it happened at the end of last week:

Short sentences

A call comes to the Eldridge police dispatcher over the 911 emergency line. The dispatcher answers and asks what the problem is.

Fragments for emphasis and drama

No response. Silence. The dispatcher can hear very heavy breathing. That's all. Pretty obvious somebody's in trouble.

Pacing: long sentence followed by short ones

Police Chief Martin Stolmeier, on patrol in the area, takes 20 seconds to get to the Frank and Paula Griggs residence, where the dispatcher's computer says the call is originating.

Key word: still for parallelism

The caller is still on the line. Still breathing heavily. Still needing help.

Short, choppy sentences to build drama Foreshadowing

Stolmeier arrives. Announces loudly that the police are there, begins a room-by-room search. Stolmeier knows somebody needs help. He enters the situation assuming someone may have broken into the house. Maybe some sort of struggle.

Stolmeier nears a downstairs bedroom. The dispatcher hears him over the phone getting closer. On the other side of the door is the situation — the burglar, killer or heart attack victim.

Cliffhanger

Right about now, if this were a movie, the camera would zoom in very close on Stolmeier's perspiring face and the music would be building to a crescendo of tension and you would be going crazy as Stolmeier at last comes face to face with . . . with . . .

Paragraph could also work as a climax kicker

Blaze. A 6-month-old black Labrador who seemed very energetic and very happy to see Stolmeier. In a fit of rambunctious puppyness, Blaze had knocked the phone off the wall and somehow dialed 911.

Circle kicker, which ties together the lead and the ending

No word on whether Blaze's phone privileges have been restricted since the incident. But they'd better not tell him about 900 numbers or the Home Shopping Network.

— PATRICK BEACH, The Des Moines (Iowa) *Register*

EXERCISES

1 Pacing exercise: Listen to classical music or other music of your choice. With your eyes closed, draw lines on a piece of paper to express the rhythm or movements of the music. Then find a story that you think has good pacing and analyze it for the mixture of short and long sentences and paragraphs.

2 Read aloud: Read aloud any story you have written and note any errors you have made. Analyze how the story sounds for pacing.

3 Endings: Take any story you have written and try different endings, using a circle kicker, quote kicker or factual kicker.

4 Analyze endings: Using any local news story from your campus or community newspaper, analyze which stories have quote endings, circle kickers or factual endings. Watch your local TV news station and note how the reporters end their stories before questions from the anchor or a sign-off ending.

5 Correction process: Take any story you have written and check it for accuracy, grammar, spelling and other factors in the correction process.

CourseMate

FEATURED ONLINE ACTIVITY Log on and visit the Writing and Reporting News CourseMate and take the interactive tutorial quiz on story organization. *Access available at www.cengagebrain.com.*

Check out the "Basketball Scandal" scenario in NewsScene for an interactive exercise that will help to reinforce many of the themes presented in this chapter.

COACHING TIPS

Consider a structure for your story **when you are reporting.**

Gather information during the reporting process for **several versions of a story:** broadcast, print and online delivery.

Consider the **form of your story for social media.**

Consider the form of your story for **delivery on mobile media.**

Alberto Zornetta/Shutterstock.com

Good structure keeps a writer's material from being like a bag of meal cut and then spilled all over the floor.

— JOHN MCPHEE, author

CHAPTER 9
Story Forms

WHEN JACK HART COACHES WRITERS, HE SOUNDS LIKE AN ARCHITECT. He talks about writing as a process and stories as structures with distinct shapes.

"Beautiful writing is built one step at a time, just like a house," he writes in his book, *A Writer's Coach: An Editor's Guide to Words that Work.*

As the former managing editor and writing coach for *The Oregonian,* Hart helped writers win Pulitzer Prizes with his methods. As a writing coach, he tells writers to think logically when they organize their stories. He calls the process "sequencing." He says writers should organize the information in a sequence that helps readers understand how one item leads to another.

Courtesy of Jack Hart

Hart also says writers should visualize a shape for their story, and he assigns names to the story shapes so writers will remember them.

Jack Hart, writing coach

"I think we are lexicon impoverished," Hart says. "We haven't had many names for story structures. I am a firm believer that if you walk through the woods and you know the names of all the plants, you'll see a lot more. A lot of writers get halfway through a story and don't realize that they are writing in a particular structure."

STORY SHAPES

The most common story structures were created for print media, but smart phones, tablets and other forms of mobile media are continuing to change the way people access information.

A recent study by the Pew Research Center revealed that the majority of Americans — 59 percent — get their daily news from online and offline resources. The research revealed that 33 percent of cell phone owners access news on their mobile phones, 37 percent contribute or disseminate news via social media sites and 28 percent of Internet users customize their home pages to access news of interest to them.

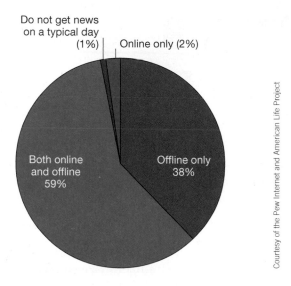

Daily news consumption: Where Americans get their news on a typical day

A majority of Americans (59%) get news from a combination of online and offline sources on a typical day

Do not get news on a typical day (1%)

Online only (2%)

Both online and offline 59%

Offline only 38%

Courtesy of the Pew Internet and American Life Project

Story forms will continue to evolve because of changes in technology and growth of social media. Stories may be shorter for cell phones, longer for tablets and online reading. Multimedia and "share" tools for social media will become standard features. But good content and good writing are still the most important factors for any platform. Here are some basic story forms that work in print and online media and may be adapted for mobile media.

INVERTED PYRAMID

Summary lead

Backup (quotes or facts)

Supporting points

Ending

Inverted pyramid structure

The inverted pyramid is one of the most basic story forms for print, broadcast and online news as well as news releases in public relations. It is used most often for hard-news stories. The story is structured with the most important information at the top of the story followed by supporting points in descending order of importance. It usually starts with a summary lead that gives some of the basics: who, what, when, where, why.

If you were watching a mystery TV show or movie, you would have to wait until the end to find out who was guilty. But with a story using the inverted pyramid, you tell the outcome in the lead.

The advantage of this form is that the reader gets the crucial information quickly. The disadvantage is that the reader may not read past the crucial information. This form is the primary structure for breaking news, and it is an important form for online journalism, where readers have unlimited choices. It is a way to let readers determine immediately whether they are interested in the story. It is also an ideal form for distribution on cell phones and other small-screen devices. To adapt this form for social media, add "share" tools — links to Facebook, Twitter, Digg, and other sites at the end of your story.

How do you decide what information should be arranged from most to least importance? Use your judgment. Some questions to ask:

- What will affect the reader most?
- What questions does the lead raise that need to be answered immediately?
- What supporting quotes are strongest?
- How does the story affect readers?

HEADLINE: FISH FRY DESTROYS 6 APARTMENTS

Summary lead: who, what, when, why, where

A woman frying fish in her apartment kitchen started a fire that destroyed six units in the complex last night and left 18 people homeless, Anchorage fire officials said.

Backup: who, how, where, when

Sheila Flister said she was just frying halibut in about an inch of oil when the whole stove was suddenly covered in flames.

Lead quote

"I don't know if it was the stove or the oil that caught fire," she said. "All of a sudden it just blew up."

Supporting facts

The fire started about 7:30 p.m. in the basement-level apartment and promptly spread through the three-story building at 5000 Lake Otis Parkway. All the residents got out safely.

Anchorage Fire Department spokesman Tom Kempton said no one appeared to be hurt, but two cats were found dead. He said six units appeared to be a total loss while another six may have been damaged by smoke. The apartment building includes 24 units.

Supporting quote

"Even though the fire department arrived within four minutes, it didn't take long for the flames to spread," Kempton said.

Kempton said it's not a good idea to use a fire extinguisher on a pan full of hot grease.

More explanation

"In some cases people take a dry chem extinguisher that's under high pressure, and they try to hit that pan of flaming oil, and it spreads all over the kitchen," he said. "What happens is that people panic and try to carry the flaming pan outside. It's best to cover it with another pan, turn the heat off and call 911."

Factual ending

Red Cross volunteer John Jones said the building was evacuated and the organization will house the displaced families. Any others who lost their apartment and need help can contact the Red Cross at 646-5400.

— Adapted from an online story by *KTUU* (Anchorage, Alaska) *Channel 2 News*

Here is an example of an inverted pyramid story for TV news; note the use of present tense to convey immediacy:

Lead	The Anchorage Fire Department is investigating an early morning fire in the Fairview neighborhood.
Supporting facts	Officials say the blaze started outside of the house in a pile of tires that were nowhere near an electrical or power source. Fire officials have also ruled out a carelessly discarded cigarette as the cause.
Background/ elaboration	Firefighters were called to the scene around 1:30 Wednesday morning, after two men walking by reported it to neighbors.

"We were standing on the corner just talking and the first thing I saw were some flames come through the house right there and we both started running and I said we need to make sure nobody's in the house, call 911."

Sound Bite (Blayne Larsson identifier on screen)

Firefighters say no one was injured in the fire.

Factual ending

— YVONNE RAMSAY, *KTUU*
(Anchorage, Alaska) *Channel 2 News*

THE WALL STREET JOURNAL FORMULA

The Wall Street Journal format starts with a soft lead, focusing on a person, scene or event. The idea is to go from the specific to the general, starting with a paragraph or two about a person, place or event that illustrates the main point of the story. The concept, whether stated or implied, is that this person or scene is one of many affected by the issue in the nut graph.

The lead can be anecdotal, descriptive or narrative. It is followed by a focus graph — nut graph — that gives the main point of the story. This paragraph should explain what the story is about and why it is important (the "so what" factor).

The story then presents backup for the lead and supporting points. The body of the story is arranged topically, with one point leading to another. The ending usually comes full circle by using a quote or anecdote from the person in the lead or a future development of something mentioned in the beginning of the story.

This structure is useful for stories about trends, major issues, features, news sidebars and news events that lend themselves to a feature approach. This technique is also effective for broadcast news because viewers relate to people, so starting the story by focusing on a person affected by a problem is a good way to hook viewers.

Although it is used in newspapers throughout the country for many news and feature stories, it is named after *The Wall Street Journal* because that newspaper originated the term "nut graph" and recommended this form to its reporters many years ago as a way to humanize business stories and make them readable for all types of readers. The technique dates back to the 1950s when *The Wall Street Journal* issued this memo to its writers about how features for the newspaper should be written:

The stories generally have one theme or point. This is usually put into a one- or two-paragraph nutshell summary high up in the story. Then the rest of the piece is made to hang together by harking back to this central theme. The story should be *clearly organized* or compartmentalized along the central thread of this theme — it should not meander around without a perceptible organization.

We want to tell the story in terms of the *specific*, not in generalized or vague terms. One way we do this is to pack the story with lots of *detail*.

Another way we reduce the general situation to the specific is to give lots of colorful examples, anecdotes or small case histories to *illustrate* the overall situation we are describing.

We also lean heavily on illustrative *quotes* — attributable if possible though not necessarily so. The quotes need not be from government officials only; they could be from businessmen, shopkeepers, men in the street, anyone who can shed some *color* on the situation or who can illustrate the general in specific, *individual terms*.

Be sure to include all *background* the reader might need. We can assume no prior knowledge by our readers of the subject or of financial lingo. We try to spell out all situations *with super-simplicity and clarity* — from how France's inflation has been brought about over the years to the recent economic history of Australia and what led up to its present economic situation. Please explain everything in clear-cut fashion.

We try to achieve very tight writing — short, punchy sentences and all essential information on the subject conveyed *concisely*.

At the same time, these leaders aim at being pretty *thorough* studies of the particular subject or trend. This means the inclusion of all detail and background and interpretation mentioned above. It also means we take pains to make sure the story contains the answers to every question that the story and its statements are likely to raise in the reader's mind. We can't use a story that raises questions it does not answer, so please re-check copy for this possible pitfall — and again, be sure all points are fully and *clearly explained*, and solidly *nailed down with fact*.

This is a very versatile formula that can be applied to many news and feature stories. It is useful for brightening bureaucratic stories. While you are reporting, seek out a person who is one of many exemplifying your point, or try to find an anecdote that illustrates the main point of your story.

In this example, the reporter uses an anecdotal lead that focuses on a person who exemplifies the problem in the focus — joblessness.

Anecdotal lead   When he graduated from Northwestern University, Marty Siewart did not anticipate that he would spend seven months unemployed, pondering the real-world value of his college degree.

Discouraged and "just about to get panicky" over his job search, Siewart finally landed with a federal poverty-fighting program in Hollywood where he tries to help others find employment.

Soft lead
Nut graph
Backup for lead and nut graph
Supporting points: quotes, facts, anecdotes
Developments: cause/effect, explanations, points of view
Circle kicker: anecdote, description, future action related to lead

The Wall Street Journal formula

Lead quote   "I've always been interested in social service, so this is a good opportunity to get a better feel for it, said Siewart, sitting in the small office from which he finds temporary jobs for teenage runaways and homeless youths. "Plus with the economy the way it is, I feel lucky to be working here."

Nut graph   Emblematic of the rise in volunteerism among college-age individuals that blends idealism with economic realities, Siewart recently began a one-year enlistment in Americorps Vista, the federal agency dedicated to alleviating domestic poverty.

A stagnant economy, changing attitudes toward volunteer work and heightened interest in world affairs have given organizations like the Peace Corps, VISTA and Teach for America a higher profile on college campuses, generating applications at an unparalleled rate.

The story continues with comments from Teach for America founder and volunteers. It ends with a quote kicker from another student contemplating volunteer service.

William Baldwin, a University of Southern California senior contemplating several volunteer options, said that many students are "learning there's more to being satisfied than making $50,000 to $60,000 a year."

"Those values may be satisfying in the short run, he said. "These programs have a lasting value that isn't going to disappear."

Quote kicker

— *Los Angeles Times*

A version of *The Wall Street Journal* formula also works well for some broadcast stories, especially when you want the lead to focus on a person to explain a larger issue, a program, a trend or a study. The structure would look like this:

- Anchor lead-in setting up the problem
- Lead focusing on a person who exemplifies a problem
- Nut graph explaining the problem
- Supporting information in sound bites, facts and other sources
- Circular ending returning to the person in the lead or main point

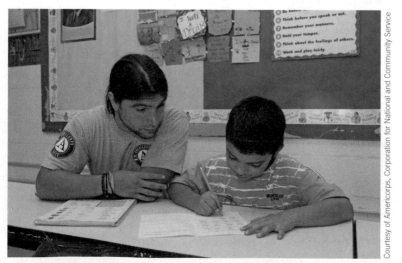

Courtesy of Americorps, Corporation for National and Community Service

A volunteer for Americorps helps a student learn reading and writing skills.

The following story, produced by students in a convergent media class at the University of Kansas, is a version of *The Wall Street Journal* structure. It would work in print or online as well by using quotes instead of sound bites and starting with the reporter's lead.

Anchor lead-in

A fast-growing trend in tobacco products may be causing more harm than first believed. KUJH-TV's Dylan Schoonover reports that college students who use hookah tobacco may be causing greater damage to their lungs than those who smoke cigarettes.

Reporter — lead focusing on a person

Smoking hookah is generally described as a social event that draws in experimental and young crowds for a so-called healthier and more arousing way of smoking tobacco. Many college students across the nation have caught on to this Middle Eastern tradition, including KU junior Pat Sullivan, who owns a hookah and uses it regularly.

Sound bite — Sullivan identifier superimposed on screen

I've read some stuff on it (hookah) and it's not a healthy alternative to smoking cigarettes, but I don't know. I think it's a lot cooler than smoking cigarettes and it's more relaxing.

Reporter — nut graph

Smoking hookah can actually be more dangerous to the lungs than cigarettes. A recent report issued by the World Health Organization claims that one 45-minute smoking session of smoking hookah exposes the user to as much as 200 times the volume of smoke inhaled in one cigarette.

Hazem Chahine, owner of the Hookah House, said customers smoking hookah generally do it for the company and relaxation of a session.

Supporting information introducing next source

People don't smoke it all time. It's not like a cigarette and you just pick it up and smoke it, you know? Customers come in one time a week; three times a week is the maximum people you've got coming in here. I see them regularly.

Sound bite with identifier of Chahine superimposed on screen

According to the American Cancer Society, nearly one third of all cancerous deaths results from tobacco use. Despite the risk hookah smoking is becoming more and more popular. Eighty-six percent of colleges and universities have at least one hookah lounge within close proximity of the school.

Reporter — more supporting information

Saudis, Egyptians, Americans, Japanese, Italians, Germans, French people; all of them have a great time. We offer them drums. Basically we give them a drum so they can loosen up a little and hit it hard.

Sound bite with Chahine

Despite the health risks, Chahine is confident that students like Sullivan will continue to frequent his Hookah House.

Reporter — circular ending

— DYLAN SCHOONOVER,
KUJH-TV News, University of Kansas

HOURGLASS STRUCTURE

The hourglass form can start like the inverted pyramid, giving the most important hard-news information in the top of the story. Then it contains chronological storytelling for a part or for the rest of the story. This approach also works for broadcast news.

CONVERGENCE COACH

BASIC STORY STRUCTURES FOR BROADCAST

When you are writing a story for print, broadcast and online publication, you will probably rely on the two most common formats: the inverted pyramid and a version of *The Wall Street Journal* formula. Basic news stories for the Web resemble print formats, but broadcast news stories must be developed around sound and images. The broadcast story structure may be interpreted as sequences, developed around a chronology:

- Lead-in tells who or what happened
- Current situation
- Background
- Ending with current or future developments.

Another version of the inverted pyramid format for broadcast is chronological storytelling. After the hard-news lead, the story may be told from beginning to end. If the story starts with a soft lead, such as a focus on a person, the structure resembles *The Wall Street Journal* formula. As with a print story, the story is organized from the specific to the general

information. It still follows a sequence developed around a basic chronology:

- Lead-in focuses on a person who exemplifies the problem
- General idea: statement of the problem or situation (equivalent to the nut graph in print writing)
- Background or past issues that led to the current situation
- Return to current or future developments

This storytelling model may be preferable for broadcast, according to Annie Lang and Deborah Potter in their article "The Seven Habits of Highly Effective Storytellers," written for Newslab, a training center for broadcasters. As they explain, "To engage your viewers, tell stories on television the way you tell them in person. Use strong, chronological narratives whenever possible. Studies have found that narrative stories are remembered substantially better than stories told in the old 'inverted pyramid' style. Whatever structure you choose, don't make viewers search their memories in order to understand your story. Give them the information they need when they need it, so they can follow each part of the story. Use words which connect the pieces of the story to each other, and which make the chronology of events clear."

Hourglass structure

Summary lead

Backup

Overview attribution

Chronological storytelling

Use the hourglass structure when the story has dramatic action that lends itself to chronological order for part of the story. The technique is useful in crime or disaster stories to recount the event.

To set up the chronological narrative, you can use an overview attribution such as "Police gave the following account" or "Witnesses described the accident this way," followed by a colon. However, this type of attribution should be used only for a few paragraphs so the reader does not forget who is speaking. All quotes still need attribution. If the speaker changes, you must attribute the new source.

Advantage: Narrative storytelling in the chronological portion adds drama to the story.

Disadvantage: The chronological portion of the story may repeat some of the key information in the top of the story, making it longer than a basic inverted pyramid.

BOY, 3, SHOOTS 16-MONTH-OLD

Summary lead
Attribution

TAMPA, Fla. — A 3-year-old boy shot and seriously wounded his 16-month-old half brother Thursday after he found a .32-caliber pistol under a chair cushion in the family's apartment, Hillsborough sheriff's deputies said.

Backup for lead

Melvin Hamilton, shot once in the chest about 9:30 a.m., was flown by helicopter to Tampa General Hospital, where he was in serious but stable condition late Thursday after surgery, hospital officials said.

Attribution

Otis Neal, who pulled the trigger, did it accidentally, authorities said.

Basic inverted pyramid structure with attribution for each point

Sheriff's officials said they did not know who owned the handgun but were still investigating. Under state law, the gun's owner could be criminally liable for leaving the gun in a place where a child could get it. . . .

Observation: no attribution needed

Hours after the accident, Otis sat bewildered on a curb outside his family's apartment as television camera crews and reporters jockeyed around him. "He is saying very little. I don't think he really knows what is going on," sheriff's spokeswoman Debbie Carter said.

Facts

Otis and Melvin live with their mother, Dina Varnes, in the Terrace Oaks Apartment complex at 6611 50th St.

Overview attribution: chronological narrative begins and continues to the end

Relatives and sheriff's officials gave this account: The two youngsters were downstairs in the living room playing Thursday morning, while a 15-year-old friend of the family slept on the couch. Ms. Varnes was upstairs.

Melvin was walking around the living room when Otis found the gun under the seat cushion. He pulled the gun out and fired one shot.

Arabell Ricks, Ms. Varnes' aunt and neighbor, said she was walking to the store when her niece ran out of the apartment screaming.

"She said, 'Melvin is shot.' She said the oldest shot Melvin," Ms. Ricks said. "I went in and looked at him, and then I just ran out of the house and started praying." She said she flagged down a sheriff's deputy who was patrolling the area.

Ending reaction quote

"I said, 'Lord, please don't let him die,'" Ms. Ricks said.

— HEDDY MURPHY, *St. Petersburg (Fla.) Times*

LIST TECHNIQUE

Lists can be useful in stories when you have several important points to stress. Think of a list as a highlights box within the story or at the end of the story. This technique works well for stories about studies, government stories such as meetings and even features about people or programs if there are several key points to list. This structure is useful for online stories and for mobile media delivery because readers often scan the text. It is also an effective technique for news releases, which should be brief.

Summary lead and backup

Key points

- •
- •
- •

Summary lead and backup

Key points

- •
- •

Elaboration

Ending

List technique

SOCIAL MEDIA

THE FORM MOST often used for writing on social media sites is the inverted pyramid, but it does not have to be the only one. This form has a definite advantage for mobile media because you get to the point quickly, which is especially helpful for small screens. But some of the other forms discussed in this chapter can work very well on social media sites: the question/answer form and the list technique are also adaptable for social media sites especially if they are geared to mobile media and small tablet screens. If you have a compelling story that will entice readers to click to another page, you could also try the sections technique especially if each section is relatively brief. The most important factor, however, is to tell a good story.

When using a list for the body and ending of a story, you can start with a summary lead or a soft lead followed by a nut graph. Give some backup for the lead with quotes, facts or both. Then itemize the main points until the ending. Investigative reporters often use the list high in the story to itemize the findings of their investigation.

Limit lists in the beginnings and middles of stories to five items or fewer; lists at the end can be longer. Parallel sentence structure is most effective, but not essential, for lists. Each item should be in a separate paragraph. Lists are often used in stories about meetings to itemize actions not related to the lead. The list is preceded by "In other business" or a similar transition or sentence ending with a colon as in this example:

Courtesy of Distraction.gov, U.S. Dept. of Transportation

Drivers using car phones are often dangerously distracted as the next example shows.

Finally, some facts to justify cursing at people with car phones.

A recent study of car phoning showed that drivers involved in car-phone conversations were 30 percent more likely to overlook potential hazards, such as your rear bumper.

"They were so engrossed in the phone call that they were oblivious to what was going on," said James McKnight, whose experiments with 51 drivers were the basis for the findings.

What McKnight found through controlled tests on driving simulators was this:

- Even casual chitchat or just dialing a car phone distracted drivers enough so that they failed to respond to hazards nearly 7 percent more often.

- When talk turned to solving simple math problems — designed to simulate business conversations — drivers failed to respond to hazards nearly 30 percent more often.

- When engaged in casual or businesslike conversations, drivers 50 or older failed to respond to hazards 38 percent more often than younger drivers.

- Drivers who had experience with car phones were as easily distracted as drivers who were using the phones for the first time.

— MARK VOSBURGH, *The Orlando* (Fla.) *Sentinel*

ETHICS

ETHICAL DILEMMA: You are covering an automobile accident in your community. When you arrive on the scene, the bodies of two victims are still on the ground. A third person covered in blood is weeping beside one of the victims. Police tell you that the accident was caused by a drunken driver, who has been taken into custody. You want to convey the deadly consequences of drunken driving in your story. Should you use the graphic images of the bodies and the blood-soaked survivor? How do you know when to use disturbing images?

The Radio Television Digital News Association suggests that before you air graphic content, consider the following questions:

- What is the journalistic purpose behind broadcasting the graphic content? Does the display of such material clarify and help the audience understand the story better? Is there an issue of great public importance involved such as public policy, community benefit or social significance?

- Is the use of graphic material the only way to tell the story? What are your alternatives?

- If asked to defend the decision to your audience or the stakeholders in the story, such as a family member, how will you justify your decision? Are you prepared to broadcast your rationale to your audience? If not, why?

QUESTION/ANSWER FORMAT

Organizing a story by questions and answers is an effective technique for print and Web stories, and it can also be effective in some news releases. It is also a useful form for mobile media stories. The Q and A, as it is commonly called, is often used for profiles, and it can be a helpful way to explain issues such as a budget increase or any controversial proposal. Even though the answer part of the story is verbatim quotes, the writer still has to be selective about which questions and answers to include from a lengthy interview. Some stories in this format just use Q for the question and A for the answer while others use names or initials for the questions and answers as in the following example. Here is an interview from the University of Alaska Anchorage college newspaper, *The Northern Light,* which used the question/answer technique in a profile of a professor:

MARIANO GONZALES, ASSOCIATE PROFESSOR OF ART

Northern Light: How long have you been teaching?
Mariano Gonzales: Full time since '88, part time since '80.

NL: How have you changed your style since you started teaching?
MG: I have much more experience now, and I have a better idea of what works in sharing knowledge and ideas with students. (Or, I'm an older guy who hates to waste time.)

NL: What have you taught at UAA and what are you currently teaching?
MG: I have taught a wide range of art subjects: drawing, painting, printmaking, metalsmithing, photography, digital art and graphic design. I am currently focusing on color and design (an arts foundation course), computer art and design, illustration and color photography.

NL: What rewards do you personally get from teaching?
MG: Teaching is like showing visitors what's cool about where you live. You get a charge out of hearing the sounds of appreciation, even if the sounds are barely audible.

NL: Where did you go to school? What was your major?
MG: I earned a bachelor's from UAA, majoring in painting (anthropology minor), and a Master of Fine Arts from the Rhode Island School of Design in metalsmithing in '79.

NL: What drew you to this field?
MG: The discipline of art, in its purest form, is an analogue or the core of all that is worthwhile in humanity. Also, I thought I could make a living at it.

NL: What was your worst or most interesting job as a student?
MG: I created Alaska "artifacts" for the tourist trade. It was good practice, not enough money and occasionally now I find these items at thrift stores. Fortunately no one has proof that I did them.

NL: Born and raised?
MG: I was born in El Paso, Texas, in '51, moved to Anchorage In '59 and have been a resident ever since.

NL: Favorite movie(s)?

MG: Anything by John Waters, Tim Burton, the Coen Bros, Jean-Pierre Jeunet and Michael Moore.

NL: Favorite book, poem or screenplay?

MG: Frankly, I can't read anything that doesn't have the word "spank" in the title.

NL: Favorite music or artist?

MG: Among my favorite artists are Miles Davis, Jimi Hendrix, Stravinsky, George Tooker, George and Robert Crumb, Robert Williams . . . the list goes on.

NL: What are your favorite pastimes and hobbies?

MG: These days my favorite pastime is stewing about the medieval darkness that has descended on my country and creating art that hopefully illuminates.

NL: What are you most passionate about in life?

MG: Finding the time to do what I need to.

Sections technique

SECTIONS TECHNIQUE

This is a technique of dividing a story into sections, like book chapters, and separating them by a graphic device such as a large dot or a large capital letter. It works best for in-depth stories such as investigations or long features. It is also useful for the Web because the story can be divided into several Web pages — one section with audio and video per page. It may also work for small-screen mobile media devices if the story is compelling enough to entice readers to click into the next section.

The most effective section stories have good leads and good endings for each section. This form lends itself to cliffhanger endings for each section or for each day's installment if the story is presented as a series. Think of the sections as separate chapters, complete in themselves but tied together by the overall focus and story plot. This technique is used often in nonfiction storytelling called "narrative writing."

One common way to organize section stories is by points of view. For example, in a story about a controversial government issue, such as a new landfill, you could arrange the story in sections for each group affected by the proposal.

The other way frequently used to organize section stories is by time frames — starting with the present, then moving to the past for background and back to present developments, and ending with the future. Although the order can be flexible, the opening section must contain a nut graph explaining why you are telling the reader this story now. This technique is very effective for stories written in narrative style.

To determine whether your story is suitable for sections, envision subheads for it. Then decide if you have enough information in each subhead group to warrant a separate section.

The following story uses a combination of points of view and time sequences to organize the sections. This is written in dramatic narrative form, using storytelling that reconstructs the event. Notice how the sections are structured as separate chapters with kicker endings.

THEY GOT OUT ALIVE, BUT NO ONE WAS SPARED

BOULDER, Colo. — For weeks after the crash, David Hooker found the love notes his fiancée had hidden around the house.

In the medicine cabinet: "David, I love you this much."

In the sock drawer: "Poo — Here's a hug for you! Susan."

In the silverware tray: "I'll miss you! Take care."

This paragraph tells why you are reading this story now

Five months have passed since Susan Fyler boarded United Airlines Flight 282. Hooker carefully stacks the yellow slips of paper into a neat pile on the corner of his dresser, next to the framed photographs of Fyler and the mahogany box that holds her ashes.

Less than a half-hour away in Denver, Garry Priest can't sleep.

He watched a movie — he doesn't even remember what it was about — and one scene stuck. A woman is thrown from a car and the pavement scrapes her skin raw.

Suddenly it was July 19 again and Priest was back in Sioux City, Ia., escaping from the plane, racing along the runway, seeing the debris, the charred metal, the boy's body.

Then he thinks of Christmas. And his eyes will not close.

***

Five months ago, they were strangers, bound only by an airplane flight.

Susan Fyler was headed to Ohio to surprise her parents with news of her engagement. Garry Priest was going to Chicago on business.

Both boarded Flight 232 in Denver. She sat in seat 31K, he in seat 15G. Fyler was one of 112 people killed in the crash. She was 32. Priest was one of 184 survivors. He is 23.

For those most directly affected — the family and friends of the victims, the survivors and their families — the holidays are proving that time has not healed all wounds. . . .

Five months later, they are strangers, but David Hooker and Garry Priest share a common grief.

This section gives the crucial information that ties the story together

***

This section is about David Hooker and how he is dealing with the loss of his fiancée

It didn't make sense. This section gives the story from Garry Priest's point of view

Every night, David Hooker walks into his bedroom, lights a candle and shares his day with Susan Fyler. Shortly after the crash, a friend admonished Hooker to stop feeling sorry for himself and to ask Fyler for guidance.

"I asked Susan to come live with me inside my body and to stay alive inside my body," he says, "and right after I did that, I felt a very dramatic change going on in me. I just felt all this energy coming over me."

After he lights the candle, Hooker may read the Lord's Prayer or flip through the love notes Fyler left him or look at the five photographs on his dresser.

***

It didn't make sense. Why, Garry Priest wondered, were people acting this way? He had survived one of the worst airplane disasters in U.S. history. He had seen horrible things, scenes that made his legs shake,

This section gives the story from Garry Priest's point of view.

pictures he will remember the rest of his life.

So why was everyone calling him lucky?

"People want to pinch you," he says. "They say, 'Let's play bingo,' or 'Let's buy a lottery ticket.' They pat your head.

"I don't feel lucky at all. If I was lucky, I wouldn't have been on that plane. Nobody would have been on the plane."

***

They are strangers, but Garry Priest would like David Hooker to know that he, too, mourns Susan Fyler.

"Could you do me a favor?" Priest asks. "Could you tell all the people who lost loved ones and all the people who survived that I wish them a merry Christmas and that my thoughts and prayers and love are with them?"

— KEN FUSON, *The Des Moines* (Iowa) *Register*

Two more sections follow before this ending section

EXERCISES

1 Inverted pyramid exercise: Organize the information for this story in the inverted pyramid order for print or broadcast. Here are your notes, based on a story from The Associated Press:

Who: Connecticut State Police

What: Ordered ban of hand-held radar guns

When: Yesterday

Where: Meriden, Conn.

Why: Because of concerns that troopers could develop cancer from long-term exposure to the radiation waves emitted by the devices. The ban was ordered as a precaution while researchers study the possible links between cancer and use of the devices.

How: The ban affects 70 radar guns, which will be withdrawn from service. State troopers will continue to use radar units with transmitters mounted on the outside of their cruisers.

Source: Adam Berluti, a state police spokesman

Backup information: "The feeling here is to err on the side of caution until more is known about the issue," Berluti said. "The whole situation is under review." The move is considered to be the first of its kind by a state police agency. It comes two months after three municipal police officers in Connecticut filed workers' compensation claims, saying they developed cancer from using handheld radar guns.

2 *Wall Street Journal* formula exercise: Here are some excerpts from a story that was originally written according to *The Wall Street Journal* formula by Matt Gowen of the *Lawrence* (Kan.) *Journal-World*. Rearrange the paragraphs to conform to *The Wall Street Journal* style. Use an anecdotal lead followed by a nut graph and a circular ending.

College students are most susceptible to online obsession, experts say

Jonathan Kandell, assistant director of the counseling center at the University of Maryland, has found that college students — especially those in the 18 to 22 age range — are quite susceptible to an Internet obsession. Kandell, an assistant professor of psychology at Maryland, recently published his theories in the journal "CyberPsychology and Behavior."

A few years ago, Stacie Kawaguchi started tinkering with the Internet. She clicked her mouse, surfed around and delved into an international pen-pal site. At the time a Kansas University graduate student in botany, Kawaguchi "met" folks from Canada, France, Japan and Brazil. Through the Internet, she even met her eventual fiancé, a Ph.D. candidate in engineering at Virginia Tech University.

"When you first start, you get really into it," said Kawaguchi, 26. "You get stuck on it for long periods of time."

The search for identity, the need for intimate relationships and the need for control often play a significant role in this potentially unhealthy behavior, Kandell said. Logging on, whether in chat rooms or through websites, can help students ranging academically from the inept to the astute cope with life's hardships. "If it's fulfilling a need, it's hard to give it up," Kandell said.

Simply put, Kawaguchi was online and over-whelmed. "You stay up late instead of going to sleep," she said. "It sucked up a lot of time." In a few months, the novelty began to wear off. "After a while, it was like, geez, this is enough," she said, adding that many of her chatmates were there night after night, even when she was gone for weeks at a time. "Basically, their whole world revolved around being there."

Studies on college campuses have shown between 6 percent and 12 percent of students may be spending too much time online, thanks in part to the ease of campus Internet access.

Kawaguchi saw the obsessive side of the Internet and managed to escape it. Others aren't as lucky.

Kandell was quick to note, however, that "addiction" was probably not the most accurate term in these cases. He compared overuse of the Internet to compulsive behaviors such as pathological gambling.

"I do see it as a psychological dependency," Kandell said. Kandell's evidence is mostly anec-dotal, culled from student clients and classrooms filled with students who say they're downloading to the point of distraction.

In one class he visited, between 70 percent and 80 percent of the students raised their hands when asked whether the Internet was their chief obstacle to concentrating on projects and pa-pers. "People are staying up all night, not going to class, not doing their homework — ultimately flunking out of school," Kandell said. "It's more pervasive than people think. There's something inherently tempting about the Internet."

For example, administrators at New York's Alfred University have found a correlation between high Internet use and a dropout rate that more than doubled. And the University of Washington has limited the amount of Internet time available to students to cut down on overuse. Several other colleges have set up support groups for Internet addiction.

Kawaguchi sees both good and bad in the Internet. The native of Oahu, Hawaii, considers it an effective communication tool but not a surrogate for human relationships. She calls it "luck" that she met her Iowa-born husband-to-be online. They traded photos and talked on the phone for a long time before tak-ing the big step of meeting in person. The couple plan to wed in June in Lawrence. "Personally, I wouldn't recommend someone going out to look for someone on the Internet," she said. "I completely lucked out."

In addition to academic problems, jobs and relationships can be affected as social isolation grows. The Internet can provide an arena for people to simulate personal contact without actually having to meet face to face.

The underlying problem may be that the Internet's many facets are still new and somewhat unfamiliar. "I think we're just kind of scratching the surface," Kandell said. "I think it'll be a good five or 10 years before people have a good understanding of everything that's going on right now."

3 **Hourglass structure exercise:** Arrange these facts in hourglass order, placing attribution where it is needed. (This story is taken from the *St. Louis Post-Dispatch* of Missouri.) Attribute information to Capt. Ed Kemp of the Jefferson County Sheriff's Department unless otherwise noted.

Who: Two bank couriers

What: Helped police capture three suspects in a robbery

When: Last night

Where: At the Boatman's Bank of Pevely, Mo.

How: One courier, Dennis Boushie, who lives near Festus, chased a suspect on foot. The other courier, Willie Moore of St. Louis, drove a bank van, chasing a getaway car.

Police have booked three people on suspicion of drug possession. The three, who were found in the getaway car, are being held in the jail at Pevely.

Backup information: "This is beyond the call of duty. They acted more like police officers than private citizens or bank couriers," said Capt. Ed Kemp.

Boushie said he had asked the teller who was robbed if the robber had a weapon, and she said he did not. He said his pursuit of the robber had been "just common sense."

A man entered the bank shortly after it opened Tuesday morning and shouted, "Give me the money or else!" The teller gave the man an envelope containing the money, and the man ran out the front door.

Boushie chased the man on foot, and when the suspect jumped into a car, Boushie pointed the car out to Moore, who pursued it in a bank van. A few minutes later, Boushie got in a police patrol car and helped police track the getaway car.

Police broadcast a description of the getaway car, which had continued north on I-55 carrying two men and a woman. Police spotted the car, stopped it and arrested three suspects.

Police said they had found several thousand dollars in the car. The female suspect had stuffed money down her pants, police said.

Police were seeking federal warrants for bank robbery.

4 **List technique exercise:** Write a brief news story in list format based on this information:

Who: Stephen J. Blumberg, health scientist and lead author of study for the U.S. Centers for Disease Control and Prevention Health Statistics

What: Report on households using only wireless phones; "Wireless Substitution: State-level Estimates from the National Health Interview Survey

When: Results of a study released today (use current date)

Why: To determine how telephone surveys for the CDC will be affected by wireless-only households

Elaboration: Oklahoma leads the nation in the percentage of households that only use cell phones.

More than a quarter of households (26.2 percent) in Oklahoma had only wireless and no landline phones. At the other end of the spectrum, only 5.1 percent of households in Vermont used only wireless phones. "These findings are important to CDC because many of our largest surveys are done on calls to landline phone numbers. All of those adults with only cell phones are being missed in these surveys," Blumberg said.

In addition to Oklahoma, states with the highest percentage of wireless–only households are Utah (25.5 percent), Nebraska (23.2 percent), Arkansas (22.6 percent) and Idaho (22.1 percent). States with the lowest percentages, following Vermont, are Connecticut (5.6 percent), Delaware (5.7 percent), South Dakota (6.4 percent) and Rhode Island (7.9 percent). Results from previous CDC reports on wireless substitution show wireless–only phone use continues to grow on a national level.

CourseMate

COACHING TIPS

marekuliasz/Shutterstock.com

Gather details and
**take notes of your
observations.**

Use **show-in-action**
techniques. Describe what
people are doing.

Use vivid **action verbs.**

For narrative writing,
**envision yourself at the
scene.**

Get a chronology to
reconstruct events as they
occurred.

Think of your story as a plot
with a beginning, middle and
climax. Envision your sources
as characters in a book;
**make your reader see,
hear and care** about them.

To write well, **read well.**
Read as much fiction and
nonfiction as you can, and
study the writing styles.

We're supposed to be
tellers of tales as well
as purveyors of facts.
When we don't live up
to that responsibility,
we don't get read.

— **BILL BLUNDELL,** *The Art and Craft
of Feature Writing*

CHAPTER 10
Storytelling and Feature Techniques

TOM FRENCH WAS FASCINATED BY KAREN GREGORY'S CASE. HE WROTE a 10-part series about her murder and the man on trial for it. It was called "A Cry in the Night."

Something very unusual happened when the series began. Readers ran out to greet the newspaper delivery trucks each day to get the next chapter in the series. Why were they so eager to read these stories? You decide.

> The victim wasn't rich. She wasn't the daughter of anyone powerful. She was simply a 36-year-old woman trying to make a life for herself. Her name was Karen Gregory. The night she died, Karen became part of a numbing statistic. . . . It was what people sometimes casually refer to as "a little murder."
>
> — TOM FRENCH, *St. Petersburg* (Fla.) *Times*

This passage was the introduction to the series. The first story began with a description of the trial of George Lewis, a firefighter who lived across the street from Karen Gregory and the person who was charged with her murder:

> His lawyer called out his name. He stood up, put his hand on a Bible and swore to tell the truth and nothing but. He sat down in the witness box and looked toward the jurors so they could see his face and study it and decide for themselves what kind of man he was.
>   "Did you rape Karen Gregory?" asked his lawyer.

"No sir, I did not." "Did you murder Karen Gregory?"
"No sir."

He heard a scream that night, he said. He heard it, and he went out to the street to look around. He saw a man he did not know, standing over in Karen's yard. The man said to go away, to not tell anyone what he'd seen. He waited for the man to leave — watched him walk away into the darkness — and then he went up to Karen's house. There was broken glass on the front walk. He knocked on the front door. There was no answer. He found an open window. He called out to ask whether anyone needed help. There was still no answer. He looked through the window and saw someone lying on the floor. He decided he had to go in. He climbed inside, and there was Karen. Blood was everywhere.

He was afraid. He ran to the bathroom and threw up. He knew no one would believe how he had ended up standing inside that house with her body. He had to get out of there. He was running toward the window to climb out when he saw something moving in the dark. He thought someone was jumping toward him. Then he realized he was looking at a mirror, and the only person moving was him. It was his own reflection that had startled him. It was George.

— TOM FRENCH, *St. Petersburg* (Fla.) *Times*

The entire series was written like a mystery novel. But it was all true, based on interviews with more than 50 people and 6,000 pages of court documents. The writing style, called narrative writing, is a form of dramatic storytelling that reconstructs the events as though the reader were witnessing them as they happened. French later turned the series into a book called *Unanswered Cries*.

French said he never believed his series would be so popular. "The way the readers responded was so gratifying," he said.

French relied heavily on dialogue throughout the series, even from the dead woman. Although most of the dialogue and description are based on interviews and his observations, Karen's dialogue was second-hand information, based on recollections about her.

"After I wrote it, I spent three weeks checking everything with all the participants," French said. "I read it to them word for word to make sure it was accurate."

In 1998 French won the Pulitzer Prize for another narrative series about murder. This time he researched 4,000 pages of police reports and court documents and conducted scores of interviews to reconstruct the chilling story of an Ohio woman and her two daughters. They were on vacation in Florida when they were raped, killed and dumped into Tampa Bay. Once again, French wrote a gripping account of their murders, the three-year search for their killer and his trial. The killer was convicted and sentenced to death.

These days French teaches narrative writing to journalism students at his alma mater Indiana University. He worked with several of the students who won honors in the writing categories of the prestigious Hearst Journalism Awards, often considered equivalent to the Pulitzer Prizes for college journalism students.

Photo by James Brosher. Courtesy of Indiana University

Tom French.

NARRATIVE WRITING

"Narrative writing" is a dramatic account of a fiction or nonfiction story. Writing in this style requires thorough reporting and descriptive detail. Dialogue also enhances the storytelling. Narrative writing for news often reconstructs events to put the reader on the scene. The sources are like characters who relive the events as they happened. But the story must include the basic factual elements of news.

Jeff Klinkenberg, a *St. Petersburg* (Fla.) *Times* writer, views the five W's this way: *Who* is character, *what* is plot, *when* is chronology, *why* is motive and *where* is place.

French uses all these elements in his stories by weaving facts with description and dramatic tension. In this section from his Pulitzer Prize-winning series, "Angels and Demons," French uses descriptive detail to reveal how the bodies of the women were found.

It was a female, floating face down, with her hands tied behind her back and her feet bound and a thin yellow rope around her neck. She was naked from the waist down.

A man from the *Amber Waves* (sailboat) radioed the Coast Guard, and a rescue boat was dispatched from the station at Bayboro Harbor in St. Petersburg. The Coast Guard crew quickly found the body, but recovering it from the water was difficult. The rope around the neck was attached to something heavy below the surface that could not be lifted. Noting the coordinates where the body had been found, the Coast Guard crew cut the line, placed the female in a body bag, pulled the bag onto the boat and headed back toward the station. The crew members had not yet reached the shore when they received another radio message: A second female body had just been sighted by two people on a sailboat.

This one was floating to the north of where the first body had been sighted. It was 2 miles off The Pier in St. Petersburg. Like the first, this body was face down, bound, with a rope around the neck and naked below the waist. The same Coast Guard crew was sent to recover it, and while the crew was doing so, a call came in of yet a third female, seen floating only a couple of hundred yards to the east.

— TOM FRENCH, *St. Petersburg* (Fla.) *Times*

In the following section, French uses dialogue to reconstruct the scene when Hal Rogers, the husband and father of the dead women, tells the boyfriend of his daughter Michelle that his wife and daughters won't be coming home:

That day, Jeff Feasby phoned the Rogers house again, hoping Michelle would be back.

Hal picked up. His voice was strange. He sounded furious.

"Who is this?" he demanded.

Jeff told him who it was and asked if he'd heard anything. With that, Hal broke down.

"They're not coming home," he said, his voice trembling.
Jeff paused for a second. He didn't understand.
So Hal told him. They were gone, he said. All of them.

— TOM FRENCH, *St. Petersburg* (Fla.) *Times*

READING TO WRITE

Good writers are good readers, and French said he was inspired to do narrative writing after he read a book by the Latin American writer Gabriel García Márquez. *The Story of a Shipwrecked Sailor* is a riveting story about a man who survived 10 days at sea without food and water.

French was also influenced by the literary journalists, a group of writers who, in the 1960s and 1970s, used the storytelling techniques of fiction for nonfiction newspaper and magazine stories. These journalists — Joan Didion, John McPhee, Tracy Kidder and Tom Wolfe — were influenced by Truman Capote's nonfiction book *In Cold Blood*. The literary journalists immersed themselves in a subject and wrote their stories with characters, scene, dialogue and plot. These were factual stories written like fiction.

Journalists often think storytelling techniques are limited to feature stories, but as you will see, you can apply this kind of writing to news about crime and courts and many other news stories.

Can storytelling survive in an age of Twitter and blogs? Stories may be shorter on some platforms and enhanced by multimedia, but good writing will endure.

REPORTING TOOLS

Good storytelling requires using observation and gathering details.

"Other people see flies; a writer sees how they move."

— WILLIAM RUEHLMANN

William Ruehlmann, author of *Stalking the Feature Story,* says writers must concentrate when they observe and then analyze what they observe. He gives this example: "Flies take off backward. So in order to swat one, you must strike slightly behind him. An interesting detail, and certainly one a writer would be able to pick up on. Other people see flies; a writer sees how they move."

During the reporting process, you don't always know what details you will need when you write your story. Ask what were people thinking, saying, hearing, smelling, wearing and feeling. Be precise. Take notes when you hear dialogue that could enhance your story.

To help you gather specific details, envision a ladder with rungs leading from general to specific. Start with the broadest noun, and take it to the most specific level, as in the adjacent diagram. Then use those details to write. For example:

> A tan and white Lhasa Apso named Joe ran onto the baseball field and interrupted the game when he stole the ball. It was only natural. After all, his namesake was Joe DiMaggio.

Lhasa apso named for Joe DiMaggio

Lhasa apso named Joe

Tan and white Lhasa apso

Lhasa apso

Dog

Ladder of details.

WRITING TOOLS

Once you have gathered all those details, what do you do with them? The better you are as a reporter, the more you will struggle as a writer deciding what information to use. The three basic tools of storytelling are theme, descriptive writing techniques and narrative writing techniques.

Theme

Before you begin writing a feature story, develop a theme — a concept that gives the story meaning.

David Maraniss, a Pulitzer-Prize winner from the *Washington Post* describes it this way:

> The theme is why readers want to read the story, not the nut graph required by many editors. To write something universal . . . death, life, fear, joy . . . that every person can connect to in some way is what I look for in every story.

DESCRIPTIVE TECHNIQUES

Too much description will clutter a story. Too little will leave the reader blank. How much is enough? First decide if the story lends itself to description of the scene or person. Then take the advice of Bruce DeSilva, a writing coach who teaches at Columbia University.

> Description, like every element in either fiction or nonfiction, should advance the meaning of your story. It would be a good idea to describe the brown house in more detail only if those details are important. Description never should be there for decoration. It never should be there because you are showing off. And when you do describe, you should never use more words than you need to trigger that mental image readers already have in their minds.

Techniques for good descriptive writing include the following:

Avoid Adjectives Write specific detail with vivid nouns and verbs, but avoid modifiers. When you use adjectives, you run the risk of inserting your opinions into the story. The late author Norman Mailer put it this way:

> The adjective is the author's opinion of what is going on, no more. If I write, "A strong man came into the room," that only means he is strong in relation to me. Unless I've established myself for the reader, I might be the only fellow in the bar who is impressed by the guy who just came in. It is better to say: "A man entered. He was holding a walking stick, and for some reason, he now broke it in two like a twig." Of course, this takes more time to narrate. So adjectives bring on quick tell-you-how-to-live writing. Advertising thrives on it. "A super-efficient, silent, sensuous, five-speed shift." Put 20 adjectives before a noun and no one will know you are describing a turd.

Use Analogies A good analogy compares a vague concept to something familiar to readers. For example, what is a "fat" man? David Finkel leaves no doubt in his story about a circus performer. How do you visualize the "World's Biggest Man" at 891 pounds? Finkel uses familiar items to help the reader see.

> Now: 891 and climbing. That's more than twice as much as Sears' best refrigerator-freezer — a 26-cubic-footer with automatic ice and water dispensers on side-by-side doors. That's almost as much as a Steinway grand piano.
>
> — DAVID FINKEL, *St. Petersburg* (Fla.) *Times*

Limit Physical Descriptions Use physical descriptions only when they are relevant to the content. They work well in profiles; in stories about crime, courts and disasters; and whenever they fit with the context. They don't work when they are tacked onto impersonal quotes.

Avoid stage directions — descriptions of people's gestures, facial expressions and physical characteristics inserted artificially as though you were directing a play. You don't need to describe what city commissioners are wearing at a meeting or how they gesture unless their clothing and movements enhance what they are saying and doing.

Effective   The 50-year-old airline pilot — who prosecutors say killed his wife by unknown means, cut up her body with a chain saw, and disposed of it with a wood chipper — testified with a voice and manner that was so calm it bordered at times on nonchalance.

> — LYNNE TUOHY, *The Hartford* (Conn.) *Courant*

Ineffective   The study shows college students are becoming more conservative, the researcher said, blinking her blue eyes and clasping her carefully manicured hands.

Avoid Sexist/Racist Descriptions When you decide to include descriptions of people, beware of sexism, racism or other biased writing. Writers often describe men with action verbs showing what they are doing and women with adjectives showing what they are wearing and how they look. One way to avoid bias is to ask yourself if you would use a similar description for both men and women or equal treatment for all racial and ethnic groups.

Consider this example:

Ineffective   Even Chandra Smith, busy being adorable in her perky non-runner's running outfit, actually looked at the track. A minute later, she was jumping around and yelling, along with most of the other 41,600 people on the old wooden benches at Franklin Field.

— *The Philadelphia Inquirer*

The story about the Penn Relay Carnival, a track meet in Philadelphia, also mentions a few men among those 41,600 people, including some volunteers who wear gray trousers and red caps. But they aren't adorable or perky.

Show People in Action One of the most effective ways to describe people or places is to show action. For example, Tom French doesn't write only about murder. In a series about life in a Florida high school, he used the show-in-action technique extensively, as in this passage about a history teacher's first day on the job. The teacher, Mr. Samsel, has given his homeroom students some forms to fill out:

The future leaders of America sit silently, some of them slumped forward, staring into space through half-closed eyes. Over to the side sits a boy. He is wearing a crucifix, blue jeans and a T-shirt. On the front of the shirt is a big smiley face. In the center of the face's forehead is a bullet hole, dripping blood. . . .

Around the room, students begin writing.

"Isn't this great?" says Samsel. "Just like real life — forms and everything."

Smiley Face looks at one of the sheets in front of him. He reads aloud as he fills it out.

"Please list medical problems."

He stops.

"Brain dead," he says.

— TOM FRENCH, *St. Petersburg* (Fla.) *Times*

Use Lively Verbs

"We report that a jumper died Monday when his parachute failed, instead of turning to action verbs such as *plummeted* or *plunged* or *streamed*."

— JACK HART

News is action, says Jack Hart, *The* (Portland) *Oregonian's* former writing coach. But writers often "squeeze the life out of an action-filled world," he says. "We write that thousands of bullet holes were in the hotel, instead of noting that the holes pocked the hotel. We report that a jumper died Monday when his parachute failed, instead of turning to action verbs such as *plummeted* or *plunged* or *streamed*."

Mitch Albom, a sportswriter and author of four best-selling books, knows the value of action verbs. Notice the ones he used in this story about the day Detroit Tigers baseball player Cecil Fielder hit his 50th home run. Also notice the analogies and the show-in-action description.

He swung the bat and he heard that smack! And the ball screamed into the dark blue sky, higher, higher, until it threatened to bring a few stars down with it. His teammates knew; they leaped off the bench. The fans knew; they roared like animals. And finally, the man who all year refused to watch his home runs, the man who said this 50 thing was "no big deal" — finally even he couldn't help himself. He stopped halfway to first base and watched the ball bang into the facing of the upper deck in Yankee Stadium, waking up the ghosts of Maris and Ruth and Gehrig.

And then, for the first time in this miraculous season, Cecil Fielder jumped. He jumped like a man sprung from prison, he jumped like a kid on the last day of school, he jumped, all 250 pounds of Detroit Bambino, his arms over his head, his huge smile a beacon of celebration and relief.

The Big Five-0.

— MITCH ALBOM, *Detroit Free Press*

Set the Scene You need to set the scene by establishing where and when. Although it is common to establish the time and weather, often in a lead, beware of using that technique unless time and weather factors are relevant to your story. "It was 2 a.m. and the wind was blowing" is akin to the cliché "It was a dark and stormy night." In this story from a California State University student newspaper, the time and weather conditions are relevant to the story:

TIJUANA, Mexico — Shivering in the mud under a 2-foot high chaparral, Jose carefully lifts his head into the cold night mist to monitor the movements of the U.S. Border Patrol.

On a ridge above a small ravine, patrol trucks scurry back and forth while a helicopter above provides the only light, turning spots of the nighttime terrain into day. In the distance, guard dogs growl, bark and yelp.

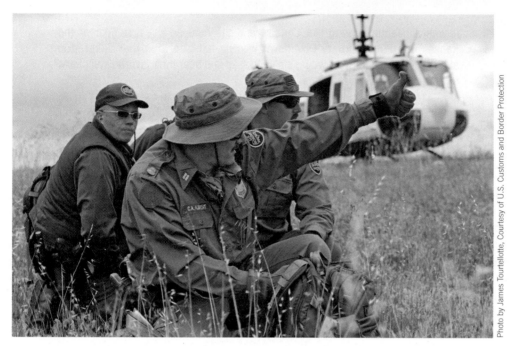

Photo by James Tourtellotte, Courtesy of U.S. Customs and Border Protection

U.S. Border Patrol.

At one point a patrol truck speeds toward Jose and his group of six Mexican farm laborers. Squatting in the brush, they quickly slide flat into the mud like reptiles seeking shelter.

Within seconds the helicopter hovers above them as its searchlight passes nearby, then at once directly over them. All their faces are turned downward to avoid detection by the brightness of the light that illuminates every detail of the soil, roots and insects that lie inches under them.

Soon, the truck and helicopter make a slow retreat. Jose and his group, safe for the moment, will remain motionless in that same muddy spot for the next three hours as the mist turns to rain and the rain turns back to mist.

Nut graphs   To those who have never passed this way before, the sights and sounds are of another world. But to the expert scouts called "coyotes," this alien land between Mexico and the United States is home.

Every weekday evening, approximately 2,000 people attempt to illegally cross the border from Mexico to the United States. On weekends the numbers can climb to between 5,000 and 10,000, said Victor Clark, director of the Binational Center for Human Rights in Tijuana, Mexico.

— BRETT C. SPORICH, (Long Beach, Calif.) *Daily Forty Niner*

In the next example, the story is about a reading program. Although the lead about the weather is backed up by a quote, the weather has nothing to do with the focus or the rest of the story.

It was a beautiful spring-like Sunday, and the heat on the first floor of the Kansas City Public Library Downtown was on full-blast. But that didn't stop about 400 people from crowding inside to read and hear their favorite selections from African-American authors.

The crowd, people of all ages and races, was there to take part in the national Read-In sponsored by the Black Caucus of the National Teachers of English.

"That is true commitment," said Mamie Isler, program director for Genesis School, which helped coordinate the event in Kansas City.

The second annual Kansas City Read-In opened with a performance by 30 students from the Genesis School choir.

— *The Kansas City* (Mo.) *Star*

Narrative Techniques Narrative writing combines show-in-action description, dialogue, plot and reconstruction of an event as it occurred. This type of writing requires a bond of faith with the reader because attribution is limited. You need to make it clear where you got the information, but you don't need to attribute repeatedly. You can also use an overview attribution for portions of the story and then attribute periodically, especially when you are quoting sources.

Before you can do narrative writing, you need to do thorough reporting. It takes a different kind of questioning to gather the information you will need to reconstruct a scene with dialogue and detail. Narrative writing is not fiction. You must stick to the facts even though the story may read like a novel. You need to ask questions like these: What were you thinking at the time? What were you feeling? What did you say? What were you wearing? What were you doing? You need to get details about colors, sounds, sights, smells, sizes, shapes, times, places.

If you were witnessing the event, you would see, hear, smell and feel — perhaps even taste — the experiences of your subject. Because you are reconstructing the event, you need to ask the questions that will evoke all those images.

Those are the kinds of questions Jane Schorer Meisner asked when she wrote this Pulitzer Prize–winning story about a woman who had been raped. The woman had agreed to use her name. In this opening part of her series, the reporter sets the scene (with relevant weather and time references) and reconstructs the woman's experience so the reader is a witness to the event:

She would have to allow extra driving time because of the fog.

A heavy gray veil had enveloped Grinnell overnight, and Nancy Ziegenmeyer — always methodical, always in control — decided to leave home early for her 7:30 a.m. appointment at Grand View College in Des Moines.

It was Nov. 19, a day Ziegenmeyer had awaited eagerly, because she knew that whatever happened during those morning hours in Des Moines would determine her future. If she passed the state real-estate licensing exam that Saturday morning, she would begin a new career. If she failed the test, she would continue the child-care service she provided in her home.

At 6 a.m. Ziegenmeyer unlocked the door of her Pontiac Grand Am and tossed her long denim jacket in the back seat. The weather was mild for mid-November, and her Gloria Vanderbilt denim jumper, red turtleneck sweater and red wool tights would keep her warm enough without a coat.

The fog lifted as Ziegenmeyer drove west on Interstate Highway 80 and she made good time after all. The digital clock on the dashboard read 7:05 as she pulled into a parking lot near Grand View's Science Building. She had 25 minutes to sit in the car and review her notes before test time.

Suddenly the driver's door opened. She turned to see a man, probably in his late 20s, wearing a navy pin-striped suit. He smelled of alcohol.

"Move over," the man ordered, grabbing her neck. She instinctively reached up to scratch him, but he was stronger than she was. He pushed a white dish towel into her face and shoved her into the front passenger seat, reclining it to a nearly horizontal position. Then he took her denim jacket from the back seat and covered her head.

He wasn't going to hurt her, the man said; he wanted money. She reached toward the console for the only cash she had with her — $3 or $4 — and gave it to him. He slid the driver's seat back to make room for his long legs, started the car and drove out of the parking lot.

"Is this guy going to kill me?" Ziegenmeyer wondered. "Is he going to rape me? Does he just want my money? Does he want my car?" She thought about her three children — ages 4, 5, and 7 — and realized she might never see them again.

— JANE SCHORER MEISNER, *The Des Moines* (Iowa) *Register*

Create Tone Hard-news stories often have an objective, factual tone, mostly an absence of mood. But in storytelling, you should create a "tone," or "mood," such as happiness, sadness, mystery, excitement or some other emotion.

You don't need to tell the reader that the mood of the place was festive or mournful. You can show it by the images you select for your story.

Saul Pett wanted to create a somber tone to reflect the mood of the nation when President Kennedy was killed. Pett chose vivid details that showed what people were feeling, and he did something else that was quite unusual. He established the reverent tone of his story by emulating biblical style.

Another way Pett created the mournful tone of his story was

The funeral procession for President John F. Kennedy leaves the White House, Nov. 25, 1963.

through the length of his sentences. Short, choppy sentences can reflect fear, excitement, anxiety or stabbing pain. Long sentences can project suffering, thoughtfulness or a quiet mood.

Pett broke many traditional journalistic rules in his article describing the four days after Kennedy was shot: His sentences were long, he used the first-person *we,* and he made no attempt to write objectively. Yet his story is one of the great feature articles of the 20th century. Here is an excerpt:

And the word went out from that time and place and cut the heart of a nation. In streets and offices and homes and stores, in lunchrooms and showrooms and schoolrooms and boardrooms, on highways and prairies and beaches and mountaintops, in endless places crowded and sparse, near and far, white and black, Republican and Democrat, management and labor, the word went out and cut the heart of a nation.

And husbands called wives and wives called friends and teachers told students and motorists stopped to listen on car radios and stranger told stranger. Oh, no! we cried from hearts stopped by shock, from minds fighting the word, but the word came roaring back, true, true, true, and disbelief dissolved in tears.

Incredibly, in a time of great numbers, in a time of repeated reminders that millions would die in a nuclear war, in a time when experts feared we were being numbed by numbers and immunized against tragedy, the death of a single man crowded into our souls and flooded our hearts and filled all the paths of our lives.

— SAUL PETT, *The Associated Press*

In this example, the writer creates a light-hearted tone by mirroring the subject matter — a profile of a hypnotist:

You will read this story.
You will hand on its every word, and you will not get sleepy.
As you proceed, you will learn about hypnosis and a Clive hypno-therapist whose work has led her to the International Hypnosis Hall of Fame.

— MARY ANN LICKTEIG, *The Des Moines* (Iowa) *Register*

Human-Interest Feature The next example is the type of human interest story that Charles Kuralt would have enjoyed reporting. It is also the type of story you might do if you work in a small community for a newspaper or TV station. Chances are you will seek stories about people who are doing interesting or unusual things in your community.

CONVERGENCE COACH

CHARLES KURALT was a consummate storyteller who wrote human-interest features for "On the Road," a series for CBS-TV's "Sunday Morning" show. Long before convergence became a buzzword for a type of journalism merging print, broadcast and the Web, Kuralt epitomized a multimedia journalist. He began his career as a print reporter for the *Charlotte News* in North Carolina, where he won the Ernie Pyle Memorial Award in 1956 for his offbeat human-interest columns. When he joined CBS in 1957, he continued producing human-interest features and later wrote several books about his adventures on the road and the people he met. He loved storytelling about people in newspapers, television and books, but he was a bit baffled by the Web.

"For most of my career I didn't do stories about things that go wrong," he once said. "I did stories about unexpected encounters, back roads, small towns and ordinary folk, sometimes doing something a little extraordinary. I would not argue that it was important to society at large; it was just fun," according to the website Annenberg/CPB learner.org, *www.learner.org/catalog/extras/interviews/ckuralt/ck02.html.*

Kuralt always found something extraordinary in the people and places he visited. "I don't know what makes a good feature story," he said. "I've always assumed that if it was a story that interested or amused me, that it would have the same impact on other people."

Kuralt learned early in his career at CBS that a good feature story for television was dependent on visuals. He said a CBS writer told him that "you must never write a sentence that fights the picture."

"If you're conveying some information that is not in tune with the picture that's on the screen, the viewer's going to be watching the picture and miss entirely what you're saying," Kuralt said. "It's always possible to fashion a sentence, it seems to me, so that it complements rather than struggles with the picture."

Whether you are writing feature stories for print, broadcast or the Web, take Kuralt's advice and find a story that interests you. Seek universal qualities of human interest such as people's hopes, fears, dreams, love, hate, the ability to triumph over adversity or the ability to achieve something special — like a story Kuralt did about a fellow in Indiana who could hold more eggs in his hand than anybody else.

Then, if you want to become a good feature writer for print or broadcast, take some tips from Kuralt, as he related in an interview with the website of Academy of Achievement: "I think good writing comes from good reading. And I think that writers, when they sit down to write, hear in their heads the rhythms of good writers they have read. Sometimes I could even tell you which writer's rhythms I am imitating. It's not exactly plagiarism, but it's just experience. It's falling in love with good language and trying to imitate it."

To read the entire interview with Kuralt, access the Academy of Achievement website at *www.achievement.org/autodoc/page/kur0int-1.*

PRINT VERSION

COOPER LANDING MAN REVELS IN CLOVER COLLECTION

KENAI — Some people believe the Kenai Peninsula is the luckiest place on Earth. Cooper Landing resident Ed Martin Sr. said he believes it is time somebody proved it.

Martin has been finding four-leaf clovers since his childhood and started to save them only two years ago. Since then he has rounded up more than 76,000 clovers.

Some people likely would ask why a person would be so concentrated on how many mutated clovers they found, especially a collection well into five figures. The answer is it has to do with a little competition and a little bit of pride.

Martin has surpassed the previously largest known four-leaf clover collection held by George J. Kaminski, who collected 72,927 clovers within prison grounds in Pennsylvania (Guinness World Records). Kaminski has held the record since April of 1995.

Although Martin's world record-breaking application still is being completed, he is confident it will stand officially. The city of Soldotna, where many of the clovers were found, is handling the paperwork.

Kathy Dawson, assistant to Mayor David Carey, is making sure the project stays within the Guinness office record guidelines. This includes clear documentation in multiple forms.

"This is just amazing. I've got file cabinets full of clovers," Dawson said. "The mayor had kids from the schools counting all these clovers, and there are still more to be counted."

Actually finding 76,000 clovers, let alone a handful, is a difficult task, so Martin shared his secret:

"I look for mutated clovers, ones with four clovers and above. Now, you're not going to believe this, but once I found 880 in one day. I found 90 percent in the Soldotna-Kenai Borough area."

It's a knack, Martin said. "People just don't see what I see," he said.

Martin expects to break a world record, but he says the accomplishment goes beyond that.

"I'm interested in the good that will come out of this," he said. "We have a wonderful country, a wonderful state and community. We are all lucky to be living here. It's just a fact of life. I really think this is the luckiest place in the world, and this will prove it. Maybe this is why the fishing is so good here."

Martin, a former member of the Matanuska-Susitna Borough Assembly, said he hasn't been as involved as he used to be — although competing for a world record in the name of your homeland seems to be a good contribution.

"When you're meeting a challenge, when you do your best in anything, there is a feeling of pride that goes with it," Martin said. "I'm going to keep looking for clovers."

— LAYTON EHMKE, *The Peninsula Clarion*

BROADCAST VERSION:

Note that the reporter's comments in this broadcast story are written around the images and sound bites. The text is written in capital letters and sound bites and the technical crew instructions are in lowercase. A TV script is normally printed in two columns with the directions on the left and text on the right. However, computer programs in broadcast newsrooms automatically format the script into two columns so the reporter just writes the text and directions above it in one column. The reporter's text is in capital letters and the sound bites are in upper- and lowercase in this example:

Anchor introduction:

THE CHANCES OF FINDING A FOUR-LEAF CLOVER ON A PATCH OF GROUND ARE SLIM.

BUT ONE ALASKAN HAS BEATEN THOSE ODDS. . . . MORE THAN 100-THOUSAND TIMES.

IN TONIGHT'S ASSIGNMENT ALASKA, CHANNEL TWO'S SEAN DOOGAN TAKES US TO COOPER LANDING TO MEET THE LUCKIEST MAN ON EARTH.

The package opens with a scene setter; shot of ground and the image of Ed Martin bending over looking for clover on the side of the road.
Reporter Sean Doogan:
WHEN YOU FIRST MEET COOPER LANDING'S ED MARTIN, SENIOR . . . CHANCES ARE YOU WON'T BE SEEING HIS BEST SIDE.

Ed Martin, Sr. (laughs and says): That crazy guy with his rear-end in the air. . . . There's a nice one. . . . I got another one.

More natural sound and image of scene
Reporter Doogan:
SURROUNDED BY A NATURAL CATHEDRAL. . . . ED PREFERS THE VIEW UNDER HIS FEET. . . . HUNTING FOR WHAT MOST PEOPLE WOULD CALL ELUSIVE QUARRY. BUT NOT SO ELUSIVE FOR ED.

Ed Martin sound bite and image of him picking clover: That's a four-leaf. . . . I got another one.

Image of Martin's home and Martin holding Guiness World Record:
Martin sound bite: I have the largest collection of four-leaf clovers in the world. It's real. . . . I didn't print it.

Reporter: MARTIN'S RECORD COLLECTION OF 111-THOUSAND AND 60 CLOVERS WOULD BE MUCH BIGGER. . . IF HE WASN'T SO DETERMINED TO SHARE HIS LUCK.

Martin sound bite: Why count them? I am going to give them away.

Reporter: MARTIN SAYS HE HAS GOTTEN MUCH MORE FROM HIS CLOVER COLLECTION . . . THAN A WORLD RECORD.

Martin sound bite: It seems when I give a four-leaf clover to anyone, I always get a smile. What's wrong with getting a smile from somebody?

Scene of town store with clover on the wall:
Reporter: CLOVER DECORATES THE TOWN STORE.

Sound bite: Glenda Mitchell, co-owner of Cooper Landing General store:
We have some on the wall here; I also have some in my wallet. I would say he's kind of like the good luck guy because when he sees you, he'll always give you one of the four leaf clovers and wish you the best of luck.

Reporter: AS LONG AS MARTIN IS AROUND, IT SEEMS . . . YOU CAN'T TRAVEL THROUGH COOPER LANDING . . . WITHOUT ENDING UP WITH SOME FRESH CLOVER.

Scene: Martin gives girl a four-leaf clover:
Martin sound bite: See . . . how many guys get to see pretty girls all the time . . . see I'm lucky . . . how lucky can a guy get?

Reporter: MARTIN CLAIMS THE CLOVER ITSELF ISN'T WHAT BRINGS GOOD FORTUNE.

Martin sound bite: I've got as many as 1000 in one day. . . . It's an attitude change. . . . When you have a four-leaf clover, you believe in luck, you believe in things happening. That's what luck is all about.

Reporter: EVEN WITH THE RECORD FIRMLY IN HAND . . . MARTIN SAYS HIS SEARCH FOR LUCK ISN'T OVER.

(Video of Martin picking clovers)

Martin sound bite: I will go 'til the good Lord pulls the chain and says, I want you up there.

Reporter:

MARTIN SAYS HE CURRENTLY HAS 165-THOUSAND FOUR-LEAF CLOVERS.

AND WITH THE ODDS OF FINDING A LUCKY PLANT AT 10-THOUSAND TO ONE. . . .

ALL THE CLOVER MARTIN HAS LOOKED THROUGH OVER THE YEARS . . . IF LAID END-TO-END . . . WOULD STRETCH MORE THAN 13-THOUSAND MILES: MORE THAN ENOUGH TO GO FROM THE NORTH POLE TO THE SOUTH POLE.

SEAN DOOGAN, CHANNEL TWO NEWS.

— *Channel 2 News, KTUU-TV,* Anchorage, Alaska

STORYTELLING STRUCTURE

Up to this point in the book, even though you have had many story structures from which to choose, you probably have been organizing your stories by focus and supporting topics or in chronological order. Even with a storytelling approach, you still need to get the focus first. A narrative story can then be arranged topically or chronologically, or it can follow a literary plot form — with a beginning, a middle and an ending called a "climax."

SOCIAL MEDIA

PEOPLE ARE EAGER to share stories. That's why social media sites like Facebook are so successful. You can use social media to enhance your reporting and writing especially when you are trying to gather details and eyewitness accounts for storytelling.

- Use Twitter to post messages about the story you are writing and ask followers to tweet any information they have about the incident, if that is the basis for your story. You can also ask people to send you any photos or videos they have on the subject.

- Use Facebook to search for sources related to your topic.

- Read blogs related to the topic. Ask sources if they have first-hand observations of your topic or a chronology if you are trying to reconstruct events of an incident for narrative writing.

- Use polls or questions with your story to encourage interactive feedback and post share icons.

Nashville resident Amy Frogge uses social media to display pictures she posted on her Facebook page about the flood damage to her home. (Courtesy of the Federal Emergency Management Agency; photo by David Fine.)

"Most news stories are endings without beginnings attached," says Jon Franklin, a Pulitzer Prize–winning writer and author of *Writing for Story*. Reporters miss the dramatic point of view when they concentrate only on the result instead of on the actions leading up to the event. Franklin says stories should be built around a complication and a resolution. In the middle is the development, how the central character gets from the problem to the solution.

If you have a story that lends itself to this kind of plot, your focus would be the complication that the main character has to overcome. The organization could be chronological, starting with the inception of the problem. The middle would be how the character wrestles with the problem, and the climax would be the resolution of the problem.

Writing coach Bruce DeSilva says the writer must determine a resolution to do narrative writing. "That's one of the most important things for people to understand about narrative storytelling: picking the problem," DeSilva said at a Neiman Conference on narrative writing. "When you get to the resolution, the story's over."

"When I write narratives, I always write the ending first. . . . You know where you're going."

— BRUCE DESILVA

DeSilva says that in narrative writing you should write the ending first. "So many people write the lead first. They slave away at the lead and spend lots of time on it before they write the rest of the story. Don't do that. It's almost always a bad idea. . . . When I write narratives, I always write the ending first. Try it. Try it. When you write the ending first, then when you go back to the top of the story and start to write it, you know what your destination is. You know where you're going."

The technique of developing the story in sections, perhaps arranged by points of view, can also work in a narrative story. You can start the story in the middle of the action, as long as you explain to the reader why you are telling this story now (the "so what" factor). This approach is somewhat like using the time frame organization — starting with the present, going to the past, back to the present and on to the future. Regardless of the technique you choose, you should plan your order before you write.

William Blundell, who spent years writing features and profiles for *The Wall Street Journal*, suggests in his book *The Art and Craft of Feature Writing* that features should be organized around "The Laws of Progressive Reader Involvement":

Stage one: Tease me, you devil. (Give the reader a reason to continue reading.)

Stage two: Tell me what you're up to. What is the story really about?

Stage three: Oh yeah? Prove what you said. (Include the evidence to support your theme.)

Stage four: Help me remember it. (Make it clear and forceful, and give it a memorable ending.)

Blundell says features should include the following elements, but not necessarily in this order:

Focus: What is the central theme?

Lead and nut graph: What is the point of the story? (Often, it is introduced anecdotally or descriptively.)

History: How did the problem develop?

Scope: How widespread is the development?

Reasons: Why is this problem or conflict happening now?

Impacts: Who is affected and how?

Moves and countermoves: Who is acting to promote or oppose the development, and what are they doing?

Future: What could happen as a result of the situation and developments?

Blundell also suggests blocking material from any one source in one place in the story, especially if the story has many sources. The organization is not as rigid as the list implies. If the material lends itself to narrative storytelling, it can be told in chronological order or natural story order: beginning, middle, climax, and ending.

Here are some reminders of good storytelling techniques:

- Use concrete details rather than vague adjectives.
- Use dialogue when possible and appropriate.
- Set a scene.
- Use action verbs.
- Observe or ask questions involving all your senses.
- Use show-in-action description.
- Tell a story like a plot, with a beginning, middle and climax. Get a chronology or sequence of events. You may want to use the chronology in all or part of your story. Even if you don't use chronological order, you need to understand the sequence of events.
- Follow Mark Twain's advice: "Don't say the old lady screamed — bring her on and let her scream."

Narrative Storytelling

Courtesy of Martha Miller

Martha Miller, writer

Martha Miller interviewed Vietnam veteran Dan Vickroy several times before she wrote this story about his injuries in the war. Each time he remembered more. She asked him to recall what he was thinking, feeling, saying and experiencing when he was injured, 25 years earlier.

Miller also reconstructed dialogue, based on Vickroy's recollections as he related them to her. The technique is acceptable if you are basing your information on documents and sources, but it is not preferable. If you can't confirm the

ETHICS

ETHICAL DILEMMA: Is it OK to make up quotes? Is it OK to reconstruct scenes in feature stories?

Tom French reconstructed scenes, quotes and dialogue in his story about the murdered woman in one story and the other women in "Angels and Demons" based on court documents and interviews with sources who knew the women. How does that differ from cases of Jayson Blair, a former reporter for *The New York Times*, and Stephen Glass, a former reporter for *The New Republic*, who were both fired in disgrace for fabricating information in their stories?

Ethical values: Credibility, truth, accuracy, fairness

---

dialogue with the original source, you can attribute it to the source who related it. If it is not controversial and you are sure it is accurate, you can reconstruct it as Miller has done.

After she finished all her interviews and filled several notebooks, Miller sat down to write the story. She was overwhelmed. She planned the story and organized it by different periods of Vickroy's life. Then she tried free-writing, just writing what she remembered to get it out of her head. After that she began refining the story, and before she revised her final draft, she read the story aloud.

The part of the story included here, the second section, contains almost no direct attribution. It is all based on Vickroy's recollections. Do you think the story needs attribution in this part? Is the story believable without it?

A SOLDIER'S STORY

BY MARTHA MILLER

Iowa City Press-Citizen

Descriptive beginning for section: sets scene

Two hands lifted the sheet that covered what was left of Dan Vickroy's body.

"You're one tough son of a bitch," the surgeon said from behind a green mask.

Reconstructed dialogue

"I'm a Vickroy," Dan said. "Take me in and sew me up." They did.

Narrative chronological storytelling through Vickroy

Vickroy regained consciousness. He figured he was in the base hospital at Cam Ranh Bay. He could see nothing through the bandages over his eyes, but he could hear the squeaks of rubber soles in the hallway and hushed conversations between doctors as they hurried from bed to bed. It sounded like a busy place.

He was scared, scared to death he was blind.

His ears wanted to believe what he heard, but his eyes would believe what they saw.

The nurses told him they were bandages and that he was strapped down. They told him he had been in bed for almost two weeks. And they told him he had a 104-degree temperature. He knew that. He couldn't stop shivering.

Clues of attribution without direct attribution (he remembered)

As he lay there, his memory returned. He knew the mine had exploded and that he was badly hurt. He remembered waking up twice in surgery. The last time, he felt a surge of pain. He saw a surgeon cutting off his leg with a bone saw.

The days and nights came and went. All the same. Dark.

Scene

This time, it was night. Someone shut off all the lights in his hospital room. The doctors were back. Slowly, they unraveled the gauze around his eyes.

Vickroy held his breath. He opened his eyes and saw a faint light. It burned, but this time it was a good sign. Doctors had worked through the night cleaning his eyes. What he saw made him want to put the bandages back on.

There were wire stitches in his stomach and his right hip. There were tubes in his nose and left arm. Instead of legs, he saw blood-soaked gauze wrapped around two stumps.

The doctors told him what happened: His right leg was blown away by the explosion and his left leg was amputated in surgery; his right arm was amputated below the elbow; and he had lost part of his stomach. Being so close to the mine saved his life; the blast threw him up and out of the way.

His face was intact, saved by that last glance back to camp. Vickroy took the news better than most.

"Psychologically, I was pretty positive." He had no legs, but he did have a wife and new baby. He had married Sharon Kay in 1968 in Tulsa. She was 8½ months pregnant when he left for Vietnam. Danny Ray was born March 28, 1969.

Direct quote with no attribution: speaker understood

Baby pictures were taped, one under the other, on the side of his bed so Vickroy could look at Danny Ray while lying on his back.

Those pictures and thoughts of heading back to the U.S. kept Vickroy's hopes up. But back home, his family wasn't so positive.

Short sentences and pacing

Dan's mother, Louise, was waiting tables in a Cedar Rapids restaurant when an Army officer handed her a telegram. She cried.

Louise had never wanted her youngest to join the service. She wouldn't sign his enlistment papers and couldn't see him off.

Vickroy had started to believe he could live without legs until the day a nurse read him a letter. It had arrived at Cam Ranh Bay several days earlier, but nobody wanted to read it to him.

It was from his wife. She wanted a divorce.

Punch ending to this section: short sentences

"She told me she didn't want half a man."

Reporting techniques: Establishing chronology, gathering detail, asking questions to get source to reconstruct specific events using all senses.

Writing techniques: Organized by sections technique in time sequences; although most of the story takes place in the past, each section deals with a different part of the character's life. Primarily follows chronological order, with cliffhanger endings for each section. Other techniques: short sentences, pacing, dialogue, definitions, description, narration.

SERIAL NARRATIVES

Stories written like novels in chapter form are called "serial narratives." The form is related to the sections technique, but each part is a separate story in a continuing saga. Tom French has been writing his stories in this form for many years.

This style of storytelling has become very popular for long stories presented in a series, with each part published on a separate day. Cliffhangers at the end of each chapter entice the reader to seek the next part of the serial. If the story is compelling enough, readers will come back for the next part. The format is well-suited for the Web, where each chapter can be presented on separate Web pages. It also could work well for reading on small screen mobile media and tablet devices.

A serial narrative needs a compelling plot with these elements:

- A character coping with a problem
- Development of the situation
- Resolution

To write a story in this form, you need to start with a good plot. Organize the story by dividing it into parts with logical breaks, just as in the sections technique. One organization technique is time frames:

- Past and present — what led to the situation and the current status to explain why you are telling the reader this story now
- Past — development of the situation
- Present — return to present
- Future — what lies ahead

Web Storytelling

The Web is an ideal medium for storytelling in many forms. Short segments are preferable to long stories that span several screens. But the Web is a perfect place to experiment with new forms of storytelling, especially nonlinear treatment with links to elements of the story, audio and video to enhance the storytelling.

Storytelling on the Web can be in multimedia format, photo essays, short chunks or serial narratives. Most of all, storytelling can be interactive on the Web. Stories can involve readers by asking them to participate in polls, blogs, answer questions, write their own endings or opinions or submit their own experiences. For examples of innovative storytelling, access Musarium (*www.musarium.com*), a site that offers stories in several creative forms. The Online Journalism Association (*http://journalists.org/*) also features examples of innovative multimedia journalism.

EXERCISES

1 Scene: Go to a busy place on campus or to the cafeteria and listen to people talking. Gather information about the scene. Then write a few paragraphs setting the scene and weaving in dialogue.

2 Analogies: Study some objects on your campus. Write similes and metaphors to describe the objects.

3 Narrative writing exercise: Interview a classmate about any experience he has had, preferably a traumatic or emotional one. If your subject can't think of one, ask him to describe the morning routine from today or yesterday. Imagine that the nut graph is "And then (your subject) disappeared and hasn't been seen since." You will need to ask specific questions, such as what was the person wearing, what color and kind of car was he driving (if a car is involved), what time of day did the events occur, what was he thinking, feeling, doing, saying. Get the person to reconstruct the event exactly as it happened by asking questions about the sequence of events and details. Then write the information in narrative style in a few paragraphs or a brief story.

4 Timed free-writing: This exercise, borrowed from Lucille deView, a former writing coach for *The Orange County* (Calif.) *Register*, requires you to write very quickly — in 10 to 15 minutes. Write a story about a personal experience and let your mind ramble, or write your thoughts about a topic. Remember that you are just getting your thoughts on paper. You can take any words that trigger thoughts — *soup, pizza, cars* — or a topic the instructor gives the class. Some topic suggestions from deView:

The happiest day of my childhood

My favorite assignment

My worst assignment

The most interesting person I interviewed (or know)

A turning point in my life

5 Read well to write well: Copy the leads or some excerpts from three news stories you read this week or copy excerpts from other fiction or nonfiction stories that you consider examples of great writing. Try to find examples of the kind of writing you wish you could write.

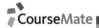

FEATURED ONLINE ACTIVITY   Log on and visit the Writing and Reporting News CourseMate   and take the interactive tutorial quiz on storytelling. *Access available at www.cengagebrain.com.*

Check out the "Sports Story" and "Theatre Feature" scenarios in NewsScene for interactive exercises that will help to reinforce many of the themes presented in this chapter.

COACHING TIPS

Mauricio Ricaldi/Shutterstock.com

Update leads: Tell **what is happening now.**

Use **conversational style** of writing.

Read your copy out loud before recording it or going on the air.

Use **active voice.**

Use **short sentences** — one idea per sentence.

Use **present tense** when possible and appropriate.

Use subject–verb–object order: **Who did what.**

Give **attribution first;** tell who said what before telling what was said.

Good writing counts for more than anything else. . . . I don't care how pretty you are; I don't care how good looking you are or how well you can chat on the air. The fundamental value around here is breaking news and reporting it well. Everything goes back to writing well.

— **ED BENNETT,** assignment editor, KTUU-TV, Channel 2, Anchorage, Alaska

CHAPTER 11
Broadcast News Writing

IT'S 9:15 ON A MONDAY MORNING AND STAFF MEMBERS OF KTUU-TV, Channel 2 in Anchorage are discussing story ideas at their daily planning meeting. It's going to be a busy day. A press conference is scheduled for 10 a.m. about a major donation for the library; a national story about MySpace needs to be localized and more than a dozen American bald eagles covered with slime are being cleaned at the bird rescue center in Anchorage. That's going to be a very visual story.

Reporter Jennifer Zilko is assigned to the eagle story. She heads to the bird rescue center with a photographer. Workers at the Bird Treatment and Learning Center are in a turmoil. They have 18 birds that were flown in by airplane from Kodiak Island, 252 miles south of Anchorage, and they are expecting 13 more in the afternoon. The eagles usually nest outside a fish processing plant in Kodiak, but when a dump truck left the plant with fish guts, about 50 eagles dove into the uncovered rear of the truck in search of an easy meal. Twenty of the eagles were crushed or drowned in the mucky guts. The others were covered with the sticky fish slime, which glued their feathers and prevented them from retaining body heat. Volunteers at the bird rescue center were trying to save the big raptors from certain death by washing them off with Dawn detergent.

Photographer Mike Nederbrock enters the small washing area to videotape the volunteers as they wash an eagle. A press conference follows. At the end of the conference, Zilko asks the director if there is anything else she would like to add.

"If I could give any advice to students, that would be the question to ask: 'Is there anything else you want to share?' And ask them (the sources) to spell their first and last name," Zilko says.

Photographer Mike Nederbrock and reporter Jennifer Zilko watch workers wash an eagle.

Zilko began working at the station while she was a student at the University of Alaska Anchorage. Her first assignment was to convert broadcast scripts into print-style stories for the station's website. "The AP Stylebook was my bible for two years." She says students really need to know AP style even if they are going into broadcast and especially if they are planning to work in public relations.

Before she could become an on-air reporter, however, she received training by shadowing a KTUU reporter on assignment. "Then I came back and wrote my own version of the story," she says. "Almost everything I know, I learned on the job."

PRODUCING A NEWSCAST

Zilko's story is only one of 14 news stories to be squeezed into a 30-minute broadcast that also includes weather, sports and commercial breaks. The process of producing a newscast is complex. It involves several editors and producers who must plan every second of the broadcast and adapt to constant changes throughout the day as news breaks.

Logging the Tape

When Zilko returns from the eagle assignment, Nederbrock hands her his videotape, and she inserts it into a machine so she can watch the video and choose the sound bites she wants to use. This process is called "logging" the tape. She types the complete sound bite with the time listed on the tape. Some TV stations require scripts that just use the first few words and last few words of a sound bite, but at KTUU reporters type the entire sound bite so it can be read on the screen as closed captions for hearing-impaired viewers. This also helps the Web editor so he doesn't have to listen to the tape when he converts her script into an online story, Zilko says.

Jennifer Zilko logs the tape to listen to sound bites.

She types quickly as she listens to the tape. "Grammar is not my best part when I'm logging, so I fix it later," she says. "The goal is not to go over 15 seconds on your bites. If they can say it in a shorter bite, that's better." Sometimes Zilko will ask the photographer to recommend his best shot to open the story, but today he has been called away to another assignment.

Planning a Rundown

The photographer shot 32 minutes of tape, but Zilko will have only one minute and 30 seconds (1:30) for her story for the 30-minute newscast at 5 p.m. and 2 minutes (2:00) for the hour-long 6 p.m. newscast. "It may not seem like very much time, but I write short so it's fine," she says.

The introduction to her story, which she writes for the anchor, will run 15 seconds before the story and 20 seconds for a question-and-answer with the anchor at the end of the story. "I sometimes come in under the time they (the producers) give me, which they like because they're always over."

The producers determine how much time each story can run. Everything is timed to the second in a television newscast. KTUU has two producers: one for the 5 p.m. newscast and one for the 6 p.m. show, but they work together throughout the day.

As soon as the morning planning meeting ends, Aniela Whah starts drafting a schedule called a "rundown" for the 5 p.m. newscast in which she allocates minutes and seconds

Producers Aniela Whah and Tracy Holenport.

for every story. Then she begins writing promotional briefs called "teasers," news briefs of about 20 to 25 seconds that will air a few times a day to encourage viewers to tune into the evening newscast. That's not always easy. A story might fall through or breaking news may force a story to be canceled. Writing teasers is an art.

"You have to keep it really short and not give too much away," says Tracy Holenport, the producer for the 6 p.m. newscast.

Scheduling the stories isn't easy either. Every story has to be timed to the second. "I would say that's the hardest part," Holenport says. If a story runs over the allotted time, she has to subtract time from another report such as weather or sports. The time allocated to news is especially limited. The 30-minute newscast at 5 p.m. has only 14 minutes and 9 seconds for news, and the hour-long newscast at 6 p.m. has 22 minutes for news. Weather runs eight minutes and sports runs six minutes. The rest of the time is allotted to teasers before the breaks and advertisements.

In addition to scheduling the rundowns and writing teasers, the producers write most of the anchor's material and some of the smaller stories, including rewrites of national stories. "I probably end up writing about 10 stories per newscast; it depends on the day," Holenport says. "If we are short of reporters, those days are tough on producers."

Before a show, the producers check all the graphics and names flashed on the screen to make sure they are accurate. The producers work closely with assignment editor Ed Bennett, whose desk is a few feet away from theirs.

Assigning the Stories

Bennett starts his day by checking his e-mail, wire stories, websites and other news media. Then he reviews the 30-day file of story ideas that he keeps in his desk. He prefers keeping paper records of news releases and other items in his "sacred file," a manila folder he keeps on his desk with a warning that it must not be removed. "That way I have an ability to cover the day's news even if the computer crashes," he says.

Page	Story Slug	Segment	Story Writer	Source Tape	Source	Key	Graphic
A16		A	JM		INTV		
A17	ANADARKO GAS DRILLING	BTS	JM		INTV		
A18		QA	JM		INTV		
A19		INTRO	JZ		ROOF	TREATING THE EAGLES	
A20		A	JZ		ROOF		
A21	EAGLE CLEAN UP	B+	JZ		ROOF		
A22		C	JZ		ROOF		
A23		QA	JZ		ROOF		
A24	5P TEASE 2	FOSTER TRIAL SETTLEMENT	AW			in court today	
A25		MYSPACE RULES	AW			myspace	
B0	COM BREAK 1						
B1	REOPEN	((BLUE))					
B2	MYSPACE RULES	A	LT			SAFETY RULES	
B3		B	LT				
B4		A	AB			CASE SETTLED	
B5	FOSTER TRIAL SETTLEMENT	BTS	AB				
B6		GFX	AB				
B7	JUNEAU SESSION ADVANCE	INTRO	WM		FIBR	LEGISLATIVE SESSION	

Courtesy of KTUU–News Channel 2, Anchorage, Alaska

This is page 2 of the rundown sheet for the 5 p.m. newscast. The story slug is Eagle Cleanup; the intro to the story is on p. A19 of the script; the writer is JZ for Jennifer Zilko, and the source is where she will report the story – on the roof of the KTUU building so that the background is outside when she is talking. A teaser to the MySpace story will come just before the commercial break.

He creates an assignment sheet as a starting point for discussion at the morning planning meeting. Then he adds or changes the story list depending on the discussion and story suggestions from the reporters, who are expected to come to the meeting with some story ideas based on their beats.

"I try to have one or two stories every day set up and ready to shoot or in certain cases ready in the can for the air," Bennett says. He can count on some stories every

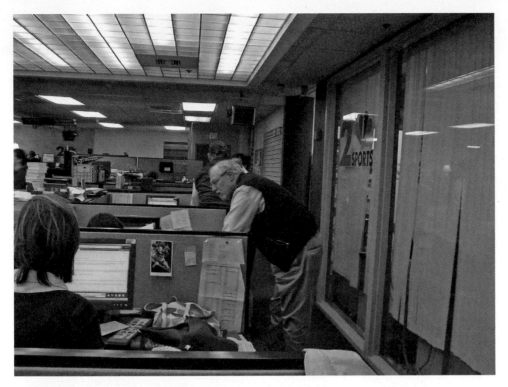

Assignment editor Ed Bennett discusses a story with a reporter.

week because the station airs regular features each day: a business story called "The Bottom Line" on Monday, health news on Tuesday, consumer news on Wednesday, movie reviews on Thursday and an unusual feature about Alaska on Fridays. And Bennett keeps his ears on the police scanner for breaking news.

"Some days it's completely slow; other days are just running and gunning from dawn to dusk so it varies a lot," he says.

He also assigns the photographers to pair with the reporters. "This is TV; the pictures often come first. The availability of a photographer determines when we go on a story or if we go on a story," Bennett says.

He says the Web doesn't affect his job too much, but if a big story breaks, he makes sure the Web editor is aware of it. "The way you cover TV news is to go quickly, go now. It's a very nice marriage with the Web because the Web is also aimed at getting information out there as soon as it comes."

But immediacy can pose problems. The Web editor might hear about a story on the police radio and want to post it, Bennett says. "Sometimes you have to wait for official confirmation. Standard journalism rules do apply to the Web and must be enforced," he says.

In addition to planning the news, Bennett edits scripts along with other newsroom managers. He looks for spelling, accuracy and completeness. He speaks emphatically when he talks about writing:

CONVERGENCE COACH

ERIC ADAMS, WEB editor for KTUU-TV, spends much of his day checking for breaking news to post on the station's website. If a major story breaks, Adams sends e-mail to the 8,000 people who signed up to receive the station's news alerts. "I want to make sure it's something that 8,000 people want in their e-mail," he says. After the reporters write their scripts for the evening newscasts, he checks them to prepare them for the Web. A style editor will rewrite them later in print format with AP style for the Web.

Adams is convinced that the future of journalism is on the Web. "I would say the biggest obstacles that broadcasters need to overcome and be aware of when they are writing stories and reporting for air is that they also need to be cognizant of online elements," Adams says. "They need to think of how they can present their story in an interactive way on a website, which is where people might see it first or might follow up for information as opposed to just writing for broadcast."

Here are some tips to help you prepare for the Web:

- Gather more information than you need for your TV story so that you can offer additional material for the Web. Consider the viewer. What information related to your story would the reader or viewer find helpful?

- When you log in your tape, consider the sound bites and video that will look good on the Web.

- Gather full text of speeches, budgets or other material that would not be in your broadcast story but could go on the Web.

- Consider an interactive question or poll that might work with your story on the Web.

Eric Adams, Web editor for KTUU-TV.

"This is the thing that people don't understand: Good writing counts for more than anything else, at least in this television newsroom — period. I don't care how pretty you are; I don't care how good looking you are or how well you can chat on the air. The fundamental value around here is breaking news and reporting it well. Everything goes back to writing it well."

Here are his recommendations for writing well:

- Clarity and brevity.

- Use plain English.

- Avoid repetition, especially between the reporter's writing and the sound bite.

- Pick sound bites that have emotion. "A reporter can give you the facts," Bennett says. "I don't need people telling you what the facts are. A reporter can do that better and faster."

It's Showtime

It's time for the 5 p.m. show. News director John Tracy heads for the studio where he anchors the 5 p.m. show. Tracy reads from the teleprompter, a machine that contains the scripts, which scroll as he reads.

Jennifer Zilko is told to go up to the station's roof to introduce her story. She's not happy about that. It's 10 degrees below zero today, but the news director likes reporters to appear against a natural background. Zilko's story comes near the middle of the newscast.

Tracy introduces the stories before the reporters deliver them, and at the end of the story, Tracy asks the reporters some questions to provide additional information. That's called a "tag." Usually the reporters write the questions, but today Tracy asks Zilko a background question about her eagle story that she didn't include. Fortunately she knew the answer regarding how many eagles had died. The show ends promptly at 5:30 to be followed by "NBC Nightly News."

News director John Tracy in the studio.

KTUU is an NBC affiliate and one of three network-affiliated television news stations in Anchorage, but it has the largest audience in Alaska. Nationally it is ranked 155 out of 210 markets for television stations.

WRITING TIPS

Here are excerpts from a booklet of writing and reporting guidelines that Tracy wrote for his reporters:

- **Why should I care?** In every story you write, think about the viewer. Why should they care about your story?
- **What's it all about?** You should be able to state your commitment (called the focus sentence throughout this book) with a simple sentence containing a subject, verb and object. Who is doing what to whom?
- **So what?** Does your story meet the "so what" test? Does it address a larger issue? Did I learn anything new by watching the story?
- **Attribution:** Who said what? If you are going to state anything but the most obvious fact, back it up with attribution. We don't use unnamed sources without the permission of the news director.
- **A good lead:**
  - Captures the viewer's attention
  - Is conversational
  - Uses active voice
  - Moves the story forward

- **Guillotine the Gimmes:** In the body of your story, get rid of the information that people already know. Focus on what they don't know. What's new?

- **Write to the corners:** It still amazes me when reporters *describe* the video to me. "The suspect was visibly upset." No kidding. I can see the picture. Your words should complement the video, not describe it.

- **Bounce the babble:** Don't write like a police report. People are caught, not apprehended.

- **Sound:** Use it whenever you can. It takes the viewers out of the studio and puts them at the story.

- **Sound bites:** Write to them. They shouldn't come out of nowhere, and they should not repeat what you said leading up to the bite.

- **The end:** All good stories build to a strong finish. You can only finish strong if you know how you are going to finish in the field. Your story should leave the viewer feeling something. A successful story evokes an emotional response. Does your story close the circle? Sometimes you can end your story by returning to the start of the story, having answered the question you posed.

BROADCAST VS. NEWSPAPER AND WEB WRITING

Good writing is crucial in every area of the media, including public relations, which involves writing for print, broadcast and the Web. Here are a few major differences between print and broadcast writing:

Attribution:

Always first in broadcast: The bird rescue center's director says one of the eagles died.

First or last for print and the Web: One of the eagles died last night, said the director of the bird rescue center.

Active Voice: Who is doing what, not what was done to whom. Active voice is preferable for print but even more necessary for broadcast.

Active: Volunteers at the center washed the eagles with Dawn detergent.

Passive: The eagles were washed with Dawn detergent by the volunteers at the center.

Present Tense: Use when possible for broadcast; past tense is more common in print and the Web.

Present: One eagle remains in critical condition.

Past: One eagle remained in critical condition.

Update Leads: Use the latest information. This technique is recommended for all media, but especially for broadcast and the Web.

Old news: Eighteen eagles were flown to the bird rescue center Saturday.

Updated: Eighteen eagles are recovering at the bird rescue center, where they were flown Saturday.

Broadcast Script Format

Broadcast scripts are written in two columns, with directions for the technical crew on the left and the story text on the right. Most newsrooms use a computer program that automatically formats the scripts. The reporter's text is usually in capital letters, while the sound bites are in uppercase and lowercase letters. Sources for sound bites are identified by a machine called a "character generator," which produces titles that are superimposed under the video to identify the speaker.

TV stations have different methods of writing directions. Some stations identify sound bites as SOT, meaning sound on tape. At KTUU each sound bite is on a different tape so the bites are identified as A roll on one tape, B roll on another tape and so on. Many of the terms previously used in scripts are changing. The script should contain a slug (a one- or two-word title), which is usually assigned by the producers. The reporter's copy is usually written in capital letters, and the sound bites are typed in uppercase and lowercase letters. While you no longer have to be concerned about typing directions in columns, you should not split or hyphenate words at the end of a sentence. Remember that the script will be read on a teleprompter, and the anchor or reporter needs to see the whole word.

Here is Jennifer Zilko's script about the eagle story; compare it with the print story that follows from the *Anchorage Daily News*.

EAGLE CLEANUP-PKG

SHOW EAGLES IN SOAP
TREATING THE EAGLES
Reporter — Jennifer Zilko
Anchor — John

                                     {***JOHN***}

Readrate 13:75   THE BIRD TREATMENT AND LEARNING CENTER IS TRYING TO SAVE THE LIVES OF MORE THAN A DOZEN EAGLES.
        SINCE LAST NIGHT 18 BALD EAGLES HAVE BEEN BROUGHT TO THE CENTER AFTER DIVING INTO THE BACK OF A TRUCK FULL OF FISH SLIME IN KODIAK…AND MORE ARE ON THE WAY.

TAKE: TAKE SPLIT

{***TAKE SPLIT***}
AND AS CHANNEL 2'S JENNIFER ZILKO TELLS US — WASHING AMERICA'S CHERISHED BIRDS IS A LENGTHY PROCESS.
JENNIFER?

<shot- EAGLE CLEANUP>

JOHN — ACCORDING TO VOLUNTEERS, IT TAKES ABOUT AN HOUR TO CLEAN EACH EAGLE.

TAKE: A ROLL (Jennifer speaking)
(also called SOT-Sound on tape)

(**A ROLL)
FIRST EACH BIRD IS DUNKED INTO A WARM BATH OF SOAPY WATER.
THE SECRET WEAPON?
DAWN DISH SOAP.
AFTER BEING METICULOUSLY SCRUBBED, THEY'RE THEN RINSED.
VOLUNTEERS GO THROUGH EVERY FEATHER ON THE EAGLE TO MAKE SURE ALL THE SOAP IS WASHED OUT.
BUT EVEN AFTER THE WASH — SOME OF THE EAGLES AREN'T DONE YET.

TAKE: B ROLL (also called SOT)
AT: 12:53
TO: 13:03
DURATION: 0:10
(This is the sound bite and the time on the tape plus the CG)
Cindy Palmatier, director of Avian care, Bird Treatment Center

{***B ROLL***}

<12:53 We have to wait until they're dry and then we go through a sniff test. If they smell like a wet eagle, you're good.

TAKE: AUDIO CUE

{***AUDIO:CUE***}
IF THE EAGLE SMELLS LIKE FISH, IT IS SPOT WASHED AGAIN.
THE REASON IT'S SO CRITICAL TO GET ALL THE OIL OFF IS THAT EAGLES REGULATE THEIR TEMPERATURE WITH THEIR FEATHERS AND THE OIL INHIBITS THAT ABILITY — MAKING THEM SUSCEPTIBLE TO HYPOTHERMIA.
BUT EVEN THOUGH IT'S GOOD FOR THEM SOME OF THESE EAGLES DON'T EXACTLY LIKE HAVING A BATH.
ONE VOLUNTEER GOT NIPPED TWICE TODAY.

TAKE: C ROLL (third sound bite)
AT: 27:31
TO: 27:38
DURATION: 0:07
CG — Gina Hollomon, volunteer, Bird Treatment Center

{***C ROLL***}

<27:31 No hard feelings, none whatsoever. If I was being manhandled, I might nip myself.

TAKE: LOSE IT

{***LOSE IT***}

THE CENTER SAYS EACH OF THESE EAGLES EATS ABOUT 400 GRAMS OF SALMON A DAY SO THEY'RE ASKING FOR PEOPLE TO DONATE IF YOU HAVE SOME EXTRA SALMON IN YOUR FREEZER.

Anchor: JOHN
Readrate 13.75

{***QUESTION***}

TAKE: QUESTION

JENNIFER — WHAT CONDITION ARE THE EAGLES IN AT THE CENTER?

TAKE: ANSWER

{***ANSWER***}

   ACCORDING TO CINDY PALMATIER, THEY'RE ALL DOING WELL EXCEPT FOR ONE OF THE BIRDS.

   THE CENTER DEEMED THAT EAGLE IN CRITICAL CONDITION BECAUSE IT'S HAVING A LOT OF PROBLEMS WITH TEMPERATURE REGULATION.

   THE CENTER WAS EXPECTING TO GET 13 MORE EAGLES IN TODAY BUT THE WEATHER IN KODIAK WAS TOO BAD TO FLY THEM TO ANCHORAGE.

Web Versions

The story posted on KTUU's website was offered in video, not text. This is how the Web page appeared after the eagle story aired.

Courtesy of KTUU-News Channel 2, Anchorage, Alaska

Courtesy of Anchorage Daily News, Anchorage, Alaska

The website for the *Anchorage Daily News* also featured the eagle story with a photo slide show:

Newspaper Version

Here is how the story was reported in the local newspaper, the *Anchorage Daily News*. Note that in the print version of the story, the reporter used description that would be unnecessary with video. Also notice that the print version is more thorough than the broadcast version, and attribution is usually at the end of the sentence.

SLIMED EAGLES GET BATHS, TLC IN ANCHORAGE

SURVIVORS: 20 others died in a truckload of fish waste.

The hot, humid air inside the warehouse smacked of fishy funk, giving away the 18 bald eagles tucked into kennels inside. They, along with 13 others still in Kodiak, were the lucky ones.

About 50 eagles swarmed into an uncovered dump truck at a Kodiak processing plant Friday, leaving 20 dead after being either crushed or drowned in the fish-gut sludge inside, according to the U.S. Fish and Wildlife Service. Now the survivors need a bath.

"We've never seen a flood of bald eagles like this before," said Megan Pool, events coordinator at Anchorage's Bird Treatment and Learning Center. "It's definitely more than we've dealt with at one time, ever."

The last batch of surviving eagles was scheduled to arrive Monday afternoon but could not get off the ground in Kodiak because of inclement weather, Pool said. The U.S. Coast Guard hopes to fly them up today, she said.

The influx has strained the resources of the center, which has three paid staff members and about 60 volunteers, Pool said. Despite the strain, volunteers were on track to finish hour-long baths for each of the raptors on hand by late Monday, she said.

Cleaning the eagles requires scrubbing them off with unscented Dawn dish detergent to remove the fish oil and slime that soaked their feathers, then rinsing them in a wood-framed structure covered in plastic to keep things hot and humid.

After they are rinsed, the birds are placed into individual kennels in a warming room, where propped-up hair dryers blow hot air on them, though they continue to need supervision.

"They can overheat, now that they're clean," said Barbara Callahan of the International Bird Rescue Research Center. "These birds are exhausted, and they really couldn't be more stressed."

After they dry, the birds are re-evaluated to see if they are completely rid of the oil, which keeps them wet and reduces their ability to retain their body heat. Those that still need scrubbing are spot-cleaned, particularly under their wings and on their upper legs, Pool said.

While most of the eagles looked understandably irritated at the process, one, No. 08-03, remained in critical condition, its listless body leaning against the back of the dog kennel where it was drying. Its blood work — yes, the eagles are having lab work done — didn't show any problems, but its body temperature remained low, Pool said.

Like all the rest, No. 08-03 is a male, said Mary Bethe Wright, a board member at the center. Nobody knows why female eagles escaped the stinky fish waste, but the women workers seemed to enjoy the gender bias.

"I don't think we have any idea. The females were smarter, maybe," Wright said with a laugh.

The opportunistic scavengers eat about a pound of salmon a day at the center, which cared for 44 bald eagles all of last year and is asking for help with heating costs — the building is being kept near 80 degrees — and donations of unprocessed salmon.

Recovered eagles should be released in a few days, Pool said, but getting them back down to Kodiak may be a challenge because of weather and expenses. Even if they make it to Kodiak, they won't be released in the same area, she said.

"We always try to release the birds as close to where we found them as possible, but we're not going to release 30 birds back at the processing plant," she said.

The fish and wildlife service is investigating to see if Ocean Beauty Seafoods will face charges because of the incident. In general, a first offense of this type would be a misdemeanor, said spokesman Bruce Woods, though intent factors into the decision about whether charges will be filed.

In a prepared statement, company spokesman Tom Sunderland said the plant adhered to its normal policies for transporting fish waste. The shipment was bound for a fish meal plant, and company procedures call for the load to be covered after the truck exits the garage, Sunderland said.

"In this case, the birds went to the waste trailer before the cover could be applied," he said.

— JAMES HALPIN, *Anchorage Daily News*

ETHICS

RADIO TELEVISION Digital News Association (RTDNA) is the largest group for electronic journalists. Although many television stations have their own codes of ethics, the RTDNA code of ethics serves as a guide for the broadcast industry. Here are a few of the main principles:

- Professional electronic journalists should recognize that their first obligation is to the public.

- Professional electronic journalists should pursue truth aggressively and present the news accurately, in context and as completely as possible.

- Professional electronic journalists should present the news fairly and impartially, placing primary value on significance and relevance.

- Professional electronic journalists should present the news with integrity and decency, avoiding real or perceived conflicts of interest, and respect the dignity and intelligence of the audience as well as the subjects of news.

- Professional electronic journalists should defend the independence of all journalists from those seeking influence or control over news content.

TEASERS AND LEAD-INS

A teaser, also called a "tease," is a short blurb to entice viewers to tune in or stay tuned to a newscast. It is broadcast during the day before the newscast or during the newscast before a commercial break. Don't tease the regular segments in general terms like weather and sports; tease something interesting or unique in your program that will affect the viewers. Write a tease as though you were telling a friend, "Guess what?" or "You won't want to miss this!" Teasers can include audio and video.

Here is a mid-day tease of two items for the 5 p.m. newscast on KTUU:

GOOD AFTERNOON. HERE'S WHAT'S GOING ON AT THIS HOUR.
LAWMAKERS ARE BEGINNING TO ARRIVE IN JUNEAU . . . AHEAD OF TOMORROW'S START OF THE LEGISLATIVE SESSION. WE'LL TAKE YOU TO THE CAPITOL FOR A PREVIEW TONIGHT.
AND, MORE THAN 45 STATES SIGN ON WITH NEW RULES TO KEEP TEENS SAFE FROM SEXUAL PREDATORS ON MYSPACE.
THE STORY . . . TONIGHT ON CHANNEL TWO NEWS.

And here is a tease that the news anchor read before the commercial break that came in the middle of the 5 p.m. newscast after the eagle story on KTUU.

SOCIAL MEDIA

THE USE OF SOCIAL media has soared in TV newsrooms in the past few years. More than 75 percent of TV newsrooms use social media on their websites and 68 percent incorporate this type of media into their storytelling, according to an annual survey conducted by Bob Papper, chair of the Department of Journalism, Media Studies and Public Relations at Hofstra University. Most of the 1,355 TV newsrooms in the survey have pages on Twitter and Facebook, Papper reported. He said that news directors use the social media sites to get viewer feedback and comments and requests for pictures from viewers. Other station directors reported that they use social media to develop tips, story ideas and contacts.

In 2010 the Radio Television Digital News Association issued a new set of guidelines for ethics relating to social media. Although social media sites pose some unique dilemmas for journalists, the association recommends that journalists should "uphold the same professional and ethical standards for fairness, accuracy, truthfulness and independence as they do on air and on all digital platforms." You can find the full set of guidelines on the association's website at *http://www.rtdna.org/ pages/best-practices/ethics.php.*

Here are some of the RTDNA guidelines unique to social media:

- "Remember that what's posted online is open to the public (even if you consider it to be private). Personal and professional lives merge online.

- "Consider whom you 'friend' on sites like Facebook or follow on Twitter. You may believe that online 'friends' are different from other 'friends' in your life, but the public may not see it that way.

- "Be especially careful when registering for social network sites. Pay attention to how the public may interpret Facebook information that describes your relationship status, age, sexual preference and political or religious views.

- "Avoid posting photos or any other content on any website, blog, social network or video/photo sharing website that might embarrass you or undermine your journalistic credibility."

> COMING UP ON THE 5 O'CLOCK REPORT . . . TWO FOSTER CARE TEENS SUED THE STATE SAYING IT DID NOT KEEP THEM SAFE. NOW BOTH SIDES AGREE TO A SETTLEMENT.
> AND KEEPING KIDS SAFE ONLINE . . . MYSPACE JOINS FORCES WITH 49 STATES INCLUDING ALASKA TO CHANGE THE RULES.

Other introductions to teasers before the commercial break can be phrases such as "Just ahead," "Still to come" or "When we come back . . . ."

Sometimes fragments can get the point across better than complete sentences.

> In a moment . . . sex behind bars. A scandal brewing in Georgia.
>
> *— CNN*

Lead-ins: The anchor reads a lead into a package by a reporter. The lead-in should give the essence of the story and sometimes the context for how it occurred. It should not repeat the reporter's lead. It ends with a statement that the reporter, cited by name, has more information or just the reporter's name as in this example:

MANY WOMEN EXERCISE HARD TO GET IN SHAPE. BUT A NEW STUDY SAYS TOO MUCH EXERCISE CAN OFTEN LEAD TO SERIOUS HEALTH PROBLEMS FOR WOMEN. ILEANA BRAVO TELLS US HOW SOME FEMALE COLLEGE ATHLETES COULD SUFFER FROM EATING DISORDERS AS A RESULT. . . .

— *NBC News Channel*

WRITING FOR RADIO

Writing for radio news follows many of the same principles as writing for television news, but the copy is shorter. Stories can be more like the TV teasers in length. A radio newscast may total about 90 seconds with six or seven stories unless it is National Public Radio, which offers longer stories. A typical story might contain fewer than 100 words. And because you can't show video; you should create word pictures by describing the scene.

Peter King, CBS News Radio correspondent, covers complicated stories in a clear, concise way. In an interview with Al Tompkins, the Poynter Institute's broadcast leader, King offers this advice for writing radio news:

"You have to be able to pick out the most important information and not get caught up in the minutiae. And you have to keep it simple. It's a big mistake to try to cram too much information into too little time, which is why you have to prioritize and do it quickly."

King says most of his sentences last only five to six seconds on the radio. "My rule of thumb is, 'If it seems awkward and long when you say it aloud, it probably sounds that way to the listener.' I try to keep each sentence focused on a single thought, and keep it simple. And keep in mind: You have to keep asking what the listener will and won't be able to digest."

Scripts for radio can be written in uppercase and lowercase letters instead of all capital letters, depending on the preference of the radio station. The following terms are used in radio:

Reader: a script that a newscaster reads without any background noise or comments from sources.

Actuality: the equivalent of a sound bite.

Natural sound: also called "ambient" sound. This is background sound, the same term that's used in television news.

Wrap: a story from a reporter that may include actualities.

Voicer: a story a reporter reads; it may contain natural sound but does not include actualities.

Here are examples of public service announcements written for radio:

30-SECOND SCRIPT

Soon, all over-the-counter medicines will have one thing in common: simplicity. That's because all over-the-counter medicines will feature new, easier-to-read labels that clearly show their ingredients, uses, warnings and directions. Because if there's one symptom we all want to relieve, it's confusion. For more information, call the Food and Drug Administration at 1-888-INFO-FDA. Again, that's 1-888-INFO-FDA. The new label — It's clearly better.

— Food and Drug Administration

15-SECOND SCRIPT

Tired of being confused when comparing over-the-counter medicines? Soon, all over-the-counter medicines will feature new, easier-to-read labels. For more information, call the Food and Drug Administration at 1-888-INFO-FDA. The new label — It's clearly better.

— Food and Drug Administration

BROADCAST STYLE

Punctuation

Avoid quotation marks. Generally, sound bites take the place of quotations. But if you want to quote someone, write out the word *quote* in this way: "She said . . . quote . . . this situation is impossible" or "and these are her exact words. . . ." Don't end the quote by saying "unquote." The reader's emphasis should make the end of the quote clear.

Limit punctuation to the comma, period, question mark and dash.

Numbers

Round off numbers when possible. Write out the numbers one through nine; use numerals for numbers over 10. Write out hundred, thousand, million, billion and trillion.

Write numbers to be read as follows: 13-hundred, two-thousand, 14-thousand, one-million, 17-million. More complicated numbers would be written this way: 320-thousand, not 320,000; 15-million-230-thousand, not 15,230,000.

Spell out fractions: one-half, three quarters.

For decimals, write out the word *point:* "It comes to 17-point-two-million dollars." Write out the word *dollars* also, instead of using the symbol.

There are some exceptions. Addresses, telephone numbers and time of day are written in numerals, even if the figures are lower than 10: "She lives at 5 Westbrooke Avenue"; "The accident occurred at 10:30 this morning" (avoid *a.m.* and *p.m.*); "The telephone number to call for information is 5-5-5-1-2-3-4" (separate the numerals with dashes so they are easier to read).

Limit the Use of Numbers They can be numbing, especially to the ear. Use percentages to give comparisons when possible. If you must use numbers, round them off and reinforce them with a graphic. Say "320-million dollars," not "320-million-122-thousand-three-hundred-44 dollars." Whenever possible, use an analogy to help viewers visualize numbers. The world's largest oil tanker is 15-hundred feet, equivalent to five football fields.

Names and Titles Spell difficult pronunciations of names and locations phonetically. Some anchors prefer only the phonetic spelling instead of the real name followed by the phonetic pronunciation. John Blum would be written as it is pronounced — John Bloom. Identify a person's title before the name: "State Attorney General John Lawmaker is pleased with the results of a crackdown on fraudulent coal dust testing," not "John Lawmaker, state attorney general, is pleased with the results. . . ."

Use Contractions with Caution Write them out. Let the anchors contract them if they want to. Avoid *can't*. It may sound too much like *can*.

Omit Needless Words Words like *that* and *which* aren't always needed.

Timing of Copy Broadcast scripts use 1:30 for one minute and 30 seconds; 2:00 for two minutes and so on.

STORY STRUCTURE

Like a newspaper story, a broadcast story needs a clear focus, a lead, a body and an ending. Unlike newspaper writing, however, broadcast writing should be geared to audio and video.

Bob Dotson, an NBC correspondent awarded more than 70 times for his good writing, calls the focus sentence a "commitment" statement. It is still a one-sentence summary of the story, but it is centered more on visual impact — what you want the audience to take away from the report. Provide the commitment visually.

In speeches he makes to journalism groups, Dotson offers these tips:

Beginning: Write to your pictures first. Build your lead around a visual that foreshadows the story to come.

Middle:

Usually no more than three to five points, which you prove visually.

Use strong natural sound to let the viewer experience what happened.

Use people engaged in compelling action that is visual.

Use surprises to keep viewers involved and lure uninterested viewers.

Use short sound bites.

Ending: Build to a strong ending throughout the story, and make it visual. Make your viewers care about the story and the people.

Here are some ways to structure each part of a package, a story that contains video and sound bites:

Leads

An anchor will introduce your story, but every story in a package needs its own lead. Max Utsler, a broadcast journalism professor at the University of Kansas, said the No. 1 consideration for a lead is that it must fit the pictures the viewer sees. "Good television writing is not the craftsmanship of words; it is the presentation of the words and pictures fitting together," he said.

Once you have decided which images to use at the beginning of your package, you can decide whether the story needs a hard or soft lead. Feature stories may take softer leads; a breaking-news story calls for a direct approach. In all cases, you must get to the focus — the nut graph — very quickly, generally by the second or third sentence.

Put a human face on the story whenever possible: Try to find someone personally affected by the issue. You can start with the specific, using a person first, and then going to the nut graph:

IRIS DUNCAN WOKE UP ONE MORNING AND SAID SHE THOUGHT SOMEONE HAD PUT WAXED PAPER OVER HER EYES.

SOUND BITE: IT WAS ALL FUZZY AND CLOUDY AND I COULDN'T SEE. I HAD NO IDEA WHAT WAS WRONG.

SHE WENT TO HER DOCTOR THAT AFTERNOON. SHE LEARNED SHE HAD GLAUCOMA. THE DISEASE STRIKES ONE OF EVERY 200-THOUSAND PEOPLE.

Starting with a general statement and going to a specific person is less effective:

GLAUCOMA STRIKES ONE OF EVERY 200-THOUSAND PEOPLE.
IRIS DUNCAN IS ONE OF THEM. SHE WOKE UP ONE MORNING AND SAID SHE THOUGHT SOMEONE HAD PUT WAXED PAPER OVER HER EYES.

The You Voice: Not all stories directly affect viewers' lives. But when possible, try to stress the impact within the first few sentences. Use an element that will make viewers care or understand why this story is important, unusual or of human interest. Don't be afraid to use the pronoun "you," especially in consumer stories, to heighten impact. Instead of writing a story about a drought in California that will cause lettuce prices to increase, try this approach:

YOU'RE ABOUT TO PAY MORE FOR YOUR SALAD. A DROUGHT IN CALIFORNIA IS RAISING THE PRICE OF LETTUCE.

Impact Leads: Lead with the effect on viewers as in the previous lead. An impact lead often uses the you voice.

IF YOU TOOK YOUR CAR TO SEARS FOR REPAIRS IN THE PAST TWO YEARS, YOU MAY GET A REFUND.

THE COMPANY AGREED TO SETTLE CHARGES THAT IT CHEATED CUSTOMERS BY DOING SHODDY OR UNNECESSARY CAR REPAIR WORK.

AN ESTIMATED 12-THOUSAND-500 MISSOURIANS WILL BE ELIGIBLE TO RECEIVE 50-DOLLAR CREDIT COUPONS FOR ANY SEARS MERCHANDISE.

Advance the Lead: When you can, advance the lead by stressing the next step to gain immediacy:

Immediacy: TWO PEOPLE REMAIN IN SERIOUS CONDITION FOLLOWING A CAR ACCIDENT THIS AFTERNOON.

No immediacy: TWO PEOPLE WERE INJURED IN A CAR ACCIDENT TODAY.

Focus on a Person: The focus-on-a-person lead works as well in broadcast as in print, especially for a feature or a news story that the anchor introduces with a hard-news lead-in. Like *The Wall Street Journal* formula, this type of lead goes from the specific to the general. The person is one of many affected by the problem.

JUDY AND JOE WESTBROOK SPENT THE MORNING CLEANING UP THE FURNITURE IN THEIR FRONT YARD. THE BLUE RIVER HAD OVERFLOWED ITS BANKS AND FORCED ITS WAY INTO THEIR INDEPENDENCE HOME.

MORE THAN 25 FAMILIES SHARE THEIR PREDICAMENT. LATE THIS AFTERNOON ALL OF THOSE FAMILIES WERE AWAITING WORD ABOUT THEIR FLOOD INSURANCE CLAIMS.

Mystery-Teaser Lead: The mystery-teaser lead is another effective soft-lead technique, as long as you don't keep the viewer wondering what the story is about for too long. You must get to the point within the first few sentences.

IN SOME WAYS IT LOOKS LIKE AN ORDINARY CAMP. IT HAS HIKING TRAILS, A SWIMMING POOL AND TENNIS COURTS.

BUT YOU DON'T HAVE TO WORRY ABOUT WHAT CLOTHES TO WEAR. IN FACT, THIS IS ONE OF THE FEW PLACES WHERE YOU'LL FEEL OUT OF PLACE WEARING CLOTHES.

AT THIS CAMP NEAR DENVER MEN AND WOMEN OF ALL AGES FROLIC IN THE NUDE.

SOUND BITE: NUDISM IS ABOUT THE ONLY RECREATION THAT ANYBODY CAN DO WHETHER THEY'RE RICH OR POOR. WE ALL SHARE IN THE SAME SATIS-FACTION, SO IT'S A VERY GREAT EQUALIZER.

— Adapted from NBC News Channel

Body of the Story

As with all story structures, you must identify your focus first. Then jot down the order of your supporting points — facts or quotes from sources in sound bites.

Limit transitions. One point should follow another one naturally. You have little time for wasted words or redundant transitions that parrot what the source will say in a sound bite. If you need transitions from the present to the past in your story, you can start the sentence with the time element — "yesterday" or "earlier today," for example.

One common transition device in broadcast news is the key-word technique, picking up on a word in the last sentence and repeating it in the next. It's also a useful technique for bridging thought from one story to the next in the newscast. In this example, the reporter uses the word "shoes" as a transition device for the next paragraph:

THE NIKE COMMERCIAL TOUTS MICHAEL JORDAN'S BASKETBALL PROWESS. SPIKE LEE SAYS IT'S GOTTA BE THE SHOES.

BUT MIKE AND HIS BUDDIES WOULDN'T EVEN HAVE TO WEAR SHOES TO WALTZ TO THE OLYMPIC GOLD.

Most of the basic news elements — who, what, when, where, how and so what — must be included in the story but not all in the same paragraph. In broadcast writing, placement of points of emphasis for these elements differs from print.

Where: Because most radio and television stations reach such a broad audience, the location of a story is even more important in broadcast than in print. Broadcast reports can superimpose the name of the location on the screen, but you also need to say it in the story. If the story follows a series of other stories from different regions, you might start this way:

IN PAWTUCKET, RHODE ISLAND, POLICE ARE LOOKING INTO THE SUSPICIOUS DEATH OF A 15-MONTH-OLD BABY.

When: Almost all broadcast stories have a "today" element. Avoid using a.m. or p.m. If the specific time element is important, say something like "An earthquake struck Southern California at 7:15 this morning"; or "earlier today" is sufficient. Place your time element after the verb, which is a more natural, conversational order.

Awkward: AT LEAST FIVE PEOPLE TODAY WERE ARRESTED IN AN ANTI-ABORTION PROTEST OUTSIDE A MILWAUKEE CLINIC.

Preferred: AT LEAST FIVE PEOPLE WERE ARRESTED TODAY IN AN ANTI-ABORTION PROTEST OUTSIDE A MILWAUKEE CLINIC.

Who: Avoid using unfamiliar names in a lead and too many names in a story. When you have video sound bites, you may not even need the name in the story. The person can be identified by a superimposed title under his image in the taped segment. For delayed identification, follow the same guidelines as for print journalism. Identify the person by an age, a location, an occupation or some other generic identifier. Then follow with the person's name. If you do have to identify a speaker, use his title before the name:

Say: BROWARD COUNTY SHERIFF JOHN LAW SAID TODAY HE WOULD NOT SEEK RE-ELECTION WHEN HIS TERM ENDS NEXT YEAR.
Do not say: JOHN LAW, SHERIFF OF BROWARD COUNTY, SAID TODAY . . .

Here are some ways of organizing broadcast stories:

Problem/Solution: The most common structure starts with a statement of the problem, provides support in sound bites and facts, offers background and discusses the solutions if any exist. It often ends with the next step in the action.

Time Sequence: A story may lend itself to order by time. Because broadcast stories need immediacy, the time sequence is usually a reverse chronology that starts with the present action, goes to the past (background) and ends with a future element. Here is an example of reverse chronology:

Present ANIMAL-RIGHTS ACTIVISTS ARE PROTESTING THIS MORNING OUTSIDE THE PITTSBURGH HOSPITAL WHERE DOCTORS TRANSPLANTED A LIVER FROM A BABOON TO SAVE A MAN'S LIFE.

Past (background) ABOUT 15 PROTESTERS CARRIED SIGNS AND CHANTED AT THE ENTRANCE TO THE UNIVERSITY OF PITTSBURGH MEDICAL CENTER.

ONE MEMBER OF THE PITTSBURGH ANIMAL ACTIVISTS SAYS THEY DON'T BELIEVE ONE SPECIES SHOULD BE SACRIFICED FOR ANOTHER.

DOCTORS SAY IF THEIR PATIENT CONTINUES TO RECOVER FOR THE NEXT MONTH OR MORE, THEY'LL DO THREE MORE OF THE SAME TRANSPLANTS. *Future*

Hourglass: This structure is a type of time sequence. However, you start with a hard-news summary lead and then rebuild the story chronologically.

Summary lead

A TOXIC CHEMICAL SPILL NEAR SUPERIOR, WISCONSIN, FORCED HUNDREDS OF RESIDENTS FROM TWO CITIES TO FLEE THEIR HOMES. AT LEAST TWO CHILDREN RECEIVED HOSPITAL TREATMENT. A HOSPITAL OFFICIAL SAYS MORE PEOPLE WILL NEED TREATMENT.

Beginning of chronology

THE PROBLEMS BEGAN THIS MORNING WHEN 13 FREIGHT CARS DERAILED JUST OUTSIDE SUPERIOR. ONE BURLINGTON NORTHERN CAR FELL INTO THE NEMADJI (NEH-MA'-JEE) RIVER, SPILLING SOME OF ITS CARGO OF BENZENE. BENZENE IS A FLAMMABLE SOLVENT, AND ITS FUMES CAN CAUSE HALLUCINATIONS, DIZZINESS AND COUGHING.

IN SUPERIOR AND NEIGHBORING DULUTH, MINNESOTA, OFFICIALS ORDERED THE EVACUATION OF HUNDREDS OF HOMES WITHIN A MILE OF THE RIVER. AND THE COAST GUARD SAYS IT'S PLACED A BOOM ACROSS SUPERIOR BAY TO PREVENT THE BENZENE FROM SPREADING.

Circle: Envision your story as a circle. The main point is the lead. All supporting points should relate to the focus in the lead. Unlike an inverted pyramid, where points are placed in descending order of importance, in a circular construction, each part of the story is equally important. Your ending can refer back to a point in the lead, as in this example about a water problem in a Kansas community:

Lead

IF YOU LIVE NEAR BALDWIN CITY, YOU MAY WANT TO AVOID DRINKING THE WATER TONIGHT.

Supporting points

THE KANSAS DEPARTMENT OF HEALTH AND ENVIRONMENT IS WARNING FOLKS IN WATER DISTRICT NO. 2 IN DOUGLAS COUNTY ABOUT THE WATER. OFFICIALS FOUND BACTERIA IN THE WATER THAT MAY BE HARMFUL.

SOUND BITE (from Greg Crawford, an official with the Kansas Department of Health and Environment):

THESE ARE INDICATOR BACTERIA, WHICH MAY INDICATE THE PRESENCE OF MORE SERIOUS BACTERIA. BACTERIA CAN CAUSE A NUMBER OF GASTROINTESTINAL PROBLEMS. AND WE WOULD LIKE PEOPLE TO PREVENT THOSE PROBLEMS BY BOILING THEIR WATER OR USING BOTTLED WATER OR PERHAPS TREATING THEIR WATER WITH CLOROX OR OTHER LIQUID BLEACH.

CRAWFORD SAYS BACTERIA COME FROM DEAD ANIMALS. UNTIL OFFICIALS CAN CLEAR UP THE PROBLEMS, PEOPLE IN THE AREA SHOULD TAKE PRECAUTIONS.

Ending referring to lead:

— *KSNT-TV*

Ending

In broadcast writing, endings are called "tags" or "wrap-ups." Newspaper stories often end with a quote from a source, but in broadcast writing, the reporter has the last word in a package, followed by his name and the station identification. Often the only time the viewer sees the reporter is at the end of the story. However, many news directors now prefer using reporter stand-ups within the story rather than at the end.

The most common endings:

- **Summary:** A fact that reinforces the main idea without repeating previous points.
- **Future:** The next step in some action.
- **Factual:** A background statement or just another fact.
- **Consumer:** Helpful items, such as where to call or go for additional information. If this information is important to the viewer, avoid giving it only one time. Warn the viewer that you will be repeating telephone numbers or locations later in the program. Plan to have phone numbers posted on the screen. You can also refer to your station's website for additional information.

REVISING STORIES

When you write the ending for your story, you are not at the end of the writing process. Revision is an important part of writing your story.

- Read your story aloud. Rewrite any sentences that sound strained.
- Check all your sources' names and titles for spelling and accuracy.
- Eliminate any bureaucratic language and replace it with simple, clear terms.
- Delete adjectives. Let the video show the viewers the scene.
- Make sure your transitions don't repeat the sound bites.
- Look at the video without the sound; then listen to your story without the video.

GLOSSARY

Here are some basic terms used in broadcast news:

Actuality: A radio term for recorded comments from a news source. Same as a sound bite, the term used in television.

Anchor: The person who reads the news on the set in the studio.

Backtiming: Exact time in the newscast that a segment will air. For example, a story that will air 12 minutes and 15 seconds into the newscast will be labeled 12:15. If the last segment in a 30-minute newscast is one minute, the backtiming will be 29, alerting the anchor that the segment must start at precisely that time or it will have to be cut.

Brief: Abbreviated news story, from 10 to 20 seconds long.

Character generator: Computer-type machine that produces the letters, numbers or words superimposed on the screen to label a visual image, such as a person or place. Also called a *Chyron,* the brand name of the machine that generates these titles.

IN: Indicates the first few words of the source's quote to start a sound bite and the time on the tape, used at stations that don't include the entire sound bite in the script.

News director: Oversees all news operations at the station.

One-man-band: Based on the definition of a musician who plays a number of instruments, in television a one-man-band refers to a reporter who shoots, tapes and writes the story — a person who does it all.

OUT: Indicates the last few words of the source's quote, ending the sound bite.

Package: Reporter's story that includes narration, visual images and sound bites from sources.

Producer: Plans the newscast and often writes teasers and some copy for the anchors.

PSA: Abbreviation for a public service announcement.

Reader: Story the anchor or radio announcer reads without visuals or sound bites.

Rip-and-read: Copy from the wire services that is read exactly as it was written instead of being rewritten.

Seg time: Length of time for a news segment. A brief may be :10, or 10 seconds; a reporter's package, including the lead-in by an anchor, may be 1:45 — one minute and 45 seconds.

SOC (standard out cue): Reporter's sign-off comments at the end of the story. For example, "This is Jennifer Zilko for KTUU Anchorage."

SOT (sound on tape): Similar to a sound bite; indicated in copy along with the amount of time the taped comments will take. For example, SOT:15 means the comments on the tape will take 15 seconds.

Sound bite: Video segment showing the source speaking.

Stand-up: A part of the story in which the reporter talks on camera at the scene; sometimes at the end of a story.

Super: Letters, numbers or words produced by the character generator and superimposed over visual images; often used to identify the person appearing on the tape. At some stations, the letters CG — for character generator — are used to indicate the super.

Tag: The closing sentence for a TV or radio story or package.

Teaser: Introduction to a story on the next newscast, to tease viewers to tune in.

Teleprompter: Video terminal that displays the script for the anchor to read. This term was previously a trademark, but AP style now considers it generic.

VO (voice over): Anchor's voice over video images. Words and images should coincide.

VOB (voice over bite): Anchor's voice over video images with a sound bite from a source.

VO-SOT (voice over sound on tape): Anchor's voice over video and sound bite; same as VOB but more commonly used.

EXERCISES

1 Write a broadcast brief, about 15 seconds, based on this information from an NBC News Channel story:

Who: A consumer group, the Florida Consumer's Federation.

What: Filed a suit charging the Publix Grocery Store chain with discrimination.

Why: Group claims that the grocery chain failed to put enough women, blacks and Hispanics in management jobs and that the company doesn't have enough stores in minority neighborhoods.

When: Today.

Backup information: Publix management agrees with some of the complaints but says it is working to overcome them, according to Publix president Mark Hollis.

2 Convert the following broadcast story into proper TV news script form.

ANCHORAGE, Alaska — Social network giant MySpace is stepping up its online security, partnering with law enforcement to make the website safer for kids.

Alaska has joined an effort with the site, along with attorneys general from 48 other states and the District of Columbia, to protect children, purge predators and get rid of inappropriate content, specifically pornography.

More than 70 million users are registered on MySpace and the site is spending big to protect those members, especially those under 18. The plans were announced Monday at a press conference in New York.

"Rather than treating the off-line and online worlds differently, our goal has been and will continue to make our virtual neighborhoods as safe as our real ones," said Hemanshu Nigam, MySpace chief security officer.

The website already makes the profiles of its 14- and 15-year-old members as "private." That designation will soon extend to 16- and 17-year-olds.

"Setting that default to 'private' definitely is a protection mechanism but it's not going to keep your child safe," said Clark Harshbarger, an Anchorage FBI agent.

Harshbarger says MySpace is making progress in its efforts to increase security but acknowledges the changes are difficult to implement.

MySpace directors also said they are working to develop technology that would help parents prevent their children from using the website. An e-mail registry would allow parents to add their children's addresses.

The website would then block the user.

Cynthia Drinkwater, an assistant attorney general for Alaska, says the partnership between law enforcement and MySpace has been two years in the making.

"It made a large step and it should be commended," she said, adding that the website made great progress last year cracking down on users who are registered sex offenders.

In July, MySpace announced that it deleted the profiles of as many as 30,000 sexual predators.

"MySpace has agreed that online identity verification is very important and that they are going to take steps to analyze the programs, that technological answers that are out there and work on developing things that might really work to make sure that people who want to use the MySpace website are who they say they are," Drinkwater said.

— LORI TIPTON, *KTUU-News,* Anchorage, Alaska.

3 Convert the following newspaper story into a TV story.

A 16-year-old boy, driving without a license, led Louisville police on a 13-minute chase yesterday afternoon, driving at up to 80 mph on streets in the Highlands sections where the sidewalks were crowded with pedestrians.

The pursuit ended at 5:05 p.m., when the boy — whose name police did not release because of his age — rammed his father's 1991 Honda Accord into the rear of Officer Bob Arnold's patrol car on Trevilian Way just east of Valley Vista.

No one was injured, and the police car suffered only a minor scrape on the rear bumper. The other car was damaged more.

Officer John Butts said the chase started near Cherokee Park when he tried to stop the boy for running over a stop sign, and the boy refused to pull over. Butts radioed for help and Arnold joined the chase.

"I was concerned, because he came close to hitting several pedestrians who were out walking because of the nice weather," Butts said last night.

"Anxiety sets in when a chase continues on for this amount of time," he added. "It's longer than any officer would prefer to be in a high-speed vehicle pursuit."

Butts said the boy forced several cars off the road during the chase, which came to an end when Arnold managed to get in front of the boy and slowed down. He said the boy will be charged with numerous felonies and traffic violations; among the charges are wanton endangerment and resisting arrest. The boy was taken to the Jefferson County Youth Center.

Butts said he did not know why the boy refused to stop, but added, "He has no license, and he was not supposed to be driving his father's car."

— *The* (Louisville, Ky.) *Courier-Journal*

CourseMate

FEATURED ONLINE ACTIVITY Log on and visit the Writing and Reporting News CourseMate and take the interactive tutorial quiz on broadcast news writing. ***Access available at www.cengagebrain.com.***

Check out the "Bank Robbery" scenario in NewsScene for an interactive exercise that will help to reinforce many of the themes presented in this chapter.

COACHING TIPS

Plan **interactive elements** such as polls, discussion questions or searchable graphics.

Provide blogs and **social media links.**

Write **short, simple** sentences.

Write **clear headlines** and summary blurbs.

Plan **photos, audio and video** elements.

Consider **summary lists** or highlights boxes.

jocic/Shutterstock.com

If you run a website that doesn't have something terrible on it, you are not trying hard enough. You have to fail and fail miserably many times.

— **ERIK WEMPLE,** editor, *TBD.com*

CHAPTER 12
Online
Journalism

WHO WAS YOUR FIRST LOVE? FROM A NINJA TURTLE TO THE BOY next door, students at the Medill School of Journalism turned that question into a multimedia storytelling experiment with print, video, photos and interactivity. You can share your first love on their site, *(www.ourfirstloves.com)*.

How safe is travel in the U.S.? Not very safe at all, according to students from 11 universities who joined forces to produce a national investigative Web project, "Breakdown: Traveling Dangerously in America." They talked to hundreds of officials, industry leaders, safety experts and victims and analyzed thousands of documents and data from the National Transportation Safety Board and federal regulatory agencies. It was part of the Carnegie-Knight News 21 project, a cooperative program among 12 universities to experiment with new forms of in-depth reporting on the Web and to foster innovation in journalism education (*http://news21.com*).

What are the concerns of people on the U.S.-Mexico border? Students at the University of Arizona's School of Journalism developed an award-winning website featuring multimedia stories, blogs and social media links about the region. The project, operated by a team of journalism seniors and an adviser, is a comprehensive collection of stories in text, audio, video and photography about life in the area. "Border Beat seeks to give people an understanding that the border is much more than a fence or a line drawn on a map," the website explains. "The border area is more than the place that two countries meet; it is a place that combines two cultures."

The projects differ in subject and scope but they all share a few qualities in common: innovation, creativity and good storytelling. For inspiration from award-winning sites by students and professionals, check the Online News Association *(www.journalists.org)*.

You don't have to create a major project to do online journalism, but you do need to master some multimedia skills to be marketable in this Web-centric society. Web skills are no longer an optional asset; they are crucial for media careers in print, broadcast and public relations.

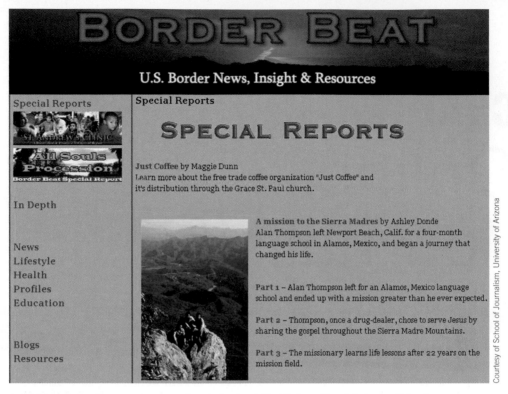

Courtesy of School of Journalism, University of Arizona

An online student-run newspaper by students at the University of Arizona School of Journalism about issues relating to the U.S.-Mexico border

You also don't have to be an expert in Web design to have a website. Many of the universities are using programs that provide free software formatted for website creation. WordPress is one of the most common (*http://wordpress.org*). The program started as a free blogging system, which has evolved into a full content management service. Web design is more complex these days because of mobile media, tablets, social media and other online tools. But some of the basic principles of online media are still essential.

QUALITIES OF ONLINE NEWS

The basic concepts for breaking news on the Web are short, fast and frequent.

Immediacy: As soon as news breaks, it should be posted on the Web. News must be updated throughout the day. It can be delivered to cell phones, e-mail, tablets such as iPads, websites via automatic updates called RSS (Really Simple Syndication) feeds or applications you choose to download.

Interactivity: Journalists aren't the only providers of news anymore. Websites feature blogs and messages posted by subscribers to the site. Interactive graphics and databases allow readers to click on a map or illustration to find the cheapest gas prices or check crime rates in their neighborhoods. And most websites offer links to share information via social media.

ETHICS

THE SOCIETY OF Professional Journalists' Code of Ethics, referred to throughout this book, is considered a standard for most media professionals (*www.spj.org/ethicscode. asp*). But no clear code of ethics exists for online journalism. However, the Poynter Institute has recommended a set of guidelines for online journalism. Some of the recommendations are:

- Journalists should avoid conflicts of interest.
- News organizations should clearly label news and opinion.
- Journalists who work for news organizations may keep personal blogs, but they should discuss their plans with an editor to avoid potential conflicts.
- Professional journalists should not write an anonymous blog or comment anonymously on other blogs. "Reporters are expected to own responsibility for their work, and commenting or blogging anonymously compromises that core principle."

Jonathan Dube, senior vice president and general manager of AOL News, proposed a blogger's code of ethics that is based on the SPJ code but addresses some specific blogging issues (*www. cyberjournalist.net/news/000215.php*). Some of his recommendations are:

- Never plagiarize.
- Identify and link to sources whenever feasible. The public is entitled to as much information as possible on sources' reliability.
- Admit mistakes and correct them promptly.
- Explain each blog's mission and invite dialogue with the public over its content and the bloggers' conduct.
- Disclose conflicts of interest, affiliations, activities and personal agendas.

That last recommendation is now a requirement of the Federal Trade Commission, which ruled that bloggers must disclose if they are getting paid or if they have received free goods from companies whose products they may have reviewed.

Multimedia: In the past, multimedia projects were limited to major projects. Now multimedia is standard on many print and broadcast websites. A multimedia story is any story that uses a variety of media such as text with photographs, video, audio and graphics.

Innovation: Storytelling on the Web can take many forms. The inverted pyramid is still preferable for breaking news stories, but you can also tell stories in many other ways. Think long and short — full-length stories or miniprofiles; question/answer instead of text; lists to itemize information briefly, blogs, quizzes and games.

ONLINE READERS

Many Web stories are versions of a print or broadcast story. But online users don't read the same way on the Web as they do in print publications.

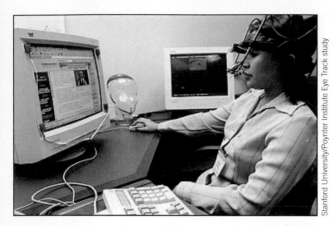

Headgear to track online readers' eye movements in the Stanford University/Poynter Institute Eye Track study.

Eye Track Studies

The Poynter Institute and Stanford University have conducted several studies to test how people read online stories. Using specially fitted glasses on the subjects, the researchers watched and recorded the readers' eye movements in these studies called "Eye Track." The original Eye Track study in 1991 tested how readers reacted to color, headlines and text in newspapers and concluded that readers looked first at headlines and photos.

A subsequent study in 2000 tested how people viewed websites, and the conclusions were opposite from those for newspaper readers. The study showed that Web viewers looked first at text and briefs, not images. Another study in 2003 concluded that the first three words in headlines and blurbs are the most important to attract Web readers. Smaller type encourages more thorough reading; larger type encourages scanning.

The last Eye Track study in 2007 compared print and online reading habits. The most significant findings were:

- People will read a story online thoroughly if they are interested in it. This is a major change from past thinking that Web readers only scanned stories.
- Both print and online readers rarely read stories to the end, but online readers read more of a story on the Web than print readers.
- Alternative story forms such as question/answer, time lines, lists and fact boxes help readers remember facts.

Several other eye track studies came to similar conclusions. The finding that most of the studies have in common is that online readers tend to scan information first by looking at headlines, key words, boldfaced terms and links, especially on mobile media. After scanning, readers will only take three seconds to decide whether to continue reading, according to a Yahoo! digital style guide. A Gomez Web performance study claimed consumers abandon slow sites between one and five seconds.

Linear vs. Nonlinear

The interactive nature of the Web makes it nonlinear, meaning users may access information in any order they choose. Conversely, print and broadcast stories are written in linear order from beginning to end, as in a straight line, offering readers no choice except to stop reading. Although many Web stories are still written in linear order, Web readers have nonlinear choices of accessing related elements linked to the story or the site.

A Web package created in nonlinear order might be divided into smaller chunks spanning several pages, or it might contain links to timelines, related stories, polls and other interactive elements.

Embedded or External Links

Should you include links within the text (embedded) of your story or at the end (external)? In the past, most Web designers and usability experts recommended that links be placed on the side or at the end of a story because a reader who clicked on an embedded link might not return to the article. However, the current thinking is that online readers have become so sophisticated that they will return to articles they want to read even if they access a link on another page, so embedded links are used regularly in news stories. If you include the actual URLs (Internet addresses), the AP Style Guide says to place them within the text if they refer to a site being discussed but at the end if they provide additional information.

STORY PLANNING

Whether readers scan or thoroughly read Web stories, the hyperlink nature of the Web changes the way writers need to plan their stories. You should plan the story *before* the reporting process so you know what information to gather. Most news organizations use formatted programs for Web stories, so you don't have to worry about designing the Web page for your story. If you plan to create a multimedia package or website, you should take a course in Web design, which is beyond the scope of this book.

Web designers plan sites by drawing a "storyboard," which is similar to an organizational chart, to show the main parts and related pieces. A storyboard can be used to plan news stories as well. You could also draft a simple outline to plan elements of the story.

First decide the best way to tell the story. Not all stories need to be written in linear text format. A story or some of its parts may be presented in alternative forms. Writing for the Web requires envisioning a story in layers. Will your story be one page of text or will you write it in chunks? Will you use photos, audio and/or video? Will you have sidebars? These are some elements to consider:

Time Lines: Does the story lend itself to background created as a timeline?

Frequently Asked Questions: Would a question/answer format or FAQ (Frequently Asked Questions) be a good way to present the story or accompany it?

Interactivity: Will the story feature a discussion question, poll, quiz, searchable databases or other information the reporter may need to gather for reader involvement?

Lists or Data for Full Coverage: Will the story be accompanied by a complete list of contest winners, school test scores or other information?

Miniprofiles: Does a story about candidates or a long feature series need short biographies of the sources?

Multimedia: Will the story include audio or video? Do you need to tape an interview for sound bites?

Related Links: Although some organizations have researchers or Web producers who find related links, when you are producing your own stories, add the relevant links.

E-mail Addresses of Reporters: Not all news sites include these addresses, but it's a good idea to add your e-mail address to your byline.

Social Media Links: Will you include social media links or related blogs?

A checklist for your story might look something like this:

- Headline
- Summary blurb
- Highlights in a bulleted list (above or on the side — optional)
- Main story — one scrolling text page or divided into chunks of several Web pages
- Timelines
- Short bios of main sources
- Links to full text of speeches, reports, budgets, lists of winners or related resources
- Photos/graphics
- Multimedia (audio or video)
- Searchable databases
- Interactive elements: polls, games, quizzes, blogs, discussion questions or places for readers to post messages
- Social media links

REPORTING FOR THE WEB

Good reporting is similar in any medium, but you need some additional tools and reporting steps for the Web.

Plan for Full Coverage: Be prepared to report your story for text delivery and for audio or video elements. Plan to get the full text of a speech, a city budget, lists of contest winners or other additional information to post on the Web.

Equipment: For basic reporting, in addition to a notebook and pens or pencils, take a tape recorder to get audio sound bites and some form of digital storage media such as a jump drive for the extended information mentioned in the previous point. Other necessities include a cell phone to call in your story, digital camera, extra batteries and a notebook computer if you are going to transmit a story from your location. You can also record and take photos with your cell phones. If you are using it to shoot video, take wipes to make sure your smart phone camera lens is clean.

Timelines: When you are covering a major disaster or crime event, mark your notes with time periods for a timeline that might be posted on the Web.

E-mail Reporting: Don't depend on it for deadline. E-mail is a good way to reach people and get limited information, but face-to-face or telephone interviewing is still preferable.

Check Accuracy and Timeliness: If you are using information from the Web, check the date of the information and the reliability of the website for accuracy. Is the information from a site by a government agency, a university, a respected media organization or is it from a personal site?

Updates and Follow-Up Stories: Plan to file your story in a brief form as soon as the news breaks. Then plan an updated version for your next print or broadcast edition. If you are covering a major breaking-news story, plan to file for the Web every time you receive new information. Think ahead. Plan to write a follow-up story for the next edition of your broadcast or print publication.

ANATOMY OF A NEWS STORY ON THE WEB

It was a major news story for *The News-Press* in Fort Myers, Fla. A 2-year-old child had discovered the bodies of his parents, both 25, who had been murdered in their home in the Gateway section of the city. It was also a chance for the newspaper to demonstrate its commitment to breaking news online. "We don't hold back anything," said Kate Marymont, then executive editor of the paper. "As soon as we know and it is verified, it goes online. It doesn't have to be the complete print story."

Marymont, now vice president of news at Gannett Company's community publishing division, explained how the paper handled this story:

- Announce the news as soon as possible. In this case, *The News Press* posted the breaking news at 4:47 p.m. and mentioned an upcoming news conference.

BREAKING NEWS: POSTED 4:47 P.M.
Suspect arrested in Gateway homicides
Lee County sheriffs officials are holding a news conference at 5:30 p.m. to announce an arrest in the Dec. 27 slaying of a young Gateway couple, news-press.com has learned.
• Gateway homicide investigation
| Readers' forum: **What do you think?** | Photo gallery: **Images from the investigation**

LATEST NEWS - POSTED 1:55 P.M.
• State ends cutting of canker-exposed trees (1:52 p.m.)
⇒ Readers' forum: **Should program have been stopped earlier?**
• Jury sees bloody knives in Cape teen murder trial (1:55 p.m.)

Lower off-peak Sanibel toll possible

Courtesy of Gannett Co. Inc.

- Update in increments. Tell when there is more to come. The next information was posted on the Web at 5:30 p.m., alerting viewers that *The News-Press* would soon be posting tapes of the police interviews shortly.

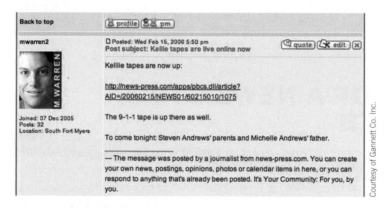

■ Promote within the site. In this case the promotion said the tapes mentioned before are live online now.

■ Post multimedia—in this case exclusive audio and video.

CONVERGENCE COACH

MOST OF THESE tips apply to online writing for print, broadcast or public relations sites.

■ Enlist "crowd sourcing," contributions from readers and viewers in blogs, messages, Twitter, Facebook or other social media.

■ Use photos, graphics, audio and video that compliment your story; don't just add multimedia for its own sake. Choose the form that best fits or enhances the content.

■ Gather more information than you need for a single story. Always plan follow-up stories, full text

of documents and other materials for the reader who wants in-depth material on your website.

■ Check the date of information from the Web.

■ Add contact information to your website. Don't just say contact webmaster. Provide a name, e-mail address, phone number and physical address, especially on corporate sites or public relations materials.

■ Add information such as "About Us," especially for corporate information or multimedia projects. Explain who created the project and other pertinent information for viewers.

■ Plan social media blogs and links to posts on Twitter, Facebook, YouTube or other popular sites.

WRITING TECHNIQUES

There is no single way to write for the Web. Choose the form that best fits the story or purpose. Is your purpose to inform or entertain or do both? If you are writing for a corporate or public relations site, determine the best way to convey information quickly and clearly. If you are writing news, consider the inverted pyramid for breaking or serious news. If you want to tell a good story, perhaps a narrative form might be suitable.

Jakob Nielsen

Jakob Nielsen, often considered the world's leading expert on Web usability, originally set the standards for online writing. He influenced a generation of Web designers and writers with his biweekly columns about Web usability (*www.useit.com/alertbox/*). Nielsen's early recommendations about how to write for the Web were based on studies he conducted in the late 1990s about how people read Web content. Many of his writing guidelines are still valid, but he admits that "because people read differently, you have to write differently."

Some of his early writing guidelines that he still espouses include:

- Write short.
- Write for readers who scan websites instead of reading thoroughly. "Users won't read your text thoroughly in a word-by-word manner. Exhaustive reading is rare," he says.
- Write to the point; avoid "fluffy marketese."
- Use common language, not made-up terms.
- State the most important information in the first two paragraphs.

"But the very best content strategy is one that mirrors the users' mixed diet," Nielsen said in a "useit" column. "There's no reason to limit yourself to only one content type. It's possible to have short overviews for the majority of users *and* to supplement them with in-depth coverage and white papers for those few users who need to know more."

In a recent eye tracking study Nielsen conducted, he reaffirmed his conclusion that the most important information in a Web page should be "above the fold," meaning information that can be viewed without scrolling. However, he said scrolling is preferable to clicking to different pages in a story. Mobile users may be forced to scroll or click to new pages if their viewing screens don't accommodate much text.

Conversely, renowned Web designer Roger Black favors paging. He is a founder of Treesaver, a program that divides content into pages instead of scrolling and automatically adjusts the layout to the size of the screen.

Here are some other writing tips that apply to most Web stories:

- Write a clear headline and subhead summarizing the main idea of the story. This is especially critical for stories distributed to mobile media. Twitter is a good way to practice writing good headlines and key words because you are limited to 140 characters; that will force you to be brief.

- Write a clear focus statement or nut graph high in the story, especially if you use an anecdotal lead. Readers should know what the story is about and why they are reading it within the first few paragraphs even if you have written a summary headline and subhead.

- Write short, simple sentences. Avoid sentences with long clauses and complex sentences. Be concise.

- Use bulleted lists to help readers scan text when the story lends itself to itemized information.

- Limit each paragraph to one idea.

- Write in active voice: Who did what rather than what was done to whom. *The student won an award,* not *An award was won by the student.*

- Avoid last name only on second reference in subsequent screens or Web pages unless the source is well known or is the main person in the story. Apply the blocking technique of restricting each source's comments to one block in the story so the reader doesn't have to scroll up and down a page or refer to a previous page to remember someone's name.

- Keep paragraphs short.

- Use conversational style. Write as though you were talking to a single reader. Borrow from broadcast writing. The "you" voice works well online. Try to let readers know what the story means for them.

SOCIAL MEDIA

"THINK OF SOCIAL media like dating. You've got to start with an introduction and deliberately work your way up toward building a sound relationship." That's the advice of Robert Niles, an online news trainer who is founder of a website about theme parks. "The easiest way for a reader to begin adding to the content on a website is by voting in a poll or other interactive feature. When readers react to your site by posting comments, now, you're dating," he wrote in *The Online Journalism Review.*

Use social media *before* you report or write your story. Tell readers about your topic and ask them to submit related information on Twitter, Facebook or message boards on your website.

Almost all websites these days include share buttons linking directly to social network sites. But limit the number of buttons to sites you think your users want the most. One designer called the overuse of these icons "the swamp" of share buttons.

Although college students are social media savvy, they don't want social networking on all the websites they visit, according to a study Jakob Nielsen conducted in 2010. He concluded that students are multi-taskers who keep many browsers open at the same time, but when a site slows them down, they switch to another tab. "Student users' high inclination to multi-task and low patience reinforce the need for quick, responsive and easy Web design," Nielsen reported. "Don't give students even the smallest excuse to check Facebook instead of staying with your site."

WRITING FOR MOBILE MEDIA

If short writing is recommended is for regular websites, shorter is even better for mobile media. Some recommendations:

- Use single column layout
- Reduce the number of links. Slow downloads will deter readers.
- Write a short, clear headline.
- Write simple sentences — the shorter the better.
- Be concise. Get to the point immediately.

Test how compatible your story will be with mobile media. If you don't have a smart phone, iPad or other tablet, you could borrow one or check your story on mobile simulation sites such as these:

- iPhone 4 Simulator *(http://iphone4simulator.com/)*
- W3c mobile OK Checker *(http://validator.w3.org/mobile/)*
- iPhoney *(http://www.marketcircle.com/iphoney/)*
- iPad Peek *(http://ipadpeek.com/)*

HEADLINES, SUMMARY BLURBS AND BRIEFS

Headlines, summary blurbs and briefs are called "microcontent," the smaller elements of a story. But they are the biggest factor in determining whether someone will click into the story. Clarity is crucial. The headline and a summary blurb of one or two sentences should accurately summarize the story. Readers in a rush want to know exactly what they're getting when they link into a story. Unlike a newspaper, which offers only a handful of stories on each page, a Web page offers scores of headlines and links competing for attention.

Most Web experts advise against writing catchy, teaser headlines because they could be misleading. A teaser headline may work if it is accompanied by a clear summary blurb. But Web pages with many headlines may not contain summary blurbs, so the headline must tell the story by itself.

Although headlines are often written *after* the story is submitted, one of the best ways of focusing your story is to write a headline and summary blurb *before* you write the full story. Because most major news organizations also require reporters to submit briefs for the Web before publication in a newspaper or on a broadcast newscast, writing a brief first is another good way to identify the essential information for a fuller story.

Here are some guidelines for Web headlines that link to the main story:

Write Brief Headlines: Fewer than six to 10 words create better links than headlines that span two or three lines:

Study: Kids are solicited online (or)

Kids are solicited online, study says

Use Strong Verbs: Some headlines may be written without verbs:

Lose 10 pounds in five weeks

(No verb) Top 10 diet tips

Put the Most Important Words First:

Cookie Monster assaulted, police say

Avoid Articles: Don't use *the, a,* or *an* at the start of a headline:

Web makes cheating easy

Not: The Web makes cheating easy

Use Question Headlines If the Subject Is Interesting Enough to Entice Readers:

Is work a pain in the neck or in the hands?

Blurbs

The majority of news sites just repeat the story lead for the blurb under the headline. That's fine if it's a summary lead. But if the lead doesn't give the main point of the story, write a clear summary or use the nut graph as the blurb.

For example, this headline from *The Tampa Tribune* online is vague standing by itself. It needs the summary blurb that accompanied it:

CHECKING IT OUT FOR THEMSELVES

LAKELAND — With a customer and brand base on its side, Publix is going after an online home-delivery market in a venture where others who tried it have seen their businesses marked down or shelved.

The next headline is somewhat catchy, but it too depends on the summary blurb for clarification:

WOMAN SEEKS DIVORCE OVER MYNAH INDISCRETIONS

A Chinese woman launches divorce proceedings after the family's pet mynah bird blabs about husband's affair. The bird began repeating words, "I love you" and "divorce" from the husband's phone calls to his lover.

Blurb Tips

Write a Clear Summary: If the lead is creative, choose the nut graph as the summary blurb. The Cookie Monster headline mentioned on this page may provoke curiosity, but it could use a blurb for clarification:

If you wanted to find out what happened to Tiny Boo, you would link to the full story, which starts the same way. You would find out that the mobile home owner who shot Tiny Boo claimed the pig tried to attack him. He was accused of cruelty to animals.

Summary Highlights

Another tool that serves as a quick summary for Web readers who are scanners is the highlights box on top of the story. For example, CNN tops its Web stories with a bulleted list of the main points in a story as in this example:

EIGHT KILLED IN SKI TOUR BUS CRASH

STORY HIGHLIGHTS

- Death toll rises to eight as tour bus runs off highway, rolls over
- Bus was carrying at least 50 people when it crashed in south-eastern Utah
- Bus was en route from Telluride, Colorado, to Phoenix, Arizona, after weekend ski trip

STORY STRUCTURE

Get to the point of the story quickly — within the first 50 words. If you picture a news website with a title image and possibly a banner advertisement at the top of the page plus the story headline, this doesn't leave you much room. In addition, text on most news sites is enclosed in tables about 4 inches wide to facilitate reading. That translates to about 100 to 150 words per screen.

Inverted Pyramid

The inverted pyramid is a favored form for Web stories because the main idea is in the lead or the first few paragraphs. The inverted pyramid form places the main point at the top of the story with the rest of the information in descending order of importance. This form is good for basic news stories, but it is too restrictive for features and other types of storytelling. As long as the nut graph expressing the main point is high in the story, writers may have as much flexibility for Web stories as for print.

The headline, blurb and lead may be repetitious, but this doesn't harm readability because it helps readers know they have accessed the correct story from the scores of others that may be linked to the site.

Headline	**COOKIE MONSTER ASSAULTED**
	Blurb Maryland dad charged with attacking Sesame Place worker. Police say the father was upset that the giant Cookie Monster would not pose for a picture with his 3-year-old daughter.

Avoid Writing Summaries that Repeat the Headline: The first sentence in this blurb is too repetitive:

Headline	**IS WORK A PAIN IN THE NECK . . . OR HANDS?**
Blurb	Has work become a real pain? If so, the problem might not be your job but your workstation. Judy Gibson, manager of the Physical Therapy department at Fairbanks Memorial Hospital, says proper ergonomics is essential to preventing problems.

Address the Reader When Appropriate: Use the "you" voice:

Headline	**GET FREE CASH FOR COLLEGE**
Blurb	You can collect thousands of dollars in scholarship money just by filling out a form.

Briefs

Blurbs are usually a few sentences. A brief can be a few paragraphs. A brief can stand alone in place of a story, while a blurb is meant to entice readers to read more. Sometimes there is not much difference between a blurb and a brief. In a majority of cases, the blurb and the brief repeat the lead or the first few paragraphs of full text. The main reason to use blurbs and briefs is to offer readers a choice of layers. Some Web readers want to read only the headline, others want a brief summary and others want the complete story.

Headline	**MISSING PET PIG TURNS UP AS MEAL**
Blurb	A woman who went looking for her family's missing pet pig says she found it — as the main course at a neighborhood barbecue.
Brief	A woman who went looking for her family's missing pet pig says she found it — as the main course at a neighborhood barbecue. Sadie Emerson said she and her 3-year-old son drove up and down their neighborhood streets, looking for the Vietnamese pot-bellied pig, Tiny Boo. They spotted a group of people having a party near a mobile home, and on the table was a mound of meat that turned out to be Tiny Boo.

— The Associated Press

Here is an example of the inverted pyramid with a summary lead:

Headline **SCHOOL OFFICIAL CUFFED, LED AWAY BY COUPLE**

Blurb Deputies arrest pair, who were unhappy with materials given students

Lead   LUCERNE VALLEY, Calif. — Two parents barged into a school superintendent's office, handcuffed him, announced he was under citizen's arrest and drove him away in their vehicle, authorities said Friday.

    Sheriff's deputies pulled them over 10 miles away, freed the school's official and arrested the couple, who said they were taking the superintendent to the district attorney's office.

— The Associated Press

This example also uses an inverted pyramid form with a creative lead, but the nut graph is in the third paragraph.

OFFICIALS SEIZE HURT ANIMALS

Lead Animal control authorities haul away more than 150 injured and neglected animals — some close to death. The sign on the stable welcomes visitors to the "Heaven and Earth" animal sanctuary.

    But authorities say the so-called animal shelter was a living hell.

    Animal Control officials spent Friday seizing more than 150 animals from the 20-acre property where they say pets and livestock were neglected, some of them almost to the point of death.

— JAMIE MALERNEE, St. Petersburg (Fla.) Times

List Format

Lists within stories break up the text and help readers scan Web stories quickly.

Headline **SOMETHING UNSPOKEN**

Blurb What not to say in an interview

    If you're a smart job candidate, you've thought about the points you want to make to sell yourself in an interview. Maybe you've even practiced your spiel. That's good, but know too that career experts caution that saying *too* much in an interview can hurt your prospects.

    You already know to avoid mentioning the office-supplies pilfering complaint filed against you in your last job — and that reprimand for arriving late on 18 days in one month. But here are some less obvious things you should avoid saying at a job interview.

- Don't address your interviewer by his or her first name, unless and until it's clearly established that the session is on a first-name basis. Here, the rule is to let the interviewer speak first.
- Don't use the wrong name. First or last.
- Don't say anything that conveys you're desperate for the job. Even if you are.

— LARRY KELLER, *CNN.com*

Question/Answer Format

A question/answer format is a good alternative form for Web writing. The story still needs an introduction. This CNN example includes an interactive poll, an ideal feature for online stories. It also has a question lead, which works better online than in print stories. Note the conversational "you" voice, also good for online writing.

→ QUICK VOTE

How well do you handle job interviews?

I'm good at them. In fact, I enjoy them. ○

I can get by, but they're no fun. ○

I really have to psych up. And sometimes I tank. ○

I'm hopeless. I fall apart as soon as I say, "Hello." ○

View Results   vote

Headline
SELLING YOURSELF AGAIN:
THE JOB INTERVIEW REVISITED

Lead
"If you were a squirrel, which commodity would you inventory first — the nuts or the berries?" May you never encounter that question in a job interview.

But the knee-knocking trial of it all, the sleepless nights leading up to it, the 18 cups of coffee before you get there, the sudden feeling that your resume belongs to someone else and your clothes do, too, for that matter . . . it's all here again for a lot of people. Some may have thought they wouldn't be facing this particular ordeal again soon, if ever.

It's a job interview. And with the wake of layoffs widening — nearly 300,000 in the United States in the first quarter of this year, according to data from Randstad North America and Roper Starch Worldwide — a lot of people are finding themselves back in that very hot seat.

CNN: So we applied ourselves to ETICON'S Ann Humphries, asking her to tell us what's important to know from the business etiquette standpoint, what to do when it's time to grip 'n grin.

And before we give you Ann, any squirrel knows the answer is berries, inventory them first — nuts have longer shelf life.

The story continues with the question/answer format from professional management consultant Ann Humphries and is accompanied by the interactive poll.

Storytelling Format

Narrative writing also can be compelling on the Web, especially if it is split into several pages with cliffhanger endings that entice readers to continue. The Web specials on the

St. Petersburg Times site offer several examples, including this narrative story, "28 Seconds," about the mystery of USAir Flight 427. The four-part Web package was organized in chunks and featured this enticing one-screen introduction:

28 . . . 27 . . .
It happened in little more than the time it will take you to read this paragraph.
19 . . . 18 . . .
It felt like turbulence at first, but then the plane twisted left, and it was clear something was wrong.
6 . . . 5 . . .
Twisting, turning.
What the hell is this?
Impact.

The rest of the story continues in dramatic storytelling.

PERSONAL STORYTELLING

Human beings have been telling stories since prehistoric man drew pictures on caves and recited stories around a fire. The Web is simply a new cave blending old and new techniques. People still want to hear, read and *share* stories. And that's how the Web can exceed any other medium in history. Personal storytelling thrives on the Web, especially in blogs, and it is increasing on news sites.

Some of the best personal storytelling sites are not traditional broadcast or newspaper sites. Musarium (*www.musarium.com*), a site devoted to photography and storytelling, is an example. "Just when you think that television has mind-numbed the brains of most people, these presentations celebrate and enforce the power of still photographs to affect people and tell great stories," the site says. The site features innovative multimedia packages with personal stories in several formats. Some of the storytelling is told in photo essays.

One of the most chilling is "Without Sanctuary," a multimedia photo essay of lynchings documented in old postcards. This story has since moved to its own site (*www.withoutsanctuary.org*).

REVISE

Don't eliminate this crucial process. Be concise. Cut every word or paragraph that does not advance the story. Short sentences, short paragraphs and active verbs make Web writing more readable. The same principles that William Strunk Jr. offered for print writing in E. B. White's *The Elements of Style* apply to the Web: "Vigorous writing is concise. A sentence should contain no unnecessary words, a paragraph no unnecessary sentences. . . . This requires not that the writer make all sentences short, or that he avoid all detail and treat his subjects only in outline, but that every word tell."

TAKE RISKS

Writing for the Web will continue to evolve as technology improves accessibility of multimedia. Basic journalistic concepts of accuracy, structure and simplicity will remain, but new forms of online writing may emerge. Start with a good story, and find an interesting way to tell it. The Web is a flexible medium.

Andrew Nachison is a risk taker in new media. He heads a media think tank and futures lab called iFOCUS, to encourage innovation in Web media. Nachison said that some of the best online storytelling is distinctly different from the typical text narrative of a newspaper story.

"The challenge is to think of the Web as a different medium, not merely an extension of the newspaper. You don't have to be an MSNBC to do great stuff. Some newspaper stories may translate perfectly well as big blocks of text. But some stories can be more compelling when they're presented in completely different ways." Nachison offered these tips:

Be Flexible: Different stories call for different approaches.

Be Smart: For some stories, you may have the luxury of time and creative people to do something innovative. For other stories, you may have to shovel text online to get the story out quickly.

Be Daring: Enjoy the creative freedom the Web offers to do great journalism. Remember the thrill of telling a great story and telling it well.

"Do great journalism whenever you can," Nachison said. "One of the great things about the Web is that you can do it all."

EXERCISES

1 Headlines and blurbs: Using your local or campus newspaper, write Web headlines and summary blurbs for news and feature stories.

2 Personal essay: Write a personal essay in chunk style on a topic of interest to you. Try to include cliffhanger endings for each chunk to entice readers to click into the next part.

3 Convert a story to the Web: Using any news or feature story you have written for this course, convert it to Web style as suggested in this chapter. Add a discussion question.

4 Web story: Write a story for the Web based on this information. Include a headline and summary blurb.

Use a bulleted list, add a discussion question to the end of your story and consider creating a poll. Use Web style — a space between each paragraph.

....

New data on marriage, divorce and remarriage in the United States show that 43 percent of first marriages end in separation or divorce within 15 years, according to a report released today by the Centers for Disease Control and Prevention (CDC). The report, "First Marriage Dissolution, Divorce, and Remarriage: United States," also shows that one in three first marriages end within 10 years and one in five end within five years.

The findings are based on data from the National Survey of Family Growth, a study of 10,847 women 15–44 years of age.

"Separation and divorce can have adverse effects on the health and well-being of children and adults," said CDC Director Jeffrey Koplan. "Past research has shown that divorce is associated with higher rates of mortality, more health problems, and more risky behaviors such as increased alcohol use."

The study also showed that duration of marriage is linked to a woman's age at first marriage; the older a woman is at first marriage, the longer that marriage is likely to last. For example, 59 percent of marriages to brides under 18 end in separation or divorce within 15 years, compared with 36 percent of those married at age 20 or over.

About 97 percent of separated non-Hispanic white women are divorced within five years of separation, compared with 77 percent of separated Hispanic women and only 67 percent of non-Hispanic black women. Younger women who divorce are more likely to remarry: 81 percent of those divorced before age 25 remarry within 10 years, compared with 68 percent of those divorced at age 25 or over. Non-Hispanic black women are less likely than other women to remain in a first marriage, to make the transition from separation to divorce, to remarry, and to remain in a remarriage.

"These data offer an important glimpse into the social fabric of this country," said Dr. Edward Sondik, director of CDC's National Center for Health Statistics, which conducted the study. "The implications of divorce cut across a number of societal issues — socioeconomics, health and the welfare of our children."

FEATURED ONLINE ACTIVITY Log on and visit the Writing and Reporting News CourseMate and take the interactive tutorial quiz on online journalism. *Access available at www.cengagebrain.com.*

COACHING TIPS

Study your audience. Find out **what kind of information they need** and how they prefer to receive it.

Find your focus. Use the focus statement as a headline or idea for your lead.

Plan visuals — charts, illustrations, photographs, diagrams and video — to make your package more appealing.

Plan video opportunities for **broadcast and online media.**

Offer delivery of press releases via **e-mail, Web, podcasts, mobile devices or social media.**

Write a fact sheet. Use it as a writing tool to make sure you have provided crucial facts in your press release or media kit.

Always **include contact information:** name, company address, telephone numbers (including cell phone and fax), e-mail and website addresses.

Marco Rullkoetter/Shutterstock.com

The overall role of public relations is to motivate a person or a group to take a specific action. No new invention or methodology can ever change the basic human characteristic of communicating ideas with the basic purpose of influencing agreement or support or otherwise.

— **HAROLD BURSON,** founder of Burson-Marsteller public relations and communications firm

CHAPTER 13
Public Relations Writing

I N 1910 AN 18-YEAR-OLD HIGH SCHOOL DROPOUT BOARDED A TRAIN FROM Nebraska to Kansas City, Mo., with two shoeboxes of postcards under his arm. He moved into the YMCA where he operated his wholesale card business until the YMCA complained about the large mail volume. He called on drugstores, bookstores and gift stores to promote his products. A few years later he opened a store and expanded his inventory to include greeting cards.

Courtesy of the Hallmark Archives, Hallmark Cards Inc.

Joyce C. Hall, founder of Hallmark, at age 18 in 1910.

Courtesy of the Hallmark Archives, Hallmark Cards Inc.

Joyce C. Hall, founder of Hallmark, chaired the company for 56 years.

A Hallmark card from the 1920s.

Now more than 100 years later, the little business that Joyce C. Hall started with a shoebox is a $4 billion company known world-wide as Hallmark Cards Inc., which includes products in 30 languages in 100 countries and 40,000 retail outlets in the U.S. Although the traditional paper cards still abound, Hallmark greetings now come with iPhone and iPad applications, recordable storybooks and cards geared to Hispanics and African-Americans.

Corporate communications have changed as well. These days information about Hallmark is on Twitter, YouTube, Facebook, blogs and several company websites. Press releases are offered online in printable formats, audio, video, and via e-mail news alerts.

"The company that defined the 20th-century greeting card is now redefining it, adding choices like e-cards and greeting card software, and exploring the possibilities for other means yet to come," according to the company's website.

A Hallmark card for the 21st century.

CHANGES IN PUBLIC RELATIONS

Hallmark is an example of how corporate communications are changing. The public relations professional today needs to be skilled in multimedia, multi-tasking and multicultural awareness.

"Writing beyond traditional media relations is required for a range of digital content, such as websites, newsletters and content-marketing related to white papers, case studies, research and journalistic-quality articles," according to Howard Sholkin, director of communications and marketing at IDG (International Data Group). "The social Web — growing at tremendous speed — requires an understanding of different platforms (LinkedIn, Twitter and Facebook) and how they can be effectively applied to public relations and marketing programs," he wrote in a blog for the Public Relations Society of America.

Defining Public Relations

Social networks are changing the way public relations practitioners reach their publics and deliver content. But the purpose of public relations transcends technology, according to Harold Burson, founder of the largest P.R. agency in the world. "My greatest frustration as a lifelong public relations professional is that so many of my fellow professionals cannot define public relations in its totality," he said in a speech at Boston University. "The overall role of public relations is to motivate a person or a group to take a specific action. No new invention or methodology can ever change the basic

ETHICS

ETHICAL DILEMMA: How truthful should you be when you are faced with a conflict between protecting your client and dealing with the media?

The case: You are the public relations director for a company that manufactures portable baby cribs. The chief executive officer of your company informs you that two babies died when their cribs collapsed. However, he is reluctant to issue a recall because more than 100,000 cribs of this particular model were sold, and it would cost the company a fortune.

He says the product development team warned him a few years ago that the sides of the crib were not secure but that to replace the design would have been too costly. He wants you to reassure the media that the cribs are safe and that there is no proof the deaths of these children were a direct result of any faulty crib parts. If the media asks, he wants you to deny that the company ever had any indication the cribs might be defective.

Will you lie or withhold information to protect your employer? What steps will you propose to the CEO?

Ethical values: Truth, credibility, fairness, loyalty to your client.

Ethical guidelines: The Public Relations Society of America offers these guidelines in its code of ethics:

- Be honest and accurate in all communications.
- Reveal sponsors for represented causes and interests.
- Act in the best interest of clients or employers.
- Disclose financial interests in a client's organization.
- Safeguard the confidences and privacy rights of clients and employees.
- Avoid conflicts between personal and professional interests.

You can find the entire code of ethics at *www.prsa.org/AboutPRSA/Ethics/*

human characteristic of communicating ideas with the basic purpose of influencing agreement or support or otherwise."

Burson, who has been described as the most influential public relations figure in the 20th century, founded Burson-Marsteller global communications firm in 1946 and now writes a blog about the changing role of public relations. He said the Internet is a powerful tool in the communications arsenal, but it is only one of many. "The public relations professional helps hone the messages that will be most persuasive to the audience and selects the media (usually a mix of media) that will deliver the messages most credibly and economically. It goes without question that this process take place within the context of uncompromised dedication to truth and transparency."

Past, Present and Future

The first press release was created in 1906 after a Pennsylvania Railroad train wreck in Atlantic City, N.J., where 50 people were killed. Ivy Lee, a publicist who represented the railroad, issued a public statement from his client, and he is credited with creating this type of public relations message. For the past 100 years, the press release didn't change much. These days the press release will probably be online or in text or video format, posted on Twitter or Facebook, or distributed to mobile media. The term "news release" is preferred by many communicators because the information is now distributed to a larger audience than the media, but the terms are interchangeable.

Press releases still play an important role in news reporting. "As the press scales back on original reporting and dissemination, reproducing other people's work becomes a bigger part of the news system," according to a report by the Pew Research Center. "We found official press releases often appear word for word in first accounts of events, though often not noted as such."

Many of the tools publicists have used in the past such as press releases and media kits will continue to have value, but their form and substance will change.

"It's pretty clear where the press release will go next: It's going to get shorter, link to more sources; be focused on simplification and explanation; and it'll come in many more flavors," according to David McCulloch, director of public relations at Cisco Systems. In an article by the social media site, Mashable, he predicted these changes: "Practically speaking, that means the press release of the future will deliver its content in text, video, SMS (short message service), microblog and podcast form, to any choice of device, whenever the reader decides, and preferably it will be pre-corroborated and openly rated by multiple trusted sources."

CONVERGENCE COACH

CONVERGENCE these days is complicated. Public relations practitioners need to target their audiences in many ways — print, e-mail, blogs, photos, audio, video, online and social media. Add information in Spanish or other languages for bilingual users and in brief formats for mobile media. The press is no longer the only target audience. Bloggers, customers and millions of social media users are consumers in the corporate communications universe.

Here are some suggestions from public relations professionals for improving convergent communications in the coming years:

- Provide a corporate blog. Follow some P.R. blogs such as these suggested by the Public Relations Student Society of America (PRSSA): *Culpwrit*, by Ron Culp focusing on guiding careers in public relations; *Edelman 6 a.m.* by Richard Edelman, CEO of Edelman PR; *P.R. 2.0* by Brian Solis, author of *Putting the Public Back in Public Relations* and other books.

- Provide multimedia. Use podcasts and video interviews to complement print and online stories. "Video is also becoming a critical part of many news sites and an important asset for PR to provide to busy reporters, particularly as publications focus on creating visually rich content for devices such as the iPad." — Levy Master Black, managing director at Sparkpr, an independent P.R. agency.

- Include more data graphics and applications for mobile media.

- Understand how to use mobile tools and provide content in various platforms.

- Provide good storytelling — no matter what platform you use. "Good content and storytelling are paramount to breaking through the clutter. Since consumers have so many competing sources from which they can receive their news, communicators must create new and interesting content using a variety of channels to capture their audience's attention." — Linda Welter Cohen, PR strategist and CEO The Caliber Group, Tucson, AZ.

WRITING SKILLS FOR PRESS RELEASES

Many press releases are not read all the way through, but most editors or recipients of your release will at least skim the releases to find out if there is some newsworthy information. Community newspapers and local television stations rely heavily on press releases about events in their area.

If you want your news event to be covered, you need to consider that you are competing with many other events and stories that these media will cover. How do you get the attention of the assignment editors? Here are some tips for writing your releases:

- **Target your audience.** Make sure that your information is newsworthy for the publication. Check the name and spelling of the person who should receive the release. Don't use nicknames (unless you are very familiar with the source), and make sure that you have the correct gender. Don't send duplicate releases to several editors. You might also send a copy to a reporter assigned to the beat covered in your press release. Ask if the publication prefers a faxed release, an e-mail release or other type of delivery via the Web.

- **Find a newsworthy angle.** If you are targeting a local newspaper or TV station, localize the angle. The qualities of timeliness, local interest, new information and unusual nature are the main factors in determining newsworthiness.

- **Identify the news element in the headline and lead.** Don't make your intended reader wade through several paragraphs to determine if the event or news you are touting should be covered.

- **Use inverted pyramid order:** Write a basic news lead that answers the most important questions — who, what, when, where and why.

- **Consider a visual element.** If you are targeting a television station, the visual impact is crucial. List photo opportunities for print and video possibilities for television and the Web.

- **Include key words that can be picked up by a search engine** (SEO–search engine optimization).

- **Relate your information to your audience.** How will readers or viewers be affected in this target area? Why is your information or event important to them?

- **Keep your information factual.** Avoid adjectives, superlatives and promotional language.

- **Provide diverse sources.** Consider how to include multicultural segments of the community in your projects, visuals and materials.

- **Allow lead time.** Send your releases in advance of the publication's deadlines. A magazine might have a lead time of several months. Some TV stations might prefer only a few days of lead time. Check with the publication or organization for preferred advance notice. Include the release date, preferably "For Immediate Release," unless there is some important reason for an "Embargoed Until . . ." date.

- **Use active voice.** Who did what, not what was done to whom.

- **Use present tense when possible.** In most cases you will want to promote an event or some information in a timely manner, not after the fact.
- **Check grammar and spelling.**
- **Make sure you include contact information for you and your company:** Your name, phone numbers, e-mail and the company address and phone contacts.

E-MAIL PRESS RELEASES

Online press releases must be shorter than print ones so the information can be seen on the first screen.

- Limit the release to one or two screens, about 600 words at most. However, if you are targeting your release for mobile media, keep it even shorter. Use single-spaced copy; a space between paragraphs is optional.
- Target your audience. Ask sources if they prefer to receive releases by e-mail. Don't send unsolicited e-mail. Personalize the release if possible.
- Write a brief summary of the topic in the e-mail subject line.
- Headings: Insert company name and contact information at the top, FOR IMMEDIATE RELEASE and date of release. Insert a space before the headline.
- Write a clear summary headline. Insert another space.
- Write a summary lead with basic information: who, what, where, when. Make sure that it is visible in the first screen.
- Use lists to itemize information when relevant.
- Avoid adjectives and superlatives. Keep the writing simple and newsworthy.
- Proofread. E-mail is notoriously filled with typos, spelling and style errors. Sloppy work is a poor reflection on you and your client.
- Don't send attachments. Your users may not be able to open your documents.
- Insert links at the bottom to relevant information. For example, if your release is about a survey the company has done, include a link to the complete survey.
- Put the contact information (office and cell phone numbers, fax, e-mail and any related website) at the bottom of the release.

SOCIAL MEDIA PRESS RELEASES

Short, substantive, scannable. Those are three essential concepts for social media messages. Make sure you have some timely, newsworthy information to share. Although some of the basic information such as contact information is the same for all press releases, messages in social media should have other qualities to encourage readers. Here are some guidelines:

- Use informal writing style.
- Write a headline and subhead that will grab attention. Keep them short and simple.
- Use a direct lead — who, what, when, where, why — and inverted pyramid style.

- Make it scannable. This means including captions, boldfaced words or subheadings that readers will focus on in a quick scan of the release.
- Use lists to itemize information quickly.
- Make it search-engine optimizable (SEO) by using key words that search engines will pick up to drive traffic to your document or website. Good headlines and subheads are among the main items for SEO documents.
- Keep it short — less than 600 words.
- Avoid adjectives, market jargon and any unnecessary information.
- Embed links to video, photos or audio if relevant and a link at the end to blogs or other content that readers might want.
- Add contact information at the end.

STRUCTURE OF PRESS RELEASES

Press releases differ very little from basic news stories. Although some press releases may have feature leads, most use a summary lead that gets to the main point quickly. If you use a soft lead, put the nut graph high in the release, preferably by the second paragraph.

These days most press releases and media kits are distributed via e-mail or online. But you may need to mail or fax a paper copy to some organizations, so you still need to know how to write a print version. Printed versions are also necessary at functions such as press conferences, speeches, product demonstrations, ceremonies, trade shows and other places where you might need to hand out information.

Here are some basics for print releases:

Style: Use one side of the paper. Double-space the body copy (or use 1.5-line spacing). Keep the release short, preferably one page and no more than two. Use Associated Press style for releases to newspapers and most magazines.

Number Pages: If the release continues to more than one page, write "more" at the bottom of the first page and number each page.

Timeliness: Send out press releases in advance of the intended publication date. Although most press releases say "FOR IMMEDIATE RELEASE," you should send them out several days or a few weeks before an event is going to occur.

Major Elements in This Order:

- **Company name:** or logo at the top and company's address (street, city, state and ZIP code) or website if the company is only on the Web.
- **FOR IMMEDIATE RELEASE:** (preferably in caps and boldface).
- **Date of release:** (This could be placed under the previous item or attached to the dateline.)
- **Contact information:** Place contact information justified on the left side of the page. Write "CONTACT": followed by the name, title, phone numbers (telephone, cell and fax) and e-mail address of the person to contact. This information can be placed on the left or right side; it can be single-spaced.

- **Headline:** Skip two lines after your contact information. Boldface is optional but suggested. Although some firms prefer writing the headline all in capital letters, websites such as PRWeb recommend that headlines be written with uppercase and lowercase letters. Limit the headline to one line, especially for Web releases.

- **Dateline:** This is the city of origin for your press release, followed by the state abbreviation if not a major city. You may put the date here, preceded by a hyphen.

- **Lead:** A direct lead is preferable, including who, what, when and where, but a feature lead immediately followed by the key information is acceptable.

- **Body:** Briefly summarize the key points. Include a quote or comment from a company official if possible. Keep paragraphs short. Use lists if you have key points.

- **Ending:** End with a brief sentence or paragraph about the company — if relevant. Repeat a contact or other relevant source for further information. Include a website if available. Skip a space and type a symbol for the ending: three # # # or — 30 — Your format should look like this:

....

ORGANIZATION NAME ON LETTERHEAD

[Heading information can be single-spaced]

For Immediate Release   Contact: (*This information can be in single space*)
Date of release   Name, title of contact person
                                                      Telephone number
                                                      Cell phone number
                                                      Fax number
                                                      E-mail address

[Leave some space before the headline]

HEADLINE

[Double-space body copy]

DATELINE — [Location for the origin of the release (in capital letters) plus a dash, followed by the first line of the lead]

Lead: Preferably start with some hard-news lead, especially on releases for news events or announcements.

Body: Write tightly. Limit copy to one page if possible, no more than two. If you have two pages, write "more" at the end of the first page and number the pages.

Ending: As part of the ending, you could tell where more information is available, such as graphics and websites. A standard ending for a corporate press release includes a few lines about the company, including the company website.

— 30 — or # # #

....

Here is an example of a press release that was sent to newspapers, including *USA Today*, which published the story on the front page.

PRESS RELEASE — PRINT VERSION

Crayola, LLC.
1100 Church Lane
P.O. Box 431
Easton, Pennsylvania 18044-0431
[company telephone number]

FOR IMMEDIATE RELEASE

Contact: Mark J. O'Brien
Media Communications
[office telephone number; cell phone number]
[e-mail address]
[date]

CRAYOLA INTRODUCES NEW CRAYONS THAT ARE LITERALLY "OFF THE WALL"

EASTON, Pa. — Parents can put away the scrub brushes and stain remover, thanks to Crayola LLC. The maker of Crayola products has introduced a totally off-the-wall product — washable crayons.

Unlike the billions of crayons produced before them, Crayola washable crayons are made from a patented formula that washes from most surfaces, including walls and fabric.

"Washable crayons address our No. 1 consumer complaint — getting crayon marks off different surfaces," says Mark O'Brien, Crayola spokesperson.

"Each year we receive thousands of calls and letters regarding crayon stains, mainly from parents of preschool children. With the introduction of washable crayons, parents can breathe a little easier when it comes to crayon mishaps."

The difference between traditional and washable crayons is in their formulas. Washable crayons contain special water soluble polymers found in many health and beauty aids. This allows them to be removed from most surfaces by simply using soap and water. Tests have shown washable crayon marks can even be removed from walls and fabric one to two months after being stained. However, crayon marks are easiest to remove if washed soon after they happen.

Crayola washable crayons are nontoxic and available in two sizes. The So Big size, for younger children, comes six to a box and has a suggested retail price of $2.99. Boxes of eight, large size washable crayons will sell for approximately $2.59.

# # #

Web Press Release

Web releases are generally shorter. A Web or e-mail press release could include contact information at the top of the screen but should repeat it or include it initially at the bottom of the release so viewers don't have to scroll back to find it.

Here is a press release on the Hallmark website that also offered photos; note that it is written in single space with embedded links:

Hallmark Launches New iPhone and iPad Apps in Time for the Holidays

One app helps find stores and store specials, the other celebrates the holidays with games and a special story.

KANSAS CITY, Mo. — Two new iPhone and iPad applications from Hallmark are set to help make holiday shopping easier and time with family merrier.

HALLMARK APP

The free **Hallmark app** launches with a Hallmark Gold Crown® store locator that will include driving directions, as well as information about products and special offers available in stores. Users also can use the app to make a call to a store located by the application.

JINGLE ALL THE WAY APP

To celebrate the holidays, Hallmark also introduces the free **Jingle All the Way app** to bring a new dimension to family story time. This app complements Hallmark's new *Jingle All the Way* Interactive Storybook and Story Buddy, a book about a husky pup that finds a home for the holidays and a plush dog with voice-recognition software that responds with barks, whimpers and other sounds when certain lines from the story are read.

Courtesy of Hallmark Cards Inc.

Hallmark "Jingle All The Way" interactive storybook.

The application includes a narrated version of the story and the option to record your own voice reading the story. The plush dog interacts with these readings as well. The app also includes kid-friendly musical games and puzzles.

To install the new Hallmark applications, users will need the most recent version of iTunes and an iPhone, iPad or iPod Touch with OS3.1.3 or higher.

This new app from Hallmark joins the existing hoops&yoyo™ **Smiles:)** and **fun@work** apps that provide a daily dose of funny from characters hoops&yoyo.

About Hallmark Cards, Inc.

Hallmark makes the world a more caring place by helping people express what's in their hearts and spend time together — a privilege few other companies in the world enjoy. Hallmark greeting cards and other products are found in more than 40,000 retail outlets in the U.S., including the network of flagship Hallmark Gold Crown® stores. The brand also reaches people online at Hallmark.com and on television through Hallmark Hall of Fame original movies and cable's top-rated Hallmark Channel. Worldwide, Hallmark offers products in more than 30 languages available in 100 countries. This privately held company is based in Kansas City, Mo., and is led by the third generation of the founding Hall family. http://corporate.hallmark.com for more details.

List Format

Another form that would work for e-mail, Web distribution or print is a simple list of the basics: who, what, when, where, why and how. Here is an example from the American Red Cross of Alaska:

PRESS RELEASE–Date

Red Cross Smoke Alarm Drive

Contact information

Photo opportunity: Anchorage Fire Department Engine Number 5 will meet Red Cross staff and volunteers for a photo opportunity at the Benson Park at 10:30 a.m. on Jan. 15. The American Red Cross emergency response vehicle will also be at the event with coffee and hot chocolate for the community and volunteers.

WHO: American Red Cross of Alaska and the Anchorage Fire Department

WHAT: Anchorage citizens will show their concern for the safety of their neighbors by helping the American Red Cross of Alaska distribute free smoke detectors and batteries. The group will visit at least 1,000 homes and will be attended by firefighters from the Anchorage Fire Department.

WHEN: Saturday, Jan. 15 (year), 10 a.m. – 1 p.m.

WHERE: Smoke detectors and batteries will be given away in the neighborhood bordered by Benson to the north, 36th Avenue to the West and C Street to the east.

WHY: Working smoke detectors are a crucial tool in the early detection of domestic fires, which can dramatically assist with the prevention of the loss of life and reduction of injuries. According to statistics, up to 50 percent of the smoke alarms in the U.S. don't work because there is not an operable battery in the smoke detector. We have chosen this time of year to distribute smoke detectors because most house fires occur during the months of December, January and February.

HOW: This event is made possible by a generous grant from the Allstate Foundation.

Note: For more information, please call Heather Adams at 907-000-0000. The American Red Cross is a humanitarian organization led by volunteers that provides relief to victims of disaster and helps people prevent, prepare for and respond to emergencies.

Contact information repeated here.

VIDEO PRESS RELEASES

The video versions of press releases are known as VNRs, which are basically news stories produced for television. They include footage with a series of video images plus sound bites of quotes from sources in the story. In many cases the VNRs are so well done that TV stations can air them as polished news stories without even editing them. And therein lies the ethical problem.

Many small stations that have limited resources have used these VNRs produced by the U.S. government without attributing the source, thus making the video sound as though the station produced the story. Because these releases are promotional in nature and not balanced news stories, if the station does not indicate the source of the release, the audience can be misled. That isn't the fault of the public relations practitioner; it's the responsibility of the station to attribute the source.

The use of VNRs without attribution became so widespread that the Radio Television Digital News Association (RTDNA) issued guidelines for use of them. "Television and radio stations should strive to protect the editorial integrity of the video and audio they air. This integrity, at times, might come into question when stations air video and audio provided to newsrooms by companies, organizations or governmental agencies with political or financial interests in publicizing the material," according to the RTNDA guidelines. The organization's code of ethics says that electronic journalists should "clearly disclose the origin of information and label all material provided by outsiders."

The advantages of these video releases are that they are cost-effective for the TV station, which doesn't have to expend resources to shoot the video, and they provide the station with images and sound bites that could be inserted into locally produced news stories.

The format for video press releases includes the following elements:

- A disclaimer giving the news organization permission to use the material without charge.
- A list of the contents, often including the timing of each element.
- B-roll, which is video footage and natural sound that news stations can insert into stories.

- Interviews and sound bites from sources.
- Contact information.

Here is a script for a video press release by the U.S. Census Bureau about the value of a college education:

BACK TO SCHOOL

More Education Means Greater Earnings
Date
Slug: College Costs
Synopsis: How and why students are handling the ever-increasing cost of college.
Video Source: The U.S. Census Bureau
Super Information: (times to be inserted after client approval)
:XX (the time for the sound bite)
Mahlet "Mimi" Goitom
College Student
University of Maryland
:XX
Dr. Sandy Baum
Senior Policy Analyst
College Board
:XX
Louis Kincannon
Director
Location: Washington, D.C.

SUGGESTED LOCAL ANCHOR LEAD-IN: DESPITE THE RISING COST OF COLLEGE, AMERICANS ARE MORE EDUCATED THAN EVER AND THE CENSUS BUREAU HAS JUST RELEASED INFORMATION THAT SUGGESTS INVESTING IN A COLLEGE DEGREE PAYS FOR ITSELF. HERE IS THE STORY.

(Open with shots of Mimi working in financial aid office)

VO: MAHLET GOITOM, (mah hoh leat goy tum), OR MIMI, A THIRD-YEAR PUBLIC HEALTH MAJOR, IS ONE OF MANY STUDENTS RELYING ON BOTH FINANCIAL AID AND WORK TO PAY THE EVER-INCREASING COST OF COLLEGE.

(Cut to Mimi on camera)

SOT: "The main way that I'm dealing with the increased finances is by taking out loans and I've also become an RA to help my parents with the burden of paying for college."

(College campus shots transition to a graphic)

VO: THE MOST RECENT CENSUS DATA SHOWS COLLEGE GRADUATION RATES AT AN ALL TIME HIGH. AT LAST COUNT, 27% OF ADULTS 25 AND OVER HAD A BACHELOR'S DEGREE. AND ACCORDING TO EDUCATION EXPERTS THAT NUMBER MAY CONTINUE RISING SINCE TODAY'S STUDENTS HAVE ACCESS TO A LOT MORE FINANCIAL AID.

(Cut to Sandy Baum, on camera)

SOT: "Over 100 billion dollars of student aid was distributed to college students last year. The reality is that grant aid is growing rapidly, loans are growing even more rapidly, and there is help out there for students to pay these rising college costs."

(College campus shots transition to Census Bureau graphic)

VO: MIMI, LIKE MANY OTHER COLLEGE STUDENTS, PUTS IN THE LONG HOURS BECAUSE SHE BELIEVES IT WILL PAY OFF IN THE FUTURE. AND THE EXPERTS SAY SHE'S RIGHT.

SOT: (Kincannon) "There's no doubt there is a strong relationship between education and earnings. The more education you have, the likelier it is you'll have a higher income. For example, high school graduates earn about $30,000 yearly, where as college graduates earn nearly 75% more."

(Shots of Mimi)

VO: AND THAT WILL HELP STUDENTS LIKE MIMI CARRY THE BURDEN OF DEBT FROM STUDENT LOANS.

(Cut to Mimi, on camera, cut to shots of Mimi walking)

SOT: "I definitely think taking out a loan is worth it, I mean, an undergraduate degree is essential for any career path, and I think it's definitely worth it to take out a loan."

THIS IS HANNAH HAINES.

(Local anchor tag)
SUGGESTED LOCAL ANCHOR TAG: FOR MORE CENSUS DATA ON EDUCATION, GO TO *WWW. CENSUS.GOV.*

PUBLIC SERVICE ANNOUNCEMENTS

Public service announcements, commonly called PSAs, are messages that TV or radio stations will air without charge, provided that the messages have noncommercial and nonpolitical content. In print media they are considered public service advertisements. Because they are used without charge, they are usually very brief. In broadcast media, PSAs generally run from 15 seconds to one minute. You should check with the stations for their requirements of formats and submission dates. In general they contain information that could be considered useful or beneficial to the audience.

- At the top of your script, write a slug, the length of time for the PSA (usually in seconds) and the agency that produced it.
- Start with a hook, a strong statement that will grab the listener's or viewer's attention.
- Read your copy aloud because the message will be heard by the audience.
- Keep it brief and include only the most crucial information.
- Include the dates and times of any event you are promoting.
- Use broadcast style of all capital letters and double-spacing for a video script.
- End with some statement that either requests an action by the listener or offers more information.
- For television broadcast of video PSAs, send your video with the PSA text.

Your format should look like this:

From: Name of organization and address

Contact: Name of contact person with phone numbers (telephone, fax and cell) and e-mail address

Length: time it takes to read the PSA

Message: Type the PSA message in paragraph form

Disclaimer: At the bottom of the page, briefly describe the organization and specify that it is nonprofit.

Here is a 15-second PSA from the Federal Trade Commission:

THE FEDERAL TRADE COMMISSION SAYS ANYONE WITH A PHONE COULD BE A VICTIM OF A SCHEMING TELEMARKETER. DON'T GIVE AWAY YOUR CREDIT CARD OR BANK ACCOUNT NUMBERS ON THE PHONE. IF YOU HAVE ANY DOUBT ABOUT AN OFFER YOU HEAR ON THE PHONE, CHECK IT OUT AND GET IT IN WRITING. A MESSAGE FROM THE FEDERAL TRADE COMMISSION AND THIS STATION.

# # #

Courtesy of the Federal Trade Commission

Video PSA.

SOCIAL MEDIA

IF YOU WANT TO get a job in public relations, you are probably going to need skills in social networking, blogging and writing for micro-blogging sites like Twitter. That's the conclusion of a survey based on interviews with more than 250 professionals who make hiring decisions in public relations and marketing firms.

"Social media skills are nearly as important as traditional media relations skills," according to the 2009 Digital Readiness Report.

Social networking is redefining the way public relations practitioners communicate with their audiences, according to Katie Winchell, marketing and communications director for the California League of Schools. "For decades, the triad of print media, journalistic standards and the AP Stylebook-driven press release meant that P.R. professionals could key in on content," she wrote in *Public Relations Tactics.*

"Because P.R. writing was aimed primarily at journalists who were in turn reporting to a passive readership, there was little motivation to understand the wants, needs and opinions of the individuals who were using a product or service. . . . Suddenly the conversation is going on all around you. Your brand is being evangelized, dismissed, measured and documented in real time online. If you haven't already done so, then it's time to join the conversation and show your company or client cares — a mission perfectly suited for the P.R. professional."

What are some of the most effective ways to write corporate content for social media? Jakob Nielsen, a world-renown authority on online usability, offers these tips based on studies he conducted of corporate use on Facebook, Twitter, MySpace and LinkedIn.

- **Post current and timely information:** If you post too rarely, you will lose users; if you post too frequently, you will crowd out other messages — a major annoyance. Post timely updates.
- **Provide useful content:** Messages with substance and timeliness scored highest.
- **Write for the medium:** The shorter the message, the more important the writing. Don't just repurpose other information.
- **Focus on one topic or subject per message.**
- **Place key words at the beginning of the message.**
- **Write in conversational, informal tone.**
- **Link to other content within the social network rather than external sites.** Make links short and readable.
- **Proofread your messages.**
- **Engage in two-way conversation.** Respond to questions from followers and fans within 24 hours.

MULTICULTURAL AWARENESS

If you want to find out how to reach 23 million Hispanics, Manny Ruiz will help you. He'll send you a daily blog at your request to keep you informed with articles and resources about publicizing and marketing to the Hispanic audience. Manny and his wife, Angela Sastaita-Ruiz co-publish the Hispanic PR Blog, a leading marketing site for Hispanic public relations and social media *(http://www.hispanicprblog.com/)*. They are also the authors of a 56-page U.S. Hispanic Social Media Guide.

"If you scour the Latino Web as often as I do, you'll notice that one of the biggest trends right now is that not only are Latinos definitely engaging more through social media but that they are producing unique content as bloggers as well," Ruiz said in the guide.

Latinos and African Americans lead all other racial groups in the use of mobile media and cell phone ownership as well, according to a study by the Pew Internet and American Life Project.

Other studies confirm that minority groups are critical audiences for public relations and marketing professionals. As mentioned previously, Hallmark has the Sinceramente line of cards and products geared to Hispanics and the Mahogany line geared to African-Americans. Most of the major U.S. government agencies offer bilingual information in English and Spanish.

PRSA also features a website devoted to articles and blogs, and a diversity toolkit to help chapters develop multicultural resources *www.prsa.org/Diversity/*.

MEDIA KITS

Public relations practitioners often use media kits to promote corporate products. Printed versions of these kits are usually included in decorative folders that contain a variety of press releases, fact sheets about the company and its products and sometimes samples of the company's products.

These days more media kits are being produced for the Web. They still contain fact sheets and news releases, but online they also offer multimedia information in audio and video, PDF files containing images of the products, plus fact sheets, backgrounders and links to other information. They may also include interactive features. If you are planning a media kit for the Web, consider how many Web pages you will need for the information and create links to each page. Most major corporate sites have a Press Room link to Web pages with information about the company, press releases, products and contacts.

A good media kit should contain these items:

Attractive Cover: The kit is usually contained in a folder with the company name and logo if it will be produced as a print product.

Brief Letter or Note: A very brief explanation of the purpose of the kit should be provided for the editor. It could be on the inside of the cover.

Press release: The first item after the editor's note should be a press release.

Fact Sheet: Present information about the organization in simple list form. You might use headings such as *Who, What, Where, When, Why* and *How*. Fact sheets might also briefly itemize vital statistics about the organization or the issue, such as statistics on obesity if you are promoting a weight-loss product.

Backgrounder: A backgrounder is information that can provide in-depth information that supplements the news, such as statistical research or historical developments that led up to the event you are promoting. Backgrounders might also include a feature story, such as a profile of a company executive. Don't include information in the backgrounder that should be in the press release. This is additional material, not a substitute for news.

Story Ideas: The story idea sheet is optional, but if you include it, try to offer suggestions for localizing the information. This sheet should be written in list form or short paragraphs. You might also include suggestions for photos, video opportunities or graphics. The cover letter for your media kit should briefly state what is included. On the Web, you can create a navigation bar or box with links.

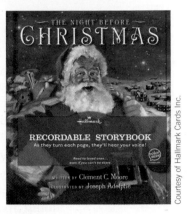

A Hallmark recordable storybook.

For example, the Hallmark online media kit for its recordable storybooks includes a fact sheet, a news release and links to multimedia. "Recordable storybooks feature exclusive voice-capture technology that enables a person to record each page of a book and have it played back over and over as the recipient turns the pages. The recording will not be lost, even when the batteries need to be replaced," according to the fact sheet. These links are included in the online media kit:

- Read and share recordable storybook stories on Facebook.
- Watch "Connecting Families, Creating Memories" on YouTube.
- View a recordable storybook video demonstration on Hallmark.com.
- Related images of storybooks in downloadable formats of low to high resolution

CORPORATE PUBLICATIONS

When you are writing press releases for the media whether in print or on the Web, use newspaper style. If you are writing a company magazine with news and features about people and events in the organization, newspaper style still applies. But when you are writing a memo or proposal to the company president or other corporate officials, you need to state your position in an analytical way.

That's where many business writers have difficulty, says Anne Baber, a writing coach who conducts seminars in corporations to improve communication techniques. She has also conducted seminars for the International Association of Business Communicators and has written books and many articles about career topics.

The key factor is to know the audience, she says: "There are some psychological problems people have when they write for folks up the ladder in management. One of my theories is that power warps communication. When people are writing for a boss, it's like a teenager talking to a parent. The parent says, 'Where are you going?' The teenager answers, 'Out.' The teen isn't saying everything he knows because of the power structure. In corporations, the power structure also affects communication. The writing becomes very formal, very passive. The writers don't want to put themselves forward as being initiators of action. They hide behind the third person. They write *the employee* rather than the word *you*."

Baber bases her theories on many years of experience in corporate communications. A former director of communications for United Telecom (now called Sprint), she now heads her own consulting firm, Baber & Associates, in Kansas City, Mo.

Many of the coaching techniques she uses are similar to those described earlier in this book. But the outcome is different. "Newswriting operates on the idea that if you give the public enough information, they will inform themselves," she says. "We're not doing that in an organization. We want to create attitudes or actions. It's much more like advertising." Here are Baber's tips for writing proposals and company plans:

Reporting Steps

Make a List: Ask what the audience — in this case, management — really wants to know. Then itemize all the points you can. (This is the same as brainstorming for a news story.)

Envision the Result: Ask yourself: What kind of action is the reader expected to take as a result of this information?

Make a Checklist of What and Why: Write a sentence beginning "I want to tell you that . . ." and then answer why. Then add this teaser to support the why factor: "This is necessary because. . . ." (This teaser is similar to the focus — "so what" — sentence at the top of your news stories.)

Writing Steps

Draw a "Mind Spill": Get all the research together. Draw a circle in the center of a large piece of paper. Put the main topic in the center circle. Then draw more circles, filling each one with an idea. With a colored pencil or highlighter, mark the key links between these ideas. Draw a line to connect one related idea to another so that all like information is grouped together. Then number the points, preferably in the order you will write them in the proposal. (This is the same technique as mapping for ideas or reporting.)

Organize the Order: Write a topic sentence (the same as a focus sentence) that completes this thought: "I believe that. . . ." For example, "I believe that we should market Mother's Day cards a different way." Then write the word *because* followed by point one, point two, point three — like the list technique. The most persuasive structure is three in parallel style.

Use Inverted Pyramid Style: Put the strongest point of the proposal in the lead, and then plan your proposal with supporting points.

Put Information in Perspective: Ask yourself: What does the reader know already, and what is new? If this is one of a series of proposals, you may need just a summary sentence referring to past information the reader already knows. The reader is going to read this proposal quickly and will get irritated if he has to wade through previously known material.

Write a Strong Conclusion: Summarize, but do not repeat, your lead. If you have written a proposal about marketing Mother's Day cards and you have given the supporting points that answer why you should change the method, the ending could be a strong statement such as "We should start marketing these new cards in six months." If that time frame is part of your proposal, you could just end with a statement telling why it is a good idea.

Check Your Verbs: After you have written your draft, go back and circle the verbs and see if they are strong action words. If not, revise.

JOB SKILLS–ADVICE FROM THE PROS

Networking is one of the most important skills for public relations practitioners. It helps to attend conferences so you can meet people face-to-face, but now you can network with hundreds of accomplished professionals without leaving your computer or smart phone. Resources for students and professionals abound on Twitter, Facebook and public relations organizations. Here are some helpful resources for public relations and marketing advice:

- PRSA (Public Relations Society of America *(www.prsa.org/)*: This is one of the most comprehensive sites offering blogs, several online magazines and perhaps most important for P.R. students, a job center with career resources and mentors to help you with resume writing, interviewing skills and job networking. You'll find complete information on how to build your portfolio.

- New pros have great advice for students in their blog, *http://prnewpros.prsa.org/*. Crystal Olig, a former chair of this blog group, offers these tips for networking: Attend events, dress smart, bring business cards, prepare questions and follow up with e-mails.

- PRSSA, the Public Relations Students Society of America, offers career guidance and internship opportunities. It also provides a skills inventory that lists effective written communication at the top of the list. Other essential skills include persuasive speaking, problem solving, multi-tasking in the list of 20. The website also gives complete advice on cover letters, resumes, and networking at *www.prssa.org*. and *http://blog.prssa.org*.

- Twitter *(http://twitter.com)*is a fast way to skim hundreds of sources and links to blogs. Just type in P.R., P.R. jobs or P.R. skills and you'll find scores of entries. Check out *pr2020* for useful tips and trends.

- Create your own list of helpful blogs and sites from Facebook, Twitter and P.R.. organizations and agencies. Find a place where you might like to work and follow that company or agency.

Here is some inspiration from Elizabeth Albrycht, author of the CorporatePR blog and an expert in new technologies for public relations: "Be prepared for the unexpected. The one constant in PR is change. Stories change, people change, clients change, jobs change, technologies change, fads change, trends change. . . . P.R. is generally NOT glamorous. There is nothing fun about stuffing press kits at 4 a.m. in a crappy conference center hotel room when you have an 8 a.m. press conference. The P.R. person rarely gets thanked when things go well and is the first to be blamed when things go badly. However, one of the great things about P.R. is you can immediately see the results of your work. You can make a difference."

EXERCISES

1 **Press release (hard-news style):** Gather information from an organization for an event on your campus or in your city. Write a press release announcing the event.

2 **Social Media:** Create an account on Twitter. Find at least five public relations sites, corporate sites or professionals to follow. Follow the discussions for at least a week. Write an analysis of each site, critiquing the good and bad information. What was helpful, annoying, a waste of time or useful? Critique the writing as well. With only 140 characters allowed, were the postings clear? What enticed you to click further?

3 **Media kit:** Study a company in your community. Devise a media kit to promote some product or aspect of the company. This activity may require some coordination so that many students do not bother the same firm. If a team of students or the whole class is studying a large company, divide the responsibilities so students are studying different aspects of the company.

4 **Press release (feature style):** As the contact, use your name, phone number and e-mail address. The company is Excaliber Entertainment Inc., 1955 Larkspur, San Antonio, Texas 78213. This information is adapted from a press release for a former online contest site owned by Excaliber. You may use a direct or creative lead. Assume that the website still exists for your press release, which should be limited to one page.

Who: www.vaultcracker.com, a contest website.

What: Sponsoring a contest, "Junkiest Dorm Room in America."

When: Use now through the next two months.

Where: www.vaultcracker.com.

Why: To promote the new website.

How: The contest will award $300 to a college student whose pictures of his or her dorm room are judged the junkiest. Second prize is $100. The contest is open to all students who are enrolled full time at a college or university in the United States.

Comments: From Richard McNairy, founder and president of www.vaultcracker.com: "We know how busy college students are and we wanted to turn a negative into a positive. I'm sure students with messy rooms get criticism from others. Now two students with junky rooms will be able to brag about the fact that they earned cash because of their junky rooms."

More information: Visit www.vaultcracker.com.

5 **E-mail press release:** Write a one-page e-mail press release (about 150 words) based on the following information; use your name, phone number and e-mail for contact information:

The U.S. Department of Commerce's census bureau released a report today about the value of various college degrees. The report is called "What's It Worth? Field of Training and Economic Status." The data are from a panel of the Survey of Income and Program Participation. College graduates who work full time and have a bachelor's degree in engineering earn the highest average monthly pay ($4,680), while those with education degrees earn the lowest ($2,802), according to the report. "Majoring in a technical field does pay off even if you don't finish a four-year degree," said Kurt Bauman, co-author with Camille Ryan of the report. "The average person with a vocational certificate earns around $200 more per month than the average high school graduate; but if the certificate is in an engineering-related field, the boost in earnings is close to $800." At the top of the earnings scale were those with professional degrees, such as doctors and lawyers ($7,224 per month), followed by full-time workers with master's degrees ($4,635), bachelor's degrees ($3,767), high school graduates ($2,279) and those without a diploma ($1,699).

Business was the most popular field of training beyond high school; 7.5 million people had bachelor's degrees in business and earned a monthly average of $3,962. An additional 1.9 million had master's degrees in business administration or other advanced degrees in business. The average monthly earnings of people with master's degrees in business was $5,579. Of people with managerial jobs, 46 percent had bachelor's or higher degrees. Of people in professional occupations, 71 percent held a bachelor's degree or higher degrees. By comparison, no more than 8 percent of those in craft, service, farm and production occupations had completed this much education. Associate degrees generally require a two-year course of study, but people took an average of more than four years to complete them. Bachelor's and higher degrees took an average of five or more years to complete.

6 **Public service announcement:** Write a 15-second public service announcement (about 65 words) based on this information:

This message is from the Federal Emergency Management Agency. It's about tornadoes. They can be deadly. Tornadoes strike nearly every year with the most powerful winds on Earth. Remember these three tornado danger signs: One — Before a tornado hits, the wind may die down and the air may become very still. Two — Tornadoes can be nearly invisible, marked only by swirling debris at the base of the funnel. An approaching cloud of dust or debris can mark the location of a deadly tornado. Seek shelter immediately. Three — Tornadoes generally occur near the trailing edge of a thunderstorm. When a thunderstorm moves through your area, be alert for tornadoes. For more information on tornado preparedness, visit the FEMA website at www.fema.gov, or contact the Red Cross. Plan ahead to survive the next tornado, and listen to this station for more emergency preparedness information from FEMA.

7 **Promote a product:** Working in small groups, create a new product and a company name and address. Use your name and contact information. Each person in the group should then write a press release promoting this product.

8 **Usability study:** Conduct your own informal usability study by visiting the websites of three to five corporations that interest you. On each site, search for basic P.R. information described in this chapter and note your findings. Do the sites contain the basic contact information that you would need, such as phone numbers, addresses and key corporate officers? Do the sites contain a good description of the company's purpose? What other information do you think these websites should contain?

COACHING TIPS

Check your story for **accuracy.**

Seek documents to **substantiate sources' claims.**

Check résumés and other **credentials** from sources.

Seek sources with **alternate points of view.**

Role-play: If you were the source or the source's attorney, what would you find **libelous or objectionable** in the story?

If you are writing about a police or court case, check for the **latest charges or disposition** in the case.

Don't copy information from a website without **attribution or permission.**

Don't use online information or social media you can't **verify, especially if it includes accusations** about a person.

zimmytws/Shutterstock.com

Congress shall make no law respecting an establishment of religion, or prohibiting the free exercise thereof; or abridging the freedom of speech, or of the press; or the right of the people peaceably to assemble, and to petition the Government for a redress of grievances.

— THE FIRST AMENDMENT TO THE
U.S. CONSTITUTION

CHAPTER 14
Media Law

TEST YOUR KNOWLEDGE OF THESE LEGAL ISSUES:

1. You are the online editor of your campus newspaper. A person using a pseudonym has posted a message on your website that could be libelous. If you don't remove the posting, the paper will be liable for the information in the message if a lawsuit is filed. True or False?

2. You have visited a website that has a graphic you want to use in your campus newspaper or your radio station's website. The site does not contain any copyright notice so you can use the graphic without permission. True or False?

3. Any columns labeled "opinion" or editorials published in your newspaper cannot be considered libelous regardless of the information they contain. True or False?

4. You are posting a video on YouTube. If you use just a portion of a popular song in your video, you will not be violating copyright laws. True or False?

Many legal issues arising from the increasing use of social networking sites, blogs and other online media do not have clear-cut answers. However, the questions posed here have legal precedents. Here are the answers to the first three questions, which are adapted from information on the Student Press Law Center (*www.splc.org*), and the answer to the last question, which is explained on the YouTube website (*www. youtube.com*):

Question 1: **False.** The paper is not liable for messages posted by a third party. The federal Communications Decency Act grants immunity to website operators and Internet providers for messages posted by a third party. But if you create part of the message by editing it, you could be considered a "content provider," and you might be liable in a lawsuit. In addition, because the Web is

1101 Wilson Blvd.
Suite 1100
Arlington, VA 22209, USA.
Telephone: 703.807.1904

Do you have questions about your legal rights and responsibilities as a student journalist or media adviser? Or are you just interested in more information about press law? The SPLC Resource Center can help you find answers.

a global medium, you could be liable in other countries. It is probably a good idea to check the postings and delete ones that you think are offensive or potentially libelous.

Question 2: **False.** All material on the Internet is copyrighted as soon as it is created. It does not need to have a copyright notice to be protected by U.S. copyright laws. However, some images may be available without permission if they are from government sites or from websites that say permission is granted for specific use. In many cases the site may grant permission to use images on personal pages but not for commercial use.

Question 3: **False.** You may express opinions without impunity, but if you publish an allegation that is false and damaging to a person's reputation, you can be sued for libel no matter where it is published in a newspaper, on a website or in a broadcast medium. You can criticize someone as a bad performer without being libelous, but if you falsely accuse the performer of being a drug addict, that would be libelous.

Question 4: **False.** You are violating copyright by using all or a portion of a song or video that you did not create yourself. The YouTube site specifically states: "Be sure that all components of your video are your original creation — even the audio portion. . . . If you use an audio track of a sound recording owned by a record label without that record label's permission, your video may be infringing the copyrights of others, and may be subject to removal."

LIBEL

"Libel is essentially a false and defamatory attack in written form on a person's reputation or character. Broadcast defamation is libel because there is usually a written script. Oral or spoken defamation is slander," according to Donald Gillmor and his co-authors in *Mass Communication Law: Cases and Comment.* The "script" is not limited to a news story, the authors explain; it can take the form of headlines, photos, cartoons, film, tape, records, signs, bumper stickers and advertisements.

Several libel suits have also resulted from messages that people posted to online discussion groups. If the defamatory statements are published — whether online or in print — they can still be considered libelous.

Truth is a defense in libel suits. Anyone can sue or threaten to sue for libel, claiming injury to his reputation. The real concern is whether the person has grounds enough to win. The key factors to consider are whether you published untrue information that hurt the reputation of an identifiable person and whether you were either negligent or reckless in failing to check the information:

- Are you publishing something that may not be truthful?
- Are you carelessly publishing something that is inaccurate?
- Are you publishing something accusatory that you haven't checked out?
- Are you publishing something that clearly identifies a person and harms that person's reputation?

If your answer is yes to any of those questions, you could be in trouble for libel.

Times v. Sullivan

Those standards were the ones the U.S. Supreme Court applied in 1964 in a landmark libel case, *New York Times Co. v. Sullivan*, and the standards have been applied since then to public officials.

The *New York Times* case stemmed from an advertisement the newspaper accepted in 1960 from a group of people in the civil rights movement. The group was trying to raise money for the Committee to Defend Martin Luther King. The ad claimed that King had been arrested seven times and that his home had been bombed. It also claimed that black students who had staged a nonviolent civil rights demonstration at Alabama State University had been the target of police brutality. The advertisement accused the police department in Montgomery, Ala., of being armed with shotguns and using tear gas to subdue students.

Even though the police commissioner, L. B. Sullivan, had not been named in the advertisement, he sued for libel. He contended that the mention of "police" in the ad referred to him as the Montgomery police commissioner, and that the ad contained factual errors that damaged his reputation. He claimed that the police did not ring the college campus or padlock the college dining hall, as the ad had claimed. Furthermore, Dr. King had been arrested four times, not seven, and three of the four arrests had occurred before Sullivan was commissioner.

Sullivan won in the lower courts and the Alabama Supreme Court. But the U.S. Supreme Court reversed the decision in its landmark ruling about "actual malice." Malice, in this context, does not mean ill will or intent to harm someone; it means that you published something knowing it was false or carelessly published information without checking whether it was true or false. As the justices wrote,

> The constitutional guarantees require, we think, a federal rule that prohibits a public official from recovering damages for defamatory falsehood relating to his official conduct unless he proves that the statement was made with "actual malice" — that is knowledge that it was false or with reckless disregard of whether it was false or not.

The court placed the burden of proving libel on the plaintiff, the person who is suing. The justices made this a constitutional issue, applying the First Amendment right of a free press to publish matters of public concern. In the ruling, Justice William Brennan wrote the following:

> Thus we consider this case against the background of a profound national commitment to the principle that debate on public issues should be uninhibited, robust, and wide-open, and that it may well include vehement, caustic, and sometimes unpleasantly sharp attacks on government and public officials.

The *Times v. Sullivan* ruling applied only to people who are public officials. The application was later broadened to include "public figures."

Public Officials

For purposes of libel law, who is a public official? Elected officials and candidates for office are definitely considered public officials. Appointed officials may or may not be. Here are the criteria: Do they have authority to set policy in the government, and are they under enough public scrutiny to have easy access to the media?

The Supreme Court defined public officials this way in *Rosenblatt v. Baer*, a case about the status of appointed officials:

U.S. Supreme Court
Justice William Brennan

> It is clear, therefore, that the "public official" designation applies at the very least to those among the hierarchy of government employees who have, or appear to the public to have, substantial responsibility for or control over the conduct of government affairs.

Is a police officer a public official? Courts in Pennsylvania are split on that decision, but most courts have ruled that law enforcement officers are public officials because they have the power to make arrests, a form of control in government. However, teachers, professors and other employees in a public education system are not usually defined as public officials because they are carrying out policies set by other officials of the school district or university. But if they achieve fame or notoriety, they may become public figures.

Public Figures

Who is a public figure, and why is the distinction between public officials and public figures important? People may be considered public figures if their achievements or notoriety places them in the public eye or if they seek attention by voluntarily thrusting themselves into a public controversy. But if they are brought into the public spotlight involuntarily, they may not be public figures. A court will usually determine whether the person qualifies as a public figure.

Like public officials, public figures also bear the burden of proving that the information in contention was libelous. The person or organization being sued does not have to disprove libel. The courts identify three types of public figures: pervasive, vortex and involuntary.

A "pervasive" public figure is a person who has gained prominence in society or great power and influence. Well-known entertainers and athletes and people who voluntarily seek public attention are in this category.

A "vortex" or "limited" public figure is a person who has voluntarily thrust himself into a public controversy to influence the outcome. The Supreme Court has stated that people in this category are not public figures for all aspects of their lives but only for the aspects that relate to their role in a particular public controversy. A key point is the "voluntary" concept. An individual does not automatically become a public figure if he is thrust into a newsworthy situation; the involvement in the controversy must be the person's choice. Access to the media is another factor in determining whether someone is a public figure. The person must have enough regular and continuing access to the media to counter criticism and expose falsehoods.

Consider the case of *Hutchinson v. Proxmire*. In 1975, when the late Sen. William Proxmire issued his annual "Golden Fleece" awards, which satirized some government-funded research projects as wasteful, he issued a press release targeting a researcher who was using monkeys to study stress. The scientist, Ronald Hutchinson, sued Proxmire for damaging his reputation and subjecting him to public ridicule by falsely claiming Hutchinson's research was wasteful. Key to the case was determining whether Hutchinson was a public figure.

Proxmire claimed the scientist was a public figure because he had received federal grants and had access to the media when they contacted him about receiving the Golden Fleece award. A federal district court agreed with Proxmire and dismissed the suit. But Hutchinson appealed.

The U.S. Supreme Court ruled that Hutchinson was not a public figure because he was not willingly involved in a public controversy until Proxmire caused it. The court said Hutchinson did not automatically become a public figure by being thrust into a newsworthy situation. Also, the court determined that Hutchinson did not have regular and continuing access to the media. He was sought out by reporters only to respond to Proxmire's criticism. Hutchinson ultimately received $10,000 from Proxmire.

The third type of public figure, "involuntary," is someone who does nothing voluntary to garner attention or to get involved in a public issue but finds himself in the middle of a public controversy anyway. Courts have found that this category rarely fits an individual in a libel suit.

Private Figures

The difference between being a public or private figure is crucial because the standards for proving libel can differ. Many states have made it easier for private persons to prove libel than for public figures. The Supreme Court has left it up to the states to determine their own standards of liability for private figures:

> We hold that, so long as they do not impose liability without fault, the States may define for themselves the appropriate standard of liability for a publisher or a broadcaster of defamatory falsehood injurious to a private individual.

The court made this ruling in a 1974 case, *Gertz v. Welch*. Elmer Gertz was a Chicago lawyer who claimed he had been libeled when a John Birch Society magazine, *American Opinion*, published an article labeling him a Communist. He sued the publisher, Robert Welch. Even though Gertz was a prominent lawyer, the Supreme Court ruled that he was a private person under the circumstances of this case. The court also declared that because private people don't have the same access to the media to defend themselves as public officials, they shouldn't be held to the same strict standards in proving libel.

In *Gertz v. Welch*, the court decided that a private individual needs to show only that the material was published with carelessness or negligence instead of proving actual malice, which means publishing with knowledge or reckless disregard of falsity. But all libel plaintiffs, public and private, have to prove the material is false and damaging to their reputation.

Even though the Supreme Court left it up to states to determine their own libel standards in cases involving private figures, the *Gertz* case paved the way for allowing private people to abide by less rigid standards than public officials and figures. Many states have followed the "simple negligence" standard in the *Gertz* case. Others require private individuals to abide by the same "actual malice" standard as public individuals. "Negligence" in this context means you failed to exercise reasonable care in doing your job as a journalist. That type of care might include talking to all sides of a controversial issue, using relevant documents, taking accurate notes and checking your information for accuracy before publishing it.

THE IMPORTANCE OF ACCURACY

Accuracy is paramount for a good journalist. Every mistake you make jeopardizes the newspaper's or broadcast station's credibility with readers and viewers. Because of that credibility factor, newspapers throughout the country print corrections every day, many for the incorrect spelling of names. That's another reason why you should always double-check the names in your stories.

The public's opinion of press accuracy has plummeted to its lowest level since 1985. A survey by the Pew Research Center for People and the Press revealed that 63 percent of Americans believe news organizations are often inaccurate and biased in their reporting compared to only 29 percent who said that news organizations "generally get the facts straight." Furthermore 60 percent of the people surveyed said news organizations are politically biased. Despite the number of corrections that news organizations print or broadcast, only 21 percent of the people surveyed said that news organizations are willing to admit their mistakes.

Accuracy in the media is also affected by the growing use of social media networks for reporting. Sources are not always reliable or identified, especially in tweets, and the rush to publish in this highly competitive news world can lead to inaccurate information. With press credibility at an all-time low, it is crucial to verify your sources when you use Twitter, Facebook and other social networking sites for reporting.

Showing Copy to Sources

Should you show your story to sources or read it to them before you publish it? Many of your sources will ask you to do that. And many editors will say you shouldn't. They claim the risks are too great that sources will recant what they have told you or ask you to delete any information that puts them in a bad light.

Steve Weinberg, former director of Investigative Reporters and Editors and a leading authority on researching records, says it's time to change that traditional way of thinking. "I am convinced that my practice of pre-publication read-backs and manuscript submission has led to more accurate, fair and thorough newspaper pieces, magazine articles and books," he wrote in *Quill* magazine. "There is no such thing as a minor mistake, not even just one or two little errors in a lengthy manuscript."

Weinberg makes it clear that the source only has the right to check for accuracy, not to make any changes.

If you don't show the entire story to your source, it is considered acceptable — even wise — to ask a source about any technical information you may not fully understand. You can read what you have written and, like Weinberg, ask the source to check its accuracy.

Corrections

The most common cause of lawsuits is carelessness. Most news media don't publish material they know or suspect is false.

Although newspapers and broadcast media get sued by people targeted in major investigative projects, the majority of libel suits stem from much less important stories. Incorrect captions, defamatory headlines, an inaccuracy in a police story or a feature can result in a libel suit.

Printed corrections or oral retractions on radio or television don't prevent libel suits. They may assuage an angered source enough to forestall a lawsuit, or they may be evidence of the news organization's good faith, but corrections do not undo the harm of inaccurate published material. It's up to a jury to decide if you were negligent, careless or reckless in your disregard for the truth.

A printed correction by the *National Enquirer* didn't stop entertainer Carol Burnett from suing the tabloid in 1976 for insinuating that she was drunk. The article said that she had an argument with Henry Kissinger, then secretary of state, at a Washington restaurant and "accidentally knocked a glass of wine over on one diner — and started giggling." Burnett denied the incident occurred, and even though the *Enquirer* apologized in a retraction, Burnett pressed her lawsuit. She was awarded a total of $1.6 million by a Los Angeles jury and ultimately settled for an undisclosed amount.

Even when you use the word *alleged*, meaning that the accusation is a charge without proof, you are on dangerous ground. This word, although widely used by reporters in police cases, does not save you from libel. It is better to attribute the information to official sources or records.

If you don't name the person against whom the accusation is made, you still can be sued for libel. A person who can claim he was identified — either by enough information to describe the person physically or by position — can then sue.

Nor does attribution save you. Say that a candidate for mayor tells you his opponent is a crook. You print the statement and attribute it to the candidate. The opponent could sue you and your newspaper. Just because you named the source of the statement, you cannot avoid responsibility for it. And if it isn't true and you haven't documented it as true, you could be considered guilty of reckless disregard for the truth.

If you are going to print any accusations that could be defamatory, you should always check with the person being accused and ask for a response. Cross-checking may not save you from libel, but it at least gives you a chance to prove you were not reckless.

There are times when you can print accusatory or damaging information, especially when you are writing about crime. You have certain privileges as a member of the press, and so do some of the officials who deal with you.

Privilege

Privilege — in a legal sense — comes in two forms: absolute and qualified.

Absolute Privilege: This means that public officials, including law enforcement officials, can make statements in the course of their official duties without fear of being sued for libel. This form of privilege extends to court proceedings, legislative proceedings, public and official meetings, and contents of public records. For example, if Senator Proxmire had announced his Golden Fleece awards on the floor of the Senate instead of in a news release, he would have had absolute privilege and could not have been sued by Hutchinson, the researcher who claimed he was libeled.

Qualified Privilege: As a member of the media, you have "qualified privilege." You may print defamatory statements made by people who are absolutely privileged as long as you are being fair and accurate and the information is from a public proceeding or public record. But if your report contains errors, you could lose that qualified protection.

If during a public meeting a city council member calls another member a crook, you may print the accusation. If the same city official makes the same comment to you during a telephone interview or after the meeting, you can't print it without risking libel. The key is that the defamatory statement must be made in an official capacity during an official proceeding. Or you may use, with attribution, something stated in court records. But you must make it clear that the accusations were made by other people in records or meetings and are not proven fact.

Suppose that a police officer tells you something about a suspect. You may print this information if the officer is acting in an official capacity and if the information is documented in a public record, such as a police report or court files. However, you still should be careful about how you word accusations in crime stories. The police officer may say the man stabbed his wife, but you may not say the same thing without attribution. If the information is not stated in a public record, such as a police report or court record, it can be libelous. Generally, statements made outside of the court by police are not privileged, but some states may extend privilege to these comments.

Never call anyone a murderer unless the person has been convicted of murder in court. Suppose that a man has been murdered and you go to the neighborhood for reaction. A neighbor says the man's wife killed him. The neighbor isn't an official acting in an official capacity, and the wife hasn't been convicted. The neighbor's comments could be libelous, and you could be sued for printing them.

Don't call suspects robbers or use any other accusatory term before they are convicted. Use terms such as "the suspect," "the man accused of murder," or "the woman charged with the robbery."

Person of Interest: In recent years police have been using another term, "person of interest," to describe someone who is being investigated in a crime but has not been arrested or charged with anything. Although the term appears to be a synonym for "suspect," it does not have any legal definition and can implicate people who are just being questioned. The term has become known as "the Richard Jewell rule," because it was used in reference to Richard Jewell, the man who was initially accused of being responsible for the 1996 Olympic Park bombing incident but was never charged. He was cleared of any wrongdoing, but when he died in 2007, news stories still associated him with the wrongful accusations in the bombing incident. The lesson from that is be careful how you characterize people in criminal investigations and think before you publish names of people who have not been officially charged with crimes.

Neutral Reportage

Another type of privilege, called "neutral reportage," has been recognized in about 10 states. It gives the news media First Amendment protection in writing accusations about a public official or public figure in a public controversy as long as the reporter states them accurately and neutrally. If one official or person considered responsible and newsworthy accuses another public figure of wrongdoing, you may print the information as long as you get reactions of the accused or other participants.

Under neutral reportage you aren't responsible for determining whether the accusations are true. However, many states don't extend this type of privilege to the media, so it's always safer to beware of printing unsubstantiated accusations.

The best defense for a reporter is the "truth" defense, proving that what you wrote is true. What you can do and what you should do may differ. You may have the right to print statements from court records or meetings, but if you think they could be untrue or unfair, should you print them? Those are the kinds of ethical decisions journalists must make. Most editors advise this: When in doubt, leave it out.

Fair Comment and Criticism

Suppose you are writing a review of a play, concert or book, and your review is very negative. Can you be sued? Yes. You can always be sued. But you are protected under the right of fair comment.

ETHICS

THE CASE: YOU are attending a school board meeting as a reporter. During the public comment portion of the meeting, a woman accuses a male guidance counselor in the high school of having had sex with students. This is a small town, with only one high school and two guidance counselors, both male. The school board says it will conduct an investigation. You are on deadline and must get the story in right after the meeting. You can't reach either guidance counselor for his reaction. The comment was made at a public meeting, and it is part of the public record. Even if you have the legal right to publish this information, what are your ethical concerns? Will you include this information in your story?

Writers of editorials, analysis stories, reviews and other criticism may express opinions, but they may not state inaccurate facts. A factual error can be grounds for libel; an opinion is protected.

To qualify as fair comment, a comment must generally be on a matter of public interest, it must be based on facts known or believed to be true, and it may not be malicious or made with reckless disregard for the truth. In this case also, truth is considered a good defense.

INVASION OF PRIVACY

Issues of privacy involve ethical decisions, not matters of accuracy. However, with the proliferation of invasion of privacy lawsuits, a journalist should understand the legal issues. Privacy is not a right guaranteed by the U.S. Constitution. In privacy cases, damage is usually considered the mental anguish that results from wrongfully revealing to the public some part of the plaintiff's life. Truth may not be enough of a defense in privacy cases.

Suppose a child drowns and a mother stands on the dock as her son's body is dragged from the river. She is hysterical. A photographer takes her picture without her consent. Has the photographer invaded her privacy? Perhaps, if the photographer was on private property. The photographer could be considered an intruder. However, it is not an invasion of privacy if the photographer was on public property. Even if a scene on private property is visible from public property, the photographer would be within his rights to take pictures.

The courts have acknowledged four grounds for invasion of privacy lawsuits: intrusion, public disclosure of private and embarrassing facts, false light, and misappropriation of a person's name or image without permission.

Intrusion into a Person's Solitude

Eavesdropping, harassing someone and trespassing on private property can be considered intrusion. So can going onto private property and using a telephoto lens, listening behind doors and using any device to enhance what the unaided eye can see or the unaided ear can hear. In other words, a journalist who uses subterfuge to obtain and publish confidential material could be risking a suit for invasion of privacy. The intrusion can be either physical or mental.

In *Dietemann v. Time Inc.*, two *Life* magazine reporters were sued for going undercover as husband and wife to do a story on a plumber, A.S. Dietemann. The plumber was believed to be practicing medicine with herbs. The so-called healer told the female reporter she had cancer and prescribed an herbal cure. The female reporter taped Dietemann's comments, and her partner took pictures with a concealed camera. Even though the plumber later pleaded no contest to a charge of practicing medicine without a license, he sued the magazine company for invasion of privacy. A California court awarded him $1,000. An appeals court upheld the award and said that the undercover methods, used without Dietemann's consent, were an invasion of his privacy. "The First Amendment is not a license to trespass, to steal, or to intrude by electronic means into the precincts of another's home or office," the court opinion said.

Unlike libel suits, publication isn't required for someone to claim invasion of privacy in this type of case. Truth isn't a defense either. After ABC-TV reporters on "Prime Time Live" used undercover techniques and hidden cameras to expose unsanitary conditions at Food Lion grocery stores, the supermarket chain sued for trespass and fraud. Reporters who had falsified employment applications to obtain jobs at Food Lion reported that the supermarket chain sold spoiled meat, fish dipped in bleach and rat-gnawed cheese. Food Lion didn't challenge the television show's findings — only the methods reporters used. In 1997 a jury awarded Food Lion $5.5 million, which was reduced to just $2 after several appeals. The rationale was the same as it was 25 years earlier in the Dietemann case: Even if the news report is true, reporters don't have license to trespass.

Public Disclosure of Private Facts

Publishing facts such as information about a person's sex life or medical history that the public considers offensive could be considered invasion of privacy, even if it's true. But if the facts are taken from the public record, such as court documents, they will probably be considered fair to publish.

In 1975 the Supreme Court ruled in *Cox Broadcasting Co. v. Cohn* that a television station in Atlanta was within its First Amendment rights to publish the name of a rape victim even though state law prohibited doing so. The victim's family had sued for invasion of privacy, claiming a private fact had been disclosed. The family had won, but Cox appealed the decision to the U.S. Supreme Court. The court said the news media had the right to report matters on the public record.

Information not on the public record is more susceptible to lawsuits. The courts have ruled that the media may be invading privacy if the private facts in question would be offensive and objectionable to a reasonable person and would not be of legitimate public concern. Community standards of what is "offensive" may vary from one place to another. That's why these are difficult cases for courts to decide.

Regarding the public concern standard, the case often cited is *Sidis v. F-R Publishing Corp.*, which involved a profile in *The New Yorker* magazine of James Sidis, a genius who had graduated from Harvard at age 16. Twenty years later the magazine wrote a profile about his life as a recluse. Sidis sued for invasion of privacy, but the courts ruled that he was a public figure who had lost his right to privacy and that his life was, therefore, newsworthy or of legitimate public concern.

Publicity that Puts a Person in a False Light

If a published story or picture gives the wrong impression and is embarrassing to the person, the possibility exists that the court will consider a "false light" verdict. For example, in one case a television station doing a story about teenage pregnancy took pictures of a young woman walking down the street. The television station did not say she was pregnant, nor did the station identify her. However, she claimed the picture put her in a false light — indicating that she was a pregnant teenager — and she won her lawsuit against the station.

False light is related to defamation, but the story or picture does not have to defame a person to be considered false light. It does have to portray the person inaccurately. Truth is a defense in these cases. Generally, the plaintiff has to prove that the media showed actual malice by knowingly publishing false information.

The case often cited here is *Time Inc. v. Hill*, because it was the first false-light case to reach the Supreme Court. James Hill, his wife and five children were held hostage in their suburban Philadelphia home by three escaped convicts in 1952. After the incident, the Hills moved to Connecticut. A few years later, *Life* magazine was planning to publish a review of a play partially based on the incident. The magazine took the cast of the play to the Hills' old home and photographed the actors in some scenes from the play. James Hill sued, saying the pictures in *Life* gave readers the impression that the scenes portrayed the family's real experiences. Hill initially won his suit. But it eventually went to the Supreme Court, which ruled that Hill would have to prove actual malice on the part of *Life* magazine. The court sent the case back for retrial to a lower court, but Hill dropped the suit.

U.S. Supreme Court

USE OF A PERSON'S NAME OR PHOTO WITHOUT PERMISSION

This doctrine applies when the picture is used for commercial purposes, such as advertising or promotion. For example, use of an athlete's photograph to promote a product without his consent could be grounds for a lawsuit. The easiest way to avoid this kind of lawsuit is to have the person sign a consent form.

Television personality Vanna White sued Samsung Electronics when an advertisement the firm used featured a robot that resembled White as she appeared on the game show "Wheel of Fortune." White claimed her image was appropriated without her permission, and a court agreed.

ONLINE LEGAL ISSUES

The Internet is spawning many new legal issues and laws regarding free speech vs. pornography, libel, copyright and privacy.

Communications Decency Act

The first major test of free speech on the Internet to reach the U.S. Supreme Court was the Communications Decency Act (CDA) of 1996, a federal law that restricted distribution of indecent material on the Internet to people under age 18. The American Civil Liberties Union challenged the law, which was ruled unconstitutional by a federal three-judge panel in Philadelphia, but the government appealed the ruling in *Reno v. ACLU*. In 1997 the U.S. Supreme Court struck down portions of the act that censored online material. In the ruling, Associate Justice John Paul Stevens wrote that the CDA's "use of undefined terms 'indecent and patently offensive' raises special First Amendment concerns because of its obvious chilling effect on free speech."

One area that was not struck down was a little section that has become a big issue for Internet providers, bloggers and other people who post messages on any Internet or social networking sites. Section 230 of the act says, "No provider or user of an interactive computer service shall be treated as the publisher or speaker of any information provided by another information content provider."

As mentioned at the start of this chapter, that means that if someone posts a libelous message to your website, you are not responsible for the content of it unless you created part of it. Courts have held that this part of the act protects you even if you edit or delete the offensive material. If you are only providing the website or service, you're safe, but if you contribute to the content, you could be held responsible.

Zeran v. America Online

Online providers can thank Kenneth Zeran for that protection. He was just at home in Seattle running his publishing business from his house in April 1995 when his phone began ringing every two minutes with callers issuing death threats. The calls began just six days after the bombing of the federal building in Oklahoma City where 168 people died.

An anonymous person had posted Zeran's telephone number on an America Online message board telling readers to call him because he was selling T-shirts, key chains and other memorabilia about the bombing with such offensive slogans such as "Visit Oklahoma . . . It's a BLAST!!!" Oddly enough, Zeran wasn't even a member of AOL, and the person who posted the message had a trial membership and was never identified because AOL didn't keep records of nonsubscribers.

To make matters worse, an announcer for a classic rock radio station in Oklahoma City read the message on air and encouraged listeners to call Zeran and tell him how they felt about what he was doing. Zeran sued the radio station on grounds of defamation, false light, invasion of privacy and intentional infliction of emotional distress, but the court ruled in favor of the radio station on all counts. The court ruled that the only charge applicable to broadcast was slander and there was insufficient evidence to establish injury to Zeran's reputation or that his emotional stress was "severe" enough to prevent him from conducting his daily affairs.

More significant was his suit against AOL on charges that the service was responsible for the defamatory messages and was unreasonably slow in removing them. This was the first libel case against an online service provider to reach the U.S. Supreme Court. Zeran's case was initially dismissed in 1997 by a U.S. District Court, which ruled that Section 230 of the Communications Decency Act of 1996 protected online service providers from liability for subscribers' material. In 1998 the U.S. Supreme Court upheld that decision. So AOL was not at fault, and Zeran got nothing for his troubles.

SOCIAL MEDIA

THE LIABILITY OF bloggers: Although the law is specific regarding protection for Internet service providers from material posted by their users, it is not as clear regarding bloggers. "Bloggers can be both a provider and a user of interactive computer services," according to "Bloggers' FAQ," an article on the Electronic Frontier Foundation website (*http://www.eff.org/issues/bloggers/legal*). "Bloggers are users when they create and edit blogs through a service provider, and they are providers to the extent that they allow third parties to add comments or other material to their blogs. Your readers' comments, entries written by guest bloggers, tips sent by e-mail and information provided to you through an RSS feed would all likely be considered information provided by another content provider," according to the EFF article. But the courts have not ruled on whether you would be responsible for defamatory material if you selected the information from other blogs to post on your site.

Liablity on MySpace: Julie Doe (known as Jane Doe in the lawsuit), was a 13-year-old teenager from Texas when she created a profile on MySpace. The next year a 19-year-old man, also from Texas, saw her profile and contacted her. They began communicating and later spoke on the phone. In 2006 the two met in person, and the man sexually assaulted her, according to a lawsuit she and her mother filed against MySpace Inc. and its partner News Corporation. The charges were negligence, gross negligence, fraud and negligent misrepresentation for failing to protect underage users from sexual predators. The court ruled that MySpace was not responsible for the content on its site and dismissed the charges against the social networking service.

The case was the first to address whether that portion of the Communications Decency Act that protects Internet providers from liability for information posted by a third party can be applied to a social networking site.

Liability on Twitter: When is a negative tweet an opinion or a potential libel suit? Amanda Bonnen posted a tweet about her landlord stating: "Who said sleeping in a moldy apartment was bad for you? Horizon really thinks it's okay." But the landlord, Horizon, didn't think the tweet was OK and filed a $50,000 lawsuit against her for defamation. A judge dismissed the case on the grounds that the tweet was "too vague." Bonnen's lawsuit was only one of several involving Twitter messages. Rock star Courtney Love was sued for libel by a fashion designer who claimed Love posted false and defamatory messages about her on Twitter and on a Facebook page. Love paid $430,000 to settle the suit. These cases show that social media messages are an emerging area for legal cases.

Privacy of text messages: If you use your employer's equipment to post text messages to a social media site while you are at work, does your employer have the right to check your messages? A case involving that issue was the first of its kind to reach the U.S. Supreme Court. A California police officer used his city-issued pager to send private text messages, some of which were sexually explicit. When his employer reviewed the messages, Officer Jeff Quon claimed his privacy rights were violated as guaranteed by the Fourth Amendment, which protects citizens against unreasonable search and seizure.

The Supreme Court was unanimous in ruling that since Quon used city equipment, he didn't have a right to privacy especially because the city had a written no-privacy policy regarding the pager. However, the Court did not apply this ruling broadly. Justice Anthony Kennedy wrote in the opinion that the Court "must proceed with care when considering the whole concept of privacy expectations in communications made on electronic equipment owned by a government employer. The judiciary risks error by elaborating too fully on the Fourth Amendment implications of emerging technology before its role in society has become clear." To be safe, you should check your employer's policy. To be even safer (and ethical), you should just work when you are at work.

 BLOGGERS' LEGAL GUIDE

Bloggers legal guide on the Electronic Frontier Foundation site.

Children's Online Privacy Protection Act

The Communications Decency Act originally contained provisions to protect children from obscene and indecent Internet material, but those parts were struck down by the Supreme Court as violations of the First Amendment's right to free speech. However, three other related efforts succeeded:

- The Children's Online Privacy Protection Act (COPPA), which took effect in 2000, makes it a federal crime — with penalties of $10,000 per violation — to collect information from children under 13 and use it for commercial purposes that could be considered harmful to minors. The law requires operators of commercial websites or online services to obtain verifiable parental consent before collecting information from preteens and to post notices on the site of how any information would be used. The law covers such information as the child's full name, home and/or e mail address, telephone number and any other information that would allow someone to identify or contact the child. One company fined for violations of this act was Bonzi Software, which markets the BonziBuddy, a purple cartoon gorilla. To download the joke-telling gorilla, registration was required. The Federal Trade Commission, which enforces COPPA, fined the company $75,000. The FTC is reviewing changes to the act to include mobile media and social networking sites.

- The Child Online Protection Act (COPA) was passed in 1998 and also went into effect in 2000, but it has been blocked by the courts as unconstitutional restriction of free speech. It attempted to protect minors from harmful material on the Internet.

- The Children's Internet Protection Act (CIPA), passed in 2000, also attempts to protect children by requiring public schools and libraries that receive federal funds to install software that would block online material considered "harmful to minors," basically pornography and obscenity. The law was challenged as unconstitutional by the American Library Association, but in 2003 the Supreme Court upheld it. In addition, more than 21 states have enacted laws to require Internet filtering software in public schools or libraries to limit children's access to sexually explicit online information.

These types of legal issues are certain to continue as the government attempts to regulate the Internet.

COPYRIGHT

If you take pictures or documents from a website that does not contain a copyright notice, are you violating copyright laws? Absolutely. The 1976 U.S. Copyright Act protects everything that you or others write the minute the information is offered in "a fixed form," which includes online or print information. The law was amended later to make a copyright notice optional on all works published on or after 1989. Works published before 1978 did require a copyright notice to be protected under the law. It's always safe to include the copyright symbol and notice on your website or material even if it isn't mandatory.

CONVERGENCE COACH

THE DAYS OF producing content only for print or only for broadcast are over. Whether the content you produce is geared to mobile phones, tablets or websites, the material will probably include print, video and social media references.

Can you include some video from YouTube or a social networking site in your material? Can you include a photo you found on the Internet or on Facebook? Is it OK to use the video or photo if you credit the source? If you read an article you like on the Internet, can you e-mail it to a friend? The simple answer to all these questions is no. However, there are exceptions.

- If the site containing the material you want to copy specifies that the information is in the public domain (allowable to everyone and not subject to copyright protection), you may use it. Works created by the U.S. federal government are in the public domain. Copyrighted works endure for the life of an author and 70 years after the author's death.

- Fair use: This is not clearly defined by law. But if you are using a portion of a work for criticism, comment, news reporting or scholarship, that could be fair use. Generally courts will decide if the use was fair based on the amount of the material you used, the purpose and whether your use would hurt the commercial value of the work.

If you use information from social networking sites or online sites for writing academic papers, blogs or any other purpose, here are a few tips on how you can prevent online legal problems:

- Don't copy material from the Internet (including images) or use it in your blog, your Facebook site or other social networking sites without permission. Many images are offered free for personal use, but check the site notices to be sure.

- Don't write any defamatory messages to an online blog or other site.

- Avoid writing defamatory or derogatory comments in personal e-mail messages. E-mail is often passed to other users without the permission or knowledge of the source.

- Consider the accuracy of material you find on the Internet. Check the site owner and organization to make sure that you are using a responsible site. You should also verify the accuracy of any information from the Internet.

- Check the posting dates of online material to determine whether the information is still accurate. Much online information may be outdated.

Although many unresolved issues remain about intellectual property rights for online materials, additional laws to protect software and online materials were enacted in the late 1990s.

- The No Electronic Theft Act, signed into law in 1997, provides penalties of up to five years in jail and fines of up to $250,000 for individuals and up to $500,000 for organizations for copying software or online materials even if you don't make a profit.

- The Digital Millennium Copyright Act of 1998 provides further penalties of up to $1 million for copying online materials for profit. More cases continue to come before the courts regarding peer-to-peer file sharing of music. Rulings are pending on other cases involving companies that furnish the software for file sharing, and these issues are likely to continue.

However, copyright laws allow you to copy portions of materials under a doctrine known as "fair use." The law favors academic use or use of portions of works if the copied material does not deprive the creator of profits.

Whether it is material for a blog, a profile in a social networking site or other online matter, most sites that host such content specify terms about posting pornography, defamatory messages or other unacceptable material that could be libelous. The nature of communication is changing rapidly, and so are the legal decisions, but the concepts of accuracy and fairness are timeless.

EXERCISES

1 Actual malice: Write a paragraph explaining "actual malice" and "reckless disregard for the truth" as defined by the U.S. Supreme Court in *Times v. Sullivan*.

2 Libel potential scenario: You are the editor of your local newspaper. A U.S. senator has decided to seek re-election. Five women who worked for him several years ago say he sexually harassed and abused them while they were in his office. The women refuse to be named. Their allegations range from stories that he plied them with drugs and alcohol and then sexually abused them to accusations of rape. All the women are reputable, including a political lobbyist and a former secretary to the senator, but none has gone to the police. As a result, you have no record of formal complaints about their allegations. However, three years ago a formal complaint by a former employee charged him with sexual molestation, but the charges were dropped. Will you print these women's allegations and use his name? If you do, will the senator have grounds for a libel lawsuit?

3 Privacy issue 1: A candidate for city council in your community had a nervous breakdown 10 years ago. The candidate's opponent has slipped you a hospital document confirming this fact. Should you print the story? Why or why not? If you do, does the candidate have any grounds to sue you for invasion of privacy?

4 Privacy issue 2: You are a photographer who went on assignment to the county fair. You snapped a picture of a woman whose skirt blew up to her shoulders, exposing her underwear, as she emerged from the fun house. Your editor decided that this picture captured the fun mood of the fair and used it. The woman is now furious and is suing the paper for invasion of privacy – disclosure of a private fact. Discuss whether she has grounds for a lawsuit and whether you think you should have taken the picture.

COACHING TIPS

Examine all your **alternatives.**

Consider all the parties who will be affected. Do you need **other points of view?**

Weigh the **benefits and harms** of your decision.

Justify why you are making this decision.

Be **careful about what you post on social networks.** Your opinions and your personal information could conflict with your job.

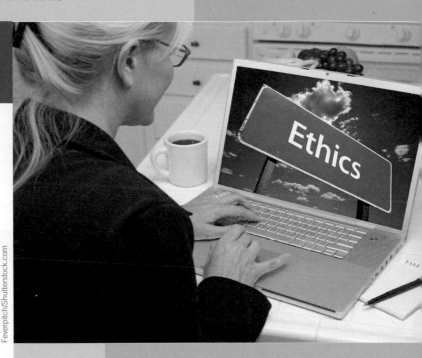

Feverpitch/Shutterstock.com

If someone is going to be hurt by what gets printed or broadcast about them, then journalists need to provide a reason — a good reason — for going with it. "That's my job," doesn't cut it. Nor do appeals to First Amendment freedoms.

— **DENI ELLIOTT,** Poynter–Jamison Chair in Media Ethics and Press Policy, University of South Florida

CHAPTER 15
Media Ethics

CASE #1: YOU ARE A REPORTER FOR YOUR CAMPUS NEWSPAPER OR TV station. A gunman entered one of the classrooms and began shooting, injuring three students before he fled. You check Facebook, where you find comments and photos from other students who were at the scene. You are on deadline and don't have much time to check the information on the site. Should you use the Facebook photos and comments if you attribute them to the names listed under the material?

The Associated Press Stylebook states: "You should never simply lift quotes, photos or video from social networking sites and attribute them to the name on the profile or feed you found them under." If you don't have time to check the accuracy of the information, don't use it.

Case #2: You are covering a campus rally on abortion issues. You have interviewed people from both sides of the issue — pro-life and pro-choice. You have also written a blog expressing your strong belief in the pro-life movement. Is it ethical for journalists to express their opinions in a blog or on social media sites if they are also covering the issue for news?

Many news organizations are developing guidelines to prohibit journalists from blogging or posting comments on social networks that might compromise their objectivity or fairness when covering news. The Radio Television Digital News Association offers these guidelines: "Be especially careful when you are writing, tweeting or blogging about a topic that you or your newsroom covers. Personal and professional lives merge online."

Case #3: You are the editor of your campus news site, and you receive a tip that a local landlord is discriminating against students of color in renting apartments near your school. You assign a black reporter and a white reporter to go undercover to investigate the situation. The black reporter applies for an apartment, and the landlord says there are no vacancies. A few hours later the white reporter applies for an apartment and the landlord shows him three vacant apartments that are available. Is it ethical to report this information without revealing that you are reporters?

Although most news organizations say deception should be used as a last resort, they still use it to a certain extent in investigative stories. However, before you publish any material you acquired in a deceptive manner, you should reveal your identity and seek comments from the sources you investigated.

Here are some other common ethical questions:

- Is it ethical for you to accept free food while you are covering a news event such as a political dinner or a sports activity?

- If you have granted confidentiality to a source, should you reveal the person's identity if the source proves to be unreliable?

- Is it ethical for a journalist to express his opinions in a blog or Facebook page about a topic that he covers for the news in an organization?

SOCIAL MEDIA

 THE OVERALL ethical guideline for social media is this one from the Radio Television Digital News Association: "As a journalist, you should uphold the same professional and ethical standards of fairness, accuracy, truthfulness, transparency and independence when using social media as you do on air and on all digital news platforms."

While that is a good suggestion, some of the ethical dilemmas created by social media pose unique situations. Because readers and viewers get their news from several sources, truth can be elusive and the lines between fact and opinion are often blurred.

One of the most common concerns in the media involves separating personal and professional material. Here are some guidelines about this issue from news organizations:

- From *The New York Times* policy on social networking sites: "Be careful not to write anything on a blog or a personal Web page that you could not write in *The Times.* Anything you post online can and might be publicly disseminated."

- From NPR: "Recognize that everything you write or receive on a social media site is public. Anyone with access to the Web can get access to your activity on social media sites. And regardless of how careful you are in trying to keep them separate, in your online activity, your professional

life and your personal life overlap. You must not advocate for political or other polarizing issues online. This extends to joining online groups or using social media in any form (including your Facebook page or a personal blog) to express personal views on a political or other controversial issue that you could not write for the air or post on NPR.org."

- From *The Roanoke Times* and the Poynter Institute, which collaborated in developing social networking policies: "Information gathered online should be independently confirmed offline. Interview sources in person or over the phone whenever possible. Verify claims and statements. Be transparent with the audience as well as sources. Let them know how you contacted people, in what context you gathered information and how you verified it (or didn't).

- From RTDNA (Radio Television Digital News Association) social media and blogging guidelines: "When using content from blogs or social media, ask critical questions such as:

  - What is the source of the video or photograph? Who wrote the comment and what was the motivation for posting it?

  - Does the source have a legal right to the material posted?

  - Has the photograph or video been manipulated?"

For other guidelines, check the Associated Press Stylebook section on social media guidelines.

Those are just a few of the typical questions the Ethics AdviceLine for Journalists receives *(www.ethicsadvicelineforjournalists.org/)*. The AdviceLine is a free service for professional journalists sponsored by the Chicago Headline Club Chapter of the Society of Professional Journalists and Loyola University Chicago Center for Ethics and Social Justice. The service will put journalists in contact with experts who will discuss the ethical dilemma on the phone at 866-345-3662. The Society of Professional Journalists also offers a hotline to provide advice about ethical issues at 317-927-8000 x208 or check online at *(www.spj.org/ethicshotline.asp)*.

Some of those ethical dilemmas have existed for many years without clear resolution, but social networks are creating new ethical problems for journalists. Ethical dilemmas have been included in every chapter, but in this chapter we'll examine some major cases and some approaches that can be used to make ethical decisions.

DECEPTION

A case of deception that generated considerable media discussion in the 1990s was the Food Lion/ABC-TV case. ABC television network reporters lied on job applications to get hired by the Food Lion supermarket chain, and they used hidden cameras and microphones to record employees processing food and discussing meat department practices. The reporters for "Primetime Live" then produced a story accusing Food Lion of selling rotten meat, fish and cheese. Food Lion didn't challenge the facts but instead sued for trespass and won a $5 million judgment. But the trial judge said that was too much and cut the award to $315,000. ABC appealed, and a federal court later reduced the award to just $2 — a dollar for trespassing and another dollar for breaching employees' legal duty of loyalty to an employer.

Could the reporters have gained the story any other way? ABC doesn't think so, but many other journalists have questioned the use of deception in this and other situations.

A classic case of deception occurred in 1978, when investigative reporters at the *Chicago Sun Times* set up a bar called The Mirage and posed as bartenders and waiters. With hidden cameras and tape recorders, they provided evidence that building inspectors, police officers and other city officials were soliciting bribes to allow them to operate the bar. Although the series won several awards, the Pulitzer-Prize board ruled that the reporting methods were unethical and rejected it for the media's highest award. The case renewed debate about deception, and today this type of reporting is considered a last resort by many editors.

Although print and broadcast media have used hidden cameras for many years, they proliferated in television news magazine shows during the 1990s. One reason was the improved technology of cameras, which could be small enough to be hidden in tie clips. But media critics charged that a more common reason for using hidden cameras was sensationalism.

More recently an NBC-TV Dateline show, "To Catch a Predator," garnered media criticism for its deceptive tactics in conducting a sting operation to lure alleged pedophiles to homes outfitted with hidden cameras for the show. The station hired a civilian watchdog group, Perverted Justice, whose members posed as underage boys and girls in online chat rooms to converse with adults seeking sex with minors. These decoys would then lure their chat-room acquaintances to the homes for a meeting, supposedly to have sex.

When the potential pedophiles entered the home and began conversing with the Perverted Justice decoys, Dateline's reporter Chris Hansen emerged and confronted them with their chat-room conversations and questions about their intentions. Police waited outside the homes to arrest them.

Over the course of three years, more than 200 potential predators were caught by the show. In one case a Texas assistant district attorney pursued by Dateline as a pedophile suspect committed suicide when police entered his home to arrest him. The TV station was criticized not only for its use of hidden cameras but also for paying Perverted Justice volunteers and for its cooperation with police. Hansen defended the show by saying that it has alerted parents to the dangers of online chat rooms, and it has resulted in convictions of many sexual predators featured in the series.

But deception remains controversial in ethical terms. Before using any form of deception, ask yourself if there is any other way to get the story. Louis Hodges, professor emeritus of ethics at Washington and Lee University, suggests that you apply three tests: importance, accuracy and safety. Ask yourself these questions:

- Is the information of such overriding public importance that it can help people avoid harm?
- Is there any way you could obtain the information through conventional reporting methods, such as standard interviews or public records?
- Are you placing innocent people at risk? For example, you should not pose as a nurse, law enforcement officer or employee in a job for which you might not be trained.

Deceptive reporting techniques are fraught with risks, such as lawsuits for invasion of privacy. On the other hand, deception may be the only way to reveal matters of great public concern. Even with such reasoning, using deception may still be unethical.

PLAGIARISM

The subjects of plagiarism and fabrication have been discussed in several other chapters in this book. Why so much attention to practices you surely wouldn't engage in? Even though technology has made it easier to plagiarize because accessibility to thousands of news sources is so easy, stealing words from someone else without attribution is not a new phenomenon. Nor is fabrication, which is making up quotes, adding false description and basically passing fictional material off as news.

Despite considerable publicity about Jayson Blair, a *New York Times* reporter who plagiarized and fabricated stories he wrote for the newspaper, journalism students and veteran journalists are apparently not getting the message that plagiarism and fabrication are serious infractions that can lead to firing and ruined careers. Blair had fabricated quotes and plagiarized several of his national stories for the *Times*, even claiming to interview sources he never contacted. The discovery of his deception led to his dismissal and a front-page story in the newspaper revealing his misdeeds. The case also resulted in the resignation of two top editors at the *Times*. This highly publicized case in 2003 brought shame to the paper and awareness of plagiarism as a major problem in the media, but it didn't prevent it from continuing — even at *The New York Times.*

Size doesn't seem to matter when it comes to plagiarism. From college newspapers and small newspapers to large newspapers, scores of journalists have been fired for plagiarism. Here are just a few examples of such ethical infractions that occurred in the last few years:

- *The University Daily Kansan* at the University of Kansas suspended a reporter who was copying material for its "Weekly Choice" calendar items from the local newspaper's website, *www.lawrence.com.*

- *The Cavalier Daily* at the University of Virginia fired two student reporters after discovering they had written movie and music reviews lifted from other publications.

- A sports editor for the *Bozeman* (Mont.) *Chronicle* was suspended without pay for plagiarizing a column taken from another columnist in North Dakota.

- A reporter from the *Sedalia* (Mo.) *Democrat* was fired after a reader called to complain about similarities between the reporter's movie review and one by syndicated movie reviewer Roger Ebert.

- *The New York Times* was at the center of other recent cases. A University of Florida student was fired from her internship at the *Colorado Springs Gazette* after editors found that she plagiarized information from the *Times* in four of her stories. A columnist for *The Collegian* at the University of Massachusetts also admitted plagiarizing material from the *Times.* And the *Times* had its own scandal recently when its business reporter was accused of plagiarism and resigned.

The list of cases involving fabrication and plagiarism could go on, and that doesn't even include plagiarism of research papers in college. Nor does it include the emerging area of plagiarism in blogs, websites and social media.

Why is plagiarism still so rampant despite the highly publicized cases of it in the media?

Lori Robertson, author of the article "Ethically Challenged" in *American Journalism Review,* concluded from a dozen interviews that the Internet was the main culprit. "It used to be that to plagiarize from another publication, you'd have to type the information letter by letter, staring at your source," she wrote. "It took a little more effort than what you can do now: cut and paste."

Using someone else's idea for a story is usually not considered plagiarism. U.S. copyright laws don't protect ideas. In the news business, it is considered good practice to localize a national story idea or use an idea from another newspaper and do original reporting. The key is "original reporting." If you use all the same sources and the same anecdotes from another publication or broadcast, it may not constitute plagiarism, but it raises ethical questions.

PRIVACY ISSUES

Some of the most wrenching ethical dilemmas the media face involve people's privacy. You may have the legal right to publish certain information, but do you have the ethical right?

To understand the ethical concerns, it may help to define "ethics." Ethics is the study of choices about what we should or should not do, whereas morality is concerned with behavior. So ethics can be considered the process of making decisions about the way a person behaves. Some of these privacy issues involve public officials, celebrities, rape accusers and photo subjects in the news.

Public Officials

Would you print information about the sex life of a politician? When is the private life of a public figure relevant? When does it serve the public interest to publish such details?

In the summer of 1987, reporters and editors at *The Miami Herald* decided that the private life of a politician was relevant. Former Sen. Gary Hart was seeking the

Former Sen. Gary Hart, D-CO (on the right), served as a U.S. Naval Reserve officer while he was in the U.S. Senate.

Democratic nomination for the presidency. Rumors of Hart's infidelity to his wife had circulated for months, and during the campaign the rumors called into question his character and credibility. When asked about the rumors, Hart challenged reporters to "follow me around. . . . They'd be very bored." Acting on a tip that Hart had a relationship with a Florida model, *Herald* reporters staked out his townhouse. They revealed that Hart spent the night with the woman, Donna Rice. Hart never admitted that the relationship with Rice was sexual. Nevertheless, he withdrew his candidacy the day before *The Washington Post* was set to reveal evidence about his involvement in another affair.

At the time of this incident, although previous presidents and presidential candidates had engaged in extramarital affairs, their private lives had not been dissected in public. The sexual affairs of President Kennedy were not revealed until long after his assassination. But the Gary Hart case changed the nature of political reporting.

The nature of sexual revelations in political reporting changed even further during Bill Clinton's second term as president when former White House intern Monica Lewinsky testified to a grand jury that she had engaged in a sexual relationship with the president during her internship. Clinton denied the allegations when he testified in a court case brought against him by an Arkansas woman, Paula Jones, who claimed sexual harassment against Clinton when he was Arkansas governor. Then the day after his testimony, in a dramatic reversal of his previous denials, he admitted on national television that he had engaged in an "inappropriate relationship" with Monica Lewinsky.

The media followed Lewinsky day and night. Competition for any tidbit of information was keen. The media published unsubstantiated rumors, including sexual details, and relied heavily on anonymous sources and other media for news.

Thus far, media references to sex were tame compared to what was about to happen. Kenneth Starr, a special prosecutor investigating Clinton for obstruction of justice and perjury, released a grand jury report that contained graphic sexual details of the Clinton-Lewinsky relationship. The majority of newspapers in the United States either printed the entire report in a special section or posted it on their websites. Many newspapers offered a disclaimer that the content might be considered offensive. This report laid the groundwork for impeachment hearings on the charges that the president had committed perjury under oath when he originally denied having an affair with Lewinsky.

In November 1998, almost four years after the case began, Clinton agreed to pay Jones $850,000 to drop the case. But it didn't prevent him from being impeached.

Despite the serious turn the case took, media critics and the public still questioned whether the media had acted responsibly in relying heavily on anonymous sources and publishing rumors in the early stages of the saga. And the debate raged about whether a politician's private life should be dissected in public. The ethical dilemmas these stories posed will continue to be debated for years.

Reporters also face other ethical dilemmas about privacy when covering politicians. For example, is it in the public interest to reveal the criminal background of a candidate if he withdraws from the race before you can print the story?

Editors at the campus newspaper of the University of Kansas faced this dilemma after they found out that a candidate for student government had been convicted of indecent solicitation of a child six years earlier. When the candidate learned that the newspaper was planning to print the information, he held a press conference to resign his candidacy. He claimed it was because he had just learned he was HIV-positive. At the same time, he resigned as director of the organization representing gays and lesbians on campus. He never referred to his criminal record, nor would he answer reporters' questions.

Was his criminal record relevant to the public now that he was no longer a candidate for office or leader of the gay rights group? What harm would the publication of his record cause him? The student's friends pressured the editor not to run the story, saying it would cause their friend immense personal suffering when he was already suffering from the HIV-positive news. In addition, they said, he had already paid his debt to society by serving time in prison.

Stephen Martino, editor of *The University Daily Kansan* at the time, said the decision was the most difficult one he ever had to make as an editor. He said he decided to run the information because it was relevant; it was why the candidate resigned. Martino said the candidate had learned about his HIV-positive status three weeks earlier and had made no attempt to resign then. "To my way of thinking, omitting the truth is the same thing as lying. Had the *Kansan* not reported the full story as it knew it, it would have been accused of a cover-up, and its credibility would have been destroyed," Martino wrote in an editorial page column the day the story ran on the front page.

Angry students protested the next day by dumping copies of the *Kansan* on the lawn in front of the newspaper offices in the journalism school.

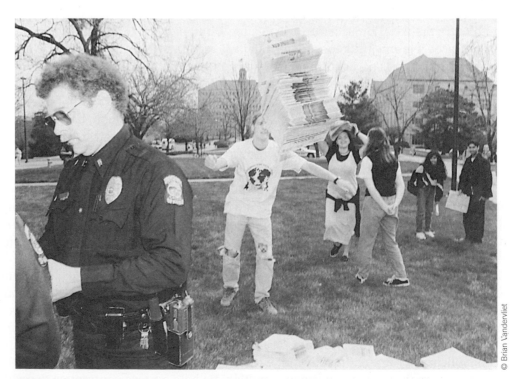

University of Kansas students dump the campus newspaper to protest a story.

Naming Suspects

Consider another case that has given the media an ethical black eye. A pipe bomb had exploded in a park on the site of the Olympic games in Atlanta on July 27, 1996. One person was killed, and 111 others were injured. Initially, a security guard at the site, Richard Jewell, was declared a hero for alerting police to the bombing. Three days later, Jewell became a suspect when law enforcement officials leaked his name to the press.

Most newspapers withhold the name of a suspect until formal charges are filed. But this was a case of great national interest. Would you have published his name? The *Atlanta Journal-Constitution* did, stating that Jewell was a "target" of the investigation. That was just the beginning.

For the next 88 days, Jewell was profiled and followed by the media, and his past, present and future were the subject of news stories. Only one factor was missing: He was never charged in the crime. On Oct. 26, 1996, the FBI apologized and publicly admitted that Jewell was no longer a suspect. Eric Rudolph, accused of this bombing and several others at women's clinics where abortions were performed, was subsequently charged with the crime, convicted and sentenced to life in prison.

But Jewell claimed that his life had been ruined. In an emotional press conference after he was vindicated, he said: "For 88 days, I lived a nightmare. . . . Now I must face

Eric Rudolph made the FBI's Ten Most Wanted Fugitives list.

the other part of my nightmare," he said. "While the government can tell you that I am an innocent man, the government's letter cannot give me back my good name or my reputation."

Jewell died in 2007, but news stories and obituaries still bore headlines identifying him as the Olympic Park bombing figure or suspect. The case has become a classic example in media ethics literature as a warning about the harm media can cause in naming or pursuing suspects before they are formally charged with a crime.

Rape Cases

Whether to name rape accusers is another continuing ethical debate in the media. Because of the stigma associated with rape, most news organizations withhold the names of people who claim they have been raped. The accuser cannot legitimately be called a "victim" until the case is decided.

That issue became apparent in a scandal involving three Duke University lacrosse players accused of rape. The case involved all the elements of a TV drama — racial conflict (a poor, black single mother with a troubled background who was earning money as a stripper vs. three white students from wealthy families), a prosecutor who refused to release evidence that would have cleared the suspects, a prestigious university protecting its reputation, and a community torn by racial tension surrounding the case.

The case began when one of two strippers hired to dance at a party for the lacrosse team accused three of the players of raping her. The three players she identified were charged with rape, kidnapping and sexual offense. But DNA tests of the three players and all the other lacrosse team members did not match the rape-kit swabs taken from the woman at the hospital where she was examined after the party.

However, Durham County District Attorney Michael B. Nifong withheld this DNA evidence from the players' defense attorney and issued statements to the press calling the athletes "hooligans." Although the accuser changed her version of the story several times, the prosecutor persisted in trying the case. After a year-long investigation, the players were exonerated and the district attorney was disbarred for unethical behavior.

"This woman has destroyed everything I worked for in my life," one of the players said on CBS's "60 Minutes" after the players were exonerated. "She's destroyed two other families, and she's brought shame on a great university. And worst of all, she's split apart a community and a nation on facts that just didn't happen and a lie that should have never been told."

The accused players were named in the press, but the accuser was not named until the case was resolved. After all the charges were dropped, one of the players said he would probably always be known as that Duke lacrosse player in the rape case. For that reason, the players' names will not be used in this textbook.

The case was reminiscent of the media treatment of Richard Jewell. Although the players were charged and Jewell was not, the intense media scrutiny of the players raises the question: Did the media act properly in the publicity it gave to this case?

Not according to Rachel Smolkin, author of "Justice Delayed," an article in *American Journalism Review*. "Unquestionably, the media too readily ran with a simplistic storyline, sacrificing a search for truth. Not only were the accused innocent of rape, the allegations of racial taunts that received so much media attention appear to have been exaggerated," she wrote.

"The lessons of the media's rush to judgment and their affair with a sensational, simplistic storyline rank among journalism's most basic tenets: Be fair, stick to the facts, question authorities; don't assume; pay attention to alternative explanations," Smolkin wrote.

Most news organizations still protect the accuser and name the suspects in rape cases, and the Duke case is unlikely to change those policies.

Geneva Overholser, director of the University of Southern California Annenberg School of Journalism, is a staunch advocate for naming both the accuser and the accused. Years ago when she was editor of *The Des Moines* (Iowa) *Register,* she wrote a column saying the stigma of rape would be reduced if it were treated like any other crime and the names of rape victims were used. As a result, Nancy Ziegenmeyer agreed to let the newspaper use her name in a story relating her ordeal as a rape victim.

Overholser still feels strongly that failing to name both parties in a rape case only prolongs the stigma of the crime for women. In a column for the Poynter Institute, she wrote: "The responsible course for responsible media today is this: Treat the woman who charges rape as we would any other adult victim of crime. Name her, and deal with her respectfully. And leave the trial to the courtroom."

Photo Subjects

Many privacy issues involve photographs. Should a photographer take a picture of a grieving mother whose son has drowned even if she doesn't want the picture taken? At what point is a photograph an invasion of privacy?

Another concern for photo editors is taste: what readers or viewers need to see versus what they want to see. For example, should newspapers, websites or TV publish pictures that depict gore and tragedy even if they would upset readers and viewers? This issue is even more relevant these days when so many photos are posted on the photo-sharing site, Flickr, and on social media sites.

The media faced those ethical decisions when they received graphic video and photographs of Iraqi prisoners who were abused by U.S. soldiers at the Abu Ghraib prison outside Baghdad during the war in Iraq. The story, initially aired by CBS on "60 Minutes," and subsequently detailed in a *New Yorker* magazine article by Seymour M. Hersh, revealed torture inflicted on the prisoners by U.S. soldiers. Although *The New Yorker* did not print the photos, CBS showed some video, and *The Washington Post* published some photos in the newspaper and more photos and video on the *Post's* website. The photos, released to newspapers around the world, showed naked prisoners being taunted and humiliated by soldiers. One of the most dramatic photos showed two U.S. soldiers smiling in front of a human pyramid of naked prisoners. Another showed a soldier holding a leash around a naked man's neck.

The *Post* posted this note on its website with the photos: "Some of these photos may be disturbing because of their graphic or violent nature." The *Post* and other news organizations cropped or blurred photos that showed the prisoners' genitals. Both *The New York Times* and *The New York Daily News* ran a front-page photo of a naked prisoner being menaced by dogs used by the soldiers. Television news anchors also gave a warning to viewers about the graphic nature of the images they were about to see.

The public was incensed, and editors throughout the country wrestled with what they should print or air. In many cases, news organizations offered more photos on their Web pages but limited images in print. In a *New York Times* article, writer David Carr wrote that "the news media are wrestling with how many and how much of the graphic photographs they should show." Some critics accused the media of promoting an anti-war agenda. But Leonard Downie, then editor of *The Washington Post,* echoed the sentiments of many other news editors when he was quoted in the article as saying "We decided that the importance of the news was the most important consideration."

The prison photographs constituted one of many ethical dilemmas that editors faced about graphic images during the war in Iraq. When Americans civilians were burned, dismembered and hanged from a bridge by Iraqis in Fallujah, editors again agonized over printing or airing photos of their charred bodies, but many newspapers printed a photo in some form on their front pages. *The Philadelphia Inquirer* received 185 complaints about showing the charred bodies. In an article for The Poynter Institute, Anne Gordon, then managing editor of the *Inquirer,* said she told the paper's staff in an e-mail: "We do our job when we give readers all the news — no matter how painful or ugly. My heart bleeds for the families of these men. But personal feelings cannot dissuade us from our mission to provide the facts upon which an informed citizenry can make decisions."

The issue of publishing gory photographs was debated again in 2011 after terrorist Osama bin Laden was killed by Americans in a military raid on his compound in Pakistan. Journalists and the public were divided about whether photos of bin Laden's body would provide proof that he was dead or incite more violence from the al-Qaida organization that he led and from other sympathizers to his cause. President Barack Obama decided not to release photos of bin Laden's body. In a statement released by his press secretary, Obama said: "We've done DNA sampling and testing and so there is no doubt that we killed Osama bin Laden. It is important for us to make sure that very graphic photos of somebody who was shot in the head are not floating around as an incitement to additional violence or as a propaganda tool. That's not who we are. We don't trot out this stuff as trophies. . . . I think that given the graphic nature of these photos, it would create some national security risk."

Such ethical dilemmas arise daily at newspapers, television stations and websites, although rarely involving photos as graphically disturbing as these. But how do editors make those decisions, and how can you decide what is ethical?

Whether it is a photo or a story, ethicist Louis Hodges suggests this guideline for privacy issues: Publish private information about public officials or public figures if it affects their public duties. But for victims of crime, publish private information only if they give their permission because these are people with special needs and vulnerability.

CONVERGENCE COACH

A YOUNG WOMAN was on the verge of jumping from a bridge in Seattle that is well known for suicides. A journalist approached the scene. First he called 911 and reported the situation to police. Then he posted a message on Twitter about the plight of the girl. Within minutes scores of other people began demanding updates on Twitter. Traffic by the bridge backed up, and one woman who complained that she had been stalled in traffic for an hour yelled, "Jump already" as did a few other drivers. The journalist tweeted minute-by-minute coverage of her actions and posted a photo of her as she stood by the bridge railing. Was it ethical for him to report her actions as they were happening?

Police negotiators came and talked the girl out of jumping. But the reporter said he knew the situation was ethically challenging and that he tried to avoid an online spectacle. However, he also felt that he couldn't ignore the situation and he got caught up in the demands for updates on Twitter.

Although the news media rarely report suicides, times have changed because of convergence of print, TV and online media, especially mobile media. News is more immediate than ever. Journalists don't need a newsroom or a computer to report breaking news; they simply need a mobile phone. If the journalists don't respond immediately, citizens will report news on social media. Speed is not synonymous with accuracy.

News will continue to be delivered across many platforms and by many "citizen journalists." In some cases, that means journalists will publish first and think later. And the purveyors of news are not limited to journalists.

Clay Shirky, a New York University professor who is a leading expert on new media, writes in his book, *Here Comes Everybody,* "The media landscape is transformed, because personal communication and publishing, previously separate functions, now shade into one another. One result is to break the older pattern of professional filtering of the good from the mediocre before publication; now such filtering is increasingly social, and happens after the fact."

As a result, it is even more important to apply the code of ethics of the Society of Professional Journalists to convergent media. Some of those basic principles state:

- Seek truth and report it. Journalists should test the accuracy of information from all sources.

- Identify sources whenever possible.

- Minimize harm. Show compassion for those who may be adversely affected by news coverage.

- Be accountable. Journalists should clarify and explain news coverage and invite dialogue with the public over journalistic coverage.

ETHICAL REASONING

Journalists use several methods to justify their decisions. In most ethical dilemmas, editors and reporters discuss the issue and the consequences of publication before making the decision. They consider how newsworthy the story is and whether the public really needs this information. The process of ethical reasoning generally involves these three steps:

1. Define the dilemma. Consider all the problems the story or photograph will pose.

2. Examine all your alternatives. You can publish, not publish, wait for a while until you get more information before publishing, display the story or photo prominently or in a lesser position, or choose other options.

3. Justify your decision. Weigh the harms and the benefits of publication, or weigh such factors as relevance and importance of the story to the public.

The Poynter Institute Model

Robert M. Steele headed the ethics program at the Poynter Institute for 14 years before joining the faculty of DePauw University as a visiting professor. While at Poynter, he developed these questions to help journalists make decisions in ethical dilemmas:

- Why am I concerned about this story, photo or graphic?
- What is the news? What good would publication do?
- Is the information complete and accurate, to the best of my knowledge?
- Am I missing an important point of view?
- What does my reader need to know?
- How would I feel if the story or photo were about me or a member of my family?
- What are the likely consequences of publication? What good or harm could result?
- What are my alternatives?
- Will I be able to clearly and honestly explain my decision to anyone who challenges it?

CODES OF ETHICS

Many news organizations have devised codes of ethics that govern the behavior of employees. These include policies about accepting gifts or freelance assignments, as well as guidelines about conflicts of interest.

Staff members who violate these policies at newspapers can be fired, and many have been. In some cases, reporters have been fired for entering into business relationships

ETHICS

THE CASE: YOUR campus newspaper has received an advertisement that promotes the revisionist point of view that the Nazi Holocaust of World War II never occurred. The ad, accompanied by a $125 check, was sent by the Committee for Open Debate on the Holocaust, an organization run by Bradley R. Smith from his home in Visalia, Calif. He sent the advertisement to colleges all over the U.S. In a cover letter he urges campus editors to run the ad to promote dialogue and to support the First Amendment.

When the University of Miami campus newspaper, *The Miami Hurricane*, ran the ad, nearly 400 students demonstrated outside the newspaper. A wealthy alumnus threatened to withdraw a $2 million gift but later recanted when the school promised to offer courses on the Holocaust. Other school newspapers have refused to print the ad. You know that this ad will offend many people on your campus and in your community, but you want to uphold the First Amendment. Will you run this ad or reject it and return the check? Justify your decision.

with a source or for using for personal gain information they get from sources. Journalism societies, such as the Radio Television Digital News Association and the Public Relations Society of America, also have basic codes of ethics to guide members.

Principles common to all the codes include adhering to accuracy, telling the truth, minimizing harm and avoiding conflicts of interest.

For links to codes of ethics, check the CourseMate for this chapter. Access is available at *www.cengagebrain.com.*

EXERCISES

1 Apply ethical reasoning, using the Poynter Institute guidelines, to the following cases (or to other cases described in this chapter):

  a An anonymous source tells you that a U.S. senator for your state has voted against many gay rights issues even though he is gay. You have heard other rumors that the senator is homosexual, but the senator has denied that the rumors are true. What will you do about this story?

  b You have heard rumors that your local nursing home is abusing its clients. However, no complaints have been filed with state regulatory agencies or with the police. You have contacted some of the clients' family members, who say they are concerned but have no proof. Will you go undercover as a volunteer aide at the nursing home (no special training required) to investigate?

2 Discuss the ethical dilemma, described in this chapter under "Public Officials," about revealing the criminal record of the student government candidate who resigned before the story could be published. What would you do if you were the editor of your campus publication or broadcast station? Do you agree or disagree with the decision made by the editor of *The University Daily Kansan?*

3 You are writing a story about problems of online pornography and the groups that oppose it. The story will be published on your campus website. Will you link to the pornography sites that the groups find objectionable?

FEATURED ONLINE ACTIVITY Log on and visit the Writing and Reporting News CourseMate and take the interactive tutorial quiz on media ethics. *Access available at www.cengagebrain.com.*

COACHING TIPS

Seek sources from **different racial and ethnic backgrounds** for all kinds of stories, not just stories about minorities.

Ask your sources **how they prefer to be addressed.**

Ask yourself if you would write the **same type of description for a man as for a woman,** for a white source as for a person of color, for a disabled person or member of any other ethnic or special group.

debra hughes/Shutterstock.com

We need to be aware of how we communicate — of our built-in biases. Language is not a neutral thing.

— **TIM GALLIMORE,** assistant commissioner, Missouri Department of Higher Education

CHAPTER 16
Multicultural Sensitivity

WHAT DO YOU THINK OF WHEN YOU HEAR THE WORD "ALIEN"? DOES it conjure up an image of a creature from outer space? Now add the word "illegal," and you get a term that the National Association of Hispanic Journalists (NAHJ) considers derogatory.

"The association has always denounced the use of the degrading terms 'alien' and 'illegal alien' to describe undocumented immigrants because it casts them as adverse, strange beings, inhuman outsiders who come to the U.S. with questionable motivations," according to the NAHJ in a news release. Even more objectionable to the association are headlines using the word "illegals" as a noun.

"Using the word in this way is grammatically incorrect and crosses the line by criminalizing the person, not the action they are purported to have committed. The NAHJ calls on the media to never use 'illegals' in headlines."

Instead of terms such as "illegal aliens" or "illegal immigrants" used by many news media, the NAHJ prefers the terms "undocumented worker," or "undocumented immigrant."

As the population of the U.S. continues to change, journalists and public relations practitioners will need to exercise sensitivity about multicultural issues.

By 2050 more than half the population in the country will be a mixture of Hispanics, Asians and blacks, with Hispanics making up nearly 29 percent of the residents, according to the U.S. Census Bureau. The Asian-American population will have

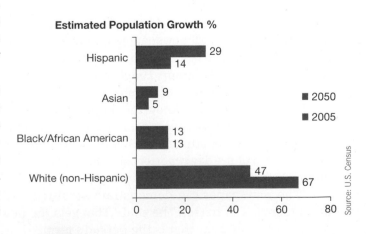

Estimated Population Growth %

Hispanic 29 / 14
Asian 9 / 5
Black/African American 13 / 13
White (non-Hispanic) 47 / 67

■ 2050
■ 2005

0   20   40   60   80

Source: U.S. Census

The U.S. Census Bureau predicts that by 2023, half of all American children will be minorities.

the next largest increase, going from 5.1 percent to 9.2 percent of the population.

Both old and young populations will also have dramatic increases. The number of people over age 65 will more than double to 20 percent of the population by 2050, but more than half of all children in the U.S. will be minorities by 2023, the Census Bureau reports.

The term "minority" has already changed. One out of every 10 counties in the country is considered a "majority-minority" county, meaning the population of nonwhites is in the majority.

THE LANGUAGE OF MULTICULTURALISM

Tim Gallimore.

Even if you choose your words carefully, you can't be sure how they will be interpreted. Gender, race and geographical and ethnic background influence interpretation, said Tim Gallimore, a former journalism professor who conducted a study about the interpretation of mass media messages. In his study, Gallimore asked students to define a number of words, including *majority, ghetto* and *inner city*. He concluded that it is hard, if not impossible, to get people to agree on one meaning for a word.

Consider, for example, the word *majority*. "It is remarkable that women view themselves as minorities although they are a majority of the population in every society," he said. "This can be explained only through the connotation of *majority* as possession of power — the white male-dominated majority."

Other loaded terms are *ghetto* and *inner city*, which Gallimore's students at the University of Missouri tended to define as an area with drugs, poverty, crime and gangs rather than as an urban geographical location. On television, when a news anchor says "inner-city youth," the phrase is almost always followed by descriptions and visuals of young blacks killing one another for crack or high-priced athletic shoes, Gallimore said. "Language is not a neutral thing."

Language changes, too. *African-American* is the term preferred by many blacks, but it is not accepted at all newspapers and television news organizations. *Chicano* is preferred by Mexican-Americans in some parts of the country, yet it is offensive to many older members of the group. *People of color* is a term preferred by many organizations with a majority of nonwhite members.

How can a journalist know the proper term to use? Any terms that might be acceptable today could be out of vogue tomorrow. Gallimore, who now is assistant commissioner of the Missouri Department of Higher Education, said that instead of memorizing the popular term of the day, reporters should ask people of different ethnic or special interest groups how they prefer to be addressed.

"The newspaper can demonstrate sensitivity with the words the person uses to define himself or herself," he said. "That gets the newspaper off the hook. If someone objects, you could say that is the person's term."

Definitions of Race

Meta G. Carstarphen, author of several books and articles about race and gender, discovered that journalists have a difficult time defining race. In a study she conducted, 40 percent of the journalists defined race as skin color or physical characteristics and 28 percent defined it as ethnicity. The remainder gave various definitions involving social and political differences.

Other terms related to race, diversity and multicultural topics are equally confusing.

"Diversity is the street where I live, and I would argue the neighborhood that all of us inhabit," Carstarphen wrote in a blog. "One definition I found online equates diversity with 'variety' and 'multiformity.' Diversity in some ways is too placid a term, connoting just the right mix of different elements, operating in a perfect balance with all of its parts. But I think the experience of diversity involves a sometimes raucous, sometimes contentious and sometimes blissful set of interactions."

Meta Carstarphen, graduate director, Gaylord College of Journalism and Mass Communication, University of Oklahoma

Racial Identifiers

The way the media identify minority groups is often considered contentious.

The Asian American Journalists Association (AAJA) conducts a "Media Watch" group to keep tabs on racial identifiers it considers offensive. The organization writes letters to editors or publishers when it finds stereotypical or negative portrayal of Asian-Americans, such as this note to *The Wall Street Journal* in reference to an article entitled "Furniture — Coping with the Asian Invasion."

> "Asian invasion" implies something ominous and dangerous; it also reinforces the bigoted belief — it continues to fester in some quarters of our society — that people of Asian descent are foreigners who are to be kept out at all cost.

The newspaper editor responded, saying no bigotry was intended but also thanking the association for calling the item to his attention.

In another case, the group objected to comments a radio station sports commentator made about Asian golfers at the U.S. Women's Golf Championship at Interlachen. "The fact of the matter is that we have these kids named Kim, Park and Lee out there . . . . It's hard to tell one of these kids from the other for us who don't follow LPGA golf real closely."

The association wrote to the radio station saying it found the comments offensive because "they reinforce the stereotype that all Asians resemble each other."

> The remarks take on a racial overtone with the implication being "well, they all look alike anyway, don't they?" Asia is a large continent with a diverse cross section of cultures, languages and physical characteristics. One could not imagine a sports columnist implying that all golfers from Europe are identical in appearance.

In a another letter to an editor at KTNV-TV in Las Vegas, Nev., the president of AAJA complained about a phrase:

We want to caution you on the use of the phrase, "yellow faces," in describing Asian-Americans. It is a misnomer and an outdated one at that. Asian-Americans are not yellow-skinned, after all.

The organization provides a stylebook for terms and issues referring to Asian-American and Pacific Islanders *(www.aaja.org/resources/apa_handbook)*.

It is not the only organization that offers a style guide for terms to improve sensitivity to a racial group. The National Association of Black Journalist (NABJ) also offers a stylebook as a resource to supplement the Associated Press Stylebook *(www.nabj.org/?styleguide)*.

When referring to African-Americans, the association says "African," "African-American" and "black" are acceptable. But it adds; "Not all black people are African-Americans (if they were born outside of the United States). Let a subject's preference determine which term to use. In a story in which race is relevant and there is no stated preference for an individual or individuals, use black because it is an accurate description of race. . . . Do not use race in a police description unless the report is highly detailed and gives more than just the person's skin color. In news copy, aim to use black as an adjective, not a noun. Also, when describing a group, use black people instead of just blacks. In headlines, blacks, however, is acceptable."

The term "people of color" is also acceptable as a synonym for minorities, according to the style guide.

For "diversity," the guidebook gives this broad definition: "Catchall term to describe a condition or environment that is multiracial and multicultural; being representative or reflective of the multiethnic society. Diversity is not synonymous with affirmative action, is not limited to race and is not government-mandated. A company can have a diverse staff mixing races, ages, sexes, sexual orientation, etc."

The National Lesbian and Gay Journalists Association (NLGJA) also aims to improve sensitivity with a style guide *(www.nlgja.org/resources/2010stylebook.pdf)*. Some of the terms that gay people prefer may be misunderstood by members of the media who are not gay. For example, when a gay and lesbian group at the University of Kansas decided to call its members "queers," students at the campus newspaper struggled with that term in a news story. But that was the term the group preferred. The NLGJA stylebook gives this advice for "queer": "Originally a pejorative term for gay, now being reclaimed by some gay, lesbian, bisexual and transgender people as a self-affirming umbrella term. Offensive when used as an epithet. Use only if there is a compelling reason."

When you are confronted with a similar dilemma, it's best to ask people how they prefer to be called, and if it does seem offensive, you can explain in the story that the term was preferred by the source.

ETHICS

ETHICAL DILEMMA: This photo was taken of the celebration at the end of a three-day conference of the Black Student Government at the University of Kansas and published in the student newspaper. African-American students at the university complained. Why? Do you think there is anything insensitive about this photo?

After students complained, the editor of *The University Daily Kansan* wrote this column:

"Newspapers have a responsibility to present the news in a way that portrays the reality of an event or issue. At the Kansan we take this responsibility seriously. But in regard to the photos used to illustrate the 16th annual Big Eight Conference on Black Student Government, our coverage was irresponsible. . . .

By including photos that represented only four hours of a three-day event, we misrepresented the conference. But even worse, we perpetuated a stereotype.

The photos were of African-Americans dancing and singing. On the sports page that same day, five African-American athletes were pictured. Those were the only photos of African-Americans in that issue.

Dancing, singing and slam dunking: These are too often the only images of African-Americans that newspapers provide to their readers. I or someone else in the newsroom should have realized before the photos were printed that we were perpetuating this stereotype of African-Americans.

My goal for this column is to help our readers understand what we did and why we were wrong for doing it. We have learned from our mistake. We hope others will learn from it, too. "

This photo caused a controversy at the University of Kansas.

Photo by Daron J. Bennett, *The University Daily Kansan*

MINORITIES IN THE NEWS

Multicultural sensitivity involves not only the sources you use but also the kinds of stories you choose. Innumerable studies have been conducted to show how women and minorities are portrayed in biased or stereotypical fashion. Minorities are often featured in stories about crime but excluded as sources in general stories about lifestyles, the economy and other stories where experts are cited. Conversely, women and minorities are often portrayed as unusual if they have operated a successful business or accomplished some of the same newsworthy feats as white males.

Mervin Aubespin, former president of the National Association of Black Journalists, said one way the media can become more sensitive to the needs of minorities is to hire more minorities. As the U.S. population becomes more diverse, the need for minority representation in the media workforce and in media coverage is only going to increase. But newspapers and broadcast media do not reflect the nation's diversity.

The big picture of minority employment in television news and newspapers has changed very little in the last 20 years, according to Robert Papper, a Hofstra University professor who conducts an annual survey of broadcast news employment. In 2010 the total minority population in the U.S. was 35.3 percent, but the minority TV workforce was only 20.2 percent. In newspapers minority employment decreased slightly that year for a total of 13.3 percent at daily newspapers, according to the American Society of Newspaper Editors survey.

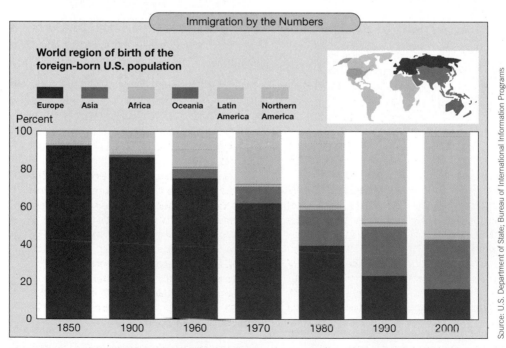

Source: U.S. Department of State; Bureau of International Information Programs

Changes in regions of origin for immigration.

Aubespin said hiring minorities is only the first step; editors have to encourage minority reporters to express their diversity. One of the problems is that white editors "really want black faces that write like whites," he said. "There is no formula, no one way to write about a minority group. The best guideline is to treat each person as an individual. We are as different as you are."

Adrienne Rivers, an NABJ member who teaches mass communication at Westchester Community College, said another problem is that reporters go to the same minority sources for all stories. "They anoint people as leaders of the community and get their voices," she said. "There may be other people of that race or ethnic origin with other points of view."

Stories about terrorism have created another problem for journalists. The media are often blamed for stereotyping Muslims and Arab-Americans in connection with these stories. The Society of Professional Journalists offers these guidelines for countering racial, ethnic and religious profiling:

- Do not represent Arab-Americans and Muslims as monolithic groups. Avoid conveying the impression that all Arab-Americans and Muslims wear traditional clothing.

- When describing Islam, keep in mind there are large populations of Muslims around the world, including in Africa, Asia, Canada, Europe, India and the United

SOCIAL MEDIA

SOCIAL MEDIA sites such as Twitter have become major communication venues for Latinos and blacks, who lead all other groups in texting and tweeting, according to a study by the Pew Internet and American Life Project. "Minority Internet users are more than twice as likely to use Twitter as white Internet users," according to the study.

Social media is "coloring the world we live in," according to Ana Roca-Castro, founder of Latinos in Social Media *(http://latism.org/)*, the largest organization of social media professionals of Hispanic origin. "Through blogging, they have planted themselves right at the epicenter of merging worlds: between tradition and modernity, between off-line and on-line, between English and Spanish, between American and Latino cultures."

One of the biggest trends now is that Latinos are not only engaging more through social media but also producing unique content as bloggers, according to Manny Ruiz, co-publisher of the Hispanic PR Blog, *www.hispanicprblog.com*, a website geared to public relations and marketing practitioners. Ruiz produces a daily blog geared to Hispanic marketers, and he has published a 57-page "U.S. Hispanic Social Media Guide" filled with articles and tips about the Hispanic market.

In one article in the guide, Paul Rand, president of the Zócalo Group social marketing agency, summed up the importance of marketing to all multicultural groups: "Across all ethnicities what consumers and customers are saying is 'We want to have a different relationship with companies we do business with' . . . . Now the question is: How do companies, brands in particular, begin operating? People under 25 years old don't call customer service lines anymore. They expect interaction through Twitter, so there's a fundamental shift in how business is being done."

States. Distinguish between various Muslim states; do not lump them together as in constructions such as "the fury of the Muslim world."

■ Avoid using word combinations such as "Islamic terrorist" or "Muslim extremist" that are misleading because they link whole religions to criminal activity. Be specific: Alternate choices, depending on context, include "al-Qaida terrorists" or, to describe the broad range of groups involved in Islamic politics, "political Islamists." Do not use religious characterizations as shorthand when geographic, political, socioeconomic or other distinctions might be more accurate.

■ Ask men and women from within targeted communities to review your coverage and make suggestions.

GENDER DIFFERENCES

Although inclusion of women on news pages and in TV broadcasts has improved, some stereotypes remain. The old stereotypes of the apron-clad housewives have given way to new ones of Superwoman moms.

"News media have long been fond of features that focus on the difficulties working mothers face when they try to 'have it all,'" Jennifer L. Pozner wrote in an article on the website for Fairness and Accuracy in the Media. "Tales of strained Superwomen can serve to reinforce the underlying notion that unlike fatherhood, motherhood and work outside the home are naturally in conflict. . . . Media never question why fathers want careers, and rarely if ever imply that their presence in the workplace is bad for their children."

Just as women are victims of stereotypes, so are men. Women are supposed to be emotional; men are supposed to be strong. More often, the men featured in the news have no feelings at all. Women have an agenda of child support and social issues; men want to read about sports.

Nonsense, says Jack Kammer, author of *If Men Have All the Power, How Come Women Make the Rules*. In an article in *Editor & Publisher,* he said it is a mistake to conclude that women have no interest in sports or business sections and that men have no interest in lifestyle sections. In fact, he says, one study showed that 84 percent of the men surveyed said family mattered most to them. Men also want a say about child care, sexual harassment and social issues.

Shifts in treatment of women and men are apparent in advertising as well. To reach the huge female buying market, advertisers have overcompensated, particularly in several television ads, by portraying men as stupid or incompetent. The use of women as sex symbols in many beer and automobile ads had declined for a while, but it appears to be returning, especially in automobile ads.

The principles for coverage of gender are the same as they are for coverage of ethnic minorities. Make an effort to include female sources as experts in general stories, not just stories geared to women. Seek diversity of opinion, but write about people as being all equal. When you write about a woman, don't include descriptive details about her appearance unless you would also include descriptive details about a man's appearance.

How can you avoid sexism and gender stereotypes? Here are some tips published in *The Gannetteer,* a magazine for employees of Gannett newspapers:

- When referring to any given person, avoid using masculine pronouns such as *he* or *his*. Instead of "Everyone should eat his own biscuit," say "Everyone should eat a biscuit." (*However, AP style says use the male pronoun "his" when it is not clear whether the antecedent is male or female*.)

- Avoid words that, by definition, refer to one sex or the other but not both. Instead of *governess*, use *tutor*.

- Avoid words starting or ending with *man*. Instead of *mailman,* use *mail carrier*. Instead of *fireman,* use *firefighter;* use *police officer* in place of *policeman*.

- Avoid stereotypes in illustrations and graphics. Not all quarterbacks are white. Not all basketball players are black. Not all single parents are women. Not all newspaper editors are men. Not all pro golfers are men.

- Avoid calling groups of people men, unless they are all male. A congressional group should be called lawmakers or members of Congress, not Congressmen.

- Avoid the stereotype of a mother. Don't say "chicken soup like your mother used to make." Maybe your father made the soup once in a while. Avoid such phrases as "old wives' tale," "tied to her apron strings" or "Dutch uncle."

- Avoid referring to women by their first names in stories. This is almost always patronizing, and not usually done to men.

- Avoid describing women with adjectives that dwell on sexual attributes. Ask yourself whether you would describe the walk of an IBM executive as "suggestive" if you were profiling a man, or would the walk just seem "confident"? Ditto for "feisty." When is the last time you saw a man described as "feisty"?

- Be careful with "first" stories: the first woman to pick up the garbage for a living, fly into space or run for the school board. (*However, if it is a first, it may be worth mentioning, but it does not have to be the focus of the story*.)

- Avoid phrases that carry an element of surprise such as "smart and dedicated woman." Is it unusual that someone who is smart and dedicated is a woman, too?

- Beware of approaching any story with the subconscious idea that it is more of a man's story or a woman's. Almost always we quote women in stories about child care. Why not men? A lack of child care is just as big a problem to them — or should be.

GUIDELINES FOR WRITING ABOUT SPECIAL GROUPS

Every group has some special needs and concerns about language. A man who uses a wheelchair probably doesn't consider himself handicapped (a derogatory term). However, he may have a disability that requires him to use a wheelchair. A person who has AIDS is not a victim but rather an AIDS patient or a person living with AIDS. And not all people over age 65 are ready for the stereotypical rocking chair.

CONVERGENCE COACH

THE INTERNET IS a multicultural mecca for sources. More than a dozen journalism organizations devoted to racial and ethnic groups offer websites with sources and research. Here are some ways you can use the Web to improve your coverage of diversity:

- Subscribe to blogs and social networking sites about diversity.

- Do a search for blogs about diversity and racial issues.
- Read ethnic newspapers online.
- Check minority journalism organizations for sources.
- Check online diversity organizations for internships, job opportunities, scholarships and guidelines to help journalists become sensitive to diversity.
- Check network and cable news stations, and analyze the coverage of people of color as well as the reporters and anchors.

You cannot be expected to memorize dictionaries for each special interest group. However, if your beat is a specialty that frequently deals with aging, disabled people, AIDS or some other minority interest, you could call an umbrella organization and ask for guidelines. Most organizations have these printed.

However, your first source should be the people you interview. Ask them how they prefer to be addressed. Next, consult the Associated Press Stylebook, which includes guidelines under such listings as *handicapped* and *AIDS*. You'll minimize trouble by avoiding the use of adjectives to describe people.

People with Disabilities

Do not characterize someone as disabled unless that condition is crucial to the story. Avoid the word *handicapped,* unless the person uses it to describe himself. If the disability is a factor, don't say "disabled people." Instead, use "people with disabilities." Avoid such terms as *crippled* and *deformed.*

Many euphemisms — such as *physically challenged, partially sighted* and *physically inconvenienced* — have come into vogue. However, disability groups object to such euphemisms because they are considered condescending. The AP Stylebook also says to avoid euphemisms such as *mentally challenged* and descriptions that connote pity, such as *afflicted with* or *suffers from* a particular disease. Just say the person has multiple sclerosis or other applicable disease.

Heather Kirkwood, a former journalism student at the University of Kansas, is legally blind but can see with the use of various aids. She doesn't like being called *visually challenged* or *partially sighted.* She prefers the term *blind.* But she says organizations representing blind people disagree with her and insist that the distinction between partially and fully blind should be made.

"As far as political correctness, my own feelings are that it isn't the word, it is what the word means," Kirkwood says. "Saying 'visually impaired' instead of 'blind' doesn't really change the way the blind are viewed in society. What matters is what comes to mind when you say the word 'blind.' Progress is changing what it means to be blind, not changing the word for it."

Kirkwood acknowledges that many stories about people with disabilities have that same "gee whiz" factor as stories about successful women.

"As far as the 'amazing factor,' that must really confuse people," she says. "Many blind people truly believe they are amazing. That is because we are taught to think that from a very early age.

"While we can expect journalists to try to understand all of this, we know the general public probably won't," Kirkwood says. "We also expect journalists to understand that we are not all representative of an entire group of people, yet we know the general public won't be as fair.

"The biggest problem we face is not blindness, but rather the public's perception of blindness."

The University of Kansas Lifespan Institute, which offers guidelines for writing about people with disabilities, says euphemisms "reinforce the idea that disabilities cannot be dealt with up front." The institute also recommends emphasizing people's abilities, not their limitations. "Show people with disabilities as active participants of society. Portraying persons with disabilities interacting with nondisabled people in social and work environments helps break down barriers and open lines of communication."

When in doubt, ask your sources how they prefer to be addressed. Here are some more tips:

- When interviewing people with disabilities, do not speak louder unless the person has a hearing impairment. A common complaint of people who have disabilities unrelated to their hearing is that everyone treats them as though they were hearing impaired. Treat people with disabilities exactly as you would any other source.

- Avoid overcompensating by writing about people with disabilities as though they were superhuman. The hidden implication is that all people with disabilities are without talent and that your source is unusual. The same principle says to avoid calling an African-American articulate or qualified, implying that other African-Americans are not.

- Avoid writing about people with disabilities as though they don't have any faults.

- Avoid using adjectives as nouns to describe a group of people with disabilities, such as *the deaf* or *the retarded.* Say "people who are deaf "or "people with mental retardation." For people who are blind, *visually impaired* is a preferred term.

- For mental illness, avoid such terms as *crazy* and *demented. Psychotic* and *schizophrenic* should be used in context — and only if they are the proper medical terms. Preferred terms are *people with emotional disorders* or people with psychiatric illness, mental problems or mental disabilities.

- Avoid "gee whiz" stories that stress how amazing it is that this person could accomplish anything special, given his disability.

Stories about Aging

If there were ever a group especially prone to "gee whiz" stories, it would have to be people over age 65. Most newspaper feature stories treat people in this age group as absolutely amazing just because they walk, run, dance or accomplish anything. People over 65 are usually described as spry, sometimes feisty, but always remarkable.

The population in the U.S. is aging and people over age 65 are among the fastest-growing group in the country, according to the U.S. Census. But for many years the journalists who wrote about them were considerably younger, and much of the coverage revealed a lack of understanding and sensitivity even though the intent may have been well-meaning.

Consider this feature:

This place hops.

The food's tame, the dance steps slower than they used to be, the stiffest drink comes from the water fountain.

Still the Gray Crowd jams the Armory Park Senior Citizens Center.

Typically, 1,200 men and women gather daily for gossip, games, and yes — even to cast some plain old-fashioned goo-goo eyes.

— *The* (Tucson) *Arizona Daily Star*

Or the story will feature a twist — surprise, surprise, they're old!

The teams, each with two rows of participants, face one another. As the blue balloon floats through the air, the two seemingly docile teams transform into aggressive competitors.

You'd think they were teenagers. They were . . . perhaps 50 or more years ago.

— *Tulsa* (Okla.) *World*

Make age a factor, not the focus of a person's accomplishments. Readers can decide for themselves if the person's accomplishments are surprising because of the person's age. Especially avoid the astonishment factor: Isn't it amazing this person can accomplish such and such at this age?

Here are some general guidelines for dealing with people of this age:

- When writing about people over age 65, avoid such adjectives as *gray-haired* or other terms unless you would use the same type of description if the story were about a younger person with blond or brown hair.

- Avoid stereotypes. Don't introduce rocking chairs or similar stereotypical images if the people in the story aren't using them.

- Avoid the *graying population, senior citizens* and other group designations unless you are writing a trend story. And then use such a term only if it is relevant, necessary and appropriate — for example, if a group uses the term in its own name, as in Gray Power.

- Avoid saying such things as "She doesn't consider herself old," unless she says it. Even though you are meaning to extend a compliment, by writing such denials you are introducing a stereotype.

AIDS Stories

In the last 20 years, medical developments have improved the life span of people living with AIDS, but the disease still carries a stigma. It is a subject that still requires the reporter to use great sensitivity.

Jacqui Banaszynski, a distinguished professor at the University of Missouri School of Journalism, says one of the reasons AIDS stories differ from other stories is the social stigma. "The disease is one story, the social context of the disease becomes another story. If you ignore the opportunity to deal with the societal revulsion, you miss the whole crux."

Banaszynski knows first-hand how difficult it can be to interview people with AIDS. She did it long before the disease was understood and before medicines existed to prolong the life of patients with AIDS. Death was the only certainty when she wrote a series that won the 1988 Pulitzer Prize for feature writing.

The rules change for this kind of story, Banaszynski says. "You have to be empathetic. On the other hand, you have to be honest and true to the reader who may be hostile to the subject. You walk a fine line between not blaming and not whitewashing."

Banaszynski, then a reporter for the *St. Paul* (Minn.) *Pioneer Press,* spent 15 months reporting how a Minnesota farmer, Dick Hanson, and his partner Bert Henningson lived and died with AIDS. She became as close to them as a family member — actually, closer than some of their family members. When Henningson was dying, his family even asked her to help decide whether they should pull the plug (she refused).

Readers don't want to read about AIDS or deal with it, she says. So she decided that the best approach was to portray these two men as two ordinary Minnesotans who had a commonality with readers. "If Joe and Suzy Reader could not relate to two gay pig farmers, they could relate to two men who plant impatiens, feed kittens and tend a vegetable garden, because that's what all Minnesotans do." In her introduction, she stresses that this is a story about people living — as well as dying — with AIDS:

> Death is no stranger to the heartland. It is as natural as the seasons, as inevitable as farm machinery breaking down and farmers' bodies giving out after too many years of too much work.
>
> But when death comes in the guise of AIDS, it is a disturbingly unfamiliar visitor, one better known in the gay districts and drug houses of the big cities, one that shows no respect for the usual order of life in the country.
>
> The visitor has come to rural Glenwood, Minn.
>
> Dick Hanson, a well-known liberal political activist who homesteads his family's century-old farm south of Glenwood, was diagnosed last summer with

acquired immune deficiency syndrome. His partner of five years, Bert Henning-son, carries the AIDS virus.

In the year that Hanson has been living — and dying — with AIDS, he has hosted some cruel companions: blinding headaches and failing vision, relentless nausea and deep fatigue, falling blood counts and worrisome coughs and sleep-less, sweat-soaked nights.

He has watched as his strong body, toughened by 37 years on the farm, shrinks and stoops like that of an old man. He has weathered the family shame and community fear, the prejudice and whispered condemnations. He has read the reality in his partner's eyes, heard the death sentence from doctors and seen the hopelessness confirmed by the statistics.

But the statistics tell only half the story — the half about dying.

Statistics fail to tell much about the people they represent. About the people like Hanson — a farmer who has nourished life in the fields, a peace ac-tivist who has marched for a safer planet, an idealist and a gay activist who has campaigned for social justice and now an AIDS patient who refuses to abandon his own future, however long it lasts.

The statistics say nothing of the joys of a carefully tended vegetable gar-den and new kittens under the shed, of tender teasing and magic hugs. Of flowers that bloom brighter and birds that sing sweeter and simple pleasures grown profound against the backdrop of a terminal illness. Of the powerful bond between two people who pledged for better or worse and meant it.

"Who is to judge the value of life, whether it's one day or one week or one year," Hanson said. "I find the quality of life more important than the length of life."

Much has been written about the death that comes from AIDS, but little has been said about the living. Hanson and Henningson want to change that. They have opened their homes and their hearts to tell the whole story — begin-ning to end.

— JACQUI BANASZYNSKI, *St. Paul* (Minn.) *Pioneer Press*

Ground Rules for Sensitive Questions

When you write about AIDS, you have to ask about dying and you have to ask about sex. How do you approach either of these sensitive questions?

"The only thing to do is to set it in context," Banaszynski says. "When I get to it, I ask as directly as I can: How many men did you sleep with? I don't warn them that this is a hard question. I set that up in the ground rules. I say, 'We're going to talk about a lot of personal things, and a lot may be embarrassing. You don't have to answer, but I'll try to get you to answer.' If you ask honestly and directly with no judgment in your voice so there is no shame involved, they will answer. If you are embarrassed, they will pick it up. I ask the question as matter-of-factly as I would about the weather."

Banaszynski says people are really very eager to tell their stories. "I think you can ask anybody any question if you are nonjudgmental and a good listener. Nobody listens anymore."

She also used another interviewing technique in her many visits with Hanson and Henningson. "I did something I don't normally do," she says. "I reminded them of my mission. They got to like me so much. My job was to be responsible and remind them that I was there as a reporter. I broke rules and invented new ones. I said when the notebook was down they could talk freely. Nothing was fair game until the notebook was out. And then I would remind them again that it was now on the record."

When she wrote the stories, she also did something that is not general practice in journalism. "I called each person involved in the story and read them their quotes, and I told them the context. For example, in one case I said, 'I set you in the context of a fight with your family.' Then I told them, if you can convince me that I have erred or been insensitive, I'll consider changing it." Only one person complained. She didn't take out any of his comments, but she added a sentence that appeased him.

She also took the newspaper to Hanson and Henningson the night before it hit the morning newspaper stands so they could see it first. "They couldn't change anything, but that's just courtesy. If they allow me to invade their privacy, I owe them that courtesy."

Banaszynski says the ground rules are different when you are writing about people who are not accustomed to dealing with the media. "These people don't know the rules. I have more responsibility to tell them what I'm going to be writing, the general thrust and what I'm trying to do."

Banaszynski predicts that it will get increasingly difficult to interest the public in AIDS stories. "The one thing you always have to remember about AIDS is that it has an overlay of homosexuality," she says. "It is a stigmatized disease that the public doesn't want to read about. You have to get past a big barrier of rejection.

"You have to focus on the common denominator. This could be your brother or neighbor or your doctor. AIDS serves as an extreme example of all the challenges in reporting more than other stories. You have got to find ways to have it connect to everyone's life."

EXERCISES

1 Multicultural story ideas: Interview members of various ethnic and racial groups in your community or on your campus about their concerns and the kinds of stories they think newspapers are not writing about them. Devise 10 story ideas based on your interviews.

2 Sexism, ageism and racism: Develop your own media watch group or become a member of one. Look for examples of language, description or other elements of stories that you think are sexist, racist or ageist. Find at least five examples in print, broadcast or online media that you think would be offensive to a minority group.

3 Gender coverage: Using highlighters of two different colors, read the news sections of your newspaper for a few days. Use one color to mark the female sources quoted and the other color for the male sources. Analyze the types of stories that feature women more than men, and vice versa. Also try to determine if multicultural sources are used in the news stories.

4 Multicultural profile: Interview a person on campus who is a member of a minority group — whether because of the person's race, ethnic background or sexual orientation. The focus should be this person's feelings about how the media treat members of his or her minority. Get some background about the person. Then ask questions related to the focus. Some questions to include might be these:

- How do you prefer to be addressed? How do you think the media portray people in your minority group? Are the portrayals positive or negative? (Ask for specific examples.) Have you ever experienced insensitivity or prejudice because of your race, ethnic background, disability or special interests? (Please specify.)

- Have you ever been interviewed by the media? Was your experience good or bad? (Please specify.) What advice would you give to reporters about coverage of minorities such as yourself? (Again, ask for specifics.) Write your findings in the form of a mini-profile.

Here are some additional questions that Meta Carstarphan asks her students to pose in similar interviews:

- Tell me about where you were born and grew up. Do you think the racial attitudes at your home are different from the ones you experience here?

- How do you describe yourself physically? When do you think about race? What makes that happen?

- Would your life be different if you were another gender or a different race? Why or why not?

If so, what ways would those differences be evident?

5 Perceptions of language: As you read the following terms, write the first descriptive words that come to your mind; then discuss whether your perceptions are stereotypes:

Texas	African-American	lesbian
ghetto	gay	truck driver
Hispanic	Asians	firefighter
Jewish	Native Americans	basketball player
Irish	Catholics	inner city
alien	immigrant	minority

6 Television shows: Discuss some of your favorite television shows. Are the characters white, African-American, Asian-American or Hispanic? What races are underrepresented in television entertainment?

7 Advertising: Watch advertisements on television for one or two days, and analyze whether they are more inclusive of racial groups than other media. Discuss which racial groups are most represented in television advertisements. Compare those ads with print ads in your newspaper or in magazines you read. Are the ads in one medium more racially diverse than in another? Discuss how men and women are portrayed in ads, especially on television. Do the ads reflect or promote stereotypes?

FEATURED ONLINE ACTIVITY Log on and visit the Writing and Reporting News CourseMate and take the interactive

tutorial quiz on multicultural sensitivity. *Access available at www.cengagebrain.com.*

COACHING TIPS

For profiles:

Observe descriptive details about the person, and **show the source in action.**

Do background research to **find unusual questions** the subject will enjoy discussing.

Check social media (Facebook, You Tube, Twitter, blogs etc.) for background.

Find a **unifying theme** that you can weave through your story.

Plan an order for your story; **consider organizing it by topics or time frames** (present, past, back to present and future).

For obituaries:

Ask yourself **what made this person memorable?**

Check the **accuracy of spellings** and information in profiles and obituaries.

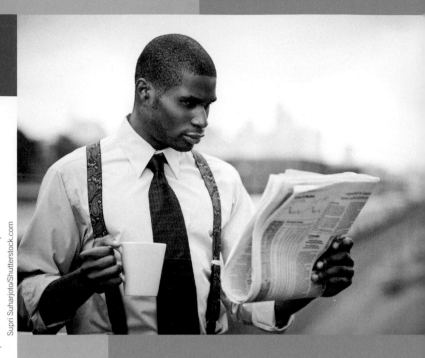

Supri Suharjoto/Shutterstock.com

Everybody's got one good story to tell. If you talk to them long enough, you'll find it. Nobody has lived a totally uneventful life.

— **ALAN RICHMAN,** writer, *GQ (Gentlemen's Quarterly)*

CHAPTER 17
Profiles and Obituaries

ALAN RICHMAN ENTERS THE DARK MANHATTAN HOTEL BAR TO AWAIT the arrival of Robert De Niro. The famous actor has agreed to meet with Richman for 15 minutes to decide whether he will grant the writer an interview for *GQ* (*Gentlemen's Quarterly*) magazine.

Richman is accustomed to writing celebrity profiles, but this time he is nervous. De Niro hates to be interviewed.

It's 6:45 p.m. The meeting is set for 7 p.m. Richman paces in the lobby. At 7:17 p.m. De Niro arrives. He startles Richman by asking him what his first five questions would be.

Richman is trying to come up with five questions the actor will like. He isn't prepared. The words don't come.

The actor says two questions will do.

I haven't said a coherent word yet and I've blown 60 percent of this interview. Later, I'm told that I should have asked him about Brando. He loved Brando in "The Freshman," wants to do character roles like that, ones in which he doesn't have to carry the film.

I don't think of that. I choke and ask the obvious. I ask him why he's agreed to consider an interview if he hates them so much.

— ALAN RICHMAN, *GQ*

De Niro says in jest that he's agreed because of the clothes he'll get by being photographed for *GQ*. Richman doesn't tell him he won't get to keep the clothes. The writer is ready to pose his second question.

He never gets the chance. De Niro says he has to go, and he leaves without agreeing to the interview.

Richman is stuck. He still has to write the profile for *GQ*. So he calls De Niro's friends and associates.

"After the interview failed, I went back and called all those people to figure how to make the story work," Richman says. "I asked them, what question could you ask that he (De Niro) would answer. Everybody told me something about De Niro you couldn't ask."

One actor who worked with De Niro said, "I don't think I'd ask him about his family or his love life. He's pretty private."

Another friend warned Richman not to talk about world politics, sports, fine wines or clothing because "he doesn't know a lot about those things."

Those and other comments about De Niro were probably more insightful than the actor would have been about himself. And that was the theme of the profile: how to interview a celebrity who doesn't like to be interviewed.

Richman had broken one of his major rules for conducting celebrity profiles. "You've got to nail them with a question they like," Richman says. "They are so bored. I always ask myself, 'What question can I ask this guy that he'll enjoy answering.' It takes thinking."

He didn't do enough thinking before he met De Niro to set up the interview. But he's had better luck with other celebrities and athletes in the 30 years that he has been a sportswriter in Philadelphia, a columnist and writing coach for *The Boston Globe*, a reporter for *The New York Times*, and a profile writer for *People* magazine.

These days, Richman has become a celebrity in his own right as the most award-winning food writer in history. As a food and wine critic for *GQ*, he has reviewed restaurants all over the world. He also teaches writing skills as dean of food journalism at the French Culinary Institute in New York. He even has a video on YouTube about a meal he cooked for a famous chef.

Richman's varied career reveals how many possibilities exist for a journalist. He tells his students that although they may be writing about food, good writing skills are more important than the subject.

Most of his articles are reviews of restaurants, but one recent story that brought him acclaim was a profile of a wannabe restaurant reviewer.

Courtesy of Alan Richman

Alan Richman,
food writer

DAVID FISHMAN suggested we meet at one of his favorite neighborhood restaurants, Hummus Place, and while I might ordinarily have complained that the locale was more convenient for him than for me, in this case I raised no objection. It wasn't because he's now the most famous restaurant critic in America. It was because he is 12 years old and his mother doesn't allow him to travel very far. . . .

The kid came in. I could tell it was him. The average restaurant critic is fat. David is seventy-nine pounds. The average restaurant critic is taller than four feet eight. He isn't. . . .

I looked at the menu. Hummus and more hummus. Hummus joints always make me feel as though I'm eating on a kibbutz. I asked him why he hung out at one.

"It's our responsibility to publicize not just the popular places but the little places that might have food just as good," he said.

Smart kid, with a conscience. That might keep him from going far in my business.

— ALAN RICHMAN, *GQ*

Celebrities — of any age — are considered worthy of profiles because they have accomplished something more special than the average citizen. However, many profiles focus on people in the community who have done something noteworthy but do not have celebrity status.

"Everybody's got one good story to tell," Richman says. "If you talk to them long enough, you'll find it. Nobody has lived a totally uneventful life."

To find that story, Richman uses what he calls the "Columbo school of interviewing," named after the deceptively naïve TV detective. "I sort of hang around looking harmless. I try to be as unthreatening as possible. Then I use a weave-and-jab style of questioning. You can't be afraid to be a little bit rude," he says. "If the point of the interview is that they were a bigamist, I'll say: 'We all want to have two wives; tell me how you got away with it.' If it's a profile of a man growing award-winning roses, I'll say: 'I can't believe someone would spend 15 years to grow a decent rose.'"

You may have a different interviewing style, but before you even get to the interviewing stage, you should research your subject's background. If possible, try to get a résumé or an academic vita if you are interviewing a professor. Check social media and online sites, but don't rely on the information.

"I don't trust press releases or clips," Richman says. "I always ask the background stuff." Sometimes background questions can be boring. So Richman just puts his subjects on notice. He tells them: "'It's that time now; I've got to ask these questions.' Basically they think I have some secret that I'm going to ask them like 'Tell me about when you were 11 years old and you slept with a goat.' Then I tell them, 'I've got to go over your life.' They're relieved. I don't mess around and pretend it's going to be fun. It's more like, do me a favor. You never know what you are going to get."

Many reporters seek background from the profile subject's friends and family *before* they conduct the main interview. In De Niro's case, Richman had no choice. He had to contact the actor's friends *after* the interview failed, but he prefers that method anyway — with this caveat:

"One of my rules is never call up friends or acquaintances of stars and ask what they think of the person, because they will always lie," Richman says. "If you were doing a profile of Hitler, most journalists would call Goebbels and Himmler and they would say, 'What a guy!' Instead, ask them for facts or anecdotes."

Terry Gross has also interviewed scores of celebrities, politicians and other people for her National Public Radio show, "Fresh Air." She is renowned for her interviewing skill. In an article for the *American Journalism Review*, Thomas Kunkel wrote: "Gross's conversational interviews are marked by intelligence, preparation and a diplomatic but firm probing of what makes people tick." She told him, "My theory of interviewing is that whatever you have, use it. If you are confused, use that. If you have raw curiosity, use that. If you have experience, use that. If you have a lot of research, use that. But figure out what it is you have and make it work for you."

"I often ask my guests about what they consider to be their invisible weaknesses and shortcomings."

— TERRY GROSS

After 25 years of interviewing people for her NPR show, Gross decided to write a book about the profiles she conducted. She explains her interviewing techniques in her introduction to the book, *All I Did Was Ask: Conversations with Writers, Actors, Musicians and Artists*.

"I often ask my guests about what they consider to be their invisible weaknesses and shortcomings," she writes. "I do this because these are the characteristics that define us no less than our strengths. What we feel sets us apart from other people is often the thing that shapes us as individuals. . . . I also violate decorum by asking questions of my guests that you usually don't ask someone you've just met, for fear of seeming rude or intrusive. Within minutes of saying hello to a guest, I might inquire about his religious beliefs or sexual fantasies — but only if it's relevant to the subject he's come on the show to discuss. Or at some point during the interview, I might ask a question about a physical flaw, the sort that we gallantly pretend not to notice in everyday life. When I do this, my purpose isn't to embarrass my guest or to make him self-conscious. I'm trying to encourage introspection, hoping for a reply that might lead to a revelation about my guest's life that might lead, in turn, to a revelation about his art. . . . I try in my interviews to find the connections between my guests' lives and their work (the reason we care about them in the first place)."

Despite the candor Gross seeks from her sources, she also says she respects her guests' privacy. "I would never pressure anyone to reveal those thoughts and experiences he desires to keep private," she writes. "That's why before beginning an interview, I tell the guest to let me know if I'm getting too personal, in which case we'll move on to something else."

Those are the kinds of questions and tips that work well in profile interviews. They are what another editor calls "turning points."

TURNING POINTS

Walter Dawson, a former editor for *The Commercial Appeal* in Tennessee, said that regardless of the profile subject, "the heart and soul of a profile is making sure the reader understands the twists and turns and intricacies of human life." Dawson said writers should consider the following universal elements:

- **Patterns:** Some lives build to a climax, as for a law school student who becomes a judge.
- **Decisive moments or turning points:** Most lives take turns along the way. Take the law school student; perhaps she wanted to be a great defense lawyer but became a prosecutor instead. Or maybe your subject was an accountant who became head of a river-rafting company.
- **Future:** Every profile subject has a future, and you need to ask your subject what could lie ahead. Let the person speculate, especially about career goals. Ask the impertinent question: If this career doesn't work out, what could you do? The answers about the future could also provide an ending for the profile.

In addition to revealing the turning points, strengths and weaknesses of the source during the reporting process for your story, here are some points to consider when you write the profile.

PROFILE PLANNING TIPS

Choose your subject:

- Why is this person newsworthy?
- What will be your focus of the profile?
- What has this person done that would be of interest to readers?
- Does this person contribute to your college or university behind the scenes?
- Has this person received an award, written a book, started a new course or program?
- Is this person new in the job?
- Is this person retiring after a long stay at your college or university?
- If the profile subject is a student, is he or she head of an organization, an athlete or has the person achieved an unusual accomplishment?

- Have a backup plan for another interview subject in case your first choice cancels the interview.

Background research:

- Check the Internet and social media sites.
- Ask for a résumé or vita.
- Get a photo.
- Ask co-workers, students or other people about the person (before the interview) to get tips on questions to ask. (You also could interview these people after the interview). Check everything you can about the person's background *before* the interview.

BASIC ELEMENTS OF PROFILES

Focus What is the main idea of the profile? What makes this person newsworthy? Why are you writing about this person now? Those questions should be answered in the nut graph.

Theme What is the difference between a nut graph and a theme? The nut graph is the reason for the story, but the theme is an angle or recurring idea that weaves throughout the story. Some general themes for profiles might be overcoming adversity; succeeding against odds; or coping with failure, illness or serious problems as in the following example, for which a Michigan State University student won first place in the profile category of the prestigious Hearst Journalism Awards program for college students:

> Sam Howell clutched the arms of his wheelchair, lips pursed, eyes wide with determination.
>
> He was going to stand.
>
> The 19-year-old MSU student focused on moving his strong arms, long legs and Adidas-adorned feet to function together — something he never struggled with nine months ago. . . .
>
> But nine months ago, the MSU freshman fell asleep while driving and woke up in a hospital bed more than two months later.
>
> Doctors predicted he'd never make it. . . .

But the "miracle boy," as Sam's family and friends call him, pulled through even when his chance for survival was estimated at less than 1 percent.

"He's got hurdles to get through, but he's such a determined human," Maureen (Howell) said. "I've never seen him not be successful just because he's so tenacious to keep going and going."

— MELISSA DOMSIC, *Michigan State University*

Background Profiles should not be written in chronological order. The subject's background should be inserted where it fits best, often in the middle of the story. But in some cases, when the background is the most interesting or crucial element, it may be the lead or in the beginning of the story, as in this example about a New Orleans detective, whose complete profile appears later in the chapter.

Background

NEW ORLEANS — The white frame house on Barrone Street is small and gated, just as it was when Jacklean Davis was a shy, serious-eyed little girl in a world of grown-up horrors.

Here, 12 blocks from the muddy brown Mississippi River, Davis was raised by a prostitute, raped by a sailor, sexually molested by an uncle and pregnant at age 16. By then, folks in the neighborhood were whispering that Davis was headed for the same hard life as the aunt who had reared her: selling herself to strangers. In a sense they were right — but in an entirely different way.

Now 34, Jackie Davis cruises the city in a police car — not just any cop but the most successful detective in New Orleans, this humid capital of good times and jazz that also happens to be one of the deadliest cities in the South, with 346 murders last year.

Nut graph

THE GOAL METHOD

To discover those turning points and other qualities of your profile subject, consider using the GOAL method (goals, obstacles, achievements, logistics). Questions about obstacles the person faced can provide some of the most interesting parts of your profile. Don't stick to any order, but consider some of these questions as they arise naturally in the conversation:

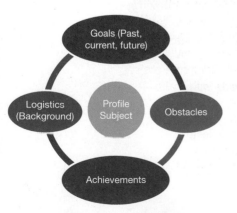

- **Goals:** What were your original goals? What are your current and future goals?

- **Obstacles:** What obstacles did you face in accomplishing your goals, and what new problems loom?

- **Achievements:** What pleasures or problems have these achievements brought?

- **Logistics:** What background (logistics of who, what, when, where) led to your current situation? How has your past influenced you?

The Goal Method

Here are some other elements to include in profiles:

Age and Physical Description: Help the reader visualize your profile subject. But use description only when it is relevant to the topic you are discussing. Make the details work for you. In this example from a profile of Willie Darden, a convicted killer who was interviewed while he was awaiting execution in a Florida prison, the writer weaves in the age and physical description by relating them to the pressure of waiting for death:

> Darden maintains a normalcy, a serenity that is surreal. His forehead is not cleaved by worry lines. His hair has not gone gray. He lifts his shackled hands and displays unbitten fingernails. "Calmness is a nice thing to have in times of stress," he says.
>
> He gives his age as 62, but prison records say he is 52. He looks 42. It's as if the man has not only cheated the executioner, but time itself.
>
> Or maybe time just stops when there is no future.
>
> "Prison does tend to sustain one's youth," Darden says with an ironic grin. "You're not doing anything that you would normally do on the outside — such as working hard every day. You've got no family problems. The wear and tear, so to speak, is on the inside."
>
> — RICHARD LEIBY, *South Florida Sun-Sentinel*, (Fort Lauderdale, Fla.)

Other Points of View: Seek anecdotes and comments from friends, family, colleagues and other people affected by the person at work, such as students for a profile about a professor or employees for a profile about a manager.

Visuals

Use graphics as a way to visualize your story in both the planning and writing stages. Outlining your profile by planning a facts (highlights) box can help you determine what topics to include in your story.

If the background is boring, break it out of your story. You can put key dates and such information as birthplace, education, career moves or similar items in a box. But if that information is an interesting and crucial part of your story, leave it in the body of the profile. You also can use a box to add information that doesn't fit well into your story but might be of interest, such as hobbies, favorite books, favorite saying or major goal. The major goal should also be mentioned in your story, but it works well in a facts box.

Several newspapers, magazines and websites use graphic devices to substitute for written profiles; others use highlights boxes to enhance profiles. For example, *The Kansas City* (Mo.) *Star* Sunday magazine profiles celebrities with blurbs following these headings:

- Vital statistics (occupation, birthday, birthplace, current home, marital status and so on)
- My fantasy is . . .

- If I could change one thing about myself, it would be . . .
- The best times of my life . . .
- Behind my back my friends say . . .
- These words best describe me . . .

Those are also good questions to ask for your profile even if you don't use the items in a visual tool. However, if you mention topics in a graphic, you don't have to repeat them in the story.

CONVERGENCE COACH

CHECK INTERNET and social media for background on your profile subject, but don't rely on the information. Make sure that you check the accuracy of anything you find in your interview with the subject. The following tips apply to profiles for print, broadcast and the Web:

- Start with a simple search for the person's name in *www.google.com* or other search engine.

- Check out any articles or books written by or about the profile subject. If the person has written books, read one, or at least read summaries in *www.amazon.com*.

- Check for personal and academic websites and online résumés the person might have — especially if you are interviewing professors.

- Check athletic records in sports sites for profiles of athletes.

- Check fan sites for celebrities or athletes. These sites may contain links to articles or other information. Use them only as a guide; don't trust information from personal sites.

- For profiles about candidates, check voting records of incumbents and campaign contributions at sites such as *www.followthemoney.org* for candidates to state offices and the Federal Election Commission (*www.fec.gov*) for candidates to federal offices.

- Check social networking sites such as Facebook, MySpace, YouTube, Twitter and others for personal pages and comments about your subject.

Broadcast Profiles

- Think visually in the planning stage before you do the reporting. Background research is essential so you can ask interesting questions that will elicit good responses from your source.

- Show and tell. Write to the video, and show your subject in action.

- Read your script aloud.

- Don't introduce your sound bites by parroting what the source will say.

Web Profiles

- Plan audio, video and graphic elements that may accompany your profile.

- Consider breaking out facts or other highlights into boxes.

- Plan links that might provide background or other elements of the profile.

- Consider writing the profile in sections; offer readers the choice of reading the parts linked on separate Web pages or on one page.

- Consider a question/answer format that is easy to read on the Web.

ORGANIZING THE PROFILE

There is no one way to organize a profile, other than having a lead, a body and an ending. Just make sure that you have a focus. Descriptive show-in-action leads, anecdotes, contrast leads and scene-setting leads work particularly well in profiles. As with any lead, make sure that you back up the lead with information that supports it later in the story.

The body of the story can be organized in many ways:

Supporting Themes: Block each concept, use all relevant material, and go on to the next concept.

Time Frames: Start with the present, go to the past, go back to the present, and end with the future. Or use some variation of the time frames, possibly starting with the past and then proceeding to the present.

Chronology: Look for a place in the story where chronological order might be useful, but don't write the entire profile in chronological order. A chronology might be helpful for the background. It might also work if you are writing the profile in narrative style. In some cases, however, the story might lend itself to chronological order if a situation unfolds in that sequence. Just make sure that your nut graph tells readers why you are writing about this person now.

Point/Counterpoint: If the subject lends itself to pro-and-con treatment, you might consider this method. It can be helpful in profiles of politicians. You can include reaction quotes from other people after each controversial point is made.

Sections: Splitting the story into separate parts may work if the profile is very complex. For example, if you are doing an in-depth profile of a politician or crime victim or crime suspect, you might organize it in sections, either by time frames of the person's life, issues or different points of view.

Q and A: The question/answer format is becoming popular as a format for profiles. It works well in print and on the Web.

Several types of endings work well with profiles. A quote kicker can be used to summarize a source's feelings about the subject or to summarize the subject's accomplishments. Or, with a circular ending, you can return to the lead for an idea and end on a similar note. An ending with a future theme tells what lies ahead for the person.

PUTTING IT ALL TOGETHER

Here is the entire profile of the New Orleans detective mentioned earlier. This profile demonstrates a variety of techniques suggested in this chapter. It has a clear focus, which is the one indispensable element of a compelling profile, and a recurring theme of overcoming adversity. It includes anecdotes, the subject's turning points and several comments from other sources. Notice that the three sections feature the present, past and future, although they are not so clearly delineated.

SHE IS THE FINEST OF NEW ORLEANS' FINEST

From a gritty past to the city's best detective

BY MATTHEW PURDY

The Philadelphia Inquirer

Descriptive lead to create contrasts with past and present

NEW ORLEANS — The white frame house on Barrone Street is small and gated, just as it was when Jacklean Davis was a shy, serious-eyed little girl in a world of grown-up horrors.

Here, 12 blocks from the muddy brown Mississippi River, Davis was raised by a prostitute, raped by a sailor, sexually molested by an uncle and pregnant at age 16.

By then, folks in the neighborhood were whispering that Davis was headed for the same hard life as the aunt who had reared her: selling herself to strangers. In a sense they were right — but in an entirely different way.

Nut graph

Now 34, Jackie Davis cruises the city in a police car — not just any cop but the most successful detective in New Orleans, this humid capital of good times and jazz that also happens to be one of the deadliest cities in the South, with 346 murders last year.

Backup for nut graph (comment from colleague)

"She was the best I ever saw at solving a murder case," said David Morales, her boss during her five-year stint in the homicide unit. "There was nobody close to her in the history of the homicide division."

More backup for nut graph

Davis solved 88 of her 90 murder cases — a record better than any other detective and all the more impressive for the first black woman to join an elite corps of mostly white men who prodded her to fail.

Specifics: anecdotes

They destroyed her case reports, told tipsters she didn't work there, placed feces in her desk drawer, posted her mistakes on the bulletin board, and decorated her mailbox with a cartoon of a mop and bucket titled "black power."

Davis reacted by putting in longer hours. In solitary moments, exhausted, she would bow her head and sob.

"Every case that I got, I was looked at under a microscope: 'Well, what is she going to do now?'" Davis recalls matter-of-factly. "My biggest accomplishment, I consider, is not cracking under the pressure."

More backup for the "so what" factor

At a time when politicians have taken to bashing the poor for dragging on society, Davis stands out as a stunning example of someone who has succeeded precisely because of her harsh past. She is now the city's most celebrated officer — and the subject of a screenplay that has caught the eye of Whoopi Goldberg. . . .

In a life full of ironies and incongruities, Davis posed as a hooker, arresting so many men in the raucous French Quarter that 20 backup officers were assigned to her and her partner. But Davis' arrest rate so riled those in the tourist trade that her superiors had her wired to prove she wasn't entrapping men. Even so, business interest prevailed, and Davis was yanked off the street.

But not before she had nailed 300 johns.

"Having lived with a prostitute all my life, there are certain things you do, certain things you say," says Davis, chuckling over her record.

•••

New section: arranged topically to reveal personal side of source

Christina Davis, 17, is a prep school senior with a B average who hopes to study engineering next year at Xavier University.

It's Wednesday night in the blond-brick ranch home where she and her mother live with Gigi and Snoopy, their two dogs. Christina Davis is alone.

Her mother, like most officers in New Orleans, earns such a modest wage — $225 a week in take-home pay — that she has to work late-night security details for extra cash, stretching her workweek to 60 hours or more.

"I'm proud of her, but she had to sacrifice time with me and a lot of things we could have done together," Christina Davis says wistfully.

Transition from show-in-action present to past, including background Physical description made relevant to job

Losing days — and really, years — with her daughter is Jacklean Davis' greatest regret, she says one evening as she steers her unmarked Chevy through the bombed-out Desire housing project.

Her career started here 11 years ago, when she was the only woman street cop in the rough-and-ready urban squad, which worked the projects. . . .

A short woman with a stocky look about her, crimped hair combed into a tight ponytail, Davis always made it a point to later return to murder scenes in street clothes. It helped, she says, that she doesn't look like a cop: being a woman, looking young, using slang.

As she rolls through the broken streets, Davis says she worries about the good people in the projects who get ground down by the force of crime and neglect. She could have been one of them.

Davis lost her father in a car accident when she was 3. Her bereaved mother squandered the insurance and had to give her children to an aunt.

As it turned out, Davis' grand-aunt was a prostitute who bedded down with sailors. But she was a protective, strong-willed woman with a heart of gold, Davis said.

Davis' aunt was married to a merchant marine. When he was home, little Jacklean lived in stifled terror. He was sexually molesting her. Her aunt didn't know until Jacklean was 14 and her uncle was dying of cancer.

Trauma set in again when Davis was raped at 12 by a sailor who visited her aunt. By 16, she was pregnant and people in her working-class black neighborhood were whispering that she had picked up her aunt's habits.

Davis' aunt died when she was 17, about the time she was about to give birth to Christina. But she still managed to graduate from high school, faltering when it came to college. A better life seemed always out of reach, she thought as she worked clearing tables at ritzy restaurants and driving a bus.

Turning point

It all hit bottom one winter when Davis found herself homeless for a two-week stretch, huddled in her parked car with Christina, danger lurking all around.

Quote kicker to section

"I knew this was it," she says. "There was no one else. I was on my own."

•••

More background to bring reader back to present and on to future

The idea to become a cop came to Jacklean Davis when she dated a rookie in the department. Problem was, when she took the exam, she flunked it — again and again and again.

It took Davis five tries to pass the test — and two to overcome her fear of guns and make it through the police academy. It was 1981 before she got her first job at the urban squad. . . .

Comment from colleague

"She puts her heart into everything," said Wayne Farve,

Anecdote

an old partner. "I've seen her at shootings where she'll kneel down in the blood right next to them and ask them who did it and where she can get more information."

Back in the old neighborhood, Davis got out of her car one night, in front of her home, eight blocks from where she grew up.

"Sssssss," a man hissed, pointing a gun.

Davis froze. Here she was, holding two bags of groceries, her own gun in her handbag, in the car. She screamed, slowly stepping away, as he closed in.

Unable to reach her gun, Davis screamed louder — and the man fled.

Davis dumped her groceries, grabbed her gun and opened fire as she chased him. Then sud

denly, he turned and fired back, hitting her in the leg.

As she recovered in a hospital, she took heart. No longer a frightened child, Jacklean Davis had fought back this time and won. A few months later, police caught the man. He had raped 14 women. Davis testified against him, helping to lock him away in Louisiana's dreaded Angola prison.

All told, it may be the stuff of movies, Davis concedes. An agent is negotiating for her, and the latest news is that Goldberg is reading the screenplay of her life.

"I don't even like to think about it," she says, admitting superstition. "I don't want to put a mojo on me."

Another turning point

Return to present

Quote kicker on future note

WRITING SNAPSHOT PROFILES

Julie Sullivan doesn't waste words. She writes snapshot profiles that let the reader see, hear and care about the character — quickly. Her skill earned her the Best Newspaper Writing Award from the American Society of Newspaper Editors for short news writing. The award was based on profiles she wrote for *The* (Spokane,

ETHICS

ETHICAL DILEMMA: How much should you reveal about a person in a profile, and what is your responsibility for the consequences? Do the circumstances differ if you are writing an obituary? What should you include if you are covering a profile or obituary of a student who committed suicide on campus? What should you do if you find that the deceased person

was on a sex offender registry or discover that the deceased had a criminal background? Should you include items in the obituary that the family would not want?

Ethical guidelines: On the one hand, the Society of Professional Journalists Code of Ethics says, "Seek the truth and report it." On the other hand, the code says, "Minimize harm." Editors disagree on this subject, especially concerning obituaries. What would you do in these cases?

Wash.) *Spokesman-Review*. They average fewer than 400 words. But she reveals a lifetime in her profiles.

Her method: short sentences, few adjectives, few quotes, many details.

Now a Pulitzer-Prize winning reporter for *The Oregonian* in Portland, Ore., she began writing at a weekly newspaper in Alaska after she graduated from the University of Montana in 1985. "I started out leaning toward brevity," she said. "My first editor in Alaska would always tell me, every time you finish a story, go back over it. Figure out what words are extraneous. What can you leave out?"

That's good advice for broadcast and Web writing as well.

Sullivan takes voluminous notes but discards about half of them. "I write everything down. I don't trust my memory," she says. That includes her observations. A cracked concrete step. An automobile battery under the sink. Cockroaches scurrying across the kitchen table. A toothless smile.

How does she know which details to include in her stories? "I write what I remember without looking at my notes. What details stand out? Like Joe Peak's teeth were so significant and personal. The contrast struck me. His place was so neat that I couldn't figure out how somebody who paid so much attention to his surroundings wouldn't take the same care personally. Then I found out how he lost his teeth."

She is equally selective about the limited quotes she includes. "I really think readers glaze over quotes," she says. "I do few quotes because I think most people are pretty plain-spoken and simple. You don't need to use it just because it's in quotes."

Her tips for writing briefly: "Trust your instincts about what is important, what struck you during the interview. The rest is chaff. I generally bounce my lead and the most important details off my co-workers, and I can gauge from their reactions if I'm on the right track."

She also stresses observation. "Pay attention to details, from the right spelling of names to finding out the date of people's birthdays."

On leads and kickers: "I tend to think readers read the beginning and the end. Never discount the lead you were throwing out. It could be a great kicker."

On structure: "You try to make a point with every paragraph."

On brevity: "Short has its place, but it won't replace more in-depth pieces; that's what a newspaper does best. I hope to continue to do both."

Julie Sullivan, reporter, *The Oregonian*

The profile that follows was part of a series about the problems of low-income residents in a deteriorating Spokane apartment building, the Merlin. Notice the details, and notice the strong factual kickers. As you read this profile, consider what information came from observations and what came from questions. And then decide how you could say it all in as few words.

It took twice as many words to describe Sullivan's style as she used in these stories.

....

DONALD 'JOE' PEAK

Joe Peak's smile has no teeth.

His dentures were stolen at the Norman Hotel, the last place he lived in downtown Spokane before moving to the Merlin two years ago.

Gumming food and fighting diabetes have shrunk the 54-year-old man's frame by 80 pounds. He is thin and weak and his mouth is sore.

But that doesn't stop him from frying hamburgers and onions for a friend at midnight or keeping an extra bed made up permanently in his two-room place.

"I try to make a little nest here for myself," he says.

Chock-full of furniture and cups from the 32-ounce Cokes he relishes for 53 cents apiece, Peaks' second floor apartment is almost cozy.

A good rug covers holes in the kitchen floor, clean-looking blankets cover a clean-looking bed. Dishes are stacked neatly in the kitchen sink.

But cockroaches still scurry across his kitchen table.

"I live with them," he says with a shrug. "I can't afford the insecticides, pesticides, germicides. I don't have the money."

With a $500 per month welfare check and a $175 rent payment, Peak follows a proper diet when he can afford it. He shops at nearby convenience stores where he knows prices are higher but the distance is right. He has adapted to the noisy nightlife in the hallways and sleeps when he is too exhausted to hear it.

Part Seminole Indian, Chinese and black, the Florida native moved to Spokane 20 years ago to be near relatives in Olympia. He quit school at 13 to help earn the family income and worked a string of blue-collar jobs. Along the way, someone started calling him Joe.

His voice is lyrical, his vocabulary huge, but Peak's experience with whites is long and bitter.

When conditions at the Merlin began worsening three months ago, junkies and gray mice the size of baby rats moved in next door. He hated to see it, but he isn't worried about being homeless.

He's worried about his diabetes. He's frightened by blood in his stool and sores on his gums. He wonders whether the white-staffed hospitals on the hill above him will treat a poor black man with no teeth.

— JULIE SULLIVAN, *The* (Spokane, Wash.) *Spokesman-Review*

Brief profiles showing a slice of life or vignettes of people are excellent formats for the Web or for a package of stories as sidebars to a main in-depth story. An idea that works well is a package of stories about diversity on campus, with profiles of international students or those from varied ethnic and racial backgrounds. A major story about an upcoming election in your town might also lend itself to mini-profiles of the candidates.

Here are some examples of vignettes written by journalism students who were following Julie Sullivan's style. The assignment was to find people behind the scenes on the campus of the University of Kansas. Students were instructed to write profiles filled with revealing details in fewer than 500 words — about one to one-and-a-half double-spaced typewritten pages. They were also told to stress show-in-action techniques. The frame was the university at work.

JOURNALISM SCHOOL LIBRARIAN

Yvonne Martinez has carefully picked out her wardrobe.

Dressed in a navy blue skirt patterned with white boxes and a white blouse with the same pattern in blue, she had come prepared for another day of work at the School of Journalism library.

However, her outfit would not be complete without her size 6 1/2 sneakers.

The 4-foot-11 librarian does not wear them simply because they help maintain a quiet atmosphere. That is just one of the added benefits.

She wears them because she is constantly on the move.

Whether it's searching for a student's request for the last two years' worth of *Folio* magazine or sorting through the seemingly endless stack of newspapers the library receives daily, she rarely has time to sit down.

Recent cuts in the library's budget and staff have increased Martinez's work load. The sneakers are crucial.

"I'd rather be comfortable than in pain," she said.

Her duties have grown during the two years she has been working behind the counter. But now her duties include repairing the copy machine.

It is the only copy machine the library can afford on its budget, Martinez said. Overuse causes it to break down at least once a day.

As she returns to the counter, she immediately is greeted by a professor who says the machine is out of ink. She reaches under the counter and pulls out a bottle of black ink.

As she pours, the bottle slips and ink covers her hands. More students who need to be helped arrive at the counter.

Martinez stands by the machine staring at her hands as if she were auditioning for the part of Lady Macbeth. She sighs and runs off to the restroom. She quickly returns to the counter and apologizes to the students.

After all, she is the only librarian on duty.

— RANJIT ARAB, *The University Daily Kansan*

BUS DRIVER

The sounds of a screaming Mick Jagger shake the windows of the bus.

A basket of Jolly Rancher's candies sits on the dashboard. And the driver in the blue and white Rolling Stones baseball cap is smiling.

This is Hank's bus — slap him a high five on the way off, please.

Hank Jones, who is in the middle of his fifth year as a (University of Kansas) bus driver, likes doing something extra for his passengers.

"Why shouldn't I," he says. "A little extra effort can go a long way."

One passenger remembers Hank stopping his bus on Jayhawk Boulevard last Valentine's Day just to give her a candy heart. She's been a regular ever since.

Hank began driving those green and white buses when he needed some extra money and he enjoyed it so much, he stayed with it.

The students are the best part of the job, but Hank is not without his complaints.

"They're not too quick sometimes," he says. "But they're good kids, most of them."

He tries to keep it interesting — he never plays the same tape twice in one day on his portable Sony stereo.

"I'm always partial to the Stones," he says, cracking open his pack of Marlboro cigarettes. "But I'll play requests, too."

Hank plans to keep driving for KU as long as he still enjoys it — or until he finds a wife. At 34, he hasn't found the right woman yet.

But he's in no hurry.

"Who knows?" he says. "Maybe someone will get on my bus."

— KATHY HILL

OBITUARIES

Obituaries are also profiles, but the subjects are dead. However, you don't write about the person's death; you write about his life. Marilyn Johnson, a magazine writer and editor, is so fascinated by obituaries that she wrote an entire book about the genre called *The Dead Beat*.

"The obituary pages, it turns out, are some of the best-read pages in the newspaper," she wrote. "Obituaries are history as it is happening. . . .Tell me the secret of a good life."

She is not alone. Alana Baranack, an obituary wrier at *The* (Cleveland) *Plain Dealer*, says in a blog that she loves the "death beat," so much so that she has written a book *Life on the Death Beat: A Handbook for Obituary Writers*.

A broadcast or Web obituary about a person who was in the news or an entertainer would include audio and video clips of the person's quotes and accomplishments as well as comments from other people.

The Associated Press has created a special editor to oversee multimedia obituary packages, which will include a written obituary accompanied by video, photos and an audio slide show when possible.

Jim Nicholson, a former obituary writer for the *Philadelphia Daily News*, became so famous for his obituaries that he was nicknamed "Dr. Death" by his co-workers. He called his obituaries "character portraits," filled with details of how the person lived, "warts and all," he says.

Obituaries tend to be flattering portraits. But Nicholson says they should be true portraits. He believes someone's bad habits and criminal background, if they exist, should be part of an obituary. Many editors would disagree. And families are not likely to be happy with unflattering material. Generally, news editors weigh whether a criminal background was a crucial part of the person's life and if the crime was

Jim Nicholson, former obituary writer for the *Philadelphia Daily News*

highly publicized. If a person was arrested at one time for shoplifting or for another misdemeanor, most editors would recommend omitting such information. When you are faced with such decisions, it is wise to confer with an editor.

"Cleaning up someone's act after he or she has died does not serve the cause of the deceased or loved ones," Nicholson says. "A sanitized portrait is indistinguishable from any other. It is the irregularities that give us identity. The ultimate acclaim may be when a reader thinks, 'I wish I had known this man or woman.'"

SOCIAL MEDIA

THE SUBJECTS are dead, so you might not think about checking their blogs. But the deceased person might have created a blog that provides insights to his thoughts. To find interesting tidbits about the people who died, you can check "twituary," an obituary list on Twitter.

Obituary writers have their own blog, the "Obituary Forum," where you can learn how they feel about their craft.

If the person had a Facebook page, it may contain posts from friends that will reveal much about the person's life. Other social media sites like YouTube might also provide information about your subject. Family members may also have personal websites worth checking. Don't copy material from these sites without permission, but use them to gather information that will reveal the kind of character portraits Jim Nicholson suggested.

Like the obituary for Lawrence Pompie "Mr. Buddy" Ellis, a retired maintenance man who was a leader in his church:

He came to be known affectionately among friends as "Dial-A-Prayer" for his unceasing availability to those who wanted him to pray with them. If he couldn't meet personally with someone, he would pray with them on the telephone, said his wife, Fannie, who shared 38 years with him. . . . At 5-foot-7 and 205 pounds, Ellis loved to eat. "He loved everything about a pig," said his wife, "and if he didn't watch out, he'd catch his grunt."

— JIM NICHOLSON, *Philadelphia Daily News*

THE IMPORTANCE OF FACTS

A misspelled name or a factual error is a major problem in any story; in an obituary it is disastrous. So you should check every fact, every name, every reference. And you should check with the funeral director and the family to make sure that the person you are writing about is dead.

Someone from the *Detroit Free Press* didn't do that. And the death of Dr. Rogers Fair turned out to be greatly exaggerated, as Mark Twain would say. Fair, a Detroit physician, woke up one morning to read in the newspaper that he had died of cancer. The newspaper had received the obituary information by telephone from a woman who claimed she was Fair's aunt. And the reporter didn't call back to check with family members or a funeral home.

Fair, 40, claimed the "aunt" was a 21-year-old woman who was infatuated with him. She had wooed him with flowers and love notes, but when he rejected her and began dating another woman, he began receiving harassing telephone calls, bomb threats and vandalism to his home.

"She is obviously an obsessed person," Fair told the *Free Press*. "She has stated that if she can't have me, nobody else can."

The follow-up story was an embarrassment to the paper:

The obituary for Dr. Rogers Fair in Tuesday's Free Press took a lot of people — especially Fair — by surprise.

"My beeper was just jumping off the hook," the 40-year-old physician said Tuesday. "My secretary called me. She was in tears. . . ."

The erroneous report of Fair's demise was the second phony obituary published by the *Free Press* in recent years. The first prompted a revision of reporting practices, requiring all obituary information phoned in by friends and relatives to be confirmed either by a funeral home or law enforcement officials.

But Fair's obituary wasn't properly double-checked, and a woman identifying herself as Fair's aunt was able to hoodwink the *Free Press* with details of his death.

— *Detroit Free Press*

Most newspapers have free or paid death notices — announcements from the family about the deceased. In addition, funeral directors and families call the newspaper to request an obituary. Almost all newspapers will publish an obituary about anyone prominent in the community.

Generally, reporters scan the paid death notices to look for interesting people, long-term residents or those active in community service. Then you make the phone calls — or double-check the validity of the ones you have received by calling a funeral home, checking the phone book, and calling the family back or calling other relatives and friends. And, as in any other story, you check newspaper clips or databases and the Internet.

Calling people about death isn't easy. But it isn't as difficult as you might expect, especially for obituaries. Most families are grateful because this is the last story — and more often the only story — printed about their loved ones. Usually, someone in the family is prepared to deal with the media.

The easiest way to start gathering information is with the funeral director, if one has been selected. The funeral director should have the basic information and should be able to tell you which family members to call and their phone numbers.

OBITUARY GUIDELINES

Obituary writing follows some basic forms, even when you are writing a special profile. All obituaries, no matter how long or short, must contain the same crucial information:

Background Research

Before you use anything from a website for background research, make sure that you check it for accuracy. Was the site dated? Does it have an author? Is the site credible? Do not use anything you can't verify. If you do include something from a website, cite your source.

Name: Use full name, middle initial and nickname if it was commonly used. Enclose the nickname in quotation marks.

Identification: How do you describe a person's life in one brief phrase? That's not so easy to do, but most obituaries start with a lead that identifies the person and summarizes the main accomplishment of his life. Usually, people are identified by occupation or community service. Always try to find something special to use following the name, such as "John Doe, a retired salesman" or "Jane Doe, a homemaker who was active in her church."

Age: In some cases, a family will request that you withhold the age. You should confer with an editor about honoring this request.

Date and Place of Death: Use the day of the week if the death occurred that week, the date if it was more than a week prior to the obituary. State the name of a hospital, if applicable, or other location where the death occurred.

Cause of Death: This fact is not required at all newspapers, especially if the cause of death was suicide or AIDS-related, or when the family requests that the cause be withheld. However, some news organizations require the cause of death, regardless of stigma or family wishes. So check your organization's policy before you gather the information. You may have to inform family members of the policy.

If a suicide occurs on a college campus, the news spreads quickly. Should it be mentioned in a campus newspaper story or obituary? That's an ethical dilemma that campus news editors and directors have debated. If it is very public and well known around the school, one approach is to do a general story about suicide, which is a significant issue on college campuses. In most cases, however, suicide is not mentioned in the obituary out of respect for the family.

Address: Tell where the person lived when he died and previous areas of residence for any major length of time. Broadcast obituaries rarely use the specific address.

Background: Specify major accomplishments, organizations, educational background, military background and any other highlights. When people are very active in their church, mosque or synagogue, this fact should be mentioned in the obituary.

Survivors: Use the names of immediate family members (husband or wife, with her maiden name, children, brothers and sisters). Grandchildren are usually mentioned only by number: "He is survived by five grandchildren." New complications are arising these days because of changes in family relationships. Most news publications still do not list unmarried partners as survivors, or "bonded" partners (homosexual couples united in a marital ceremony), but that rule is changing. In the future, these relationships may also be a standard part of obituaries.

Services: Specify the time, date and location.

Burial: Name the place, and provide memorial information when available. When the death occurred a week or more ago, it is customary to start with information about the service or a memorial if that has not yet been conducted.

This example about the death of a local citizen follows all the basic guidelines; it also includes information about contributions:

Lucy Davis Burnett, a Dallas native and longtime civic leader, died of cancer Saturday at her home. She was 79.

A graduate of Woodrow Wilson High School in Dallas and Mary Baldwin College in Staunton, Va., Mrs. Burnett was active in numerous cultural and civic affairs.

She was past president of the Southern Methodist University Lecture Series, vice president of the Dallas Junior League and president of the Junior League Garden Club.

She was a founding member of the Dallas Slipper Club and also held memberships in the Dallas Women's Club, the Dallas Arts Museum League, the women's division of United Way of Dallas and Highland Park United Methodist.

She is survived by her husband, F.W. Burnett of Dallas; a daughter, Lucy Chambers of Vancouver, British Columbia; a son, F.W. Burnett Jr. of Dallas; and six grandchildren.

Services for Mrs. Burnett will be at 2 p.m. Tuesday at Highland Park United Methodist Church.

Memorials may be made to Children's Medical Center of Dallas, the Dallas Chapter of the American Cancer Society or a charity of the donor's choice.

— *The Dallas Morning News*

Here are some style tips:

Names of Services: Mass is celebrated, not said. The word is capitalized. Find out the exact wording you should use for the particular mass, such as Mass of Christian Burial. Likewise, ask for the proper wording of a service for other denominations.

Courtesy Titles: Although many newspapers and TV news organizations have eliminated courtesy titles (*Mrs., Mr., Ms., Miss*) for news stories, several keep them for obituaries. Again, you must check your newspaper's or broadcast station's policy.

Titles for Religious Leaders: Check the proper title for a rabbi, minister or priest. When writing about a priest, do not use *Father* or *Pastor* for the title. Use *the Rev.* (the reverend) followed by the priest's name: "the Rev. Vince Krische." For a rabbi, use *Rabbi* before the name on first reference: "Rabbi Jacob Katz." On second reference for clergy, including priests, use only the last name. But for second reference to high-ranking clergy, use "the cardinal," "the archbishop" and so on. Check The Associated Press Stylebook for specific religious titles.

Here is a feature obituary for Dr. Seuss that follows the guidelines. The story begins with the writer's death, some basic information about his accomplishments and then a chronology of his life. It ends with information about survivors. No information was available about services at the time, but if it had been, it would have been included at the end.

Theodor Seuss Geisel, alias Dr. Seuss, whose rhymed writing and fanciful drawings were loved worldwide and helped teach generations to read, died Tuesday night at his home in La Jolla.

Geisel's stepdaughter, Lea Dimond, told reporters the world-famous author died with his family around him. No other information was released regarding the cause of death, but Dimond said Geisel, 87, had been ill for several months.

In the 1950s and '60s, Geisel's books gave millions of children relief from the drab textbook adventures of Dick and Jane. His 48 children's books were translated into 18 languages and sold more than 100 million copies.

Geisel also drew most of the fanciful illustrations in his books, creating a menagerie of Whos, grinches, ziffs and zuffs, talking goldfish and loyal, sweet elephants. He was awarded a special Pulitzer Prize in 1984 for his contribution to children's literature.

Geisel's tales were filled with his own moral concerns, particularly for the environment and world peace. "The Lorax" warns against polluting the environment, while "The Butter Battle Book" tells of an arms race between creatures who disagree about whether it is better to eat bread with the butter side down or up.

When asked recently whether he had any final message, Geisel told a reporter from the *San Diego Union*: "Whenever things go a bit sour in a job I'm doing, I always tell myself, 'You can do better than this.' The best slogan I can think of to leave with the USA would be 'We can do this and we've got to do better than this.'"

Geisel was born in Springfield, Mass. His father was a brewer and superintendent of parks, which included the zoo, where Geisel said he started drawing animals.

He graduated from Dartmouth College in 1925, having drawn cartoons for the school humor magazine. He went to England to study literature at Oxford University, but dropped out, in part, after receiving encouragement in his artistic ambitions from another American student, Helen Palmer. She became his first wife a few years later.

Geisel spent a year in Paris, where he got to know Ernest Hemingway, James Joyce and other writers. He returned to the United States in 1927, hoping to become a novelist.

He wrote humor for the magazines *Judge* and *Life*, adopting his now-famous pen name, Dr. Seuss, as a spoof of scientific developments.

Among his most famous books are "The Cat in the Hat," "Green Eggs and Ham" and "Horton Hears a Who!" which was made into a popular TV special, as was "How the Grinch Stole Christmas!"

He moved to La Jolla soon after the end of World War II. During the latter part of the war he served in the Army, helping director Frank Capra make training and documentary films. Two Geisel documentaries, "Hitler Lives?" and "Design for Death," co-written with his wife, won Academy Awards for their producers in 1946 and 1947.

After the war, Geisel's work continued to be translated to movies, with his cartoon short "Gerald McBoing Boing" winning an Oscar in 1951. He turned his attention to television in the 1950s, designing and producing cartoons, including the Peabody Award–winning "How the Grinch Stole Christmas!" and "Horton Hears a Who!". . .

Geisel did not have any children of his own. His first wife died in 1967. He later married Audrey Dimond, who has two daughters from a previous marriage. He also is survived by his niece, Peggy Owens, and her son, Theodore Owens, of Los Angeles.

— LAURA BLEIBERG, *The Orange County* (Calif.) *Register*

EXERCISES

1 Snapshot profile: Write a short profile about someone on your campus, using Julie Sullivan's style. Plan it as a vignette, considering it part of a package or a larger subject so it has a frame of reference. For example, consider a package of multicultural profiles, new professors or alumni.

2 Celebrity profile: Plan a celebrity profile of someone you would like to interview. If you enjoy sports, plan a profile of an athlete on your campus. Use Alan Richman's tips, and plan an interesting question you would use to begin the interview, as well as a preliminary theme you might pursue.

3 Profile coaching: Coach a classmate on writing a profile. Ask your classmate some of the basic coaching questions: What's it about? What is the focus? Do you have a theme? Were there any patterns, any turning points? What anecdotes do you remember as most interesting? What is the point — why should the reader care? What order are you considering? As the writer discusses the profile, you as the coach can ask questions that occur to you.

4 Slice-of-life snapshots: Using the theme of "A Day in the Life" of your campus or your community, write vignettes about people and places. Each person in the class can take a different part of the campus or community.

5 Personal profile: Write a blog or memo about a turning point in your life or a significant experience that might make you worthy of a profile. Pairing up with a classmate, exchange your memos and interview each other for a profile. Then write your profiles and share the results with your partner.

6 Obituary: Gather information from news clips, magazines, online sources and social media about a celebrity or otherwise prominent person in your community who is still alive. Write an obituary, including comments the person has made and comments about the person.

Check out the "Extended Profile/Obituary" scenario in NewsScene for an interactive exercise that will help to reinforce many of the themes presented in this chapter.

COACHING TIPS

Do your homework. **Check clips and online sources** for background about the speaker or issue.

Listen for **what the speaker doesn't discuss.** Then ask questions to find the answers that the readers or viewers will want.

Include audience reactions and responses to questions at speeches, meetings and news conferences.

Try to get as many good quotes and sound bites as possible. **Favor full quotes** over partial ones.

Write a **highlights box** to accompany your story or to organize your story especially for the Web.

Get the **full text of speeches** and documents from meetings to post on websites.

Record audio or video to post on the Web.

R. Gino Santa Maria/Shutterstock.com

The comments officials make during a meeting are for public posturing. Some of the best quotes you get are after the meeting when you ask them to explain why they did or said something.

— **MARK FAGAN,** reporter

CHAPTER 18
Speeches, News Conferences and Meetings

HE TWEETS, HE BLOGS, HE BROADCASTS AND HE WRITES NEWSPAPER
stories. Mark Fagan calls himself a "converged reporter." Although he is primarily
a print reporter for the *Lawrence Journal-World* in Kansas, when the newspaper's editors
asked print reporters to appear on its cable TV station as well, Fagan took to it naturally.
He says if you are a print or broadcast reporter, you are still applying the reporting and
writing skills you already have. You're just learning a new way to use them. These days
he also tweets news updates and writes a blog about his beat as a transportation and
community news reporter.

In the *Journal-World* newsroom, reporters from the partner TV station, 6 News, and
the print newspaper work side by side. A multimedia desk in the center of an open
atrium in the newsroom is the headquarters for coordinating stories for the newspaper,
TV and websites.

When Fagan covers local government, he gets most of his news stories at meetings.
But he gets most of his best quotes when the meetings end. Fagan says the most important part of a meeting story is what you cover before and after it.

One night the city commission was debating a zoning change. A business owner
wanted to expand his electrical shop in a residential neighborhood. Commissioner Jo
Andersen was angry. More business would bring traffic and crime to the neighborhood,
she said.

Fagan headed straight for Andersen after the meeting. "Why were you so upset?"
he asked.

"What I really wanted to say was that even if Jesus Christ himself wanted to expand
his carpenter's shop in East Lawrence, we would respectfully request that he find
another area that is more appropriate," she said.

"You can still say that," Fagan said. This is the beginning of the story he wrote the next day:

Not even divine intervention could help a proposal to expand an East Lawrence electric shop onto vacant lots next door.

During their meeting Tuesday night, Lawrence city commissioners denied a request from Patchen Electric & Industrial Supply Inc. to expand its 47-year-old business at 602 E. Ninth onto two lots zoned for apartments.

In the end, the request never had a prayer.

"If Jesus Christ himself wanted to expand his carpenter's shop in East Lawrence, we would respectfully request that he find another area that is more appropriate," Commissioner Jo Andersen said after the meeting. "It has nothing to do with a person's personality. It has everything to do with zoning."

— MARK FAGAN, *Lawrence* (Kan.) *Journal-World*

The story continued with explanations of how zoning had changed from commercial to residential use since the business was built and why residents objected to its expansion.

"The comments officials make during a meeting are for public posturing," Fagan says. "Some of the best quotes you get are after the meeting when you ask them to explain why they did or said something."

That advice also applies to someone from the public who speaks at a meeting. "A person may speak for 30 seconds and afterward she'll tell you, 'My kid needs a safe place to walk because he was attacked two years ago,'" Fagan says. "Don't just sit in the meeting if the person leaves; follow him or her out and get those additional comments."

What you write before the meeting is even more important, Fagan says. He writes at least one story to tell readers what officials will discuss at their next meeting. He also provides timely tweets about meetings and events on his beat before, during and after the events. If people don't know what officials plan to do, they won't get a chance to participate in government.

For example, to inform readers of an accident in his community he posted these tweets starting at 2:59 p.m.: "KS Turnpike: Multiple vehicle accident E/B milepost 205.5 east of Lawrence. Traffic stopped in both lanes." At 4:26 he tweeted: "Ref the accident e/b mm 205 all lanes are open but traffic is moving slowly." And at 6:06 p.m., he tweeted: "KS Turnpike: E/B mm 205 traffic has resumed normal speed."

Reporting these days is a job that takes place anytime, anywhere and in any medium.

Although many newspapers and TV news programs are curtailing meeting coverage because the news is sometimes dull, Fagan thinks that's a mistake. Meetings are where officials make decisions that affect the public.

Reporter Mark Fagan interviews a city commissioner.

"I'll write stories sometimes and no one (from the public) will show up at a meeting, and I wonder if what I do makes a difference. Then a city commissioner will say, 'I got about 20 phone calls after your article.' So I know people are reading them."

Even if people don't read his stories or attend the meetings, Fagan thinks it's important for reporters to be there as watchdogs for the public. He says the officials know he is really there for 20,000 other people: his readers.

"I put the commissioners' comments in the paper, and everyone knows where they stand," Fagan says. "That's a great power of the press."

Whenever you are covering a meeting, it's important to look beyond what officials say publicly. Fagan says reporters should ask questions before and after the public event to find out how the story affects readers.

"An item on a meeting agenda may say they are going to award bids for highway improvements on North Second Street," he says. "I look at that and say, 'What does that mean?' Are they going to widen the street? This is the only artery that connects downtown and an old neighborhood. Are they going to close the road to traffic for eight months? This is how officials plan to spend taxpayers' money. You need to find out how it affects readers."

MEDIA MANIPULATION

Sources who give speeches or conduct news conferences are often using the media to further their own causes. There's nothing wrong with that. It's a way of presenting news. But a responsible reporter should ask good questions after the speech or news conference and add points of view from opposing sources when possible.

For example, Operation Rescue, an anti-abortion group, waged massive demonstrations to close an abortion clinic in Wichita, Kan. The sources from that group had a definite agenda; they were clearly trying to manipulate the press, said Steven A. Smith, former managing editor of *The Wichita* (Kan.) *Eagle*. One of the leaders of Operation Rescue conducted a news conference during which he held up a fully developed fetus, which supposedly had been aborted at about seven or eight months. Smith said the situation posed a difficult ethical dilemma for the *Eagle* staff. The leader's actions were news. But there was no evidence that the fetus had been aborted at the Wichita clinic. The result: The *Eagle* published news about the protest and the leader's actions, including the statement that there was no proof the fetus came from the Wichita clinic. But the paper did not publish a picture of the fetus. Smith said he was convinced the situation was staged to manipulate the press. Television stations also refused to show the fetus.

Richard Hernandez, *The Wichita Eagle*. Tribune Media Services, Inc.

A Roman Catholic priest, leader of the pro-life group called the Lambs of Christ, is arrested after attempting to block the entrance to the Women's Health Care Center in Wichita.

Protesters on both sides of the abortion issue came from around the nation to converge on Wichita, and 2,600 of them were arrested for violating city laws and defying court orders prohibiting them from blocking the abortion clinic. Both sides sought to manipulate the press.

The problems of manipulation were even greater for the three local television stations. Operation Rescue leaders staged their news conferences shortly before the 5 p.m. newscasts in hopes of receiving live coverage from television. News directors, concerned about issues of accuracy and fairness, limited the live coverage. They edited the tape to be shown at the end of the 5 p.m. newscasts or only on the 10 p.m. programs so that they could have more control and present balanced viewpoints.

PREPARATION

Most speeches, news conferences and meetings do not pose such severe problems. Still, reporters always need to do more than listen and repeat what they hear. As Mark Fagan suggests, reporters need to ask good questions after the event as well.

To ask good questions, however, you must prepare for the event. You need to find out all you can about the speaker and the issue. Be sure to check the clips, blogs and online databases.

With a prominent speaker, you can often get the text of the speech in advance. But be careful not to rely on it. The speaker may depart from the prepared text. However, you can still use the prepared text. Just say, "The speaker said in prepared remarks" or "in a written text." Reporters sometimes have to rely on the written version, especially if their deadlines come before the speech or news conference is over.

During the speech, try to get full quotes of the important points (especially if they vary from the written text), and jot down reactions of the speaker and the audience. Note when and if the speaker shows emotion and how the audience responds. Write follow-up questions to ask the speaker after the speech or news conference.

Try to get an aisle seat. If someone asks a good question after the speech or meeting and then leaves, you should follow that person out of the room quickly so you can check the name and get more information.

STORIES ABOUT SPEECHES

Your story should always include some basic information:

- Size of the audience
- Location of the speech
- Reason for the speech
- Highlights of the speech, including good quotes
- Reaction of the audience, especially at dramatic points during the speech

Although you need to include this basic information, don't clutter the top of your story with it — unless it is crucial to the event. Write the story just as you would any other good story.

You can lead with a hard-news approach that emphasizes a main point the speaker made or a soft-news approach that describes the person or uses an anecdote from the speech. Just don't lead with a no-news approach: Someone made a speech. Tell the reader what the speaker said.

For example, here is the kind of lead to avoid; this one appeared on a story in a campus newspaper:

> Students from Gay and Lesbian Services spoke yesterday to a psychology class about their lives and experiences.

What did they say? It's better to focus on some interesting point they made.

Speakers usually don't make their strongest points first and follow in chronological order, so your story shouldn't be written in that order. Put the most emotional or newsworthy information first. Then back it up with quotes and supporting points.

Sometimes the most interesting information isn't what happens during the speech. It can be what happens after the speech or outside the place while the person is speaking, especially if there is a protest or other major reaction to the speech.

You can also use storytelling techniques for speeches. In the next example, a journalism student used narrative and descriptive writing to convey the drama of a speech by a survivor of the Holocaust. Notice where the writer put the basic information: when, where and how many people attended the speech.

Zev Kedem huddled in silence with his grandparents in a pigeon coop above his family's apartment while soldiers searched for them. His grandparents were prepared to swallow vials of poison as the soldiers tried the metal door they hid behind.

The door held. And the soldiers went on.

The year was 1942, and so begins Zev Kedem's story of survival that began over 70 years ago as Adolf Hitler orchestrated the Holocaust.

A "Schindler's List" survivor, Kedem spoke for over an hour as he told the story of his childhood in a Nazi concentration camp to 750 people in the Union Ballroom last night.

— GAIL JOHNSON

Here is a basic speech story that starts with a summary lead followed by a backup quote in the third paragraph. Note that the basics of location, audience size and reaction are lower in the story.

REPORTER NOTES LOWER STANDARDS IN JOURNALISM

Half of the reporting duo that unearthed the Watergate scandal, which led to the downfall of President Nixon, railed Saturday against what he characterized as another downfall: the media's fascination with the "loopy and lurid."

Former *Washington Post* reporter Carl Bernstein took aim at trash television, inaccurate reporting and media monopolies, primarily that of mogul Rupert Murdoch. The media are fascinated with celebrity, gossip and manufactured controversy, and pander to viewers and readers, adding to the "triumph of trash culture," he said.

"The greatest threat to the truth today may well be in our own profession," said Bernstein, who spoke for more than an hour at Budig Hall. His speech was sponsored by Kansas University's Student Union Activities.

Although every society has an "idiot subculture bubbling beneath the surface," Bernstein said a constant diet of certain television talk shows could cause it to boil over.

The problem needs to be addressed at the root level, with reporters refusing to limit their horizons and keep digging for the "best obtainable version of the truth," he said. "Really great reporting almost always comes from the initiative of the reporter, not the editor," said Bernstein.

— CHRIS KOGER, *Lawrence* (Kan.) *Journal-World*

STORIES ABOUT NEWS CONFERENCES

News conferences are like speeches, except that the questions reporters ask after a news conference are often more important than the prepared comments the speaker makes. The answers to those questions are an important part of the story — and sometimes are the story. Consider news reports after the U.S. president conducts a news

CONVERGENCE COACH

WHEN YOU COVER speeches, meetings and news conferences, plan to provide additional coverage on the Web, including audio and video if possible.

■ Write or broadcast a story advancing coverage of meetings and post highlights or a complete meeting agenda on the Web.

■ Tape the event to post sound bites or the entire speech or news conference on the Web.

■ Get a complete copy in digital form of budgets, proposals, speeches or other documents to post on the Web.

■ Be prepared to post a breaking news story of the event online and plan a more complete follow-up story for the next print or broadcast edition of the news.

■ Focus on the significance of a news conference or meeting; find people who are affected by the news before, during or after a meeting or news conference.

■ Plan a highlights box of the key points in a speech, news conference or meeting for print, broadcast or Web publication.

conference. His prepared remarks often are less interesting than his answers to the press corps.

Do your homework. Before or after the news conference, research the issue. If the conference is about a local crime, check files or background to provide perspective. How many other crimes of this nature have occurred? If the conference is about a city issue, how does the information affect your readers and viewers? Don't just recite the news; interpret it so that your audience can understand how the issues affect them.

Courtesy of the Federal Emergency Management Agency
Photo by Leif Skoogfors.

Media covering a news conference about Hurricane Katrina.

Stories about news conferences must include the following information:

- Person or people who conducted the news conference
- Reason for the news conference and background
- Highlights of the news, including responses to questions
- Location, if relevant
- Reaction from sources with similar and opposing points of view

Stories about news conferences are like most other news stories. Although reporters' questions may prompt the most interesting information, the answers are usually incorporated into the story without references such as "In response to a question" or "When asked about. . . ."

Summary lead–main point; reason for press conference

Location

College students today called on Congress to cut student loan interest rates as a first step to making college more affordable.

At a Capitol Hill news conference, students offered their personal stories and support of the House bill to cut subsidized Stafford loans in half as well as, a further agenda to reduce the rising cost of higher education and the impact of rising student debt.

Supporting quotes-reactions

"Paying for college is a major concern for millions of American students and their families," explained Jennifer Pae of the United States Student Association. "We need Congress to take concrete steps to make college affordable by lowering the burden of student debt, increasing Pell Grant funding and cutting excessive subsidies to private lenders."

The proposed legislation, which would cut interest rates in half for subsidized Stafford loans, offers important relief for middle class families. The average borrower would save $4,420 dollars in college loan payments.

At the press conference, participants noted that tuition has risen 40 percent in the last five years and that the average student graduates with an estimated $23,000 in total student loan debt. Each year, this translates into 400,000 qualified students enrolling in community colleges rather than four-year institutions, and 200,000 qualified students not enrolling in any higher education institution.

The groups are seeking the following measures:

- Increasing need-based grant aid by raising the maximum Pell Grant award to $5,100.

  Highlights

- Making student loans more affordable by lowering interest rates, limiting the percentage of income students spend repaying loans, expanding loan forgiveness programs for critical public service careers and reinstating the refinancing of existing loans.

- Cutting waste in the student loan programs by passing the Student Aid Reward Act to give money to students and parents, not banks.

"Higher education is the ticket to good jobs and a good future, said Anthony Daniels, an education student. And it's a ticket that many Americans can't afford."

— Adapted from Campaign for College Affordability

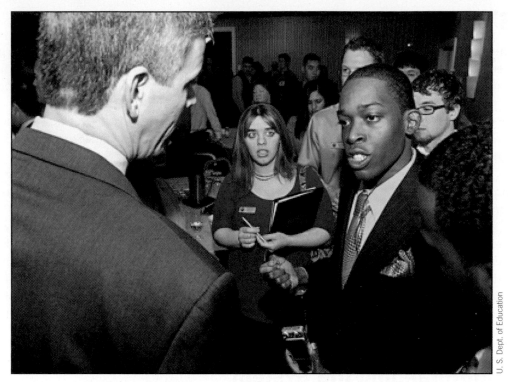

U.S. Secretary of Education Arne Duncan meets with students at the American Student Association of Community Colleges in Washington, D.C.

SOCIAL MEDIA

SOCIAL MEDIA tools are ideal for reporting and delivering information about speeches, news conferences and meetings.

- Use Twitter to post updated information during a news conference or meeting. Encourage readers to tweet about the issues.

- Post video of a speech or interesting news conference on YouTube.

- Encourage readers and viewers to blog about the issues in a news conference or meeting, especially if the subjects are controversial.

- Follow community, business or government agencies on Facebook, MySpace, Twitter and other popular social media sites.

- If you are a public relations practitioner, post tweets and news releases on social media sites

- Add share tools to your story to encourage reader and viewer communication.

STORIES ABOUT MEETINGS

The decisions that affect readers' daily lives — such as where they take their trash, get their water and send their children to school — are made by local government officials at meetings. Yet meeting stories are often written without explaining their real impact on the reader.

Countless surveys conducted by news organizations reveal that local news is near or at the top of the list of the kinds of stories readers and viewers want. Sometimes they don't read or listen past the lead, especially when the lead is dull.

The stories don't have to be boring. They may not be as compelling as a story about a murder trial. But they can be written with flair and with an emphasis on the meeting's significance to readers.

All states have open-meeting laws requiring officials who have the authority to spend public funds to conduct their business in public. These boards may conduct executive sessions behind closed doors for certain discussions, such as personnel matters or collective bargaining, but all decisions must be made in a public meeting. Although open-meeting laws vary from state to state, most of them require public agencies to give advance notice — usually 48 hours — of their meetings and to conduct public hearings.

Understanding the System

When a board makes a decision at a meeting, you need to understand what kind of authority that board has. Suppose you are covering a zoning board meeting. The board is discussing a zoning application from a developer for a major shopping center. If the board approves a zoning change, is that the final decision? Probably not. Most zoning boards are advisory and must submit their recommendations to a city or county board of officials for final approval. That is essential information to include in your story.

If you are covering meetings of your university administration, find out who can make the decisions and which boards are advisory. Who can raise the tuition — school officials or a board of regents? Is the action taken at a meeting a recommendation or a ruling? You need to explain the system as well as the next step in an action.

Writing the Advance

Many times, knowing what is going to happen at a meeting is more important to readers than knowing what did happen. A story that tells readers what is being proposed can alert residents to make their concerns known before a measure is adopted by local officials. A pre-meeting story is called an "advance."

An advance is especially crucial if local officials are planning to conduct a public hearing about an issue. If the public doesn't know about it, how can the public be heard? You can tweet about an advance, but you need to link it to a full story for important issues.

City and school boards usually publish an agenda in advance of their meetings. This agenda lists the items to be discussed, although new items can and usually are presented.

When you receive an agenda, look through it for items that might be of special interest to readers. Call board members and ask for comments, or ask them to discuss the items they expect to be most interesting or controversial. If the issue has been in the news previously, check clips or blogs and call other interested parties. If you are writing an advance for a public hearing, make sure that you give the time and location of the hearing.

Here is an example of an advance with an impact lead:

For the first time in its 107-year history, Temple University may require all undergraduates to take a course related to race and racism.

The proposal, which grew out of black students' demonstrations at Temple, is to be debated by the school's faculty senate on Friday.

Among the faculty, however, the proposal has already sparked intense discussion. The debate mirrors that of other campuses — including Stanford, Wisconsin, Michigan and Berkeley — where courses related to race are required.

— HUNTLY COLLINS, *The Philadelphia Inquirer*

The following excerpt from an advance includes the time and location of the meeting:

The stage is set for changing the city's human relations ordinance to include protections for homosexuals.

Lawrence city commissioners agreed to set ground rules for public comment on a proposal to add the words "sexual orientation" to the city's anti-discrimination ordinance.

The ground rules — such as how long people will be allowed to speak — will be determined during next week's meeting, which begins at 6:35 p.m. Tuesday at City Hall, Sixth and Massachusetts streets. A draft form of the ordinance is planned for a vote one week later on April 25.

— MARK FAGAN, *Lawrence* (Kan.) *Journal-World*

Covering the Meeting

Arrive early. Find out the names of board members (usually they have nameplates), and find out who is in charge.

Ask board members, especially the head of the board, if you could talk to them after the meeting. If you know people in the audience who are leaders of a group favoring or opposing a controversial issue, greet them and tell them you would like to get comments after the meeting.

Check items on the agenda, and get any background that you need.

Check the consent agenda, a list of items on the agenda that the board will approve without discussion. They may include bids for approval or other points the board may have discussed in work sessions. A "gem" of a story may be buried in the consent agenda.

One reporter wondered why the school board had approved $30,000 in "token losses." That's a lot of money to be considered "token" losses. She discovered that it represented losses of bus tokens that the school board sold to students who had to ride public buses because there were no school buses in the city. Why $30,000 in losses? The school district had no system of monitoring the sales, and the money had been stolen at several schools. By school officials! The board didn't want to discuss this item publicly, so it was buried in the consent agenda. But the reporter discussed it — in a front-page story.

Don't remain glued to a seat at a press table. When members of the audience give public comments, get their names and more comments. Many times they will leave immediately after their testimony. Follow them out of the meeting. You can catch up with the action inside later. Or sit in the audience. Sometimes the comments of people attending the meeting are more interesting than the ones the board members make.

Stay until the end, unless your deadline prohibits staying. The most important issue could emerge at the end of a meeting when the board asks for new business or public comments. Or something dramatic could happen. The mayor could resign. Violence could erupt. You never can tell, especially if you're not there.

Writing the Story

First, how not to write it: Do not say the city council met and discussed something. Tell what they discussed or enacted. This is the kind of lead to avoid:

> The 41st Annual Environmental Engineering Conference met yesterday at the Kansas Union to discuss solutions to environmental problems.
> Representatives of the Kansas Department of Health and Environment, the Environmental Protection Agency and other organizations spoke to about 180 people who attended the conference.

So what did they say? This lead reveals nothing.

Some meetings are long. They can be boring. Avoid telling the reader how much you suffered listening to board members drone on and accomplish nothing in a long meeting. The reader doesn't care how much you suffer. The reader wants the news. If the length of the debate is crucial to the story, you should include it. But if the meetings are usually long and the time element is not a major factor related to the focus, don't mention it.

Here are some points to include in your story:

Type of Meeting and Location: Give this information, but if the city council or school board meets all the time in the same building, don't mention the location.

The Vote on Any Major Issue: For instance, say "in a 4-1 vote. . . ." If the issue is particularly controversial, say who voted against it — or for it, if an affirmative vote was more controversial. If the measure was approved unanimously, say so. However, don't give the vote for every minor item.

The Next Step: If a major issue or ordinance cannot be adopted until a public hearing is conducted, tell readers when a hearing is scheduled or what the next step is before the action is final.

Impact on Readers: Explain how the decision will affect them.

Quotes: Use only quotes that are dramatic, interesting or crucial to the story.

Background of the Issues: What do readers need to know to understand what has happened?

To write the story, select one key issue for the focus. If the board approved several other measures, add them at the end: "In other business." If several important actions occurred, consider breaking another key issue into a separate story, if possible. If not, try a lead mentioning both items, or put the second key point in the second paragraph and give supporting background later, after you have developed the first point — for example, "City commissioners yesterday approved plans for the city's first shopping mall but rejected plans for a new public golf course." Then proceed with the discussion about the shopping mall.

Although many meeting stories are written with summary leads, especially if the news is significant, they do not have to follow that form. If you think a softer lead is appropriate for the type of news that occurred, you can use it. Try an impact lead that emphasizes how readers and viewers are affected by the action or lack of action that occurred at a meeting.

Here are a few matters of style for meeting coverage:

- *Board* is a collective noun and therefore takes a singular verb: The board discussed the issue at *its* meeting, not *their* meeting. If this approach seems awkward in your story, say that the board *members* said *their* next meeting would be Tuesday.

- Capitalize *city council, city commission* and *school board* when they are part of a proper name — such as the Rockville City Commission — and when the reference is to a specific commission in your town — the City Commission. If you are not referring to a specific city commission but just saying most municipalities have city commissions, use lowercase letters.

- Capitalize the titles of board members or other officials when they come before the name, as in *Mayor John Corrupt.* If the title follows the name — *John Corrupt, the mayor* — use lowercase letters.

- For votes, use *3-1,* not *3 to 1.*

Stories about meetings can take a hard, soft or advance-impact approach. Whichever one you use, make the story relevant to readers. Here's how:

Summary lead: what happened

LAGUNA BEACH, Calif. — Despite neighbors' objections, a North Laguna Beach couple were given permission Tuesday to adorn their home with a 17-foot-high outdoor sculpture of 30 water heaters and two house trailers.

Vote

The City Council, after viewing a scale model of the artwork, voted 3-1 to endorse the sculpture. It will climb around a pine tree in the back courtyard of Arnold and Marie Forde's home.

Dissenting vote

Mayor Neil Fitzpatrick dissented, saying the sculpture infringed on neighbors' views. Councilwoman Martha Collison was absent.

Reaction

"It's a victory for the freedom of expression," said Los Angeles artist Nancy Rubins, who will craft the sculpture. "It would have been a sad day if a community that sees itself as supporting the arts struck down an artwork in a private yard."

Impact: so what

The sculpture had been the focus of an intense neighborhood battle.

Residents who live near the Fordes have called the sculpture junk and complained that the artwork would block their view and spoil the neighborhood character.

More reaction

David DeLo, who lives across Cliff Drive from the Fordes, said he was considering challenging the council's action in court.

Next step

"If the council wants to place a piece of junk in a residential neighborhood, that's their prerogative, but this council has been overturned before," he said.

Backup: conditions of council action

To appease neighbors, the council approved the sculpture on the condition that the Fordes place it as low as possible in the yard and landscape the area with another tree and a hedge. The additional plants should hide the sculpture from neighbors, officials said.

Future kicker

The $5,000 sculpture will take a week to build. Rubins said she did not know when it will be finished.

— HARRISON FLETCHER, *The Orange County* (Calif.) *Register*

EXERCISES

1 **Speech story:** If possible, cover a speech on campus or in the community.

2 **Online speeches:** Go to YouTube and search for speeches. A recommended speech is "Steve Jobs' 2005 Stanford Commencement Address" but you can find many others, including Martin Luther King's famous "I have a dream" speech, which is also available on other online sites.

CourseMate

FEATURED ONLINE ACTIVITY Log on and visit the Writing and Reporting News CourseMate and take the interactive tutorial quiz on speeches, meetings and news conferences.

Access available at www.cengagebrain.com.

Check out the "City Council" and "Big Fire" scenarios in NewsScene for interactive exercises that will help to reinforce many of the themes presented in this chapter.

COACHING TIPS

Use **impact leads** to explain how readers and viewers are affected.

The more complex the information, **the simpler your sentences** should be.

Avoid **jargon**.

Write for your readers and viewers, not your sources.

Use quotes that **advance the story,** not the egos of the bureaucrats.

Use analogies to help readers understand numbers.

Think about graphics before you write your story. **Use charts** for numbers.

Post digital versions of budgets and government proposals on the Web.

Haywiremedia/Shutterstock.com

There are no boring government stories, but there are a lot of boring reporters and editors.

— **JAMES STEELE,** investigative reporter

CHAPTER 19
Government and Statistical Stories

JENNIFER LAFLEUR WASN'T LOOKING FOR A DATE, BUT SHE WANTED to find the best places to meet single people. Using a census database, she found the information she needed — and something she didn't want. "I threw out the data for prisons," she said. "They had a high level of single men, but not men I'd want to date." Combining the statistics with some old-fashioned reporting, she discovered that the best place to meet single men was in grocery stores.

"After I did the story, an 85-year-old woman called me and said, 'I loved your story, honey, but could you do it by age?'" LaFleur said.

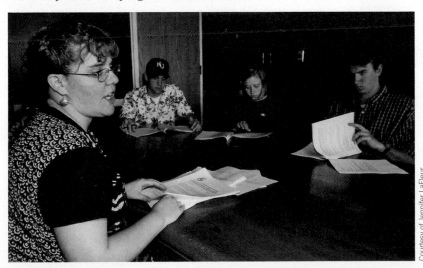

Courtesy of Jennifer LaFleur

Jennifer LaFleur, trains students in computer-assisted reporting at the University of Kansas.

LaFleur is director of computer-assisted reporting for the investigative reporting site, ProPublica, a nonprofit newsroom for journalism in the public interest. She also trains journalists throughout the country how to use databases and the Internet. She reels off stories she has reported from databases — for example, what color cars get the most tickets, how many dead people voted in an election, what names are most popular for the dogs in a community. And more serious stories about bus drivers with drunken-driving records, campaign finance records and foster parents with criminal records. As the former computer-assisted reporting editor for *The Dallas Morning News,* she even investigated Santa Claus by using public records.

Courtesy of the U.S. Air Force. Photo by Capt. Guy Hayes.

A Santa, who has no criminal record, gives a gift to a Native Alaskan child as part of the Alaska National Guard program.

Who's been naughty and will likely end up with a stocking full of coal?

It might just be Santa Claus or Kris Kringle.

Public records show that nationally, someone named Santa Claus has been convicted at least a dozen times during the past decade.

Mr. Claus' indiscretions include a 1996 arrest for driving while intoxicated in Jefferson County, Texas.

And Mr. Kringle has a lengthy criminal record in Oregon.

Even the Christmas crew appears to have had some troubles: Rudolph Reindeer violated a restraining order in 2004.

But don't plug the chimney and forgo the cookies and milk just yet.

Skilled backgrounders know that you can't just put someone on the naughty list based on a name. Many people have the same name, but other information would distinguish them — such as their date of birth or home address.

Unless Santa has a summer home in Beaumont, it's unlikely the Texas drunken driver with the same name is the Santa Claus. None had an address at the actual North Pole, according to public records. But several residents of North Pole, Alaska, have criminal records.

And yes, in Virginia there is a Santa Claus. In fact, there are at least four — two of whom are women. But no public records showed criminal records for those Clauses.

— JENNIFER LAFLEUR, *The Dallas Morning News*

"I'm convinced there's not a beat that you can't use database reporting for," she said. "The biggest shortage in journalism is people with computer-assisted reporting skills."

Search.USA.gov

This is the website for searching for information from the U.S. government.

The term *computer-assisted reporting* often refers to the use of databases, but it also refers to use of the Internet to find sources, documents and information about millions of topics. You can download many government databases directly into your computer and analyze them in a spreadsheet program such as Excel or in a relational database program that allows you to find and compare data.

A staggering amount of federal government data is available on the Web. But some of the state or local information you want might not be accessible online, especially in small communities. You have to ask officials for it, and they may be reluctant to give it to you.

LaFleur says reporters should try to find the person in a government agency who knows about computers and data. "It's usually a guy named Leon who works in the basement," she says. "I go to whatever agency I'm covering to find out how they do what they do. I also try to be overly cheery. I never first go in and demand a computer file."

After you get and analyze your data, don't flood your story with statistics. LaFleur bristles when people say computer-assisted stories are about numbers. They may contain only a paragraph or two of numbers, which could make the difference in the focus, but the stories still require good reporting and writing techniques.

CONVERGENCE COACH

WHEN YOU COVER government agencies, think in multimedia terms. Don't just plan to write a story or script for a print or broadcast publication: Plan to provide complete versions of proposals and budgets on the Web. Get a digital version of a local government budget, school district test scores, government proposals and important statistics to accompany stories on the Web.

Here are some other tips for using the Web for government statistics and information:

- Check the date the information was posted; many reports may not be current. Contact the agency by phone or e-mail to find out if more current information is available.

- Check your city, school district and state sites for background information on government stories.

- Check if advocacy agencies and other groups in your community have websites. Use these sites for sources in reaction stories and human interest.

- Add graphics to explain statistics or digital maps to identify locations in your stories.

SOCIAL MEDIA

GOVERNMENT affects people's lives, but too many stories just parrot news releases or report coverage of meetings. If you don't help readers and viewers understand how the information affects them, chances are that they won't read or watch the information you are trying to convey. Social media tools provide journalists with more ways than ever before to connect with their communities and devise stories that will reflect people's concerns.

Reporters used to go to barber shops or beauty parlors, local beer halls and other gathering places to find out what people in the community were discussing. That's still a good idea, but now the gathering places are online. With social media such as blogs, Twitter, Facebook and others, you can reach far more people and engage them in issues that concern them. You can also use social media sites to follow blogs or Twitter sites of politicians, governmental agencies and citizens who are interested in community issues.

Many of the federal government agencies post information on social media sites, including the U.S. Census Bureau, which is a treasure trove of statistical information.

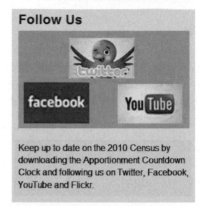

Follow Us

Keep up to date on the 2010 Census by downloading the Apportionment Countdown Clock and following us on Twitter, Facebook, YouTube and Flickr.

The U.S. Census Bureau uses social media for news releases and updates to its data.

REPORTING TIPS

Here are some tips for covering local government:

Human Interest: Make government relevant to readers by finding people who are affected by the actions of government agencies. Using social media tools, you can find sources to contact. But don't forget the old-fashioned reporting technique of going into the community and talking to people face-to-face.

Bulletin Boards: Check them for job offerings and other announcements that could result in stories.

Memos and Letters to and from City Officials: Check with the city clerk or administrative assistants for access to files about any issue involving public funds. Most of these — except for personnel and labor matters — are public records.

Planning Commission: Check agendas for meetings, and develop sources in planning offices. Seek information not only about future plans but also about the past. Some great stories can result from plans gone awry.

Consultants: Check who gets consulting contracts and fees, and investigate previous studies on the same subject.

Zoning Meetings: They can be full of human interest. People care about what is going up or down in their neighborhood.

Legal Notices: Check them for bids and other notices. Government agencies must advertise for any major purchases. Check with disgruntled bidders for major contracts. Many good stories lurk behind these seemingly boring subjects.

Audits: Read them carefully. They can reveal misuse of public funds.

Union Leaders: Cultivate heads of unions in school districts and cities as sources. They know what is going on behind the scenes.

Nonofficials: Talk to the people who do the work. Get into the schools and write about what teachers and students are doing or talk to people working in government offices. Spend some time learning about what they do, how they do it and whether they do it. Many good stories can result from finding out how lower-level employees work in government.

The System: Learn how it works. Are officials in your town following the laws? If you don't know how government is supposed to operate, you won't be able to find out if it is working properly.

Records: Check expense accounts, purchasing vouchers and other records pertaining to issues or officials you are covering.

Offices: Check all the offices in your government building, and find out what kind of work the people in them do. For example, do you know the function of every office in your campus administration building? You could find features or great news stories just by checking what the people in these offices do.

The Internet: Many communities, local police departments and school districts have Web pages offering a wealth of information and documents. You can find sources, news releases and databases on their sites. In addition, websites for state and federal government agencies abound.

VISUALS

Before you write your story, think not about what you can put in it; think about what you can pull out of it, especially when you are writing stories with statistics. Use highlights boxes, facts boxes and charts to break out key concepts of a proposal or budget. Then you don't need to clutter the story with the same information.

Consider empowerment boxes, information that tells readers what the story means to them and what they can do. These boxes should contain information about where they can call for help, more information or other facts that would be useful. Once you have decided what can be displayed visually, you can present the remaining information verbally.

Here's an empowerment box from the *Reno* (Nev.) *Gazette-Journal* that accompanied a story about overdue parking tickets. The city adopted late fees that would add $30 to tickets not paid within a month.

TO PAY

- Pay at the city clerk's cashier office, using cash, check or Visa or Mastercard.

TO PROTEST

- Make an appointment. The hearing officer is setting aside time in Room 204 at City Hall. Call 334-2293.
- Hearing times are from 5-8 p.m. on Nov. 4 and Nov. 6; 1-4 p.m. on Nov. 8; 5-8 p.m. on Nov. 13 and Nov. 14.

ETHICS

THE CASE: YOU are the news producer for your campus television station. Spring Break is approaching, and every year at this time sexually transmitted diseases become rampant. The Centers for Disease Control and Prevention offers a video explaining the types of diseases and how to treat them. The video quality is excellent, and it features unidentified students and a doctor explaining risks and treatment. You don't have the staff or time to produce your own video on the subject, and the one you have seems perfect. After all, it's a news release, so you are entitled to use it without any copyright violation. Will you use the video news release? Will you identify the source as the CDC?

Guidelines: The Radio Television Digital News Association says this in its code of ethics: "Clearly disclose the origin of information and label all material provided by outsiders." However, a *New York Times* investigative story revealed that many television stations are using video news releases from the government without identifying them as government sponsored. The problem has become such a concern that the Boston University Department of Journalism adopted a resolution condemning the practice. It states in part: "We find particularly objectionable the use of 'phony reporters' hired by one agency or another who deliver complete reports, including sign-offs, without ever mentioning their affiliation and, in some cases, misrepresenting it. We also condemn those stations that knowingly run news segments, written, shot and recorded by the government with no identification as to the source of the material. We regard these practices as unethical journalism that run the high risk of confusing or even deceiving the public."

Centers for Disease Control and Prevention media tools.

WRITING TIPS

After you have found good information for your stories, how can you make them readable?

One way is to avoid "jargon," stilted or technical words and phrases that officials use but readers don't. Writing coaches call this artificial language "journalese," long words or phrases instead of short ones that would be clearer. Examples: *medication* for *medicine, restructuring* for *changing, funds* for *money*. When you need a loan from a friend, do you ask to borrow "funds"?

Clichés are another common form of journalese in government stories. Journalists love to use words related to heat and cold: *heated debate, hotly contested, blasted, chilling effect, cooling-off period*. In this example, the reporter strained the lead by picking a holiday that had nothing to do with the story just so she could use these "heated" terms:

> The Fourth of July is four months away, but insults and accusations exploded like fireworks at the tumultuous Board of Supervisors meeting yesterday.
>
> The firecracker was Republican Supervisor John Hanson, who blasted his colleagues by calling them "crooks."

Here are some other tips:

Use Short, Simple Sentences: The more complex the information, the simpler and shorter the sentences should be:

Complex	*Simpler*
The City Commission last night approved a resolution to authorize the city staff to apply for funding through the systems enhancement program of the state Department of Transportation for a $3.6 million project for the expansion of U.S. Highway 77 from two to four lanes for 2.2 miles between Interstate 70 and Kansas Highway 18.	The City Commission last night agreed to apply for $3.6 million from the state Department of Transportation to expand a portion of U.S. Highway 77 from two to four lanes. The project would widen the highway for 2.2 miles between Interstate 70 and Kansas Highway 18.

Keep the Subject and Verb Close Together: Long clauses and phrases before the verb make it hard for the reader to remember what the subject is — who said or did what. Use subject–verb–object order.

Complex	Rather than having government inspectors sweep through businesses, finding violations and imposing fines, in Maine, officials at the federal Occupational Safety and Health Administration, in an effort to improve work conditions and save the government money, are urging employers to identify health and safety problems and then to work with the agency to correct them.	A federal agency is urging employers in Maine to find and correct health and safety problems in their businesses instead of having government inspectors seek violations and impose fines. The move is an attempt by the federal Occupational Safety and Health Administration to improve work conditions in businesses and save the government money.	*Simpler*

Use Vigorous Verbs: Whenever possible, replace *to be* verbs and other bland verbs with words that help to paint a picture of the activity you are reporting.

A 42-year-old St. Joseph man <u>escaped</u> a blazing house without serious injuries when he <u>grabbed</u> a coffee table, <u>hurled</u> it through a picture window, and then, like a movie stunt man, <u>leaped</u> through the jagged glass to escape the heat and flames.

— TERRY RAFFENSPERGER, *St. Joseph* (Mo.) *News-Press*

Avoid Starting Sentences with There: The word *there* forces you to use a weak *to be* verb, such as *is, are, was* or *were*.

Weak	There was sadness expressed among local people gathered Thursday night to watch their team lose by two points in the NCAA finals.	Local people expressed sadness as they gathered Thursday night to watch their team lose by two points in the NCAA final.	*Strong*

Interpret Information: Tell readers how they are affected.

The value of real estate in the county jumped roughly $83 million in one year — an increase of about 27 percent.

What does all that mean to the average homeowner? Most likely a lower tax rate — called a mill levy — and perhaps a lower tax bill for some, Douglas County Administrator Craig Weinaug said.

Translate Jargon: Explain terms in concepts or comparisons that the reader can understand.

A spot inventory of Jeanne Johns' freezer shows the usual stuff. Ice cream. Frozen peas. TV dinners.

Acid rain.

Acid rain? You bet.

Johns, who lives in Haslett, is one of four Michigan volunteers in the Citizen Acid Rain Monitoring Network. The network has more than 300 stations nationwide to monitor acid rain. . . .

She measures the acidity on a pH scale ranging from 0 to 14, with 0 being the most acidic. The scale increases tenfold, meaning a 4.0 reading is 10 times more acidic than 5.0.

Normal precipitation is usually about 5.6. A pH of 5.0 is equal to the acid content in cola. Frogs die if placed in water with a pH of 4.0. Battery acid is 1.5.

— KEVIN O'HANLON, *Lansing* (Mich.) *State-Journal*

Vary the Pace: Avoid writing huge blocks of complicated concepts and complex sentences. Follow long sentences and long paragraphs with a short sentence as in this example:

MAT-SU — When Mat-Su school board members voted to cut three sports and millions of dollars in jobs and services earlier this spring, they said they hoped they would be able to restore some of those cuts once the borough and state budgets were finalized.

Their wish has come true.

Between the Mat-Su Borough and the state, local schools will get around $3 million more next year than district officials originally anticipated.

— *The* (Wasilla, Alaska) *Frontiersman*

Focus on a Person to Explain Impact: The way an issue affects one person makes it clear to many. That's the concept of the *Wall Street Journal* formula, and it can be used effectively in government stories. Lead with an anecdote about a person; then go from the specific to the general. It's the "one of many" technique.

Linda Green paid $42,000 in 1982 for a house on a half-acre lot in Fontana, banking on the equity that would build over the years.

But if Fontana's new general plan is approved, Green is fearful her property may be worth no more than the day she bought it.

The proposed plan would change the zoning on her half-acre so no additional homes could be built on it, making the site less attractive to buyers.

Green is not alone in her fears. She was among several landowners complaining Monday that the revised general plan — a blueprint for Fontana's growth — will put their properties in less profitable zoning areas.

"I bought my land as an investment. If they zone it down, I will lose my money, and I worked hard to put my money into it," Green told the planning commission during the first public hearing on the new 20-year plan.

More than 130 people attended the hearing.

— TONY SAAVEDRA, *The* (San Bernardino, Calif.) *Sun*

Use an Impact Lead or Explain Impact in the Story: Tell how the reader will be affected by a bureaucratic action or proposal.

A $10,000 car would cost $25 more in taxes, a $40 power saw an extra dime and a $4 six-pack of imported beer a penny extra in Rockford if Alderman Ernst Shafer, R-3rd, gets his way.

Shafer wants Rockford to join the push in Springfield for a 0.25 percent increase in the sales tax. Locally the sales tax would rise from 6.25 to 6.5 percent under the proposal.

— BRIAN LEAF, *Rockford* (Ill.) *Register Star*

Avoid Boring Quotes: You don't have to quote an official to prove you talked to him. If you can express the official's point better in your own words, do so. You could say that park repairs included cutting trees, removing sand, adding soil for a seed bed and repairing a shelter. But one reporter quoted an official instead:

"The total project involved tree takedowns, removal of some of the sand and replacement with some soil that would actually provide a seed bed," he said. "We also had to make some repairs on a shelter."

Use the Pull-Quote Test: Are your quotes strong enough to be broken out as pull quotes? That's one way of testing whether they are worth using in a story.

"I'm convinced there's not a beat that you can't use database reporting for. The biggest shortage in journalism is people with computer-assisted reporting skills." — Jennifer LaFleur

Use Conversational Style: Write the story as though you were having a conversation with a friend. Here is how one reporter used the conversational style in the lead of a government story:

How'd you like an airport for a neighbor? Or maybe a landfill or an incinerator?

Probably about as much as government officials like trying to find a site for these things.

But what if you could negotiate noise insulation for your airport-area home? Or an agreement requiring the incinerator to douse its fires if it didn't burn hot enough to eliminate most pollutants?

Those alternatives were offered Wednesday to a roomful of Twin Cities area public officials frustrated by their protracted and often doomed efforts to make people accept controversial facilities they don't want.

In an area where officials are looking for places for new landfills, a new airport, light-rail transit routes and other public works projects, the Metropolitan Council sponsored yesterday's conference in an effort to see if there's a better way.

There is, they were told by a specialist in how to make the risks of such facilities more acceptable to their neighbors.

— STEVE BRANDT, (Minneapolis) *Star Tribune*

Use Lists: Use them in the middle or at the end of the story, especially to explain key points of an issue. Lists are particularly helpful in stories with numbers or explanations of proposals. They are also helpful for stories distributed on mobile media because readers can scan the information quickly.

Avoid the City-Dump Syndrome: Be selective. Use only quotes and facts that you need. Don't dump your notebook into the story.

Use the Blocking Technique: If you have more than three speakers, block the comments from each one, and then do not use the sources again unless you reintroduce them. The reader can't remember all the officials by second reference only.

Read Aloud: If you read all or parts of your story aloud, you will catch the cumbersome phrases.

STATISTICAL STORIES

Jennifer LaFleur writes about numbers all the time, but they rarely appear in the leads to her stories. She knows how to relate to readers and make sense of statistics. Here are some of the techniques you can use in stories with statistics:

Use Analogies: Whenever you are referring to large numbers, comparisons with something familiar to readers are especially helpful. This is an analogy from a story about pollution in Alabama's rivers:

Each minute, about 30 million gallons of Alabama river water, or the equivalent of what it would take to fill 60 Olympic-sized swimming pools, flush into Mobile Bay, washing over oyster beds in the northern part of the bay closed to harvesting.

— DAN MORSE, *The* (Montgomery) *Alabama Journal*

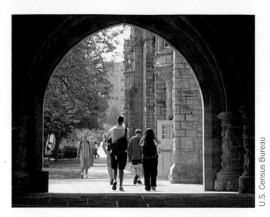

University enrollments might offer clues for dating prospects.

U.S. Census Bureau

Round Off Numbers: In most cases it is better to round off numbers — for instance, to $3.5 million instead of $3,499,590. Make it easy for the reader to grasp large numbers. This is especially important in broadcast stories.

Avoid Bunching Numbers in One Paragraph: Spread numbers out over a few paragraphs rather than glutting one sentence or paragraph with them. Another good technique is to present numbers in lists.

Interpret Numbers: Show the impact on readers in terms they can understand.

A 10-year analysis of enrollment patterns at Kansas University and five other state universities revealed two dating tips for college students:

- Men hoping to improve dating prospects might consider attending Emporia State University, where 60 percent of students are women.

- Women interested in more dating opportunities should look to Kansas State University, the only state university in the area with more men than women.

— TIM CARPENTER, *Lawrence* (Kan.) *Journal-World*

Use Storytelling Techniques: Even statistical stories can lend themselves to storytelling. In this example, the writer uses an anecdotal lead and limits the use of statistics, which were presented in a graphic accompanying the story:

James Frazier walked across the stage at Civic Arena on May 31 and picked up his diploma from Central High School. On Aug. 24, he'll head off to college.

Not bad for someone who dropped out of school in 1996.

He's one example of why the dropout rate in St. Joseph has fallen by half since 1989.

He's part of a trend that no other urban Missouri city can match. Not Columbia. Not Springfield. Certainly not Kansas City or St. Louis.

With a dropout rate of 13.4 percent, according to figures released Thursday, the St. Joseph School District tops the list.

Figures for this year aren't in for the other school districts, but last year's dropout rate for Columbia was 31.5 percent. For Springfield it was 29.6 percent. The state average is the closest figure — 22.8 percent.

Announcing the results, United Way cited its program, Profit in Education, started in 1989 to reduce the dropout rate. Barbara Sprong, coordinator for Profit in Education, credited the efforts of the entire community in lowering the dropout rate. Those efforts included innovative programs at the St. Joseph School District, such as the Learning Academy.

That program, Frazier said, made the difference for him.

"The way I was going, I would have been dead or in jail," he said. He spent a rough two years in high school, missing classes and taking drugs. Academically he was on the edge.

"The Learning Academy basically turned that all around," he said.

— DIANNA BORSI, *St. Joseph* (Mo.) *News-Press*

Use Graphics: Try to get the numbers out of your story and into a separate graphic. You need to mention some of the numbers, but always consider whether a chart, graph or diagram could convey the information better.

This site offers data on federal government spending by agencies, for states and for companies.

BUDGET STORIES

Budget stories are hard to write and even harder to read if you flood them with a lot of numbers. And in broadcast stories, numbers are worse to hear. You can't avoid using numbers in all stories, but don't put several numbers in the same sentence or paragraph. Whenever you are writing about numbers, you must analyze what they mean. Most reports list numbers in comparison to a previous year or time frame. Always put numbers in perspective in two ways:

- **Explain change:** Do the numbers show an increase or decrease from a previous period?
- **State the significance:** What do the numbers mean, and why are they important? Explain what is interesting or important about these statistics in a way that will make readers care. You can even use a transition such as "Here's what this means to you."

Consider these basic questions:

Who: Who is most affected by the budget? Who are the winners and losers?

What: What are the major changes in a budget? How does it compare with previous years? Don't just say the budget or tuition has increased by 10 percent; give the figures; what is the current tuition.

When: When do the new proposals go into effect? Not all budgets have immediate ramifications.

Where: Where are the increases and decreases in the budget?

Why: Why are the cuts or additions to the budget being proposed?

Budget planning starts several months before the budget is approved. Learn how to interpret the proposed budget by asking a financial officer of the city, school or agency to explain it to you before the budget is released. If he can't brief you on this

Employees of the U.S. Government Printing Office prepare the federal budget.

Courtesy of the U.S. Government Printing Office

year's proposal, use last year's budget to learn the system. In most cases, officials will be willing to cooperate because they want you to present the facts accurately.

Basically, budgets have two sections:

Revenues: The income, usually derived from taxes — primarily property taxes in municipalities. But there also are sales taxes, income taxes and fees. Look for clues about how the revenue will be raised. Will property taxes increase? If you are covering a university budget, will tuition be increased? Find out how the revenue source will affect your readers.

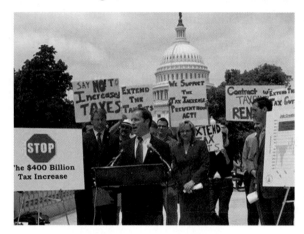

Congressman Peter J. Roskam (R-Ill) speaks to supporters of the Tax Increase Prevention Act that he helped introduce.

Expenditures: Where most of the money will be spent. Will some departments be increasing expenses more than others, such as police or fire departments? If so, why? Will salaries be increased or more people be hired? How do the expenditures for this year compare with those of the past few years?

Generally, budgets include figures from the previous year or past few years. Look for major increases and decreases in revenues and expenditures.

Before a government agency can adopt a budget, it must conduct public hearings, where the public can comment about the budget. If the budget proposal is at the hearing stage, be sure to include the dates of the hearings in your story.

Taxpayers often want to attend hearings to protest cutbacks, tax increases or to request money for programs they support.

Budget and Tax Terms

If you want to explain budgets, you must know what these terms mean:

Assessments and Property Taxes: Common in municipal budgets, where taxes are based on real estate. Homeowners pay taxes based on an assessment, or estimated value, of their property. This value is determined by a city property appraiser based on a number of factors: size of the property, number of bedrooms, construction and so on. For example, suppose you decide to buy a condominium or a house selling for $160,000. That is its "market value," the price it sells for on the market. Some communities base their tax on the full market value, but most use only a percentage of the total value. The property is given an "assessed value," a value for tax purposes. If your community bases its tax on half the market value, your house would be assessed for $80,000. Your annual property taxes equal some percentage of the assessed value.

Capital Budget: Money used to pay for major improvements, such as the construction of highways or new buildings. Capital is often raised by selling bonds, and people who buy the bonds receive interest. The government then uses the money and repays the bonds, plus interest, over a period of years in what is called "debt service." The process is much like buying a house: The bank lends you money; you live in the house and repay the loan plus interest on a long-term basis, often over 30 years.

Deficit: When government spends more money than it receives. Most municipalities and states require a balanced budget: The expenses must be the same as the income. The difference between the expenditures and the income is the deficit, or debt.

Fiscal Year: Year in which budgeted funds will be spent. In government, the budget term often starts on July 1 and goes to June 30, instead of the calendar year. So if you use a fiscal year, give the dates: "in this fiscal year, which starts July 1." Or if you are writing about when the money will run out: "in this fiscal year, which ends June 30."

Mean: An average; the sum of all the figures divided by the number of items in the survey. If the salaries of 100 journalists total $3 million, they have a mean salary of $30,000. The salaries of the 100 journalists in the survey would be added and then divided by 100 to get the mean.

Median: An average; the value in the middle of a range. If 15 journalists in a survey earn from $20,000 to $65,000, you would list all the salaries in numerical order and find the one in the center of the list. The eighth number in the list would be the median.

Mill: Unit equal to $1 for every $1,000 that a house is assessed. Local school and city taxes are based on mills. Explain the impact of these taxes clearly. If the school tax rate is 25 mills, your story should say, "The tax rate is 25 mills, which equals $25 for every $1,000 of assessed property valuation." Or you could insert a definition: "A mill equals $1 for every $1,000 of assessed value on a property." Then give an example: "Under this tax rate, a homeowner whose property is valued at $80,000 (multiplied by 0.025) would pay $2,000 in school taxes." Try to avoid using the term *mills*; just say the tax rate will be $25 for every $1,000 of assessed property value. Follow with a specific example so residents can figure out how much their tax will be.

Operating Budget: Money used to provide services (police, fire, garbage removal and so on) and to pay for the operation of government. Most of the money for this budget comes from taxes.

Other Taxes: Wage tax, income tax and sales tax. Cities and states often charge these additional taxes. Check when you write your budget stories to determine whether they will be increased or decreased. If they will stay the same, say so.

Per Capita: The rate per person. For example, if a community has 50 murders and a population of 175,000 people, the per capita murder rate would be determined by dividing 50 by 175,000, to yield 0.000286. However, such a small number is hard to comprehend, so it might be multiplied by 100,000 to give a number per 100,000. In this case the rate would be 28.6 murders for every 100,000 people.

Reappraisal: State or local decision to re-evaluate properties in the community, usually to increase their values. This action almost always generates good stories because it affects people dramatically. For example, Kansas had not reappraised properties for 20 years. When the state decided to do it, property values soared, and a tax revolt resulted. People who had been paying $200 in taxes on their homes were suddenly paying $1,000. A similar situation occurred in Atlanta:

A groundswell of protest over the mass reappraisal of Atlanta and Fulton County property is threatening to become a wholesale tax revolt.

Thousands of homeowners have turned out at meetings throughout the city and county to express displeasure with their new assessments, in some cases more than double last year's.

At the South Fulton County Annex, more than one thousand people gathered Monday to talk about fighting the assessments.

"My assessment went up 190 percent and I'll gladly sell my home to the county for what they think it's worth," said Mitch Skandalakis, a leader of the Task Force for Good Government, as the crowd roared.

— MARK SHERMAN, *Atlanta Constitution*

Writing Techniques

Impact is crucial in budget stories. So are graphics. A chart or list of key numbers can make a story more presentable. Also get reactions from city officials, residents at public hearings or the people most affected by budget cuts. If you are writing about university budgets, get reactions from administrators, students, professors and the officials whose departments will be affected most.

Here are some key points to include in a budget story, not necessarily in this order:

- Total amount of the budget (rounded off when possible — $44.6 million instead of $44,552,379). Most budgets are supposed to be balanced, so the figure applies to both revenues and expenditures.
- Amount of increase or decrease
- Tax or tuition levy, or how funds will be raised (impact on reader, comparison to current tax)
- Major expenditures (major increases and decreases in department funds)
- Consequences (impact on the government or agency — cuts in personnel, services, and so on)
- Historical comparisons (how budget compares with previous year and past few years)
- Reactions from officials and people affected by increases or decreases
- Definitions and explanations of technical terms

Here is an example of the kind of budget story you should avoid writing. It is flooded with statistics but doesn't clarify how the budget will affect the reader.

The recommended Rockville Centre city budget would require a 2.56-mill property tax increase.

City Manager Joan Weinman recommended to Rockville City Commission a budget of $55,672,309, which would require a local levy of 42.59 mills. Last year's budget of $50,322,409 required a levy of 42.03 mills.

A mill is $1 of tax for every $1,000 of assessed property valuation.

Weinman is recommending a 3 percent across-the-board salary increase for city employees. She is also recommending an addition of five police officers to the public safety department.

Here is the lead on another budget story, but this one explains the impact on homeowners:

HACKENSACK, N.J. — A $39.2 million budget that offers residents their first property-tax break in 20 years has been adopted by the City Council.

The budget, which includes $4 million in new state aid, was approved by a 4-1 vote following a public hearing Monday. No residents commented.

Despite a 6 percent increase in spending, the boost in state aid means that total property taxes for the owner of a home assessed at $180,000, the borough average, will drop $54 a year.

— TOM TOPOUSIS, *The* (Hackensack, N.J.) *Record*

Here is another way of explaining impact in a lead that is not cluttered with statistics:

Pinellas School Superintendent Howard Hinesley has proposed a list of budget cuts for the next school year that will mean fewer textbooks, fewer teachers and fewer administrators if School Board members approve them next Wednesday.

— PATTY CURTIN JONES, *St. Petersburg* (Fla.) *Times*

Don't forget that budgets affect people. So when you are writing advances and reaction stories, you can use feature techniques. Here is an example of an anecdotal-narrative approach to an advance on the city budget:

It was 8:05 on a Monday in August, Rosemary Farnon remembers, when her husband, Tony, called the police to report that their rowhouse in the Juniata Park section had been ransacked.

Amid a shambles of overturned furniture, scattered papers and food taken from the fridge, the Farnons nervously and angrily waited nearly five hours before an officer appeared. He explained apologetically that the local police district had no cops to spare.

Theirs is one story, from one neighborhood, but it typifies what is happening across Philadelphia:

Taxes are up and services are down — and residents are unhappy about it.

So Rosemary Farnon and hundreds of thousands of taxpayers will be listening closely Thursday when the mayor proposes the budget for the coming fiscal year, which begins July 1.

— DAN MYERS AND IDRIS M. DIAZ, *The Philadelphia Inquirer*

EXERCISES

1 Census for dating prospects: David Cuillier, a professor at the University of Arizona, created this exercise to teach students how to find the best and worst places for dating prospects by U.S. Census data. It is similar to the research Jennifer LaFleur did for her story, but now you can tailor the material for your own interests. Here's a variation of his exercise:

- Go to Census.gov. Find the best states with the highest male to female ratio.

- Click on American Factfinder on the left. Click on "People."

- Click on "Age and Sex." Access a map of the male-female ratio.

- Now access the "Sex ratio for all states" data list.

- Go back to the left panel and click on "Relationships." Click on "Marital Status." Then click "Change" and get the statistics for your state or any other state where you want to find a percentage of never-married or divorced people in an age group that interests you. You can keep narrowing down the fields by changing the geographical locations. You can also use these tables to find out information about the population estimates, racial composition, economic factors and other data for your state.

2 Taxes: Figure your taxes using the following method:

a You own a home that is worth $100,000 on the market. The city appraises residential property for tax purposes at 11.5 percent of its market value. What is the assessed value of your property?

b Using your assessed value as calculated in **a**, figure your tax rate as follows:

 1 Write your assessed value:

 2 Divide the assessed value by 1,000 because a mill is a $1 tax on every $1,000 of assessed property value. Write that figure:

 3 The tax levy in your community is 125 mills. Multiply the amount in **b–2** times the tax levy to figure your tax bill. Write the result:

c Last year your taxes were $1,250. Using the answer from **b–3** for this year's taxes, figure your tax percentage increase.

d The city had a tax rate of 125 mills last year and is raising it to 137.5 mills this year. What is the percentage increase?

3 Your dream home: Envision the home you would like to own. How much will it cost? If you want a swimming pool, sauna and other amenities, make sure that you figure them into the price along with the land value in your community or wherever you want to live. When you figure the selling price, that's the market value.

Now figure your taxes. Your community assesses property at 30 percent of its market value for tax purposes. The tax rate for city and schools combined will be 75 mills. How much will you pay in taxes?

4 Statistics: Analyze the following information, and write a story about which sandwiches are healthiest (lowest in fat and sodium). These statistics are based on a study by the Center for Science in the Public Interest, a nonprofit consumer nutrition organization. The organization analyzed 12 sandwiches for fat, saturated fat and sodium. Daily limits of fat recommended by the Food and Drug Administration for adults are 65 grams of total fat, 20 grams of saturated fat and 2,400 milligrams of sodium.

Turkey with mustard: 6 grams fat, 2 grams saturated fat, 1,407 milligrams sodium

Roast beef with mustard: 12 grams fat, 4 grams saturated fat, 993 milligrams sodium

Chicken salad: 32 grams fat, 6 grams saturated fat, 1,136 milligrams sodium

Corned beef with mustard: 20 grams fat, 8 grams saturated fat, 1,924 milligrams sodium

Tuna salad: 43 grams fat, 8 grams saturated fat, 1,319 milligrams sodium

Ham with mustard: 27 grams fat, 10 grams saturated fat, 2,344 milligrams sodium

Egg salad: 31 grams fat, 10 grams saturated fat, 1,110 milligrams sodium

Turkey club: 34 grams fat, 10 grams saturated fat, 1,843 milligrams sodium

Bacon, lettuce and tomato: 37 grams fat, 12 grams saturated fat, 1,555 milligrams sodium

Vegetarian (cucumbers, sprouts, avocado and cheese): 40 grams fat, 14 grams saturated fat, 1,276 milligrams sodium

Grilled cheese: 33 grams fat, 17 grams saturated fat, 1,543 milligrams sodium

Reuben: 50 grams fat, 20 grams saturated fat, 3,268 milligrams sodium

Background: Interview with Jane Hurley, nutritionist for the center. She analyzed 170 sandwiches from Washington, New York, Los Angeles and Chicago delicatessens: "People tend to think of a sandwich as just a bite to eat, but many shops are giving you a dinner's worth of fat and calories. Tuna itself is fat free, but in sandwiches, it's drowning in one-third cup of mayonnaise. That's the equivalent of three McDonald's Quarter Pounders, fat-wise."

The center also did studies showing fat in Mexican, Italian and Chinese food. One of its most controversial studies showed that one bag of popcorn popped in coconut oil, as served in movie theaters, has as much saturated fat as six Big Macs.

5 Crime statistics: Access the website for the crime statistics on your campus. It should be on your college or university website, but if you can't find it there, go to the Security on Campus website (*www.securityoncampus.org*) and find the statistics. They may not be as recent as they should be on your university site. You might also compare the statistics for your campus with those from a neighboring or similar-size school. Look for patterns — increases and decreases. Write a news story. If possible, call your campus police department for comments.

Check out the "City Council" scenario in NewsScene for an interactive exercise that will help to reinforce many of the themes presented in this chapter.

COACHING TIPS

Liv friis-larsen/Shutterstock.com

Role-play: Ask yourself what you would want to know if you were affected by this crime.

Gather enough details to **recreate the crime scene** as though you were witnessing it.

Avoid the jargon of police or other legal authorities. If you don't understand a term, chances are the reader may not know it either.

Always include the **background of the case,** no matter how many days a police story or trial continues.

Be careful. **Double-check your story for accuracy,** and make sure that you don't convict someone of a crime before a judge or jury does.

Check the Internet and sex offender registries for **background searches** of suspects.

The police beat is all about people, what makes them tick, what makes them become heroes or homicidal maniacs. It has it all: greed, sex, violence, comedy and tragedy.

— EDNA BUCHANAN, former police reporter, *The Miami Herald*

CHAPTER 20
Crime and Punishment

THE POLICE BEAT, WHICH OFTEN INCLUDES THE FIRE DEPARTMENT, is considered an entry-level job. Most reporters move on to other beats after a few years of covering crime stories. Edna Buchanan did not. She covered the police beat at *The Miami Herald* for more than 20 years before resigning to write books. But while she was at the *Herald*, she turned police reporting into an art form and won a Pulitzer Prize.

A soft-spoken woman, she writes with a strong punch. One Pulitzer-Prize juror said, "She writes drop-dead sentences for drop-dead victims. She is never dull." Consider:

> There was music and sunlight as the paddle wheeler Dixie Bell churned north on Indian Creek Thursday. The water shimmered and the wind was brisk. And then the passengers noticed that the people in the next boat were dead.

Buchanan is most famous for the lead she wrote on a story about a man who shoved his way to the front of a line at a fried chicken restaurant. The counter clerk told the man to go to the end of the line and wait his turn. He did. But when he reached the head of the line again, the restaurant had run out of fried chicken. He battered the clerk fiercely, and he was shot fatally by a guard in the restaurant. Her lead: "Gary Robinson died hungry."

"In truth, Edna Buchanan doesn't write about cops. She writes about people," *Herald* editors wrote in the Pulitzer entry. Buchanan is the first to admit that. "You learn more about people on the police beat than any other beat," she said in a speech at a convention of investigative reporters.

She said she had reported more than 5,000 violent deaths. How did she keep from getting upset by them and burned out on the job? "The thing that keeps you going is that you realize you can make things better. You may be affected like everyone else by a terrible tragedy, but you're in a position to do something about it. That's the real joy of this job. We can be catalysts for change. We can bring about justice. Sometimes we are all the victim has got. Police stories do make a difference.

"You've got to be accurate and fair and very, very careful, particularly in crime reporting. A news story mentioning somebody's name can ruin their lives or come back to haunt them 25 years later. It is there in black and white on file. It's like a police record; you never outlive it. You can do terrible damage. So you knock on one more door, ask one more question, make one last phone call. It could be the one that counts."

When Buchanan made those phone calls and someone hung up on her, she just redialed the number and said, "We were cut off." The second time, she might have gotten a relative or someone else who was willing to talk, or the first person might have changed his mind. But she didn't try a third time; that would be harassment, she said.

CRIME STORIES

Buchanan gathered her information from interviews and records. And then she wove them into stories with leads that hooked the reader. She said that crime reporters need to talk to witnesses and get color, background, ages and details — what people were wearing, doing and saying when they became crime victims or suspects.

Police have the right to protect the crime scene and limit access to the press. If the crime scene is on public property, reporters and photographers can get as close as police will allow. If the crime scene is on private property, access is at the discretion of the police or the owners of the property.

Records

If you have the police beat, you should check the daily police log, also called the "blotter," to see the list of all crimes recorded by police for that day. The log will list the names of the victims and the nature of the crimes. This is public record and should be available to the press and anyone else. However, the reports filed by the officer at the scene and records to cases under investigation may not be available.

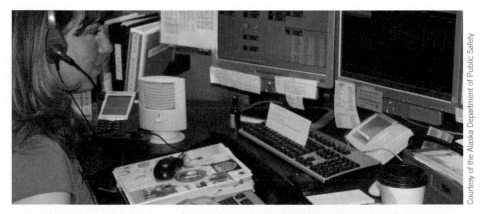

Courtesy of the Alaska Department of Public Safety

A police dispatcher takes calls and communicates with the police. The dispatcher is often the person who answers reporters' phone calls about daily crime reports in some police departments.

Although the incident reports contain the names of the officers who filed them, many police departments with a public information officer do not allow reporters to talk to the arresting officers. However, if access is permitted, try to talk to the arresting officers, especially in a major crime.

For details about arrests, check the jail log, which should contain the suspect's name and address, birth date, sex, race, occupation, place of arrest and charges.

Previous Criminal Records Check to see if a suspect has a previous criminal record. If someone has been convicted of a crime, that court record should be available in the court jurisdiction where the person was convicted — unless the record is sealed by order of a judge. If the person was charged with a crime and found not guilty or charges were dropped, that record is also public. You need to look up the court file (and get the case file number) under that person's name and probably the year of the court case.

The court file should contain all pertinent information, including names of the lawyers involved, description of the crime and all motions filed in the case. Most important, it will tell what happened — the disposition of the case — including specific terms of the sentence or probation or dismissal. Many court records are posted online in searchable databases.

In some cases, a person convicted of a minor crime can have his record erased — "expunged" — after a number of years, with permission of the court. In other cases, a judge may permit certain records to be sealed, meaning that they will be withheld from the public and available only to law enforcement officers.

University Records In 1986 Jeanne Ann Clery, a 19-year-old student, was raped and murdered in her third-floor dormitory at Lehigh University. Her parents later learned that 38 violent crimes had been committed on the Lehigh campus in the previous three years, but the university was not required to divulge those statistics. Connie and Howard Clery wanted to make sure that their daughter's death was not in vain.

As a result of their efforts, a landmark federal law was enacted requiring all colleges and universities that have federal student financial aid programs to publish an annual report listing three years of crime statistics. The law, originally called the Campus Security Act, was amended in 1998 and renamed the Clery Act in memory of Jeanne Clery.

However, universities may withhold names on crime reports because of another federal law. The Buckley Amendment to the Family Educational Rights and Privacy Act prohibits government agencies from releasing any personal data about students and employees in institutions that receive federal funding. But in 1992, a new federal law exempted campus records from the restrictions of the Buckley Amendment. Universities are still not compelled to release information on crime records, but they will no longer risk losing federal funds if they do release the names. Another change added to the act after the shootings at Virginia Tech in 2007 requires institutions to have a plan notifying the campus as soon as an emergency is confirmed.

Records of Juvenile Offenders All states have laws restricting the release of records that identify "juvenile offenders," people under age 18. The names are withheld by all branches of the juvenile justice system, including the social services system, but a judge can authorize their release. If a juvenile is being tried as an adult — a decision that is made by a judge — or if the juvenile's name is mentioned in open court, the name can be used. This sometimes happens when the crime is particularly heinous or the juvenile has an extensive criminal record.

Most newspapers and broadcast stations have policies to withhold the names of juveniles, but that is more of an ethical decision than a legal one. The media may use the name if they receive it by legitimate means.

Use of Names   Many newspapers and TV news stations also withhold the names of suspects in crime stories until they have been formally charged with the crime. Being arrested means only that someone has been stopped for questioning in a crime. The person becomes an official suspect after charges are filed in a court, usually at a hearing called an "arraignment." (The process will be explained in the section about courts.)

Person of Interest: In recent years, police have begun releasing the name of a suspect as a "person of interest" before actual charges are filed. This term is used most often when police have good reason to believe the suspect will soon be charged with the crime, but it is controversial because it casts suspicion on someone who may not be involved in the crime.

Some news organizations also withhold the names of crime victims to protect their privacy. A growing controversy at newspapers and television stations is whether to withhold the names of complainants in rape cases. Again, the policy varies, but most of the media do not publish the names.

When names are used in crime stories, always get the full name, including the middle initial, and double-check the spelling. Do not rely on police reports; many names on reports are spelled incorrectly. Check the names in telephone directories whenever possible. If a discrepancy exists between the name in the phone book and the one the officer gave you, call the officer again or go with the information from the police.

Using full names with initials helps reduce confusion and inaccuracies; there could be a dozen John Smiths in the community. John T. Smith is more specific, especially when followed by age and address.

Wording of Accusations   Remember that all people are innocent until they are proved guilty in court or until they plead guilty. When a suspect is arrested, the person is not officially charged with anything. A person can be arrested after an officer gets a warrant or on suspicion of a crime. But the police cannot charge anyone with a crime; a member of the district attorney's office must file the charge officially with the court (more about that later). As a result, you must be careful with wording so you don't convict a person erroneously. Most media wait until the person has been charged with the crime, except in sensational cases when the arrest is important news.

If you are writing about an arrest before the official charge, do not say, "Sallie R. Smith was arrested for robbing the bank" (that implies guilt). Do say, "Sallie R. Smith was arrested in connection with the bank robbery." If you are writing about the suspect after charges have been filed, say, "Sallie R. Smith was charged with bank robbery" or "Sallie R. Smith was arrested on a charge of bank robbery."

Also be careful before you call anyone a crime victim. If a person was killed or visibly injured during a crime, it is probably clear that the person is a crime victim. In other cases, the suspect has to be proved guilty before you can say the other person is a victim. You can say "the *alleged* victim," or, if applicable, you can call the other person the accuser — for example, "The accuser in the rape trial . . . ."

Use the official charges when possible. If they are very awkward, and they often are, don't use them in the lead. For example, one man who was accused of robbing a jewelry store was also accused of carrying a gun. But police didn't charge him with possession of a gun. They charged him with possession of an instrument of crime. And there are varying degrees in the charges, such as first-degree murder, which should be cited. But don't cite the other qualifications, such as Class E felony (a category for the crime), unless you are going to explain what they mean and why the reader must know. If categories are used at all, it is for explanation of the penalties: "The crime is a Class E felony, which carries a penalty of . . . ." It is still preferable to explain the penalty without the category, which is meaningless to readers.

Alleged: The word *alleged* is dangerous, so avoid it whenever possible. It means to declare or assert without proof. If you allege carelessly, you can be sued. Do not say, "Smith allegedly robbed the bank." You, the writer, are then the source of the allegation — and a good candidate for a libel suit. You can say, however, "Police accused Sallie R. Smith of robbing the bank" or "Police said Smith robbed the bank. An accusation is OK if it comes from police (and they are citing charges on record), not if it comes from you. Other permissible uses include "The bank was allegedly robbed" or "the alleged robbery," although such uses are not preferable.

Here's an example of the proper use of *alleged*:

When basketball star Kobe Bryant was accused of rape, it would be accurate to say the "alleged rape" when referring to the incident because it was never established that the accuser was actually raped; Bryant claimed that the sex was consensual. The case was dismissed when the woman who accused Bryant of sexual assault decided not to testify. The woman also had to be considered an "alleged victim" because the charges were never proved.

Also be careful when using the word *accused*. Follow the Associated Press Stylebook guidelines: A person is accused *of,* not *with,* a crime. In addition, you should not say, "accused bank robber Sallie R. Smith" (this convicts her). Instead, say, "Sallie R. Smith, accused of the bank robbery . . . ."

Attribution

In crime stories, make sure that you attribute all accusatory information and much of the information you received secondhand (not by direct observation). Factual information does not need attribution. For example, the location of a crime is usually factual. If someone has been charged with a crime, you can state that as a fact.

To reduce the use of attribution after every sentence, you can use an overview attribution for part of your story, especially when you are recounting what happened: "Police described the incident this way."

Newspaper or Television Archives

The first thing you should do before you write your story is check newspaper clips in your library, TV file tape or online archives. They may make a big difference in your story.

A reporter for *The Hartford* (Conn.) *Courant* covered the case of a man arrested on a charge of rape. Small story for a big paper. But the reporter checked clips and discovered that the man had been previously arrested on rape charges and was free on bail when he was charged with this other rape — a much bigger story. Three months later, a different reporter was making police checks. A man had been accused of rape. The reporter checked the clips. It was the same man charged with a third rape, which occurred when he was free on bail still awaiting trial in the first rape case — a very big story. And this story led to a major front-page follow-up story on the system in Connecticut that allows rape suspects to be released on bail, no matter how many times they have been arrested and charged with that type of crime. ("Bail" is the amount of money, set by a judge, that the suspect has to deposit with the court to be released from jail pending a hearing or trial. If the suspect flees, the bail money goes to the court.)

One caution: Clips and tape on file in your news organization's database may not be up to date. They may contain stories of someone's arrest but not the disposition of the case. Always check to see if charges were dropped, or if the person is still waiting trial or was convicted.

Guidelines for Reporting Crime Stories

In any story you will seek good quotes and answers to the five W's. Here are the basic questions to ask and the basic information to include in crime stories:

Victims: Get full names, ages, addresses and occupations, if available (use if relevant).

Suspects: Get full names, ages and addresses, if available; if not, get a description. Guidelines about whether to include race or ethnic background are changing. Check your organization's style. A general rule is to avoid mentioning race or ethnicity unless it is crucial to the story or to a description of a suspect.

Cause of Fatalities or Injuries: Also describe the injuries, where injured people have been taken and their current condition (check with hospitals). In stories involving property, specify the causes and extent of damage.

Location of Incident: Don't forget to gather specific information for a graphic.

Time of Incident: Be as specific as possible.

What Happened: Make sure that you understand the sequence of events; always ask about any unusual circumstances.

Arrests and Charges Filed: If people have been arrested, find out where they are being held, when they will be arraigned (a hearing for formal charges) or when the next court procedure will be. If they have already been arraigned, find out the amount of bail.

SOCIAL MEDIA

SOCIAL MEDIA has changed the nature of crime reporting. It does not replace the need for checking with police and other sources, but it is an invaluable additional tool for police and reporters.

The Boynton Beach Police Department in Florida was one of the first local police agencies to use Facebook, YouTube and MySpace to inform citizens about crimes and to seek their help in solving crimes. The department later added a Twitter page to post updates to the daily reports on its website. "We can also showcase dramatic video from our police cars. . . . That's where YouTube comes in. There we can post all of our videos and put links to those videos on our MySpace and Facebook pages," according to the department's website.

It is one of many police agencies using social media to seek citizen tips for solving crimes. The FBI uses Twitter, Facebook and YouTube as well. "To reach out to the public, we need to be where people are — and we know tens of millions of people spend their time in social media sites," said John Miller, former head of FBI Public Affairs. "Adding our fugitives, missing kids, threat and scam warnings, and other information into these sites is an extension of what we've done for decades — enlisting the help and support of concerned citizens around the globe to keep communities safer."

John Miller, former head of FBI public affairs.

Courtesy of the FBI.

Social media is even more valuable for reporters. Journalists can follow police agencies' social media sites for reports, tips and documents that were not accessible online in the past. But another indispensible use of social media is the ability to acquire sources. With social media, you can invite readers to submit leads, tips and personal stories about a crime or subject. If you are covering a breaking news crime, Twitter, Facebook and Flickr and other social media sites can provide on-the-scene reactions from sources. However, in this age of instant news, you need to exercise caution about publishing information you get from social media without checking it for accuracy and validity. You also need to avoid using information you receive from anonymous sources on social media sites.

Eyewitness Accounts: Comments from neighbors may also be relevant. Be careful about using accusations against named individuals. When in doubt, leave them out.

In addition to gathering the basic information, you may want to try some of these other reporting techniques:

Role-Play: Imagine that it is your car in the accident, your home that was burglarized or burned in a fire, your friend or relative injured in a crime. What information would you want to know if you were personally affected by the story?

Play Detective: What information would you want to gather to solve the crime?

Gather Graphics: What information would you need to diagram the car accident, draw the crime scene or a locator map, write a highlights box or a chronology of events or design a chart or graphic depicting how and where the crime occurred? Ask questions to gain the information you will have to convey to the artist who will draw the graphics for your story or for locating the crime scene on a Google map or other online mapping program.

Use the Telephone: Often you will gather information for crime stories over the telephone. Usually you will get the information from a dispatcher or public information officer who was not at the scene and is just reading a report to you. Make sure that you ask police officials to repeat any information you did not hear clearly. Also ask the police officer releasing the information to give you his full name and rank. Police often identify themselves only by title and last name, such as Sgt. Jones. Ask the officer to spell the names of all people involved; you can spell them back to double-check the accuracy.

Stories about Specific Types of Crimes

For the first version of a major crime story, a hard-news approach is preferred. With the instant changes that mobile and online media provide, be prepared to update the leads continually. For follow-up stories and sidebars, consider some of the storytelling techniques.

Motor Vehicle Accidents Vehicle accident stories usually are hard-news stories, unless there is an unusual angle. In addition to following the basic guidelines, make sure that you have this information:

- Speed, destination and directions of vehicles and exact locations at the time of the accident

Courtesy of the Alaska Department of Public Safety

A fatal traffic accident on a snowy highway in Alaska.

- Cause of accident, arrests, citations and damages
- Victims' use of required equipment, such as seat belts and bicycle or motorcycle helmets
- Weather-related information, if relevant
- Alcohol- or drug-related information, if relevant
- Rescue attempts or acts of heroism

It is customary to lead the story with fatalities and injuries. This example is very basic, structured in inverted pyramid form:

Summary lead: delayed identification, fatality and cause

A Santa Ana boy was killed when a van rear-ended the car he was riding in while it was stopped at a turn signal, police said. The van's driver was booked for vehicular manslaughter.

Identification

Robert Taylor, 10, died at UCI Medical Center in Orange.

When, where, other injured people

The 3:17 p.m. accident at First and Bristol streets in Santa Ana also critically injured the boy's mother, Griselda Taylor, 29, and his sister, Lynelle, 8. An 8-year-old boy in the car sustained minor injuries, police said. His name and relation to the Taylors were not released.

What happened and who was involved

Taylor was waiting on the eastbound side of First, in the left-turn lane, at a red light when a van driven by Don Currie Edwards, 49, struck the back of her car, police said. The impact pushed her car into the intersection, and it was then struck by a westbound car driven by Phillipe Hernandez, 18.

Taylor sustained a broken neck. She was in guarded condition at Western Medical Center in Santa Ana, hospital officials said. Lynelle sustained critical head injuries, police said.

Condition of injured people; hospital sources

Edwards was treated for minor injuries and arrested, police said. Hernandez was not injured.

— *The Orange County* (Calif.) *Register*

Here is a broadcast accident story with similar crucial information in a brief form:

Summary lead: delayed identification, fatality

A man is dead after a traffic accident at Mile 66 of the Glenn Highway yesterday.

Identification and cause

Alaska State Troopers say 50-year-old Spencer Ricketts of Anchorage was northbound on his Harley Davidson motorcycle when he crossed the double yellow line and struck a Winnebago.

Condition of victim

Ricketts was evacuated by helicopter to Mat-Su Regional Medical Center, where he was pronounced dead on arrival.

The driver of the Winnebago, 61-year-old Robert Nastri of Arizona and his wife, who was a passenger, were not injured.

Who was involved

Ricketts' next of kin has been notified.

Troopers are still investigating the crash.

— *KTUU, Channel 2, Anchorage, Alaska*

Burglaries and Robberies A burglary involves entry into a building with intent to commit any type of crime; robbery involves stealing with violence or a threat against people. If you are away and a person enters your home and steals your compact disc player, that's a burglary. If you are asleep upstairs and the person is downstairs stealing the player, that's still a burglary. But if the person threatens you with force, that's a robbery. A burglary always involves a place and *can* involve violence against a person; a robbery *must* involve violence or threats against a person.

For both burglaries and robberies, ask the basics: who, what, when, where, why and how. Then add the following:

- What was taken and the value of the goods
- Types of weapons used (in robberies)
- How entry was made
- Similar circumstances (frequency of crime or any odd conditions)

In burglary and robbery stories, mention in the lead any injuries or deaths. Keep the tone serious when the story involves death or serious injuries. In other cases, use your judgment and lead with any unusual angles. If there are none, stress what was taken or how the burglars entered the building, if that is the most interesting factor.

Whether you write a hard or soft lead depends on how serious the crime was, whether it is the first story on the crime and whether you have enough interesting information to warrant a soft approach.

Here's a hard-news version of a burglary story:

> FAIRBANKS, Alaska — A Fairbanks man was charged with burglary after he broke into a home, took off his clothes and fell asleep in the homeowner's bed, police said.
>
> Jordan Anderson, 28, will be arraigned today in district court where he will also face a criminal mischief charge.
>
> Alaska State Troopers said Anderson told them he had been smoking synthetic marijuana, a legal substance that is a blend of spices and herbs sold in head shops. They said Anderson claimed he went to bed in the house on Goldhill Road because "God had told him to."

In this burglary story, the tone is lighter and a soft lead is used because of the subject matter:

> Someone took Burger King's "Have It Your Way" slogan too literally this week and stole a three-foot-wide Whopper hamburger display costume from a van parked in northeast Salem.
>
> Shannon Sappingfield, a marketing representative for local Burger Kings, said the missing burger was made of sponge.
>
> The Whopper was in a van parked at Boss Enterprise, 408-A Lancaster Drive NE. The company owns nine local Burger Kings.
>
> When Sappingfield came to work about 6 a.m. Tuesday, she saw that the van's window had been broken. The cardboard box containing the Whopper

costume was missing; two other boxes containing a milk shake costume and a french fry costume were untouched.

"I'm not convinced they realized what they had until they were away from the site and opened the box," she said.

She estimated that the costume was worth about $500. But to get another one, the company would also have to buy another milk shake and french fry costume, which cost $500 each.

— (Salem, Ore.) *Statesman-Journal*

Homicides   *Homicide* is the legal term for killing. *Murder* is the term for premeditated homicide. *Manslaughter* is homicide without premeditation. A person can be arrested on charges of murder, but he is not a murderer until convicted of the crime. Do not call someone a murderer until then. Also, don't say someone was murdered unless authorities have established that the victim was murdered — in a premeditated act of killing — or until a court determines that. Say the person was slain or killed. Some additional information to gather:

- Weapon (specific description, such as .38-caliber revolver)
- Clues and motives (from police)
- Specific wounds
- Official cause of death (from coroner or police)
- Circumstances of suspect's arrest (result of tip or investigation, perhaps at the scene)
- Lots of details, from relatives, neighbors, friends, officials, eyewitnesses and your own observations at the crime scene

For many first-day stories about death, you may choose to use a hard-news approach. You should get the news about the death in the lead. But if there is a more compelling angle, you could put it in the second or third paragraph. Again, you must use judgment in deciding whether the story lends itself to a hard-news or a storytelling approach.

This is a hard-news approach to a homicide story:

A 32-year-old man was charged Tuesday with killing his former girlfriend when she wouldn't leave the back porch of his home.

Lester Paul Stephens of 3357 N. 2nd St. was charged with first-degree intentional homicide while armed in connection with the death of Ruby L. Hardison, 42. Hardison was shot in the head Saturday.

According to the criminal complaint, Stephens told police that he and Hardison recently had ended their relationship. But Hardison came to Stephens' home Saturday and began knocking and banging on the door and front window.

Stephens told police he got upset about the noise, and went to the back door to tell her to leave him alone. Then he went back inside and got a .32-caliber semiautomatic pistol and walked back to the porch, the complaint says.

Stephens told Hardison to get off the porch and go home, then fired one shot in the air to scare her away.

The complaint says that he then put the pistol to the right side of her head, and after they continued to argue, the gun discharged.

Stephens, who faces life plus five years in prison if convicted, was being held on $50,000 cash bail. A preliminary hearing was scheduled for April 30.

— The Milwaukee Journal

Here is an excerpt from a homicide story written in a storytelling style. This story includes reporting done according to most of the guidelines: interviews with neighbors, description based on observation, information from the police report and from officials. Remember that if you can't get to the scene, you can use your cross-directory to find neighbors to contact by telephone.

Soft lead

MELBOURNE, Fla. — June Anne Sharabati had planned every aspect of her children's lives, from their tasteful clothes to their exposure to classical music.

She missed only one detail: She forgot to plan a bullet for herself.

Backup for previous statement

The woman charged in the slaying of her two children Thursday night told deputies she would have committed suicide but she ran out of ammunition.

Basic news (five W's)

When deputies were called to her home at 2410 Washington Ave., they found Stephen Faulker, 14, dead on the floor of his bedroom. The Central Junior High School student had been shot in his stomach and head with a .38-caliber revolver.

Type of weapon

Two-year-old Aisha Sharabati was in her mother's bedroom dying from similar wounds.

Possible motive (note attribution)

Sharabati, who divorced Aisha's father in 1989, told deputies that Stephen had been a discipline problem, but she gave no explanation for her daughter's death, said Brevard County sheriff's spokeswoman Joan Heller.

Stephen's father died about nine years ago. Sharabati's former husband, Mohamad, lives in Canada and is en route to Melbourne, deputies said.

The first sign of the shootings came to light shortly before midnight Thursday with Sharabati's frantic calls to police and neighbors.

John Marrell said he was sleeping when the phone rang.

Narrative based on interview with neighbor

The call was from Sharabati, his 32-year-old neighbor. He had known her for 11 years and had helped her from time to time.

Dialogue

"She said, 'Didn't you hear the shots?' and I asked, 'What shots?'" Marrell said.

"And then she said, 'You need to get over here and get these kids. They've suffered enough.'"

Marrell said he grabbed a gun and a flashlight, thinking maybe a prowler was threatening the single parent and her children.

Instead, Sharabati met him at her screen door and told him she had "killed the kids."

Marrell said he ran home and called police, not knowing they had already been called.

Information from officials

When deputies arrived at the house, Sharabati met them unarmed on the doorstep and said, "Kill me. Kill me," Heller said. Sharabati was taken into custody, and deputies went in to find the bodies.

Police report

In the investigation report, Deputy Scott Nyquist said the suspect shot her son "in a fit of rage."

Reaction from neighbors

On Friday, many neighbors in the middle class neighborhood were struggling to understand how a seemingly "ideal mother" could have committed the slayings.

Occupation of neighbor (relevant to statement)

"She was the kind of mother who would attend parent-teacher conferences," said Frances Edwards, a retired high school guidance counselor who lives across the street from Sharabati. "She often said her children were her life. I sure didn't see this coming."

Observations

Sharabati's light blue, one-story home — like most in the wooded, spacious subdivision — was well maintained. In the back yard, three lawn chairs were lined up alongside Aisha's child-sized chair.

Edwards said Sharabati wanted only the best for her children.

Backup for lead

"She bought them Mozart records to listen to and dressed them beautifully," she said. . . .

Reaction from relative

"We are in deep shock — very, very deep shock," said Helen Faulker, Sharabati's mother.

Where suspect is, next step in court process

Sharabati is being held in the Brevard County jail, where she is scheduled to make her first court appearance at 9 a.m. today.

— LAURIN SELLERS AND LYNNE BUMPUS-HOOPER, *The Orlando (Fla.) Sentinel*

ETHICS

ETHICAL DILEMMA: An 18-year old student at your university has accused three men on the college football team of raping her at a party on campus. The men have been arrested and arraigned on rape charges. You are the editor of your campus newspaper's website. Your website and other print and broadcast media on campus have a policy against naming accusers in rape cases, but they do not prohibit naming the accused parties after they have been arraigned. However, the local newspaper has published the names of the suspects, and their names are being posted on several social media sites.

The Twitter site for your campus is buzzing with tweets about the incident. Several of the tweets are ranting about why the media publish the suspects' names but not the name of the accuser. The tweets are also defending the basketball players and questioning whether the woman is telling the truth. The case is even getting national attention.

At this point you have not named any of the parties involved, but the pressure is mounting, particularly because the suspects' names are all over the Internet and they are on the police records.

Do you think it is fair to publish only the suspects' names but not the accuser's name? Will you withstand the pressure from the public and your followers on social media? What will you decide?

Epilogue: This scenario is adapted from a case at Hofstra University, where five men were accused of raping a female student in a dormitory bathroom. The men's names were published in local and national media. After police obtained a cell phone video of the incident, the woman recanted her story and admitted that she had sex with the men but it was consensual.

Firefighters battle a blaze south of Anchorage, Alaska.

Courtesy of the Alaska Department of Public Safety

Fires

Although fire stories may not be crime stories, unless arson or other criminal behavior was involved, police reporters are often responsible for fire stories. Here are the important elements:

- Time fire started, time fire companies responded, time fire was brought under control

- Number of fire companies responding, number of trucks at scene

- Evacuations, if any, and where people were taken

- Injuries and fatalities (make sure that you ask if any firefighters were injured)

- Cause (ask if arson is suspected — intentional setting of fire), how and where fire started

- Who discovered the fire, extent of damage, insurance coverage

- Description of building

- Estimated cost of damages

- Presence and condition of smoke detectors or sprinkler system (especially in a public building or apartment building, if city requires them)

- Fire inspection record, fire code violations (usually for a follow-up story, especially in public buildings)

When fatalities or injuries occur in a fire, they should be mentioned in your lead, preferably a hard-news lead. If no one is injured or if heroic rescue attempts are involved, a soft lead may be appropriate. Follow-up stories and sidebars provide many opportunities for storytelling techniques.

These examples follow most of the guidelines for reporting fires:

Print version

Child alerts family to duplex fire

A child in an East Anchorage duplex alerted his family that the house was on fire Tuesday morning, leading to a safe evacuation and only minor injury to one person.

The family of four — one adult and children ages 6, 8 and 12 — were at their rented duplex unit on Northwind Avenue, near Muldoon Road, when the child roused everyone as smoke detectors started sounding, said Tom Kempton, Anchorage Fire Department spokesman.

The first firefighters arrived on the scene about three minutes later, at 7:43 a.m., Kempton said. Crews found smoke streaming from an upstairs window and the family waiting outside. The adult had a minor burn to the hand but didn't have to go to a hospital, Kempton said.

Firefighters had to wake residents in the attached duplex unit and get them out, Kempton said. But that half of the building wasn't damaged.

The fire apparently started in an upstairs bedroom. Crews kept the blaze to that area, though the rest of the unit had smoke damage, Kempton said. Firefighters declared the scene under control just before 8 a.m. Damage is estimated to be $40,000 to $50,000, and the cause of the fire is under investigation.

The occupants reportedly do not have renter's insurance. The Alaska chapter of the American Red Cross is providing the family with food, clothes, shoes and lodging.

— KATIE PESZNECKER, *Anchorage Daily News*

Broadcast version posted on the station's website.

Family left homeless after fire

Anchorage, Alaska — Two Anchorage families are safe, but one is homeless after a duplex fire this morning in the Muldoon area.

The Anchorage Fire Department says the blaze broke out about 8 a.m., in a child's bedroom at 8151 Northwind Ave. The child alerted the rest of the family while fire crews went to the adjoining unit to make sure neighbors escaped safely. Firefighters were able to safely evacuate all people and pets from the home.

The cause of the fire is not yet known.

The American Red Cross of Alaska is assisting the family who was displaced. They did not have renters insurance.

— MARIA DOWNEY, KTUU

COURT STORIES

Court cases are full of drama. They are the stuff of television series and movies. Yet print and online stories about them are often dull. Even if you use a hard-news approach to report a conviction or testimony, you can still use storytelling techniques of dialogue, description and narrative writing for portions of the story so the reader can experience the human drama that filled the courtroom.

To cover courts, you need a basic understanding of the process and the terminology that is used. Court procedures vary from state to state and even in counties within states. You need to find out how the system works in the area where you are working.

U.S. Dept. of State, Bureau of International Information

Whenever you hear a term you don't understand, seek a definition. Go by this guideline: If you don't understand something, chances are the reader won't either. It's up to you to make the story clear.

Here are some basic guidelines for writing court stories:

- Get reactions, facial expressions and gestures of the defendant and the accusers, attorneys, relatives and other people affected by the case, especially in trial stories and verdict stories.
- Use descriptive detail and color — lively quotes, dramatic testimony and dialogue.
- Translate all jargon, and avoid legal terminology.
- State exact charges in the story.
- Give the background of the crime, no matter how many stories have been published about this case.

CONVERGENCE COACH

USE THE WEB TO DO background research and put stories in perspective.

- Check the Web for background of criminal suspects. Start with a basic search engine and check sex offender registries — even if the person is not charged with a sex crime.

- Check the Web for perspective on issue stories. For example, if you are writing about a local school shooting, check online for a listing of recent school shootings or similar statistics in other crimes.

- Search blogs, and social networking sites for messages suspects may have sent.

- Include the name of the court where the trial or hearing is being held.
- Get comments from defendants, prosecutors, defense attorneys, plaintiffs (the people who brought suit or filed charges), relatives, and jurors in all verdict stories.
- In verdict stories, include how long the jury deliberated. Also include how many jurors were on the case; not all cases have 12-member juries, the most common number. In all cases, however, the length of deliberations is part of the story.
- Write the next step — the next court appearance or, in verdict stories, plans for an appeal if the defendant is found guilty.

Criminal and Civil Cases

Court procedures fall into two categories: criminal and civil cases. Criminal cases are violations of any laws regulating crime. If you are arrested on suspicion of drunken driving, you could be charged in a criminal case.

Civil cases involve lawsuits between two parties. If your landlord says you have not paid the rent or you have damaged your apartment, he can bring a civil lawsuit against you. Divorces, malpractice, libel, contract disputes and other actions not involving criminal law are civil cases.

FEDERAL COURTS AND STATE COURTS

The court system functions on two levels: a federal level and a state level. Federal courts have jurisdiction over cases involving matters related to the U.S. Constitution (such as civil rights), federal tax and antitrust matters and any other federal laws. Federal courts also hear cases between people from different states. Here is the hierarchy of the federal court system:

U.S. District Court: This is the lowest level of the federal judicial system, where most cases involving federal issues are first heard.

U.S. Court of Appeals: There are 12 of these courts for geographical areas, plus the U.S. Court of Appeals for the D.C. (District of Columbia) Circuit. It is the intermediary court, where cases from the federal district courts are appealed.

U.S. Supreme Court: This is the highest court in the nation. Cases may be appealed to this court, but the justices do not have to rule on all the cases.

Most states also have three levels of courts: a trial court, an appeals court and a state supreme court for appeals of the last resort on the state level. Cases from the state's highest court may be appealed to the U.S. Supreme Court if there is a federal angle, such as a constitutional matter — a First Amendment issue, for example — or a civil rights violation.

The names of the state courts can be confusing. In one state a superior court may be a trial-level court, whereas in others it may be an appellate court.

There also are municipal courts, where violations of local laws, such as traffic laws or city ordinances, are heard.

In addition, within the state system there are juvenile courts (for cases involving people younger than age 18) and probate courts, where disputes involving wills and estates are heard.

When you write your court story, find out the proper name of the court — whether it is called a district court, a circuit court or a common pleas court — and write that in the story.

Criminal Court Process

Crimes are classified as misdemeanors or felonies. *Misdemeanors* are considered minor offenses that carry a potential penalty of up to a year in jail and/or a fine. *Felonies* are more serious crimes punishable by more than a year in prison. Criminal procedures differ from state to state, but there are some general processes in the court system that you should understand. The diagram outlines court procedures for both criminal and civil cases.

Court procedures

Crimes are defined as misdemeanors or felonies. The path through the judicial process is different depending on the type of crime. However, criminal justice is just one of the types of cases that courts hear. More common, but less prominent, are civil disputes, which are usually resolved in civil court.

Misdemeanors
Misdemeanors are considered minor offenses that carry a potential penalty of up to a year in jail and/or a fine.

- **ARREST**
- **BOOKING / BOND SET**
- **ARRAIGNMENT** — Case usually disposed at this time and sentence issued
- **POSSIBLE TRIAL AND VERDICT**

Felonies
Felonies are serious crimes punishable by more than a year in jail.

- **ARREST**
- **BOOKING**
- **ARRAIGNMENT**
- **PRELIMINARY HEARING**
- **TRIAL**
- **SENTENCING IN GUILTY VERDICTS**

Civil cases
In civil cases, a plaintiff files a suit against another party — a person or a company — seeking damages or some compensation. Divorce cases are examples of civil matters. The court procedures can be lengthy. Usually, after a suit is filed, numerous motions are filed by attorneys for both parties. Eventually the case can go to trial if it is not resolved in an out-of-court settlement.

- **SUIT FILED**
- **VARIOUS MOTIONS**
- **TRIAL**
- **RULING BY JUDGE OR JURY**
- **SENTENCING IN GUILTY VERDICTS**

© Bill Skeet

Process of criminal and civil cases.

Terms Used in Court Reporting

You should become familiar with these terms so you can better understand and explain court proceedings:

Acquittal: Finding by a court or jury that a person accused of a crime is not guilty.

Adjudicate: To make a final determination or judgment by the court.

Affidavit: Sworn statement of facts.

Appeal: Plea to ask a higher court to review a judgment, verdict or order of a lower court.

Appellant: Person who files an appeal.

Arraignment: Court hearing in which a defendant in a criminal case is formally charged with the crime and given a chance to enter a plea of guilty, not guilty or no contest (nolo contendere). At this time, bail is usually set.

Bail: Amount of money set by the court that the defendant must guarantee to pay if he does not show up for a court trial. If the defendant can't raise the money through a bail bond company or personal sources, he stays in jail.

Bond: Written promise to pay bail money on the conditions stated. The bond for bail is usually 10 percent of the total amount of bail set. The term is often used interchangeably with bail. Very often, a person will borrow money from a bond company. Then if the person flees, the bond company loses the money.

Brief: Legal document filed with the court by a lawyer, stating the facts of the case and arguments citing how laws apply to this case.

Change of Venue: Procedure to seek a change of location of the trial, usually when defense attorneys contend that the defendant can't get a fair trial in the current location because of too much pretrial publicity.

Charge: Official allegation of criminal wrongdoing.

Civil Suit: Lawsuit to determine rights, duties, claims for damages, ownership or other settlements in noncriminal matters.

Complaint: Formal affidavit in which one person accuses another of violating the law.

Condemnation: Civil action to acquire ownership of property for public use. When a municipality wants to build a road or sidewalk, the government will condemn the property to gain right of way.

Contempt: Action that disregards the order or authority of the court. A lawyer who screams obscenities at the judge will probably be found in contempt of court.

Defendant: In a civil case, the person being sued. In a criminal case, the person charged with breaking the law.

Deposition: Written statement of testimony from a witness under oath.

Discovery: Pretrial examination of a person (including depositions), documents or other items to find evidence that may be used in the trial.

Dismissal: Order to drop the case.

Docket: List of cases pending before the court. A trial docket is a list of cases pending trial.

Extradition: Procedure to move a person accused of a crime from the state where he is residing to the state where the crime occurred and where the trial will be conducted.

Felony: Major crime punishable by a sentence of a year or more. Crimes such as robbery, homicide and kidnapping are felonies; lesser crimes such as shoplifting are misdemeanors. Legally, a felony is defined as a crime punishable by death or imprisonment in a state prison.

Grand Jury: Group of citizens selected by the court to investigate whether there is enough evidence or probable cause that a crime occurred and that the person should be charged, or indicted.

Hung Jury: Jury that cannot reach a unanimous verdict, a requirement in most criminal trials.

Indictment: Recommendation by the grand jury that there is enough probable cause to charge a person or group of people with the crime under investigation. The grand jury hands up an indictment to the judge (because the judge sits on a platform higher than the jury); the judge hands down rulings. It's preferable to use the word *issued*.

Injunction: Order by the court instructing a person, group or company to stop the action that was occurring, such as picketing. For example, an injunction can order a group to stop marching outside an abortion clinic.

Innocent: The term "not guilty" is preferable in court cases. The Associated Press Stylebook previously recommended using the term "innocent" in case the "not" in "not guilty" was dropped from typesetting, but that is no longer the case. AP now recommends using "not guilty."

Misdemeanor: Crime less serious than a felony; crime punishable by less than one year in jail and/or fines.

Mistrial: Trial that is set aside or declared invalid because of some mistake in proceedings or, in a criminal trial, because the jury cannot reach a unanimous verdict.

Motion: Request for the court to make a ruling or finding.

Nolo contendere: Latin for "I will not contest it" (no contest). This plea has the same effect as a guilty plea, but it is not an admission of guilt. It means the person will not fight the charge. If you agree to pay a fine for a traffic ticket but do not agree that you were speeding, you are pleading no contest. This type of plea is used as a form of bargaining to get the defendant a reduced charge in exchange for his agreement not to protest and to eliminate the need for a trial. Use the English term *no contest* in a story, and explain briefly that it is not an admission of guilt.

Plaintiff: Person who sues in a civil case. The defendant is the one being sued.

Plea: Defendant's response to a charge, stating that he is guilty, not guilty or not willing to contest the charge.

Plea bargain: Agreement between the prosecutor and the defendant (or defense attorney) to accept a lesser charge and a lesser sentence in return for a guilty or no-contest plea. Plea bargaining is used extensively as a way to eliminate court trials. Once the defendant pleads guilty or no contest, there is no need for a trial. However, a plea bargain must be approved by the court.

Probable Cause: Determination that there is enough evidence to prosecute a criminal case. Police officials also need probable cause — enough reason to believe a crime is being committed — when they seek a search warrant or any other warrant for a person's arrest.

Probation: Condition in which the person is released from serving a jail sentence if he meets certain terms, such as serving in the community, entering drug treatment or accepting whatever restrictions the judge decides.

Recognizance: Literally, "recognition." A person may be released from jail based on his own recognizance — meaning the recognition of a previously good reputation. This ruling is essentially the judge's way of saying that, because of the person's reputation, he is not considered a high risk for skipping the next court hearing or trial.

Subpoena: Court order commanding a person to appear in court or to release documents to the court.

Summary judgment: Procedure in a civil suit asking the court to give final judgment on the grounds that there are no further questions and no need for a trial.

Summons: Document notifying a defendant that a lawsuit or complaint has been filed against him.

Suspended sentence: Court order stating that the punishment of the defendant will be suspended if certain conditions are met. A person who receives probation gets a suspended sentence.

Temporary injunction: Court order to stop an action, such as a protest, for a specific amount of time until a court hearing and ruling whether the action should be enjoined, or stopped permanently.

Tort: Civil case involving damages, pain, suffering or other allegations of wrongdoing.

True Bill: Indictment issued by a grand jury.

Verdict: Decision by a jury about guilt or innocence.

Warrant: Court order directing law enforcement officials to arrest a person. A search warrant gives officials authority to search a premises.

U.S. Judge Howard Matz with a student counterpart in a mock trial in federal court in Los Angeles.

Court Story Examples

A court case is a continuing saga. From the time a person is arrested until the case is resolved, whether in a trial or a settlement, you will write many stories about it. But never assume that the reader is familiar with the case, no matter how sensational it may be. Always include the background.

Whether you take a soft or hard approach, make sure that your nut graph explains who is being accused of what, and place it high in the story.

If information is part of a court record, you may use it as fact — but it still may not be true. It's up to a judge or jury to decide whether the claims in court documents and trials are true. So you need to attribute your information, although not necessarily in the lead.

Unlike other stories, many court stories do not appear balanced. On any given day, one side in the case may present its arguments, so you won't always have a story that seems fair to both parties. The testimony will be biased; you should not be.

Some reminders:

- Explain charges and background.
- Describe defendants and witnesses.
- Specify the court where the proceeding takes place.
- Tell how long the jury deliberated in verdict stories.
- Tell a good story.

When the verdict is issued in a major trial that has garnered interest locally or nationally, a hard-news story is appropriate. A soft lead also may work, but make sure that you put the verdict very high in the story. The following example uses a hard news lead and includes all the major points needed for a court story at the end of a trial.

INTERNET ROMANCE KILLER GETS 30 YEARS

Summary lead

A judge gave confessed Internet romance killer Theodore Manning 30 years in prison Thursday after a jury found him guilty of voluntary manslaughter, not murder, in the death of Nikki McPhatter, a Charlotte airline employee.

Length of deliberations and charges

The Richland County jury of seven men and five women deliberated for almost 10 hours over two days before finding Manning guilty of the lesser charge. Murder would have meant life in prison without parole.

Jury reasoning and background

But the jury sided with the defense, accepting the argument that the 2009 killing was a spur-of-the-moment action during a lovers' quarrel and not premeditated. They focused on the couple's wrestling over the gun that killed McPhatter, instead of what Manning did next: looting McPhatter's ATM accounts, stuffing her body in the trunk of her car, driving the car to rural Fairfield County and setting it on fire to try to cover up his crimes. Still, in the end, Judge Thomas Cooper could have given Manning from two to 30 years behind bars. He chose 30.

"I have no sympathy for you whatsoever," a grim-faced Cooper told Manning in front of more than a half-dozen of McPhatter's weeping friends and family members who asked for the maximum sentence.

The verdict was a defeat for 5th Circuit Solicitor Barney Giese, whose office earlier had turned down a request for a plea agreement while trying to persuade the jury to return a verdict of murder.

And the verdict came despite Giese's argument that McPhatter had been shot "execution-style," in the back of the head.

Under South Carolina law, Manning, 30, will be eligible for parole after serving 85 percent of his sentence, or 25½ years.

Manning had confessed to the killing, taking the witness stand to defend himself. But he told the jury that although he shot and killed McPhatter, it happened during a quarrel and that he never meant to do it.

Moreover, Manning testified, another girlfriend pressured him into disposing of McPhatter's body in the way he did.

There were no witnesses, and by Manning's own admission, he lied repeatedly to law officers trying to gather information about what happened to McPhatter.

Length of trial

The verdict climaxed a hard-fought, nine-day trial over in one of the most sensational, widely publicized murder cases in Richland County in recent years. It illustrated the perils of Internet dating where two people can use cyber dating services to link up with romantic partners who are completely outside a person's normal circle of friends and family.

Background

Manning and McPhatter met on Tagged.com and had no mutual friends. When she disappeared in May 2009, police had few immediate leads. McPhatter's frantic friends only knew that she had been seeing a man named "Teddy" in Columbia.

Deputies were able to crack the case by using high-tech and shoe leather investigative techniques that led to another Manning girlfriend, Kendra Goodman, who told police where McPhatter's body was and who had killed her.

Confronted, Manning confessed but said it was an accident, that McPhatter was angry because she wanted more from their relationship. Manning told police he didn't want a more extensive relationship with McPhatter — that he had been seeing six girlfriends simultaneously, keeping each one in the dark about the others.

Reactions More than a half-dozen family and friends of McPhatter rose to speak before Cooper's sentencing. Each cried or choked back tears.

Latoya McPhatter, McPhatter's oldest sister, her words punctuated by sobs, said: "My sister was a very sweet, jolly person. She was my biggest fan. She used to tell me when she was a little girl that she wanted to be like her big sister. I will always miss her. My heart is so heavy now."

She added, "I don't have any hatred in my heart for nobody, but just please — give her some justice." She collapsed sobbing into her seat.

An aunt, in angry tones, recalled how Nikki was missing 23 days and told the judge that she had been killed twice — first, "shot in the back of the head, then killed a second time — burnt up to a crisp…I beg your honor, please, serve the maximum penalty."

Trial highlights Manning's burning of the body and his looting of McPhatter's bank accounts were admittedly despicable acts but had nothing to do with the killing itself, argued Manning's attorneys,

Richland County assistant public defenders Jim May and Luke Shealey.

The defense attorneys also stressed that Manning had no prior criminal record and was an Air Force veteran who held a steady job working the night shift at the Bluff Road Westinghouse nuclear fuel plant, making more than $31,000 a year with overtime.

Giese and his deputy, Luck Campbell, sought to convince the jury that Manning's treatment of the body was so horrific, and his attempted cover-up so extensive, that he should be convicted of murder.

Ironically, Cooper is known for often giving criminals less than the maximum penalty so they can have hope to rehabilitate themselves.

But, in this case, Cooper said, he agreed with Giese.

The soon-to-be-retired Giese had just told the judge that Manning's coverup and burning of McPhatter's body was perhaps the worst crime he had seen in his 30 years in the solicitor's office, first as an assistant and then as elected solicitor.

Manning's "desecration of the body" made him think the same as Giese, Cooper said, giving Manning the maximum time behind bars.

— JOHN MONK, *The State*,
Columbia, S.C.

Stories about upcoming court trials lend themselves to storytelling techniques. If the story is important enough to "advance" the trial, it probably has a good story behind it. A narrative writing technique was used to advance this trial in a story that uses almost no direct attribution, except for quotes. The story is based on court records and previous admissions by the defendant. If the defendant had not admitted the crime, this story would be too accusatory.

MIAMI — He was a distraught man that day, a man who sang lullabies and wept. With one hand, he held a gun. With the other, he stroked the smooth face of his daughter, a 3-year-old existing in limbo between life and death.

An hour before, he had given her what he thought was a fatal dose of Valium. But here she was still breathing, her tiny chest rising and falling rhythmically, if ever so slightly.

She was in a crib at Miami Children's Hospital, lying on her back. She had been there for eight months, since the day she nearly suffocated. He leaned over the crib railing and looked at her eyes. They were open. They stared ahead, mirrored, no emotions, saw nothing. It was the same for her other senses. The damage to her brain was total and irreversible, and because of it, she couldn't hear his weeping, and she couldn't feel his last touch goodbye before he aimed the gun at her heart.

He shot her twice. He dropped the gun. He prayed that her suffering was over. He fell into a nurse's arms, cried and said he wanted to die. He said, "Maybe I should get the electric chair to make things even. I killed my daughter. I shot her twice. But I'm glad she's gone to heaven."

On Tuesday morning in a Miami courtroom, almost five months after the death of his daughter, Joy, Charles Griffith is scheduled to go on trial for murder. The defense, says Griffith's attorney, Mark Krasnow, will be mercy. "It was an act of love," Krasnow says, "not an act of malice."

— DAVID FINKEL, *St. Petersburg* (Fla.) *Times*

Most court stories are serious, but some have a humorous angle. Here is a light-hearted story in a conversational style that tries to involve the reader. It is an example of how a plea bargain works — or in this case, how it didn't work out very well. This story is written in storytelling form with the clincher at the end; unfortunately, the headline gives the twist away.

MAN GAMBLES ON PLEA, LOSES

He admits guilt, then is acquitted

You're the defendant. You make the call:

You're Marvin E. Johnson, 40, convicted three times of drug possession.

You're facing a minimum 15 years in prison without parole if convicted of being a felon in possession of a handgun.

On Wednesday, the jury at your federal trial in Kansas City deliberates three hours without reaching a verdict. On Thursday, the jury deliberates three more hours and announces it is hopelessly deadlocked. A hung jury and a new trial loom on the horizon.

The prosecutor, Assistant U.S. Attorney Rob Larsen, offers a deal. If you plead guilty, he'll reduce the government's sentencing request to a range of 15 to 22 months.

While you ponder that deal, the jury buzzes. It has a verdict.

Do you:

A) Sign the plea agreement and serve at least 15 months in prison? Or

B) Roll the dice with the jury's verdict? If it's guilty, you get at least 15 years; if it's not guilty, you walk away.

On Thursday afternoon, Marvin E. Johnson signed the plea agreement.

Five minutes later, the jury found him not guilty.

"I'm sure glad I struck that plea agreement," Larsen said.

"I can't win for losing," said Johnson's defense lawyer, John P. O'Connor.

— TOM JACKMAN, *The Kansas City* (Mo.) *Star*

EXERCISES

1 Crime story: Although the police report shown on the next page is labeled "Standard Offense Report," it is not. Each state has its own form; however, this one is similar to many. Most of the report is self-explanatory, with some exceptions. The case number is important for reporters; if you want to follow the case through the court system, you need this number, which stays the same for all actions in the case. Time is computed as military time, from one to 24 hours. Where the stolen property is listed, codes are used to signify the type of property. A complete code sheet is usually on the back of the police report. Write a story based on the report on the next page.

You called the police to ask more about the theft of the bird because that was unusual. The police told you that the bird was valuable and that was probably the reason it was stolen. They told you there is no rash of bird burglars, although there had been some thefts of birds several months ago. But this bird theft does not appear to be related to those because other items were taken, the police said. Police are still investigating. Use yesterday as your time frame for the date of offense and today as the date reported.

2 Fire story: You are making a routine call to the fire department to find out if any fires occurred overnight. Fire Battalion Chief Stephen McInerny gives you this information:

A fire occurred in a ground-floor apartment in the 2700 block of Northeast 30th Place in your town at 1:12 a.m. today. Four fire engines and 16 firefighters responded at 1:15 a.m. Cause of fire: A stove was turned on, and some cookbooks and towels on the stove ignited. When firefighters arrived, they found a 2½-year-old cocker spaniel at the front door. Estimated damage: $9,000 smoke damage to apartment. Other units not affected. Apartment is uninhabitable. Dog's name is Tito. McInerny said the dog apparently started the fire by jumping on the stove, using one of the knobs for foothold. The setting on the burner was on medium high. The dog was apparently looking for food. The dog crawled to the front door. "The dog was clinically dead; it had no pulse and no respiration." McInerny said firefighter Bill Mock took the dog outside and gave it cardiopulmonary resuscitation and oxygen, and the dog came back to life. The dog was taken to the animal hospital and treated for smoke inhalation. McInerny said it is not unusual for dogs to be caught in house fires, but it is unusual for them to be revived from the dead. "That's twice in a little more than a year we've revived dogs that have been clinically dead as a result of a fire. We're getting pretty good at it."

You interview Mark Alan Leszczynski, who rented the apartment and owns the dog. He said he and a house guest went to a bar before midnight and left the dog alone. "The dog is a little mischievous. I've caught him doing this before. He has a never-ending appetite. I had just reprimanded him for going into my house guest's suitcase and stealing some candy."

STANDARD OFFENSE REPORT
FRONT PAGE OPEN PUBLIC RECORD

On View √ Dispatched √ Citizen	Name of Agency Your town police dept.	Agency No. 0230100	Case No. 03-123456

Incident

Date offense started Use yesterday's date	Time 0700	Date offense ended Use today's date	Time ------	Date of report Today's date
Location of Offense 2339 Felony Lane	Time reported 22:36	Time arrived 22:40	Time cleared 22:55	

Offense

Description Burglary	Premise	Method of Entry Force √ No Force	Type of Theft From building	Type of Force Unknown

Victim

Name of Victim Last First Middle Smith Jon J.	Address Street 2339 Felony Lane	City Your town	State Yours	ZIP Yours	Telephone no. 555-1234

Type of victim Individual	Race W	Sex M	Age 22	Ethnicity ----	Height 6-0	Weight 195	Hair Blond	Eyes Blu	License -----	Social Security No 131-300-0123

Reporting Person

Last First Middle Doe James Brian	Address Street 2337 Felony Lane	City Your town	State Yours	ZIP Yours	Telephone no. 555-4321

Type of victim Individual	Race W	Sex M	Age 25	Ethnicity ----	Height 5-10	Weight 170	Hair Br	Eyes Br	License -----	Social Security No 171-009-0554

Property Description - Type of Loss
1=None 2=Burned 3=Counterfeit 4=Destroyed/damaged /vandalized 5=Recovered 6= Seized 7= Stolen 8 = Unknown

Type Loss	Property Code	Description	Est. Quantity	Value	Date Recovered
7	0618	Zenith VCR	1	300	-------------
7	0618	Sharp CD player	1	350	-------------
7	1002	Cockatoo (bird)	1	1,500	-------------

Reporting Officer John Law	Badge No. 733	Date Today	Copies to Property Total 2,150	

Description of incident

At 22:56 the office was contacted by Mr. James Doe, next-door neighbor of the victim. He was watching Mr. Smith's house while Smith was away. Doe checked the door to Smith's residence at 07:00 before he went to work. When he returned home at 22:30, he again checked Smith's residence and noticed that someone had pried the deadbolt lock on the front door. I was dispatched to the residence. I searched premises but did not find any suspects. When Mr. Smith returned home, he advised that items missing were VCR, CD player and cockatoo, who answers to the name of Homer. Owner described bird as white and 10 years old. He said the bird could say his name and had limited vocabulary of "damn," "rotten" and a few curse words.

3 Court terms: You may use your imagination for this exercise. The point of it is to see if you can use court terminology in the proper context and spell the words correctly. Use the following terms: *change of venue, affidavit, felony, misdemeanor, subpoena, mistrial, bond, arraignment, suspended sentence, plea bargain.*

Use the terms to write a story about this situation: A college student, 19, named Gold E. Locks, has been charged with a felony: breaking and entering into the home of Pa Pa Bear and his wife, Ma Ma Bear, who live at (you decide the address) with their child, Bay B. Bear.

4 Civil court case: Write a brief story about the following case, a petition for a name change, which was filed in the civil section of a county court (use your county court).

IN THE CIRCUIT COURT OF (YOUR COUNTY, YOUR STATE)

Joseph Weirdo, Petitioner   Case No. 99 C638

PETITION

Comes now the petitioner, Joseph Weirdo, and prays his cause of action and states as follows:

1 That he resides at 700 Louisiana St., Your City, Your State.

2 That the petitioner requests a change of name from Joseph Weirdo to Joseph Weir.

3 That the current name of the petitioner has caused him great embarrassment and suffering.

4 That petitioner is a citizen in good standing and the request for the name change is not to avoid any legal actions against said petitioner.

5 That petitioner is not seeking for redress as a means of avoiding any debts owed to any parties.

6 Wherefore, petitioner prays for favorable judgment from the court.

Joseph Weirdo
City, State, ZIP Code
On behalf of himself

You call Joseph Weirdo, and he tells you he was tired of being kidded about his name. "I didn't want to go through life being a Weirdo," he says.

You check with Circuit Court Judge Jack Musselman, who approved the petition. He says he signs hundreds of these, but most of them are name-change petitions from divorced women, foster children who want to take the name of the family they have stayed with or people with "an extremely ethnic name." "I can't recall anyone looking to play games. A lot of times people are trying to avoid creditors. There's no way of checking that out."

The court clerk tells you that more than 300 people filed to have their names changed this year. It costs $200 to file the papers.

Check out the "Trial" and "Music Download Lawsuit" scenarios in NewsScene for interactive exercises that will help to reinforce many of the themes presented in this chapter.

COACHING TIPS

Seek **human-interest stories** and anecdotes.

Check **social media** for Twitter, Facebook, blogs and other citizen journalism accounts.

Get information to **reconstruct a chronology of events.**

Use **descriptive and narrative** techniques for sidebars.

Double-check all information; initial reports and statistics will change quickly.

Use **role-playing** reporting techniques: If you were a relative of someone in a tragedy, what would you want and need to know?

Plan **highlights boxes** and empowerment boxes to provide survival tips.

Check the Internet for **weather and disaster resources.**

Use online sources for **background perspective**.

jam4travel/Shutterstock.com

Death is always and under all circumstances a tragedy, for if it is not, then it means that life itself has become one.

— THEODORE ROOSEVELT

CHAPTER 21
Disasters, Weather and Tragedies

DAVID HANDSCHUH WAS BURIED ALIVE. A PHOTOGRAPHER FOR THE *NEW YORK Daily News,* Handschuh was driving to New York University to begin his first day as an adjunct professor of a photojournalism class. It was the morning of Sept. 11, 2001. He looked up and saw a mass of smoke. He turned on his police scanner and heard a voice screaming: "Send every piece of apparatus; the World Trade Center is on fire."

He called his newspaper and then called NYU to tell them to post a note that he would be "a little late this morning."

"All we knew is that it was an accident," Handschuh recalled. He said he turned his car around and crossed over the center divider of the highway to head toward the towers. As a photographer who had shot hundreds of fires, he knew many of the city's firefighters. He passed a fire truck with 11 firefighters who were waving to him. "All 11 firefighters in that truck died," Handschuh said. "They were on their way to their own funeral, and they didn't know it."

It was just one of many traumatic moments Handschuh would experience on that day and long after the terrorist attack of Sept. 11, 2001, in which 2,749 people died when two hijacked planes crashed into the World Trade Center towers in New York City. Terrorists had also hijacked two other commercial jetliners on that day and crashed one of them into the Pentagon; a fourth plane, headed toward Washington, D.C., plummeted into a field outside of Pittsburgh, Pa.

Although many other tragedies have occurred since then, the terrorist attack on 9/11 will endure as one of the most significant events in U.S. history. In 2011, after 10 years of searching for

David Handschuh.

Osama bin Laden, the leader of the al-Qaida terrorist organization responsible for the attack, a U.S. military team succeeded in finding and killing him at the compound where he was hiding in Pakistan. In announcing his death, President Barack Obama said, "For over two decades, bin Laden has been al-Qaida's leader and symbol and has continued to plot attacks against our country and our friends and allies. The death of bin Laden marks the most significant achievement to date in our nation's effort to defeat al-Qaida. Yet his death does not mark the end of our effort. There's no doubt that al-Qaida will continue to pursue attacks against us. We must — and we will — remain vigilant at home and abroad."

For many of the families who lost loved ones and for survivors of those attacks, bin Laden's death does not erase the pain or memories of that September day in 2011.

The first attack in New York was at 8:46 a.m., and Handschuh arrived at the scene at 8:48 a.m., one of the only times he remembers that day. "At that time only one plane had hit the towers," Handschuh said. "The streets of New York were eerily quiet, as though somebody had pressed a mute button." Eighteen minutes later the second plane slammed into the south tower.

Handschuh kept shooting photos. About an hour later the south tower started to collapse. "I was standing across the street," Handschuh said. "A voice in the back of my head said, 'Run.' It was like a wave at the beach. I was running one second and flying the next. The impact of the building tossed fire trucks. I wound up partially under a fire truck. I was buried alive. I never lost consciousness, I don't think. I couldn't move my legs. A fireman came and said, 'Don't worry, Brother, we'll get you out. You're hurt but you're alive.'"

For the next nine months he went through physical therapy. "I had to learn how to walk again," he said. His right leg had been completely crushed, and his left leg had also been "messed up." His nose and mouth had been clogged with ashes. His breathing and his lungs remain only at 50 percent capacity. But even now, several years after the 9/11 tragedy, that experience scarred him in less visible but equally significant ways. He still pauses when he hears a plane overhead.

"I never want to photograph anyone dead or dying again," Handschuh says. So these days he is a food photographer.

Working with the Dart Center for Journalism & Trauma (*www.dartcenter.org*), Handschuh spends some of his time coaching journalists on how to deal with post-traumatic stress disorder, which can result from reporting and photographing tragedy. The center, based at the University of Washington, provides tips and tools to help journalists understand how to cover tragedies and how to cope with their own emotional stress that can result from this type of

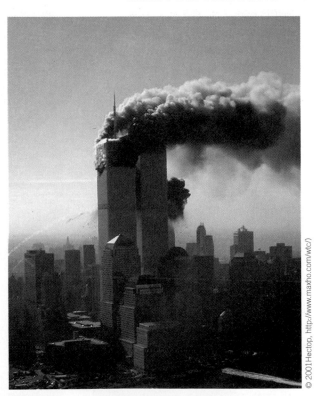

© 2001 Hectop, http://www.maxho.com/wtc/)

The World Trade Center towers shortly after planes crashed into them.

Cleanup at the world Trade Center disaster area in New York.

journalism. Until recently, little attention had ever been paid to the toll that disaster coverage can take on journalists who have to stifle their own emotions as they report and photograph the trauma of tragedy victims. But during these tragedies, journalists excel and suppress their own feelings to fulfill their mission to inform the public. Despite the personal toll, Handschuh stresses the crucial role of journalists by saying, "Our work became history."

Images from that tragedy will be seared in people's minds and in history. "We have to take those pictures," Handschuh says, "but we don't have to publish them. These were some very tough calls."

Associated Press photographer Richard Drew captured a haunting image of a man falling headfirst from one of the twin towers of the World Trade Center. His photo became the subject of ethical discussions in newsrooms around the country as editors debated whether to use it. Many did.

Bill Marimow, former editor of *The Philadelphia Inquirer,* was one of them. "The horror of the event determines the use of the photos," he wrote in an article for The American Press Institute. "There are so many other things that we can adjust to minimize the sensitivity aspect, but we must not minimize the horror of the event."

After bin Laden was shot and killed, the media again debated the ethics of whether they should publish gory photos of his body. However, President Obama decided that the photos should not be released. "It is important for us to make sure that very graphic photos of somebody who was shot in the head are not floating around as an incitement to additional violence or as a propaganda tool," he said.

But in 2001 reporters and editors faced a more difficult task: how to convey the significance and the emotional toll of the attacks that destroyed thousands of lives.

Of the 2,749 people who died in the 9/11 attacks, the remains of more than 1,000 victims were never identified, and efforts to analyze the DNA from remains have ended. The pain has not ended for families of the victims, and their stories explain the tragedy that lingers behind the numbers.

> The news was disheartening for many families who say they can't find closure when they don't have a body part to place in a coffin and bury in a grave.
>
> Joan Greene, 72, of Staten Island, said she knew in her heart that the chances of getting back remains of her daughter Lorraine Lee were not good, but had held out hope.
>
> "This is very hard," Greene said. "I just wish I could have something of her. It's hard to put into words but I need something to go to in the cemetery to think that part of her is there. It feels very empty."
>
> — LINDSAY FARBER AND CAROL EISENBERG, *New York Newsday*

In 2004 a natural disaster usurped the death toll of 9/11. More than 180,000 people were believed to have died and another 100,000 were missing in more than 12 Southeast Asian countries bordering the Indian Ocean when an earthquake spawned a massive wall of water called a "tsunami" that swept entire towns and their inhabitants into the sea. It happened the day after Christmas in 2004, and months later, the search continued for victims of one of the world's worst natural disasters in 100 years. The final death toll may never be known.

But again the story was best told not by numbers but by the human toll on individuals — some searching for loved ones and others who witnessed the devastation and lived to describe it. Like this excerpt from a *Tampa Tribune* story:

> HAMBANTOTA, Sri Lanka — When T.D. Kamaldeen's toddler son asks where his Mama is, he tells him she's working abroad, making money to buy him chocolate. Or maybe a bicycle.
>
> Sometimes the 3-year-old boy with big brown eyes wants to call and talk to Mama. Kamaldeen doesn't know what to say. How do you tell a child his mother, grandmother, aunt, uncle and cousins — nine people in all — died in the ferocious water that he saw take his house?

Throughout the U.S., news organizations sought local angles for the story by writing about disaster-relief efforts in their area and finding people personally affected by the tragedy.

Joe Hight, director of information and development at *The Oklahoman* in Oklahoma City, stressed the importance of covering tragedy with sensitivity. In an article for the Dart Center for Journalism & Trauma, he reflected on the bombing of a federal building in his city.

"The bombing aftermath taught me the impact of your coverage on the victims, community and journalists," he wrote. "It taught me that a tough journalist could be a sensitive journalist. And it taught me that we live in a world in which violent acts can occur anywhere at anytime, even on a nice and sunny spring day in your community."

It was in that unlikely place that journalism students at the University of Oklahoma learned how to cover a disaster that was not a class exercise.

Joy Mathis was sitting at her desk in *The Oklahoma Daily* newsroom at 9 a.m. on April 19, 1995, when someone ran in and said there had been a bomb explosion in Oklahoma City. Terrorists had bombed a nine-story federal building in Oklahoma City, 20 miles from the campus in Norman, Okla.

As managing editor of the campus newspaper, Mathis tried to find reporters to send to the scene. "No one realized what a big deal it was," she said. But within an hour after the news broke, reporters started calling Mathis and asking what they could do. Mathis didn't have a specific plan. "I was just screaming at people. I was saying, 'Get University of Oklahoma angles.' That's the kind of story I knew we could do better than anyone else."

At that time, it was the worst-known terrorist attack in the United States. Timothy McVeigh, the terrorist who bombed the building, was later convicted and executed. His accomplice, Terry Nichols, was sentenced to life in prison. The federal building was razed, and a permanent memorial and museum have been erected on the site. The memorial site includes a reflecting pool and 168 empty metal chairs, one for each of the bombing victims, each on a glass base inscribed with the name of a victim.

Like the indelible inscriptions for the victims, that tragedy remains etched in the memories of the Oklahoma students, and their coverage still serves as a lesson on how to report and write about tragedy. Within hours after the bombing occurred, Mathis had at least 20 reporters and photographers gathering news on the scene in the city and around the campus. The coverage wasn't organized at this point.

ETHICS

YOU ARE THE NEWS editor for a newspaper or television station in your community, and the photographer has shot images of dead bodies along with several other photos of an airplane disaster scene. The photos of the bodies strewn around the crash site are the most dramatic. Until the disasters of 9/11 and subsequent images from the war in Iraq, most U.S. media did not run photos of dead bodies. However, that changed after the 9/11 terrorist attack. Will you print or air these photos? If so, how will you justify it to the victims' families? Would you have published a photo of Osama bin Laden's body if it had been released?

Guidelines: The National Press Photographers Association's code of ethics states, "Photographic and video images can reveal great truths, expose wrongdoing and neglect, inspire hope and understanding and connect people around the globe through the language of visual understanding. Photographs can also cause great harm if they are callously intrusive or are manipulated. Treat all subjects with respect and dignity. Give special consideration to vulnerable subjects and compassion to victims of crime or tragedy. Intrude on private moments of grief only when the public has an overriding and justifiable need to see."

Courtesy of the Federal Emergency Management Agency.

Alfred P. Murrah building after it was bombed.

By 7 p.m., most of the reporters and photographers had returned. Mathis and Tiffany Pape, editor of the newspaper, began organizing the stories and planning the pages.

"I was feeling a little panicky because we were just getting organized, and the reporters were freaking because they didn't have much time to write," Mathis said. "But by 8 p.m. we had every editor reading stories." Their 16-page newspaper included six pages of explosion news and photographs, graphics and information boxes about where to donate blood or get more information.

Photo by Anita Amarfio, Courtesy of The Oklahoma Daily.

Omar L. Gallaga (left) and Joy Mathis work on a story about the Oklahoma City bombing.

Omar L. Gallaga had kept his emotions in check most of the day. Now he was tired. He returned to the newsroom and then headed for Norman Regional Hospital and the Norman Red Cross. But coverage wouldn't be easy.

"At the hospital a doctor said they had their first explosion victim," Gallaga said. "The man had been walking into an elevator when the building exploded. This was exactly what I'd been waiting and hoping for. Just when I felt it was time to approach the slightly wounded man, the (public relations) woman came in. She forbade me to speak to any patients." Everyone else was too busy to speak to him.

He headed for the Red Cross. He had better luck there. People were lined up for about two hours to give blood. He went to the waiting room. "In that waiting room I saw a poster whose content would become the lead for one of my bombing stories. It read ominously, 'A disaster can happen in any place, at any time!' WOW. I scribbled it down. I talked to some students who were getting ready to donate and left the scene. I returned to the newsroom where I would spend the rest of the day and night."

Gallaga was emotionally composed until he read Rudolf Isaza's story about a grandmother who was awaiting news about her two grandchildren, ages 5 and 3, who had been in the federal building's daycare center. The woman had told Isaza about the youngest one:

> "He liked to draw," she said. "Just the other day he showed me a drawing of a tall and short man. I asked him who it was. He said it was Shaquille O'Neal and me."
> Seconds later, she was rushed into the hospital with the hope that there was some news of her grandchildren. After looking through pages of hospital fatalities and treated people, there came a tragic cry.
>
> — RUDOLF ISAZA, *The Oklahoma Daily*

"I began to cry when I read that," Gallaga said. "As the night wore on, we all pitched in to edit stories, and the stress was starting to wear us down."

It was close to deadline. Midnight came and went. By 12:30, only a half hour after deadline, the paper was ready for the printer.

The techniques of reporting and writing these stories are the same as for any other story. But there are some differences in how you gather the information.

REPORTING TECHNIQUES

Before you venture out of the newsroom to report on a disaster, you should find out a few facts and take emergency precautions and supplies. Many major metropolitan newspapers have plans for covering disasters.

Cities also have disaster plans, and police and fire departments frequently conduct drills to test them. If you have a municipal beat, find out if the government has such a plan, and get a copy of it. If a disaster occurs, a good follow-up story is to check whether the plan was effective.

These tips are not only crucial for reporters in print and broadcast media, they also apply to public relations practitioners who might work for nonprofit organizations such as the American Red Cross or other agencies.

In the event of a disaster, you should follow these basic procedures before leaving your office or home:

- Check a map or use your GPS application on your mobile phone to see what routes lead to the scene. Are there alternative routes in case major arteries are blocked?

- Find out if temporary headquarters have been established for officials and media.

- Make sure that your cell phone is fully charged. Make sure that you have the right e-mail addresses and phone numbers stored in your computer or cell phone. If you are calling in your story on deadline, remember that information changes frequently, and you will need to keep updating your editors.

- Take proper clothing, if necessary: boots, rain gear, a change of clothes (in cases of flood coverage) and emergency rations — food and beverages if you think you'll be stuck somewhere for an extended period, flashlight and so on. You could be reporting for a long time in an area without utilities. It's a good idea to have this emergency kit of supplies in your car at all times.

- Make sure that you have a full tank of gas for your vehicle.

- Take plenty of notebooks, pens and even pencils, which are better than pens or electronic gear in rainy weather. Don't rely on electronic equipment — cell phones, notebook computers, tablets or other e-media, at the scene of a disaster.

When you are covering the breaking news of a plane crash or earthquake or you are in the middle of a major storm, the sources of information are disorganized and unreliable. The news changes momentarily. The death toll often changes radically within the first few hours and even weeks or months later in a major disaster. Chaos reigns. You get the best information you can from eyewitnesses and officials at the scene. And then you check back repeatedly.

How do you know what to ask? You always need to ask the basics: who, what, when, where, why and how. But another way of thinking about questions is role-playing, the "what if" technique of reporting. What if I were in this person's place? What if I were waiting to find out about a relative? What would I want to know?

For example, what if it is spring or winter break and you are expecting friends or relatives to visit you? Suddenly you hear over the radio that a plane has crashed at the international airport closest to you. What do you want to know? Make a list. Chances are that the information you want to know is the kind of information any reader would want to know. What airline, what plane, how many people died, who died, who survived, what caused the crash, how did it happen, where did it crash? Those questions will produce information for your lead and the top of your story. Then you gather details.

Think statistics. You need specifics: numbers of people killed or injured or evacuated for the story and for graphics that your newspaper or TV news program might display.

Think human interest. How did people cope? How did they survive? What are their losses? What are their tragedies? Three hundred people could die in a plane crash, but the human-interest stories of a few people make that crash vivid and poignant for the reader.

Think about narrative storytelling techniques for sidebars. How would you reconstruct the incident — what was the chronology? Try to gather information about the sequence of events if the story involves such disasters as explosions, plane crashes and other events that are not acts of nature. However, even with tornadoes, earthquakes, floods and hurricanes, it helps to get the sequence of events — specific times that events occurred, the minutes involved in destruction.

Think about helpful information for empowerment boxes. Where can people get more information, donate blood, volunteer their services and so on?

SOCIAL MEDIA

SOCIAL MEDIA sites have changed the ability of journalists to report breaking news and to gather information from citizens who are witnessing the events or are affected by them. You can tweet updates constantly to inform your readers of moment-by-moment changes in a disaster or tragic event. Other social media forms that are being used effectively during tragic events include Facebook, YouTube, Flickr for photos and Twitter to engage the community of readers and viewers in a breaking news event. Although on-site reporting is still crucial in a disaster, social media sites make it easier to gather human interest stories and sources for follow-up stories.

Government and disaster agencies also use social media to post information via tweets, Facebook pages and other sites to provide people with helpful information during a disaster. You can follow agencies like the Red Cross on their website, Twitter, blogs and Facebook for information about their relief efforts. One Red Cross survey found that the more than half of the respondents said they would use social media sites to seek help or send messages if other people needed help.

Sidebars

Sidebars are not synonymous with soft news. Many sidebars are human-interest stories, but they also can be hard-news stories or informational self-help stories. A sidebar is basically a story that gives the reader some new information or more information than the main story, called a "mainbar," can provide. The main story in a disaster story is comprehensive; each sidebar should be very narrowly focused on one topic. The mainbar can allude to information that is in the sidebar, such as a quote from an eyewitness, but the sidebar should not be repetitive. A mainbar without emotional quotes from people would be boring. However, an entire sidebar about the people who have been quoted extensively in the mainbar is too repetitive.

Here are some ideas for sidebars and some questions you can ask to determine whether you need them:

Helpfulness: If I were the reader, what information would I find helpful? For example, if a disaster affects utilities, as in a flood, consider a sidebar on how to cope without electricity or fresh water. If it affects roads, consider a story about alternate routes or when homes and businesses are destroyed, plan a story about how to get government aid.

Human Interest: Is there a human-interest story that the reader might find compelling? Does someone have a story that is unusual?

Perspective: Would the reader find it interesting to know the history of other disasters of this type?

The Location: Is there a color piece that is compelling about the scene or a location affected by the disaster, such as a story about the hospital scene or the shelters where evacuated people were taken?

Other Angles: Is there enough information worth telling about a specific angle of the story, such as the rescue efforts, the efforts of investigators or previous problems with that type of aircraft?

Analysis: If your community has been working on a disaster plan, is there a need for an analysis piece about how rescue or government workers coordinated the disaster operations?

In most cases, especially in human-interest sidebars, you can use all the feature techniques of descriptive and narrative writing that you have studied. You should try to make the story vivid and compelling.

A sidebar still stands alone as a story, so you need to insert a reference to the main news — a brief line about the disaster or crash — especially if you have only one sidebar. If you have a huge package of several sidebars, you don't need to rehash the news statement in each one. You need to coordinate with the editor just how much of the main news needs to be in your story.

Here is an excerpt from a sidebar to the students' Oklahoma City bombing package:

EXPLOSION PROMPTS BLOOD DRIVES, DONATIONS

An ominous poster hangs in a room of the Cleveland County Red Cross. It reads, "Disaster can strike anywhere, at any time!"

As Norman residents lined up to donate blood and supplies, conversation kept going back to the explosion that ripped through downtown Oklahoma City, leaving fatalities and shock in its wake.

When the Red Cross opened its doors at 10:30 a.m., about 100 people were waiting to give blood, said Kelly Walsh, director of Red Cross donor services in Cleveland County. Kelly said her organization will continue to accept blood of all types. "We'll need blood tomorrow, the next day and next week." Particularly, the Red Cross is looking for type O blood, which can be used universally. However, Walsh said, "We need all types because all types of blood can be used for platelets."

The Red Cross will stay open until people stop coming in and as long as the staff lasts, Walsh said. Extended hours will be kept for the remainder of the week.

Those donating blood waited an average of two hours while volunteers and about 20 staff members took donations and brought in food and supplies.

Anthony Johnson, an OU microbiology sophomore, waited to donate with a group of friends. Johnson said he was angered by the bombing. "It was a big mistake. You just don't do that. Not in this country. Not in this state."

— OMAR GALLAGA, *The Oklahoma Daily*

Graphics

Think in multimedia terms. Almost all disaster stories in print, broadcast and on the Web, are accompanied by graphics — maps, illustrations, charts — to help the reader visualize where, when and how. The job of supplying information to the graphic designer or artist falls to the news reporter.

You need to gather details. Use a mapping application to pinpoint exact locations: cross streets and measurements in yards or feet of where the accident, explosion or plane crash occurred. Consider whether the incident lends itself to a graphic using the time of the accident. Get a chronology in minutes or hours.

Disaster Basics

Whether you are a covering a natural disaster, such as an earthquake, or another kind, such as a plane crash or explosion, you need to gather some basic facts. With the exception of the five W's, which come first, the rest of the items are not listed in order of importance.

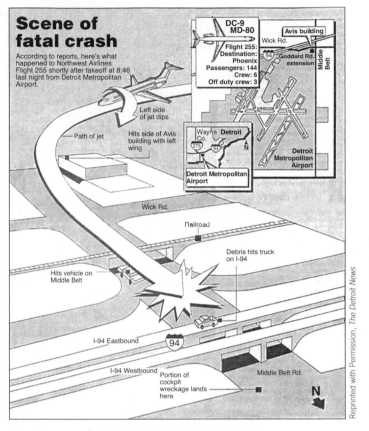

Graphic accompanying story about a plane crash.

Who: How many people died or were injured, and how many survived? These numbers will change constantly, but "who" should be one of your first questions. In a plane crash, get the name of the airline, the flight number and type of aircraft, takeoff and destination sites and the number of passengers and crew members on board.

What and Why: In many disasters, particularly airplane crashes, the cause is not immediately known. However, you should always ask and keep asking for follow-up stories. In natural disasters, get statistics about the height of rivers in floods, the intensity of earthquakes, the velocity of winds in hurricanes and similar information.

When and Where: Find out exactly what time the disaster occurred and the location. Consider graphics and a reconstruction of the event.

Weather: For a weather-related disaster, get the specifics. If it is a plane crash, always find out about the weather, which could have been a factor.

Where People Go: In case of evacuation — as in floods, hurricanes and earthquakes — find out where people are finding shelter.

Hospitals: Whenever people are injured, check hospitals.

CONVERGENCE COACH

WHEN 33 PEOPLE died at Virginia Polytechnic Institute in 2007 during the worst campus shooting in U.S. history, social networking sites and blogs became a primary source for parents, students and other people desperately seeking information about their loved ones. The first video of the shooting was sent to CNN by a student who took the images on his cell phone. Other images of the campus after the shooting were posted on a photo-sharing site, Flickr.

The shooter, Seung-Hui Cho, a senior English major at Virginia Tech, began his rampage about 7 a.m. on April 16, and almost two hours later, he went to a classroom building and shot 32 students and professors before killing himself. The university was widely criticized for failing to alert students via text messages or other means after the first shooting. The tragedy prompted many universities to examine ways of notifying students, faculty and staff members in such crises. The event also emphasized the role that social networking sites play in conveying information during a tragedy.

Virginia Tech students posted messages on Facebook, blogs and other sites to find and provide information. And journalists turned to these sites as well to find sources for first-hand accounts of the tragedy.

This tragedy offers a lesson in how you need to think in multimedia terms when you cover a disaster.

- Plan to post information immediately to your organization's website.
- Check social networking sites and blogs for information, but don't trust the material as accurate. Check with the sources if possible.
- Provide links on your company's website to consumer information such as the Red Cross and other agencies.
- Offer ways to have citizen journalists contribute to your reports.
- Provide perspective about similar tragedies by creating time lines or lists of other disasters.
- Use the Web to provide interactive graphics if possible.

Disaster Scene: Gather every detail of sight, sound, emotion and other sensory feelings. You will need them for description in your stories.

Estimated Cost of Damages and Property Loss: Initially, these accounts — from insurance agents, fire departments, police officials or state offices — are often inaccurate, but they add an essential element to the story.

Eyewitness Accounts: Get accounts from eyewitnesses and survivors. People make the story real and emotional. You need them for quotes in the main story and for sidebars. Ask people to reconstruct where they were and what they were doing at the time of the disaster.

Government Agencies Involved: In plane crashes, the Federal Aviation Administration and National Transportation Safety Board always get involved in investigations. In major disasters, find out whether the National Guard is helping and which federal, state and local agencies will provide relief.

Consumer Information: Find out where to go to give blood, to get help with insurance or rebuilding, to get further information. Consumer information may be included in your story or in empowerment boxes.

Red Cross and Shelters: Always check with the Red Cross and other relief agencies for their role and their needs.

Safety Precautions: Check with police and fire departments and with electric, gas and water utility companies to find out about the precautions people should take. You could refer to dangerous conditions in the main story or in a separate story.

Roads: Check highway departments to find out which roads are closed or dangerous and what alternate routes people can take.

Survivors: List those who are known to be alive.

Victims: The names of people who were killed are often not released for days, but try to obtain them from officials.

Crime: Check with police to find out about looting or other post-disaster crimes or arrests in cases of human-created disasters.

Perspective: Was this the worst, second-worst or ninth-worst disaster of its kind in a certain period of time? Check online sources or an almanac to find out how this disaster ranks against previous disasters of its kind. If it is the worst of its type, that information should appear high in the story.

Background: Check the background of the airline involved in a plane crash or a business involved in a disaster. Readers will be interested in any history that may apply to this disaster.

Medical Examiner: Check for information about progress in the identification of victims.

Here is how many of those basic elements worked in *The Oklahoma Daily's* first-day story by Rudolf Isaza about the bombing in Oklahoma City. Many descriptive human-interest stories were in sidebars or some of the 14 other stories.

BOMB CRIPPLES OKLAHOMA CITY

Explosion leaves 31 dead, 300 missing

At least 31 people died and 300 were still missing Wednesday after a car bomb gouged a nine-story hole in a federal office building.

A 9:04 a.m. explosion ravaged the north side of the Alfred Murrah Federal Building at 200 NW Fifth St. in downtown Oklahoma City. Most of the more than 500 employees were in their offices.

As of midnight Wednesday, the confirmed death toll was 31 people, 12 of those children.

About 300 people were missing. At least 200 people were injured, 58 critically, said Fire Chief Gary Marrs. Many more were feared trapped in the rubble.

"Firefighters are having to crawl over corpses in areas to get to people that are still alive," said Jon Hansen, assistant fire chief.

Gov. Frank Keating has called a state of emergency. Nationwide bomb experts from federal agencies have been called in to decipher the cause of the bombing. The Oklahoma National Guard was called in.

Keating said he was told by the FBI that authorities were initially looking for three people in a brown pickup truck. The Oklahoma Highway Patrol put out an all-points bulletin for three individuals, described as of Middle Eastern descent. One was described as being between the ages of 25 and 30. Another may have been between 35 and 38.

Bob Ricks, head of the Oklahoma City FBI office, said the blast left a crater 20 feet long and eight feet deep directly outside the building, meaning the source of the explosion was probably outside.

An architect said the building was stable and was not in immediate danger of falling over. Ricks said the shock was felt 50 miles away. Glass was reported shattered in businesses and homes within a 30-mile radius.

The search for people trapped in the rubble started as soon as the blast occurred, starting from the top floors down. People frantically looked for loved ones, including parents whose children were in the building's day-care center. Rescuers had problems initiating the search because the elevator shaft was destroyed in the blast.

"The only way up the building is one staircase," Marrs said.

Ricks would not speculate on any suspects. "We are making no assumptions at this point," he said. "We've had hundreds, if not thousands, of leads." By midday, the government had received calls from six people saying they were from Muslim sects and asserting they were responsible for the bombing.

A police source, who requested anonymity, said FBI agents were trying to piece together a van or truck that was believed to have carried the explosives. An axle of the vehicle was found about two blocks from the scene, the source said.

General concern was that this was a direct attack on the FBI. Ricks said although the FBI did not have an office in the building, 13 brother agencies did, including the Secret Service and the Bureau of Alcohol, Tobacco and Firearms.

Also destroyed, on the second floor on the northwest side, was America's Kids, a day-care center for federal and county employees. Seventeen children had been treated as of 10 p.m. Three were treated and released, and 20 were still unaccounted for.

Oklahoma City Chief of Police Sam Gonzalez said the Oklahoma City Police Department was in charge of perimeter control and monitoring streets, and has roped off four blocks in each direction.

Oklahoma City Mayor Ron Norick requested that all people who were in the building at the time of the explosion call 297-2424 or 397-2345 to get an accurate number of people inside the building.

— RUDOLF ISAZA, *The Oklahoma Daily*

Death Tolls

The day after the Oklahoma City bombing, the death toll had risen to 57. Each day thereafter, the number of dead and injured increased. The final toll was 168 people, including 19 children. The opposite situation occurred in the World Trade Center tragedy, where the death toll dropped from initial reports of more than 6,000 to about 3,000 a few months later and ultimately to 2,752.

In disasters, dealing with numbers of victims is difficult because they change constantly. The first day you can report the facts as Isaza did, saying "At least . . . ," or use the words "an estimated" with the specific number. The following day your lead can state that the death toll has increased, or you can just write the new death toll. You don't need to correct previous information. Readers know you haven't made an error; you are just giving the facts as they become available.

Interviews with Grief-Stricken People

You have a list of people who died. Your editor wants you to call the families of victims to get biographical data and reactions. What do you do? Quit your job? Cry? Get sick? Many reporters feel like doing all three. But there are sensitive ways to cover grief. And it's difficult, if not impossible, to avoid dealing with such situations if you are going to be a reporter. So here are some concerns students have expressed and some suggestions about how you can cover such stories.

What If the Person Hangs Up on Me? You could try calling back or try calling someone else. Another suggestion is to call a neighbor and ask if he knows someone in the house who might talk to you. You don't have to ask for the person who is in the greatest pain. If you are on the scene and the person does not want to talk to you, you might give him card (or a note with your name and phone number) and ask if you could talk at another time.

What Questions Do I Ask? Don't ask, "How do you feel about your son's death?" Obviously, the person feels terrible. You might instead ask specific questions about what the person was like — in other words, biographical questions. What was the person planning, or where was he going when the accident happened? Then you could ask for memories about the person.

What Is the First Thing I Should Say? Introduce yourself and state your purpose. You might also express your condolences.

What If I Start to Cry? You can be empathetic and even a little teary. Try not to weep. But be sincere. Do not fake your emotions.

What If the Person I'm Interviewing Starts to Cry? Stop interviewing and ask if you can get the person a glass of water or a tissue, or just be quiet for a while. You might also ask if the person would prefer you to come back another time, depending on the severity of the situation.

What If I Say Something Insensitive Without Knowing It? Apologize.

Why Do I Have to Interview People in Times of Grief? Because these types of stories make a news event more significant and real to readers. Because people relate to other people, not to vague generalities. And remember, for some people, talking about their pain is a form of catharsis. For others, grief is a very private matter. So some people will talk to you, and others won't. Respect their needs. You won't get every story, especially if reporters from other newspapers and television stations have already talked to them. But the ones you do talk to can be wonderful.

Here is an example of how reporters interviewed friends and relatives of people who died in a plane crash. Notice from the quotes that reporters did not ask "How do you feel?" The quotes and backup information contain specific memories and details about the people who died.

GRIEF CUTS WIDE SWATH

Relatives draw close as horror sinks in

BY JON PEPPER AND RACHEL REYNOLDS

The names of the dead trickled out slowly.

Among them was a professional basketball player. A weight lifter. A high school cheerleader and a successful businessman. A nursery school teacher from St. Clair Shores.

There were boyfriends and girlfriends, granddaughters and grandsons, husbands and wives.

None of the dead were positively identified by this morning. The few names that trickled out came from friends and relatives.

Kurt Dobronski, 28, vice-president of a Scottsdale, Ariz., construction firm and a former star football player at Dearborn Edsel Ford High and Central Michigan University, had come home to Dearborn for the wedding of a friend and found his 10-day visit "the best vacation he ever had," said brother Karl Dobronski.

"Things were going great for him," Karl Dobronski said. "This is a shock." Things were also going well for Nick Vanos, a 7-foot-2 center for the Phoenix Suns basketball team. After playing only sparingly in his first two years in the National Basketball Association, Vanos was expected to start for the Suns this fall. He had come to Detroit to visit a girlfriend and boarded Flight 255 for his return to Arizona, team officials said.

"Nick Vanos was a young man who was just beginning to come into his own as a professional athlete and was about to take a giant step," said Suns general manager Jerry Coangelo. "It was very sad because he gave everything he had with his abilities. . . ."

Bill Horton of Phoenix lost his wife, Cindy, 37, who had been visiting her parents in Wisconsin. She had flown to Detroit to catch a flight to Phoenix. At midnight Sunday, he tried to calm his two stepchildren, aged 11 and 7. "They're hysterical," Horton said, sobbing. "How do you explain something like this to them?"

— *The Detroit News*

Follow-Up Stories

All major disasters require follow-up stories for many days. The second-day story should attempt to explain the cause, if that was not clear the first day. If the cause still isn't clear, you can lead with what officials are investigating. If there isn't any new information, you can describe cleanup attempts at the scene. The death toll should remain in the lead, especially if it has changed from earlier reports, or should be in the first few paragraphs. Other follow-up stories may focus on rescue efforts, human-interest elements, cost of rebuilding or any other related news.

In follow-up stories, you still need to mention what happened — when and where the plane crashed, when the earthquake occurred and so on. In successive stories, that information can go a little bit lower. But it should still be high in the story on the second day.

Here is the second-day lead on the mainbar about the plane crash in Detroit:

Loose and broken parts caused the breakdown since mid-1985 of four jet engines like those on Northwest Flight 255, which crashed Sunday at Detroit Metropolitan Airport.

At least 154 people were killed after witnesses saw an explosion in or near the aircraft's left engine. However, the head of a National Transportation Safety Board team investigating the crash said other witnesses saw no such fire and "very preliminary" findings are that there was no failure or fire in the left engine.

Documents describing the engine failures, known to the Federal Aviation Administration (FAA) and the National Transportation Safety Board (NTSB) since April, were obtained in Washington Monday.

A U.S. Department of Transportation source claimed Monday that a serious fuel leak problem with the jet was reported by crew members less than two weeks ago. FAA officials refused to confirm such a report.

In Romulus, workers began the soul-bruising task of collecting human remains from the crash site for identification by pathologists, friends and relatives.

— RIC BOHY, FRED GIRARD, MIKE MARTINDALE AND JOEL SMITH,
The Detroit News

AIRPLANE CRASHES

You may never have to cover a major airplane crash, but small plane crashes occur in almost every community. The principles for writing and reporting the news are the same, regardless of the size of the crash.

Almost all the disaster-related information listed earlier also applies to an airplane crash. One of your first concerns should be the number of dead or injured people. Initially, you will get only estimates, and most likely they will be wrong. But some accounting of the death and injury toll should be in the lead.

Although an actual cause may not be known for months, ask anyway because you need some idea.

You should also seek the names, ages and hometowns of victims and survivors. In major plane crashes, the list of passengers and their status is usually not released for a day or more, until the relatives have been notified. The names and status of the pilots and crew members may be available sooner.

In addition to getting accounts from eyewitnesses, reactions from relatives or people at the airport and other human-interest stories, make sure that you get the following specifics: name of the airline and flight number of the plane; the type of plane and number of engines, especially for small planes; the origination and final destination sites.

Check for comments from the air controllers. The pilot's last words are usually not available until investigators get the plane's "black box" recording, but keep it in mind for follow-up stories.

Don't forget the perspective: how many plane crashes of this type have occurred in recent years or how this crash ranks in severity.

Here are excerpts from a plane crash story that illustrates most of the guidelines for disaster coverage in the first four paragraphs:

> A Northwest Airlines jet with 153 people aboard crashed just after takeoff Sunday night at Detroit Metropolitan Airport, killing at least 152 aboard and two people on the ground.
>
> A 4-year-old girl, found in the wreckage under the body of a woman assumed to be her mother, is thought to be the only surviving passenger.
>
> Witnesses said the airborne plane, Northwest Flight 255, burst into flames before coming down at the intersection of Middle Belt and Wick roads. Several cars were hit on the ground and at least two motorists were killed.
>
> The Northwest jet was carrying 151 passengers and six crew members when it departed from Metro runway 3-center at 8:46 bound for Phoenix.
>
> — *Adapted from The Detroit News*

NATURAL DISASTERS

All disaster stories should include the same basic information: death toll, survivors, eyewitness accounts, human-interest quotes from survivors and details of the scene and of recovery efforts. For natural disasters, add information about the natural forces at work, such as weather conditions.

Any time you are writing about a weather-related disaster, be sure to include a weather forecast. If you are covering floods, find out how high the river crested — if that was a factor — or the height of water in feet. If winds were a cause of the destruction, get the specific miles per hour of the wind velocity. In the case of an earthquake, find out the magnitude and the location of the epicenter. Explain in simple terms how the natural phenomenon occurred. A graphic may be better than words.

Tornadoes, earthquakes, hurricanes and floods all cause extensive damage and leave people homeless. Find out where people are finding shelter and what is being done to help them. Insurance is also a big factor in natural disasters. Include consumer information, such as areas that readers should avoid and the names of impassable streets, or how people can cope. Utilities are often affected, so make sure that you check about the safety of drinking water, food supplies and electricity.

Many of these consumer elements may be in sidebars. But when you write the first-day story, the format is similar to that of a plane crash or any other disaster. Give the basic facts and a death or injury toll in the lead.

FERNDALE, Calif. — A powerful earthquake rocked California's remote North Coast on Saturday, knocking brick facades off buildings, sparking fires that destroyed several businesses and two post offices and sending at least 35 people to hospitals with cuts, broken bones and chest pains.

— *Los Angeles Times*

Here are excerpts from a weather disaster story that include all the basic information and human elements. Note the vivid verbs, descriptive writing, pacing of long and short sentences and details of observation.

NAPA, SONOMA HIT BY FLOODS — AGAIN

Basic news lead

For the second time this winter, rain-swollen rivers flooded Napa and Sonoma county towns and vineyards Thursday, creating a colossal mess where weary residents were just getting their lives in order after fierce January storms.

Weather specifics

Howling out of the central Pacific, the storm slammed into the state late Wednesday with steady, torrential rain and winds blasting to 60 mph. And weather forecasters expect more of the same today.

But for a few brief respites, the relentless battering continued all day Thursday.

Power problems

Torrential rains overpowered small streams and larger rivers throughout the region, triggering floods and mudslides. High winds snapped electrical power to 540,000 customers from Big Sur to Eureka, closed highways and shut down shipping in San Francisco Bay. New snow blanketed the Sierra Nevada.

Numerous rivers and streams were at or near flood stage throughout Northern California.

Among communities threatened by the rising water were Susanville, Tehama and Hamilton City along the Sacramento River.

Forecast

The National Weather Service warned residents to brace for another wave of rain spinning in from a strong low-pressure system in the northeastern Pacific before dawn today.

Forecaster Brandt Maxwell at the National Weather Service's Monterey office said some areas could get as much as two inches of rain today. "Of course, any amount is going to aggravate flooding."

The rain is forecast to taper off this afternoon, with showers tonight and Saturday.

A winter storm warning was issued for the Sierra Nevada with snow levels forecast to range from 5,000 to 6,000 feet today. As much as three feet of snow could fall above the 7,000-foot elevation, according to the National Weather Service.

History/ perspective

It's starting to look like January, when a disastrous series of storms caused widespread flooding and $300 million in damage, killed 11 people and displaced thousands throughout California.

For residents of Napa and Sonoma counties, still recovering from the floods of January, it was an all too-familiar story.

In St. Helena, a small town in the Napa Valley wine country, the Napa River flooded vineyards, homes, apartments and a mobile home park. Firefighters evacuated more than 1,000 people as the river rose to 19 feet — six feet above flood stage.

Several hundred others were rescued from the Vineyard Valley Mobile Home Park, which survived the January floods. On Thursday, two-thirds of the 300 mobile homes were under water.

Emergency workers in small boats evacuated people through waist-deep water that blocked access to apartment complexes. But even the rescuers had troubles. One rowboat, caught in the swift current, floated down the Napa River for five miles before another boat came to its rescue.

Human interest

Malia Barron Hendricks, about to give birth to her second child, and her husband, Charles, found the road to the hospital blocked by floodwaters. So they drove to a fire station where firefighters helped deliver a healthy baby girl. The woman and her newborn, Hope Bridget Hendricks, eventually were taken to St. Helena Hospital by an ambulance that had to negotiate flooded streets.

Shortly after the birth, the firefighters shared a bottle of expensive Napa Valley sparkling wine with the new mother and father.

By late afternoon, a sheet of water four feet deep covered much of the eastern Napa Valley, isolating flooded farmhouses in inundated vineyards.

Farther south in Napa, the river was expected to rise four feet above flood level, flooding Soscol Avenue, a main business artery. Helpless onlookers watched water creep into the street, growing deeper by the minute.

Mark Townsend, 41, owner of Soscol Antiques, hurriedly tried to waterproof his store, sealing the doors with tape and sandbags, putting his wares as high on shelves as he could, and hauling away the most valuable items in pickup trucks. He lost $10,000 worth of antiques in the flood two months ago.

"It's a little hard, but you have to remember we are going home tonight, and home will have booze and an espresso machine," Townsend said, "and there are a lot of people who don't get to go home tonight."

— FRANK SWEENEY, JANET RAE-DUPREE AND MICHAEL DORGAN, *San Jose* (Calif.) *Mercury News*

WEATHER STORIES

Not all weather stories involve disaster coverage. Weather stories can be news or features about prolonged hot, cold, wet or dry spells or just a statistical roundup of rain or snow totals for the month or year. They also can be features about interesting aspects of the weather and the ways it affects people. When a major snowstorm or thunderstorm hits an area, a weather story is expected.

Weather stories also provide drama. In 2005, *Chicago Tribune* reporter Julia Keller won the Pulitzer Prize for reconstructing the terror created by a tornado that struck one block in downtown Utica, Ill., where eight people who huddled in the basement of a bar were killed. Keller was initially reluctant to do the feature story after the event because it had been so thoroughly covered by the media as breaking news. But she persevered for seven months as she pored over weather documents and conducted hundreds of interviews to write a compelling narrative account of just 10 seconds when the "wicked wind" had ripped through the town nearly a year before. The Pulitzer judges called it a "gripping, meticulously constructed account." Here is the lead on the first of three stories:

> Ten seconds. Count it: One. Two. Three. Four. Five. Six. Seven. Eight. Nine. Ten. Ten seconds was roughly how long it lasted. Nobody had a stopwatch, nothing can be proven definitively, but that's the consensus. The tornado that swooped through Utica at 6:09 p.m. April 20 took some 10 seconds to do what it did. Ten seconds is barely a flicker. It's a long, deep breath. It's no time at all. It's an eternity.
>
> If the sky could hold a grudge, it would look the way the sky looked over northern Illinois that day. Low, gray clouds stretched to the edges in a thin veneer of menace. Rain came and went, came and went, came and went. . . .
>
> The survivors would henceforth be haunted by the oldest, most vexing question of all: whether there is a destiny that shapes our fates or whether it is simply a matter of chance, of luck, of the way the wind blows.

Here are some other ideas for features about weather stories:

- Unusual patterns in weather for your area. Include why the weather patterns are occurring.
- Effects of weather on pets, businesses, people's moods, health. For example, many people suffer from seasonal affective disorder, a depressive state usually related to a lack of light in the winter.
- Insect infestation because of weather patterns.
- People whose occupations force them to work outside during very hot or cold spells.
- Effects of snow removal on city budgets: price of salt, sand, overtime for employees and so on.
- Excessive costs of air conditioning or heating on your school or city during hot or cold spells.
- Features about upcoming seasons.
- Consumer stories or sidebars about coping with extreme heat, cold, tornadoes, hurricanes, floods or earthquakes.

Regardless of whether you are writing a feature or a breaking-news story, include these elements in all weather stories:

Forecast: Always include the forecast for the next day or for an extended period, especially when you are writing about floods, droughts, weather-related fires, or hot or cold spells.

Unusual Angles: If the weather is unusual for your area or for the time of year, include explanations from weather forecasters.

Human Interest: Tell how people are coping. Focus on one or a few people who have interesting stories.

Warnings: Explain how extremely hot or cold weather affects people, especially very young or old people. Tell how to cope with or prevent problems. Also include warnings about keeping animals safe. Include any road or traffic information, such as road or bridge closings and alternate routes.

Records: Explain if the weather has broken any records or come near to breaking records, especially if you are doing a roundup of statistics or a story about unusual weather. Even if no records have been broken, put the weather statistics in perspective by comparing them to other months or years or using a graphic for the statistics.

Terms: Check your Associated Press Stylebook for definitions of weather terms. If you use such a word as *blizzard* or *hurricane,* define it by explaining how high the winds must be. In any flood story, explain the flood stages of a river and how far above or below flood stage the river is or when it is expected to crest to its highest level.

Here is a basic weather feature about an excessively hot day. It includes all the basic information, such as the forecast and human-interest elements. The writer, Cheryl Wittenauer, said she checked with the guard to make sure that she wouldn't get him fired by writing that he wasn't standing at the entrance he was supposed to guard. She also said she wanted to use the "screw it" quote "because that's the way people talk," but she cleared it first with her editor.

WEATHER FORECAST BLAZES ON

Temperatures to soar throughout weekend

At 5 o'clock, security guard Shawn Brown was halfway through his shift watching over a parking lot under construction at the downtown post office.

The Wells Fargo employee, beads of sweat popping from his brow, is supposed to take his post at the Edmond Street entrance, where the only shelter from the sun was the bill of his cap.

Nudged by the discomfort of a 102-degree heat index Wednesday, the outdoor worker deferred to his own judgment.

"Screw it," he said. "I'm staying here in the shade. . . . This is the only post without an air conditioner. It's my second day here in a row."

The day ushered in what is forecast to be a series of blazers with above-normal temperatures and wind.

"It's blast furnace-type weather," Weather Data meteorologist Jeff House said.

Today will be sunny with a high of 96. But it will only get worse. Temperatures Friday and Saturday will soar to a searing 99, with at least 50 percent humidity.

There could be slight relief Sunday and Monday if a "cold front" produces thunderstorms. Even with the cold front, highs would hover in the middle 90s.

The above-normal temperatures are the result of a strong ridge of high pressure in the upper levels of the atmosphere.

The average high for June 24 is 87 degrees. A record high of 103 was set in 1937.

Cooper, a black poodle mix, was one of seven lucky dogs that lost a winter coat Wednesday at Jeanne's Dog Grooming, 922 Alabama St.

"They come in miserable from the heat, but they're bouncing when they leave here," groomer Colleen Whitson said. "They love it. They feel so much better."

The steamy temperatures also drew people in search of quick relief to stores and social service agencies that could supply them with fans and air conditioners.

"Sales usually hit a peak when it turns hot like this," Sears salesman Bill Patrick said. "They're replacing ones that finally gave up on them."

The Economic Opportunity Corp., 817 Monterey St., has given away more than 100 air conditioners in a four-county region since June 1. The agency has fielded many additional requests from low-income clients the last few days.

AFL-CIO Community Services, 118 S. Fifth St., is seeking donations of fans and 110-volt air conditioners that plug into a standard outlet — and are in good working condition. The agency won't accept 220-volt air conditioning units because they require electrical wiring most clients' homes lack.

— CHERYL WITTENAUER, *St. Joseph* (Mo.) *News-Press*

EXERCISES

1 Grief reporting: How can you ask questions about grief? Try this classroom exercise: In groups of three or four, list all the fears and anxieties you have about interviewing people who are grieving. Then discuss some reporting techniques you can use to deal with each of these concerns. After compiling your concerns and solutions, discuss them with the class as a whole.

2 Disaster coverage: Brainstorm a package of stories about a disaster in your community. If you live in an area prone to weather disasters, such as earthquakes, tornadoes or floods, plan that type of coverage. Or you can brainstorm how you would cover a plane crash or an explosion in your community. List the stories you would do and places

you should go for reporting on the type of disaster you have identified.

3 Disaster plan: Develop a plan for how you would cover a weather disaster in your area. Make a list of agencies and sources you should contact. Write a list of key questions. Develop a sidebar of consumer information with links that you would post on your campus or community newspaper or news station's website.

4 Social media: Check Twitter, Facebook, YouTube and any other social media sites you think would be helpful to you in covering a disaster. Make a list of agencies that use social media sites you might follow. Note the type of information you can gather from these sites.

Check out the "Tornado" and "Big Fire" scenarios in NewsScene for interactive exercises that will help to reinforce many of the themes presented in this chapter.

COACHING TIPS

Adam Gregor/Shutterstock.com

Call the employer to ask who should receive your application. Find out the **person's title and gender** and how to spell his or her first and last name.

Research the companies to which you are applying by checking the Web or library resources. Find out if the prospective employer prefers a **printed or online application.** Many companies have online application forms.

Limit your cover letter to **one page.**

Proofread your application carefully for spelling and typographical errors.

Make a **follow-up telephone call or e-mail** a few weeks after you send your application.

Be careful about information you post in blogs or social networking sites that potential employers can find.

Check **online job sites,** journalism organizations and public relations associations for internships and career opportunities.

I guarantee that a prospective employer who doesn't already know you (and maybe one who does) will check you out online before calling your references, or possibly even before reading your résumé. . . . Through a blog, social networks and/or your personal website, make it easy for me to see how good you are.

— **STEVE BUTTRY,** journalism blogger and director of community engagement, *TBD.com*

CHAPTER 22
Media Jobs and Internships

ONCE UPON A TIME IF YOU WERE LOOKING FOR A JOB, YOU HAD TO submit an application letter and résumé on paper. You still do for many media jobs. But these days employers don't limit their search for candidates to the printed applications they receive. They might also search Facebook, YouTube, Twitter and similar sites. So beware of what you post on social networking sites. Potential employers might check out your blogs and social networking postings to find out more about who you really are. A video on YouTube showing your antics during Spring Break might be fun to share with friends but not with potential employers.

It's an asset to have multimedia skills. Video résumés may be desirable for some jobs, and many employers prefer online applications and résumés that include your websites. But don't forego the old-fashioned methods of applying for a job with a letter and printed résumé. That's especially important for media jobs, where writing well matters.

Good communication topped the list of most-desired skills sought by employers, according to recent surveys by the National Association of Colleges and Employers, a nonprofit association for college career services. Employers also cited the lack of communication skills as the major problem with new graduates.

"Many employers reported that students have trouble with grammar, can't write and lack presentation skills," according to a survey by the association. "Poor communication skills are often evident in the interview, where students are unable to articulate how what they have done relates or contributes to the position they are seeking."

In addition to good verbal communication skills, respondents to the 2011 survey cited a strong work ethic, teamwork, analytical skills and initiative as traits they seek most in new college graduates they would hire.

As students in media classes, you probably have an advantage in gaining good communication skills. But you may not know how to market yourself well. Unless you know how to write a good cover letter and résumé, even the best grade point average may not get you the job. You may also need to market yourself with digital skills especially in large corporations that circulate applications among their properties and companies that have a significant online operation.

Steve Buttry, a writing coach and journalism blogger who is also director of community engagement for the Washington, D.C., local news site *TBD.com*, stressed the importance of having a good profile on social media networks and websites. "The first thing most people are going to do if they check you out is Google you," he wrote in his blog "The Buttry Diary." "If I want to learn about someone, I am going to pay more attention to what I can find about that person online by myself than to what he or she sends me or tells me. So you should investigate your online profile and see how you look to others. . . . The image you present online is not more important than the work you can do. But you may not get to show what you can do if you don't show someone first in your digital profile."

If you had 140 characters to describe yourself on Twitter, what would you say? That's one way of creating a good headline or lead for your digital profile. You can also use the concept for a printed cover letter and résumé. Now think about how you would describe yourself to a prospective employer in one sentence in print or online. How would you persuade an employer that you are special and worth hiring? How can you tailor your application to the organization where you want to work? And how do you find jobs or internships?

These are some of the questions and answers this chapter will cover to help you find and apply for media jobs.

FINDING JOBS AND INTERNSHIPS

Q: How do you find internships and jobs?

A: The journalism and mass communications program at your school is a good starting place. It may list job and internship opportunities on bulletin boards or your department website. Professors in your department usually have good contacts in your field of study, so check with them as well. If you are seeking an opportunity at a specific news or public relations organization, check the website for that company. If you don't want to be limited to media jobs, the Associated Collegiate Press, (*www.studentpress.org*), offers a more inclusive job site as well as general sites like *jobster.com* and *monster.com*. The next step is to check several of the websites offering jobs and internships in media careers, some of which are mentioned in the next few answers.

Don't limit your search to media jobs sites even if you want to work in print, broadcast or public relations companies. Jobs abound for people with good writing and editing skills and media training — many in unlikely places. Consider some of these job ads:

- Online communications and community coordinator. Develops content on the company website, manages online discussions, pitches to bloggers. Must follow AP writing style and have ability to rapidly produce editorial and technical content.

That was an ad from a national chain that sells pet products.

- Writer/editor and reporter with a nose for news, a flair for creatively conveying it in writing and a talent for online and offline research skills. Writes news briefs for two weekly e-newletters and posts content on the association's Facebook and Twitter profiles.

That was an ad from the Society of American Florists.

- Social media strategist. Responsible for the company's engagement through social networks primarily with consumers and also employees.

That was from a dental services company.

The iPhone and iPad application for the U.S. federal government job site.

As you can see, media-related jobs are available in many companies. In addition, the U.S. government offers an extensive list of media-related jobs ranging from $50,000 to more than $150,000. Just access *www.usajobs.gov* and search for "media" to find hundreds of job opportunities. In addition, the website offers a special section for students and tutorials on how to write good résumés and applications.

Q: How do you find internships and jobs in newspapers?

A: If you want a job or internship at a particular newspaper, first check the newspaper's website. Most newspapers list jobs and internship openings on their sites. Several umbrella websites list searchable jobs and internships by state. The American Society of Newspaper Editors, *(asne.org)*, is one of them. Another excellent searchable site for jobs and internships is journalismjobs *(www.journalismjobs.com)*. These sites and others listed on our website for this chapter will give you more specific information than a general search in Google or Yahoo, which will refer you to these sites anyway. In addition, AOL Inc. is hiring hundreds of reporters and editors for its "hyperlocal" news operation Patch. Reporters and editors, who can work from home, produce local news information that does not usually get covered for communities. The company has operations in 800 towns and expects to continue adding more.

Q: How do you find internships and jobs in television or radio?

A: Some of the advice in the previous answer applies to broadcast jobs as well. First check the website of a specific station to see if job or internship opportunities are listed. The Radio Television Digital News Association, *(www.rtdna.org)*, the main organization representing the broadcast industry, is a good place to start. It offers a searchable job base as well as information about scholarships and career resources. Some websites specific to the broadcast industry also provide a searchable job databases. For example, TVJobs, *(www.tvjobs.com)*, contains an extensive list of jobs in television and radio as well as an e-résumé database where you can post your résumé. Others include TV Newser Jobs, (*www.mediabistro.com/tvnewser-jobs*), tvandradiojobs, (*www.tvandradiojobs.com*) and more linked to social media sites.

Q: **How do you find internships and jobs in public relations?**

A: The public relations field is so broad that you can find opportunities in government, corporations, marketing and public relations firms. A good place to start your search is with the umbrella organizations representing public relations such as The Public Relations Society of America, (*www.prsa.org*), and the International Association of Business Communicators, (*www.iabc.com*). Both have searchable databases by location or position. If your school has a chapter of the Public Relations Student Society of America, (*www.prssa.org*), you should consider joining because many student chapters offer networking and local job opportunities. Even if you don't

Job fairs are good places to network for jobs and internships.

Courtesy of the Peterson Air Force Base

have a local chapter, you can check the PRSSA site for internships and jobs. In some communities advertising and marketing firms combine with public relations positions, so you can check under advertising as well. For example, talentzoo, (*www.talentzoo.com/*), contains a searchable site for advertising, publishing, marketing and broadcasting.

If you want a public relations job in government, which offers many opportunities in local and national agencies, check your state government site or the U.S. Web portal, (*www.usa.gov*), which has links to state and federal sites. Think broadly. Many organizations need publicists including hospitals, companies and nonprofit agencies, so you should consider opportunities in the location you desire.

APPLYING FOR A JOB OR INTERNSHIP

Q: **How can you find out the name of the person to whom you should send your job or internship application?**

A: Start by checking the organization's website, a search engine or telephone book to find a phone number for the company. Even if the name of the person in charge of hiring is listed on a website or in a publication, call the organization and find out who should get your application anyway. Accuracy matters in media. Websites may not be up to date and printed directories are frequently incorrect because people change jobs before publications are reprinted. Get a specific person's name and title and ask how to spell the person's name and whether the person is male or female. Don't make the mistake of addressing a letter to a female executive as Dear Mr. or worse, Dear Sir. Also make sure you spell the person's name correctly.

Q: Should you contact the editor or hiring officer first by e-mail?

A: Sure, but be careful. Check your grammar and spelling before you send any e-mail. Dan Lovely, a former metro editor at a Florida newspaper, said he liked to correspond with applicants by e-mail so he could see how they communicate. He said if their e-mails were filled with typos or poor grammar, he wouldn't hire the applicants.

Q: Should you send your application via e-mail?

A: Send an e-mail application only if the organization requests it in that form. You can send an e-mail query to find out if the organization has a job or internship, but send a written cover letter and résumé as well unless the company specifies that it prefers e-mail résumés. If so, make sure you take a print copy of your résumé with you if you get to the interview stage.

Many organizations request that you apply by filling out a form on their websites. If you are applying to a company that has a major online operation and publishes primarily in digital formats, you should apply with an online application, links to your website and social media sites.

Q: Should you use your school e-mail address or a personal one?

A: Use the e-mail address you check frequently, and don't use a school address if you are graduating. Use a professional e-mail login. If you have been using an address with a login like "sexybabe," "cuteblondechick" or "studguy," change it unless you are applying for a sex-related job. Don't use smileys or other emoticons and Internet abbreviations that are often used in chats or e-mails.

Q: How many résumés should you send out?

A: Apply to as many organizations as you like, but don't send a form cover letter. Make sure you target your cover letter (in print or digital form) to the specific organization. Later in the chapter, we'll discuss how to write résumés and cover letters.

Q: Should you just send a résumé to a company on speculation without contacting an editor or hiring officer?

A: If the organization has posted a job ad, you can apply without an invitation from someone in the company. You can also post your résumé on a job or résumé site, but if you are seeking a job from a company that isn't advertising a position, it is preferable to contact someone there who has requested your material before sending it.

Q: Should you include your websites and blog addresses in a résumé?

A: Yes. These days so much information is online that you need to illustrate that you are capable of corresponding online and that you have knowledge of social media. If you have a media-related blog that is relevant to the job or internship you are seeking, it is a good idea to include a reference to it. Otherwise, keep your personal websites and blogs to yourself and your friends.

Q: Should you post your résumé on social networking sites such as Facebook, MySpace or YouTube?

A: It doesn't hurt to post your résumé on social networking sites, but you need to be careful about other material you have on these sites. Prospective employers might check out applicants who have applied to see what other information they might learn about them. If you do post a video résumé on YouTube or other site, make it professional as though you were speaking to the prospective employer.

Q: How many clips, scripts, graphics or other examples of your work should you include in a job or internship application?

A: In general, newspaper editors suggest at least six articles, preferably showing variety in styles such as features and hard news. For a broadcast job, enclose a few tapes, and for a Web job, make a copy of the sites you have created and include working links. For a public relations job, enclose a few samples you have created of news releases, brochures or other materials, especially examples of your writing ability.

Q: If you are a member of a minority ethnic or racial group, should you mention this in your cover letter or résumé?

A: A racial or ethnic minority background may be an advantage in some media jobs, particularly if the organization is in a community with a large population of minorities, such as Hispanics, Asians or African-Americans. Most news organizations are eager to increase the number of minorities on their staffs. You can refer to your racial or ethnic background judiciously in a cover letter and résumé by mentioning organizations or activities in which you have engaged that reflect this diversity or by explaining how your racial or ethnic background may help you in the job that you are seeking.

Q: What skills or qualities would be especially important to cite in your résumé?

A: Multimedia and social media skills are valuable for most media organizations. In addition, if you are bilingual or multilingual, that could be an asset in many media jobs. However, if you make that claim, make sure you are fluent in the languages you mention; do not exaggerate. If you say you are bilingual in English and Spanish, you could be interviewed by an employer in Spanish to test your fluency.

SOCIAL MEDIA

SOCIAL MEDIA can help you find a job or lose one. You can search for jobs or post your résumé on social media sites or you can post embarrassing photos and videos that will hurt your job chances.

Some of the social media sites you need for job hunting and posting your professional profile are LinkedIn, Facebook and Twitter. You also need an online portfolio with links to your website or blogs.

Twitter: You can post your résumé on the Twitter jobsite, (twttjobs). Use Twitter to follow media organizations and leaders in your field. A Twitter bio can be 160 characters, not the usual limit of 140 characters. Find hashtags such as #journalism_jobs, #prwork, #media_pros or just input a term for the jobs you seek in the Twitter search box.

Facebook: You can search pages and groups for jobs, and you can also use the Facebook Marketplace for job searching. Follow a company or organization on Facebook to learn more about it before you apply. Use a professional photo and include the same information in your Facebook profile as on your LinkedIn profile. Be careful about what you post on Facebook in the first place. Although you can remove information from your profile, copies may have been shared with other people and distributed. Check your privacy settings.

LinkedIn: This is a professional profile site that is useful for finding contacts and especially for posting your profile for job searches and related information. It is wise to post your photo, but you should choose one that looks professional. Avoid the party photos, full-body shots and dramatic poses.

Joe Grimm, who wrote a job recruiting blog for the Poynter Institute, says you should avoid some buzzwords such as "innovative" in your profile. When he searched LinkedIn for "innovative," it turned up 527,000 results. He offers this advice:

- Use phrases such as "innovative editor" instead of single words.
- Better yet, look for untapped words. Do a LinkedIn search for adjectives to find out which ones are overused.
- Use LinkedIn as a network by asking and answering questions that will end up circulating your name.
- Check your posts on any of these networks for spelling and accuracy.

WRITING COVER LETTERS

Your cover letter gives employers their first impression of you. You may get all A's in your news writing and public relations classes, but do you know how to market yourself? That is the purpose of a cover letter, which is often more difficult to write than a news story because it is hard to write about yourself without appearing egotistical. However, you can use some of the same techniques that you use in a news story. Just as you need a focus in a news story, you need to get to the point of your cover letter quickly. Explain within the first three paragraphs that you are applying for a job or internship at this organization.

Paul Salsini, former staff development director and writing coach for the *Milwaukee Journal Sentinel*, said he evaluated cover letters carefully when he was reviewing job applications. "I can't stress how important it is for the applicant to write a cover letter that is both clear and interesting and tells me this person is a good reporter and writer," he said. "If they're just saying they want a job, that doesn't excite me. I want a letter to entice me into their clips and résumé. The cover letter is the only original thing they send."

One of the worst mistakes applicants make is that they fail to change the text in their word processors when they are sending out multiple applications, Salsini said.

He also was appalled by the mistakes in these job applications. One applicant misspelled *Milwaukee* throughout her application. Another said, "I've always wanted to work at the *Minneapolis Star*."

"Good for her," Salsini said. "Why should I care?" He also stressed that applicants should attach some explanation to their clips about how they wrote the story. "If they would just write a couple of sentences to explain whether this was their story idea and why the story was important, it would help to put the clip in context. It helps an editor understand the story. That doesn't take a lot of work and it is so important."

The same principles apply to broadcast jobs. When you submit a tape, you should include an explanation of how and why you did the story.

Cover letters can start with a straightforward approach like a hard-news lead or a more creative feature-type lead. Most important, avoid writing a form letter that you send to several employers. Each letter should be tailored to the company where you are seeking a job. To do that, you need to do research. Check out the organization's website. If it is a newspaper site, read the paper online for a few weeks. For a broadcast job, check out the station's site for news stories and personnel. For public relations, familiarize yourself with the material that company produces or clients the firm represents.

In addition, the Public Relations Student Society of America, (PRSSA), offers career advice on its website about how to write cover letters and résumés *(www.prssa.org/ Career/career_tools/)*.

Internships and experience on campus newspapers, radio and television stations are important. Editors want evidence of how you report and write or what you can do as a copy editor, broadcast producer or reporter. They want clips of stories you have written or edited.

Technology has further complicated the job application process in the past few years. Many employers now scan applications into databases, so you need to keep your format simple and brief, preferably limited to one page each for the cover letter and the résumé. In addition, employers expect you to include an e-mail address or cell phone number, whichever way you would be most accessible.

Cover Letter Tips

Make your first impression on the editor a good one. Use proper business letter form, and keep it brief — no more than one page. Editors and other employers are busy people. Double-check and triple-check your spelling. Make sure that all the names and titles are correct. A misspelled name, typo or other mechanical error can disqualify you for consideration.

Be straightforward — not cute, not boring. Start with why you are applying to this organization or something about yourself that makes you worth noticing. But get to the point quickly about why you are applying. Specify whether you are seeking an internship or full-time job.

Here is some advice from an article that Judith G. Clabes, president emeritus of Scripps Howard Foundation, wrote for *Quill* magazine when she was editor of the *Kentucky Post:*

I'm editor of a medium-sized daily, and being deluged with letters to the editor comes with the territory.

Believe me, by the time I've shuffled through the "Dear Stupid" letters to the editor, the "Dear Employee" memos from corporate, and the really important "Dear Resident" mail that somehow pours into the office, I'm in no frame of mind for a job-seeker's "Dear Mr. Clabes" letter.

"Dear Mr. Judith Clabes" really ticks me off.

Now, this may seem quirky, but we editors are entitled to an eccentricity or two.

Idiosyncrasies aside, we editors do seem to agree on the issue of introductory letters from job-seekers. We prefer:

- Straightforward, one-page letters
- Simple résumés
- Well-selected clips (yes, college newspaper clips are fine)

In the end, the clips speak loudest. But the introductory letter may determine whether a busy editor will even bother to listen. . . .

The following will automatically turn off an editor:

- Grammatical errors
- Typographical errors
- Misspelling the name of the newspaper
- Misspelling the name of the editor
- Form letters
- Incorrect titles, including courtesy titles
- Cutesy letters
- Bad writing, including poor sentence structure
- Phony sales pitches
- Lengthy, self-centered letters . . .

Typos are killers. "I can't remember bothering to interview an applicant whose letter contained typos or grammatical errors," says Dee W. Bryant, former editor of *The Leaf-Chronicle* in Clarksville, Tennessee. "If a person is that careless with letters, it raises the question about carelessness as a staffer."

Bryant's pet peeve, however, is the automatic — and mindless — "Mr." greeting. "If an applicant is seriously interested, he should have taken the time to find out. It irritates me that people make the invalid assumption that editors are men." . . .

Though we editors have our own pet peeves as well as hiring strategies, we shudder over the cute stuff, the gimmicks, the overzealous attempts at creativity. . . .

What will work is a simple, professional approach. Throw away fuchsia paper and the gimmicks. Invest time in investigating the newspaper. Write a simple, well-crafted (and proofread) one-page letter that demonstrates your interest in journalism generally and in that particular newspaper specifically. Include a brief résumé and five or six well-selected clips.

Before you write your cover letter and résumé, do some research about the organization to which you are applying. If you are seeking a job at a newspaper or magazine, read the publication. You can check the Web or online databases, such as LEXIS/NEXIS, or get copies of the publication.

If you are applying to a corporation for a public relations or advertising position, check databases, such as Standard & Poor's Register of Corporations, and business publications to learn something about the organization. Don't just cite facts about the company; weave the information into the paragraph in your cover letter that explains why you want to work for the organization. Most good websites have an "About Us" page, which will give you some good background about the company.

Content of Cover Letters

Try to limit the cover letter to one page. Always address it to a specific person, never "Dear Sir" or "Dear Madam." Write a good lead that tells something about you, but don't make it too flowery. Follow with a nut graph — your reason for writing. If you prefer a direct approach, lead with your reason for the letter.

In the middle of your letter, explain why you are eager to work for this particular organization. Even though you are including a résumé, mention its high points. Make special note of any unusual skills you may have, such as fluency in a second language or relevant experience. If someone at the organization has encouraged you to apply, mention this person's name. The adage "It's not what you know but who you know" has some validity.

Write a few more paragraphs briefly explaining your experience, if any, and your major assets — why anyone should want to hire you — and why you want to work for this company. Then wrap it up with a brief paragraph thanking the editor for his attention.

Consider the lead to your cover letter as carefully as you would consider the lead to a news story. It's the attention getter.

A cover letter that starts "I am graduating in May from journalism school, and I am seeking an internship (or job)" will most likely land in the trash. Thousands of other applicants are also graduating from journalism schools. That lead reveals nothing special about you.

Here are some effective types of leads:

Direct Approach: "Please consider me for a reporting internship (or job — and specify the type of position and the name of the organization) this summer." Follow with a line or two about who you are and why you are interested in this company. This approach does not reflect any creativity, but it is preferable to a strained lead.

Experience Approach: If you had a good internship or have previous journalism-related experience, consider starting with a paragraph about what your experience was and why you are interested in or qualified for this job. If you are a graduate student or nontraditional student, you might refer to your previous experience and your reasons for studying journalism.

For example, Michael Strong was a nontraditional student who was once a massage therapist. His job application began, "How many reporters do you know who have experience meeting people when they are nude? That isn't exactly traditional training for a reporter, but I'm not a traditional candidate for a reporting job."

Although clichés aren't a good idea, Tiffany Hurt made one work to describe herself, and she inserted her race subtly. "Good things definitely do come in small packages. Even though I only look 10 because I am 4-feet, 7-and-a-half inches, I am actually twice that age with the responsibilities and leadership of an ambitious college student....On campus I am a member of the editorial board for the newspaper. In addition, I am the chairperson and editor of the newsletter for the Black Student Union."

Reference Approach: The adage of who you know, not what you know, is still somewhat true when you are applying for a job or internship. If someone in the organization referred you to the company or if you have spoken to the recruiter, you can begin your cover letter by referring to that person or conversation.

Preferably by the second paragraph, explain the purpose of your letter — similar to a nut graph in a news story. State what type of job or internship you are seeking and why you are applying to this organization.

In the body, mention some highlights of your résumé or special skills that make you qualified or valuable for the position you seek. Elaborate briefly on any experience you've had related to this position. Try to tailor your comments to this organization rather than writing a form letter with a generic tone.

At the end, mention any enclosures, such as clips or videos. You may thank the person for attention to your application or provide any contact information that you think is necessary.

Autobiographical Approach: Start with something about your background that made you want to become a journalist, public relations professional (or whatever type of career position you are seeking). If you use this technique, keep it short. Don't give your life story. (See the example that follows.)

Student's home mailing address
City, State, ZIP code
Student's e-mail address
Phone numbers (including cell phone)
Date

Maureen Murray, Recruiter for Account Executives
Leo Burnett Company Inc.
35 W. Wacker Drive
Chicago, IL 60601

Dear Ms. Murray:

The basket of apples in your company logo indirectly led me to seek a career in advertising and to write this letter seeking a job in your agency. When I was growing up in Chicago, my grandparents told me a story about how your company used to hand out apples to people on the streets during the Depression as a good public relations gesture. I was impressed. I thought that your company would be the kind of place where I would like to work someday. Every time I see your logo, I remember that story.

Now, as a journalism student at the University of Kansas, I am even more impressed with the Leo Burnett Company, which is ranked the No. 1 advertising agency in the Midwest. Please consider me for a position as an assistant account executive in your client services division. I will graduate in December with a bachelor's degree in journalism. I have taken several advertising, public relations and news-writing courses. I would be eager to work on any of your accounts, such as Nintendo, Reebok, Hallmark Cards or Pillsbury. Any opportunity in your agency would be challenging, but a chance to assist on the Walt Disney account is my idea of the perfect job.

Although I have gained many skills from my academic training, I believe that my internships have offered me the best education. Currently I am a public relations intern for the Nelson-Atkins Museum of Art in Kansas City. I recently promoted and publicized the autobiographical exhibit of artist Andrew Wyeth. I also gained valuable experience last winter as an advertising intern for The Pioneer Press, a suburban Chicago newspaper chain. In that position, I created target account booklets, wrote reports and assisted sales representatives. When I worked in the advertising department of my college newspaper, *The University Daily Kansan,* I won an award as the best account executive.

I work well with people, and I am a good problem solver. In addition to my sales and advertising skills, I have written news stories for the university newspaper. I understand that you are seeking applicants with a broad educational background, and I believe that the media experiences I have had make me a good candidate for your firm. Although I have much to learn, I offer boundless enthusiasm and a positive work ethic.

I will call you within the next two weeks to see if you will grant me an interview. I can be reached at (913) 000-0000. I am enclosing a résumé and some examples of my work. Thank you for your consideration.

Sincerely yours,

[Signature]

Shelly Falevits
E-mail address

ple cover letter with an autobiographical approach

Here is a more straightforward approach by another journalism student:

Student's home address
City, State, ZIP code
e-mail address
Phone numbers (including cell phone)
Date

Name and title of person to whom you are applying
Name of organization
Address of organization
City, State, ZIP

Dear Mr. or Ms. Name of person (don't use generic Dear Sir or Dear Madam):
I am seeking the position of a graphic designer for the Web pages produced by Information Network of Kansas. After corresponding with you by e-mail, I realized that my skills and training fit the needs of your state agency. My background in Web design and my experience with layout of newspapers and business communications make me a qualified candidate.

I can benefit your organization with my knowledge of several computer graphic design packages and programming languages. I have lived and worked in many different towns in Kansas and will use this knowledge to help develop services for the people who use your network. My internship with the Kansas Public Policy Institute also gave me an in-depth view of our state government and the politicians who represent the people.

The Information Network of Kansas is providing cutting-edge information, and I am interested in working for an agency that refuses to stagnate. I am also interested in working for an agency that provides an essential service to its community. I hope that my skills and your services will benefit both of us.

I appreciate your consideration. I can be reached by e-mail at .... or by phone at ....

Sincerely yours,

Erin Rooney
Enc. Résumé

Sample cover letter with a straightforward approach

ETHICS

CASE 1: YOU HAVE an internship at a local newspaper or television station. A few weeks after you start working, your supervisor asks you out on a date. You like your supervisor and think you could get romantically involved. Should you go on a date? What are the ethical problems of dating your supervisor?

Case 2: You have been hired by the newspaper or television station where you have wanted to work for a long time. You have established some roots and really enjoy your job. You've been on the job for about a year. You are very attracted to your editor, and he or she feels the same attraction to you. Should you get romantically involved? If so, what are the ethical problems and alternatives?

Case 3: You face a similar situation as in Case 2, but this time you are attracted to a source on your beat. Can you or should you get romantically involved? Do you have to give up a romantic relationship for your job? What are the ethical issues, and what alternatives are open to you?

ONLINE APPLICATION EXAMPLES

Check online application forms or instructions from major companies to get examples of the type of information companies are seeking. For example, Burson-Marsteller, the largest public relations company in the world, offers an internship application procedure on its website *(www.burson-marsteller.com/)*. In addition to submitting a resume and cover letter, the company asks for the following:

- **Press release:** You've just been hired by Burson-Marsteller. Write a press release announcing your hire. Be creative.
- **Essay:** Write a one- to three-page essay on one of the topics listed such as this one: How might you use research and insights to make a public relations campaign more impactful.

An application for a writing and editorial internship at Hallmark also requires a cover letter and resume and responses to some questions that demonstrate your creative skills. For example, one question asks you to create a new product (cards or gifts) and follow it from conception to retail display as follows: "Identify your market, briefly describe your new product, give it a name, copy ideas and design descriptions for packaging if needed and copy ideas and design direction for the retail display."

These are just a few illustrations of how companies in public relations and other media organizations expect you to demonstrate your skills. As indicated above, in print and broadcast journalism, your clips and videos show your abilities in those fields.

RÉSUMÉS

Limit your résumé to one page, with a possible second page for references. Arrange your topics from most recent to previous, such as current experience followed by previous jobs. White paper is preferred. Content is more important than appearance. If you have a home page and online résumé, add the Web address to your résumé.

Bring copies of your resume to job fairs where you could be interviewed.

If your experience in previous internships or jobs is more interesting than your education, put the experience category first. If you have no experience or awards, eliminate the category; don't write "none."

You can start your résumé with an objective, a sentence that explains your job goal or a summary, a paragraph that highlights your skills and accomplishments. Summaries are gaining favor with employers these days because they offer more information in a quick format than a vague objective.

Objective: Limit your objective to one sentence. Tailor the statement to the type of job you are seeking.

- **Vague:** "Seeking to use my skills in public relations."
- **More specific:** "To use my journalism training at a small, community newspaper to gain experience in several types of reporting and writing assignments."
- **Specific: "**To use my communication skills and my background in graphic arts in a public relations and marketing firm with opportunities for creative expression and growth."

Summary: The summary should be limited to a paragraph that highlights your skills and/or experience:

- "Campus newspaper editor and journalism major with internships at two major metropolitan newspapers. I am seeking a reporting position at a small to midsize newspaper with opportunities for advancement. Versatile skills include reporting, writing, copy editing and page design."

Here are some other tips:

- List your experience, education and other items in order of the most recent first.
- Make sure that your résumé is free of typos and spelling errors.
- List two or three references, and include phone numbers and e-mail addresses where your references can be reached. Do not say "References available on request." Do everything you can to help the employer. By withholding references, you force the employer to spend more time checking on you. Make sure you ask the people you list if they agree to be references for you. Don't assume or just list their names.
- Skip the fancy paper. Scannable résumés should be as simple as possible on plain white paper with black type of at least 12 points. Your headings can be in larger type, but don't mix fonts. Also eliminate borders and underlining.
- Include five or six clips (or videotape for broadcast journalists, although scripts help in this area as well). Choose clips with good leads. Editors rarely read past a bad lead. Try to include a variety: features and hard news, short and long. Short is better, unless you have a major project. If you have some good enterprise stories, those you developed through your own ideas, include them. The significance of the news event is not important to editors; they want to see how you wrote more than what you wrote.

- When you copy your clips, don't reduce them in size. Cut them so they fit on standard-sized paper, even if you have to use more than one page for a story.

- Templates such as those offered in Microsoft Word are acceptable provided that you adapt them by adding or eliminating categories that don't apply to you. Consider using "Education" as your first topic heading if you are just graduating, but if you have considerable experience, list that heading first. Interests are optional, but references are not. Make sure that you add a heading for references because one is not included in the templates. Then list your references' titles, phone numbers and e-mail addresses if they agree to be listed.

- Follow-up phone call: A week or two after you have sent your letter and résumé, call the organization to ask if they were received and if you may come for an interview. Find out when the editor you are calling is on deadline or in meetings, and try to avoid these times.

CONVERGENCE COACH

ONLINE RÉSUMÉS
Reading a résumé online is more difficult than reading it in print, so keep your Web résumé even shorter than your print one. Try to limit it to three screens. Don't just transfer the print résumé to an online version.

Use a different format, perhaps paragraphs or lists. Don't use the column structure you might use in print; online reading is vertical, not horizontal. If you use a one-screen design, don't offer too many links to separate categories for education, experience and so on. Endless clicking can be tedious for a potential employer. Put the basic information on one page, and link to clips or your portfolio.

Here are some other tips for Web résumés:

- **Background:** Don't use a dark background with white or light type. The type may not show up if an employer wants to print your résumé. If you really prefer this type of design, offer a printable version as well, with white background and black type.

- **Privacy:** Protect your own privacy and that of your references. Consider eliminating your address and phone number in online documents, especially if you post your photograph on your site. The same is true for your references. Although providing contact information for references is preferable in print, for online sites you may have to write "References available on request."

- **Create your own online résumé:** Many websites include résumé forms. Unless you are applying to a company that prefers you to use its online résumé form, create your own résumé so you can demonstrate your ability to express yourself — a major qualification for media jobs.

- **Identify yourself:** If you are creating your own Web résumé, make sure that you put your name and e-mail address on every page of your site. Don't use "I" or "Nancy's résumé" as an identifier.

- **Offer a printer-friendly résumé:** If you have a fancy website, offer a simple printer version. Recruiters will need to print your résumé and keep it on file.

- **Use key words:** Include terms that search engines will pick up.

YOUR NAME

E-mail: name@ . . .
Cell phone number

Permanent Address
[If home address differs from address during the semester]
Street
City, state, ZIP code
Phone number with area code

Present Address

Street
City, state, ZIP code
Phone number with area code

Objective or summary List your career objective or a brief summary paragraph of your achievements and goals

Education:

| Years | University of . . . | Location |

[Give dates, from most recent to previous.]
Degree expected: B.A. in journalism, [Date]
Major: Journalism with emphasis in magazine

Other colleges attended [If any]   Location

High school attended [Optional]   Location

Experience: [List any full-time or part-time jobs, particularly any related to your field, in order starting from the most recent. Give the dates. You may add a line or two explaining your job duties.]

January–May [Year]
Reporter, *The Daily Campus* newspaper; covered university administration

July–August [Year]
Reporting internship with *City Newspaper;* covered general news for city desk and features

May–August [Year]
Server Starving Students, [City, state]

Special skills and awards: [Omit this category if you have no special skills.]
Skilled in graphics programs and computer-assisted reporting
Fluent in Spanish
Scripps Howard Scholarship for College Journalism

Activities: [List only important activities and memberships, especially those that show leadership or skills related to the job you are seeking. This category may be omitted.]

References: [List only two or three people who have given you permission to list them. References may be listed on a separate page if you run out of room. List people's titles, addresses and phone numbers. Do not write "Available on request."]

Sample of scannable résumé.

ONLINE PORTFOLIOS

Even if you submit a printed resume and cover letter, it's a good idea to have an online portfolio linked to the digital profile you should be creating. You don't have to know Web design to create your online portfolio; WordPress and Blogger, free online publishing tools, can do the work for you. Check out online portfolios of some successful professionals in your field for inspiration. One site that offers creative online portfolios of journalists is 10,000 words at *www.mediabistro.com/10000words/*. Here are some suggestions about what to include:

- **Home page:** Include your name and e-mail address. Many people just label their home pages "MyPage" and they fail to provide a name and contact information. Include a link to your online resume.
- **Writing and/or video examples:** Link to clips or video, brochures or public relations materials you have produced. You can provide the text in PDF format if that is preferable.
- **Social media links:** Provide links to your LinkedIn site, Facebook, Twitter or other social media sites which contain your professional information.
- **Blogs:** Link to blogs you have written if they demonstrate your media skills.
- **Update:** Keep your online resume and other items up to date. List items in order of the most recent one first.

INTERVIEWS

The interview is your chance to explain how much you want to work for the employer and why you would be a good choice. It is also your chance to find out more about the employer and to assess whether you would really like to work there.

Here are some tips:

Dress Conservatively: Wear the type of clothing that employees at that organization would wear to work. Women might wear casual attire such as a skirt and blouse or more businesslike outfits such as a suit or dress, depending on the company. Men should wear a suit or sport jacket with a shirt and tie. No jeans and no sneakers!

Be Prompt: Be on time for your interview. You may arrive 15 minutes early, but don't get there too early. Never be late. That's equivalent to missing a deadline. And that's equivalent to saying you are not fit for the job.

Be Prepared: Be informed about the publication, organization or station. Read copies of the publication, particularly the most recently published ones, or view video on the station's website if possible. Public relations applicants should try to gather research about the company and the types of promotions the firm does. Memorize the names of key editors in advance.

Understand the Costs: Some organizations will pay for your transportation and hotel. If not, be prepared to pay for them yourself. Small newspapers and other

© Gannett Co. Inc.

Newspaper newsroom.

organizations may not have the budget for your travel costs. You have to decide if the cost is worthwhile to you. If the organization is out of state, it's fair to ask if your transportation and lodging costs will be reimbursed.

Concentrate: When you are introduced to people, try to remember their names, especially those of key editors — such as the city editor or, if you are applying for a sports job, the sports editor. Homework helps.

Be Enthusiastic: Your enthusiasm is your best asset, especially if you don't have experience. Show that you're interested in the job. Smile and enjoy the interview just as if you were doing an interview for a story. If you don't really want to work for the firm, don't waste everyone's time.

Be Polite: Thank the editor or key person for granting you an interview, and thank the person at the end of it as well.

Be Pleasant: Even if you are frightened, smile and be responsive.

Be Yourself: Do not try so hard to make a good impression that you are insincere. Be honest about what you can and cannot do and what you want to learn. Never try to give a false impression of yourself.

Ask Questions: The questions you ask are as important as the ones you answer. They show your curiosity and your concern about the job — qualities of a good reporter, editor or publicist.

Editors have their favorite questions, so it is hard to prepare for the interview. However, almost all of them will ask why you want to work for their organization and why you want to be a journalist. Try to be creative but sincere. "I've always wanted to write" is such a boring answer.

Here are some other questions that are popular with newspaper editors (similar questions are often asked in other fields):

Why Do You Want to Work for This Organization? The answers are up to you: because you grew up in the area, want to remain in the area, are familiar with the community and so on. It's best to specify something you like about the organization if you are familiar with it. Or you could say you are seeking a variety of experiences, particularly if it's a small newspaper or television station, where reporters tend to do all types of stories. If it's a large organization, you could say you're attracted by the prestige of the publication or station or the chance to learn from very experienced journalists. If you are so eager that you will work anywhere, it's OK to say so. Just be honest.

Why Did You Want to Become a Journalist or Public Relations Practitioner? Because it's more interesting than selling used cars, because you seek adventure, because you love the language, whatever. Here is your chance to give your real reason. It could be that someone influenced you or that you just like the type of work.

What Are Your Goals As a Journalist? A preferred answer might be because you like the work of this paper or station and you are familiar with the community (if that's true). If your goal is to be a foreign correspondent, at this point you might consider joining the Navy. Small papers don't have much use for foreign bureaus. Again, be sincere.

What Books, Magazines and Newspapers Do You Read? Editors love this question. It tells them something about you.

What Other Interests Do You Have? This is another favorite question.

What Can You Do for this Organization, or Why Should I Hire You? Don't say you can turn the organization around or make it wonderful. But do say something about the types of stories you would like to do, or say that you would be willing to do all types of stories. Don't be arrogant.

What Do You Think of This Newspaper, TV Station or Public Relations Firm? Be cautious with this one. Don't say it's terrible and you can save it. Point out something good first. Then you might point out some weakness or area that you think could be improved. Perhaps you think it could use more human approaches to stories or more hard news. If you've read it, you have a right to your opinion. Just be diplomatic.

What Was Your Favorite Story (or Public Relations Project) That You Wrote or Produced, and Why Did You Like It? This is another question that gives insight into you — as well as your professional interests.

How Would You Cover This Issue? The editor might give you an example of a topic that is of concern in that community. You'll have to think and do the best you can to come up with some interesting approaches.

What Questions Do You Have? This question is very important. Here's where you get your chance to ask about the company, the workload, perhaps what the editors want or expect from reporters and copy editors. You could ask about a probationary period. You could also ask about salary, benefits and other compensation; generally, however, that shouldn't be your first question.

At the end of the interview, don't forget to thank the interviewer for his or her time and interest.

Interview Follow-Up After you have had an interview, wait a few weeks and then call to let the editor know you are aggressive and interested in the job. But don't be a pest.

Even if you are not interested in the job, send a note thanking the editor for the interview. That's just basic courtesy. And if you are interested in the job, the thank-you note lets the editor know something else about you: You're thoughtful.

EXERCISES

1 Tell your story in six words: This exercise comes from Anne McNeilly, an assistant professor at the School of Journalism, Ryerson University. (A similar exercise is in the social media chapter based on the website *www.sixwordstories.net/*.) However, Professor McNeilly uses the concept to ask students to write a six-word bio and include an image or photo that illustrates the concept. Although she used the exercise to create a multimedia show, you can use this concept to create your home page of an online portfolio or resume. Here are some of the examples from her students: "I want money, but chose journalism;" "Waiting for a sign. Still hopeful," "Missing mornings of Oreos with milk," "University degree: bad credit, $40,000 debt."

2 Interview people in your field: Depending on your field of interest, interview three newspaper editors, television news directors, magazine editors or public relations employers about the qualities they seek in job candidates and the kinds of applications they want.

3 Describe yourself: Write a few descriptive paragraphs about yourself in the third person (*she* or *he*). This exercise will give you a clue to what makes you special, and it may help you find a lead for your cover letter.

4 Cover letter and résumé: Write a cover letter and a résumé for a job or internship you would be interested in getting.

5 Online résumé. Write an online résumé.

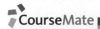 CourseMate

Appendix

GRAMMAR AND USAGE

The difference between the right word and the nearly right word is the same as that between lightning and the lightning bug.

Mark Twain

Mark Twain.

Library of Congress

Test Your Knowledge:

Whom or *who* should you contact for jobs and internships?

Will grammar have an *effect* or *affect* on your career?

Do you expect to go *further* or *farther* in your career if you get a good journalism background?

Do you know how the media *is* or *are* changing the way news is covered?

Does this sentence look *alright* to you? If it does, you need to study this chapter well.

The correct usage is in this paragraph: *Whom* should you contact for an internship? Check directories in your field. A good grasp of grammar will have a beneficial *effect* on your career, but poor grammar will *affect* your chances of getting a good job. You will go *further* in your career if you understand how the media *are* changing the way news is covered. It is never *all right* for you to write *alright*.

Despite the abbreviations and new language of tweets, u need 2 master grammar 2 b a gd writer. Whether news is delivered to your smart phone, tablet device, computer or in print form, it still must be well written and adhere to the principles of good grammar and style, preferably Associated Press style for most news organizations.

Should you send an e-mail or an email? Do you have a website or a Web site? Do you have a smart phone or a smartphone?

The AP Stylebook recently changed Web site to website, but it still insists that Web page is

COACHING TIPS

When in doubt, **check it out.**

***

Don't depend on computer spellers and grammar checkers.

***

Don't turn in copy without **checking it for grammar,** spelling and style.

***

Keep a **dictionary and stylebook** on your desk as you write. Use them.

***

Check your **Associated Press Stylebook** for usage.

two separate words and the Web when used alone should be capitalized. These words are joined and in lower case: website, webcam, webmaster and webcast. As media terms keep changing or being created, the style for writing about them will inevitably evolve as well. But most news organizations and public relations firms still follow the AP Stylebook for print and online writing. Recently the Stylebook added sections on social media and food writing as well. You can follow the AP Stylebook on social media sites, Facebook and Twitter.

Many news organizations require you to take a grammar and style test if you are applying for a job as a reporter or copy editor. Public relations practitioners also need good writing skills. If you don't have a good grasp of grammar and usage, you won't be considered a good writer. And you can't rely on an editor or your computer to catch all your errors.

Now that you understand how to write a news story, this chapter will help you avoid these common errors in grammar, spelling and usage:

Advise/advice: *Advise* is what you do; *advice* is what you receive.

I advise you to study this chapter. If your professor has *advised* you to buy an Associated Press Stylebook, she gave you good *advice.*

Affect, effect: *Affect* is an active verb, and *effect* is a noun. Think of *affect* with an *a* for action and *effect* with an *e* for the end result. *Effect* can be used as a verb with *to,* as in "to effect change," but that is not a common use.

Failing your style tests will *affect* your grade. But the *effect* on your writing will be more serious.

Aggravate/annoy: *Aggravate* means to make a condition worse; *annoy* means to irritate. People don't get aggravated; conditions do.

If you continue to smoke, you will *aggravate* your lung disease.

If you don't turn off your cell phone in class, you will *annoy* me.

A lot, alot: Two words, please. Always. If you can't remember, use *many* instead of *a lot.*

Alright: *Alright* is listed in the dictionary as all right in informal dialogue, but it is not all right, according to the Associated Press Stylebook, which says *never* use that spelling. Use two words, *all right,* to mean OK.

It is not *all right* to use *alright.*

Altogether/all together: *Altogether* means completely or thoroughly. *All together* means people or items are all gathered in one place.

Among, between: *Among* is used with more than two items; *between* is used with two items.

The conflict was *between* two students. The pay increases were divided *among* 10 employees.

Ampersand: Do not use the ampersand (&) as a substitute for *and.* This symbol should be used only when it is part of a company's name, such as Dun & Bradstreet.

Anxious, eager: *Anxious* means you are worried; *eager* means you are excited or looking forward to something.

In your cover letter, don't say you are *anxious* to work for a company.

Even if you are worried about the job, you are probably *eager* to get it.

As, like, as if, as though: Use *as, as if* or *as though* to introduce a sentence or clause with a verb. *Like* means "similar to" and should be used only to compare nouns or pronouns. Whenever you are confused, just see if *similar to* would fit in the sentence. If the sentence or clause contains some action, use *as.* Think *a* for *as* for action.

As I said (not *like I said*), she plays basketball *like* a professional. It looks *as if* she will become a professional basketball player.

Bad, badly: *Bad* is an adjective that modifies a noun, as in "You wrote a *bad* paper." *Badly* is an adverb that modifies a verb, as in "You played *badly* in the game." These words are used *badly* most of the time when used with the linking verb *feel.* "You *feel bad*" means that your health, emotional or mental state is bad. "You *feel badly*" means that your sense of touch is poor. (See *Linking verbs* for more explanation.)

Don't *feel bad* if you have made this common mistake, but don't write *badly* anymore in this context.

Before, prior to: *Before* is appropriate and less formal for most uses. *Prior to* is appropriate when the connection between the two events makes it clear that one event must precede the other.

Every passenger must show identification *before* a ticket will be issued. Every passenger must show identification *prior to* boarding the plane. (*Before* would also be acceptable here.)

Between, among: See *among.*

Between you and I or between you and me: Never use *I* in this case. *Between* is a preposition that must be followed by a pronoun in the objective case: *me, her, him, them, us.* Every time you are tempted to use *I,* mentally substitute *he* or *we.* You're not as likely to say "between you and he" or "between they and we."

Biannual/semiannual/biennial: *Biannual* means twice a year. So does *semiannual.* *Biennial* means every two years. Note that these words are not hyphenated.

Bimonthly/semimonthly/biweekly/semiweekly: *Bimonthly* means every other month; *semimonthly* means twice a month. Same with biweekly — every other week — and semiweekly — twice a week.

Board with singular verb: A reference to a board of directors or a board of education or any other board followed by a phrase describing it takes a singular verb, such as *is, was* or *votes.* The board is considered a singular entity; it's still one board even if it has 30 members. Ignore the modifying phrase.

The *Board of Education is* meeting tonight. The *Board of Regents votes* on the issue tomorrow. (If that sounds awkward, you might say "*Members of the Board of Education are meeting* tonight.")

Can, may: *Can* means you are capable of doing something; *may* means permission or the chance to do something.

You *may* get a promotion if you *can* create Web pages or a complete website.

Clause, phrase: A clause is a group of words containing a subject and a verb. An independent clause forms a complete sentence; a dependent one depends on the rest of the sentence to make sense. Use a comma after an introductory clause. A phrase is a group of words without a subject or a verb. If you want to write well (that's a dependent clause), don't interrupt your subject and verb with a long clause.

Poor: The student, who was fond of writing long, complicated sentences with clauses between his subject and verb, was an English major.

Better: The student, who was an English major, was fond of writing long, complicated sentences.

Phrase: After the game, the fans celebrated at a local pub.

Comma: Use a comma between two independent clauses joined by a conjunction — *and, but, for, or, no, so, yet* — unless the clauses are short. Use a comma after an introductory clause unless it is short. Always put commas inside the quotation marks in a direct quote. Check the Associated Press Stylebook for a more complete discussion.

"When a sentence includes a direct quote (that's an introductory clause), the comma always goes inside the quotation marks," the professor said. "So does the period."

Comma splice: Never join two sentences with a comma. That's called a comma splice. Learn to love the period. If the sentences are closely related, you might use a semicolon.

People who use commas to join sentences are making a dreadful mistake; comma splices indicate bad writing.

Compared to/compared with: Use *compared to* when you liken one thing to another. Use *compared with* when you examine the similarities and differences of two or more items.

She is very smart *compared to* her sister. *Compared with* all the other students in her class, she is the best writer.

Complement, compliment: *Complement,* with *e,* means "to complete," also with *e. Compliment,* with *i,* means to flatter or praise.

"If you can't get a *compliment* any other way, pay one to yourself," Mark Twain said.

If you want a scarf to *complement* your outfit, buy one.

CONVERGENCE COACH

ONLINE SITES WITH poor grammar and spelling errors lack credibility. Online news stories use Associated Press style. TV "crawls," the print that scrolls across the bottom of a screen, must also adhere to good grammar and usage even though these headlines are brief.

- Proofread your copy carefully before you post anything online.

- Most people's e-mail messages are notoriously sloppy. Check spelling and grammar before you send your e-mail messages, particularly if you are sending an e-mail for an interview, an online résumé or other career-related activities.

- Although broadcast journalists also use Associated Press style, the medium features the spoken word. Therefore, you may want to use a phonetic spelling of a name that is difficult to pronounce. But anything that is shown on the screen, such as a name or a title, should be checked for accurate spelling and grammar.

Consensus: This word means an agreement of opinion, so do not say *"consensus of opinion."* That's redundant.

After six hours of debate, the board of commissioners reached a *consensus* about building a new parking garage.

Council/counsel: A *council* is an appointed or elected group of people who give advice or make decision. *Counsel* is the advice or consultation you receive.

Credible/creditable: *Credible* is believable. *Creditable* is deserving of credit, honor or esteem. He gave a *credible* explanation for his absences.

He is doing a *creditable* job in the department, but it would be better if he were just doing a good job. The use of *creditable* in this case is awkward.

Criteria, criterion: *Criteria,* referring to the factors that will be used to judge something, is plural. If only one factor is involved, it is a *criterion.*

The *criteria* to get an A in this class are good writing, spelling, grammar and punctuation. The *criterion* for expulsion from the journalism school is plagiarism.

Currently, presently, now: *Currently* means now; *presently* means soon, although it can mean now. If you are confused, just use *now.*

Dangling modifier: A phrase or a participle (an adjective made from a verb ending in *ing*) is said to dangle if it is not placed directly before the noun or pronoun it modifies.

Dangling participle: After *studying* for three hours, the *test* was canceled. (The test did not study for three hours. The student did.)

Correct: After *studying* for three hours, the *student* learned that the test was canceled.

Desert, dessert: A desert is a barren place; a dessert is something to eat.

You probably won't find a delicious *dessert* in a *desert.*

Directions/regions: Capitalize regions of the country — *Midwest, North, South, West, Northeast, Southwest, East Coast* and *West Coast.* Use lowercase for directions: Go *west* and turn *east.*

She is hoping to get a job on the East Coast, but right now she lives in the Midwest.

He said the party is about five blocks east of the university.

Either, neither: Each of these words requires a singular verb and a singular pronoun. Think of *either one* or *neither one.* But if *either* joins a singular word and a plural word, the verb agrees with the closer subject.

Either student *is* qualified for the position.

Neither the president nor the vice president *is* available for comment.

Neither of the students *plans* to present *her* project tomorrow.

Either the president or several members *are going* to attend *their* fraternity's philanthropic event.

Embarrassment, harassment: These words are often spelled incorrectly. *Embarrassment* has two *r*'s and two *s*'s; *harassment* has just one *r.* You are probably embarrassed more than you are harassed, so give it the extra *r* for being a regular occurrence.

Etc.: This is an abbreviation for the Latin word *et cetera,* meaning "and other things." You can substitute *and so on* or *and so forth,* but it is best to avoid this term. It leaves the reader wondering what else should follow. As the late John B. Bremner, a renowned authority on usage, wrote, "Above all, don't use *etc.* as a cover for ignorance when you have run out of ideas."

Everyone, everybody, every one, each: Each of these words takes a singular verb and a singular pronoun. If the previous sentence sounds strange to you, mentally eliminate the prepositional phrase (of these words). The phrases that intervene between everyone, each and everybody and the verb or pronoun are what cause the confusion. If you really get confused, substitute all or another plural word for everyone, each or *everybody*.

> *Every one* of the students is seeking a good job in his or her field. (Stress the one in this sentence. You wouldn't say everyone are or everybody are seeking.)

Farther, further: *Farther* is distance; *further* involves length of time, quantity or intensity.
> How much *farther* do we have to drive?

> I'll give this *further* thought.

Feel: This word indicates a state of being or a sense of touch. Don't use it to mean "think" or "believe."
> You will *feel* bad if you don't get an A on the quizzes at the end of the chapter.

> You *think* or *believe* you are doing well (not you *feel* you are doing well) in the course.

Fewer, less: Use *fewer* to refer to a specific number of items that you can count; use *less* to refer to a collection of items, a period of time or a quantity. *Less* is often used with a sum of money.
> *Fewer* than 10 graduates took jobs in which they made *less* than $15,000.

Fragment: An incomplete sentence, sometimes just a word or phrase. (That is a fragment.) Fragments can be effective as a writing technique for emphasis but should be used cautiously and rarely.

Full-time/full time: Use the hyphenated version when you are using the word to describe something such as a *full-time* job. But use two words without a hyphen when it is not followed by a noun. *He works full time.*

Goes without saying: If it does *go without saying,* then why say it? This is a stupid expression often used in corporate memos.

Half-mast, half-staff: On naval ships and at naval stations, flags are flown at *half-mast.* Other flags are flown at *half-staff,* usually to commemorate a person or tragic event.

Hyphenate compound modifiers: When two or more adjectives are used together to modify a noun that follows them, use a hyphen. Don't use a hyphen for *very* or adverbs ending in *ly*. Do not use a hyphen if a compound adjective follows an action verb.
> The *3-year-old* child had a chronic ear infection. But: The child is 3 years old.

> She was an *honor-roll student* in high school (compound adjective modifying *student)*. But: The student was on the honor roll in high school (no modifier).

> The *part-time job* pays well (compound adjective modifying *job*). But: I work *part time* in the office (compound adjective after an action verb).

> The student had a *poorly furnished apartment* (no hyphen after *ly* adverb).

> A *very strong wind* blew off the roof (no hyphen after *very*). Limit the use of *very* in your writing; it's a weak modifier.

I, me: *I* does the action; *me* receives it. The same rule applies to the pronouns *he, she* and *we*. Don't use these words after the prepositions *to* or *with. I, he, she* and *we* are in the nominative case, meaning they should be used as subjects. *Me, her, him, us* and *them* are in the objective case and should be used as objects in sentences.

Whenever the newspaper needs someone to work overtime, Julie and *I* always get picked.

The chancellor gave the report to several journalism students and *me* to review before he made a decision.

If I were: Do not use if I was. If is a word used in the subjunctive mood, meaning it expresses a condition; it should always be used with *were*.

If I were you, I'd learn to use were with if when I mean it in a conditional sense. If I were he, I'd probably reword the sentence, because it is correct but it sounds weird. If she were in my reporting class, she wouldn't use was in a sentence starting with if.

Irregardless: There is no such word, *regardless* of what you may believe and regardless of the fact that it is listed in the dictionary as nonstandard usage. Don't use it.

It's, its: Wordsmith John B. Bremner calls the misuse of *it's* and *its* "possibly the most sickening example of literary ignorance." *It's* is a contraction for *it is; its* is a possessive word meaning "belonging to it."

It's going to cost more to attend college next year because the university raised *its* tuition.

Join, not join together: *Join* means to connect. Can you *join* something apart? *Together* is superfluous.

Judgment: No *e*. There is no judge in *judgment*.

Lay, lie, laid, lain: *Lay* means to place or put something somewhere; it always takes an object when used in this sense. If you can substitute the verb *place,* use *lay. Laid* is the

SOCIAL MEDIA

IF YOU WANT TO join, not join together, a social media network such as Facebook, you can find a lot (not alot) of grammar resources. Just log onto Facebook, search for "grammar," and you will find GrammarGirl, who has many interesting posts. Additional entries in Facebook and other social media sites where you can find answers to some grammatical questions include:

- *The Elements of Style* or its authors William Strunk Jr. and E. B. White. This book, written in 1918, is one of the classic reference books for writers.

- Associated Press Stylebook. The style authority for most journalism organizations. You'll find posts on Facebook and Twitter.

- YouTube: If you are a visual learner, go to YouTube and search for English grammar and style. A number of entries will show you videos on proper punctuation or grammar issues.

- ACES — American Society of Copy Editors. Follow this organization on Twitter. You'll find timely posts and links to the society's blogs, which discuss many journalism issues and editing guidelines.

past tense. *Lie* means to recline. Its past tense is *lay,* and therein lies the confusion. It might help you to mentally use *down* with *lie* or to substitute *recline. Lain* is the perfect tense of *lie.*

> Please *lay* the book on the desk. She *laid* the book on the desk yesterday.

> *Lie* down and take a nap for a few hours. She *lay* on the beach for three hours yesterday and was badly sunburned. (This still sounds awkward, and it might be preferable to say, "She *was lying* on the beach" or "She *had lain* on the beach for three hours. . . .")

> He *had lain* on the sofa for three hours.

Layoffs/lay off: *Layoffs* without a hyphen is one word when used as a noun. When you lay off people as a verb, you must do it in two words.

> Newspapers had many *layoffs* this year. The station was forced to *lay off* several reporters.

Less than/under: When you are using a collection of items rather than a specific number of items, *less than* or *under* is acceptable. For a comparison of a specific number, use *fewer than* (see *fewer*).

> She makes *less than* $20,000 per year.

> She makes *under* $20,000 per year.

> He weighs *less than* 200 pounds.

> He weighs *under* 200 pounds.

Like, as: See *as, like.*

Linking verbs: The *to be* verbs are linking verbs: *am, is, are, was, were, have been.* Verbs expressing the senses are also considered linking verbs: *appear, feel, smell, sound, taste, look.* Linking verbs join the subject with a predicate nominative, meaning a noun or pronoun in the same case as the subject. The pronoun that follows a linking verb could be used as a subject. The adjective after a linking verb modifies the subject and is called a predicate adjective.

> It *is* she. She *is* it. (You wouldn't say "Her *is* it.") The food *tastes good* and the music *sounds good,* but I still *feel bad.* (*Good,* a predicate adjective, modifies *food* and *music,* not the verb. You wouldn't say "The food *tastes well* and the music *sounds well,* but I still *feel badly.*")

Lose, loose: If you *lose* your assignment, you're in trouble. If your pants fall down because they are too *loose,* you'll be embarrassed. You might also be in trouble. You'll certainly be in trouble if you mix up the spelling of these two words.

Media: This word is plural and takes a plural verb for agreement. Television is one *medium,* but newspapers, magazines and television are the *media.*

> The *media are planning* major coverage of the election. The *media are changing* the way *they* cover news.

Memento/not momento: If you want to give students something to remember at their graduation, you will give them a *memento.* There is no such word as a momento although your graduation might be a *momentous* occasion, meaning it was of great moment or something to remember.

ETHICS

ETHICAL DILEMMA: Should you clean up quotes? If a speaker uses poor grammar, should you fix the grammar?

Ethical values: Accuracy, fairness, sensitivity.

Ethical Guidelines: The Associated Press Stylebook says, "Never alter quotations even to correct minor grammatical errors or word usage. . . . Do not routinely use abnormal spellings such as *gonna* in attempts to convey regional dialects or mispronunciations."

The guidelines reinforce the concept that a quote must be someone's exact words. However, what is stylistically correct may not be ethically sensitive. If you are trying to convey that a politician uses poor grammar and if that concept is relevant to a profile or to the person's way of speaking, you may want to use the ungrammatical language. However, if you are interviewing someone who may be an immigrant and does not speak English well, it could be insensitive to quote exactly. Instead of using the exact quote, consider paraphrasing or using a partial quote. Avoid using too many partial quotes because they disrupt the flow of a sentence and cause the reader to wonder what was left out.

Morale/moral: *Morale* means a mental or emotional attitude; *moral* is the distinction between right and wrong.

In his ethics course, he studied *moral* reasoning methods, but when he failed the course, his *morale* plummeted.

More than, over: *More than* is better when referring to numbers; *over* is better when referring to spatial relationships, as the opposite of *under*. In some cases, *over* can be used with numbers, such as ages or amounts of money.

More than 300 people attended the hearing.

The car went *over* the bridge. He is *over* 20. She earns *over* $400 per week. (This last sentence is acceptable, but so is *more than* $400 per week.)

Needless to say: If it's *needless to say,* don't say it. This is another stupid expression.

None: When you use *none* as in *not one,* use a singular verb. Use a plural verb when you mean *no two or more* or *not any* in a collective sense.

None (*not one*) of these students *is* going to graduate school.

None (*not any*) of the student fees *are* being used for health care.

Nonprofit/not-for-profit: A *nonprofit* organization is not supposed to make any profits, nor is it supposed to have a hyphen. The term *not-for-profit* can mean the same thing. If you are using it as an adjective to describe an organization, join the words with hyphens.

Off of: *Off* is enough. *Off of* is unnecessary and ugly usage.

The manager took 10 percent *off* the regular price.

Part-time/part time: When this term is used as an adjective to describe another word, treat it as one word by hyphenating it, such as your *part-time* job. When you say you work only part time, meaning part of the time, use two words.

Passive voice, active voice: Avoid passive voice whenever possible. You are using passive voice when you indicate that something has happened to you or the subject. You are using the active voice when you indicate that you or the subject is doing the action. The action verbs that characterize the active voice have more impact than passive verbs. But sometimes you need the passive voice. Place the most important information first in the sentence, and that will determine if you need active or passive voice. Active voice is preferable for print media and essential for broadcast media.

> *Active voice:* Three students *received* scholarships.

> *Passive voice:* Scholarships *were received* by three students.

> *Appropriate use of passive:* The serial killer *was sentenced* to death by the judge. (That's probably better than saying "The judge *sentenced* a serial killer to death today" because the emphasis should be on the killer, not the judge.)

Pleaded, pled: *Pled* as the past tense of *plead* is considered acceptable in English usage, but the Associated Press Stylebook considers it colloquial and prefers *pleaded*.

> The defendant *pleaded* guilty, but if he *pled* guilty, he would still go to jail regardless of whether the Associated Press style gurus approved of the term he used.

Precede/proceed: *Precede* means what goes before; *proceed* means to go ahead or continue.

Proved/proven: *Proved* is the past tense of an action. *Proven* is an adjective and should be used to describe someone.

> You have *proved* that you are ready to graduate.

> He is a *proven* leader.

Prerequisite/perquisites: If you have to take a beginning reporting course before you can take magazine writing, the first course is a *prerequisite,* meaning it is required to precede something. You know that because you have many prerequisites (without hyphens). If you get a good job, you might get some *perks,* which is really an abbreviation for *perquisites.*

Publicly, not publically: If you want to run for president of the student government, you should announce your intentions *publicly.* Be careful not to commit the common mistake of omitting the *l* from the word.

Restaurateur: No *n* as in restaurant. Think of a *restaurateur* as the person who manages the place where you ate, not a place for an ant.

Seasons: Use lowercase for seasons — spring, summer, autumn and fall. That goes for springtime and summertime, too. However, if the season is part of a formal title such as *Spring Break* or *Winter Olympics*, capitalize it.

Should have, not should of: *Of* should never be used as a verb. Also wrong: *could of* and *would of* in place of *could have* and *would have.*

> By the time you are in college, you *should have* learned never to write *should of.*

Stationary, stationery: *Stationary* means something stays the same (note the *a*'s); *stationery* is the paper you use for letters (note the *e*).

Subject–verb agreement: The verb must agree with the subject. If the subject is singular, the verb must be singular as well. Plural subjects take plural verbs. Here's why that is not as easy as it seems:

The number of students who drop classes *is* increasing. The subject is *number,* not *students.* When you have a noun, *number,* followed by a prepositional phrase with a plural word such as *students,* identify the subject. Don't be misled by the phrase. When *number* is the subject, it always takes a singular verb.

The rate of dropouts *is* increasing. The subject is *rate,* not *dropouts.*

There *are* fewer students enrolled in the print journalism program. The subject is *students,* not the expletive *there.* Avoid starting sentences with *There* because you are forced to use a weak verb. Better: Fewer students are enrolled in the print journalism program.

A singular subject, followed by the phrase *as well as,* takes a singular verb. The city budget, as well as the tax proposal, *was* approved. Better to say: The city budget *and* the tax proposal *were* approved.

Everyone, each, either, neither, every take singular verbs. Imagine the word *one* as the subject when you use those words. *Each* (one) of the students *is* creating a Web page. If that sounds awkward, use *All* of the students *are* creating a Web page.

When a compound subject (two or more subjects) is joined by *and,* it takes a plural verb. The *professor and the students were* sick.

Singular or plural: When a compound subject is joined by *or, nor, but, either, neither,* the verb agrees with the subject closest to it. *Neither* the mayor *nor* the council members *have* proposed a solution. The desk *or* the computers *have* to be sold to raise the money.

Collective nouns such as *audience, jury, board* take singular verbs. The *Board of Commissioners is* scheduled to meet after the holidays. If that sounds awkward, just say The *commissioners are* scheduled to meet after the holidays.

The audience *was* enthusiastic about the performance.

See other entries for *none, board, everyone.*

Than, then: *Than* is used for comparison; *then* is used for time. Think of *then* and *when.*

That, which: When a clause is essential (or restrictive), meaning the sentence won't make sense without it, use *that.* If the sentence can stand alone without the clause (if the clause is nonessential or nonrestrictive), use *which.* Use a comma before a clause with *which;* don't use a comma to precede a clause with *that.* And don't use either word to refer to people. Use *who.*

The committee *that* banned reporters from the hearing was fined. (What committee was fined? The clause is essential to the meaning of the sentence.)

The Lawrence School Board, *which* meets regularly on Tuesdays, will discuss changing school boundaries this week. (The sentence is clear without the clause telling when the board meets.)

The school board members, *who* will vote next week, were elected to two-year terms. (Use *who* when referring to people.)

Their, there, they're: *Their* means "belonging to them"; *there* means "where" or is sometimes used to begin a sentence; *they're* is a contraction for *they are*.

Students who did not qualify for *their* loans this year said *they're* going to file new applications while *there* is still time.

There is or there are: Avoid starting sentences with these words. They always force you to use the weak *to be* verbs. Turn the sentence around and insert an active verb.

Poor: There are no internships being offered at that newspaper.

Better: That newspaper is not offering any internships.

Toward, towards: Use *toward* without the *s*.

Unique: *Unique* means "one of a kind, incomparable." You cannot have something that is more unique or most unique or very unique. If it's unique, it is beyond comparison or qualification.

Who, whom: *Who* is the subject; *who* does the action. *Whom* is the object and receives the action. These words are confusing in clauses. Try to reverse the sentence or clause and see if *who* can be the subject. Deciding on the right word is even trickier when *who* or *whom* is the subject of a clause.

Are you the person *who* called me about the job? (*Who* is the subject of this clause; *who* does the action; *who* called.)

Are you the student *who* is seeking the job? (*Who* is the subject of the clause *is seeking*.) Are you the student *whom* I hired last week? (*Whom* is the object of *I hired*; *whom* received the action.)

Whom do you wish to see about the job opening? (*You* — the subject — wish to see *whom* — the object, the person who receives the action of your wish.)

The personnel director will choose *whoever* she thinks is the most qualified. (She thinks *whoever* is qualified; *whoever* is the subject of the clause *whoever is most qualified*.)

Who's, whose: *Who's* is a contraction for *who is*; *whose* is a possessive meaning "belonging to whom."

Whose team project was late, and *who's* responsible?

Your, you're: *Your* is possessive, meaning "belonging to you," and *you're* is a contraction for *you are*.

Now *you're* ready to test *your* skill by doing the following exercises.

ZIP code: ZIP should be all in capital letters and code should be in lowercase. It is a trademark of the U.S. Postal Service, and it stands for Zone Improvement Program.

EXERCISES

1 Grammar A–K: Study the grammar and usage tips from A to K, and correct the errors in the following sentences. Not all sentences contain errors; some may contain more than one error. Type the errors and the corrections, or type the entire sentence in correct form if your instructor prefers.

a She felt bad about missing the school board meeting, but her editor fired her irregardless of her excuse.

b We will all join together in prayer for the students who died in the shooting, and we will fly the flags at half-mast.

c It's alright if you miss class for a job interview, you can make up the test tomorrow.

d We'll divide the workload between three students.

e The St. Joseph Board of Commissioners are planning to submit a proposal for a bond issue to pay for road improvements, and they are hoping the election committee will reach a consensus of opinion to put the issue on the ballot.

f I know you are anxious to get this job, but each of the applicants will have a chance to discuss their strengths and weaknesses with the personnel director.

g Based on your writing skills, it looks like you could be a good journalist.

h Each of the students is going to receive a plaque with their diplomas at graduation.

i She was embarrassed that she had less than five answers correct on the quiz.

j After the boss read the report, he gave it to Jim and I to rewrite and said its due back by Monday.

2 **Grammar L–Y:** Study the grammar and usage tips from L to Y, and correct the errors in the following sentences. Not all sentences contain errors; some may contain more than one error, and some of the errors may include information from A to K. Type the errors and the corrections, or type the entire sentence in correct form if your instructor prefers.

a The people that attended the gay rights rally said it was one of the most unique events the school had sponsored.

b However, the participants in the rally said the media was annoying when they converged on the speakers with cameras and microphones.

c Some of the speakers felt badly that the crowd became unruly and the organizer said he was embarassed when some of the participants complained.

d Needless to say, next year the rally will be planned better.

e None of the five students involved in the fracas is going to be punished.

f The first-place award, that was an engraved silver bowl, was received by the class valedictorian.

g The three top restauranteurs in the city provided food for the banquet, but over 200 people got sick after the event.

h The City Board of Health, that investigates such cases, said the food smelled and tasted well, but they are withholding judgement on the cause of the illness until the food can be tested.

i Irregardless, alot of people were laying on the ground, holding their stomachs in pain.

j The city health inspector wanted to know who he should blame, and he said he was moving towards a solution to the mystery of revealing whose responsible for the food poisoning outbreak.

3 **Edit a story:** The following poorly written story would never be accepted for publication. Ignore the wordiness, and edit it only for grammar and usage errors. When you retype the story, underline, circle or use boldface to identify the errors, and type in the corrections.

In 1918 William Strunk Jr. produced a little book for his English course at Cornell University, it had a great affect on his students. E.B. White, one of the students who the professor taught, published the book in 1957. Today, the book, that was originally known as "The Little Book," is still having a great effect on writers. Its called *The Elements of Style.* Like I said, it's still popular, and every writer should have their own copy. It's presently available on the World Wide Web.

Strunk never thought it was alright to use alot of unnecessary words. One of his famous sayings are "Omit needless words". Between you and I, that advice is still good today, and I feel badly that this story is filled with errors that would of made Strunk cringe. It goes without saying that Strunk would have been embarrased if I was in his class. None of these sentences are perfect, and if this was the way a student wrote, Strunk would have issued stern judgement. Poor grades were received by students who wrote this badly.

Their is no excuse for writing badly, Strunk might have said. "Vigorous writing is concise", Strunk wrote. The media does not always follow Strunk's advice. He was the most unique teacher of his time. If your anxious to be a good writer, you'll check out his book online.

FEATURED ONLINE ACTIVITY Log on and visit the Writing and Reporting News CourseMate for the grammar appendix and take the interactive quizzes on grammar and spelling.
Access available at www.cengagebrain.com.

Index